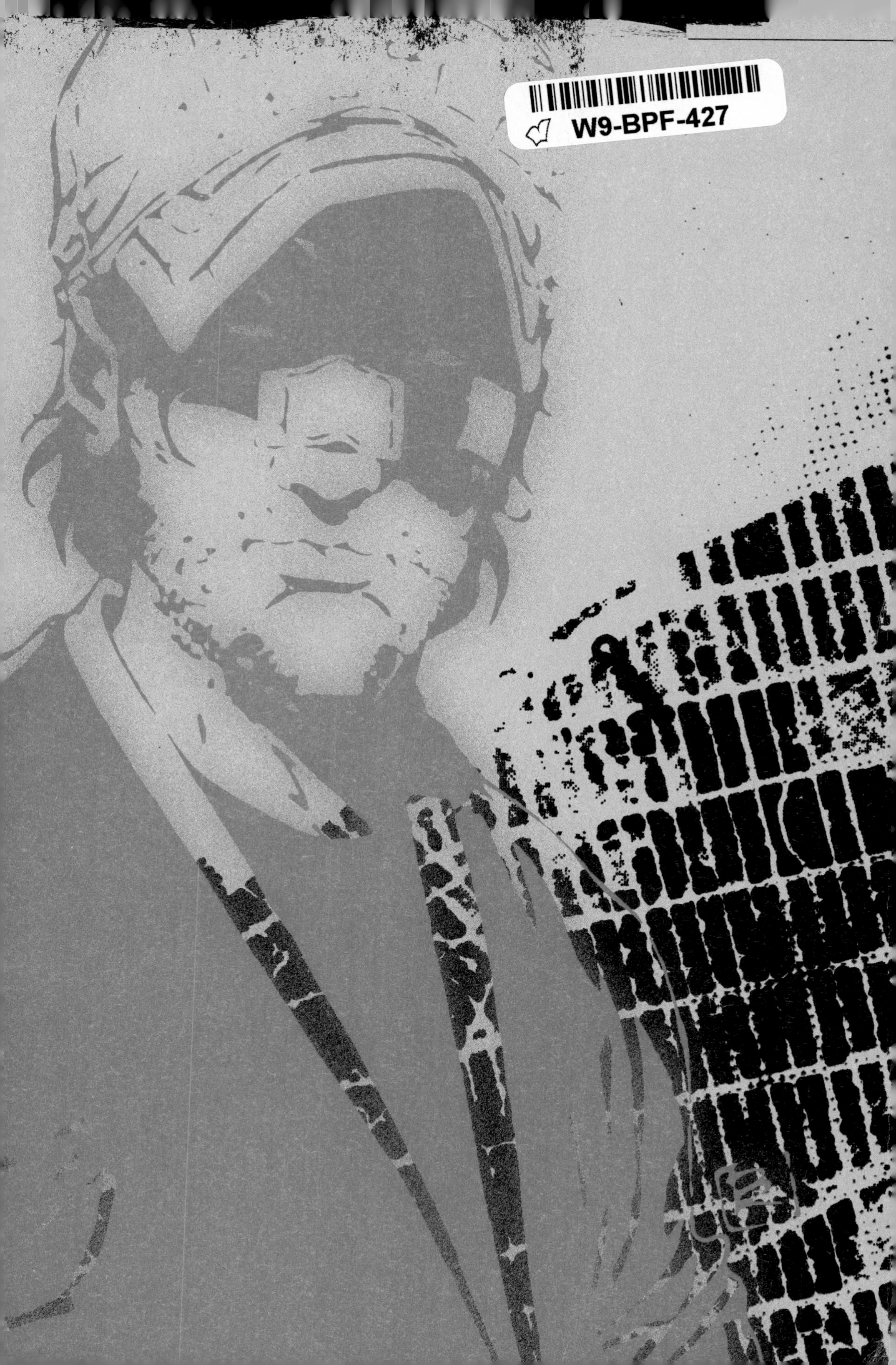

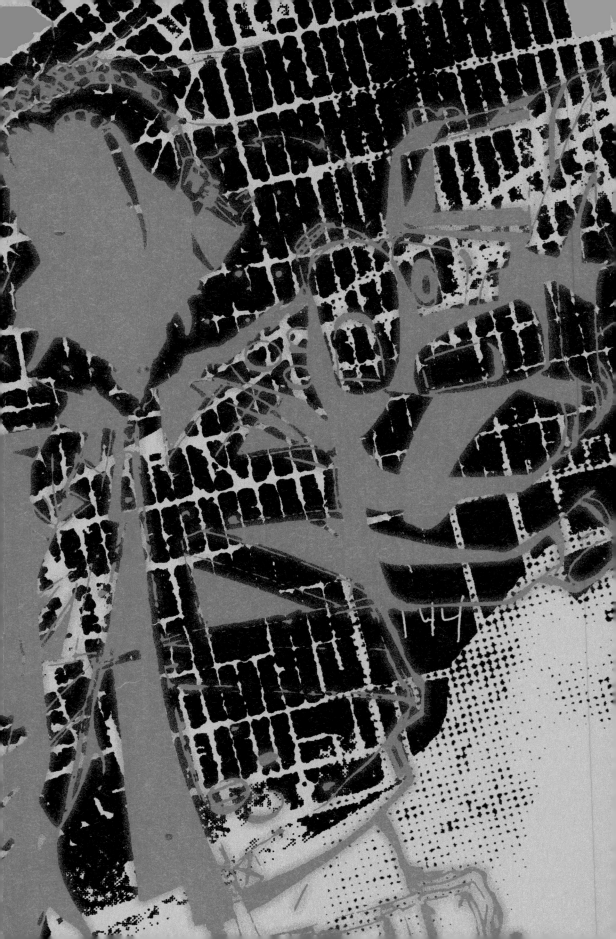

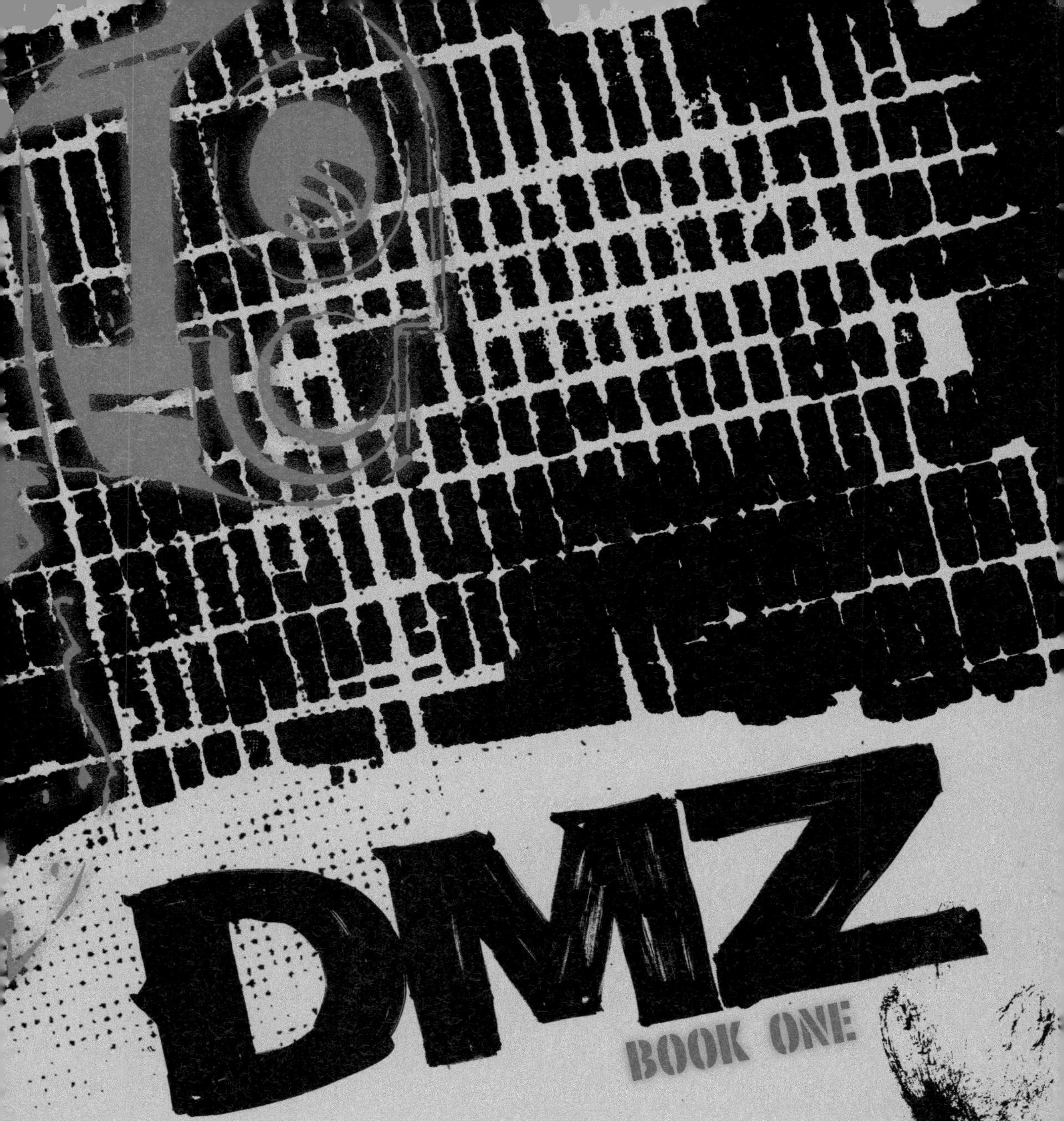

DMZ

BOOK ONE

BRIAN WOOD WRITER

RICCARDO BURCHIELLI
BRIAN WOOD KRISTIAN DONALDSON ARTISTS

JEROMY COX COLORIST

JARED K. FLETCHER LETTERER

BRIAN WOOD COVER ARTIST

DMZ CREATED BY BRIAN WOOD AND RICCARDO BURCHIELLI

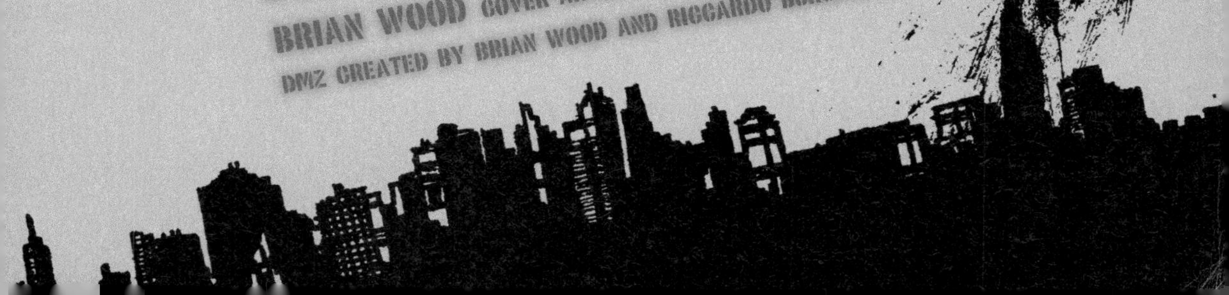

Will Dennis Editor – Original Series
Casey Seijas Assistant Editor – Original Series
Jeb Woodard Group Editor – Collected Editions
Peter Hamboussi Editor – Collected Edition
Steve Cook Design Director – Books
Louis Prandi Publication Design

Shelly Bond VP & Executive Editor – Vertigo

Diane Nelson President
Dan DiDio and Jim Lee Co-Publishers
Geoff Johns Chief Creative Officer
Amit Desai Senior VP – Marketing & Global Franchise Management
Nairi Gardiner Senior VP – Finance
Sam Ades VP – Digital Marketing
Bobbie Chase VP – Talent Development
Mark Chiarello Senior VP – Art, Design & Collected Editions
John Cunningham VP – Content Strategy
Anne DePies VP – Strategy Planning & Reporting
Don Falletti VP – Manufacturing Operations
Lawrence Ganem VP – Editorial Administration & Talent Relations
Alison Gill Senior VP – Manufacturing & Operations
Hank Kanalz Senior VP – Editorial Strategy & Administration
Jay Kogan VP – Legal Affairs
Derek Maddalena Senior VP – Sales & Business Development
Jack Mahan VP – Business Affairs
Dan Miron VP – Sales Planning & Trade Development
Nick Napolitano VP – Manufacturing Administration
Carol Roeder VP – Marketing
Eddie Scannell VP – Mass Account & Digital Sales
Courtney Simmons Senior VP – Publicity & Communications
Jim (Ski) Sokolowski VP – Comic Book Specialty & Newsstand Sales
Sandy Yi Senior VP – Global Franchise Mangagement

DMZ BOOK ONE
Published by DC Comics. Compilation, cover and
all new material Copyright © 2016 Brian Wood and
Riccardo Burchielli. All Rights Reserved. Originally
published in single magazine form in DMZ 1-12 ©
2006, 2007 Brian Wood and Riccardo Burchielli. All
Rights Reserved. All characters, their distinctive
likenesses and related elements featured in this
publication are trademarks of DC Comics. VERTIGO
is a trademark of DC Comics. The stories, characters
and incidents featured in this publication are entirely
fictional. DC Comics does not read or accept unsolic-
ited submissions of ideas, stories or artwork.

DC Comics, 2900 West Alameda Ave.
Burbank, CA 91505
Printed by RR Donnelley, Salem, VA, USA. 4/1/16.
First Printing.
ISBN: 978-1-4012-6135-1

Library of Congress Cataloging-in-Publication Data

Wood, Brian, 1972-
  DMZ, Book one / Brian Wood ; [illustrated by]
Riccardo Burchielli.
   pages cm
   ISBN 978-1-4012-6135-1
1. Militia movements--United States--Comic books,
strips, etc. 2. New York (N.Y.)—Fiction. 3. Graphic
novels. I. Burchielli, Riccardo, illustrator. II. Title.
  PN6727.W59D5766 2014
  741.5'973—dc23

                              2013035933

"I'll see you later," he said, and I could taste the disgust. "I'm gonna catch a ride back to Brooklyn with these guys." I tried to grin, though I'm sure the bruises made my mouth look like it was doing something vile. "I didn't get to say enough," I coughed while sizing up the "these guys," not sure whose side they were on, and watched Brian Wood fade away into the New York night with them.

Another missed opportunity, I thought to myself, making my way back into the bar I used to like, a bar like so many in a great city that had caved. At a table filthy with Italians I looked around for Riccardo Burchielli, thinking maybe I could tell him what I was feeling about his and Brian's book, but that opportunity was missed as well. Riccardo had a sentimental thing for breakfast, meaning he was long gone.

So I fled the bar that used to be something, and I started walking east. My handler was nervous, but then given my mood, she had every right to believe I was going to war. Ah, yes, war...I tried to imagine New York the way Brian and Riccardo were presenting it to me in DMZ. A New York smack dab in the middle of America's Second Civil War. A New York where around every corner was a discovery, a story, a shock to the system.

New York, a great big unruly beauty, brimming with iconoclasts, artists and visionaries who couldn't dream of living anywhere else, no matter how shitty things get in the city. Full of humanity without the means to go anywhere else, and those who at the first whiff of trouble would get mean and get out.

And it was on those streets, looking at the lights behind windows, that I realized Brian and Riccardo weren't trying to make me see their vision; they were pointing out what already was there. New York defines itself. Put a Gap on every corner, and a Starbucks across the street, it'll still be New York.

Put it at ground zero, it won't change what it is.

Brian Wood and Riccardo Burchielli's DMZ caught me off guard. On Lafayette and Houston, I came across a couple of New York's Finest, but at that moment, I needed them to be the two men who created this book in your hands. I wasn't about to miss another opportunity.

"You guys—the two of you—do good work. Thank you."

They looked at me like they couldn't care less about my opinion.

Azz 03.24.06

Brian Azzarello is the Eisner and Harvey Award winning author of 100 BULLETS and SPACEMAN for DC/Vertigo. He's left his mark on SUPERMAN, BATMAN, WONDER WOMAN and HELLBLAZER. He lives in Chicago and twitters only when he has something to say.

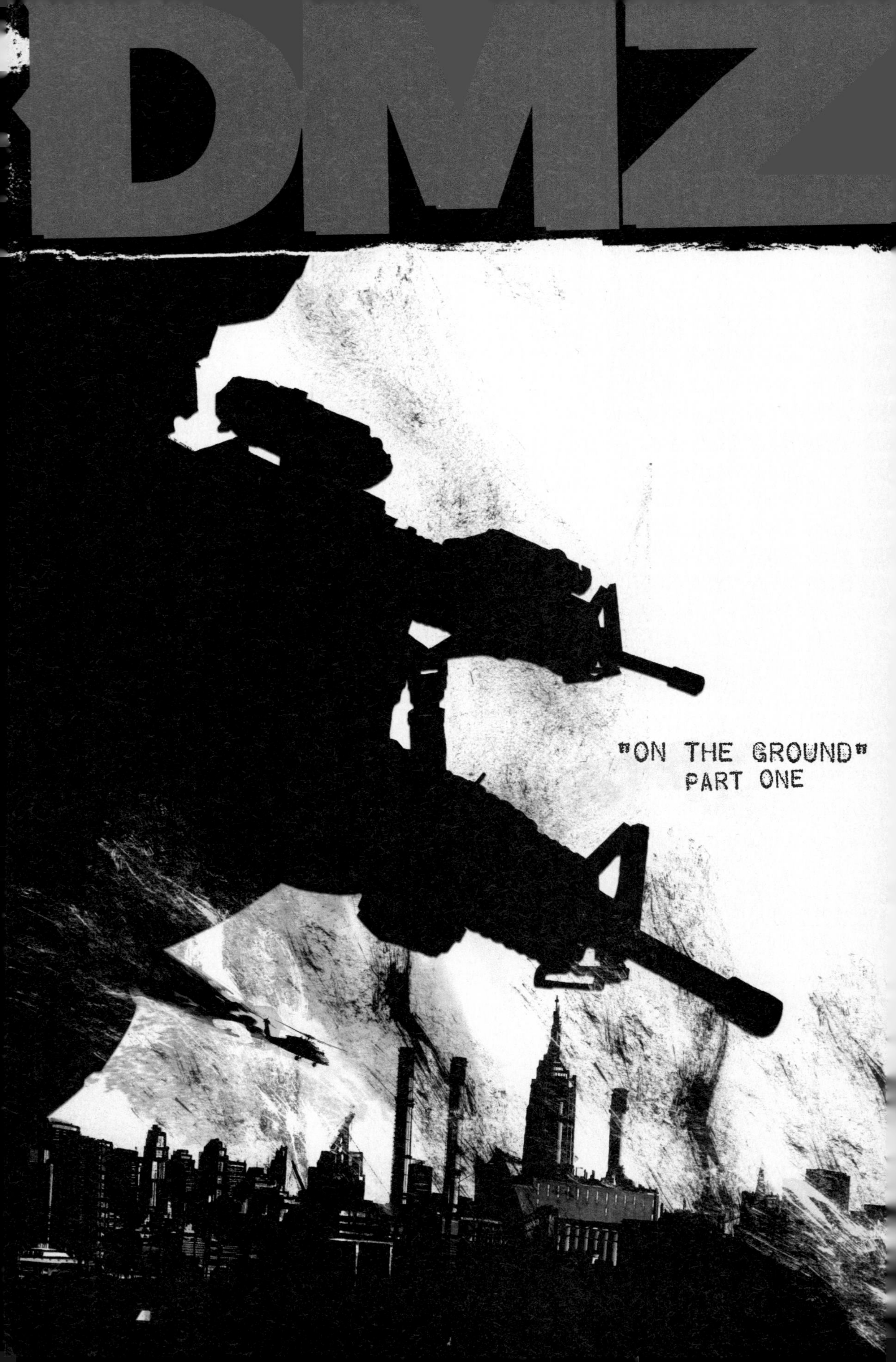
DMZ
"ON THE GROUND"
PART ONE

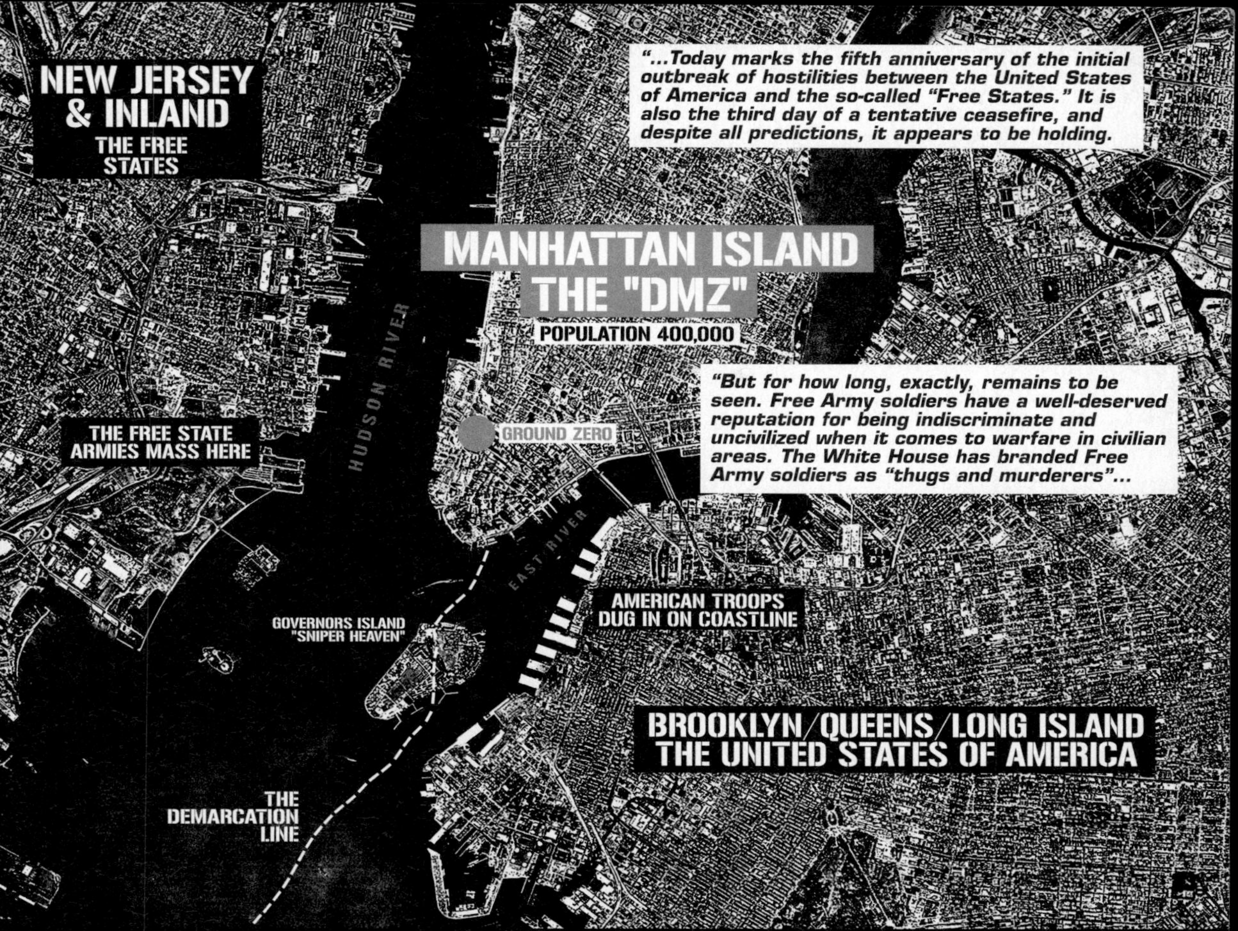
NEW JERSEY & INLAND
THE FREE STATES
"...Today marks the fifth anniversary of the initial outbreak of hostilities between the United States of America and the so-called "Free States." It is also the third day of a tentative ceasefire, and despite all predictions, it appears to be holding.
MANHATTAN ISLAND
THE "DMZ"
POPULATION 400,000
HUDSON RIVER
"But for how long, exactly, remains to be seen. Free Army soldiers have a well-deserved reputation for being indiscriminate and uncivilized when it comes to warfare in civilian areas. The White House has branded Free Army soldiers as "thugs and murderers"...
THE FREE STATE ARMIES MASS HERE
GROUND ZERO
EAST RIVER
AMERICAN TROOPS DUG IN ON COASTLINE
GOVERNORS ISLAND "SNIPER HEAVEN"
BROOKLYN/QUEENS/LONG ISLAND
THE UNITED STATES OF AMERICA
THE DEMARCATION LINE

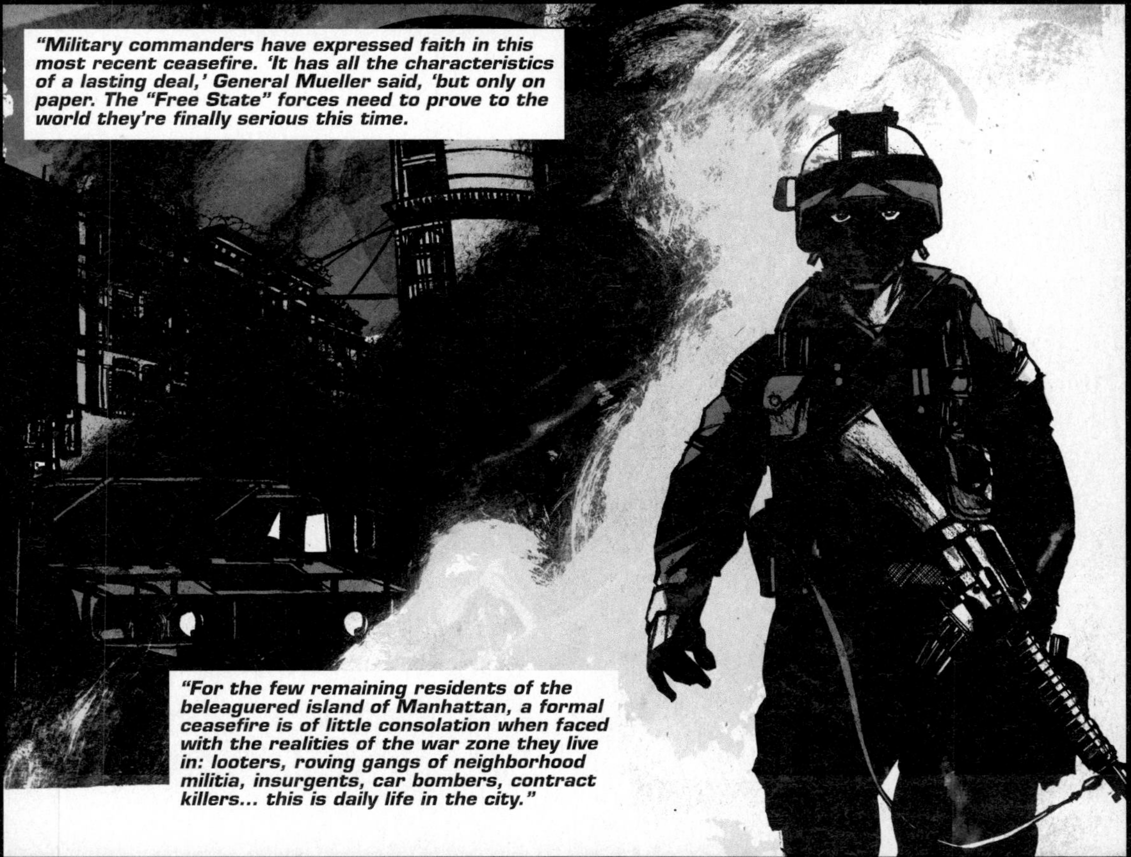
"Military commanders have expressed faith in this most recent ceasefire. 'It has all the characteristics of a lasting deal,' General Mueller said, 'but only on paper. The "Free State" forces need to prove to the world they're finally serious this time.
"For the few remaining residents of the beleaguered island of Manhattan, a formal ceasefire is of little consolation when faced with the realities of the war zone they live in: looters, roving gangs of neighborhood militia, insurgents, car bombers, contract killers... this is daily life in the city."

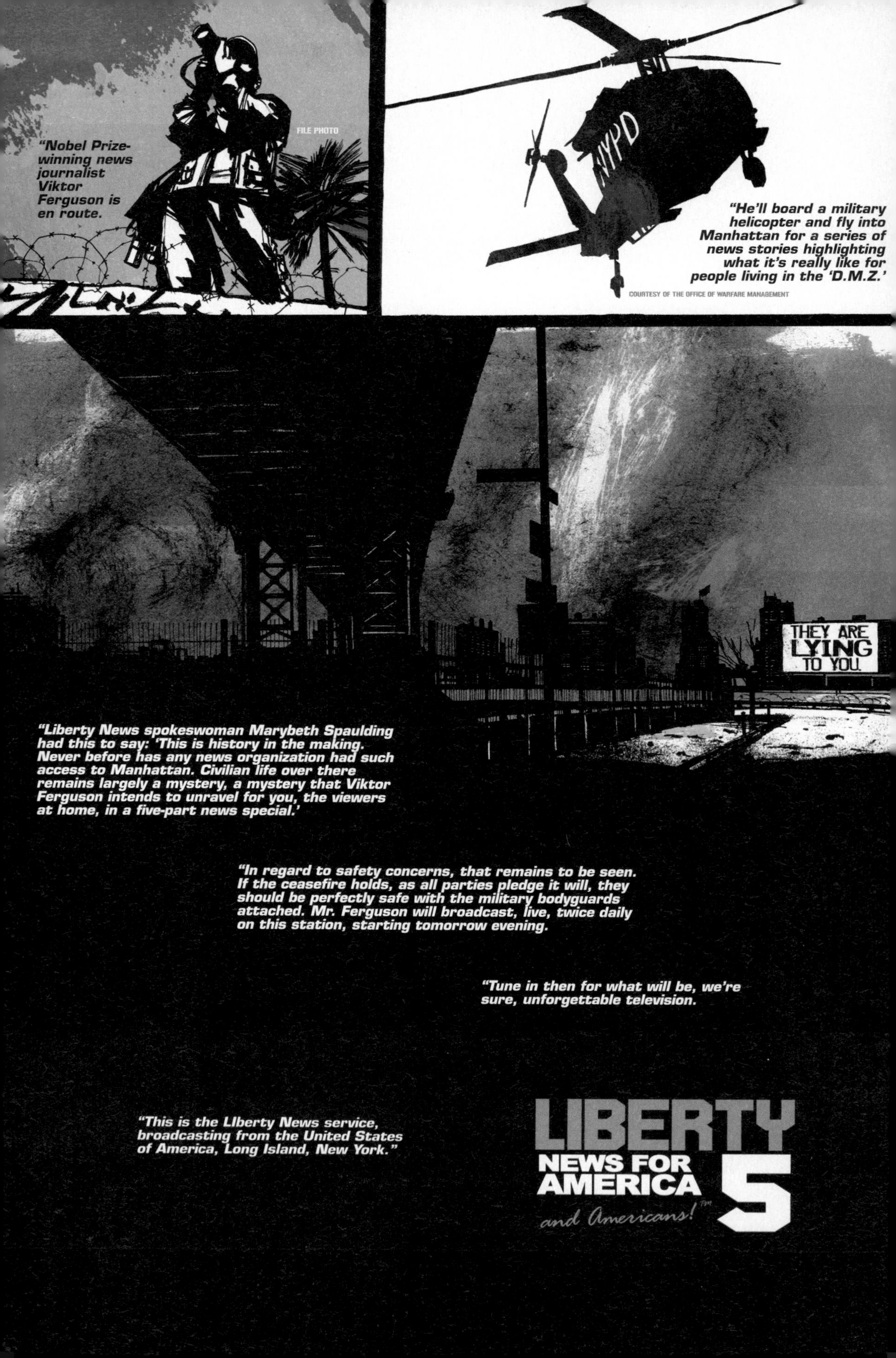
FILE PHOTO
"Nobel Prize-winning news journalist Viktor Ferguson is en route.
"He'll board a military helicopter and fly into Manhattan for a series of news stories highlighting what it's really like for people living in the 'D.M.Z.'
NYPD
COURTESY OF THE OFFICE OF WARFARE MANAGEMENT
THEY ARE LYING TO YOU.
"Liberty News spokeswoman Marybeth Spaulding had this to say: 'This is history in the making. Never before has any news organization had such access to Manhattan. Civilian life over there remains largely a mystery, a mystery that Viktor Ferguson intends to unravel for you, the viewers at home, in a five-part news special.'
"In regard to safety concerns, that remains to be seen. If the ceasefire holds, as all parties pledge it will, they should be perfectly safe with the military bodyguards attached. Mr. Ferguson will broadcast, live, twice daily on this station, starting tomorrow evening.
"Tune in then for what will be, we're sure, unforgettable television.
"This is the LIberty News service, broadcasting from the United States of America, Long Island, New York."
LIBERTY
NEWS FOR AMERICA
5
and Americans!™

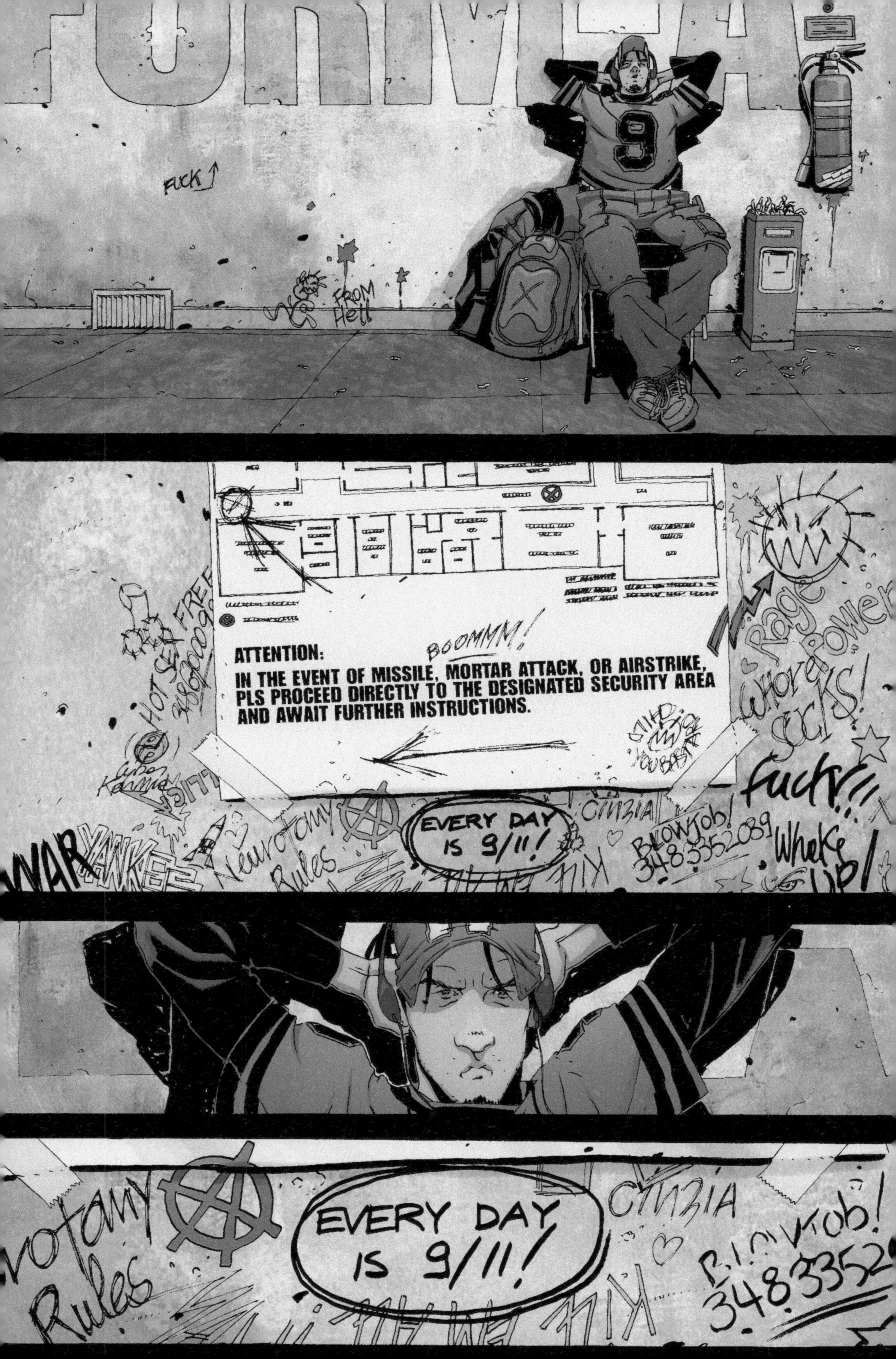
FUCK ↑
FROM Hell
BOOMMM!
ATTENTION:
IN THE EVENT OF MISSILE, MORTAR ATTACK, OR AIRSTRIKE, PLS PROCEED DIRECTLY TO THE DESIGNATED SECURITY AREA AND AWAIT FURTHER INSTRUCTIONS.
HOT SEX FREE
Rage
Whore Power
SUCKS!
fuck!!!
WAR
YANKEES
Neurotomy Rules
EVERY DAY IS 9/11!
CINZIA
BLOWJOB! 3483352089
Whake UP!
EVERY DAY IS 9/11!

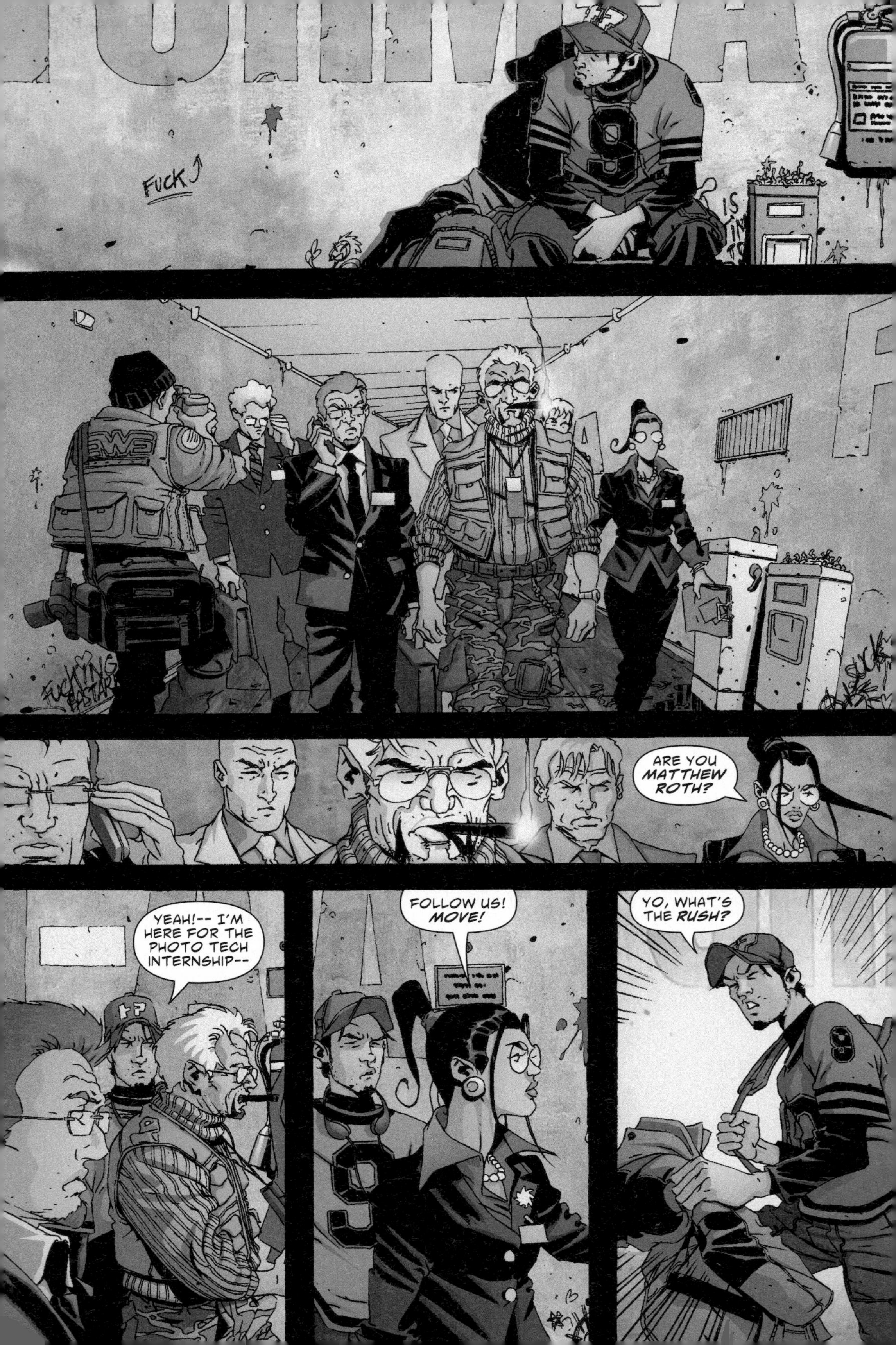
FUCK
FUCKING BASTAR
ARE YOU MATTHEW ROTH?
YEAH!-- I'M HERE FOR THE PHOTO TECH INTERNSHIP--
FOLLOW US! MOVE!
YO, WHAT'S THE RUSH?

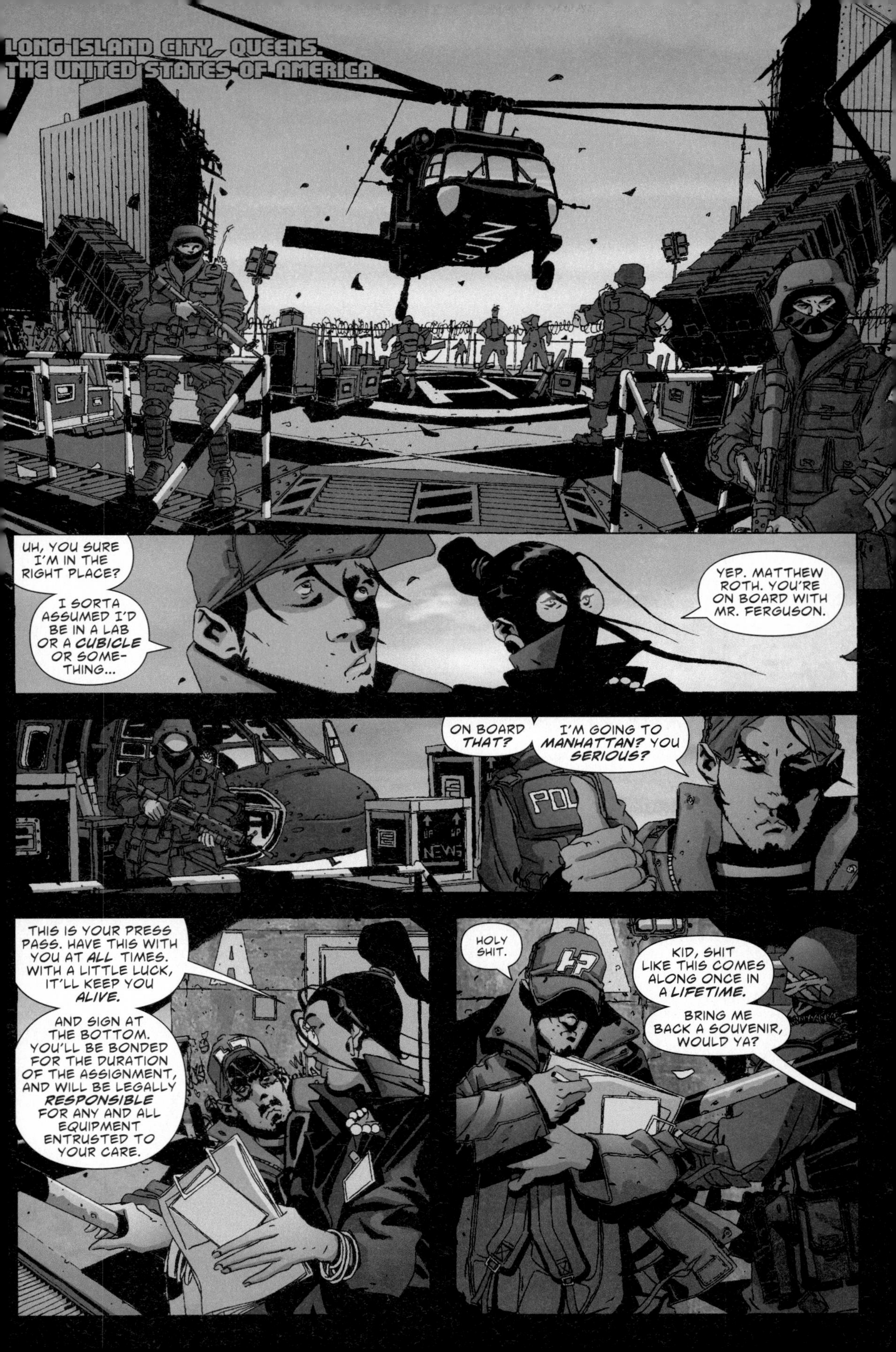
LONG ISLAND CITY, QUEENS.
THE UNITED STATES OF AMERICA.
UH, YOU SURE I'M IN THE RIGHT PLACE?
I SORTA ASSUMED I'D BE IN A LAB OR A CUBICLE OR SOME-THING...
YEP. MATTHEW ROTH. YOU'RE ON BOARD WITH MR. FERGUSON.
ON BOARD THAT?
I'M GOING TO MANHATTAN? YOU SERIOUS?
POL
NEWS
THIS IS YOUR PRESS PASS. HAVE THIS WITH YOU AT ALL TIMES. WITH A LITTLE LUCK, IT'LL KEEP YOU ALIVE.
AND SIGN AT THE BOTTOM. YOU'LL BE BONDED FOR THE DURATION OF THE ASSIGNMENT, AND WILL BE LEGALLY RESPONSIBLE FOR ANY AND ALL EQUIPMENT ENTRUSTED TO YOUR CARE.
HOLY SHIT.
KID, SHIT LIKE THIS COMES ALONG ONCE IN A LIFETIME.
BRING ME BACK A SOUVENIR, WOULD YA?

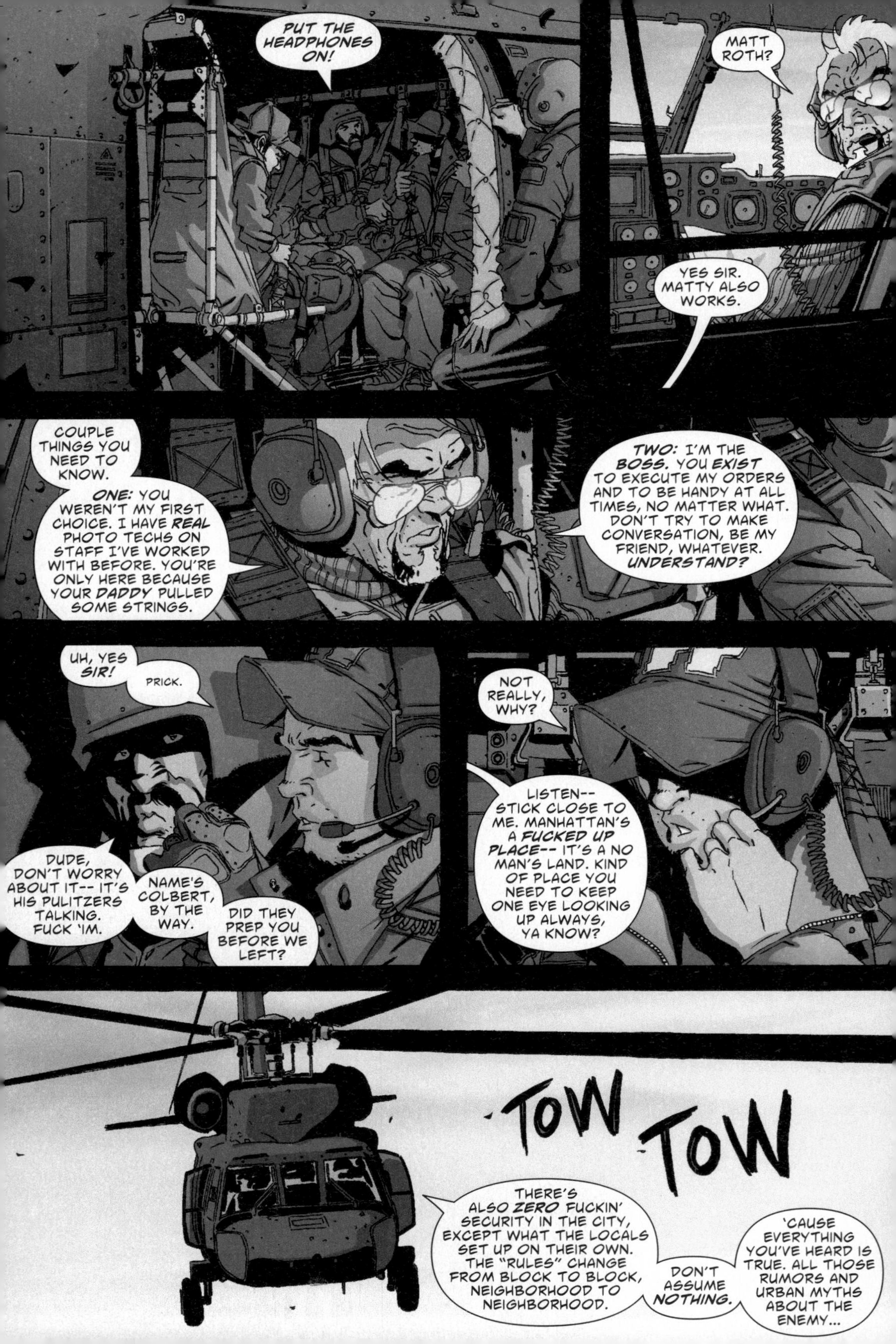
PUT THE HEADPHONES ON!
MATT ROTH?
YES SIR. MATTY ALSO WORKS.
COUPLE THINGS YOU NEED TO KNOW.
ONE: YOU WEREN'T MY FIRST CHOICE. I HAVE REAL PHOTO TECHS ON STAFF I'VE WORKED WITH BEFORE. YOU'RE ONLY HERE BECAUSE YOUR DADDY PULLED SOME STRINGS.
TWO: I'M THE BOSS. YOU EXIST TO EXECUTE MY ORDERS AND TO BE HANDY AT ALL TIMES, NO MATTER WHAT. DON'T TRY TO MAKE CONVERSATION, BE MY FRIEND, WHATEVER. UNDERSTAND?
UH, YES SIR!
PRICK.
DUDE, DON'T WORRY ABOUT IT-- IT'S HIS PULITZERS TALKING. FUCK 'IM.
NAME'S COLBERT, BY THE WAY.
DID THEY PREP YOU BEFORE WE LEFT?
NOT REALLY, WHY?
LISTEN-- STICK CLOSE TO ME. MANHATTAN'S A FUCKED UP PLACE-- IT'S A NO MAN'S LAND. KIND OF PLACE YOU NEED TO KEEP ONE EYE LOOKING UP ALWAYS, YA KNOW?
TOW
TOW
THERE'S ALSO ZERO FUCKIN' SECURITY IN THE CITY, EXCEPT WHAT THE LOCALS SET UP ON THEIR OWN. THE "RULES" CHANGE FROM BLOCK TO BLOCK, NEIGHBORHOOD TO NEIGHBORHOOD.
DON'T ASSUME NOTHING.
'CAUSE EVERYTHING YOU'VE HEARD IS TRUE. ALL THOSE RUMORS AND URBAN MYTHS ABOUT THE ENEMY...

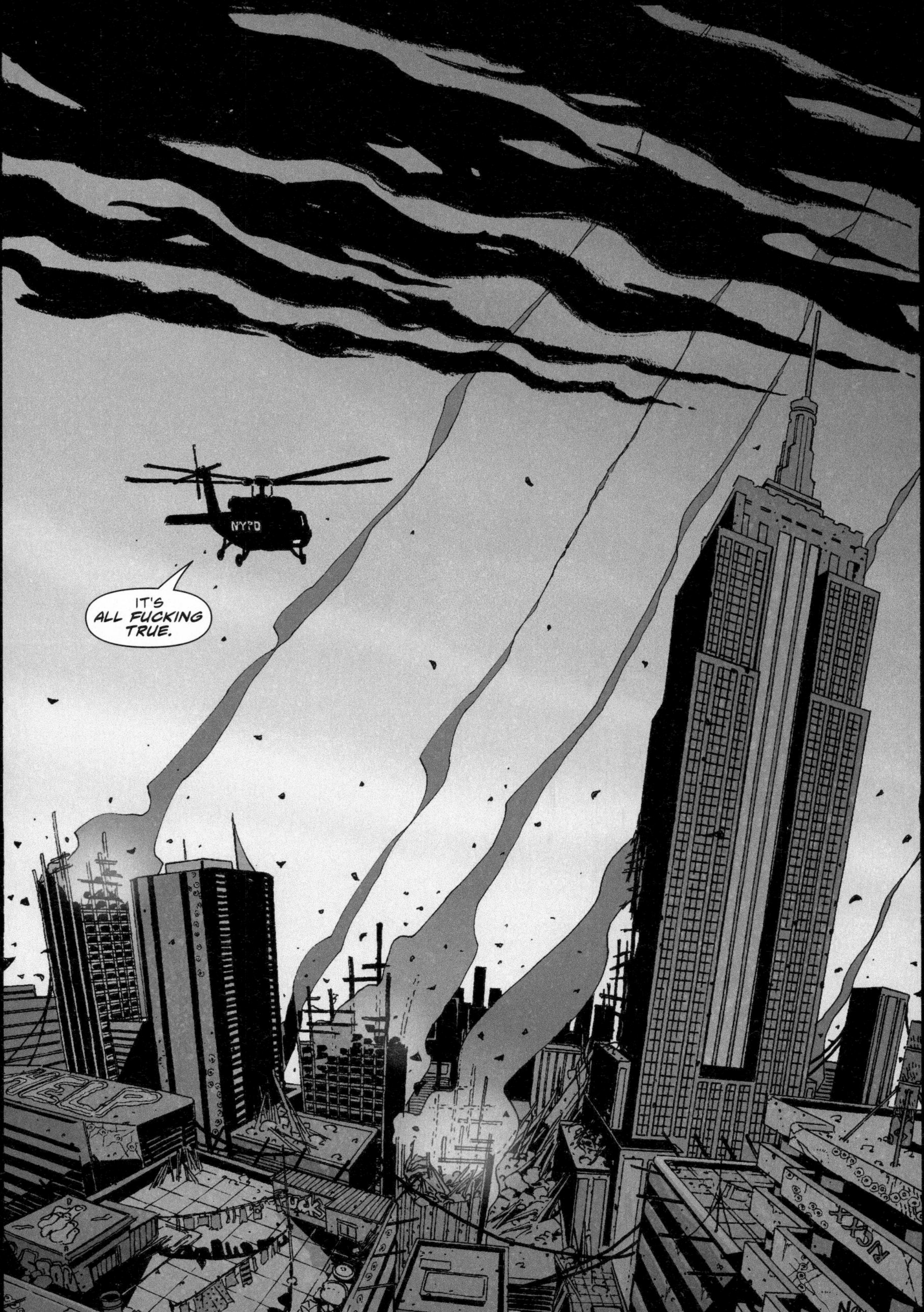
NYPD
IT'S ALL FUCKING TRUE.

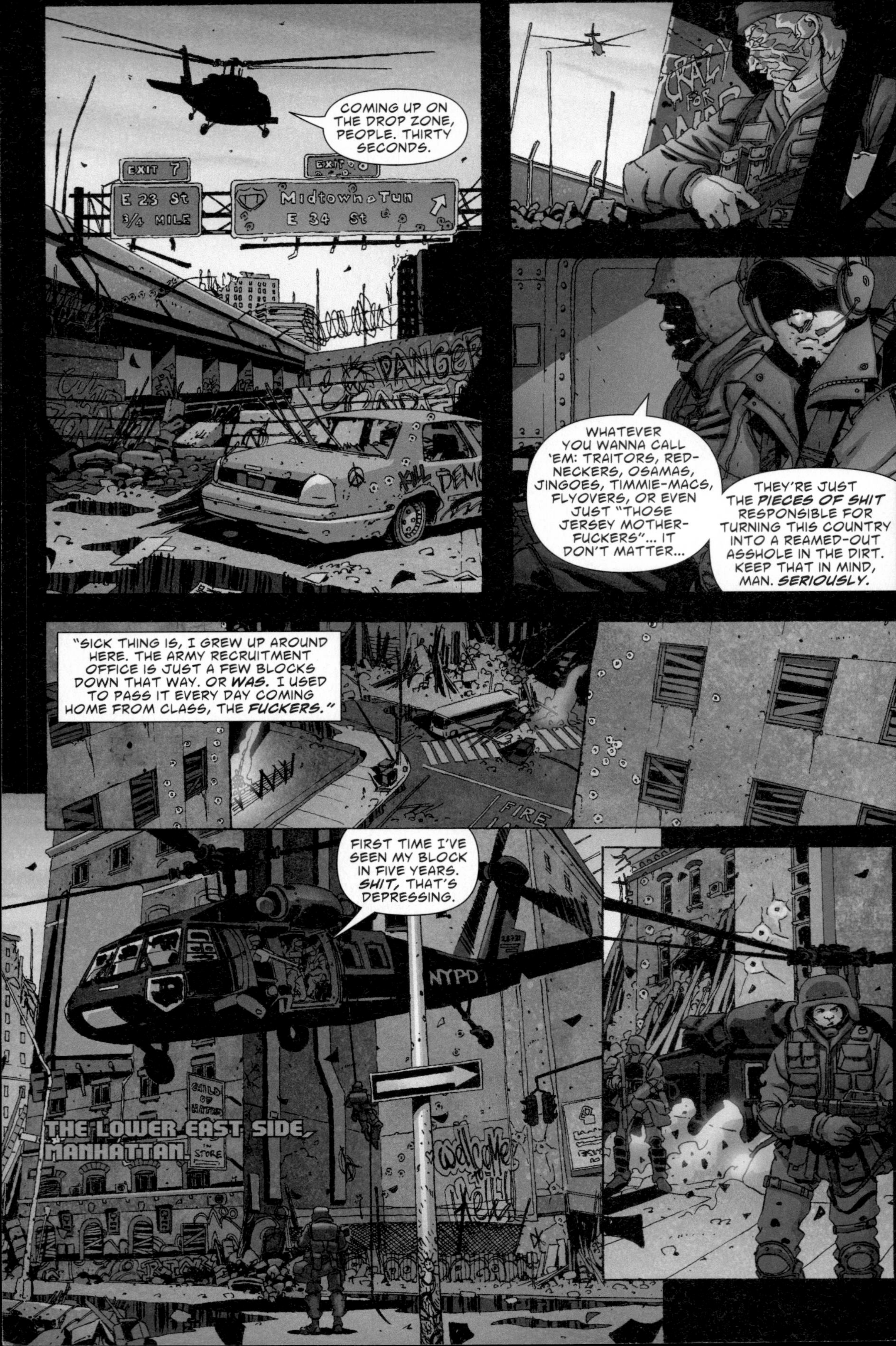
COMING UP ON THE DROP ZONE, PEOPLE. THIRTY SECONDS.
EXIT 7
E 23 St 3/4 MILE
Midtown Tun E 34 St
WHATEVER YOU WANNA CALL 'EM: TRAITORS, RED-NECKERS, OSAMAS, JINGOES, TIMMIE-MACS, FLYOVERS, OR EVEN JUST "THOSE JERSEY MOTHER-FUCKERS"... IT DON'T MATTER...
THEY'RE JUST THE ***PIECES OF SHIT*** RESPONSIBLE FOR TURNING THIS COUNTRY INTO A REAMED-OUT ASSHOLE IN THE DIRT. KEEP THAT IN MIND, MAN. ***SERIOUSLY.***
"SICK THING IS, I GREW UP AROUND HERE. THE ARMY RECRUITMENT OFFICE IS JUST A FEW BLOCKS DOWN THAT WAY. OR ***WAS.*** I USED TO PASS IT EVERY DAY COMING HOME FROM CLASS, THE ***FUCKERS.***"
FIRST TIME I'VE SEEN MY BLOCK IN FIVE YEARS. ***SHIT,*** THAT'S DEPRESSING.
NYPD
THE LOWER EAST SIDE, MANHATTAN.

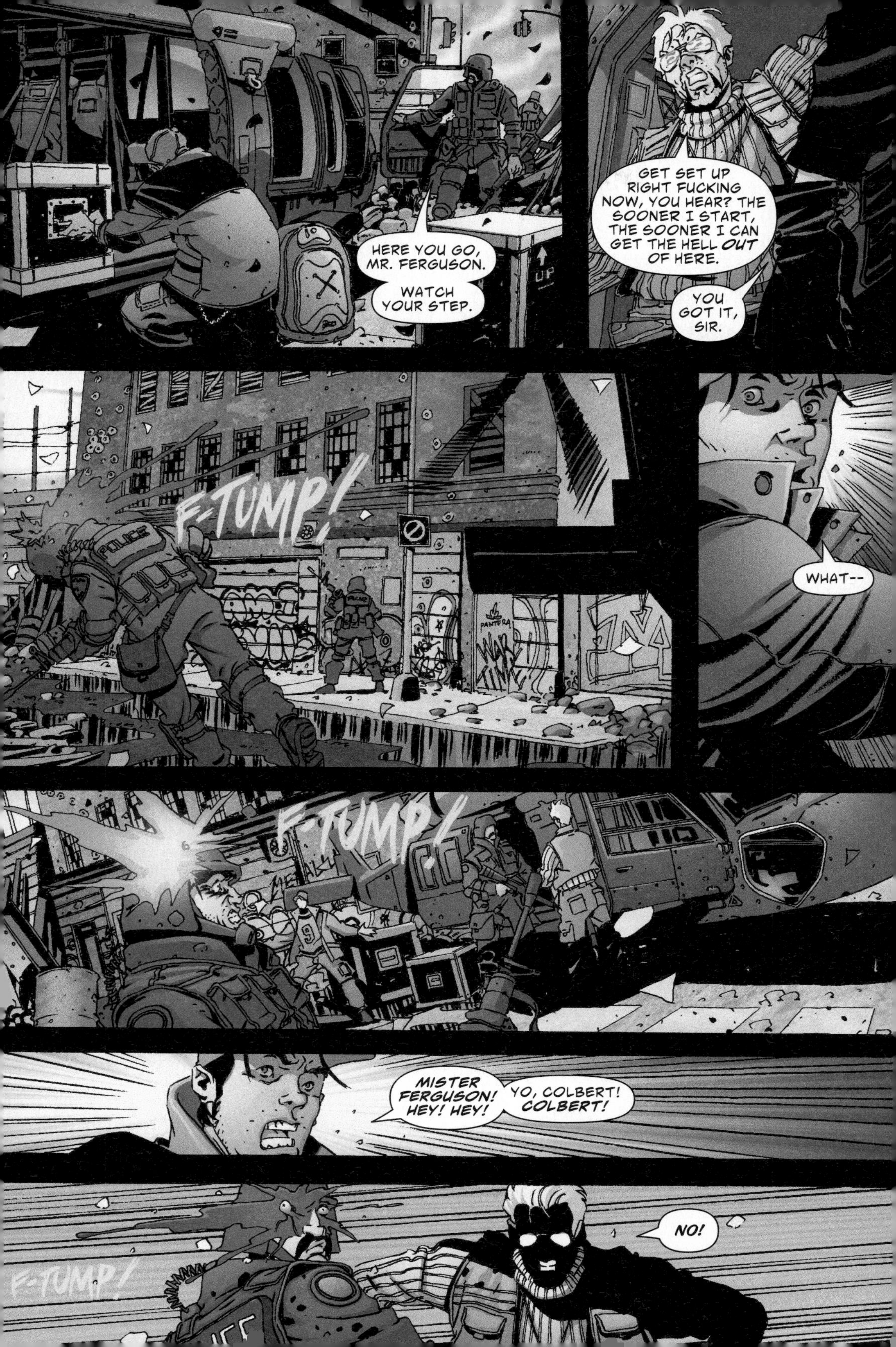
HERE YOU GO, MR. FERGUSON.
WATCH YOUR STEP.
GET SET UP RIGHT FUCKING NOW, YOU HEAR? THE SOONER I START, THE SOONER I CAN GET THE HELL OUT OF HERE.
YOU GOT IT, SIR.
F-TUMP!
POLICE
WHAT--
F-TUMP!
MISTER FERGUSON! HEY! HEY!
YO, COLBERT! COLBERT!
NO!
F-TUMP!

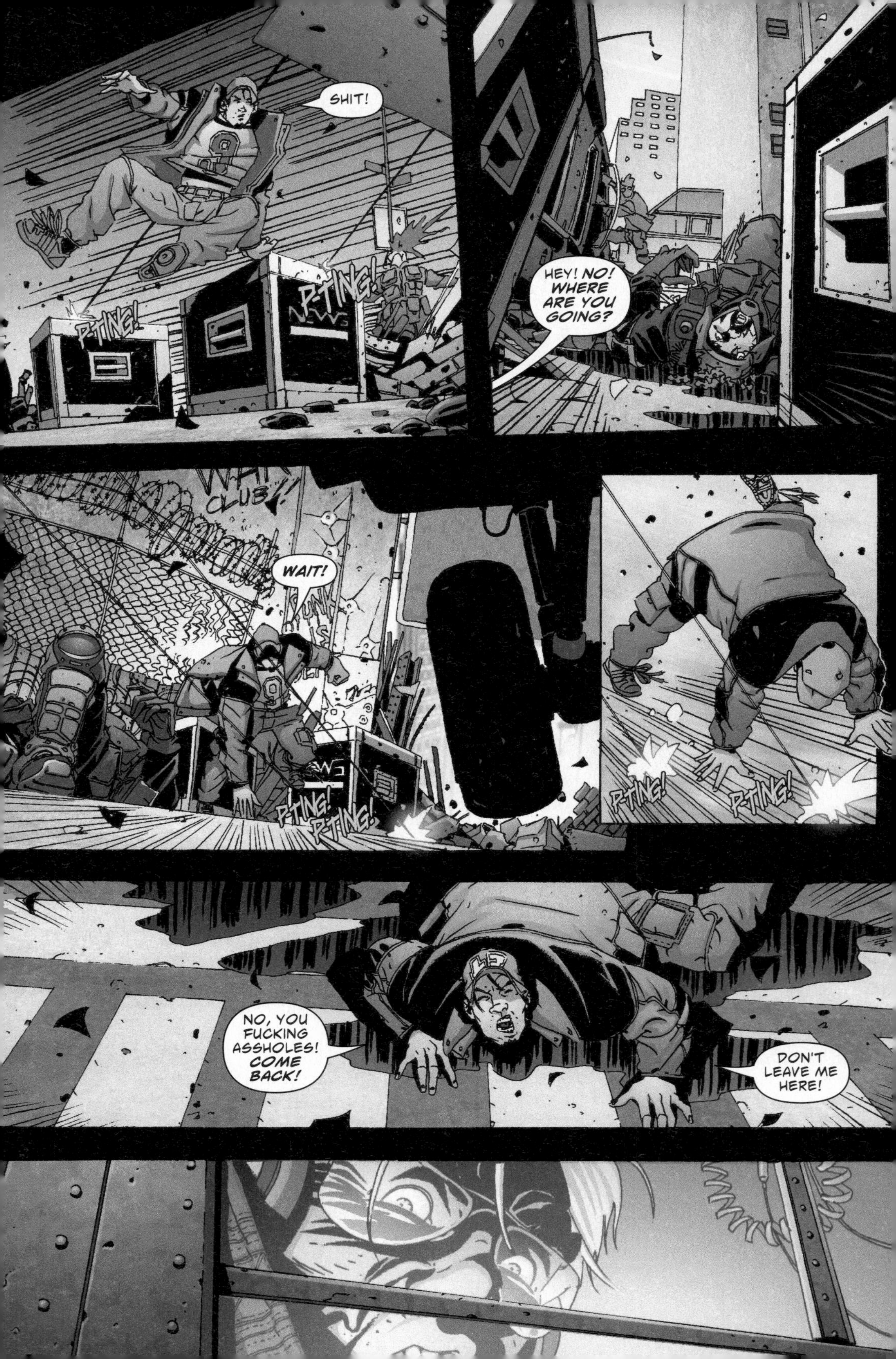
SHIT!
P-TING!
P-TING!
HEY! NO! WHERE ARE YOU GOING?
WAIT!
P-TING!
P-TING!
P-TING!
P-TING!
NO, YOU FUCKING ASSHOLES! COME BACK!
DON'T LEAVE ME HERE!

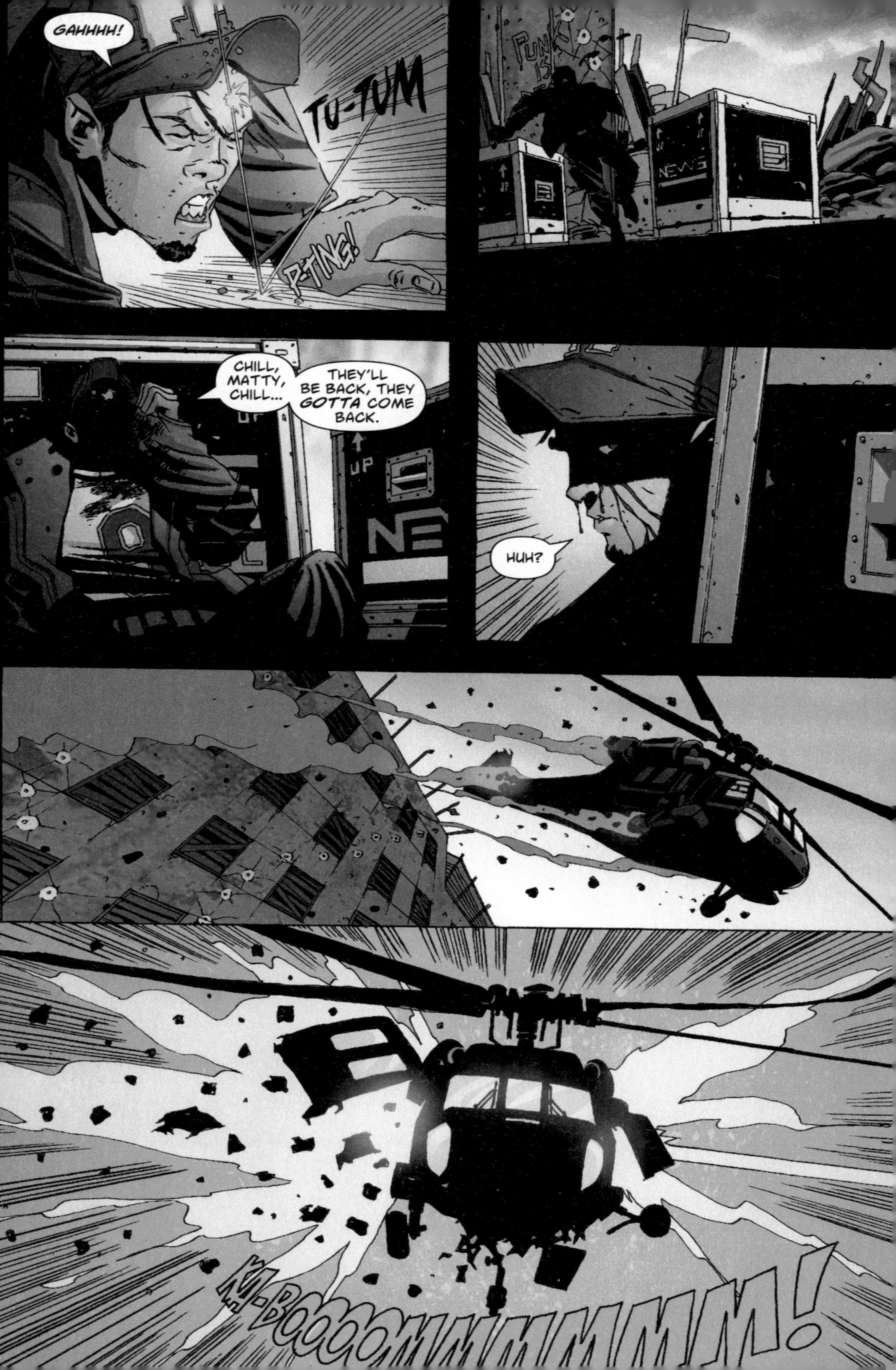
GAHHHH!
TU-TUM
P-TING!
PUNK IS
NEWS
CHILL, MATTY, CHILL...
THEY'LL BE BACK, THEY GOTTA COME BACK.
UP
HUH?
KA-BOOOOMMMMMMM!

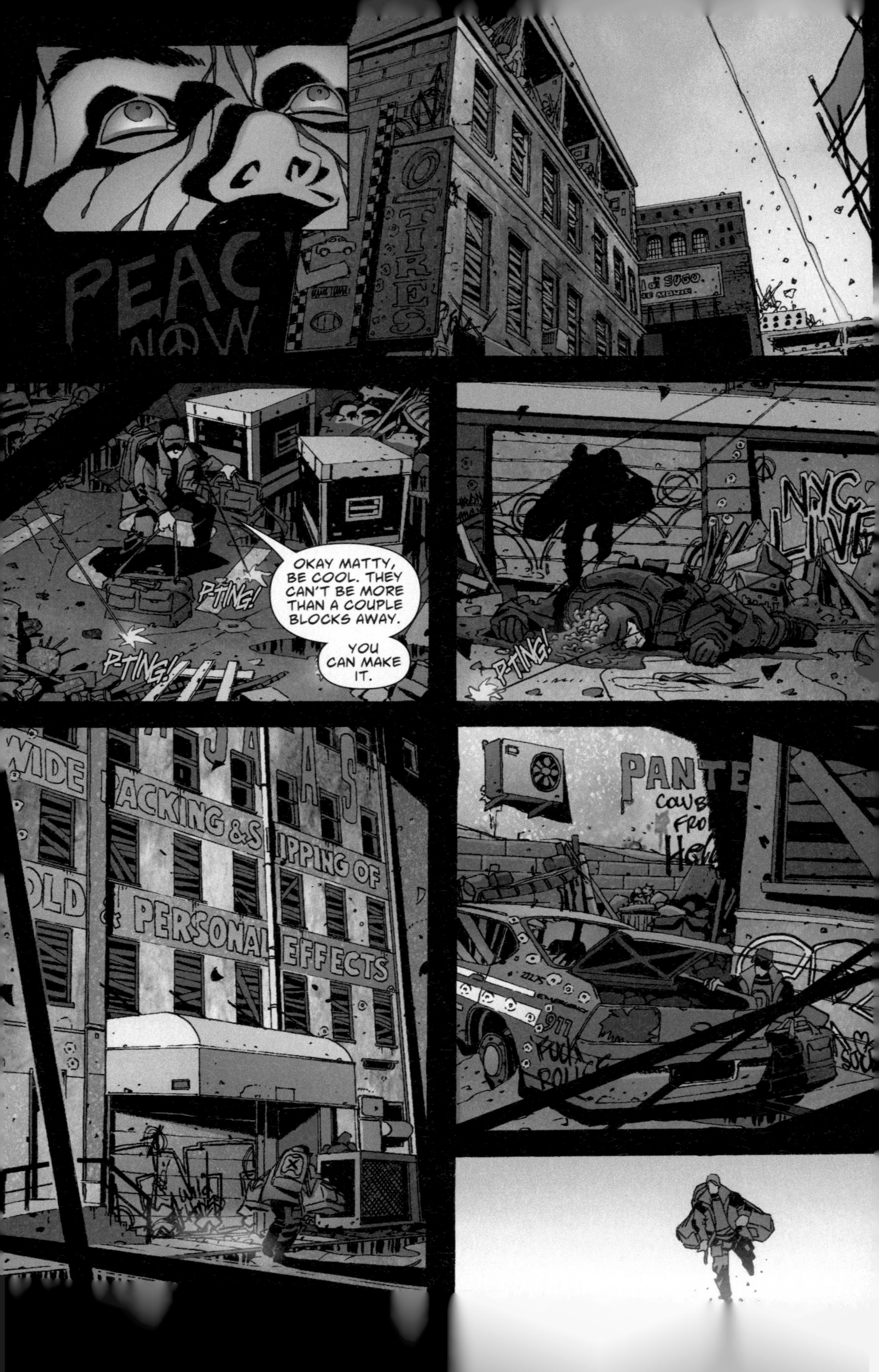
PEACE NOW
TIRES
OKAY MATTY, BE COOL. THEY CAN'T BE MORE THAN A COUPLE BLOCKS AWAY.
YOU CAN MAKE IT.
P-TING!
P-TING!
NYC LIVE
P-TING!
PACKING & SHIPPING OF
PERSONAL EFFECTS
PAN
911

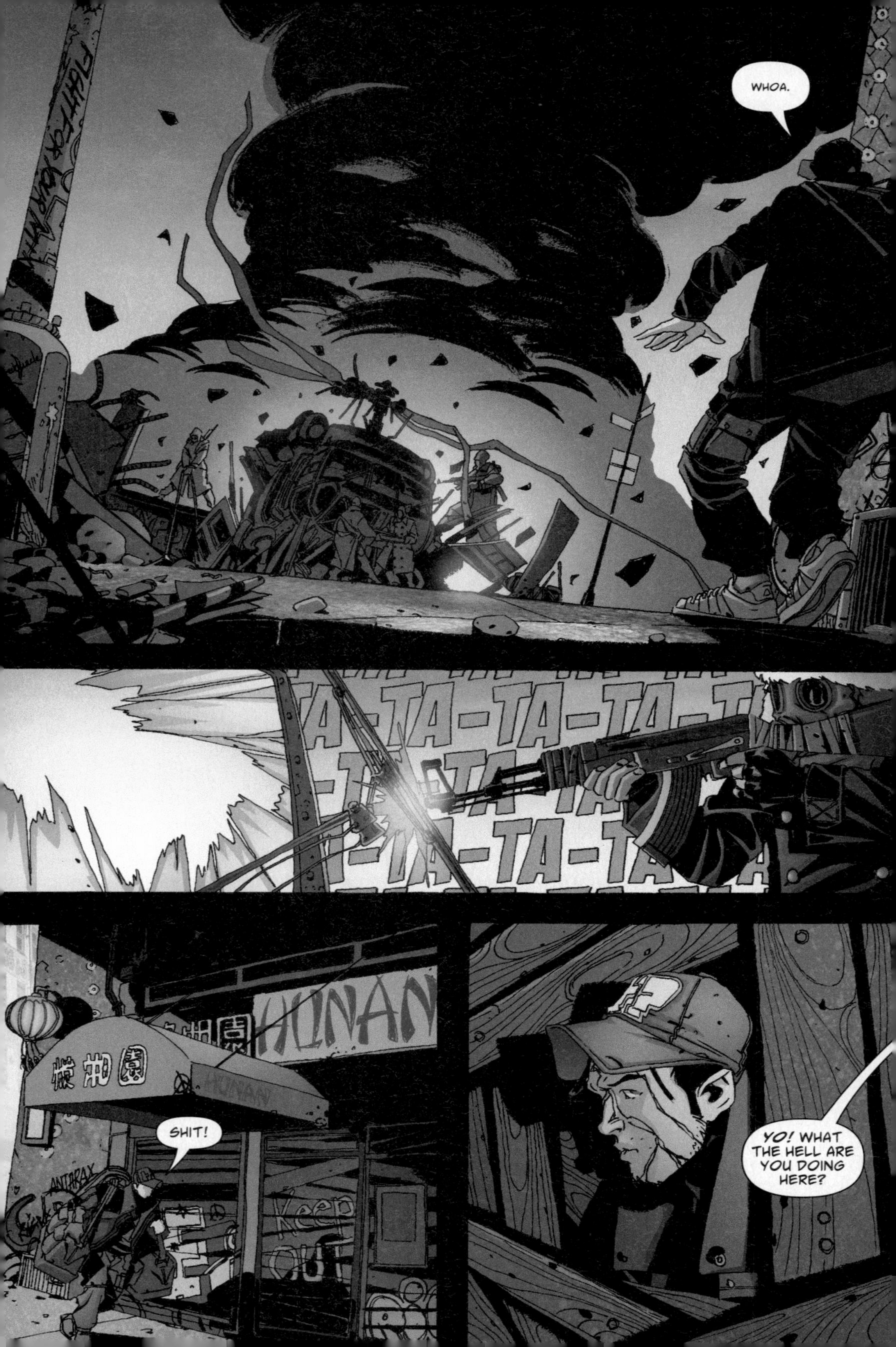
FIGHT FOR YOUR CITY
WHOA.
TA-TA-TA-TA-TA
TA-TA
TA-TA-TA-TA
HUNAN
HUNAN
SHIT!
ANTIFAX
Keep
OUT
YO! WHAT THE HELL ARE YOU DOING HERE?

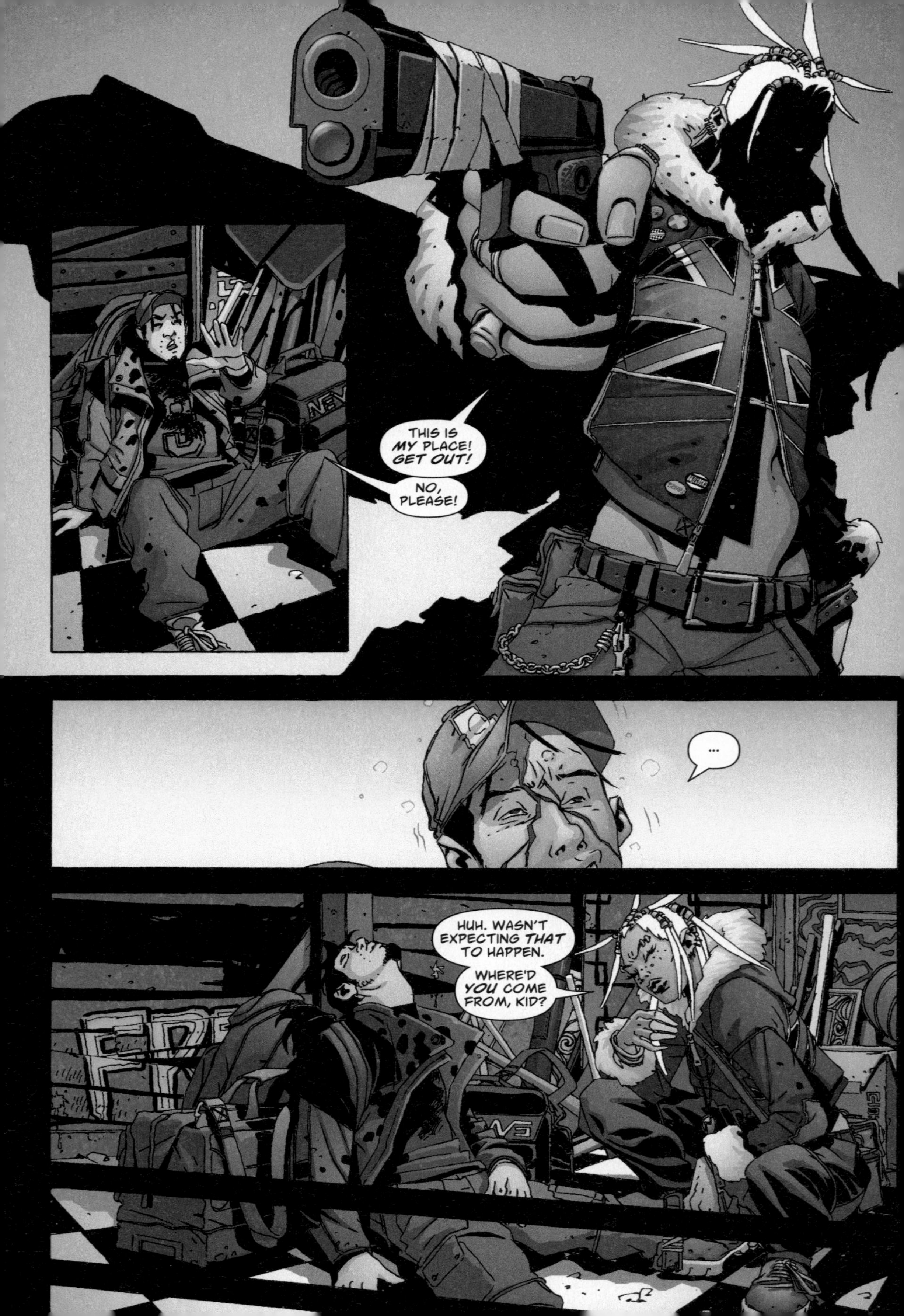
THIS IS MY PLACE! GET OUT!
NO, PLEASE!
...
HUH. WASN'T EXPECTING THAT TO HAPPEN.
WHERE'D YOU COME FROM, KID?

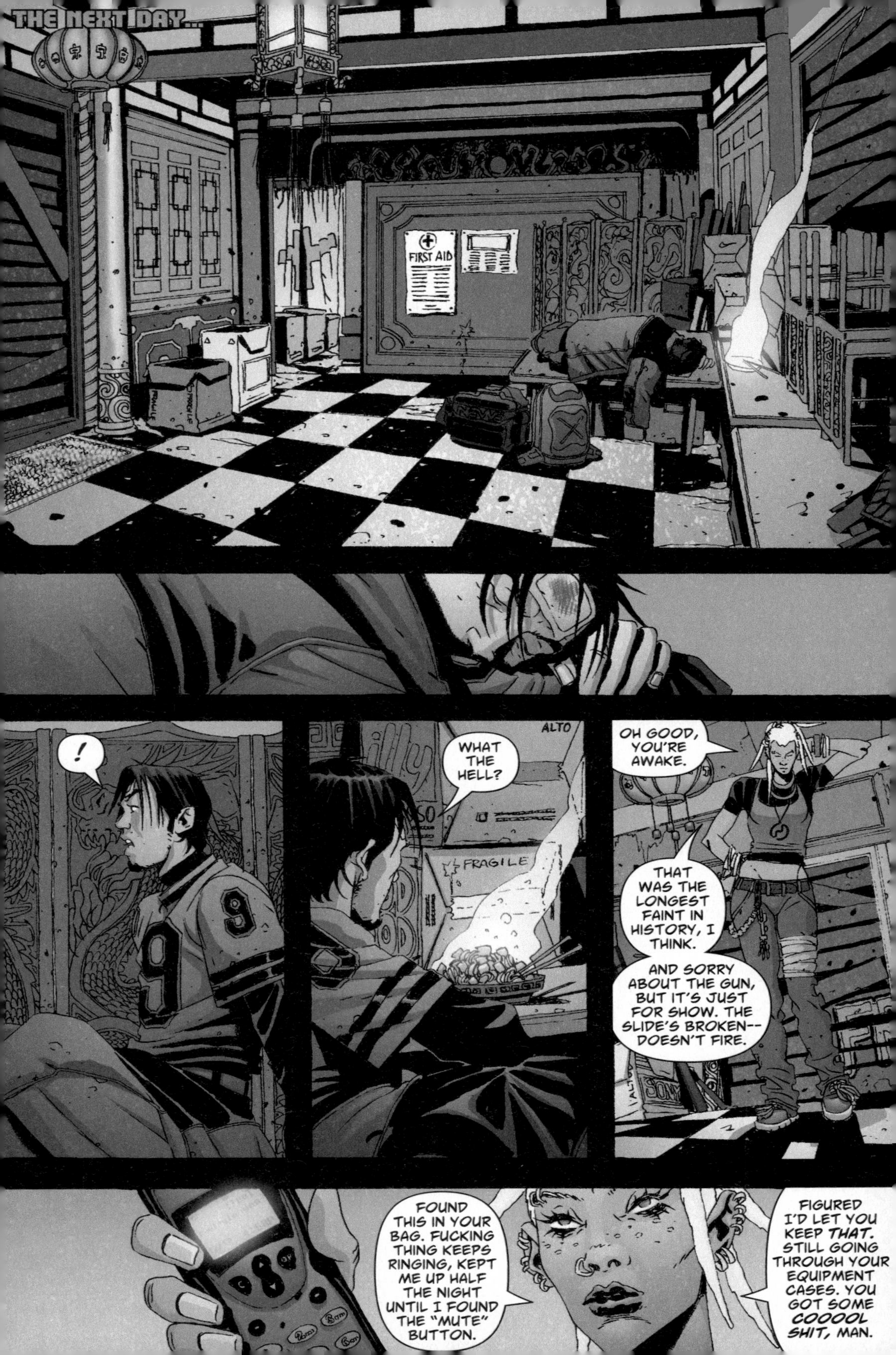
THE NEXT DAY...
FIRST AID
FRAGILE
!
WHAT THE HELL?
FRAGILE
ALTO
OH GOOD, YOU'RE AWAKE.
THAT WAS THE LONGEST FAINT IN HISTORY, I THINK.
AND SORRY ABOUT THE GUN, BUT IT'S JUST FOR SHOW. THE SLIDE'S BROKEN-- DOESN'T FIRE.
SONY
FOUND THIS IN YOUR BAG. FUCKING THING KEEPS RINGING, KEPT ME UP HALF THE NIGHT UNTIL I FOUND THE "MUTE" BUTTON.
FIGURED I'D LET YOU KEEP *THAT*. STILL GOING THROUGH YOUR EQUIPMENT CASES. YOU GOT SOME ***COOOOL SHIT,*** MAN.

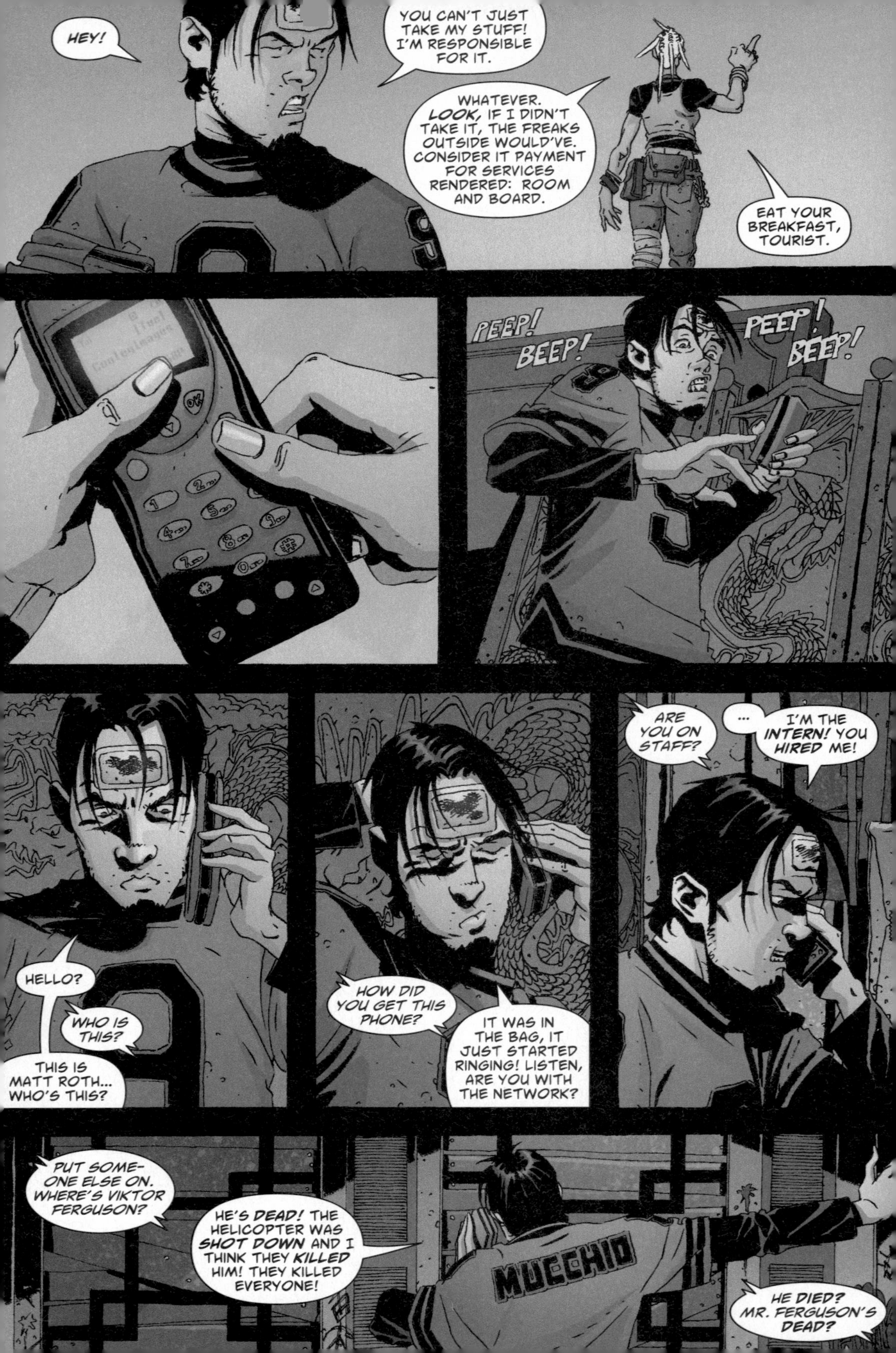
HEY!
YOU CAN'T JUST TAKE MY STUFF! I'M RESPONSIBLE FOR IT.
WHATEVER. LOOK, IF I DIDN'T TAKE IT, THE FREAKS OUTSIDE WOULD'VE. CONSIDER IT PAYMENT FOR SERVICES RENDERED: ROOM AND BOARD.
EAT YOUR BREAKFAST, TOURIST.
PEEP! BEEP!
PEEP! BEEP!
HELLO?
WHO IS THIS?
THIS IS MATT ROTH... WHO'S THIS?
HOW DID YOU GET THIS PHONE?
IT WAS IN THE BAG, IT JUST STARTED RINGING! LISTEN, ARE YOU WITH THE NETWORK?
ARE YOU ON STAFF?
...
I'M THE INTERN! YOU HIRED ME!
PUT SOME-ONE ELSE ON. WHERE'S VIKTOR FERGUSON?
HE'S DEAD! THE HELICOPTER WAS SHOT DOWN AND I THINK THEY KILLED HIM! THEY KILLED EVERYONE!
MUCCHIO
HE DIED? MR. FERGUSON'S DEAD?

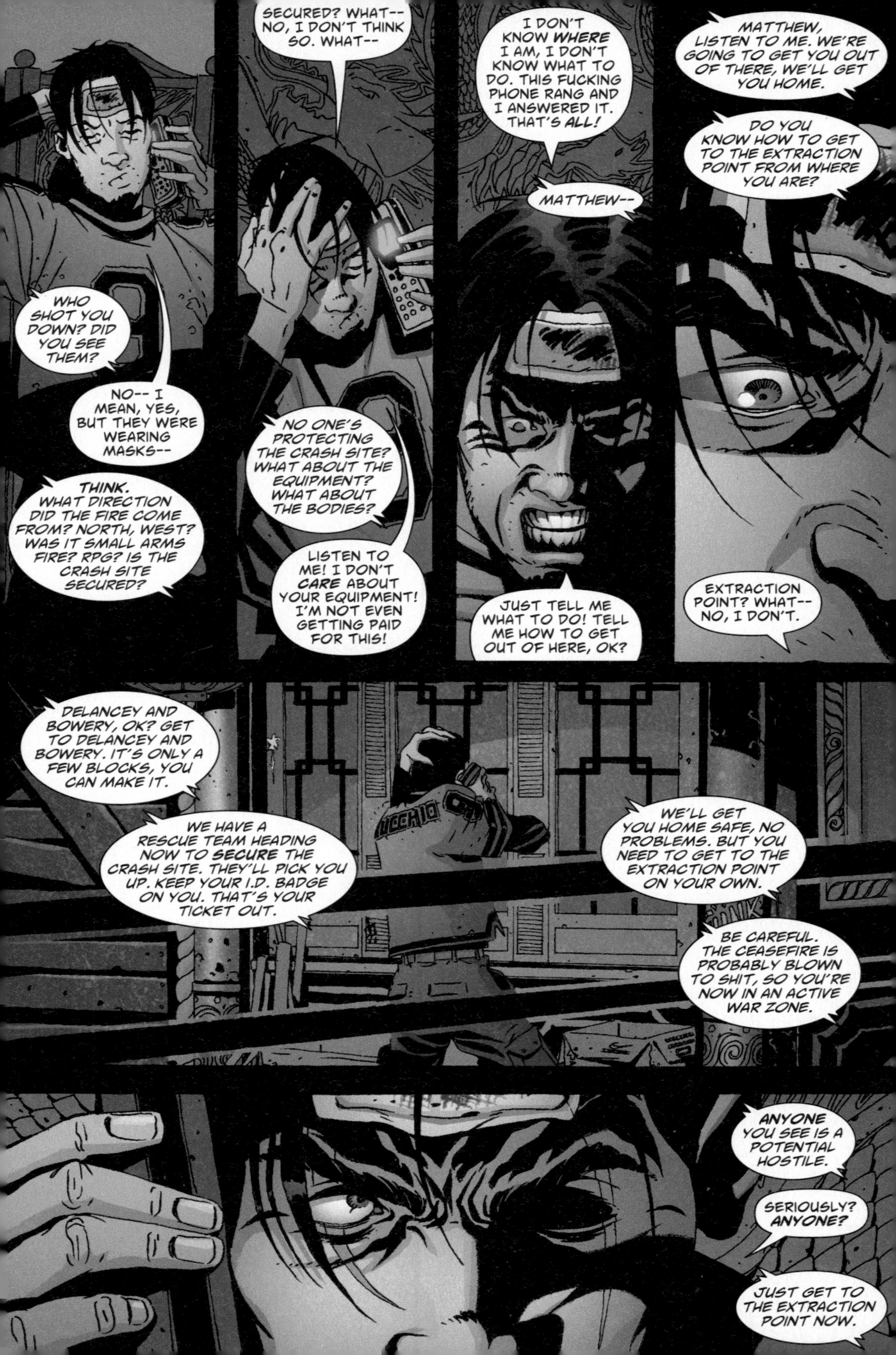
WHO SHOT YOU DOWN? DID YOU SEE THEM?
NO-- I MEAN, YES, BUT THEY WERE WEARING MASKS--
THINK. WHAT DIRECTION DID THE FIRE COME FROM? NORTH, WEST? WAS IT SMALL ARMS FIRE? RPG? IS THE CRASH SITE SECURED?
SECURED? WHAT-- NO, I DON'T THINK SO. WHAT--
NO ONE'S PROTECTING THE CRASH SITE? WHAT ABOUT THE EQUIPMENT? WHAT ABOUT THE BODIES?
LISTEN TO ME! I DON'T CARE ABOUT YOUR EQUIPMENT! I'M NOT EVEN GETTING PAID FOR THIS!
I DON'T KNOW WHERE I AM, I DON'T KNOW WHAT TO DO. THIS FUCKING PHONE RANG AND I ANSWERED IT. THAT'S ALL!
MATTHEW--
JUST TELL ME WHAT TO DO! TELL ME HOW TO GET OUT OF HERE, OK?
MATTHEW, LISTEN TO ME. WE'RE GOING TO GET YOU OUT OF THERE, WE'LL GET YOU HOME.
DO YOU KNOW HOW TO GET TO THE EXTRACTION POINT FROM WHERE YOU ARE?
EXTRACTION POINT? WHAT-- NO, I DON'T.
DELANCEY AND BOWERY, OK? GET TO DELANCEY AND BOWERY. IT'S ONLY A FEW BLOCKS, YOU CAN MAKE IT.
WE HAVE A RESCUE TEAM HEADING NOW TO SECURE THE CRASH SITE. THEY'LL PICK YOU UP. KEEP YOUR I.D. BADGE ON YOU. THAT'S YOUR TICKET OUT.
WE'LL GET YOU HOME SAFE, NO PROBLEMS. BUT YOU NEED TO GET TO THE EXTRACTION POINT ON YOUR OWN.
BE CAREFUL. THE CEASEFIRE IS PROBABLY BLOWN TO SHIT, SO YOU'RE NOW IN AN ACTIVE WAR ZONE.
ANYONE YOU SEE IS A POTENTIAL HOSTILE.
SERIOUSLY? ANYONE?
JUST GET TO THE EXTRACTION POINT NOW.

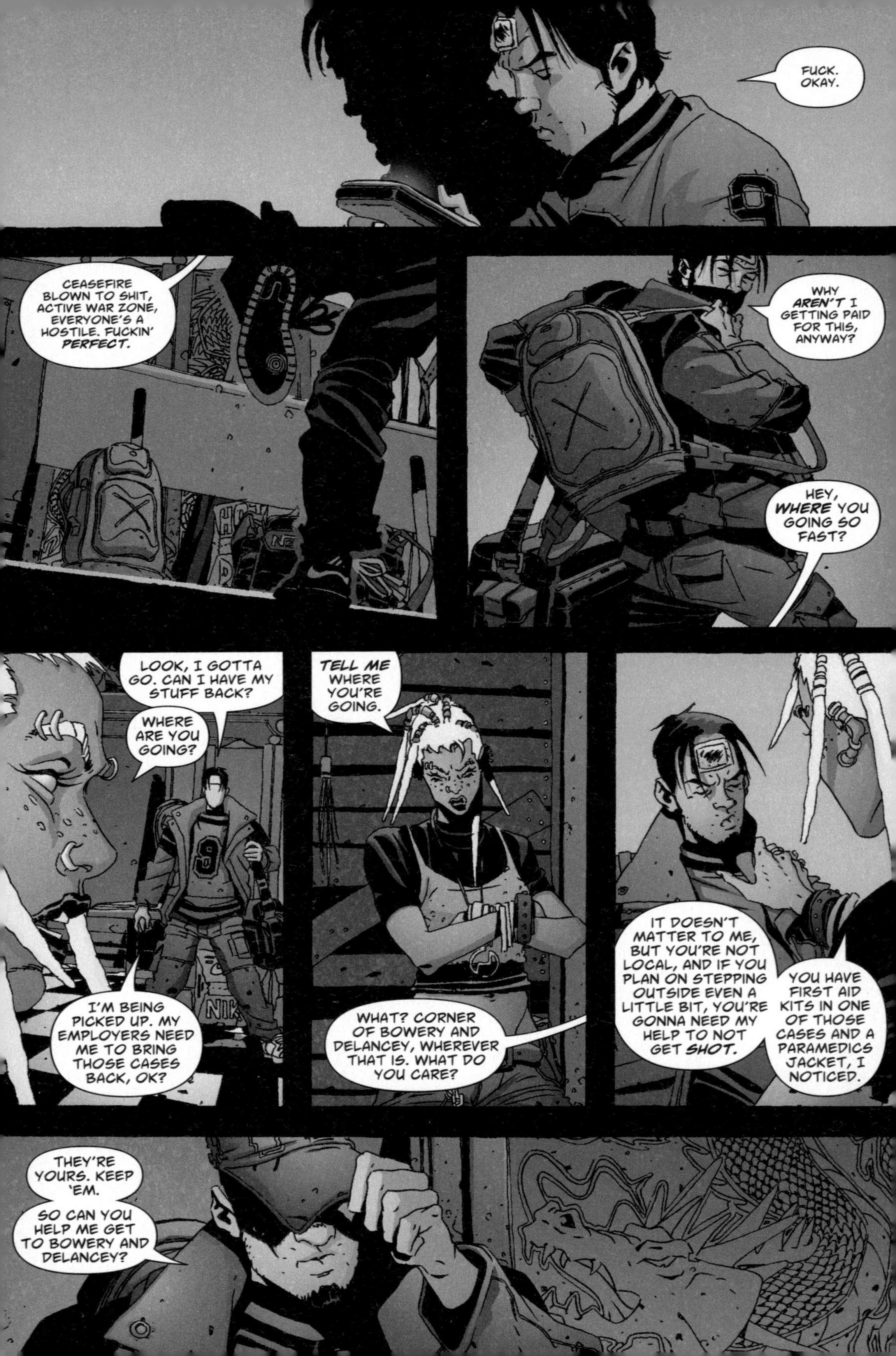
FUCK. OKAY.
CEASEFIRE BLOWN TO SHIT, ACTIVE WAR ZONE, EVERYONE'S A HOSTILE. FUCKIN' *PERFECT*.
WHY *AREN'T* I GETTING PAID FOR THIS, ANYWAY?
HEY, **WHERE** YOU GOING SO FAST?
LOOK, I GOTTA GO. CAN I HAVE MY STUFF BACK?
WHERE ARE YOU GOING?
I'M BEING PICKED UP. MY EMPLOYERS NEED ME TO BRING THOSE CASES BACK, OK?
TELL ME WHERE YOU'RE GOING.
WHAT? CORNER OF BOWERY AND DELANCEY, WHEREVER THAT IS. WHAT DO YOU CARE?
IT DOESN'T MATTER TO ME, BUT YOU'RE NOT LOCAL, AND IF YOU PLAN ON STEPPING OUTSIDE EVEN A LITTLE BIT, YOU'RE GONNA NEED MY HELP TO NOT GET *SHOT*.
YOU HAVE FIRST AID KITS IN ONE OF THOSE CASES AND A PARAMEDICS JACKET, I NOTICED.
THEY'RE YOURS. KEEP 'EM.
SO CAN YOU HELP ME GET TO BOWERY AND DELANCEY?

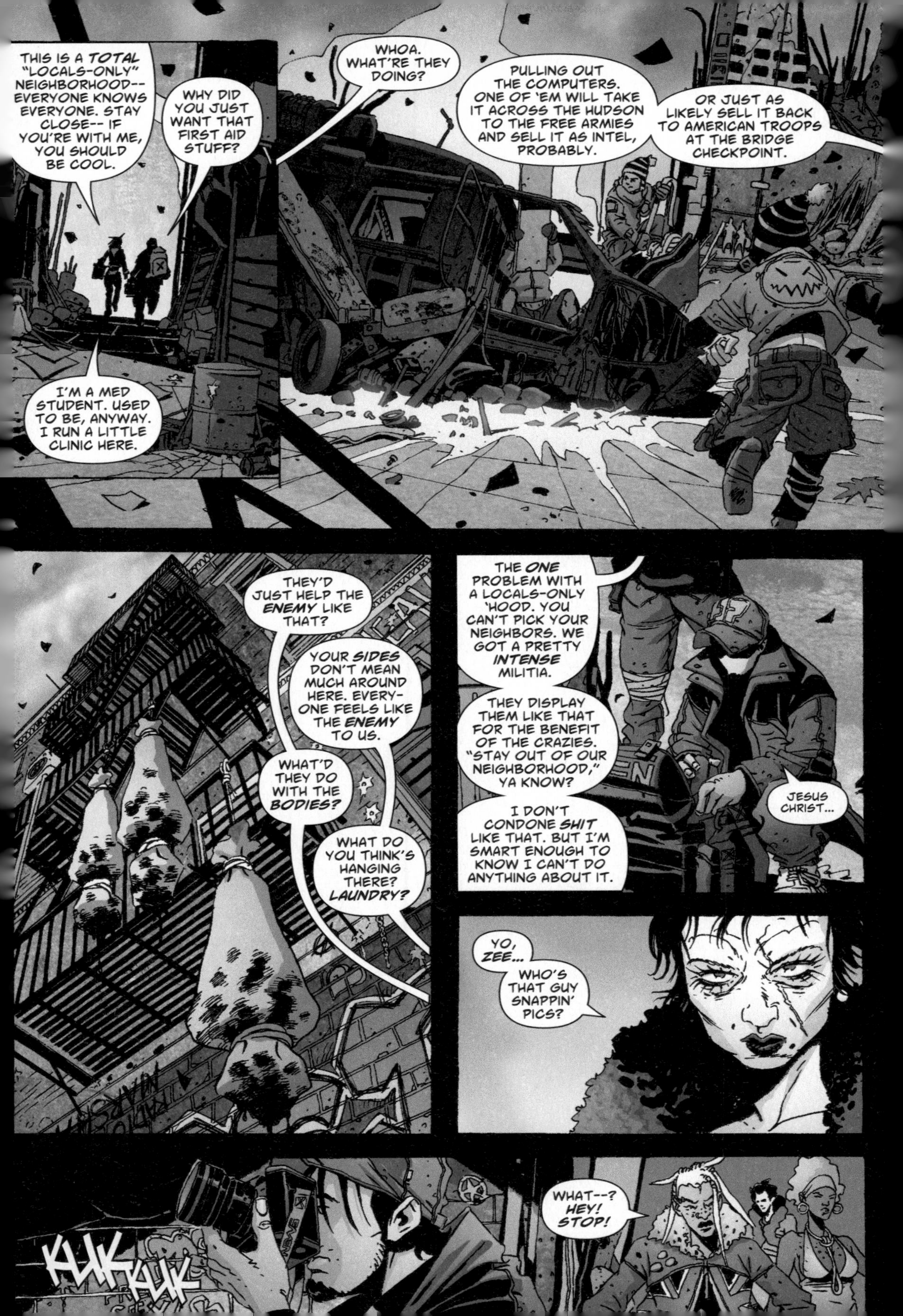
THIS IS A *TOTAL* "LOCALS-ONLY" NEIGHBORHOOD-- EVERYONE KNOWS EVERYONE. STAY CLOSE-- IF YOU'RE WITH ME, YOU SHOULD BE COOL.
WHY DID YOU JUST WANT THAT FIRST AID STUFF?
I'M A MED STUDENT. USED TO BE, ANYWAY. I RUN A LITTLE CLINIC HERE.
WHOA. WHAT'RE THEY DOING?
PULLING OUT THE COMPUTERS. ONE OF 'EM WILL TAKE IT ACROSS THE HUDSON TO THE FREE ARMIES AND SELL IT AS INTEL, PROBABLY.
OR JUST AS LIKELY SELL IT BACK TO AMERICAN TROOPS AT THE BRIDGE CHECKPOINT.
THEY'D JUST HELP THE *ENEMY* LIKE THAT?
YOUR *SIDES* DON'T MEAN MUCH AROUND HERE. EVERY-ONE FEELS LIKE THE *ENEMY* TO US.
WHAT'D THEY DO WITH THE *BODIES?*
WHAT DO YOU THINK'S HANGING THERE? *LAUNDRY?*
THE *ONE* PROBLEM WITH A LOCALS-ONLY 'HOOD. YOU CAN'T PICK YOUR NEIGHBORS. WE GOT A PRETTY *INTENSE* MILITIA.
THEY DISPLAY THEM LIKE THAT FOR THE BENEFIT OF THE CRAZIES. "STAY OUT OF OUR NEIGHBORHOOD," YA KNOW?
I DON'T CONDONE *SHIT* LIKE THAT. BUT I'M SMART ENOUGH TO KNOW I CAN'T DO ANYTHING ABOUT IT.
JESUS CHRIST...
YO, *ZEE*...
WHO'S THAT GUY SNAPPIN' PICS?
KLIK KLIK
WHAT--? *HEY! STOP!*

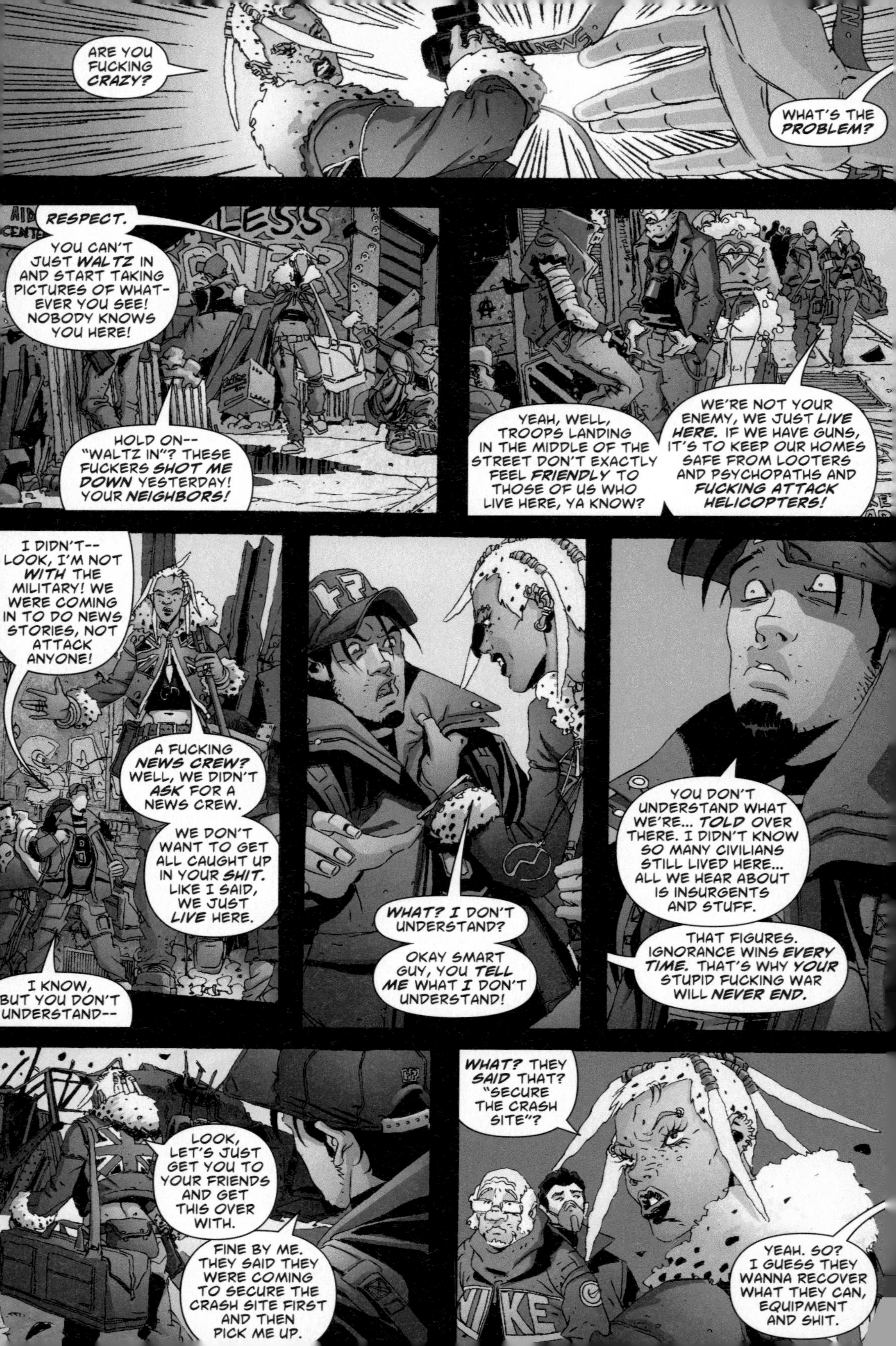
ARE YOU FUCKING CRAZY?
WHAT'S THE PROBLEM?
RESPECT.
YOU CAN'T JUST WALTZ IN AND START TAKING PICTURES OF WHATEVER YOU SEE! NOBODY KNOWS YOU HERE!
HOLD ON-- "WALTZ IN"? THESE FUCKERS SHOT ME DOWN YESTERDAY! YOUR NEIGHBORS!
YEAH, WELL, TROOPS LANDING IN THE MIDDLE OF THE STREET DON'T EXACTLY FEEL FRIENDLY TO THOSE OF US WHO LIVE HERE, YA KNOW?
WE'RE NOT YOUR ENEMY, WE JUST LIVE HERE. IF WE HAVE GUNS, IT'S TO KEEP OUR HOMES SAFE FROM LOOTERS AND PSYCHOPATHS AND FUCKING ATTACK HELICOPTERS!
I DIDN'T-- LOOK, I'M NOT WITH THE MILITARY! WE WERE COMING IN TO DO NEWS STORIES, NOT ATTACK ANYONE!
A FUCKING NEWS CREW? WELL, WE DIDN'T ASK FOR A NEWS CREW.
WE DON'T WANT TO GET ALL CAUGHT UP IN YOUR SHIT. LIKE I SAID, WE JUST LIVE HERE.
I KNOW, BUT YOU DON'T UNDERSTAND--
WHAT? I DON'T UNDERSTAND?
OKAY SMART GUY, YOU TELL ME WHAT I DON'T UNDERSTAND!
YOU DON'T UNDERSTAND WHAT WE'RE... TOLD OVER THERE. I DIDN'T KNOW SO MANY CIVILIANS STILL LIVED HERE... ALL WE HEAR ABOUT IS INSURGENTS AND STUFF.
THAT FIGURES. IGNORANCE WINS EVERY TIME. THAT'S WHY YOUR STUPID FUCKING WAR WILL NEVER END.
LOOK, LET'S JUST GET YOU TO YOUR FRIENDS AND GET THIS OVER WITH.
FINE BY ME. THEY SAID THEY WERE COMING TO SECURE THE CRASH SITE FIRST AND THEN PICK ME UP.
WHAT? THEY SAID THAT? "SECURE THE CRASH SITE"?
YEAH. SO? I GUESS THEY WANNA RECOVER WHAT THEY CAN, EQUIPMENT AND SHIT.

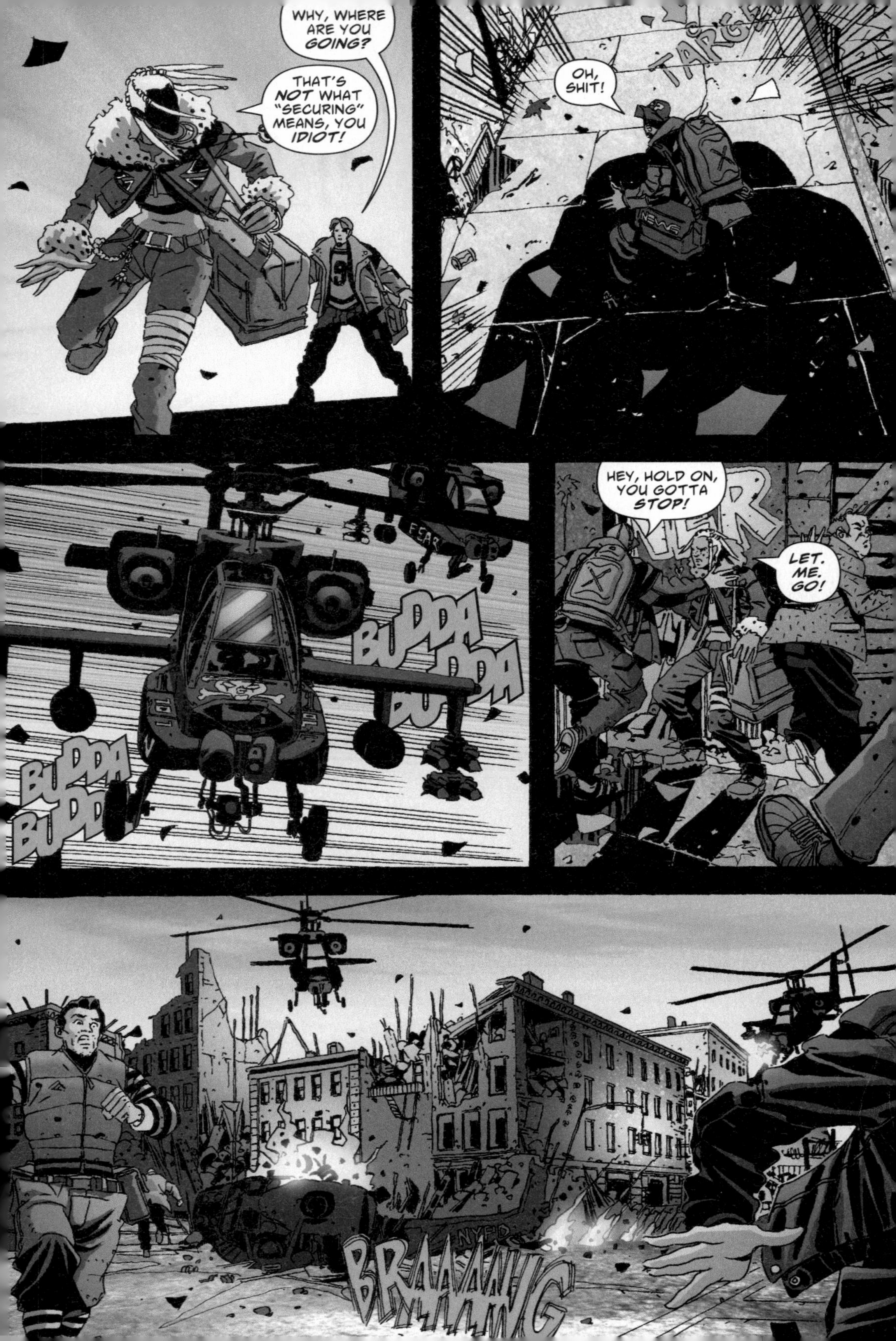

WHY, WHERE ARE YOU GOING?
THAT'S NOT WHAT "SECURING" MEANS, YOU IDIOT!
OH, SHIT!
BUDDA BUDDA
BUDDA BUDDA
HEY, HOLD ON, YOU GOTTA STOP!
LET. ME. GO!
BRAAAANG

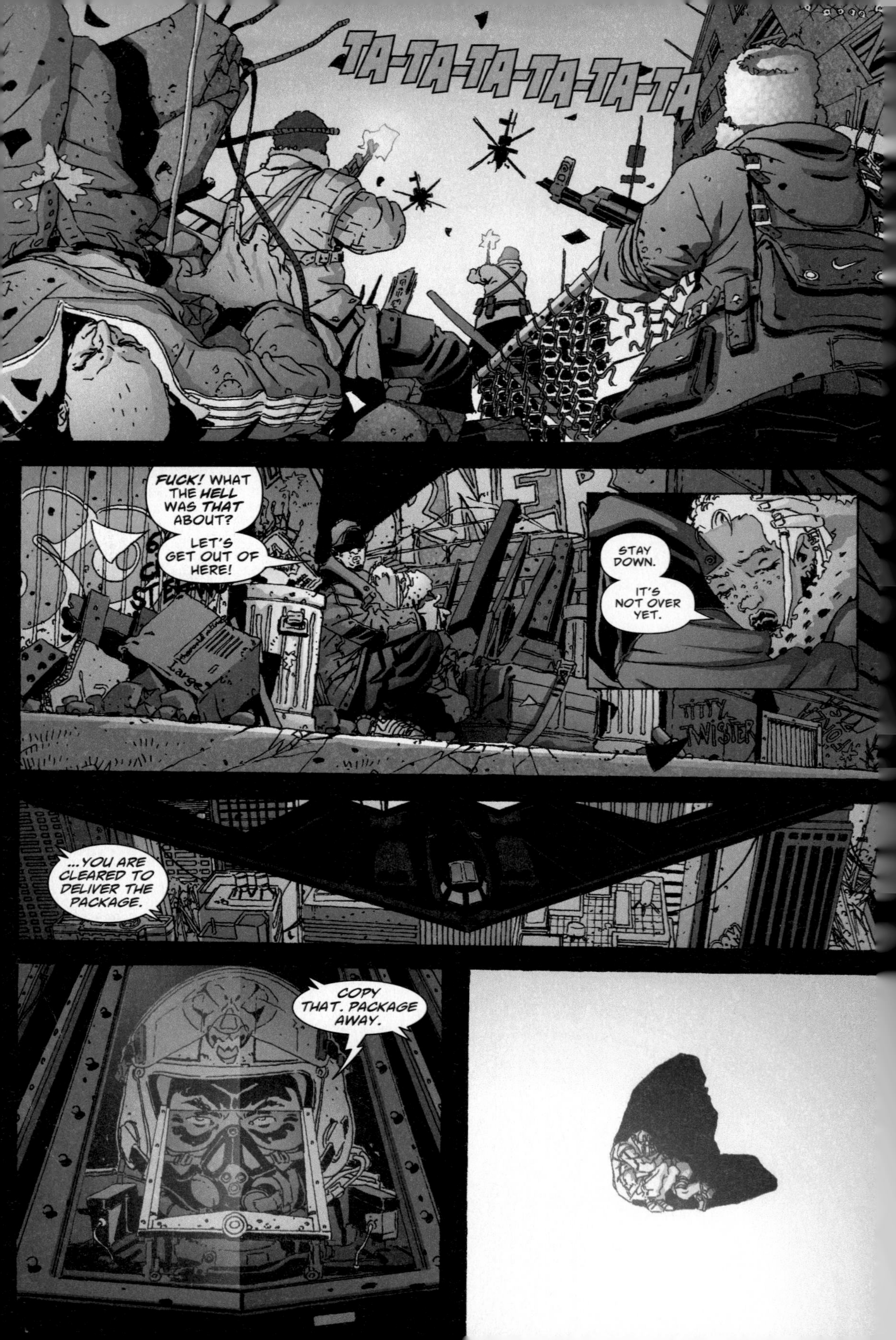
TA-TA-TA-TA-TA-TA
FUCK! WHAT THE HELL WAS THAT ABOUT?
LET'S GET OUT OF HERE!
STAY DOWN.
IT'S NOT OVER YET.
TITTY TWISTER
...YOU ARE CLEARED TO DELIVER THE PACKAGE.
COPY THAT. PACKAGE AWAY.

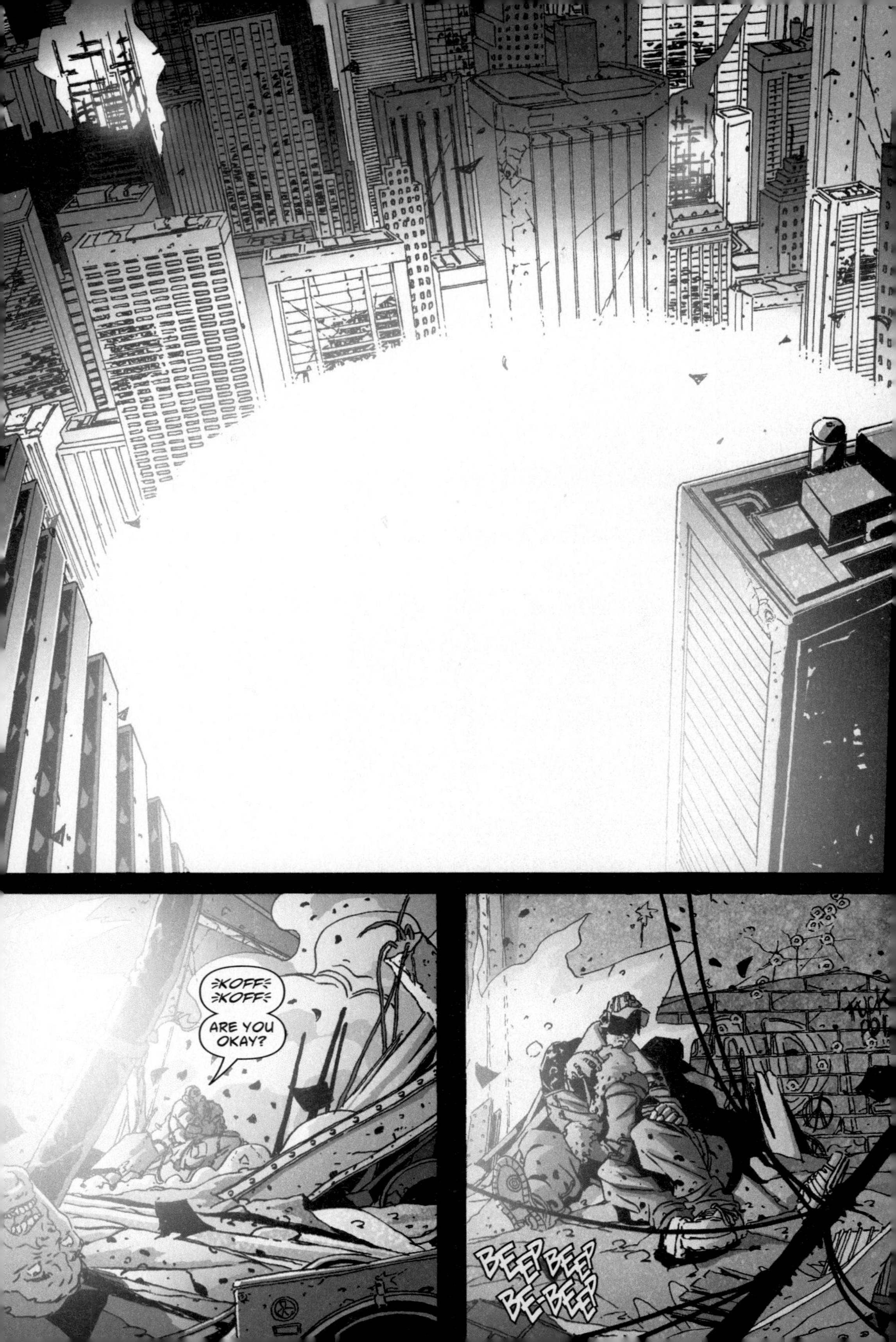

KOFF KOFF
ARE YOU OKAY?
BEEP BEEP BE-BEEP

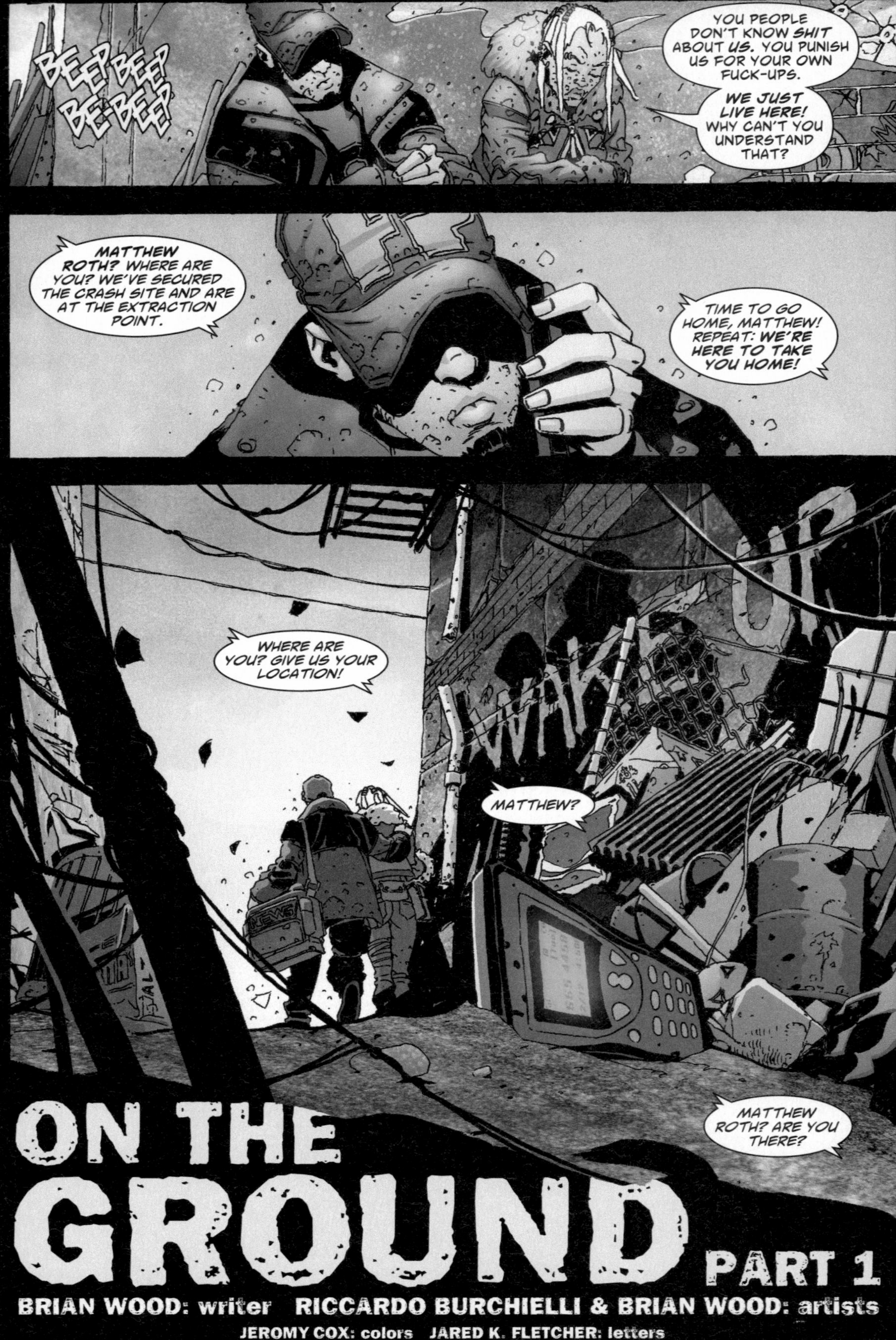
BEEP BEEP BE-BEEP
YOU PEOPLE DON'T KNOW SHIT ABOUT US. YOU PUNISH US FOR YOUR OWN FUCK-UPS.
WE JUST LIVE HERE! WHY CAN'T YOU UNDERSTAND THAT?
MATTHEW ROTH? WHERE ARE YOU? WE'VE SECURED THE CRASH SITE AND ARE AT THE EXTRACTION POINT.
TIME TO GO HOME, MATTHEW! REPEAT: WE'RE HERE TO TAKE YOU HOME!
WHERE ARE YOU? GIVE US YOUR LOCATION!
MATTHEW?
MATTHEW ROTH? ARE YOU THERE?
ON THE GROUND PART 1
BRIAN WOOD: writer RICCARDO BURCHIELLI & BRIAN WOOD: artists
JEROMY COX: colors JARED K. FLETCHER: letters

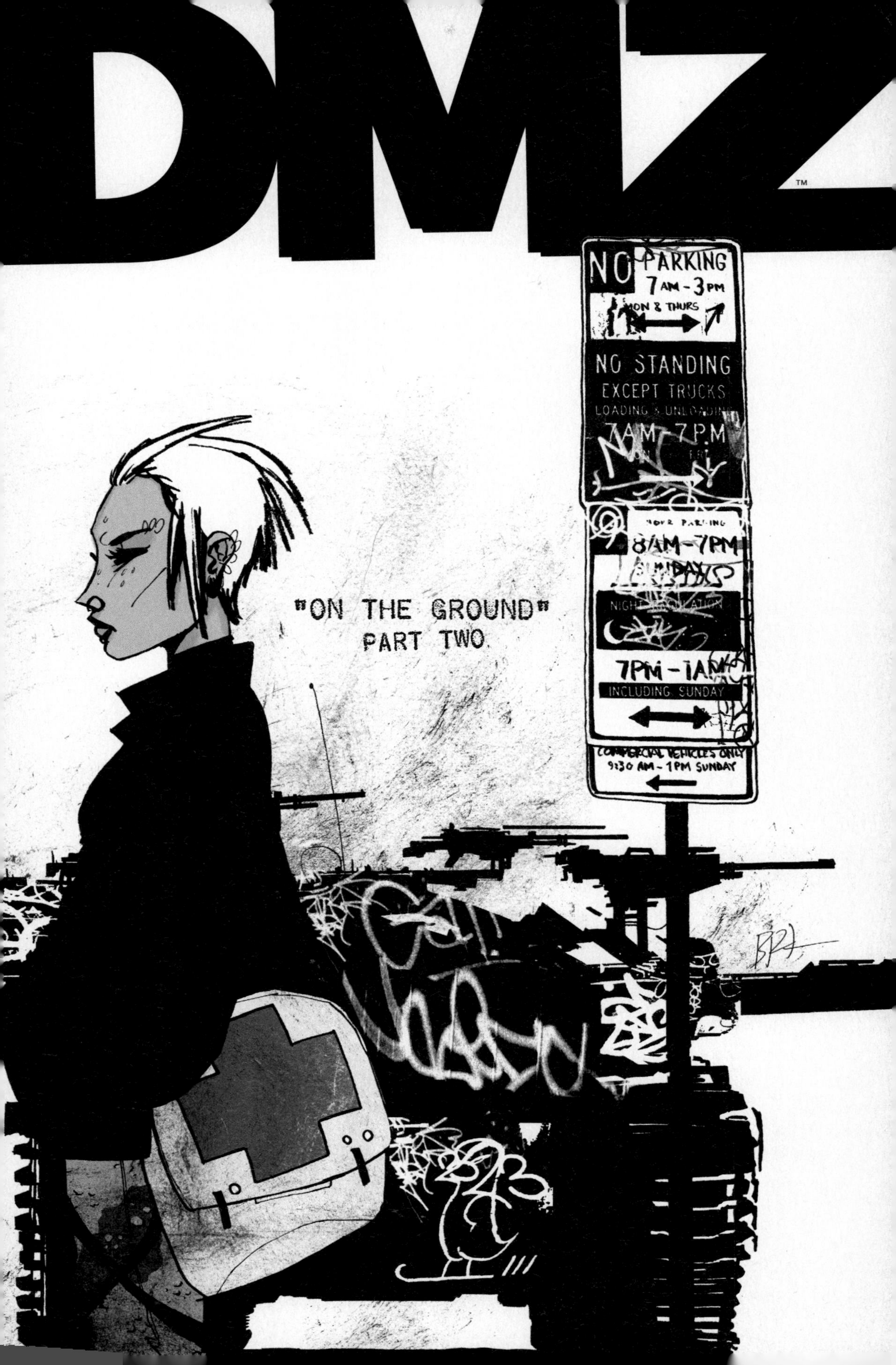
DMZ™
"ON THE GROUND"
PART TWO
NO PARKING
7AM - 3PM
MON & THURS
NO STANDING
EXCEPT TRUCKS
7AM-7PM
8AM-7PM
7PM-1AM
INCLUDING SUNDAY
COMMERCIAL VEHICLES ONLY
9:30 AM - 1PM SUNDAY

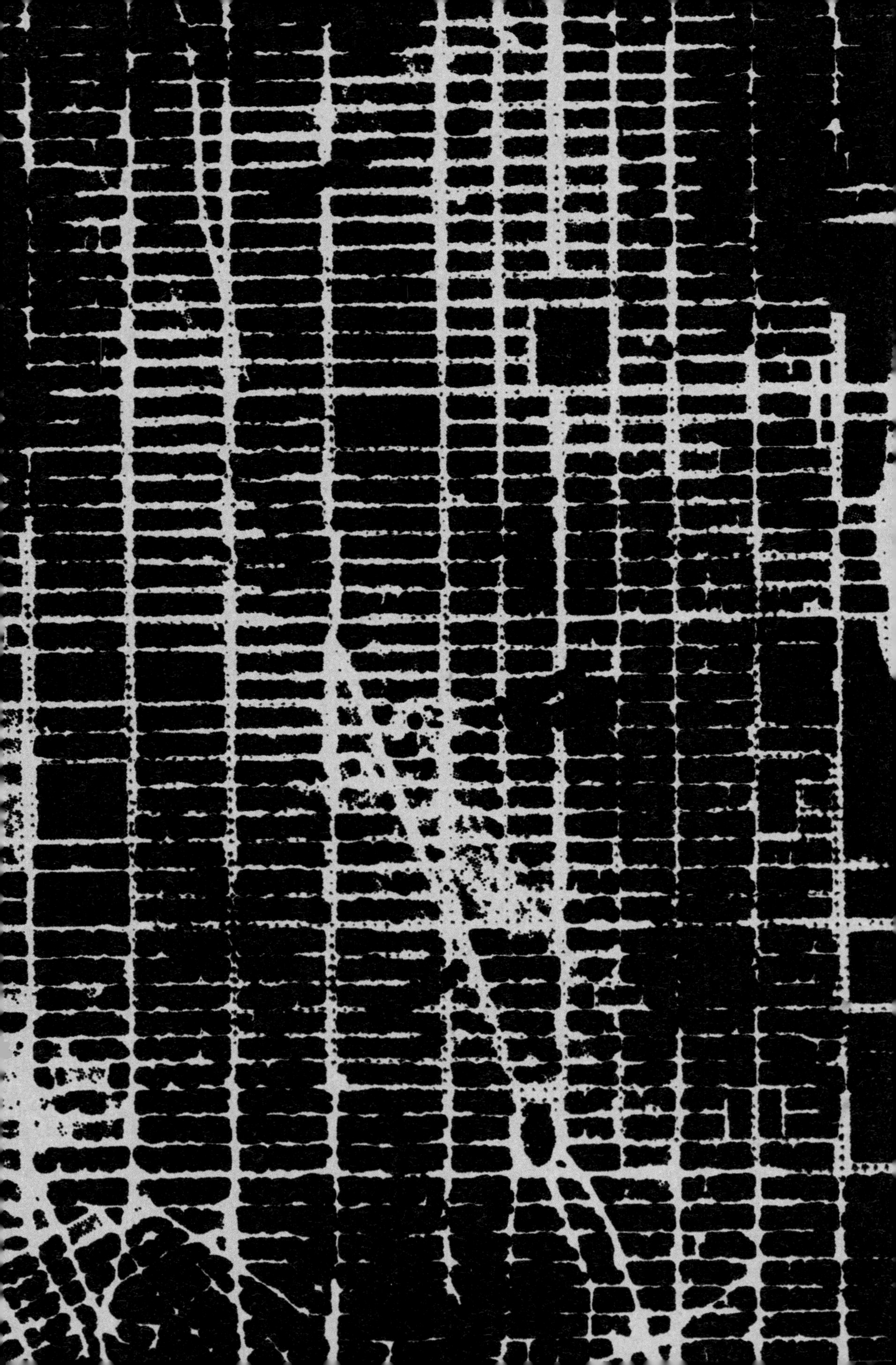

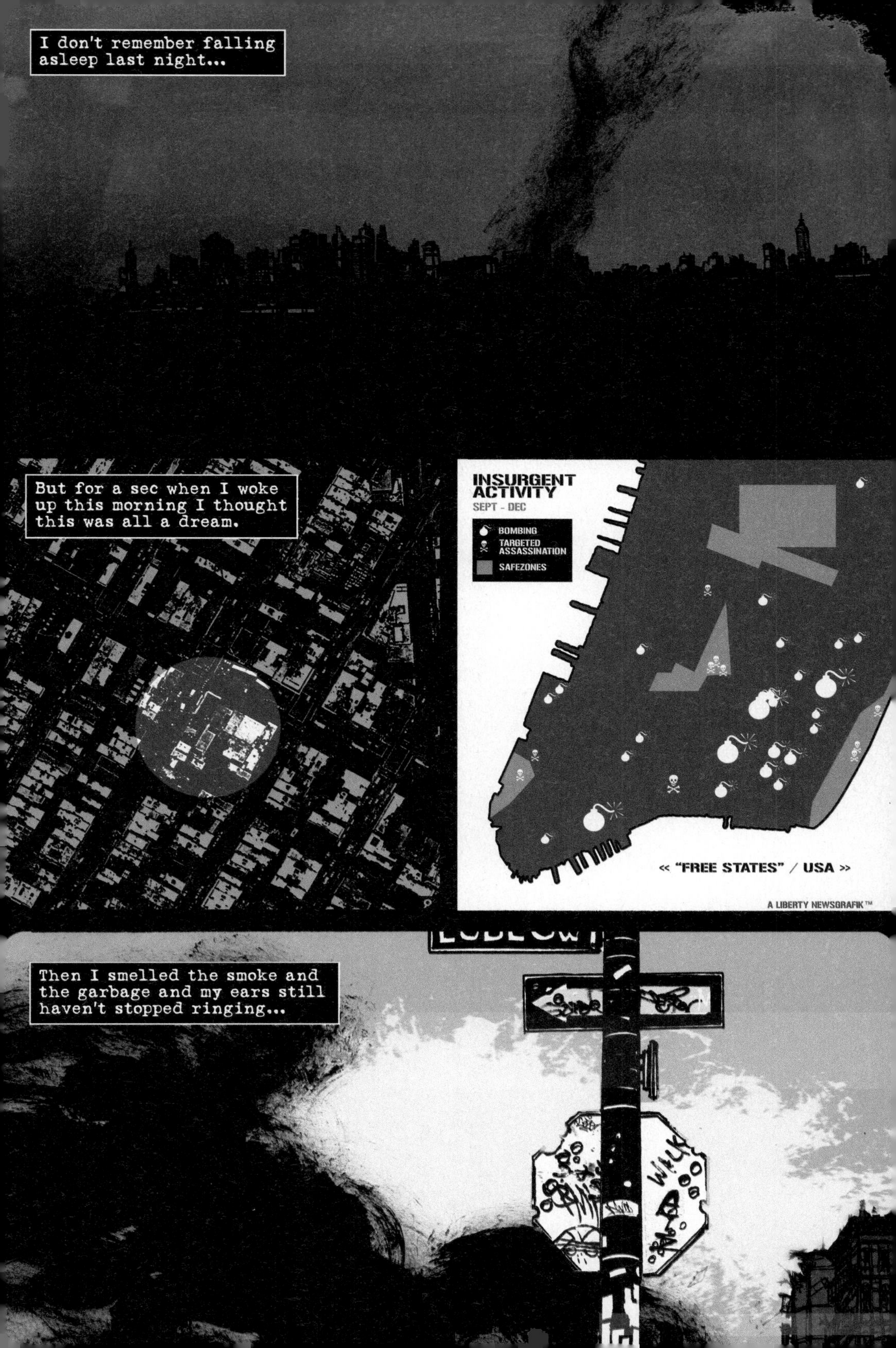
I don't remember falling asleep last night...
But for a sec when I woke up this morning I thought this was all a dream.
INSURGENT ACTIVITY
SEPT - DEC
BOMBING
TARGETED ASSASSINATION
SAFEZONES
« "FREE STATES" / USA »
A LIBERTY NEWSGRAFIK™
Then I smelled the smoke and the garbage and my ears still haven't stopped ringing...

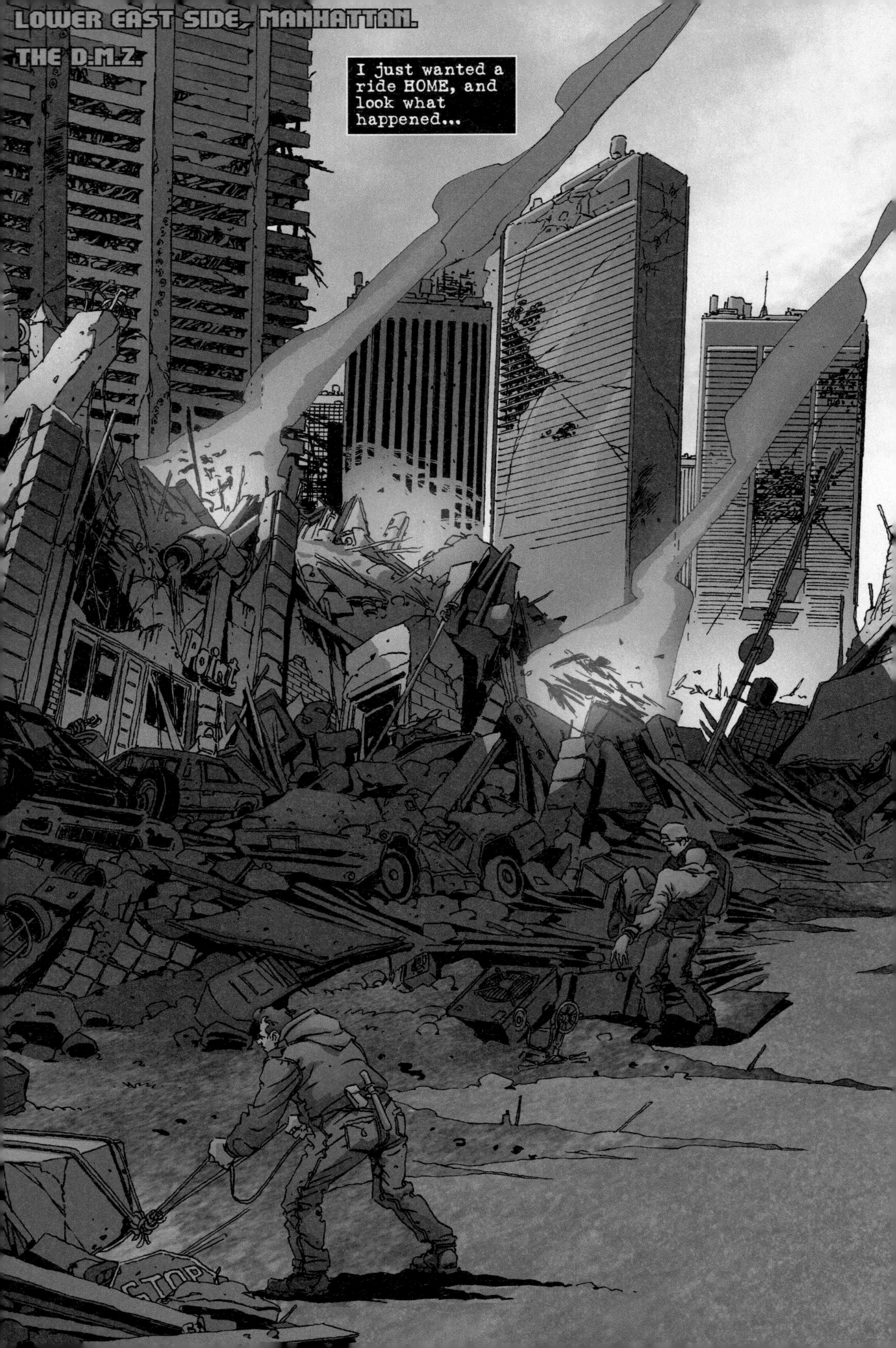
LOWER EAST SIDE, MANHATTAN.
THE D.M.Z.
I just wanted a ride HOME, and look what happened...
Point

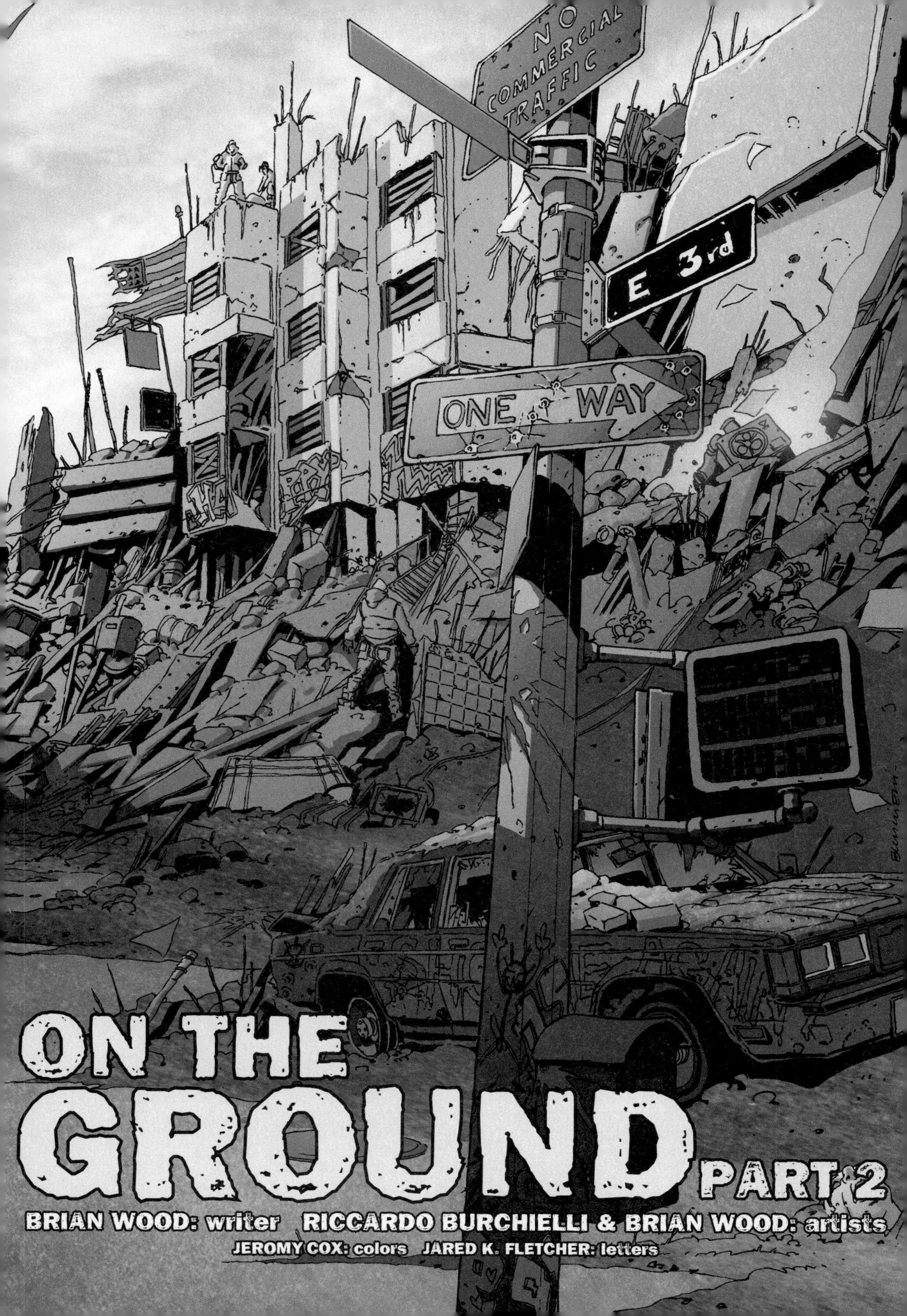
NO COMMERCIAL TRAFFIC
E 3rd
ONE WAY

ON THE GROUND PART 2

BRIAN WOOD: writer RICCARDO BURCHIELLI & BRIAN WOOD: artists
JEROMY COX: colors JARED K. FLETCHER: letters

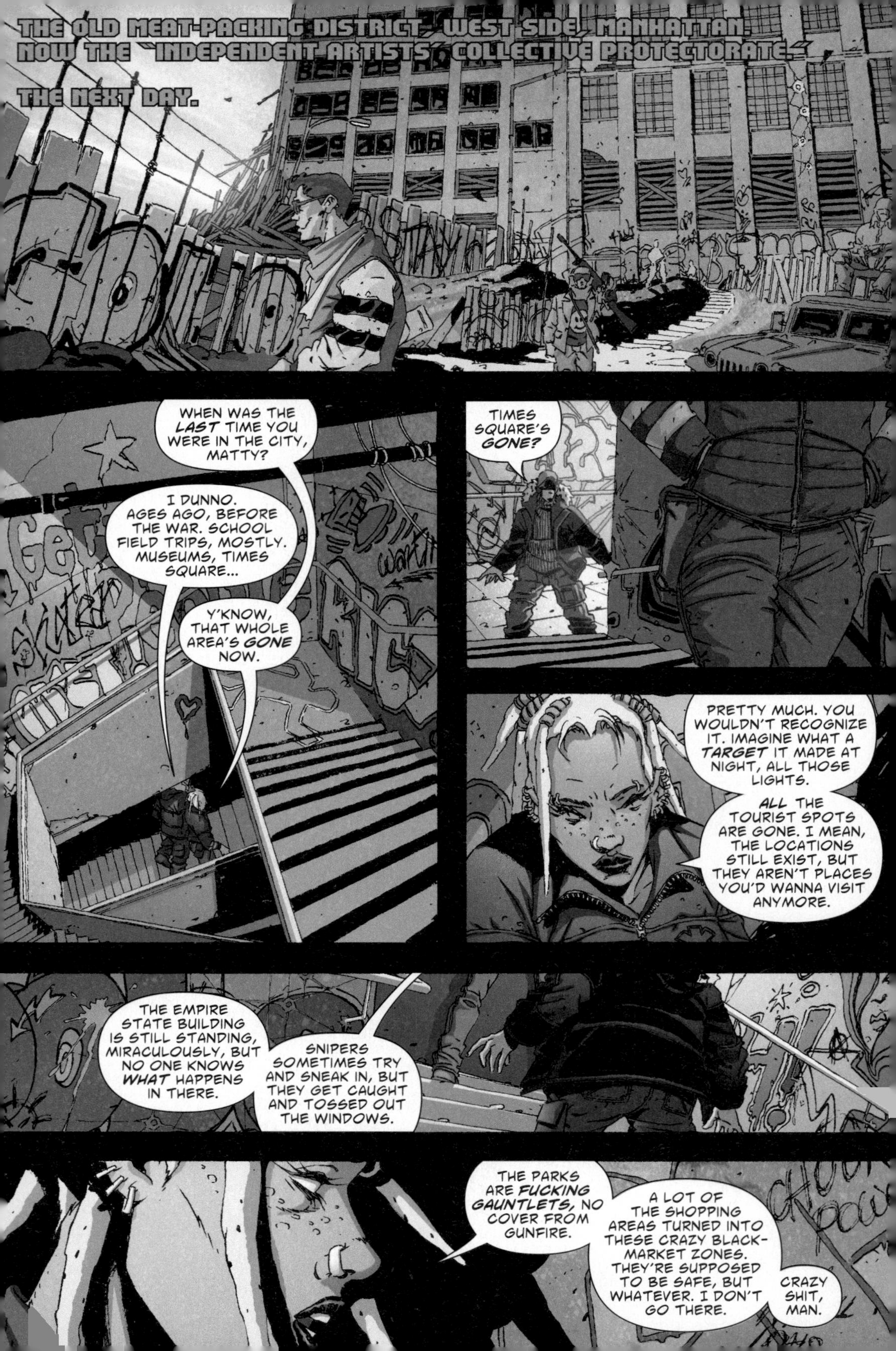
THE OLD MEAT-PACKING DISTRICT, WEST SIDE, MANHATTAN. NOW THE "INDEPENDENT ARTISTS' COLLECTIVE PROTECTORATE."
THE NEXT DAY.
WHEN WAS THE LAST TIME YOU WERE IN THE CITY, MATTY?
I DUNNO. AGES AGO, BEFORE THE WAR. SCHOOL FIELD TRIPS, MOSTLY. MUSEUMS, TIMES SQUARE...
Y'KNOW, THAT WHOLE AREA'S GONE NOW.
TIMES SQUARE'S GONE?
PRETTY MUCH. YOU WOULDN'T RECOGNIZE IT. IMAGINE WHAT A TARGET IT MADE AT NIGHT, ALL THOSE LIGHTS.
ALL THE TOURIST SPOTS ARE GONE. I MEAN, THE LOCATIONS STILL EXIST, BUT THEY AREN'T PLACES YOU'D WANNA VISIT ANYMORE.
THE EMPIRE STATE BUILDING IS STILL STANDING, MIRACULOUSLY, BUT NO ONE KNOWS WHAT HAPPENS IN THERE.
SNIPERS SOMETIMES TRY AND SNEAK IN, BUT THEY GET CAUGHT AND TOSSED OUT THE WINDOWS.
THE PARKS ARE FUCKING GAUNTLETS, NO COVER FROM GUNFIRE.
A LOT OF THE SHOPPING AREAS TURNED INTO THESE CRAZY BLACK-MARKET ZONES. THEY'RE SUPPOSED TO BE SAFE, BUT WHATEVER. I DON'T GO THERE.
CRAZY SHIT, MAN.

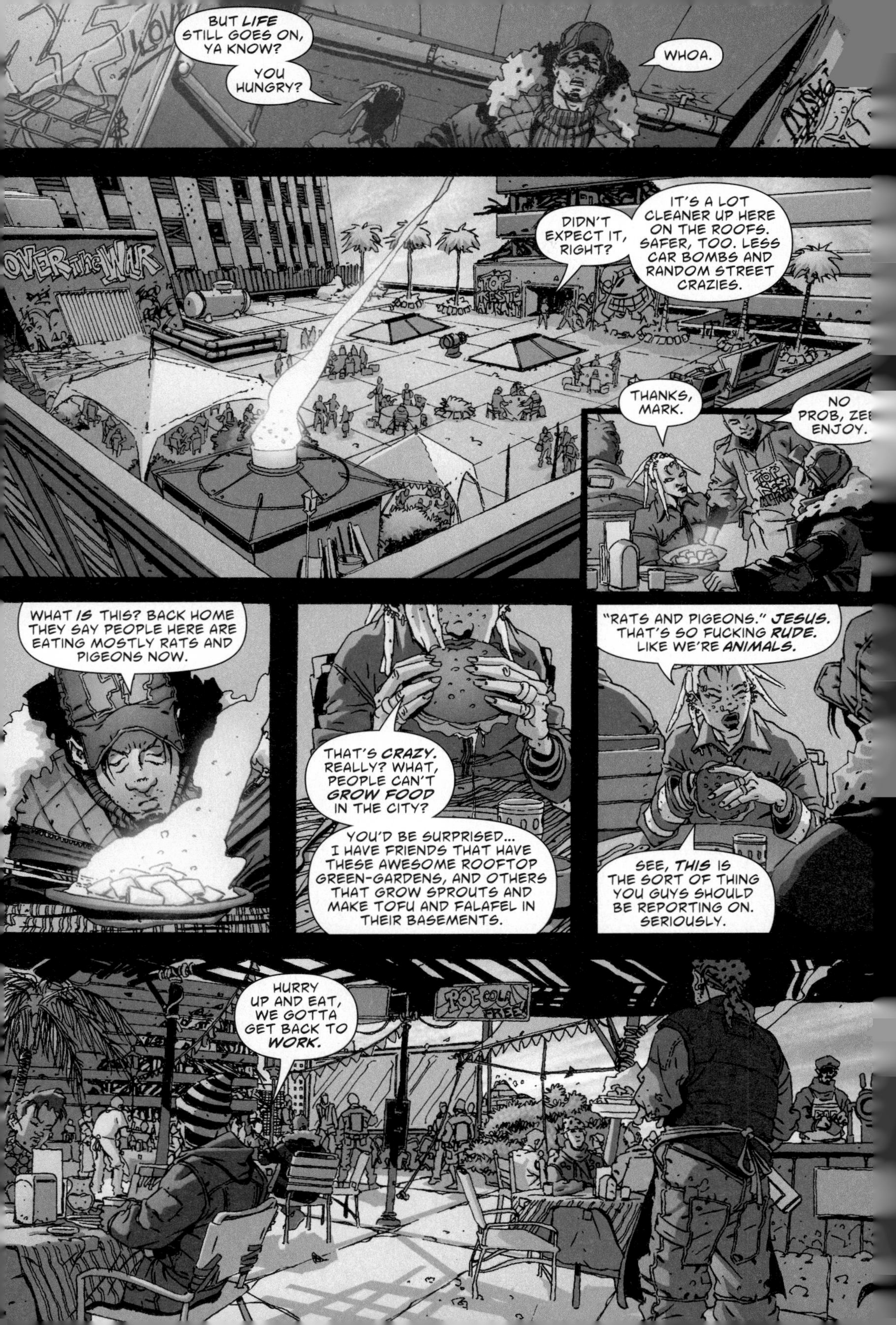
BUT *LIFE* STILL GOES ON, YA KNOW?
YOU HUNGRY?
WHOA.
DIDN'T EXPECT IT, RIGHT?
IT'S A LOT CLEANER UP HERE ON THE ROOFS. SAFER, TOO. LESS CAR BOMBS AND RANDOM STREET CRAZIES.
OVER the WAR
THANKS, MARK.
NO PROB, ZEE ENJOY.
WHAT *IS* THIS? BACK HOME THEY SAY PEOPLE HERE ARE EATING MOSTLY RATS AND PIGEONS NOW.
THAT'S *CRAZY.* REALLY? WHAT, PEOPLE CAN'T *GROW FOOD* IN THE CITY?
YOU'D BE SURPRISED... I HAVE FRIENDS THAT HAVE THESE AWESOME ROOFTOP GREEN-GARDENS, AND OTHERS THAT GROW SPROUTS AND MAKE TOFU AND FALAFEL IN THEIR BASEMENTS.
"RATS AND PIGEONS." *JESUS.* THAT'S SO FUCKING *RUDE.* LIKE WE'RE *ANIMALS.*
SEE, *THIS* IS THE SORT OF THING YOU GUYS SHOULD BE REPORTING ON. SERIOUSLY.
HURRY UP AND EAT, WE GOTTA GET BACK TO *WORK.*
POP COLA FREE

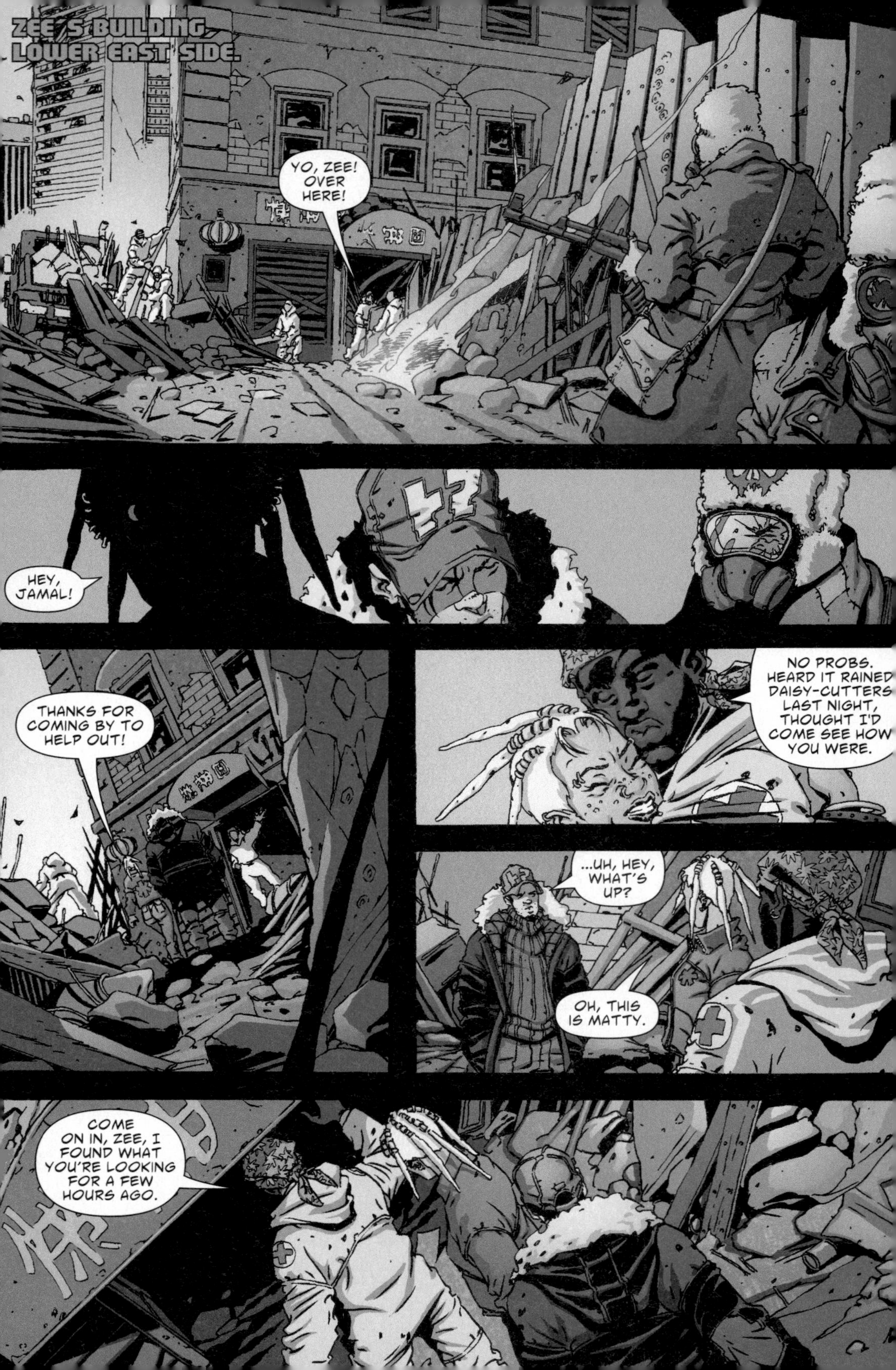
ZEE'S BUILDING, LOWER EAST SIDE.
YO, ZEE! OVER HERE!
HEY, JAMAL!
THANKS FOR COMING BY TO HELP OUT!
NO PROBS. HEARD IT RAINED DAISY-CUTTERS LAST NIGHT, THOUGHT I'D COME SEE HOW YOU WERE.
...UH, HEY, WHAT'S UP?
OH, THIS IS MATTY.
COME ON IN, ZEE, I FOUND WHAT YOU'RE LOOKING FOR A FEW HOURS AGO.

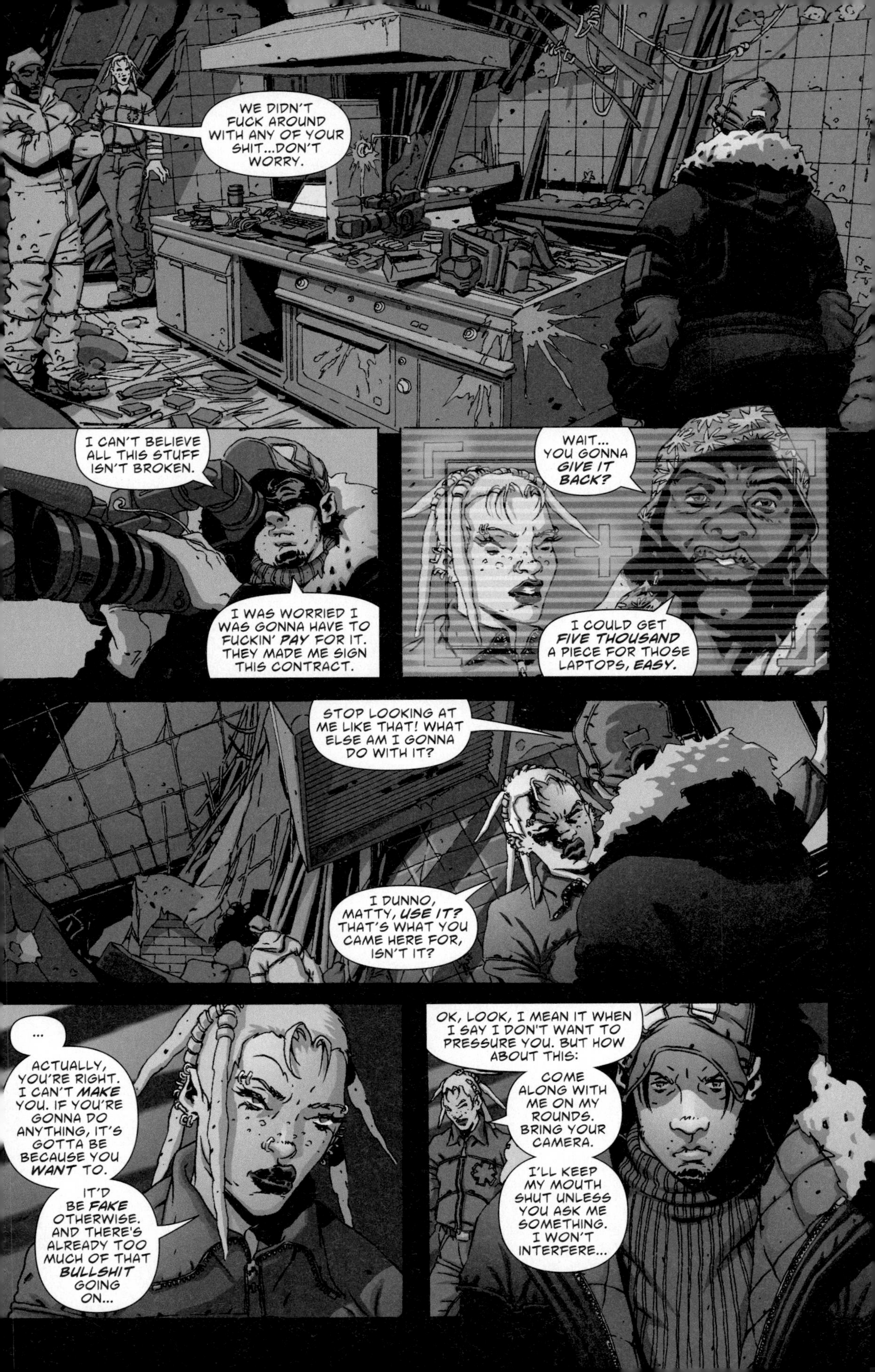

WE DIDN'T FUCK AROUND WITH ANY OF YOUR SHIT...DON'T WORRY.
I CAN'T BELIEVE ALL THIS STUFF ISN'T BROKEN.
I WAS WORRIED I WAS GONNA HAVE TO FUCKIN' PAY FOR IT. THEY MADE ME SIGN THIS CONTRACT.
WAIT... YOU GONNA GIVE IT BACK?
I COULD GET FIVE THOUSAND A PIECE FOR THOSE LAPTOPS, EASY.
STOP LOOKING AT ME LIKE THAT! WHAT ELSE AM I GONNA DO WITH IT?
I DUNNO, MATTY, USE IT? THAT'S WHAT YOU CAME HERE FOR, ISN'T IT?
...
ACTUALLY, YOU'RE RIGHT. I CAN'T MAKE YOU. IF YOU'RE GONNA DO ANYTHING, IT'S GOTTA BE BECAUSE YOU WANT TO.
IT'D BE FAKE OTHERWISE. AND THERE'S ALREADY TOO MUCH OF THAT BULLSHIT GOING ON...
OK, LOOK, I MEAN IT WHEN I SAY I DON'T WANT TO PRESSURE YOU. BUT HOW ABOUT THIS:
COME ALONG WITH ME ON MY ROUNDS. BRING YOUR CAMERA.
I'LL KEEP MY MOUTH SHUT UNLESS YOU ASK ME SOMETHING. I WON'T INTERFERE...

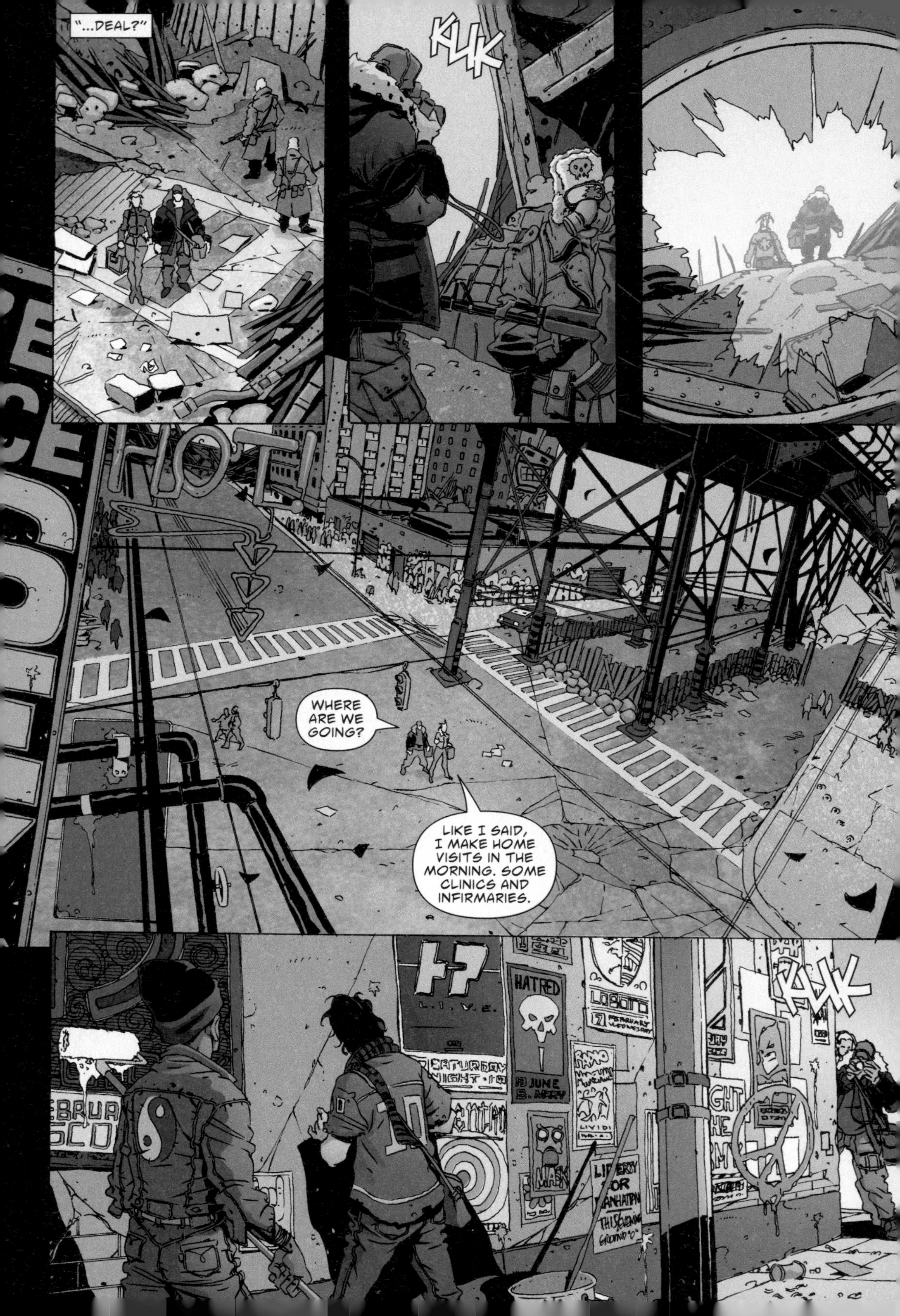
"...DEAL?"
KUK
WHERE ARE WE GOING?
LIKE I SAID, I MAKE HOME VISITS IN THE MORNING. SOME CLINICS AND INFIRMARIES.
KUK

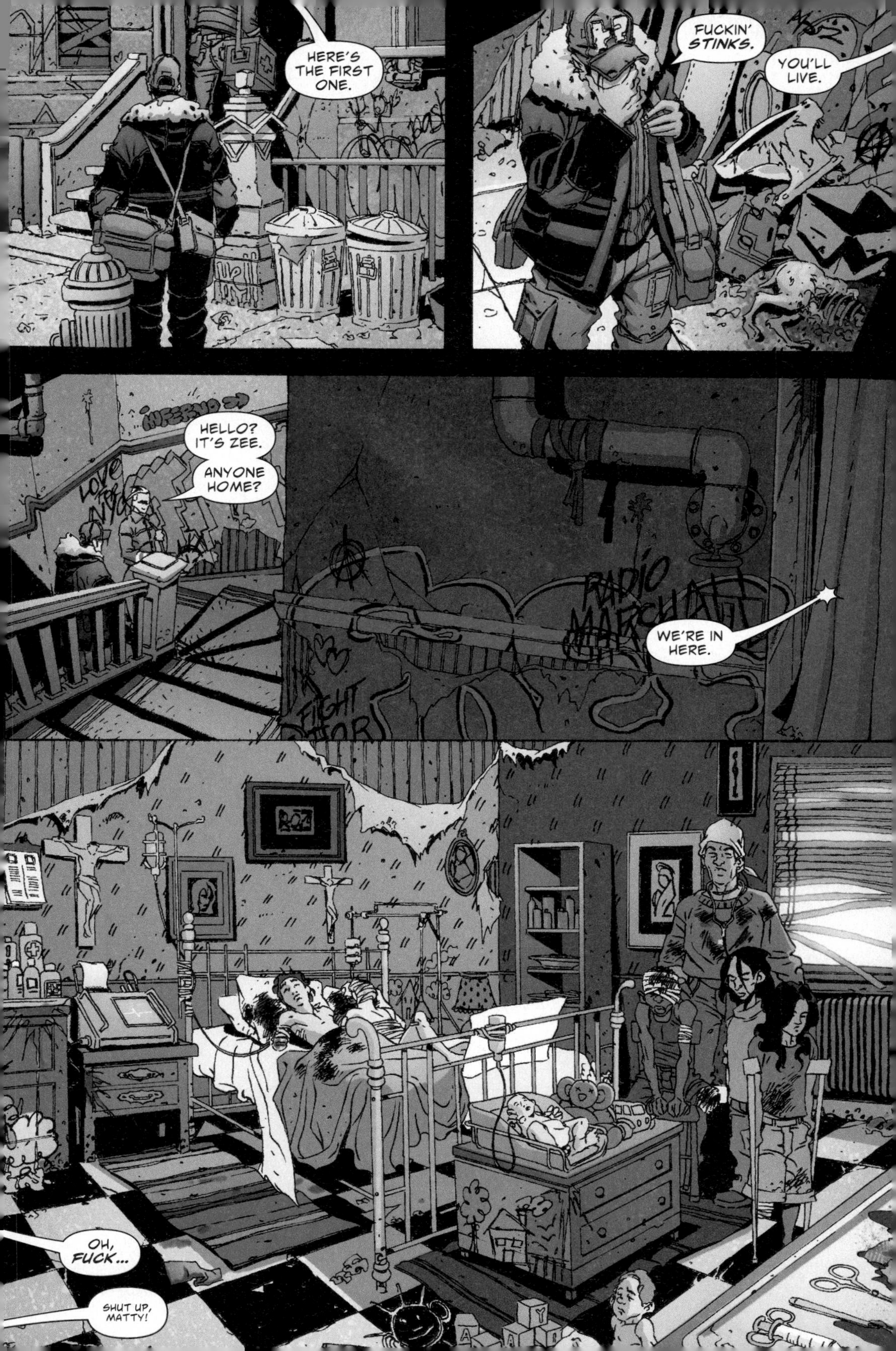
HERE'S THE FIRST ONE.
FUCKIN' STINKS.
YOU'LL LIVE.
HELLO? IT'S ZEE.
ANYONE HOME?
WE'RE IN HERE.
OH, FUCK...
SHUT UP, MATTY!

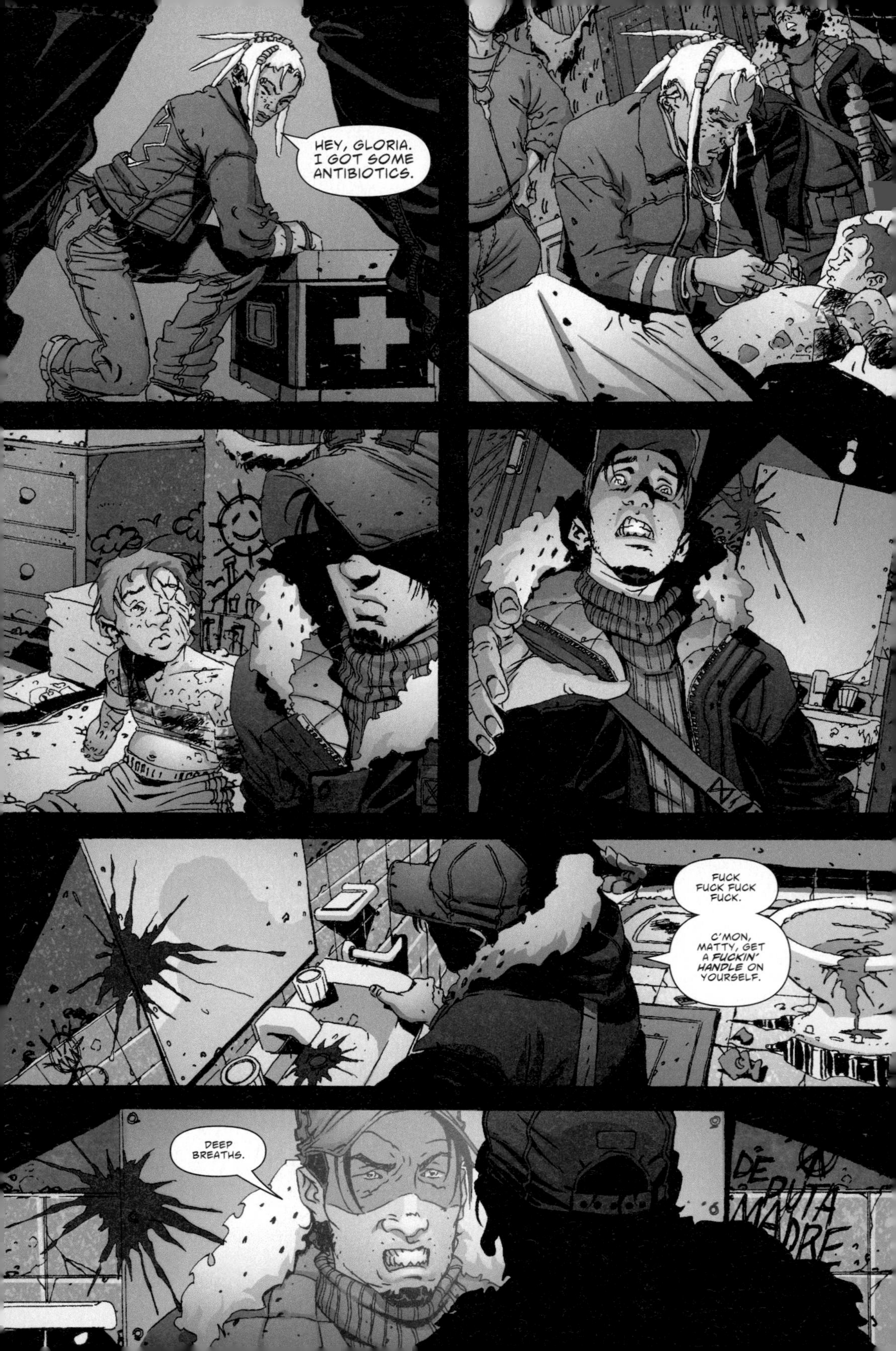
HEY, GLORIA. I GOT SOME ANTIBIOTICS.
FUCK FUCK FUCK FUCK.
C'MON, MATTY, GET A *FUCKIN'* *HANDLE* ON YOURSELF.
DEEP BREATHS.
DE PUTA MADRE

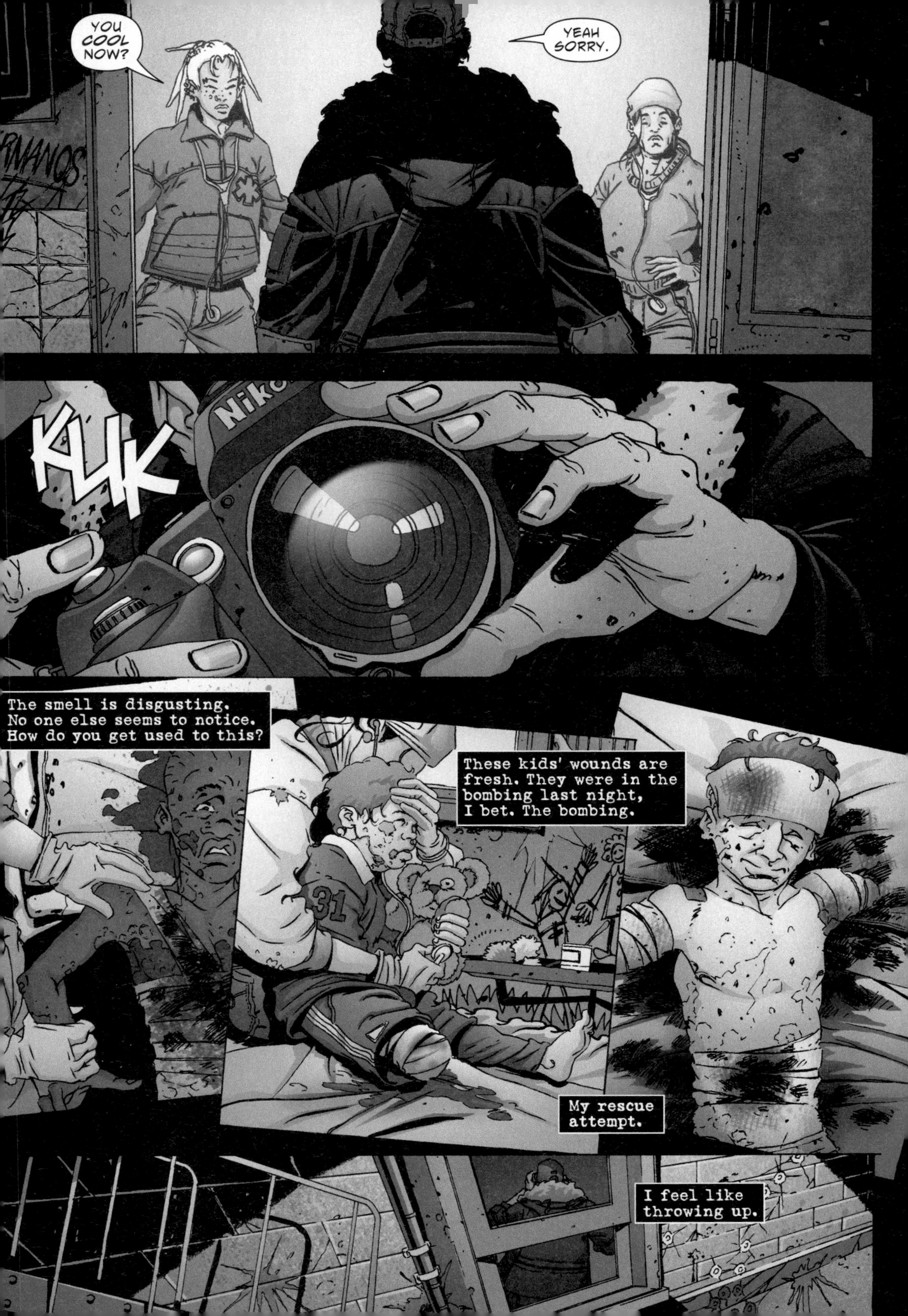
YOU COOL NOW?
YEAH SORRY.
KLIK
The smell is disgusting. No one else seems to notice. How do you get used to this?
These kids' wounds are fresh. They were in the bombing last night, I bet. The bombing.
My rescue attempt.
I feel like throwing up.

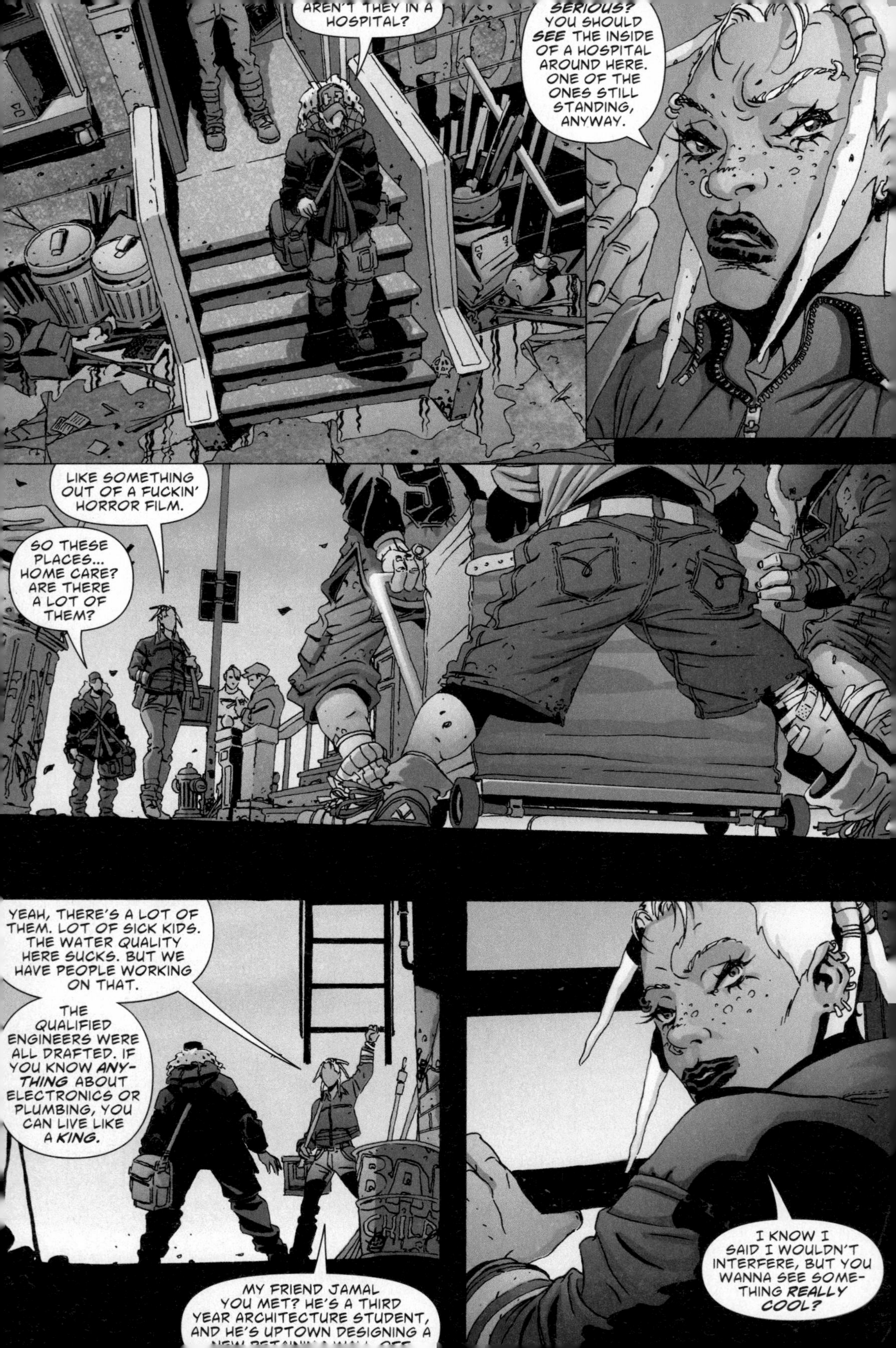
AREN'T THEY IN A HOSPITAL?
SERIOUS? YOU SHOULD SEE THE INSIDE OF A HOSPITAL AROUND HERE. ONE OF THE ONES STILL STANDING, ANYWAY.
LIKE SOMETHING OUT OF A FUCKIN' HORROR FILM.
SO THESE PLACES... HOME CARE? ARE THERE A LOT OF THEM?
YEAH, THERE'S A LOT OF THEM. LOT OF SICK KIDS. THE WATER QUALITY HERE SUCKS. BUT WE HAVE PEOPLE WORKING ON THAT.
THE QUALIFIED ENGINEERS WERE ALL DRAFTED. IF YOU KNOW ANYTHING ABOUT ELECTRONICS OR PLUMBING, YOU CAN LIVE LIKE A KING.
MY FRIEND JAMAL YOU MET? HE'S A THIRD YEAR ARCHITECTURE STUDENT, AND HE'S UPTOWN DESIGNING A
I KNOW I SAID I WOULDN'T INTERFERE, BUT YOU WANNA SEE SOMETHING REALLY COOL?

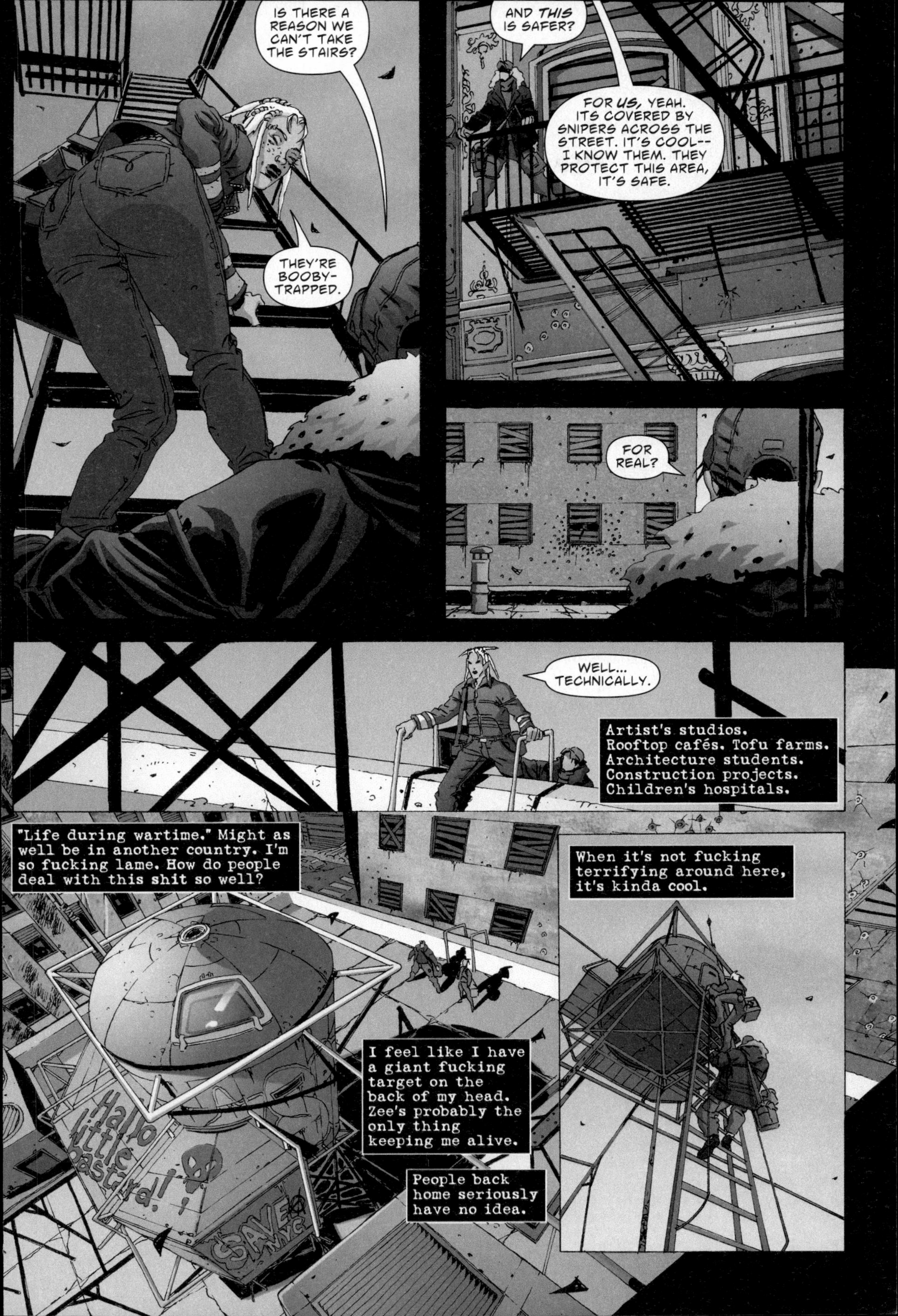
IS THERE A REASON WE CAN'T TAKE THE STAIRS?
THEY'RE BOOBY-TRAPPED.
AND THIS IS SAFER?
FOR US, YEAH. ITS COVERED BY SNIPERS ACROSS THE STREET. IT'S COOL-- I KNOW THEM. THEY PROTECT THIS AREA, IT'S SAFE.
FOR REAL?
WELL... TECHNICALLY.
Artist's studios. Rooftop cafés. Tofu farms. Architecture students. Construction projects. Children's hospitals.
"Life during wartime." Might as well be in another country. I'm so fucking lame. How do people deal with this shit so well?
I feel like I have a giant fucking target on the back of my head. Zee's probably the only thing keeping me alive.
People back home seriously have no idea.
When it's not fucking terrifying around here, it's kinda cool.
Hallo little bastard!
SAVE NYC

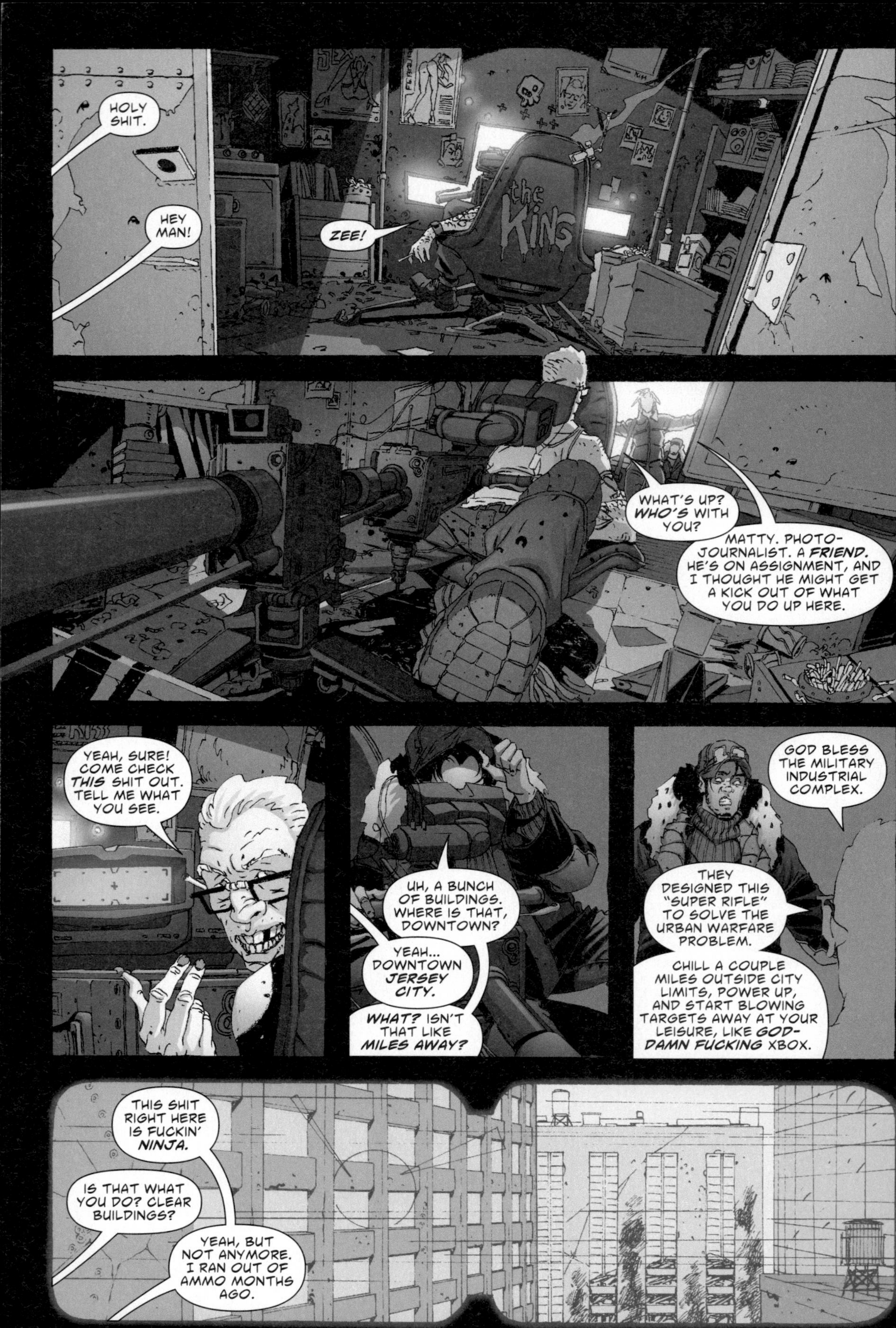
HOLY SHIT.
HEY MAN!
ZEE!
the KING
WHAT'S UP? WHO'S WITH YOU?
MATTY. PHOTO-JOURNALIST. A FRIEND. HE'S ON ASSIGNMENT, AND I THOUGHT HE MIGHT GET A KICK OUT OF WHAT YOU DO UP HERE.
YEAH, SURE! COME CHECK THIS SHIT OUT. TELL ME WHAT YOU SEE.
UH, A BUNCH OF BUILDINGS. WHERE IS THAT, DOWNTOWN?
YEAH... DOWNTOWN JERSEY CITY.
WHAT? ISN'T THAT LIKE MILES AWAY?
GOD BLESS THE MILITARY INDUSTRIAL COMPLEX.
THEY DESIGNED THIS "SUPER RIFLE" TO SOLVE THE URBAN WARFARE PROBLEM.
CHILL A COUPLE MILES OUTSIDE CITY LIMITS, POWER UP, AND START BLOWING TARGETS AWAY AT YOUR LEISURE, LIKE GOD-DAMN FUCKING XBOX.
THIS SHIT RIGHT HERE IS FUCKIN' NINJA.
IS THAT WHAT YOU DO? CLEAR BUILDINGS?
YEAH, BUT NOT ANYMORE. I RAN OUT OF AMMO MONTHS AGO.

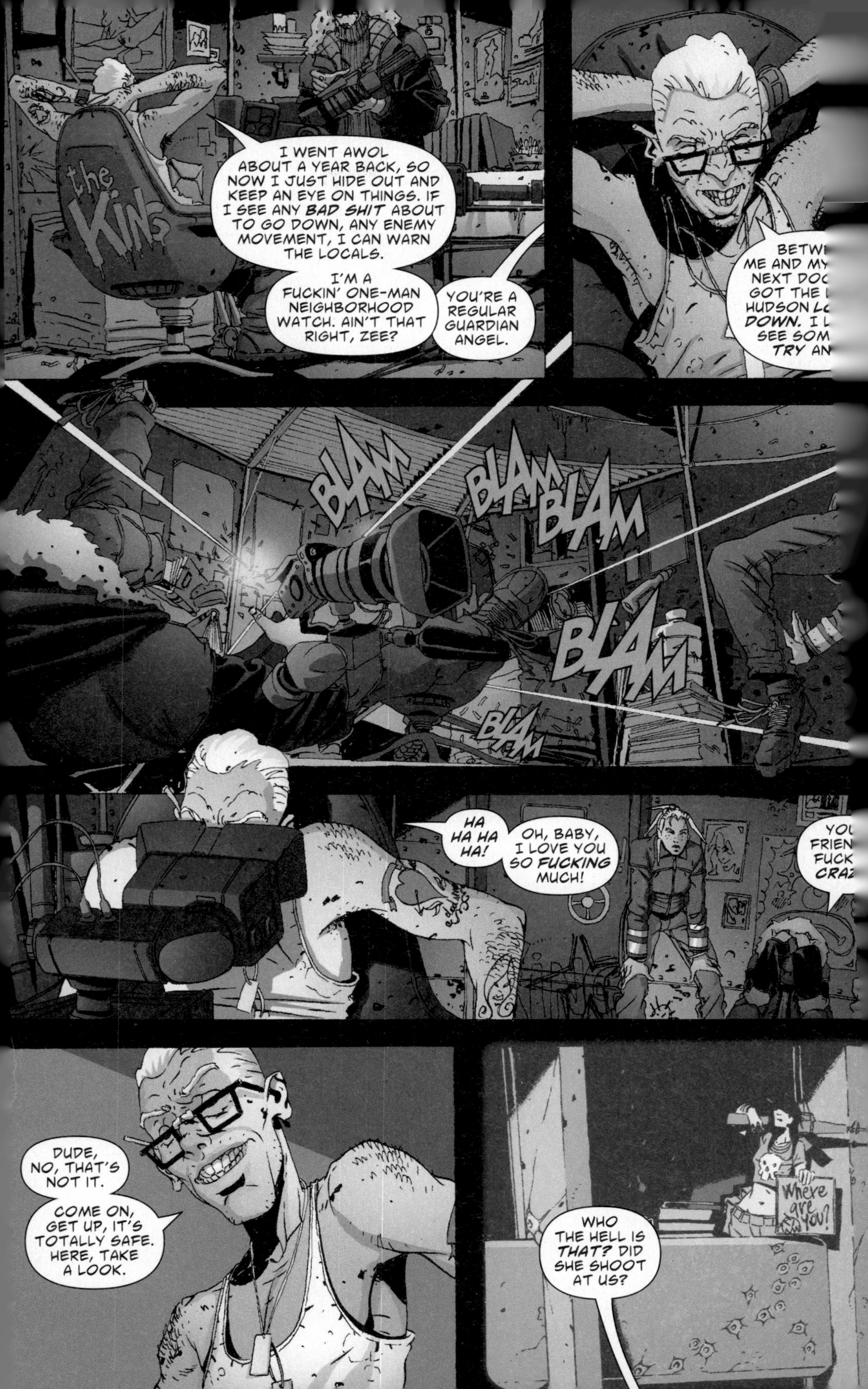
I WENT AWOL ABOUT A YEAR BACK, SO NOW I JUST HIDE OUT AND KEEP AN EYE ON THINGS. IF I SEE ANY BAD SHIT ABOUT TO GO DOWN, ANY ENEMY MOVEMENT, I CAN WARN THE LOCALS.
I'M A FUCKIN' ONE-MAN NEIGHBORHOOD WATCH. AIN'T THAT RIGHT, ZEE?
YOU'RE A REGULAR GUARDIAN ANGEL.
the KING
BETW ME AND MY NEXT DOO GOT THE HUDSON LO DOWN. I L SEE SOM TRY AN
BLAM
BLAM BLAM
BLAM
BLAM
HA HA HA HA!
OH, BABY, I LOVE YOU SO FUCKING MUCH!
YOU FRIEN FUCK CRAZ
DUDE, NO, THAT'S NOT IT.
COME ON, GET UP, IT'S TOTALLY SAFE. HERE, TAKE A LOOK.
WHO THE HELL IS THAT? DID SHE SHOOT AT US?
Where are you?

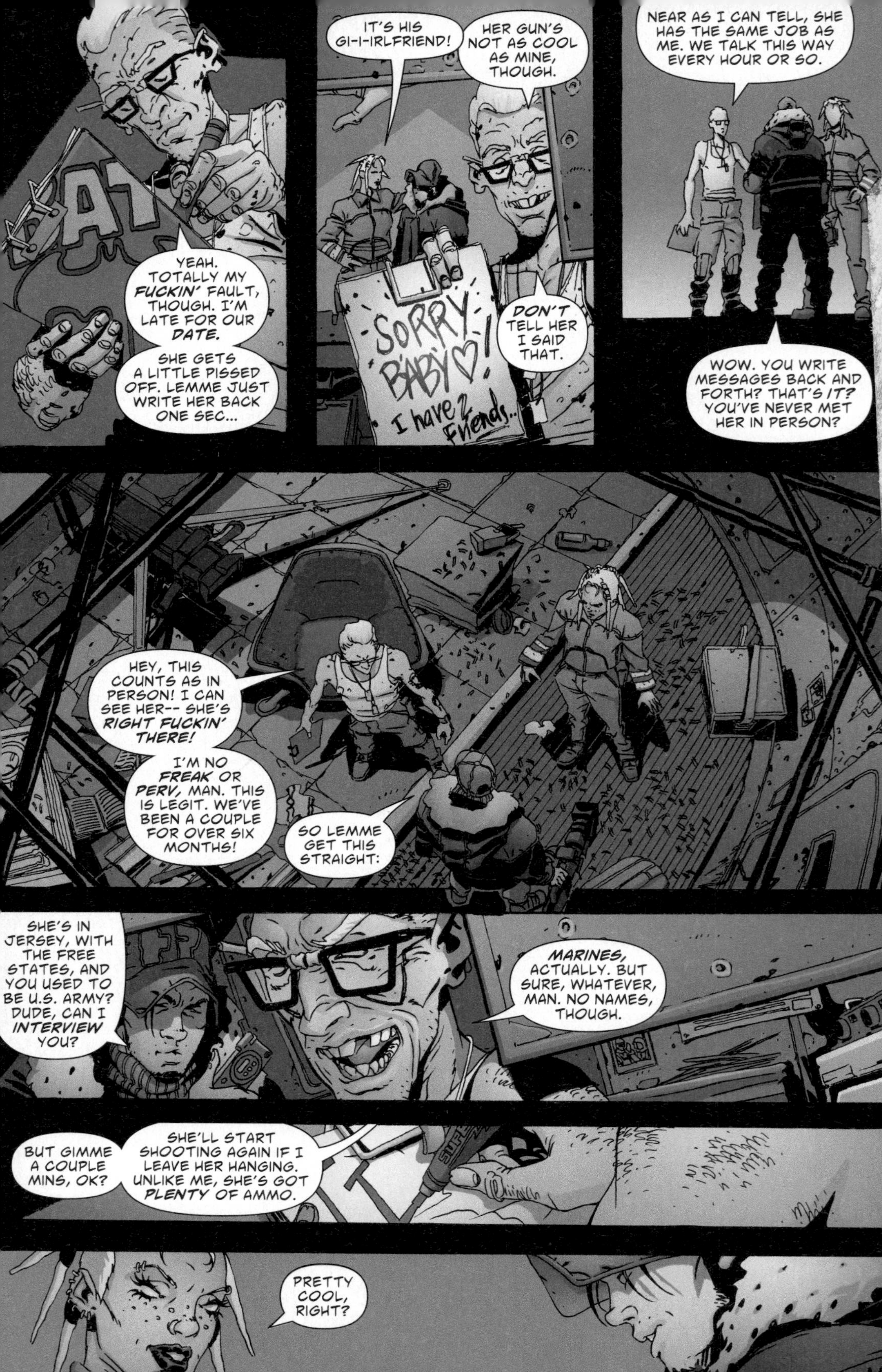
YEAH. TOTALLY MY FUCKIN' FAULT, THOUGH. I'M LATE FOR OUR DATE.
SHE GETS A LITTLE PISSED OFF. LEMME JUST WRITE HER BACK ONE SEC...
IT'S HIS GI-I-IRLFRIEND!
HER GUN'S NOT AS COOL AS MINE, THOUGH.
SORRY BABY ♡ I have 2 Friends...
DON'T TELL HER I SAID THAT.
NEAR AS I CAN TELL, SHE HAS THE SAME JOB AS ME. WE TALK THIS WAY EVERY HOUR OR SO.
WOW. YOU WRITE MESSAGES BACK AND FORTH? THAT'S IT? YOU'VE NEVER MET HER IN PERSON?
HEY, THIS COUNTS AS IN PERSON! I CAN SEE HER-- SHE'S RIGHT FUCKIN' THERE!
I'M NO FREAK OR PERV, MAN. THIS IS LEGIT. WE'VE BEEN A COUPLE FOR OVER SIX MONTHS!
SO LEMME GET THIS STRAIGHT:
SHE'S IN JERSEY, WITH THE FREE STATES, AND YOU USED TO BE U.S. ARMY? DUDE, CAN I INTERVIEW YOU?
MARINES, ACTUALLY. BUT SURE, WHATEVER, MAN. NO NAMES, THOUGH.
BUT GIMME A COUPLE MINS, OK?
SHE'LL START SHOOTING AGAIN IF I LEAVE HER HANGING. UNLIKE ME, SHE'S GOT PLENTY OF AMMO.
PRETTY COOL, RIGHT?

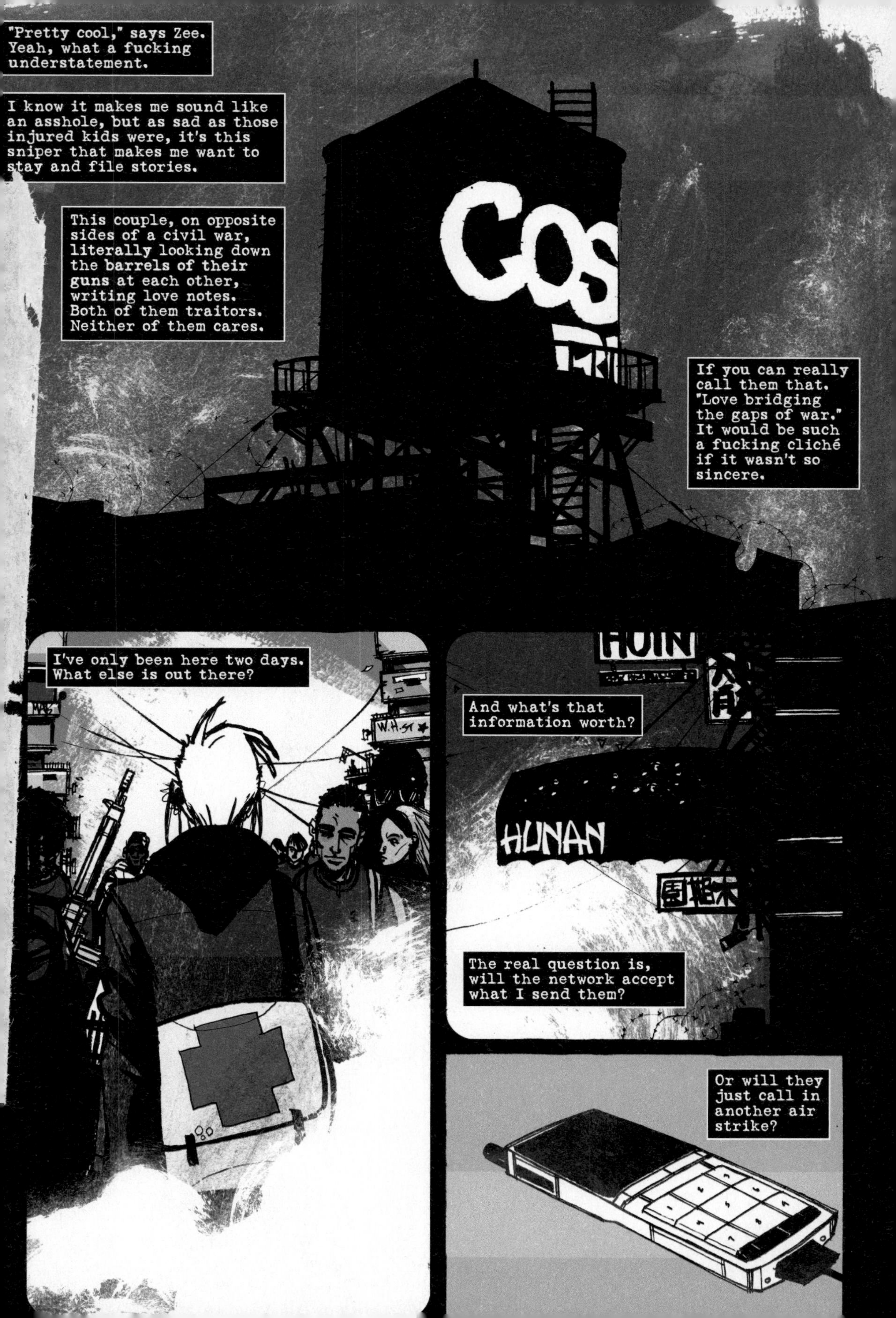
"Pretty cool," says Zee. Yeah, what a fucking understatement.
I know it makes me sound like an asshole, but as sad as those injured kids were, it's this sniper that makes me want to stay and file stories.
This couple, on opposite sides of a civil war, literally looking down the barrels of their guns at each other, writing love notes. Both of them traitors. Neither of them cares.
If you can really call them that. "Love bridging the gaps of war." It would be such a fucking cliché if it wasn't so sincere.
COS
I've only been here two days. What else is out there?
And what's that information worth?
HUNAN
The real question is, will the network accept what I send them?
Or will they just call in another air strike?

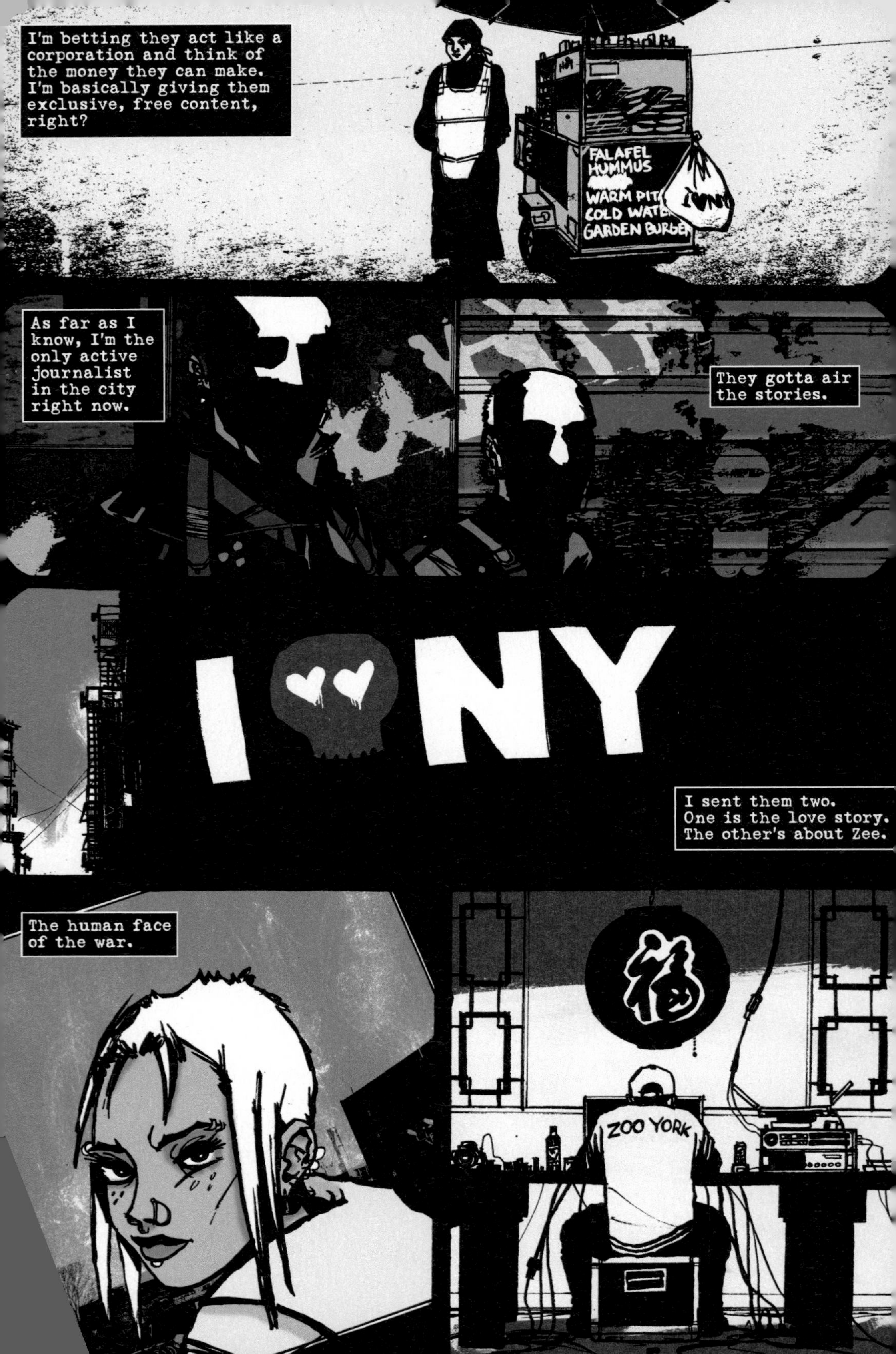
I'm betting they act like a corporation and think of the money they can make. I'm basically giving them exclusive, free content, right?
FALAFEL
HUMMUS
WARM PIT
COLD WATE
GARDEN BURGE
As far as I know, I'm the only active journalist in the city right now.
They gotta air the stories.
I NY
I sent them two. One is the love story. The other's about Zee.
The human face of the war.
福
ZOO YORK

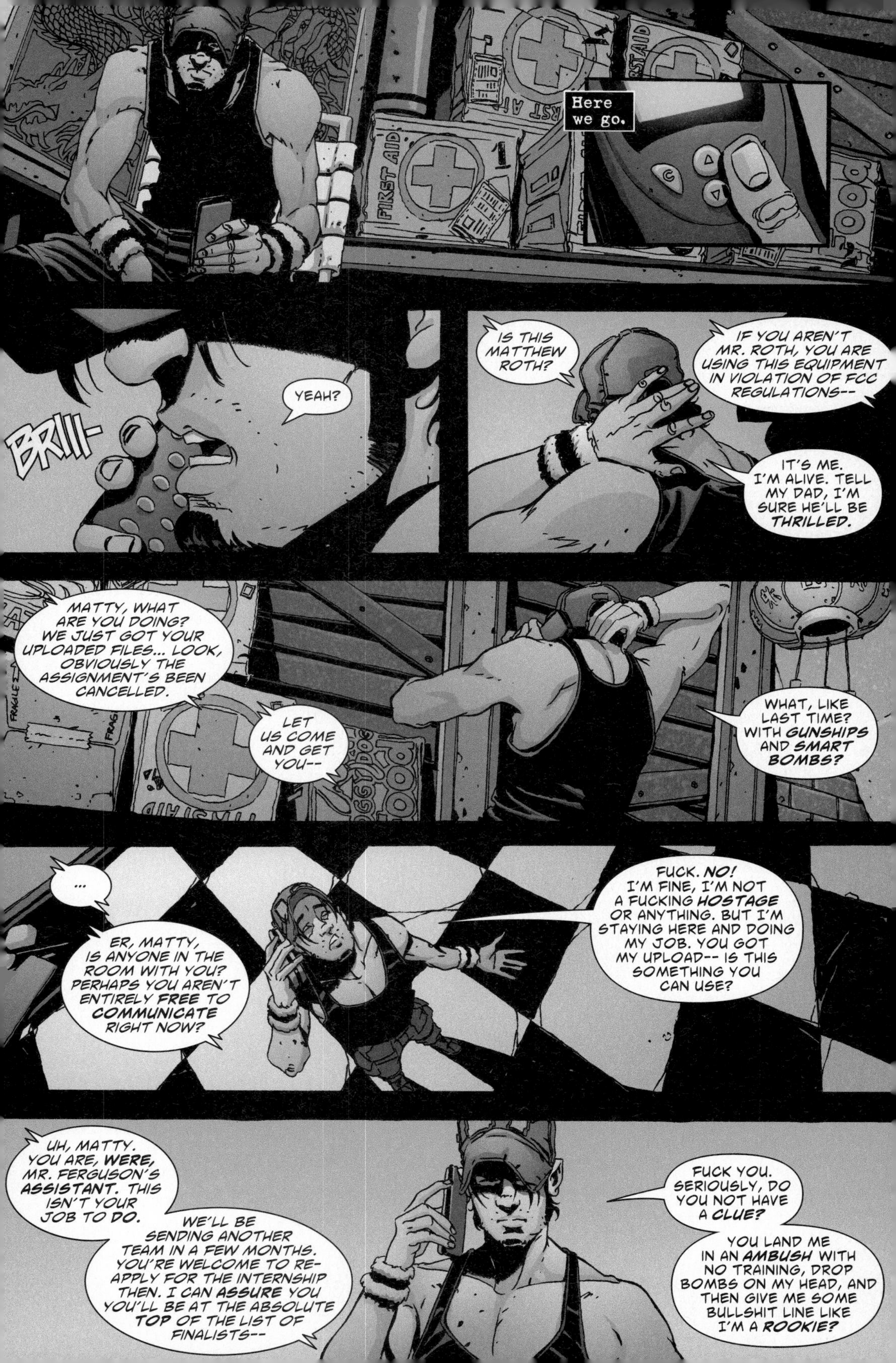
Here we go.
BRIII-
YEAH?
IS THIS MATTHEW ROTH?
IF YOU AREN'T MR. ROTH, YOU ARE USING THIS EQUIPMENT IN VIOLATION OF FCC REGULATIONS--
IT'S ME. I'M ALIVE. TELL MY DAD, I'M SURE HE'LL BE THRILLED.
MATTY, WHAT ARE YOU DOING? WE JUST GOT YOUR UPLOADED FILES... LOOK, OBVIOUSLY THE ASSIGNMENT'S BEEN CANCELLED.
LET US COME AND GET YOU--
WHAT, LIKE LAST TIME? WITH GUNSHIPS AND SMART BOMBS?
...
ER, MATTY, IS ANYONE IN THE ROOM WITH YOU? PERHAPS YOU AREN'T ENTIRELY FREE TO COMMUNICATE RIGHT NOW?
FUCK. NO! I'M FINE, I'M NOT A FUCKING HOSTAGE OR ANYTHING. BUT I'M STAYING HERE AND DOING MY JOB. YOU GOT MY UPLOAD-- IS THIS SOMETHING YOU CAN USE?
UH, MATTY. YOU ARE, WERE, MR. FERGUSON'S ASSISTANT. THIS ISN'T YOUR JOB TO DO.
WE'LL BE SENDING ANOTHER TEAM IN A FEW MONTHS. YOU'RE WELCOME TO RE-APPLY FOR THE INTERNSHIP THEN. I CAN ASSURE YOU YOU'LL BE AT THE ABSOLUTE TOP OF THE LIST OF FINALISTS--
FUCK YOU. SERIOUSLY, DO YOU NOT HAVE A CLUE?
YOU LAND ME IN AN AMBUSH WITH NO TRAINING, DROP BOMBS ON MY HEAD, AND THEN GIVE ME SOME BULLSHIT LINE LIKE I'M A ROOKIE?

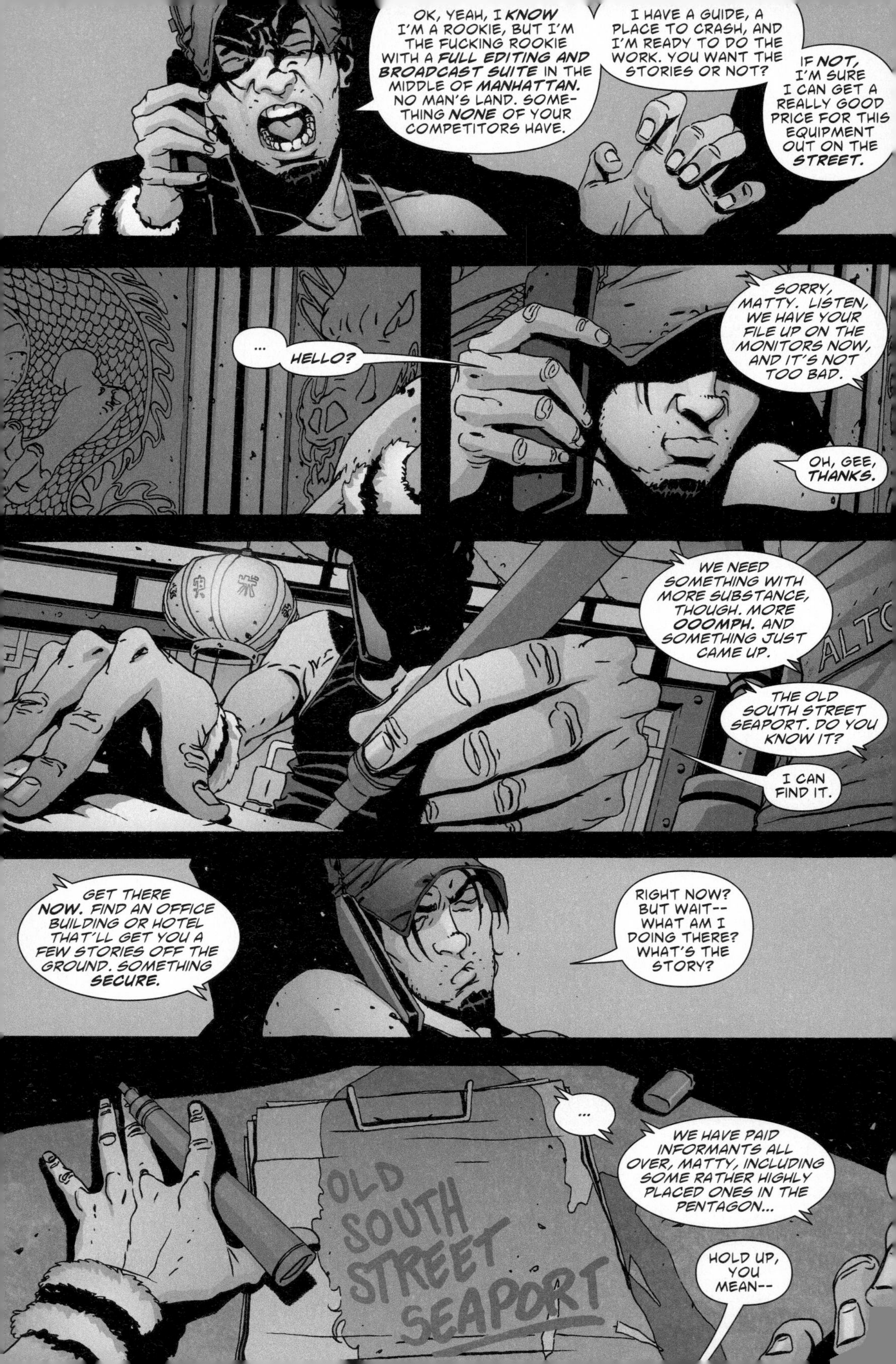

OK, YEAH, I KNOW I'M A ROOKIE, BUT I'M THE FUCKING ROOKIE WITH A FULL EDITING AND BROADCAST SUITE IN THE MIDDLE OF MANHATTAN. NO MAN'S LAND. SOMETHING NONE OF YOUR COMPETITORS HAVE.
I HAVE A GUIDE, A PLACE TO CRASH, AND I'M READY TO DO THE WORK. YOU WANT THE STORIES OR NOT?
IF NOT, I'M SURE I CAN GET A REALLY GOOD PRICE FOR THIS EQUIPMENT OUT ON THE STREET.
...
HELLO?
SORRY, MATTY. LISTEN, WE HAVE YOUR FILE UP ON THE MONITORS NOW, AND IT'S NOT TOO BAD.
OH, GEE, THANKS.
WE NEED SOMETHING WITH MORE SUBSTANCE, THOUGH. MORE OOOMPH. AND SOMETHING JUST CAME UP.
THE OLD SOUTH STREET SEAPORT. DO YOU KNOW IT?
I CAN FIND IT.
GET THERE NOW. FIND AN OFFICE BUILDING OR HOTEL THAT'LL GET YOU A FEW STORIES OFF THE GROUND. SOMETHING SECURE.
RIGHT NOW? BUT WAIT-- WHAT AM I DOING THERE? WHAT'S THE STORY?
...
WE HAVE PAID INFORMANTS ALL OVER, MATTY, INCLUDING SOME RATHER HIGHLY PLACED ONES IN THE PENTAGON...
HOLD UP, YOU MEAN--
OLD SOUTH STREET SEAPORT

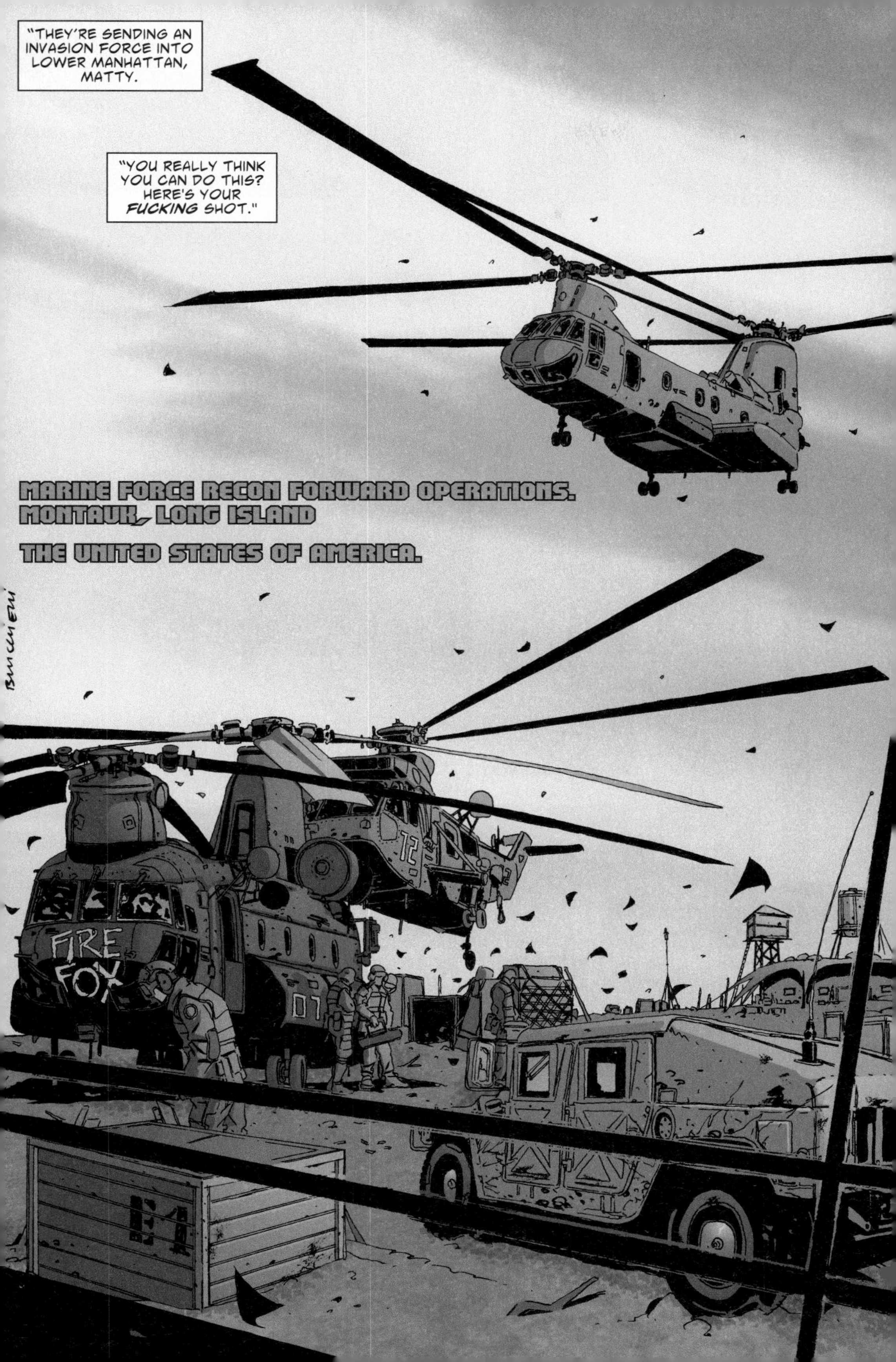
"THEY'RE SENDING AN INVASION FORCE INTO LOWER MANHATTAN, MATTY.
"YOU REALLY THINK YOU CAN DO THIS? HERE'S YOUR *FUCKING* SHOT."
MARINE FORCE RECON FORWARD OPERATIONS. MONTAUK, LONG ISLAND
THE UNITED STATES OF AMERICA.
72
FIRE FOX
07

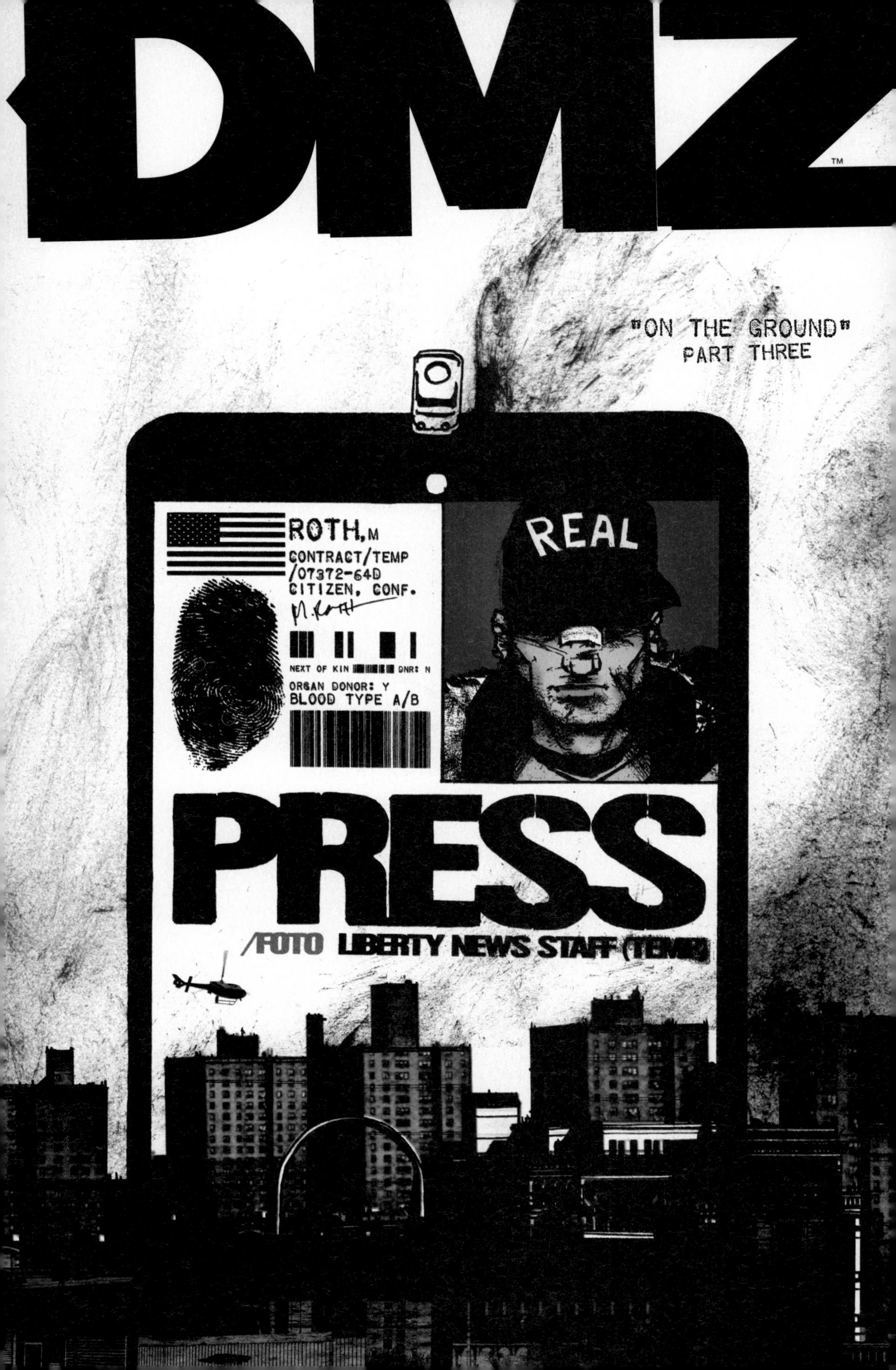
DMZ™
"ON THE GROUND"
PART THREE
ROTH, M
CONTRACT/TEMP
/07372-64D
CITIZEN, CONF.
NEXT OF KIN [redacted] DNR: N
ORGAN DONOR: Y
BLOOD TYPE A/B
REAL
PRESS
/FOTO LIBERTY NEWS STAFF (TEMP)

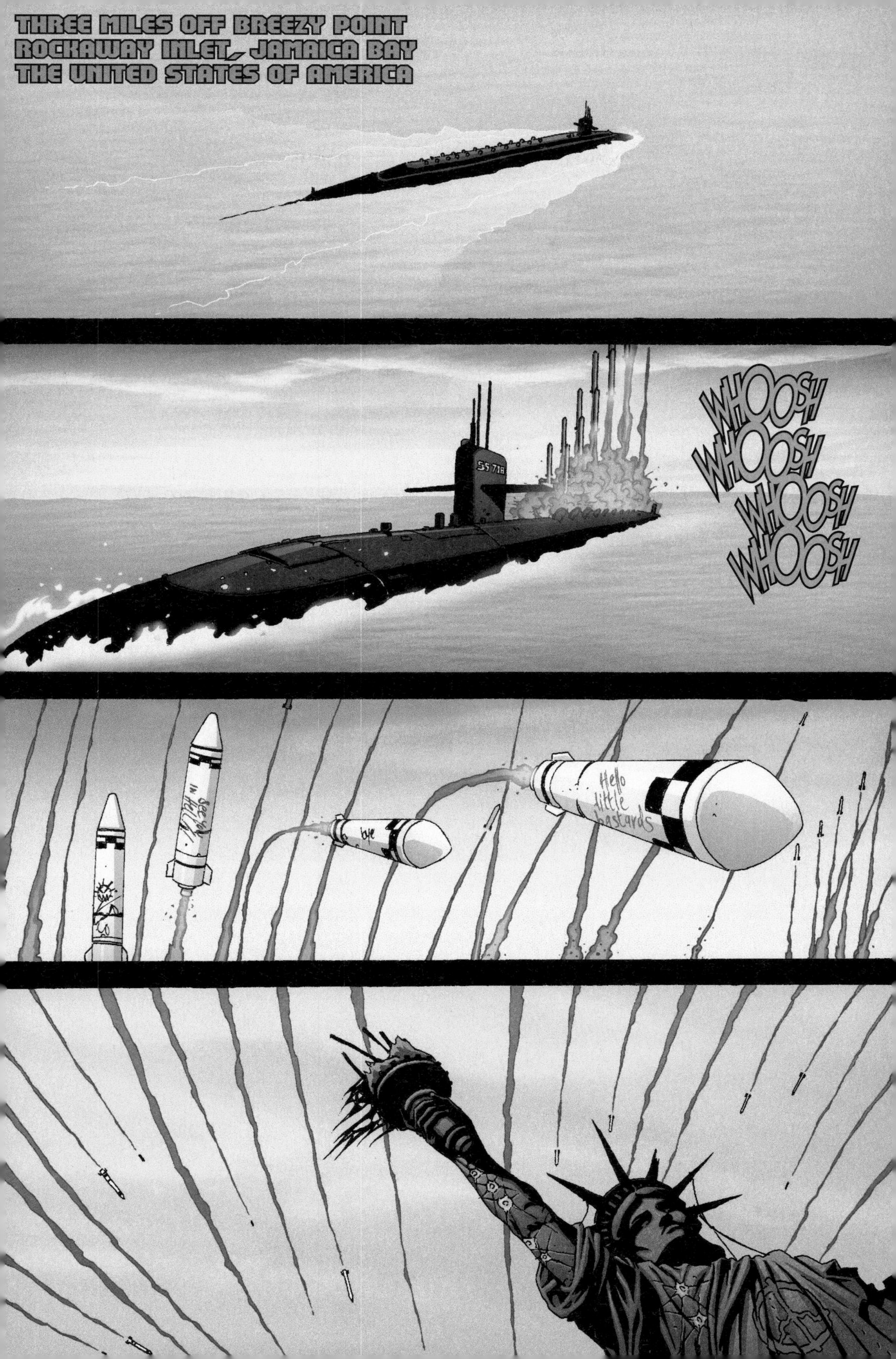
THREE MILES OFF BREEZY POINT
ROCKAWAY INLET, JAMAICA BAY
THE UNITED STATES OF AMERICA
WHOOSH
WHOOSH
WHOOSH
WHOOSH
see you in HELL
bye
Hello little bastards

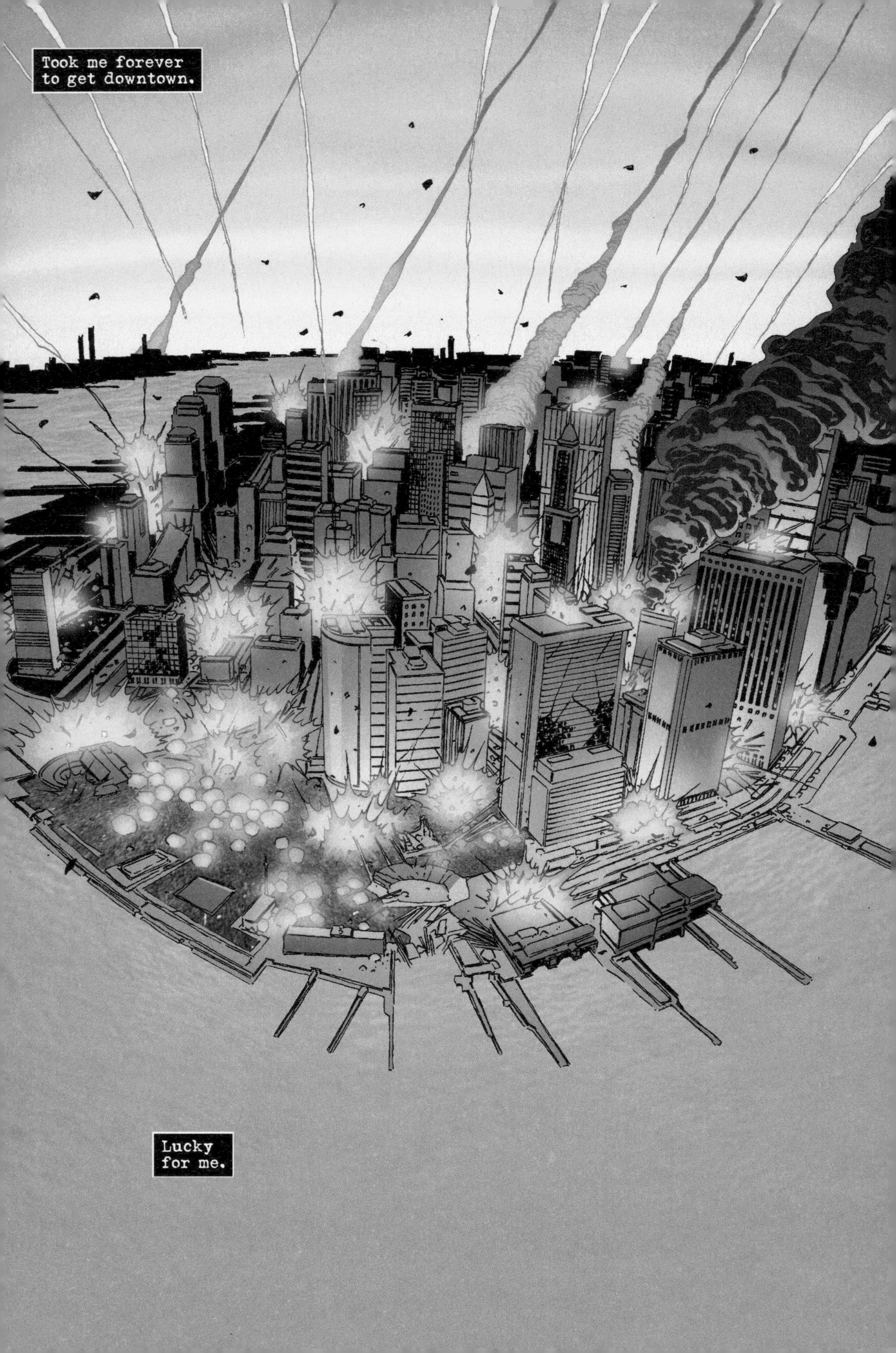
Took me forever to get downtown.
Lucky for me.

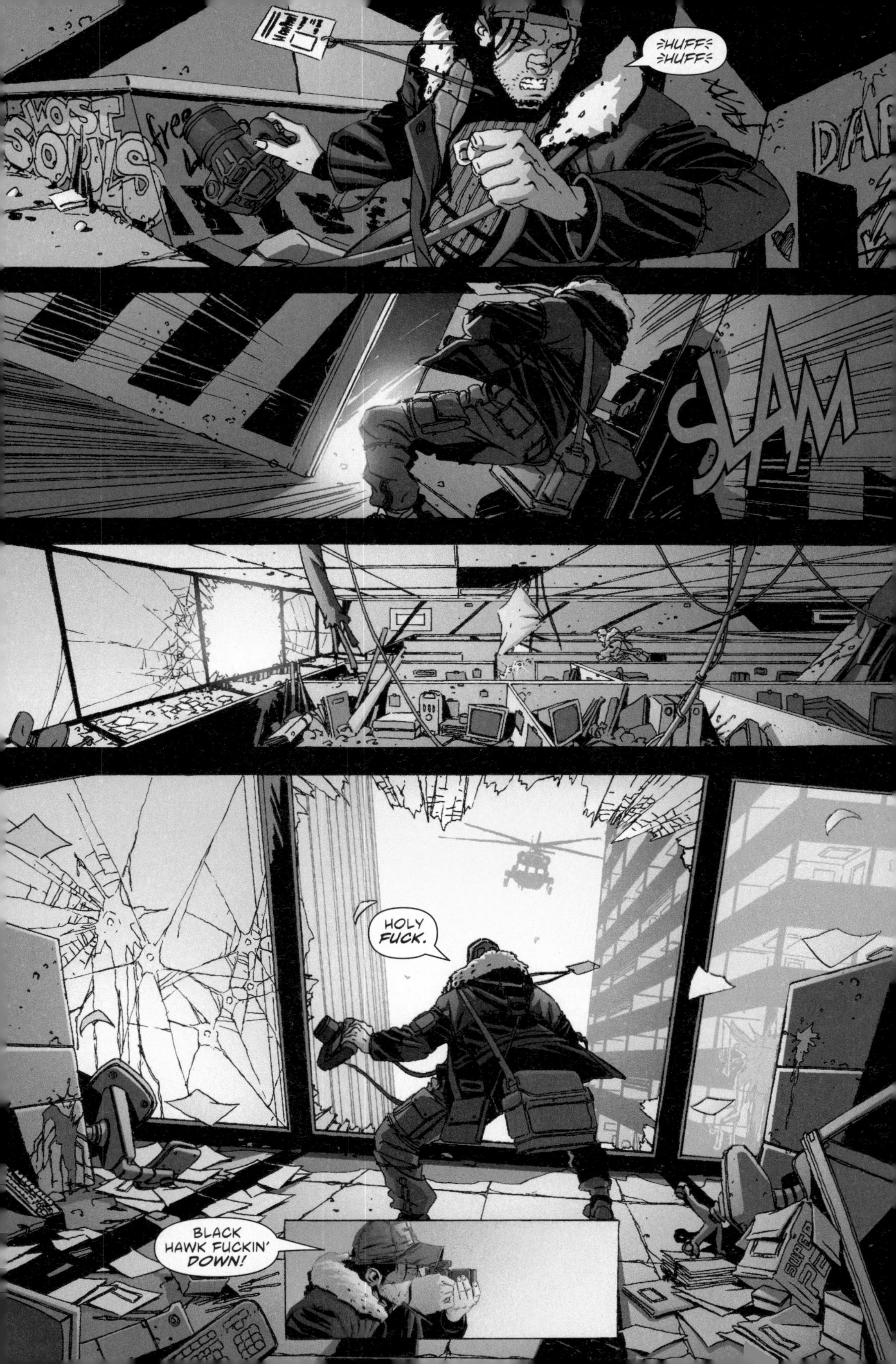
HUFF HUFF
WOST SOULS
free
SLAM
HOLY FUCK.
BLACK HAWK FUCKIN' DOWN!

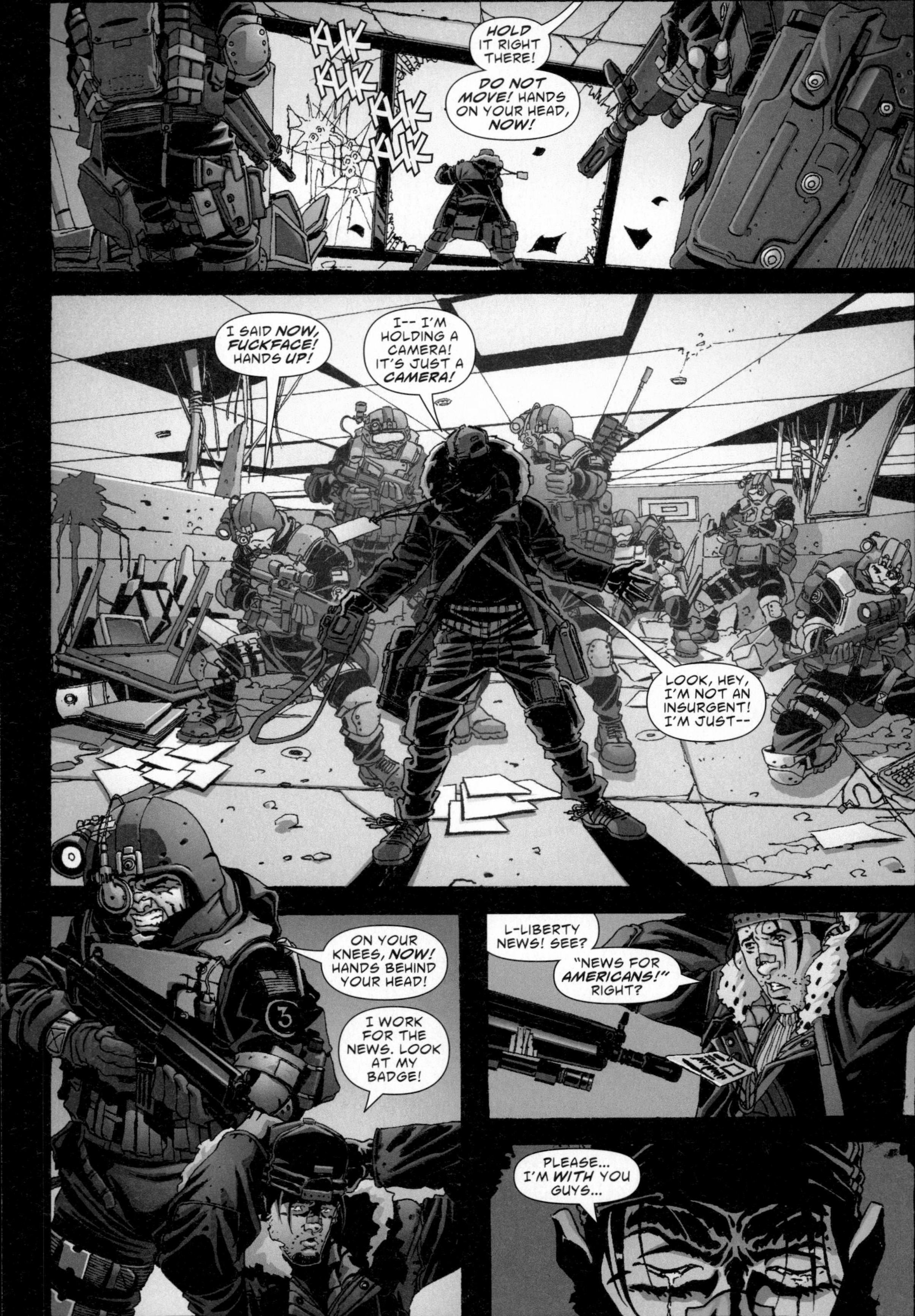
KUK KUK KUK KUK
HOLD IT RIGHT THERE!
DO NOT MOVE! HANDS ON YOUR HEAD, NOW!
I SAID NOW, FUCKFACE! HANDS UP!
I-- I'M HOLDING A CAMERA! IT'S JUST A CAMERA!
LOOK, HEY, I'M NOT AN INSURGENT! I'M JUST--
ON YOUR KNEES, NOW! HANDS BEHIND YOUR HEAD!
I WORK FOR THE NEWS. LOOK AT MY BADGE!
L-LIBERTY NEWS! SEE?
"NEWS FOR AMERICANS!" RIGHT?
PLEASE... I'M WITH YOU GUYS...

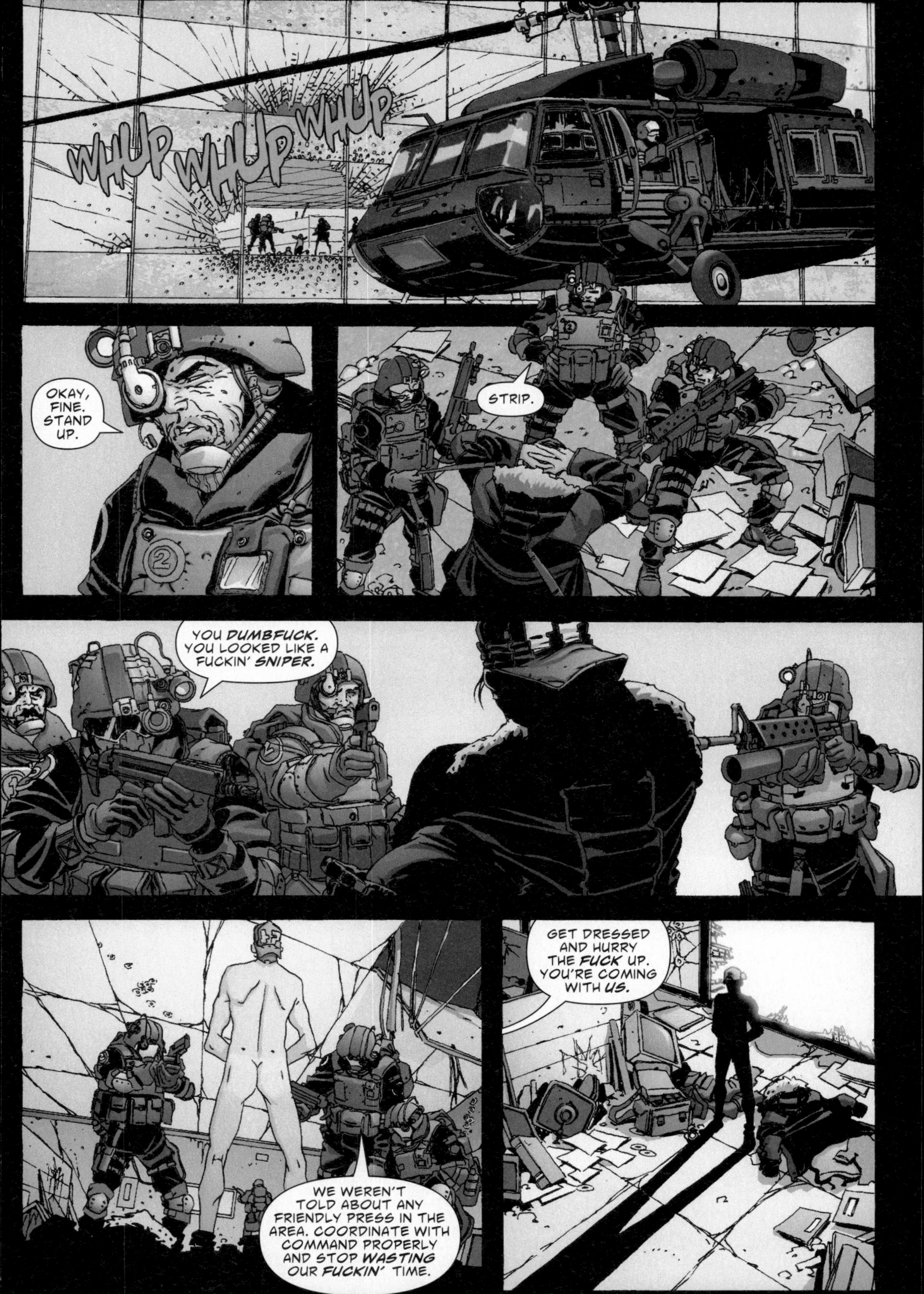
WHUP WHUP WHUP
OKAY, FINE. STAND UP.
STRIP.
YOU DUMBFUCK. YOU LOOKED LIKE A FUCKIN' SNIPER.
WE WEREN'T TOLD ABOUT ANY FRIENDLY PRESS IN THE AREA. COORDINATE WITH COMMAND PROPERLY AND STOP WASTING OUR FUCKIN' TIME.
GET DRESSED AND HURRY THE FUCK UP. YOU'RE COMING WITH US.

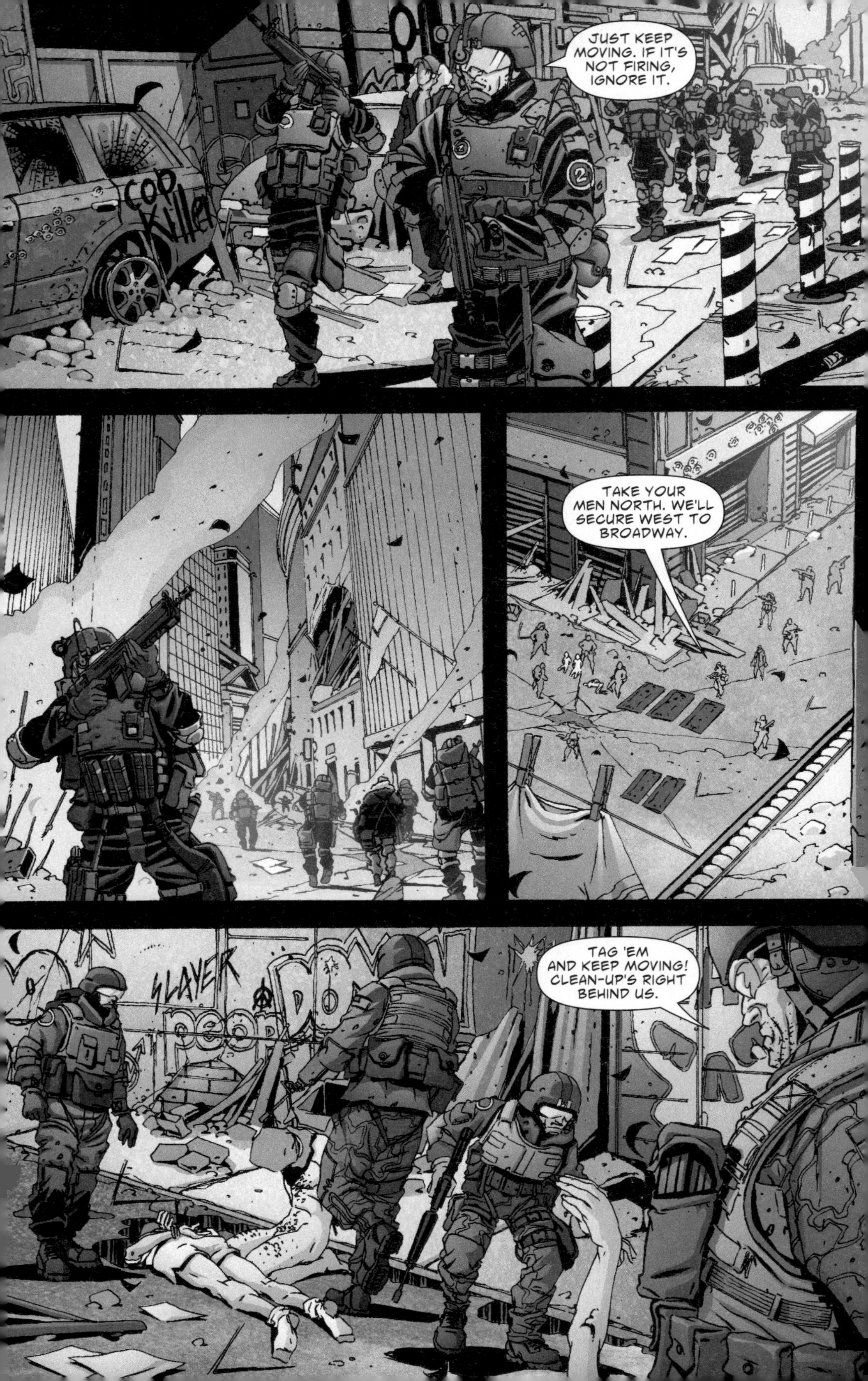
JUST KEEP MOVING. IF IT'S NOT FIRING, IGNORE IT.
COP Killer
TAKE YOUR MEN NORTH. WE'LL SECURE WEST TO BROADWAY.
SLAYER
TAG 'EM AND KEEP MOVING! CLEAN-UP'S RIGHT BEHIND US.

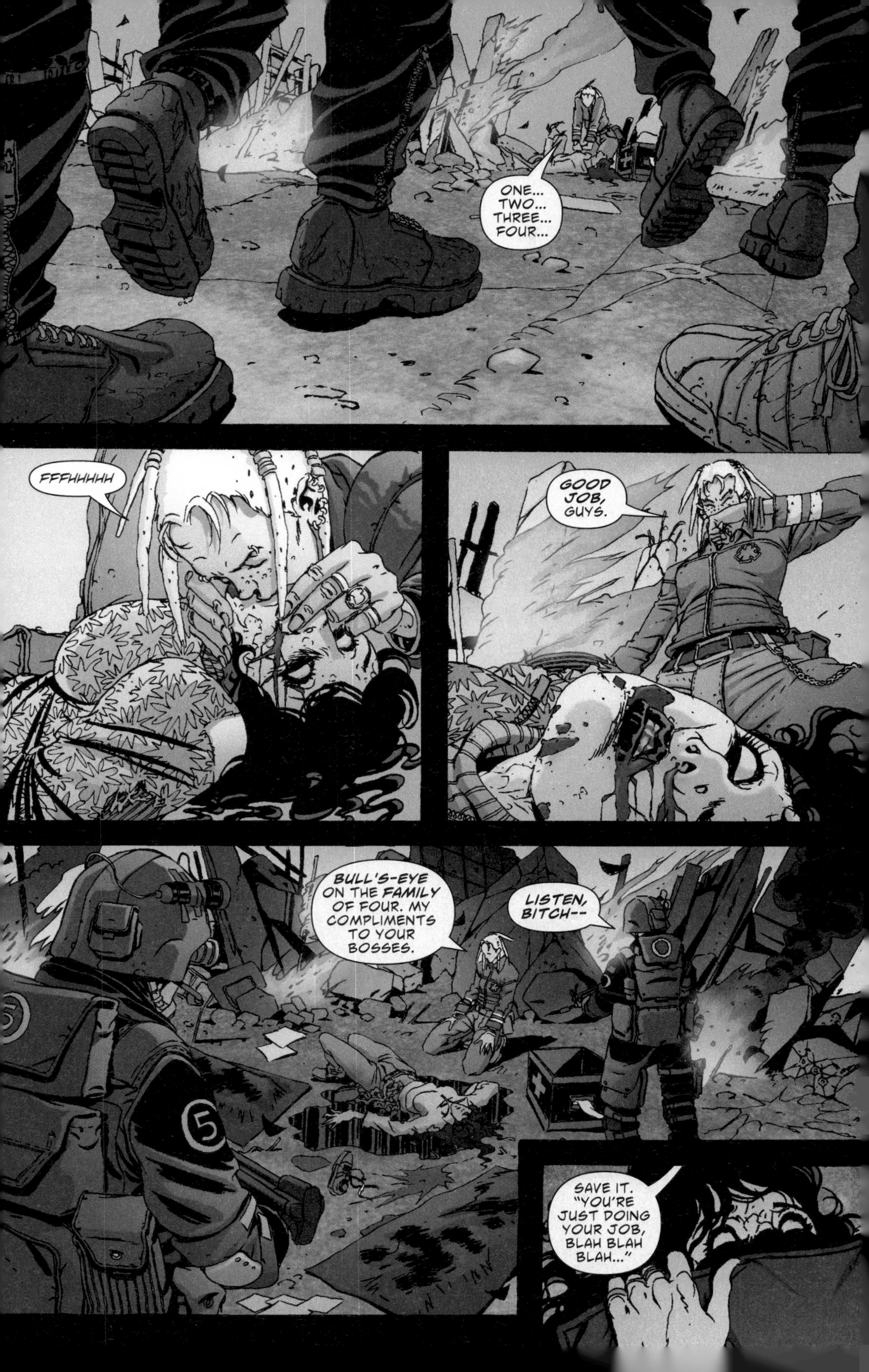
ONE... TWO... THREE... FOUR...
FFFHHHHH
GOOD JOB, GUYS.
BULL'S-EYE ON THE FAMILY OF FOUR. MY COMPLIMENTS TO YOUR BOSSES.
LISTEN, BITCH--
SAVE IT. "YOU'RE JUST DOING YOUR JOB, BLAH BLAH BLAH..."

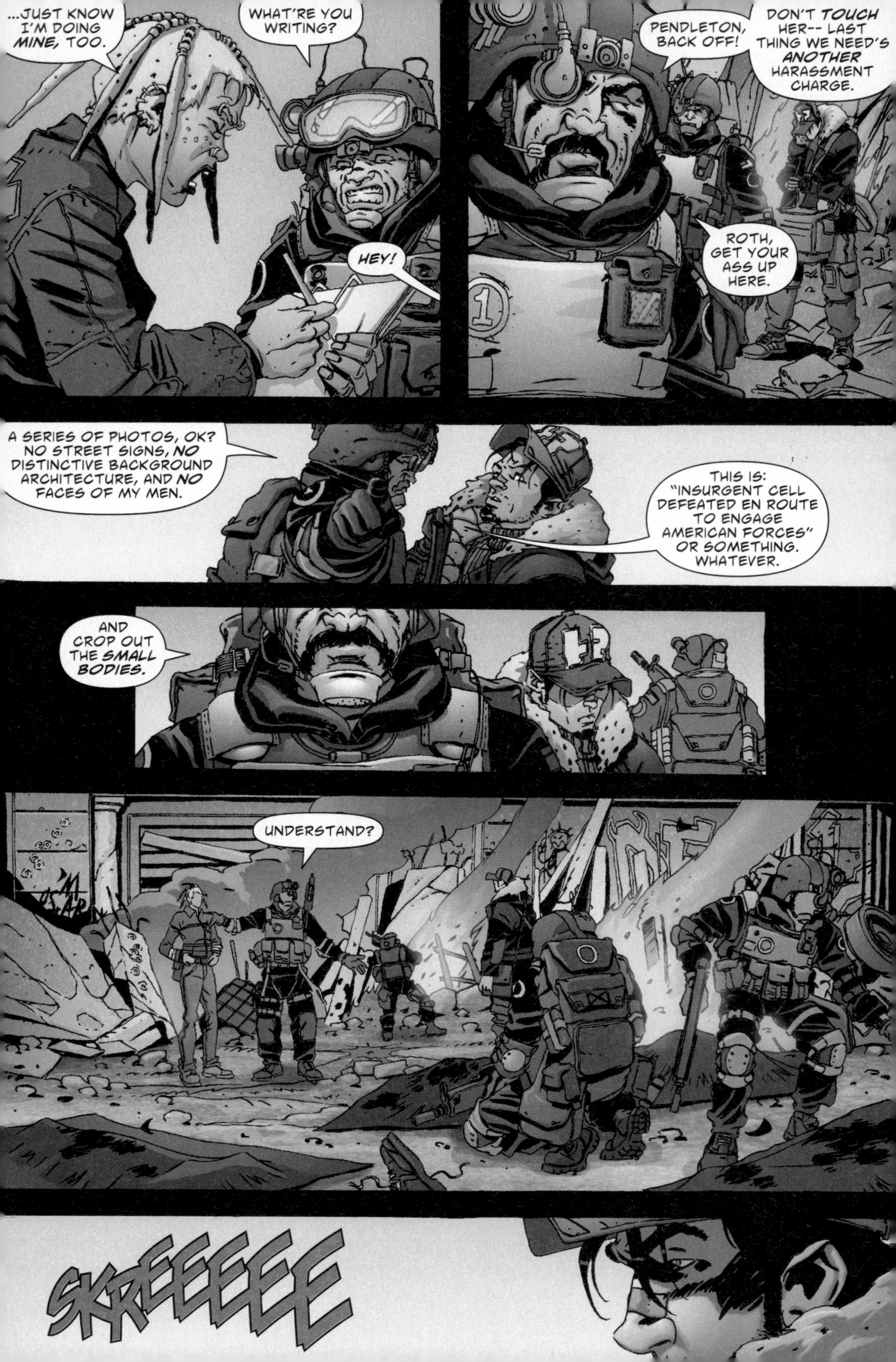
...JUST KNOW I'M DOING MINE, TOO.
WHAT'RE YOU WRITING?
HEY!
PENDLETON, BACK OFF!
DON'T TOUCH HER-- LAST THING WE NEED'S ANOTHER HARASSMENT CHARGE.
ROTH, GET YOUR ASS UP HERE.
A SERIES OF PHOTOS, OK? NO STREET SIGNS, NO DISTINCTIVE BACKGROUND ARCHITECTURE, AND NO FACES OF MY MEN.
THIS IS: "INSURGENT CELL DEFEATED EN ROUTE TO ENGAGE AMERICAN FORCES" OR SOMETHING. WHATEVER.
AND CROP OUT THE SMALL BODIES.
UNDERSTAND?
SKREEEEEE

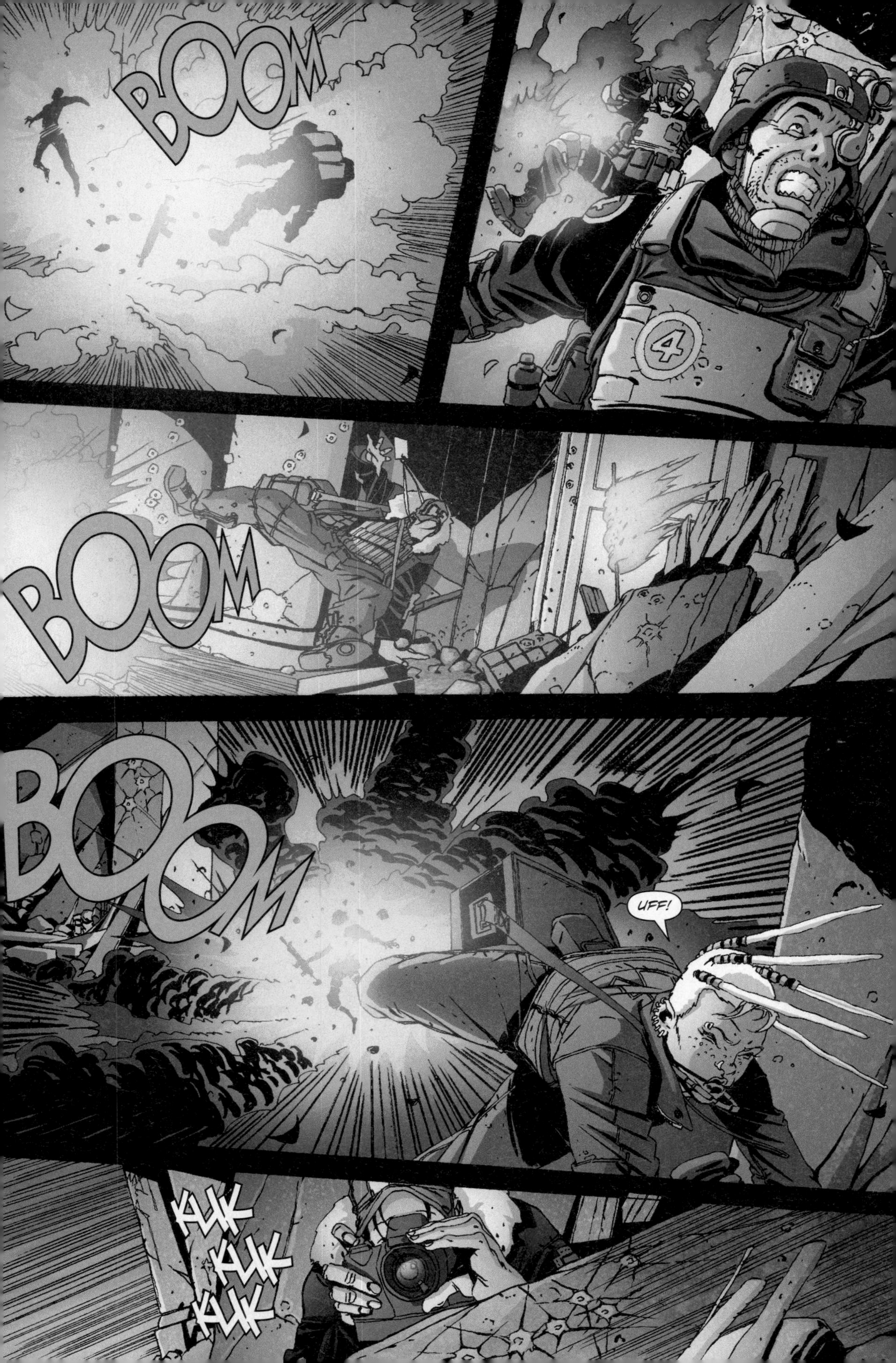
BOOM
BOOM
BOOM
UFF!
KLIK
KLIK
KLIK

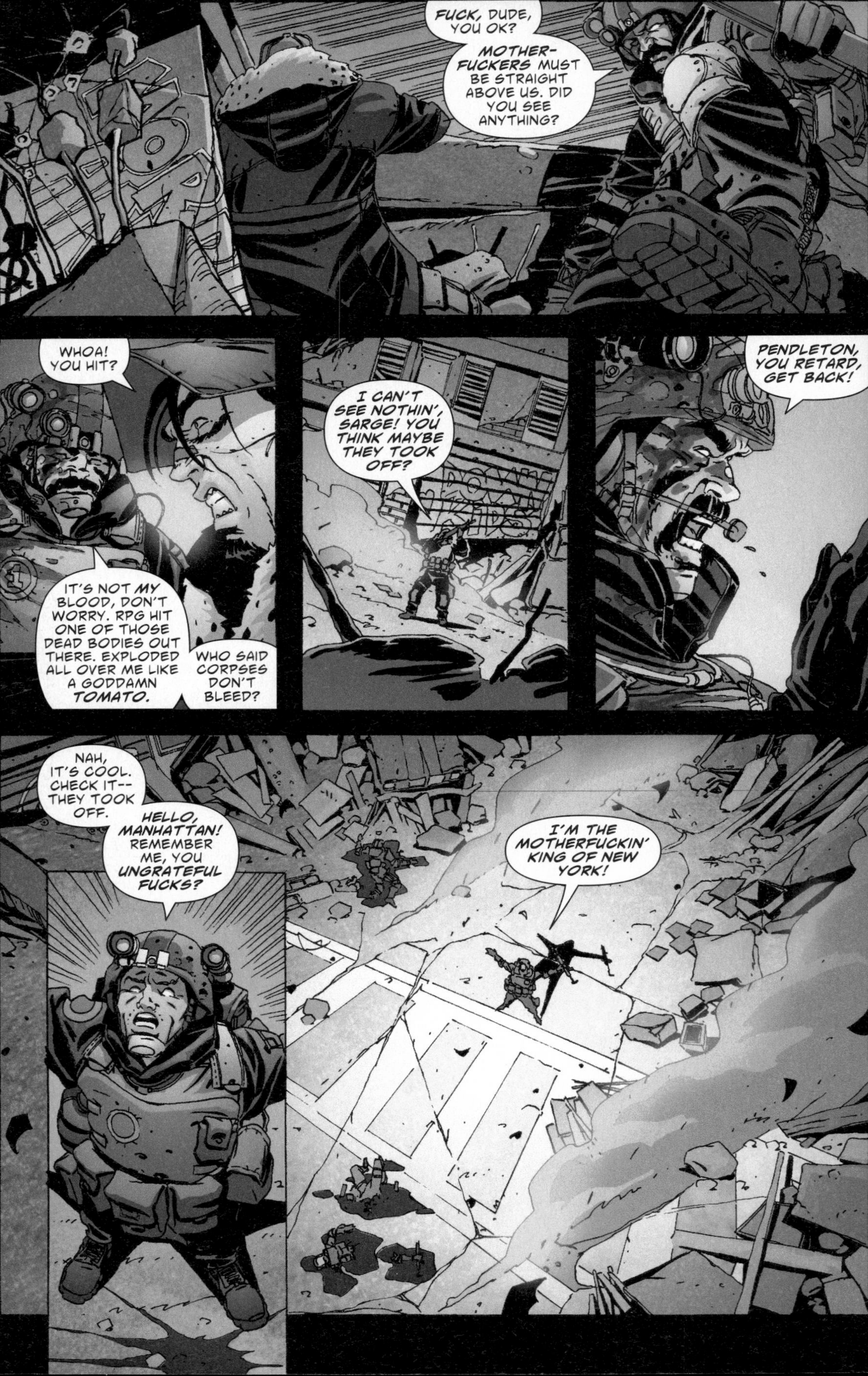
FUCK, DUDE, YOU OK?
MOTHER-FUCKERS MUST BE STRAIGHT ABOVE US. DID YOU SEE ANYTHING?
WHOA! YOU HIT?
IT'S NOT MY BLOOD, DON'T WORRY. RPG HIT ONE OF THOSE DEAD BODIES OUT THERE. EXPLODED ALL OVER ME LIKE A GODDAMN TOMATO.
WHO SAID CORPSES DON'T BLEED?
I CAN'T SEE NOTHIN', SARGE! YOU THINK MAYBE THEY TOOK OFF?
PENDLETON, YOU RETARD, GET BACK!
NAH, IT'S COOL. CHECK IT-- THEY TOOK OFF.
HELLO, MANHATTAN! REMEMBER ME, YOU UNGRATEFUL FUCKS?
I'M THE MOTHERFUCKIN' KING OF NEW YORK!

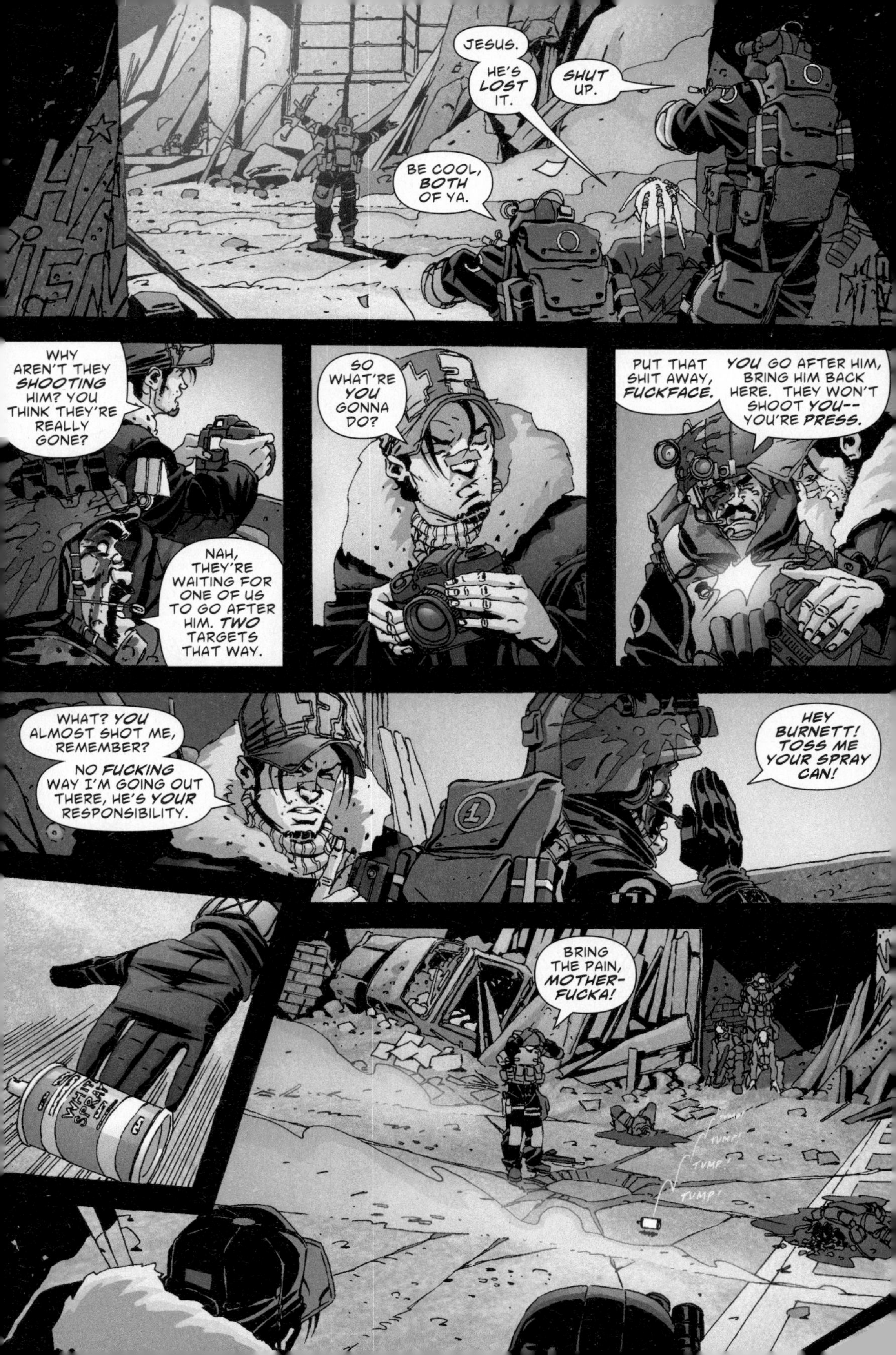
JESUS.
HE'S LOST IT.
SHUT UP.
BE COOL, BOTH OF YA.
WHY AREN'T THEY SHOOTING HIM? YOU THINK THEY'RE REALLY GONE?
NAH, THEY'RE WAITING FOR ONE OF US TO GO AFTER HIM. TWO TARGETS THAT WAY.
SO WHAT'RE YOU GONNA DO?
PUT THAT SHIT AWAY, FUCKFACE.
YOU GO AFTER HIM, BRING HIM BACK HERE. THEY WON'T SHOOT YOU-- YOU'RE PRESS.
WHAT? YOU ALMOST SHOT ME, REMEMBER?
NO FUCKING WAY I'M GOING OUT THERE, HE'S YOUR RESPONSIBILITY.
HEY BURNETT! TOSS ME YOUR SPRAY CAN!
BRING THE PAIN, MOTHER-FUCKA!
TUMP!
TUMP!
TUMP!

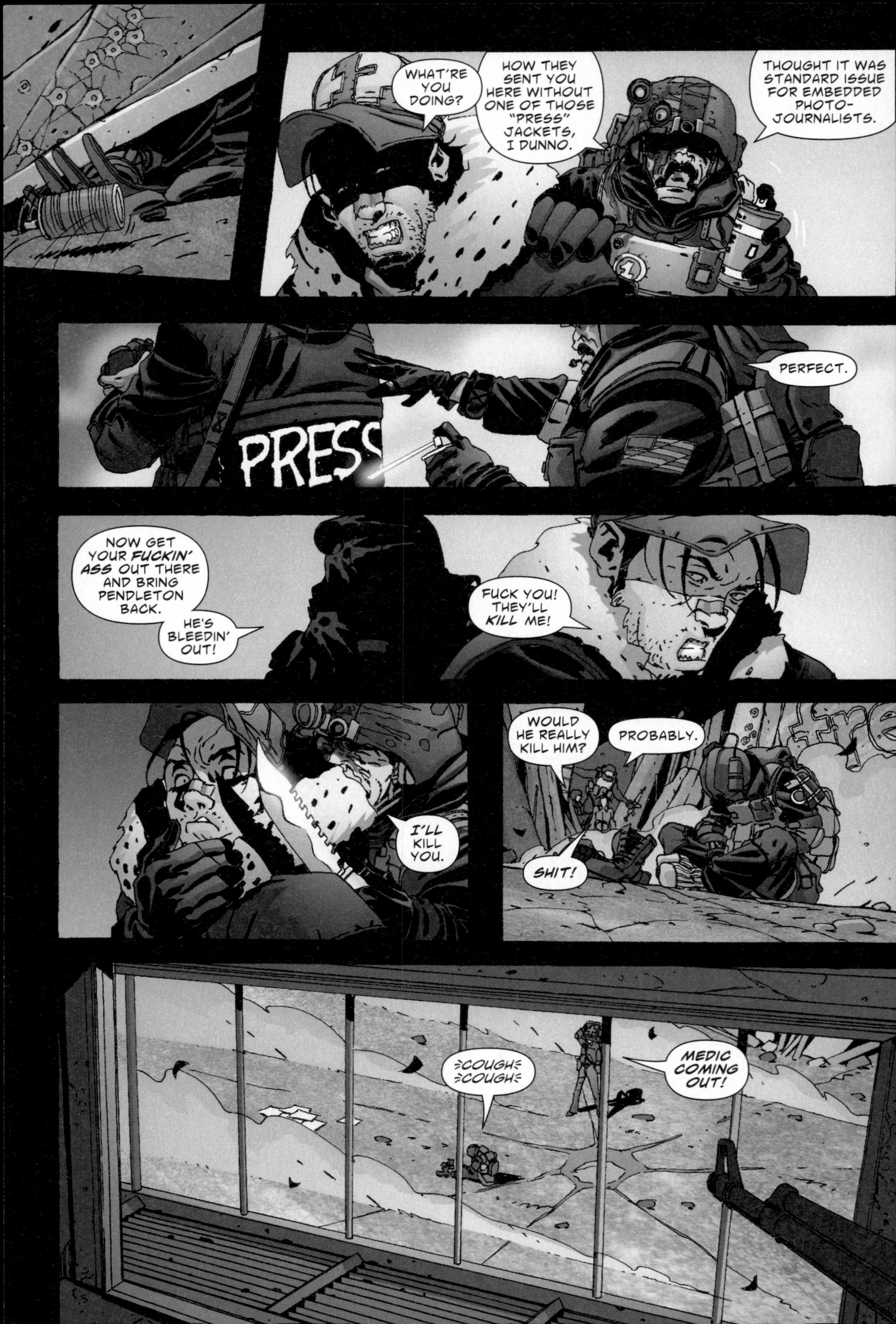
WHAT'RE YOU DOING?
HOW THEY SENT YOU HERE WITHOUT ONE OF THOSE "PRESS" JACKETS, I DUNNO.
THOUGHT IT WAS STANDARD ISSUE FOR EMBEDDED PHOTO-JOURNALISTS.
PERFECT.
PRESS
NOW GET YOUR FUCKIN' ASS OUT THERE AND BRING PENDLETON BACK.
HE'S BLEEDIN' OUT!
FUCK YOU! THEY'LL KILL ME!
I'LL KILL YOU.
WOULD HE REALLY KILL HIM?
PROBABLY.
SHIT!
COUGH COUGH
MEDIC COMING OUT!

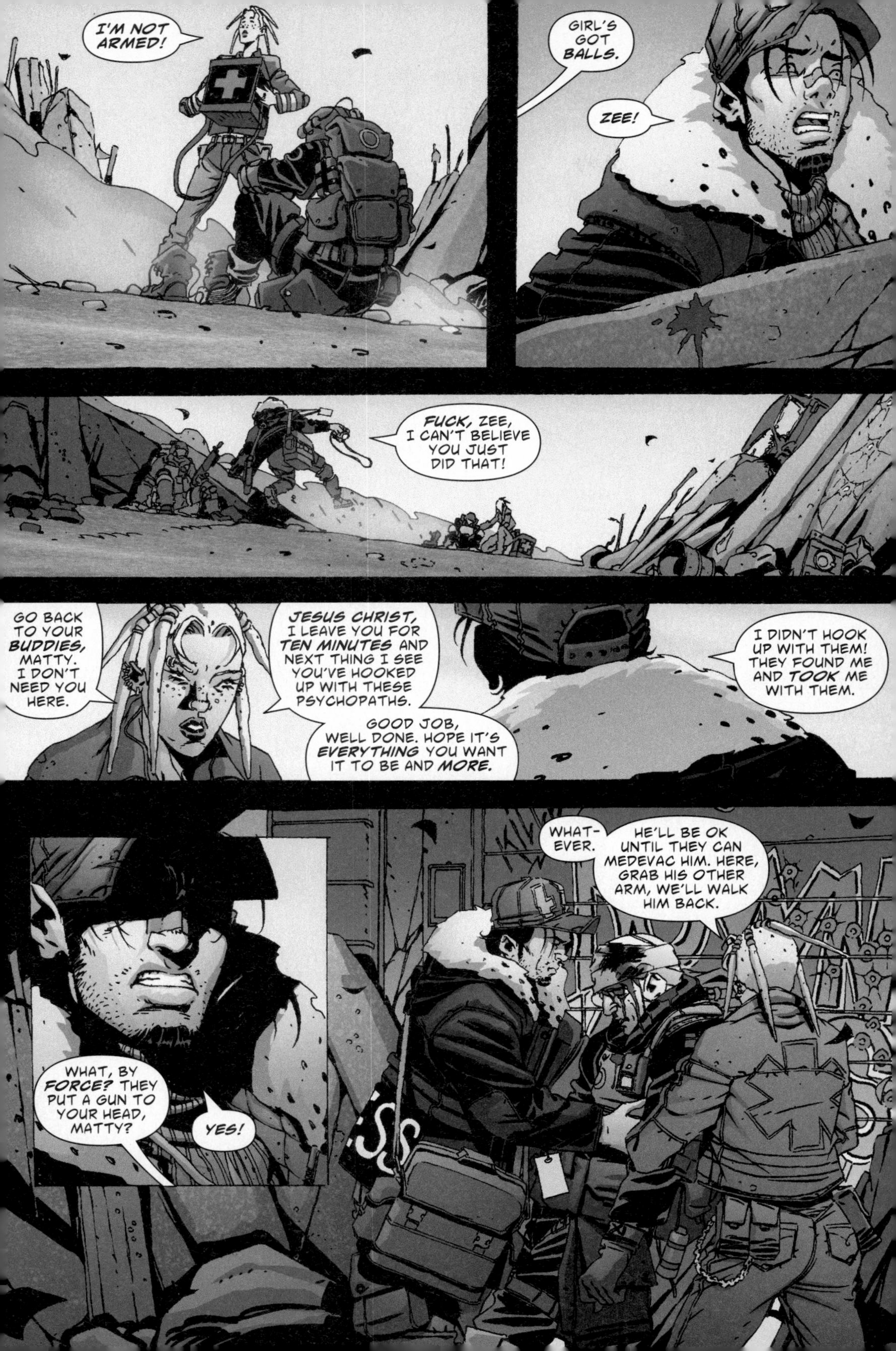
I'M NOT ARMED!
GIRL'S GOT BALLS.
ZEE!
FUCK, ZEE, I CAN'T BELIEVE YOU JUST DID THAT!
GO BACK TO YOUR BUDDIES, MATTY. I DON'T NEED YOU HERE.
JESUS CHRIST, I LEAVE YOU FOR TEN MINUTES AND NEXT THING I SEE YOU'VE HOOKED UP WITH THESE PSYCHOPATHS.
GOOD JOB, WELL DONE. HOPE IT'S EVERYTHING YOU WANT IT TO BE AND MORE.
I DIDN'T HOOK UP WITH THEM! THEY FOUND ME AND TOOK ME WITH THEM.
WHAT, BY FORCE? THEY PUT A GUN TO YOUR HEAD, MATTY?
YES!
WHAT-EVER.
HE'LL BE OK UNTIL THEY CAN MEDEVAC HIM. HERE, GRAB HIS OTHER ARM, WE'LL WALK HIM BACK.

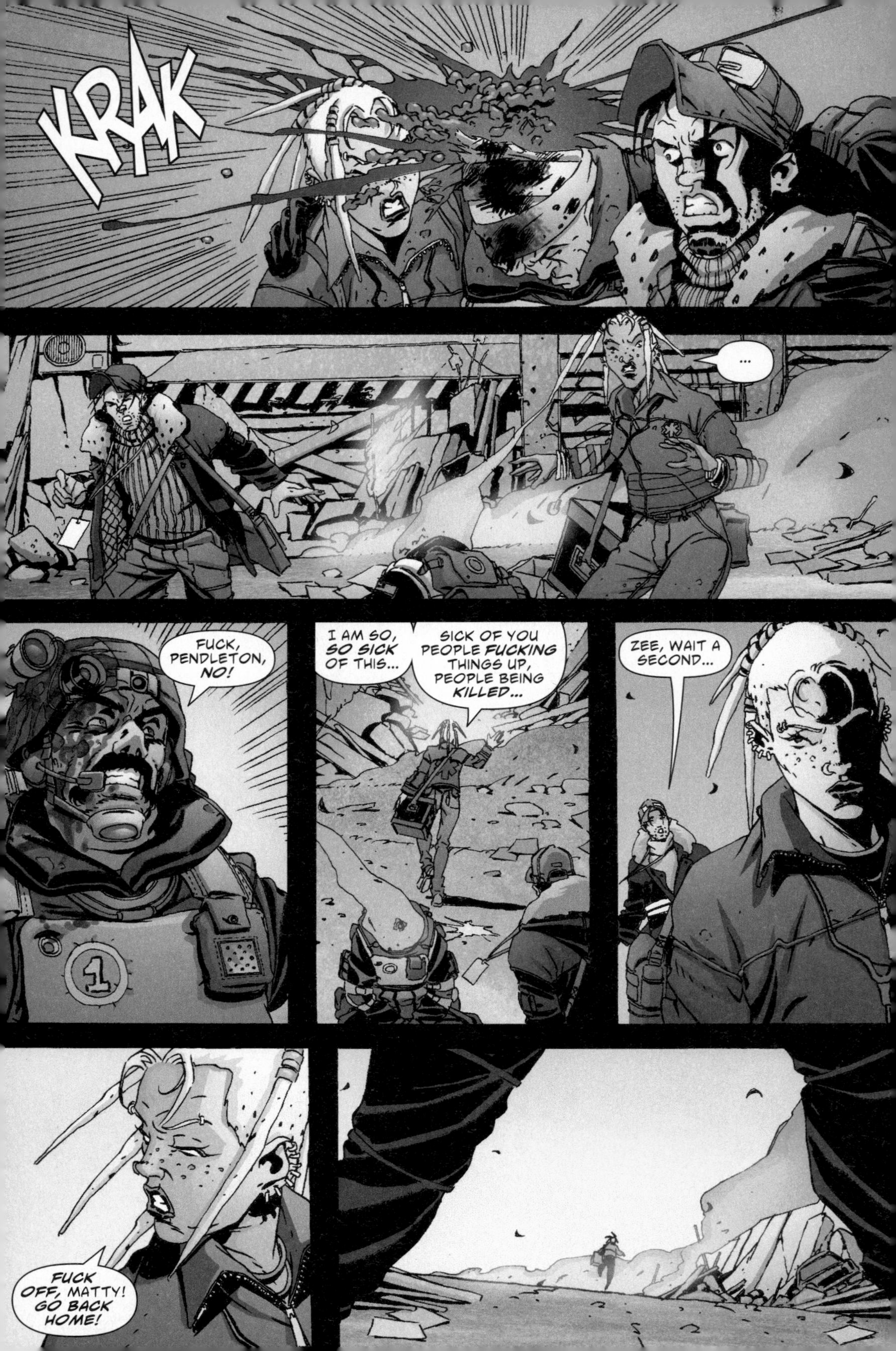
KRAK
...
FUCK, PENDLETON, NO!
I AM SO, SO SICK OF THIS...
SICK OF YOU PEOPLE FUCKING THINGS UP, PEOPLE BEING KILLED...
ZEE, WAIT A SECOND...
FUCK OFF, MATTY! GO BACK HOME!

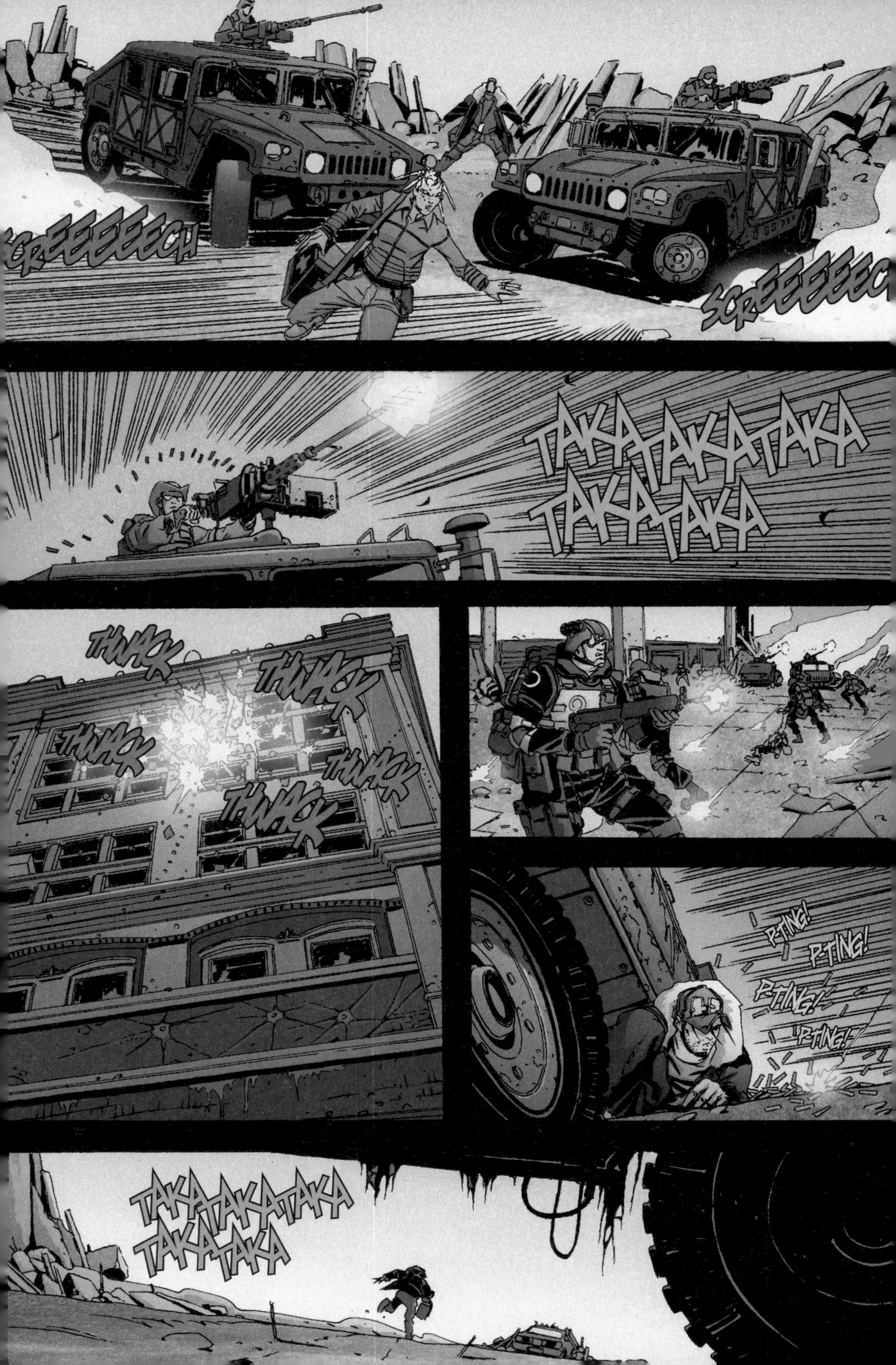
SCREEEEEECH
SCREEEEEECH
TAKATAKATAKA TAKATAKA
THWACK
THWACK
THWACK
THWACK
THWACK
P-TING!
P-TING!
P-TING!
P-TING!
TAKATAKATAKA TAKATAKA

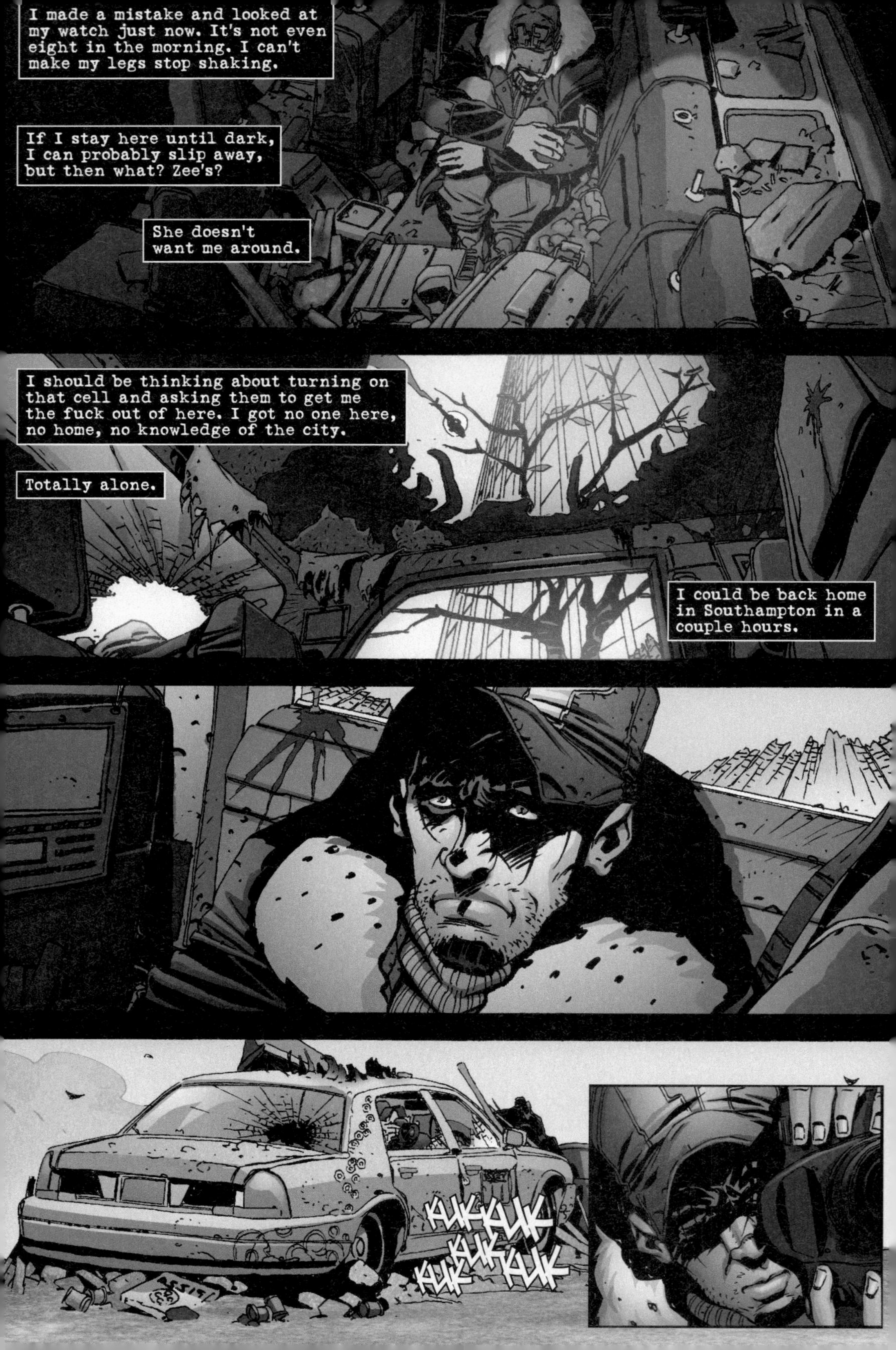
I made a mistake and looked at my watch just now. It's not even eight in the morning. I can't make my legs stop shaking.
If I stay here until dark, I can probably slip away, but then what? Zee's?
She doesn't want me around.
I should be thinking about turning on that cell and asking them to get me the fuck out of here. I got no one here, no home, no knowledge of the city.
Totally alone.
I could be back home in Southampton in a couple hours.
KUK KUK KUK KUK KUK KUK

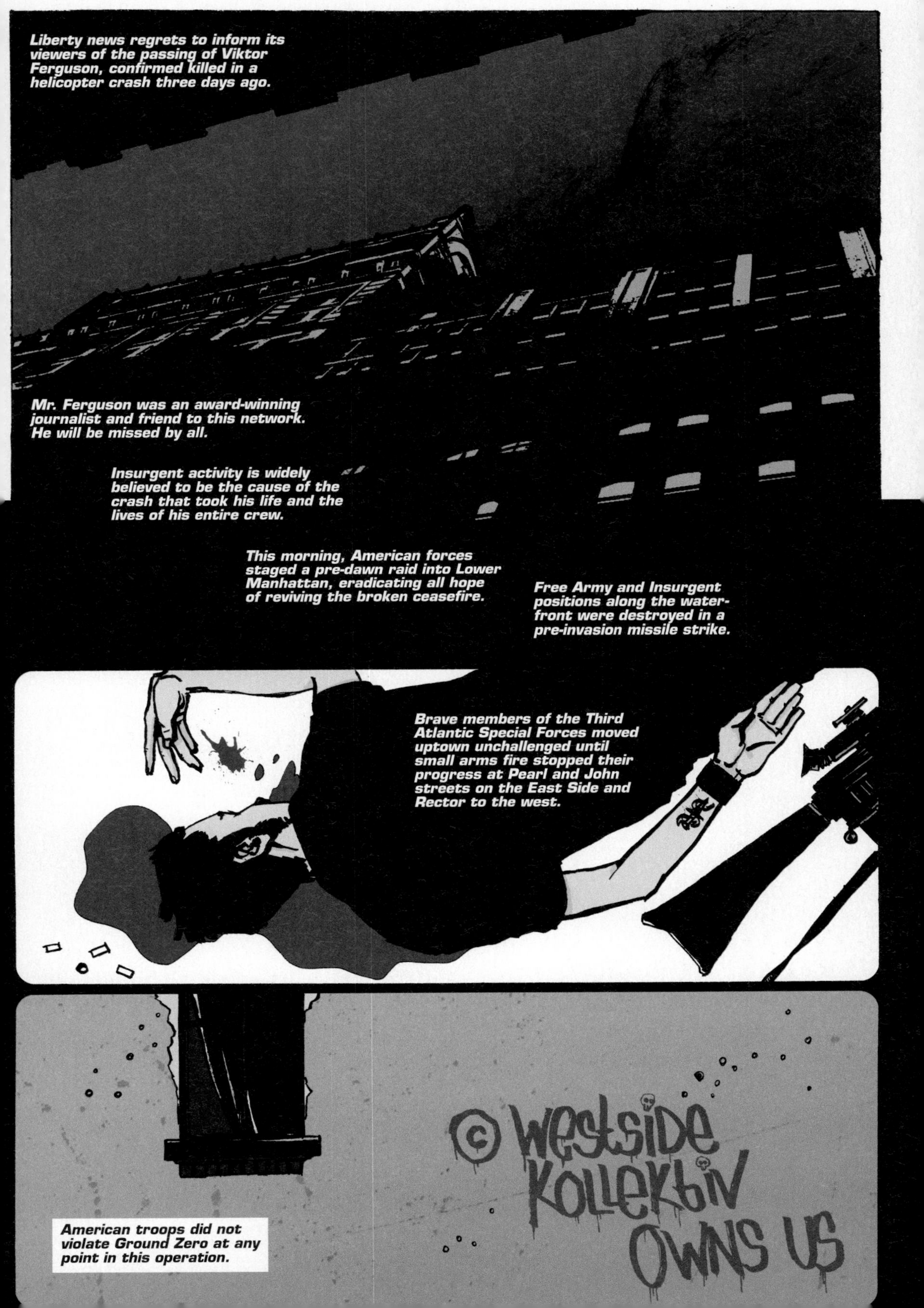

Liberty news regrets to inform its viewers of the passing of Viktor Ferguson, confirmed killed in a helicopter crash three days ago.

Mr. Ferguson was an award-winning journalist and friend to this network. He will be missed by all.

Insurgent activity is widely believed to be the cause of the crash that took his life and the lives of his entire crew.

This morning, American forces staged a pre-dawn raid into Lower Manhattan, eradicating all hope of reviving the broken ceasefire.

Free Army and Insurgent positions along the water-front were destroyed in a pre-invasion missile strike.

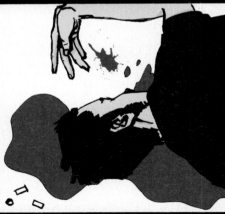

Brave members of the Third Atlantic Special Forces moved uptown unchallenged until small arms fire stopped their progress at Pearl and John streets on the East Side and Rector to the west.

© WESTSIDE KOLLEKTIV OWNS US

American troops did not violate Ground Zero at any point in this operation.

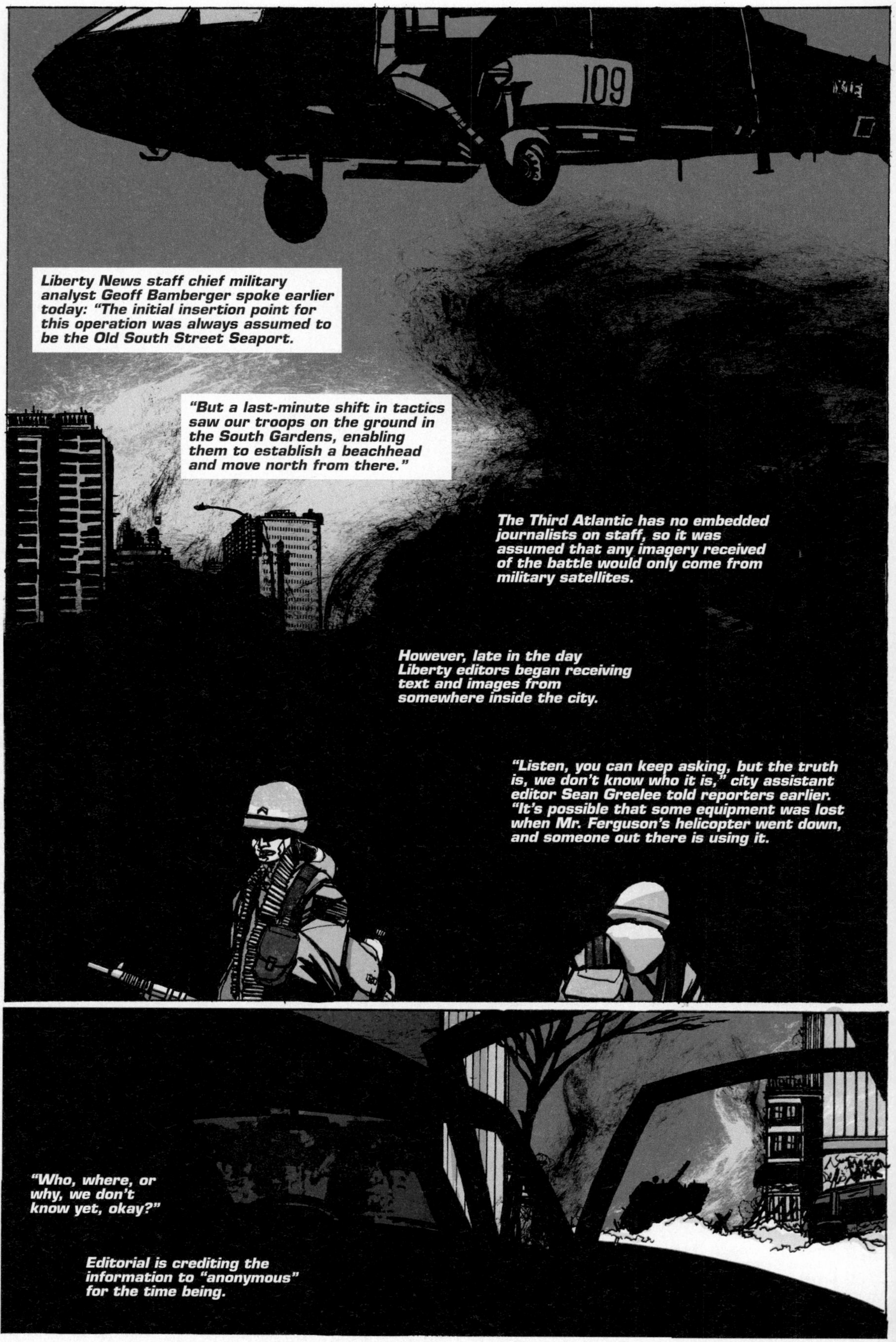
109
Liberty News staff chief military analyst Geoff Bamberger spoke earlier today: "The initial insertion point for this operation was always assumed to be the Old South Street Seaport.
"But a last-minute shift in tactics saw our troops on the ground in the South Gardens, enabling them to establish a beachhead and move north from there."
The Third Atlantic has no embedded journalists on staff, so it was assumed that any imagery received of the battle would only come from military satellites.
However, late in the day Liberty editors began receiving text and images from somewhere inside the city.
"Listen, you can keep asking, but the truth is, we don't know who it is," city assistant editor Sean Greelee told reporters earlier. "It's possible that some equipment was lost when Mr. Ferguson's helicopter went down, and someone out there is using it.
"Who, where, or why, we don't know yet, okay?"
Editorial is crediting the information to "anonymous" for the time being.

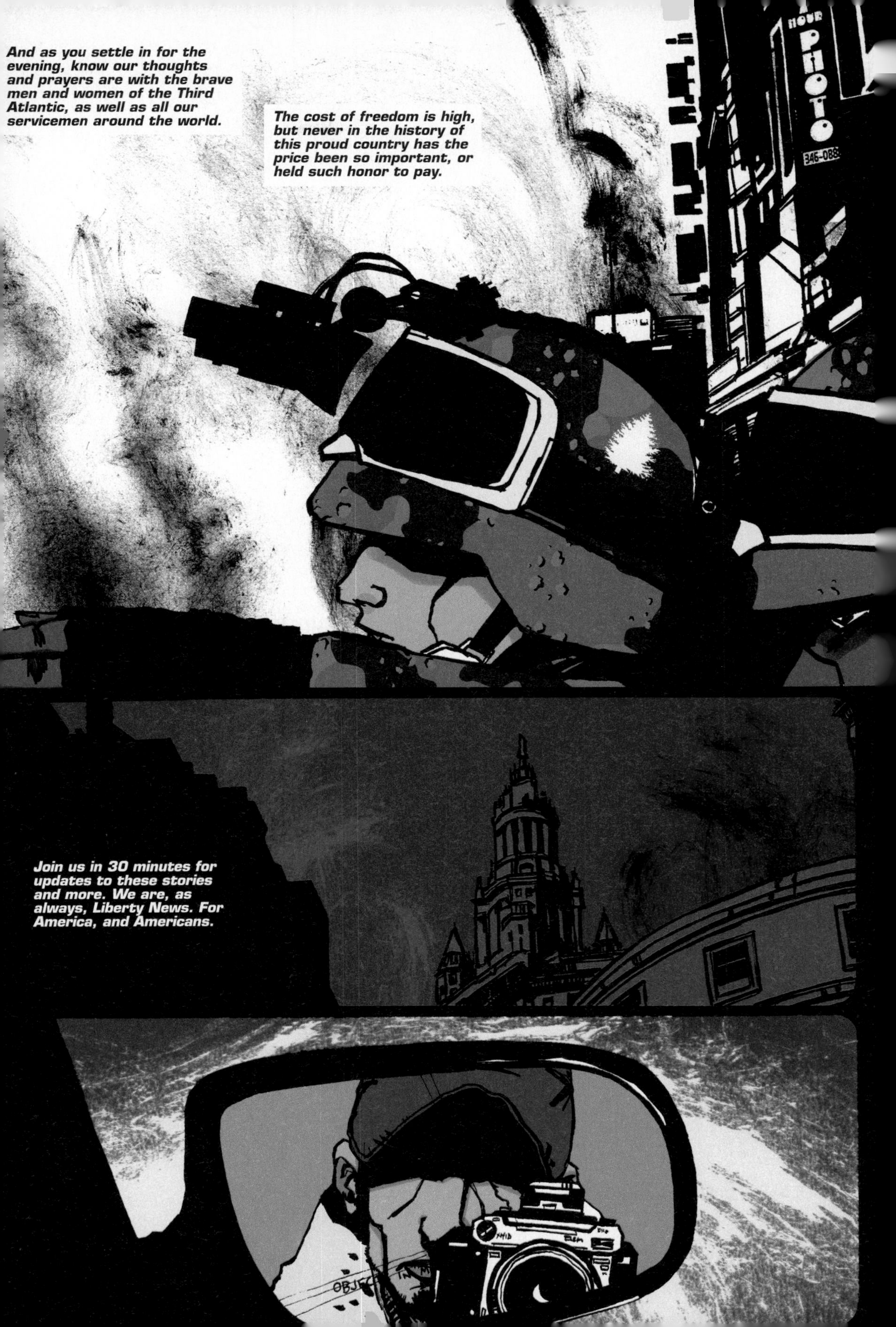
And as you settle in for the evening, know our thoughts and prayers are with the brave men and women of the Third Atlantic, as well as all our servicemen around the world.
The cost of freedom is high, but never in the history of this proud country has the price been so important, or held such honor to pay.
HOUR PHOTO
Join us in 30 minutes for updates to these stories and more. We are, as always, Liberty News. For America, and Americans.

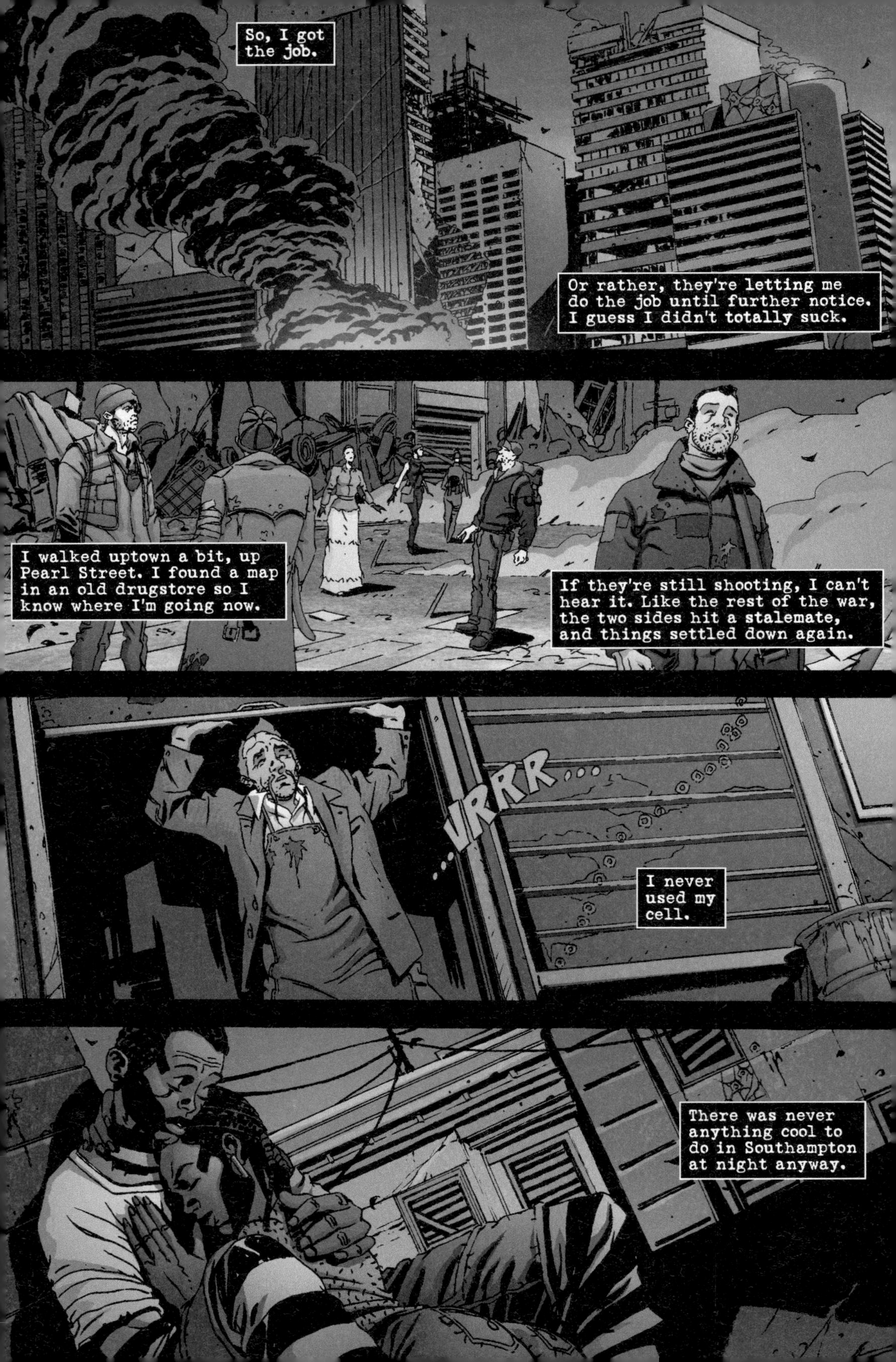
So, I got the job.
Or rather, they're letting me do the job until further notice. I guess I didn't totally suck.
I walked uptown a bit, up Pearl Street. I found a map in an old drugstore so I know where I'm going now.
If they're still shooting, I can't hear it. Like the rest of the war, the two sides hit a stalemate, and things settled down again.
VRRR...
I never used my cell.
There was never anything cool to do in Southampton at night anyway.

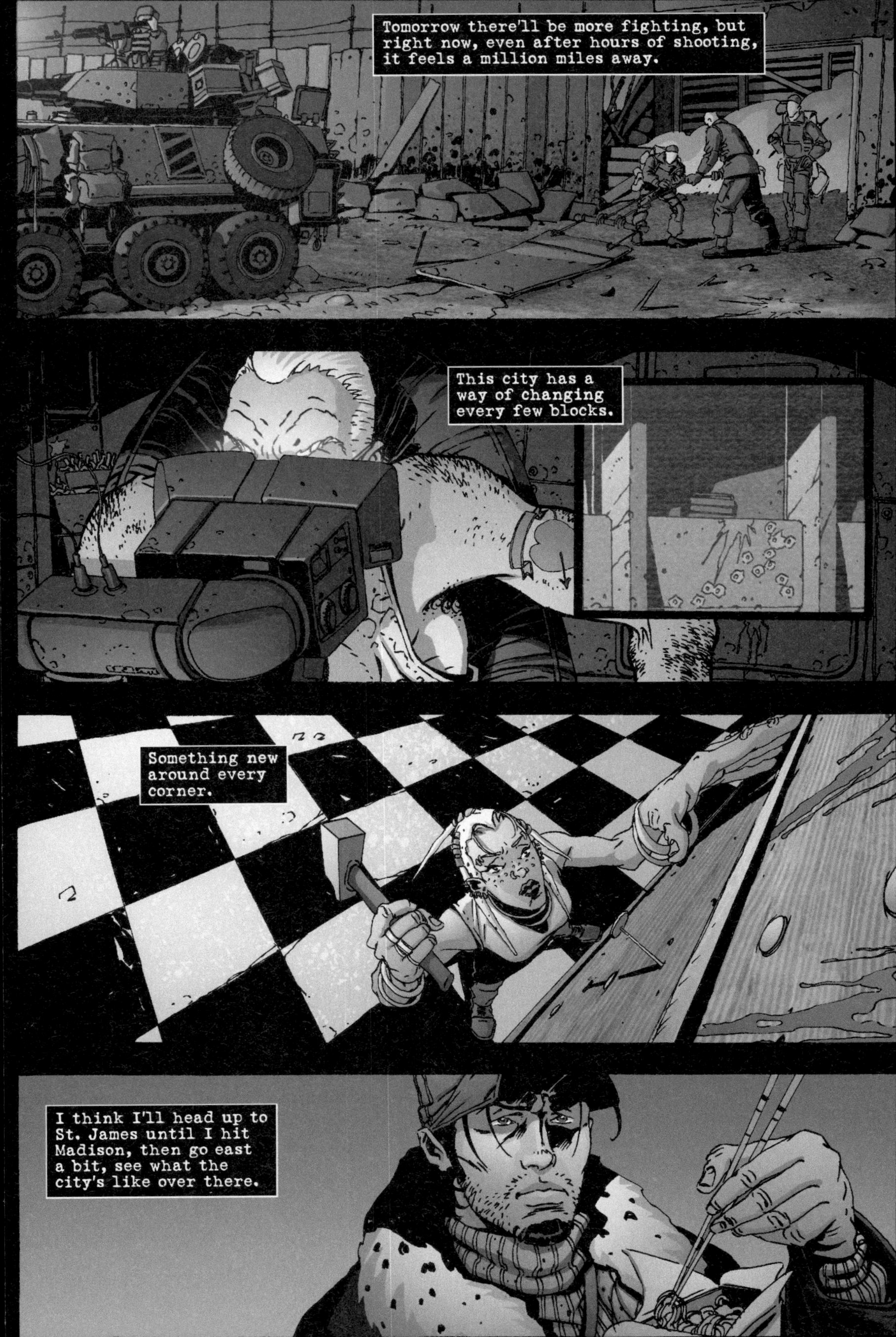
Tomorrow there'll be more fighting, but right now, even after hours of shooting, it feels a million miles away.
This city has a way of changing every few blocks.
Something new around every corner.
I think I'll head up to St. James until I hit Madison, then go east a bit, see what the city's like over there.

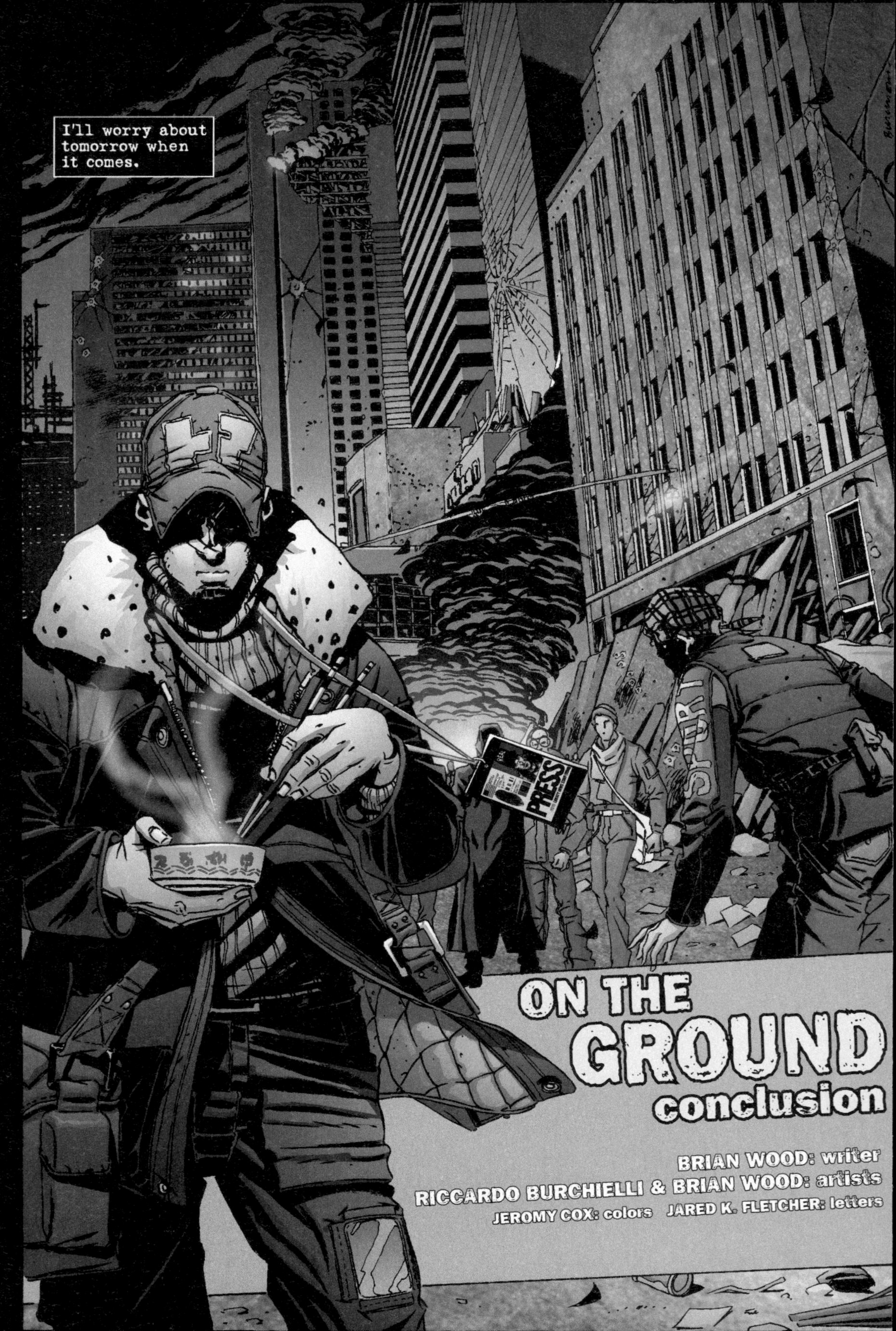
I'll worry about tomorrow when it comes.
PRESS
ON THE GROUND conclusion
BRIAN WOOD: writer
RICCARDO BURCHIELLI & BRIAN WOOD: artists
JEROMY COX: colors JARED K. FLETCHER: letters

DMZ
"GHOSTS"

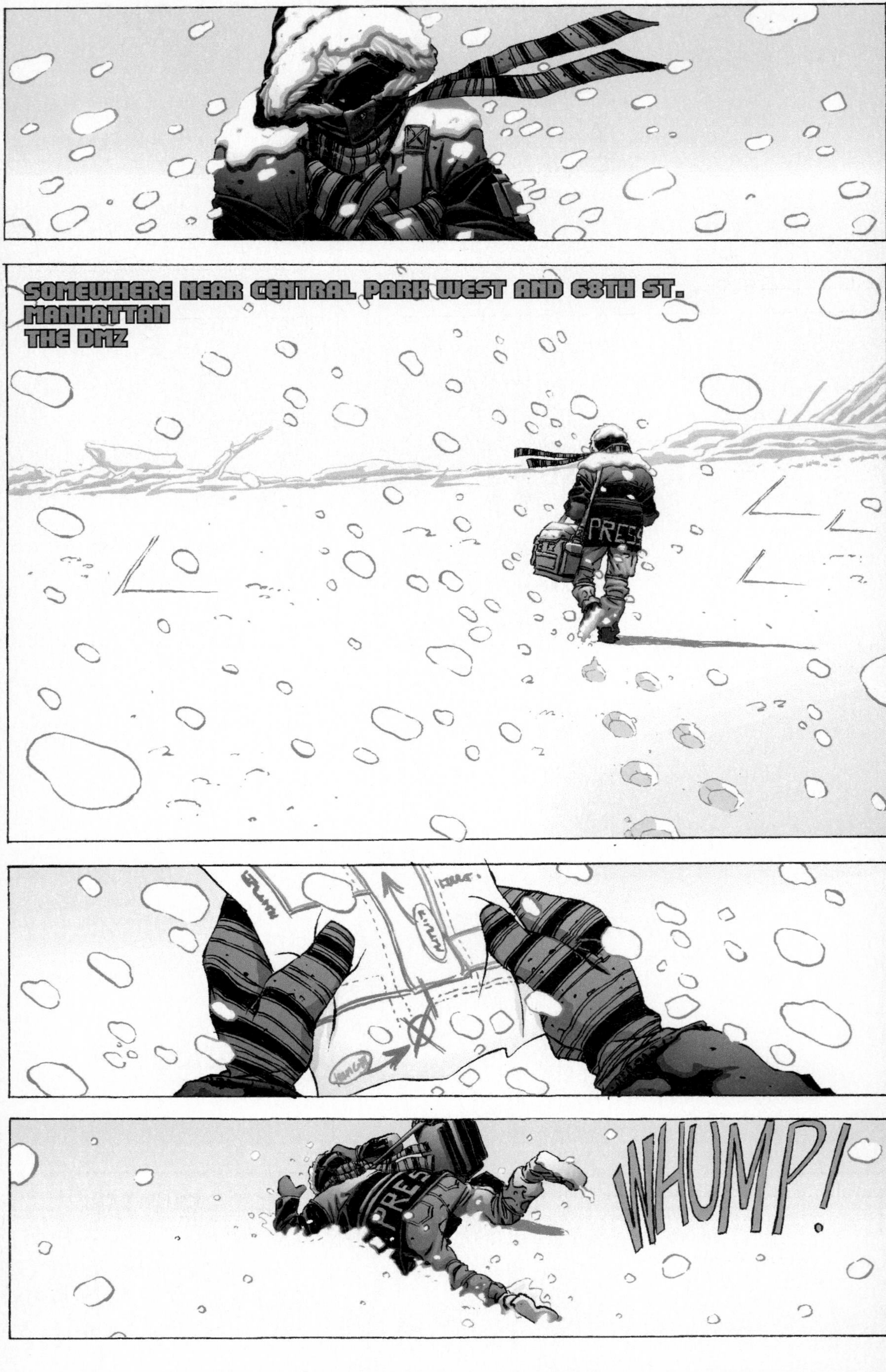
SOMEWHERE NEAR CENTRAL PARK WEST AND 68TH ST.
MANHATTAN
THE DMZ
PRESS
PRESS
WHUMP!

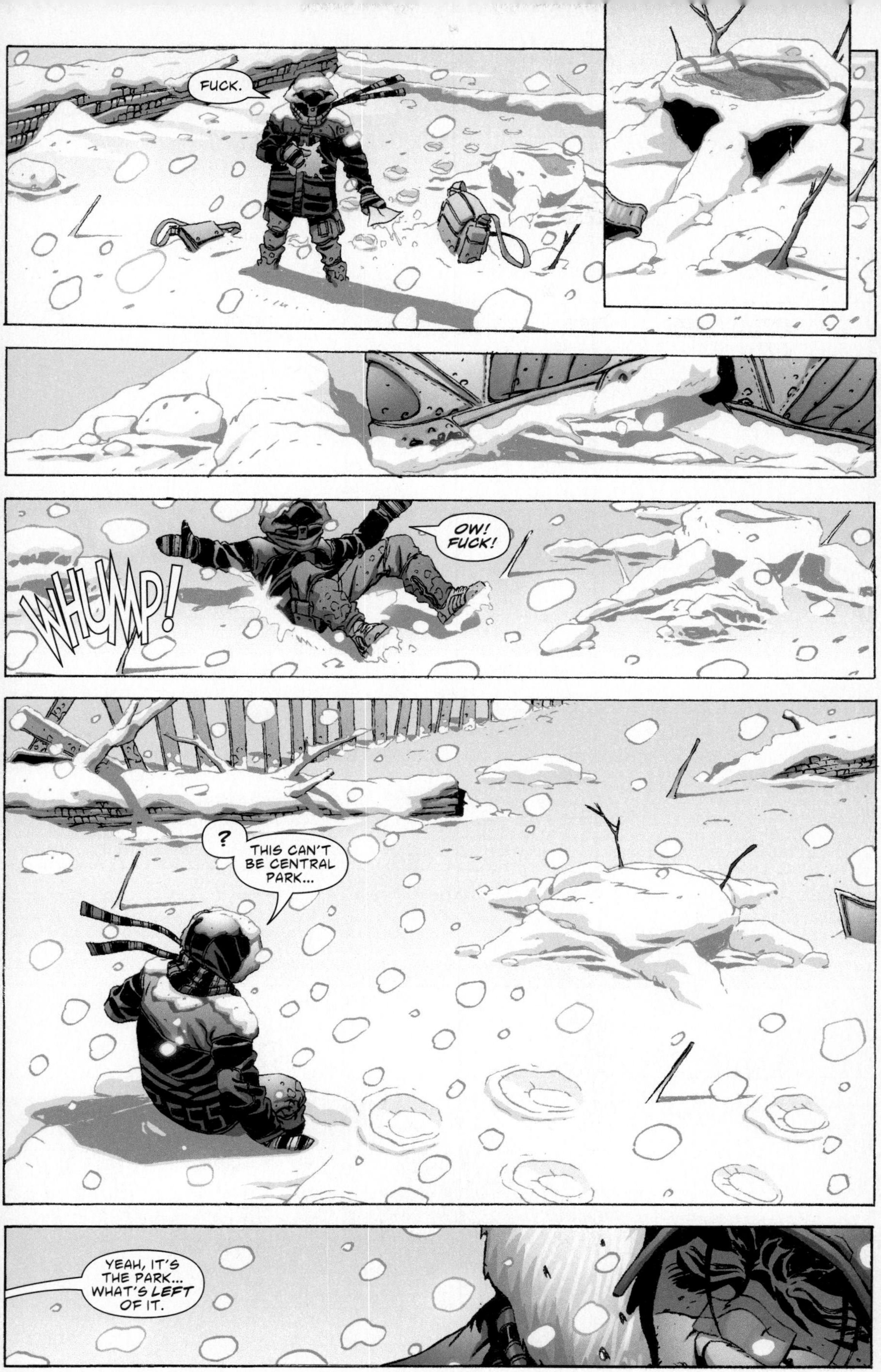
FUCK.
OW! FUCK!
WHUMP!
?
THIS CAN'T BE CENTRAL PARK...
YEAH, IT'S THE PARK... WHAT'S LEFT OF IT.

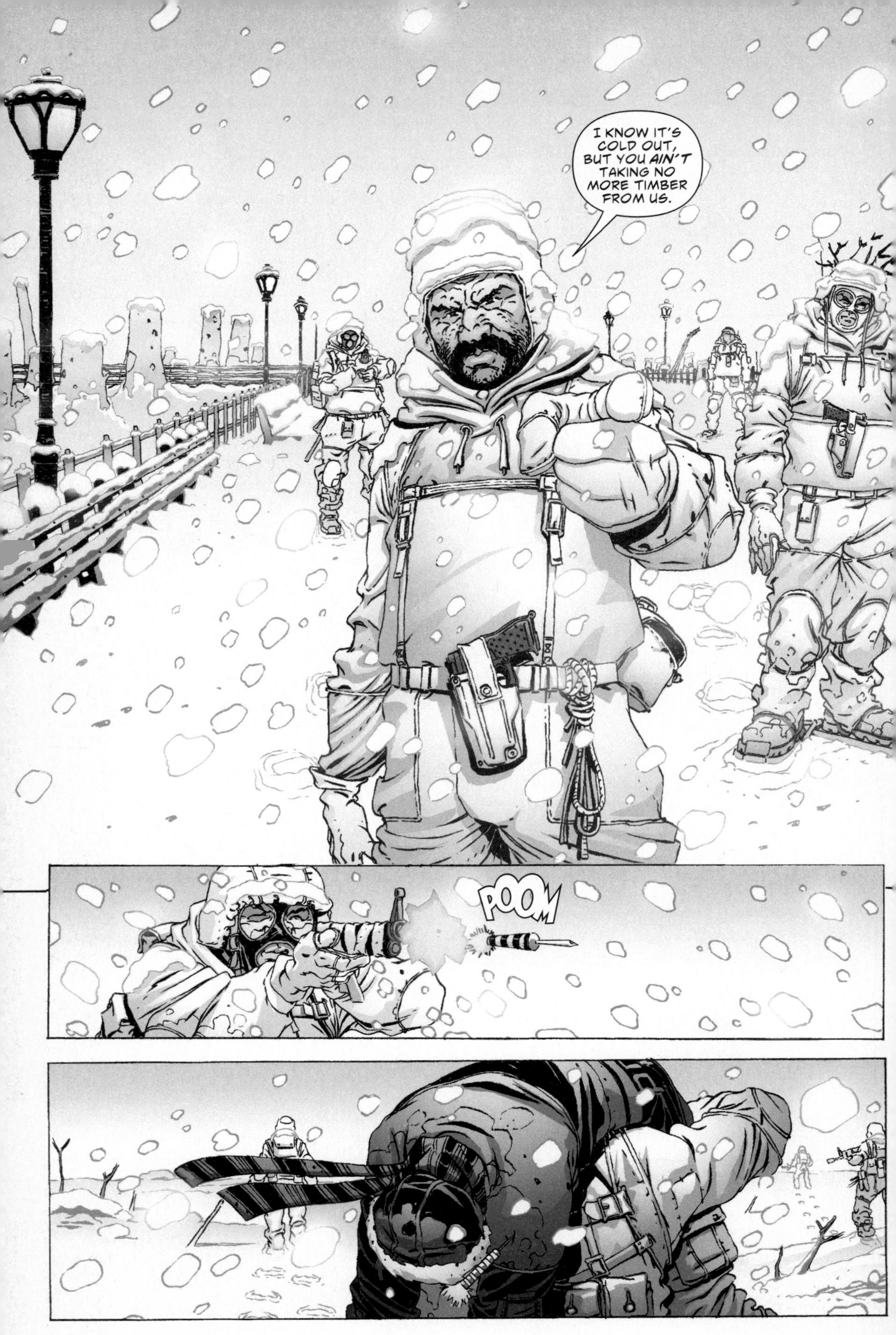
I KNOW IT'S COLD OUT, BUT YOU AIN'T TAKING NO MORE TIMBER FROM US.
POOM

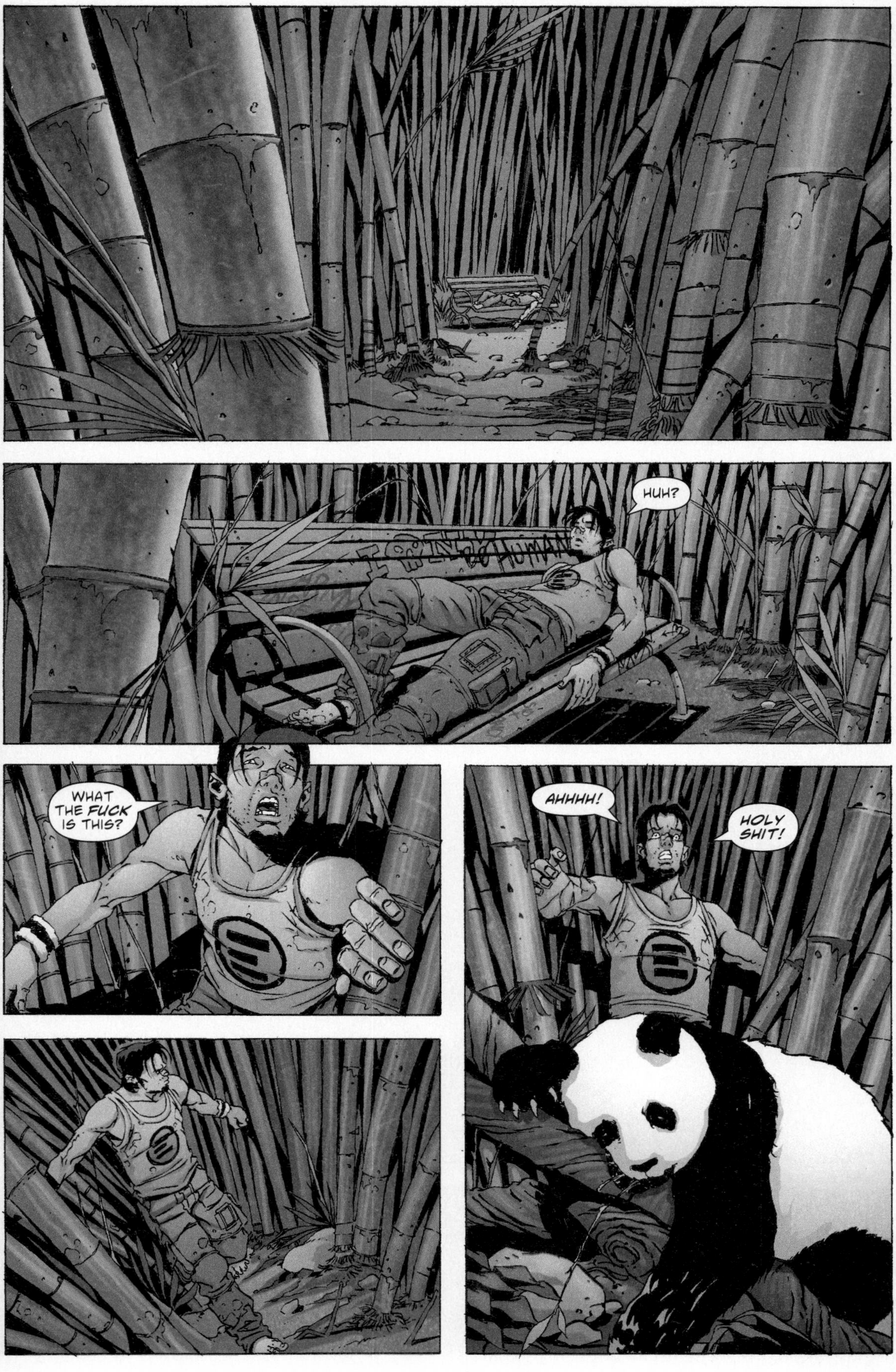
HUH?
WHAT THE FUCK IS THIS?
AHHHH!
HOLY SHIT!

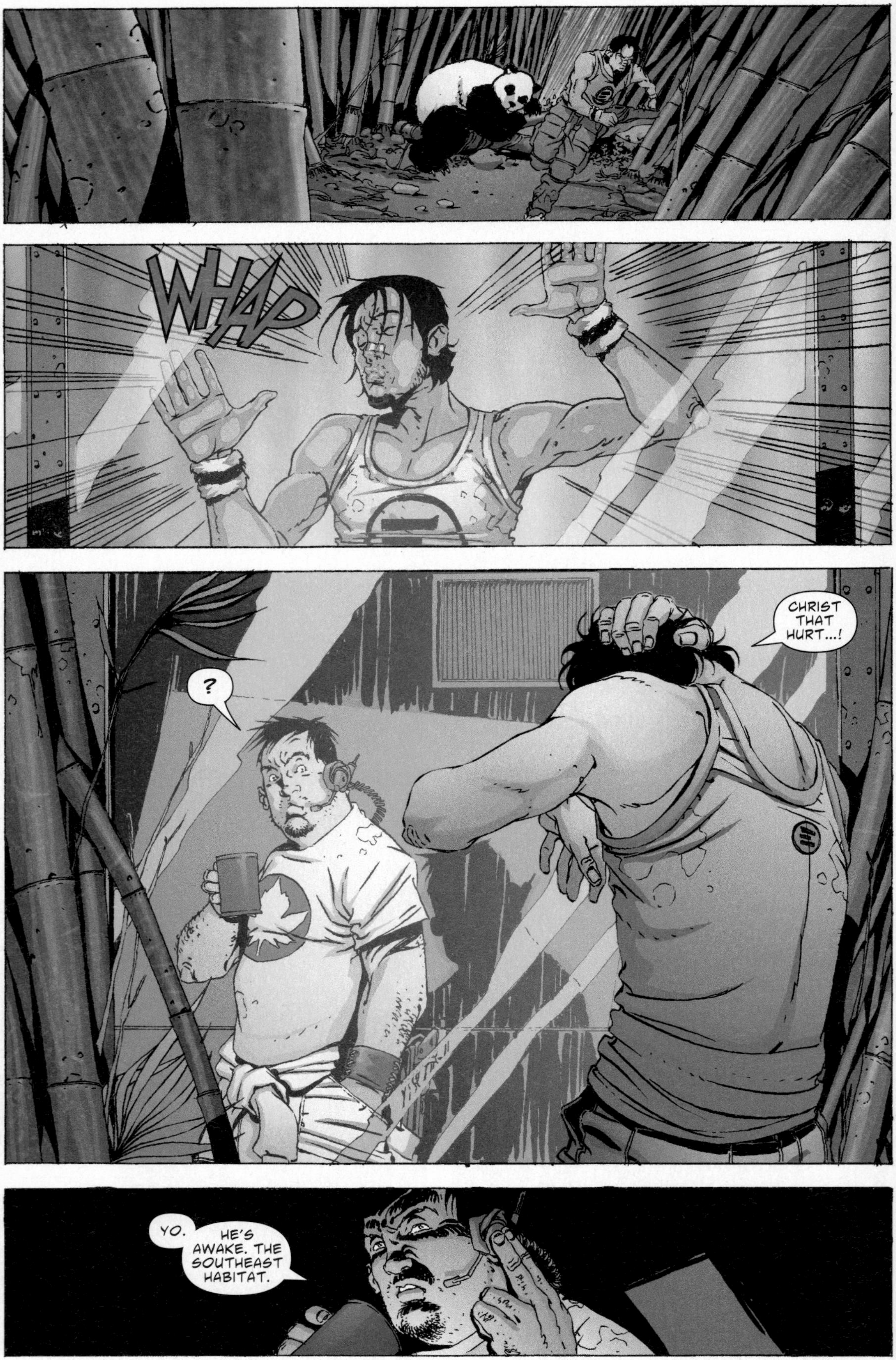
WHAP
CHRIST THAT HURT...!
?
YO.
HE'S AWAKE. THE SOUTHEAST HABITAT.

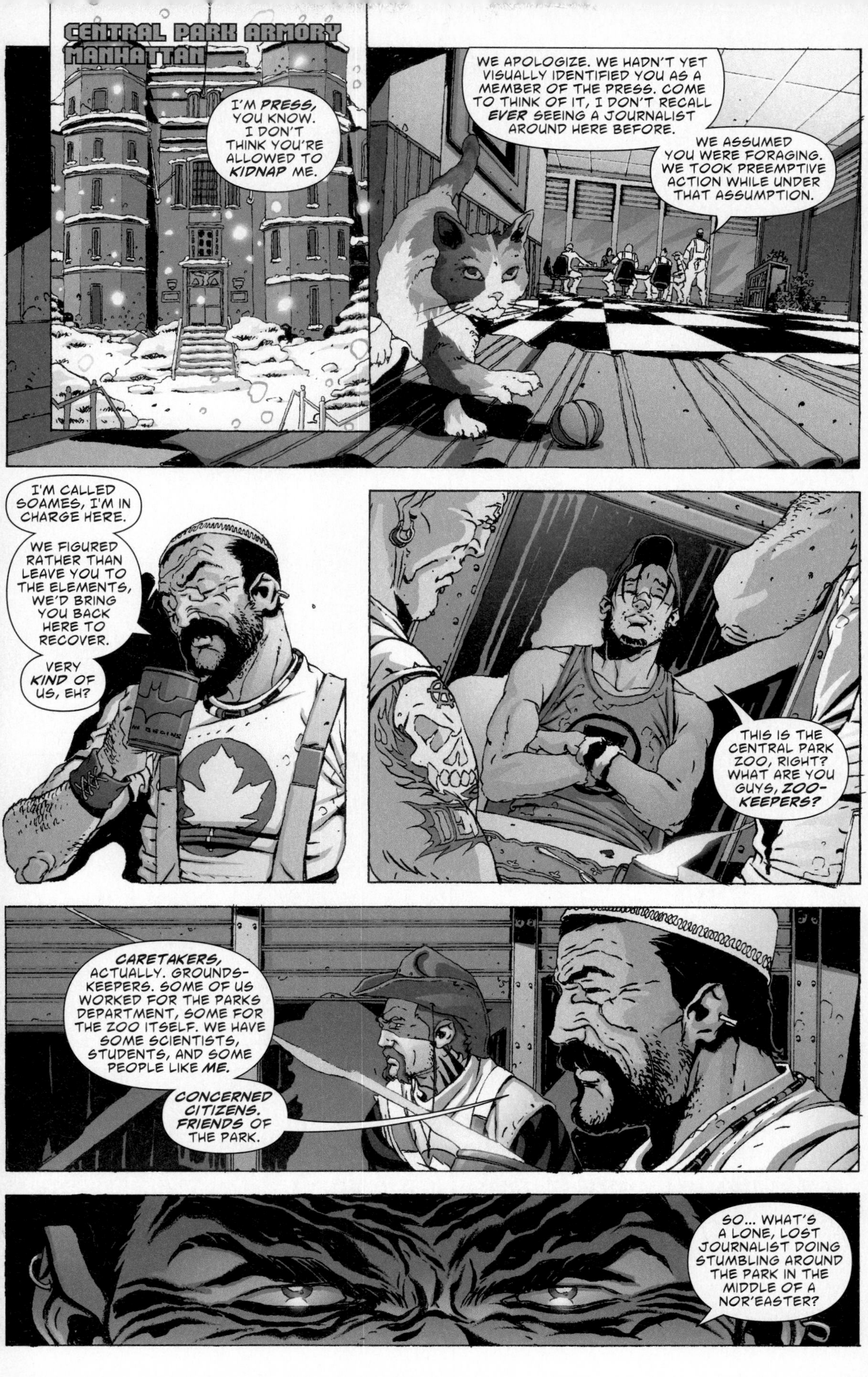
CENTRAL PARK ARMORY
MANHATTAN
I'M PRESS, YOU KNOW. I DON'T THINK YOU'RE ALLOWED TO KIDNAP ME.
WE APOLOGIZE. WE HADN'T YET VISUALLY IDENTIFIED YOU AS A MEMBER OF THE PRESS. COME TO THINK OF IT, I DON'T RECALL EVER SEEING A JOURNALIST AROUND HERE BEFORE.
WE ASSUMED YOU WERE FORAGING. WE TOOK PREEMPTIVE ACTION WHILE UNDER THAT ASSUMPTION.
I'M CALLED SOAMES, I'M IN CHARGE HERE.
WE FIGURED RATHER THAN LEAVE YOU TO THE ELEMENTS, WE'D BRING YOU BACK HERE TO RECOVER.
VERY KIND OF US, EH?
THIS IS THE CENTRAL PARK ZOO, RIGHT? WHAT ARE YOU GUYS, ZOO-KEEPERS?
CARETAKERS, ACTUALLY. GROUNDS-KEEPERS. SOME OF US WORKED FOR THE PARKS DEPARTMENT, SOME FOR THE ZOO ITSELF. WE HAVE SOME SCIENTISTS, STUDENTS, AND SOME PEOPLE LIKE ME.
CONCERNED CITIZENS. FRIENDS OF THE PARK.
SO... WHAT'S A LONE, LOST JOURNALIST DOING STUMBLING AROUND THE PARK IN THE MIDDLE OF A NOR'EASTER?

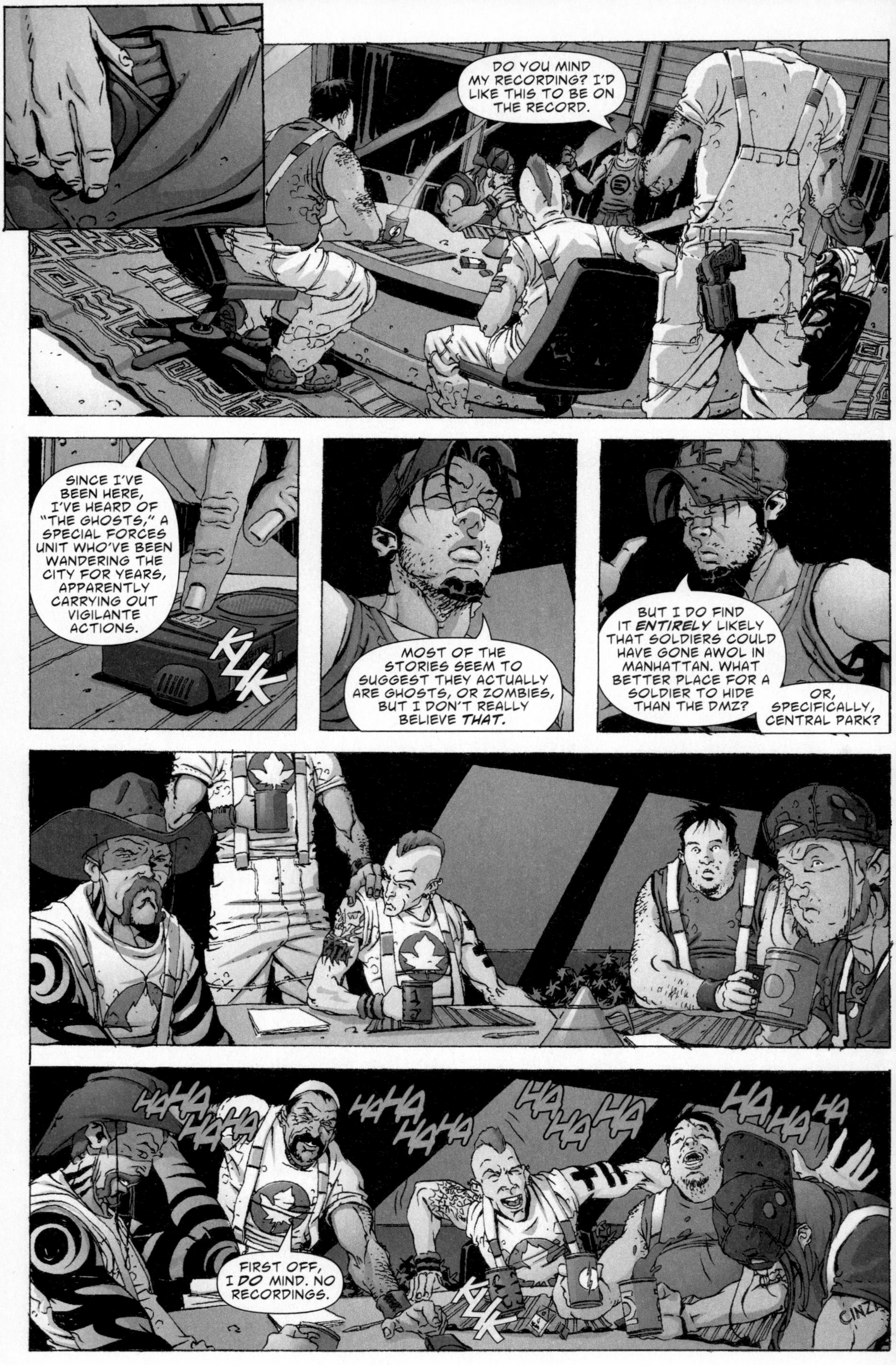

DO YOU MIND MY RECORDING? I'D LIKE THIS TO BE ON THE RECORD.
SINCE I'VE BEEN HERE, I'VE HEARD OF "THE GHOSTS," A SPECIAL FORCES UNIT WHO'VE BEEN WANDERING THE CITY FOR YEARS, APPARENTLY CARRYING OUT VIGILANTE ACTIONS.
KLIK
MOST OF THE STORIES SEEM TO SUGGEST THEY ACTUALLY ARE GHOSTS, OR ZOMBIES, BUT I DON'T REALLY BELIEVE *THAT.*
BUT I DO FIND IT *ENTIRELY* LIKELY THAT SOLDIERS COULD HAVE GONE AWOL IN MANHATTAN. WHAT BETTER PLACE FOR A SOLDIER TO HIDE THAN THE DMZ?
OR, SPECIFICALLY, CENTRAL PARK?
HAHA HAHA HAHA HAHA HAHA HAHA HAHA HAHA HA
FIRST OFF, I *DO* MIND. NO RECORDINGS.
KLIK
CINZ

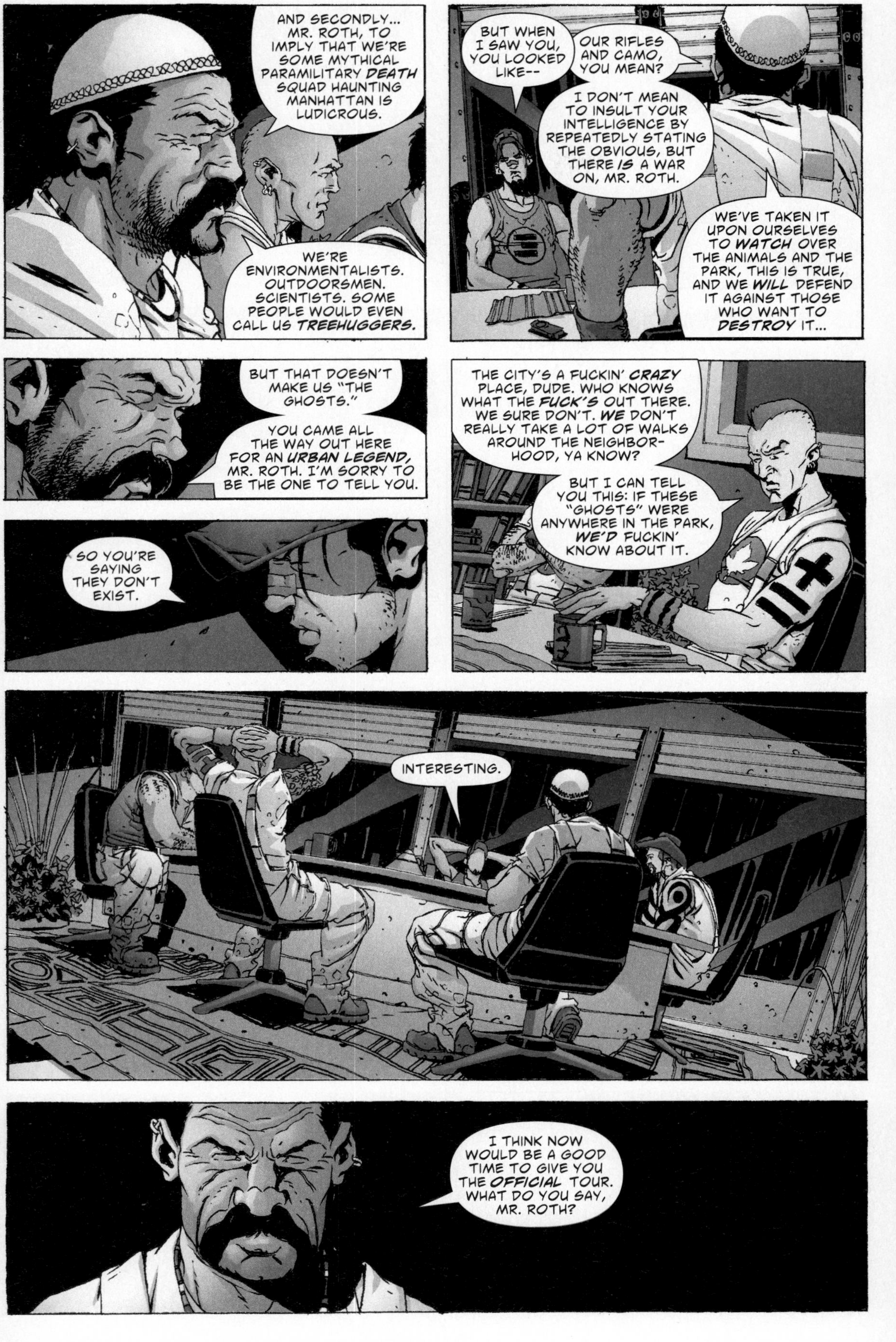
AND SECONDLY... MR. ROTH, TO IMPLY THAT WE'RE SOME MYTHICAL PARAMILITARY DEATH SQUAD HAUNTING MANHATTAN IS LUDICROUS.
WE'RE ENVIRONMENTALISTS. OUTDOORSMEN. SCIENTISTS. SOME PEOPLE WOULD EVEN CALL US TREEHUGGERS.
BUT WHEN I SAW YOU, YOU LOOKED LIKE--
OUR RIFLES AND CAMO, YOU MEAN?
I DON'T MEAN TO INSULT YOUR INTELLIGENCE BY REPEATEDLY STATING THE OBVIOUS, BUT THERE IS A WAR ON, MR. ROTH.
WE'VE TAKEN IT UPON OURSELVES TO WATCH OVER THE ANIMALS AND THE PARK, THIS IS TRUE, AND WE WILL DEFEND IT AGAINST THOSE WHO WANT TO DESTROY IT...
BUT THAT DOESN'T MAKE US "THE GHOSTS."
YOU CAME ALL THE WAY OUT HERE FOR AN URBAN LEGEND, MR. ROTH. I'M SORRY TO BE THE ONE TO TELL YOU.
SO YOU'RE SAYING THEY DON'T EXIST.
THE CITY'S A FUCKIN' CRAZY PLACE, DUDE. WHO KNOWS WHAT THE FUCK'S OUT THERE. WE SURE DON'T. WE DON'T REALLY TAKE A LOT OF WALKS AROUND THE NEIGHBOR-HOOD, YA KNOW?
BUT I CAN TELL YOU THIS: IF THESE "GHOSTS" WERE ANYWHERE IN THE PARK, WE'D FUCKIN' KNOW ABOUT IT.
INTERESTING.
I THINK NOW WOULD BE A GOOD TIME TO GIVE YOU THE OFFICIAL TOUR. WHAT DO YOU SAY, MR. ROTH?

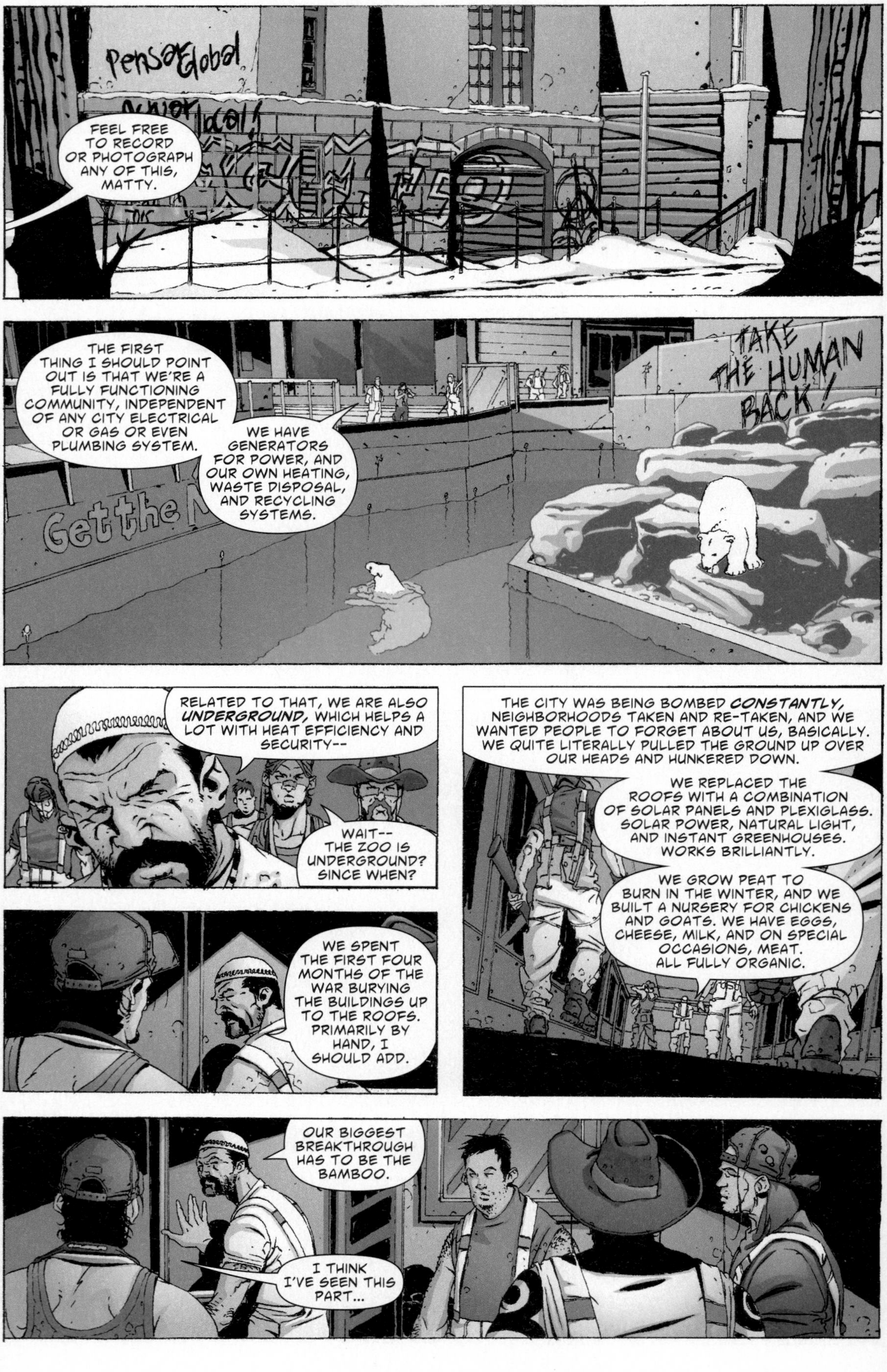
Pensar Global
Actuar local!
FEEL FREE TO RECORD OR PHOTOGRAPH ANY OF THIS, MATTY.
TAKE THE HUMAN BACK!
THE FIRST THING I SHOULD POINT OUT IS THAT WE'RE A FULLY FUNCTIONING COMMUNITY, INDEPENDENT OF ANY CITY ELECTRICAL OR GAS OR EVEN PLUMBING SYSTEM.
WE HAVE GENERATORS FOR POWER, AND OUR OWN HEATING, WASTE DISPOSAL, AND RECYCLING SYSTEMS.
Get the
RELATED TO THAT, WE ARE ALSO ***UNDERGROUND,*** WHICH HELPS A LOT WITH HEAT EFFICIENCY AND SECURITY--
WAIT-- THE ZOO IS UNDERGROUND? SINCE WHEN?
WE SPENT THE FIRST FOUR MONTHS OF THE WAR BURYING THE BUILDINGS UP TO THE ROOFS. PRIMARILY BY HAND, I SHOULD ADD.
THE CITY WAS BEING BOMBED ***CONSTANTLY,*** NEIGHBORHOODS TAKEN AND RE-TAKEN, AND WE WANTED PEOPLE TO FORGET ABOUT US, BASICALLY. WE QUITE LITERALLY PULLED THE GROUND UP OVER OUR HEADS AND HUNKERED DOWN.
WE REPLACED THE ROOFS WITH A COMBINATION OF SOLAR PANELS AND PLEXIGLASS. SOLAR POWER, NATURAL LIGHT, AND INSTANT GREENHOUSES. WORKS BRILLIANTLY.
WE GROW PEAT TO BURN IN THE WINTER, AND WE BUILT A NURSERY FOR CHICKENS AND GOATS. WE HAVE EGGS, CHEESE, MILK, AND ON SPECIAL OCCASIONS, MEAT. ALL FULLY ORGANIC.
OUR BIGGEST BREAKTHROUGH HAS TO BE THE BAMBOO.
I THINK I'VE SEEN THIS PART...

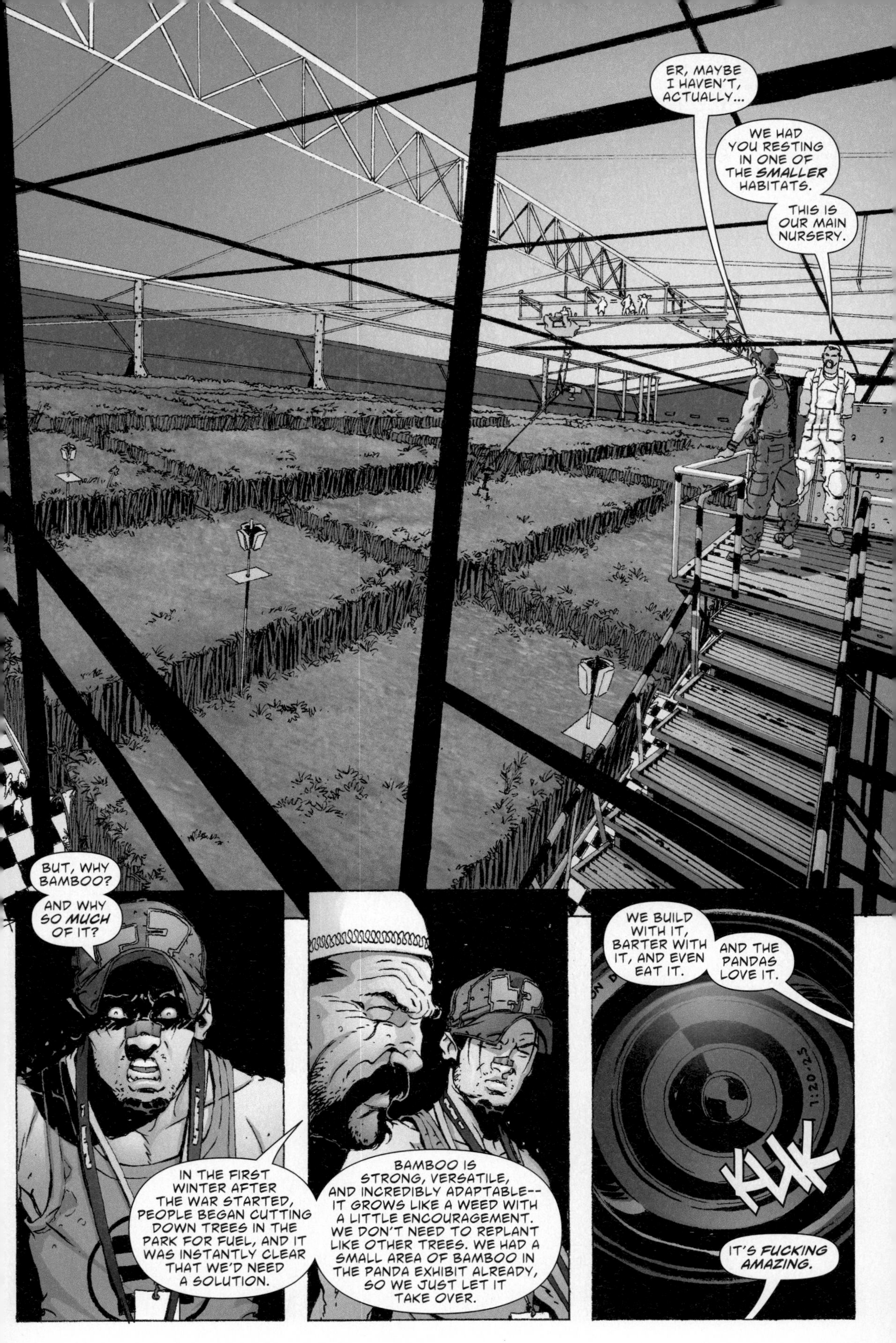
ER, MAYBE I HAVEN'T, ACTUALLY...
WE HAD YOU RESTING IN ONE OF THE SMALLER HABITATS.
THIS IS OUR MAIN NURSERY.
BUT, WHY BAMBOO?
AND WHY SO MUCH OF IT?
IN THE FIRST WINTER AFTER THE WAR STARTED, PEOPLE BEGAN CUTTING DOWN TREES IN THE PARK FOR FUEL, AND IT WAS INSTANTLY CLEAR THAT WE'D NEED A SOLUTION.
BAMBOO IS STRONG, VERSATILE, AND INCREDIBLY ADAPTABLE-- IT GROWS LIKE A WEED WITH A LITTLE ENCOURAGEMENT. WE DON'T NEED TO REPLANT LIKE OTHER TREES. WE HAD A SMALL AREA OF BAMBOO IN THE PANDA EXHIBIT ALREADY, SO WE JUST LET IT TAKE OVER.
WE BUILD WITH IT, BARTER WITH IT, AND EVEN EAT IT.
AND THE PANDAS LOVE IT.
KLIK
IT'S FUCKING AMAZING.

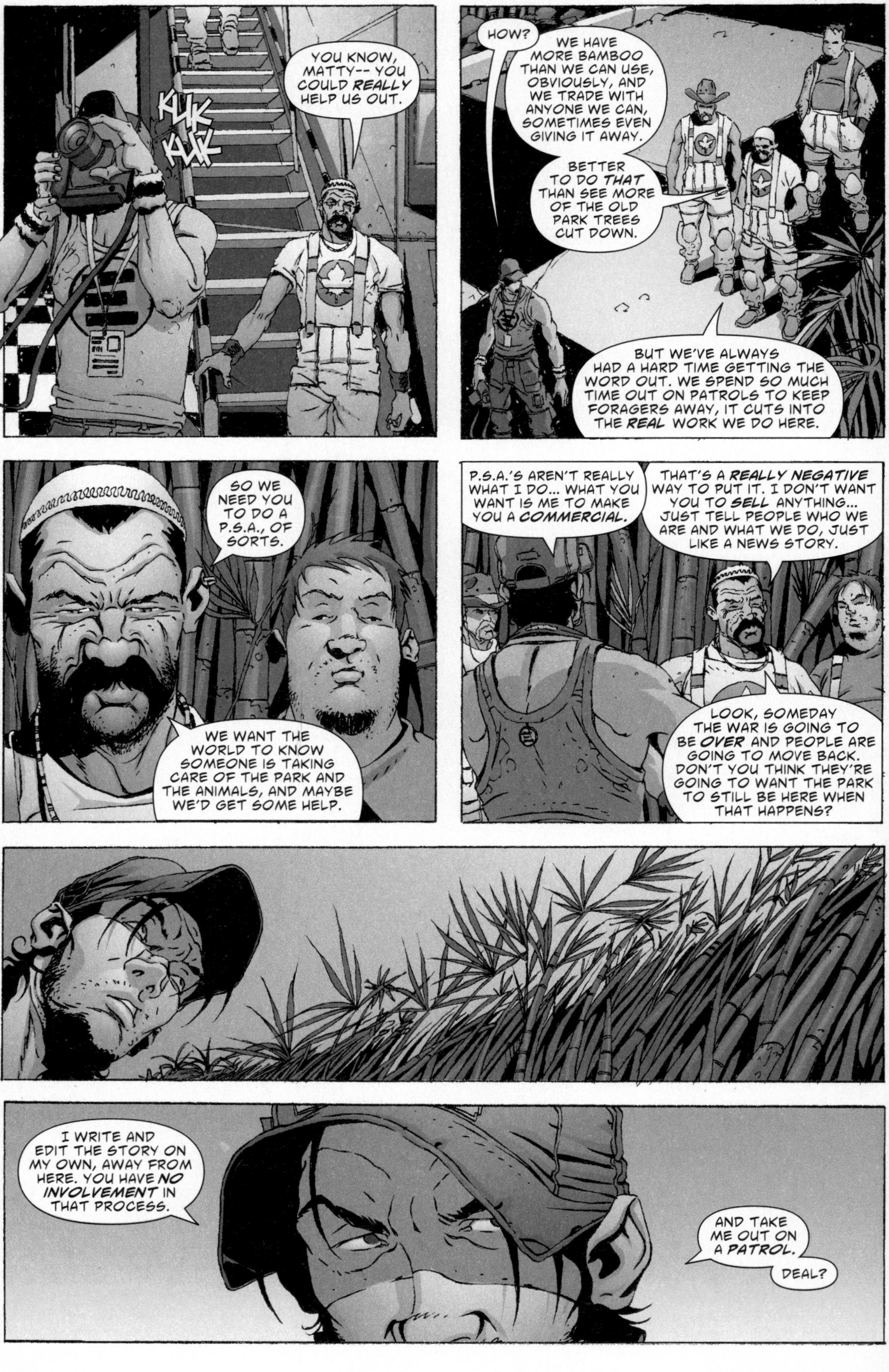
YOU KNOW, MATTY-- YOU COULD REALLY HELP US OUT.
KLIK KLIK
HOW?
WE HAVE MORE BAMBOO THAN WE CAN USE, OBVIOUSLY, AND WE TRADE WITH ANYONE WE CAN, SOMETIMES EVEN GIVING IT AWAY.
BETTER TO DO THAT THAN SEE MORE OF THE OLD PARK TREES CUT DOWN.
BUT WE'VE ALWAYS HAD A HARD TIME GETTING THE WORD OUT. WE SPEND SO MUCH TIME OUT ON PATROLS TO KEEP FORAGERS AWAY, IT CUTS INTO THE REAL WORK WE DO HERE.
SO WE NEED YOU TO DO A P.S.A., OF SORTS.
WE WANT THE WORLD TO KNOW SOMEONE IS TAKING CARE OF THE PARK AND THE ANIMALS, AND MAYBE WE'D GET SOME HELP.
P.S.A.'S AREN'T REALLY WHAT I DO... WHAT YOU WANT IS ME TO MAKE YOU A COMMERCIAL.
THAT'S A REALLY NEGATIVE WAY TO PUT IT. I DON'T WANT YOU TO SELL ANYTHING... JUST TELL PEOPLE WHO WE ARE AND WHAT WE DO, JUST LIKE A NEWS STORY.
LOOK, SOMEDAY THE WAR IS GOING TO BE OVER AND PEOPLE ARE GOING TO MOVE BACK. DON'T YOU THINK THEY'RE GOING TO WANT THE PARK TO STILL BE HERE WHEN THAT HAPPENS?
I WRITE AND EDIT THE STORY ON MY OWN, AWAY FROM HERE. YOU HAVE NO INVOLVEMENT IN THAT PROCESS.
AND TAKE ME OUT ON A PATROL.
DEAL?

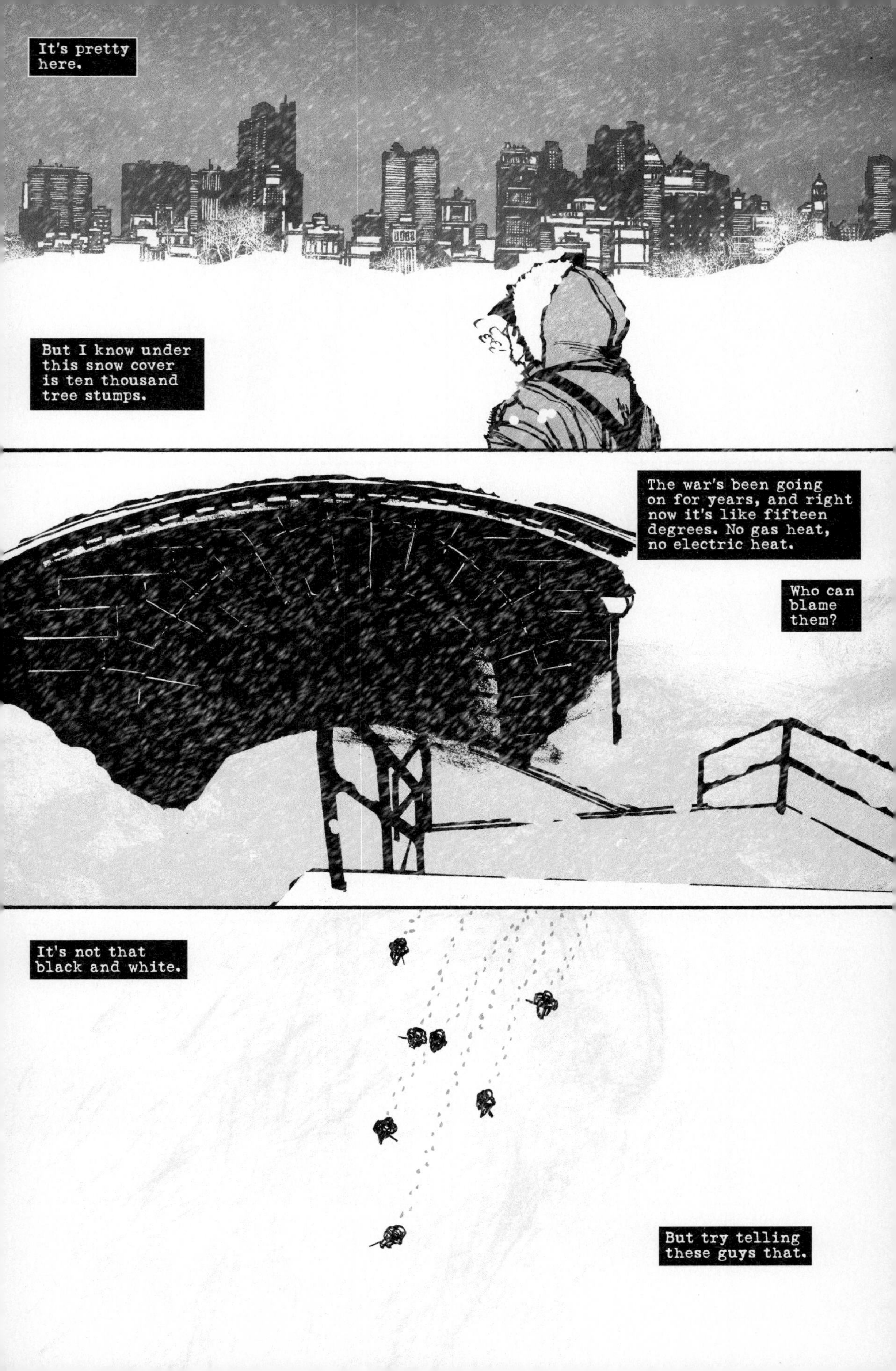
It's pretty here.
But I know under this snow cover is ten thousand tree stumps.
The war's been going on for years, and right now it's like fifteen degrees. No gas heat, no electric heat.
Who can blame them?
It's not that black and white.
But try telling these guys that.

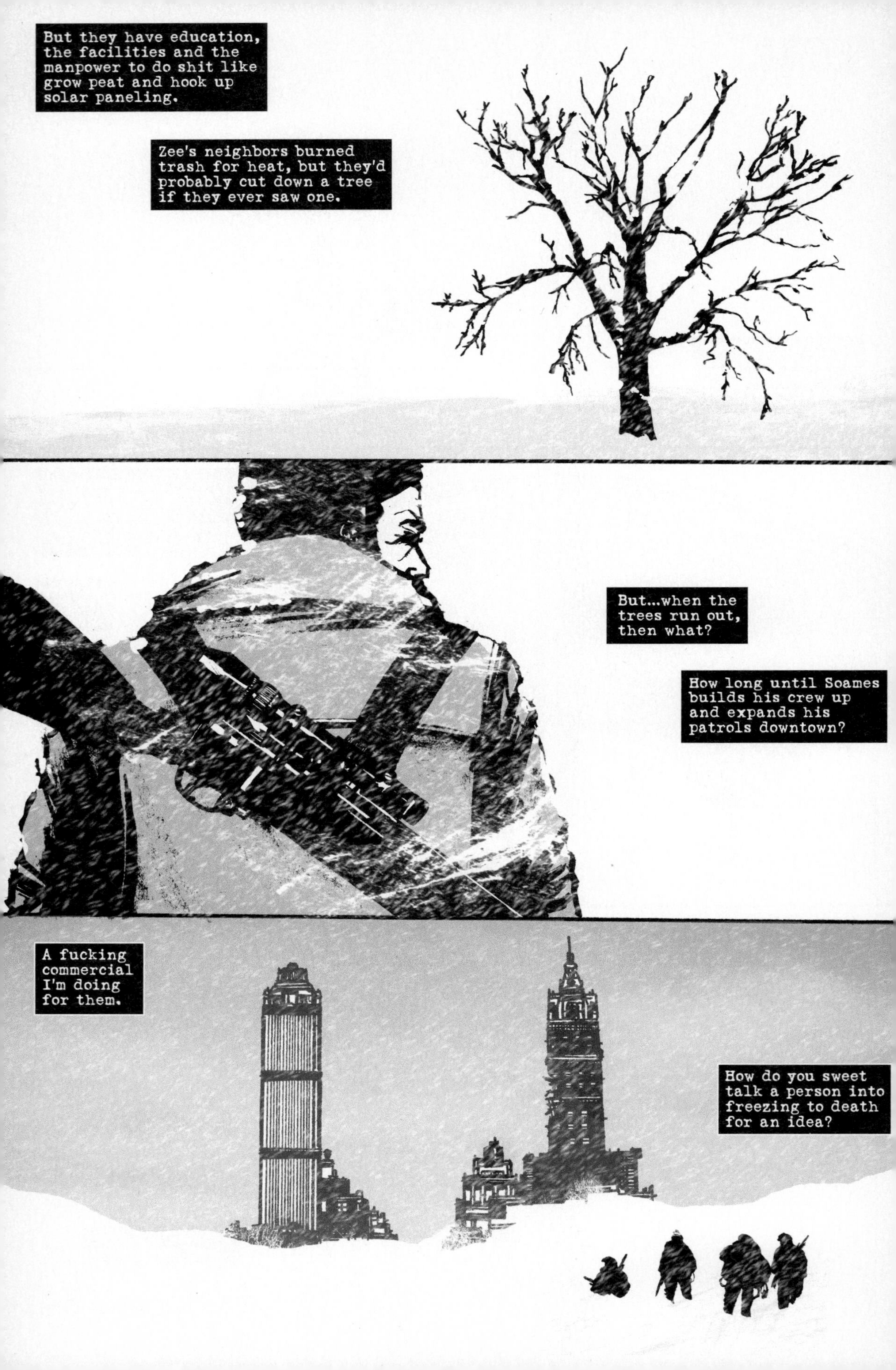
But they have education, the facilities and the manpower to do shit like grow peat and hook up solar paneling.
Zee's neighbors burned trash for heat, but they'd probably cut down a tree if they ever saw one.
But...when the trees run out, then what?
How long until Soames builds his crew up and expands his patrols downtown?
A fucking commercial I'm doing for them.
How do you sweet talk a person into freezing to death for an idea?

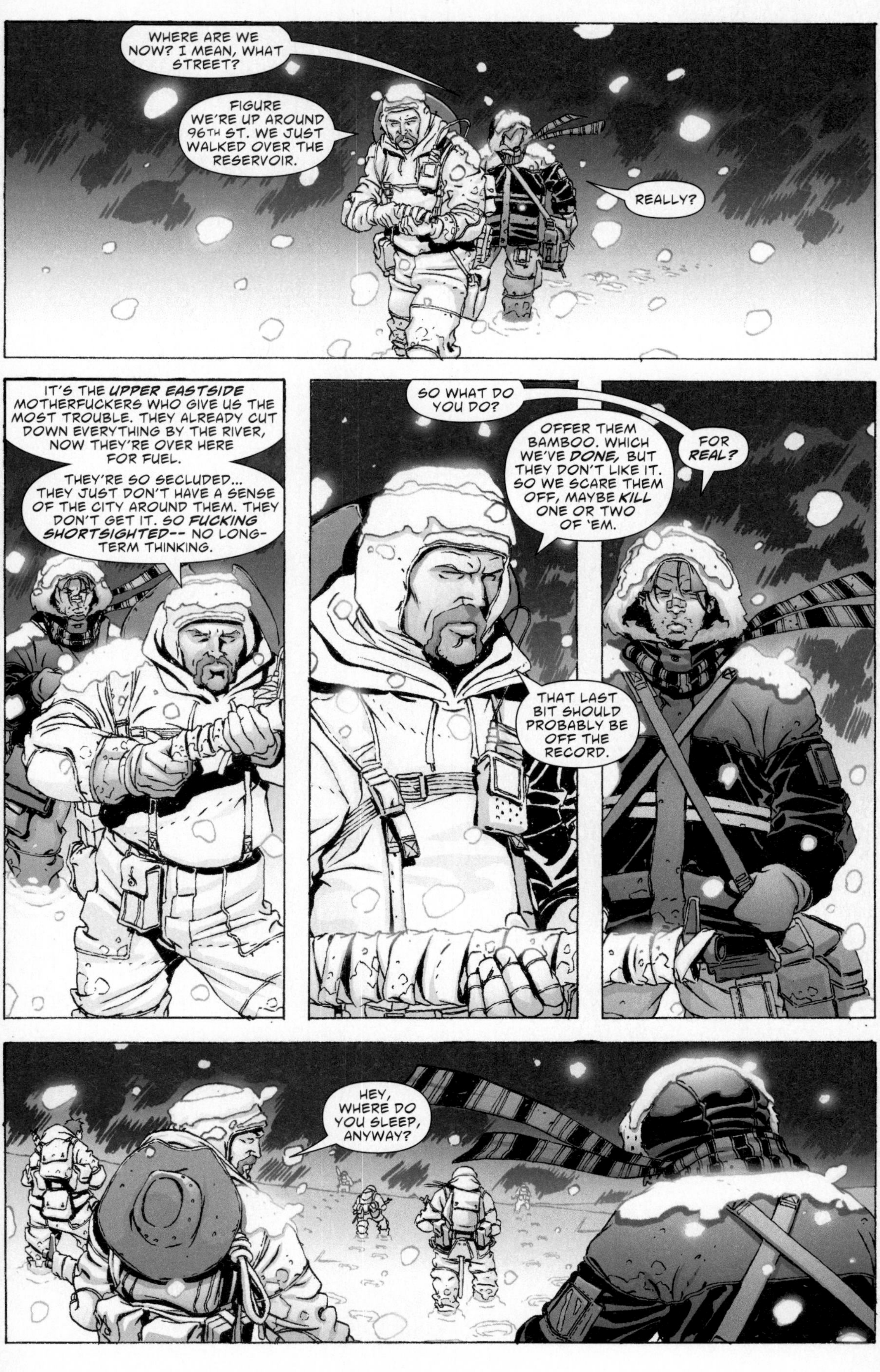
WHERE ARE WE NOW? I MEAN, WHAT STREET?
FIGURE WE'RE UP AROUND 96TH ST. WE JUST WALKED OVER THE RESERVOIR.
REALLY?
IT'S THE *UPPER EASTSIDE* MOTHERFUCKERS WHO GIVE US THE MOST TROUBLE. THEY ALREADY CUT DOWN EVERYTHING BY THE RIVER, NOW THEY'RE OVER HERE FOR FUEL.
THEY'RE SO SECLUDED... THEY JUST DON'T HAVE A SENSE OF THE CITY AROUND THEM. THEY DON'T GET IT. SO *FUCKING SHORTSIGHTED*-- NO LONG-TERM THINKING.
SO WHAT DO YOU DO?
OFFER THEM BAMBOO. WHICH WE'VE *DONE,* BUT THEY DON'T LIKE IT. SO WE SCARE THEM OFF, MAYBE *KILL* ONE OR TWO OF 'EM.
FOR *REAL?*
THAT LAST BIT SHOULD PROBABLY BE OFF THE RECORD.
HEY, WHERE DO YOU SLEEP, ANYWAY?

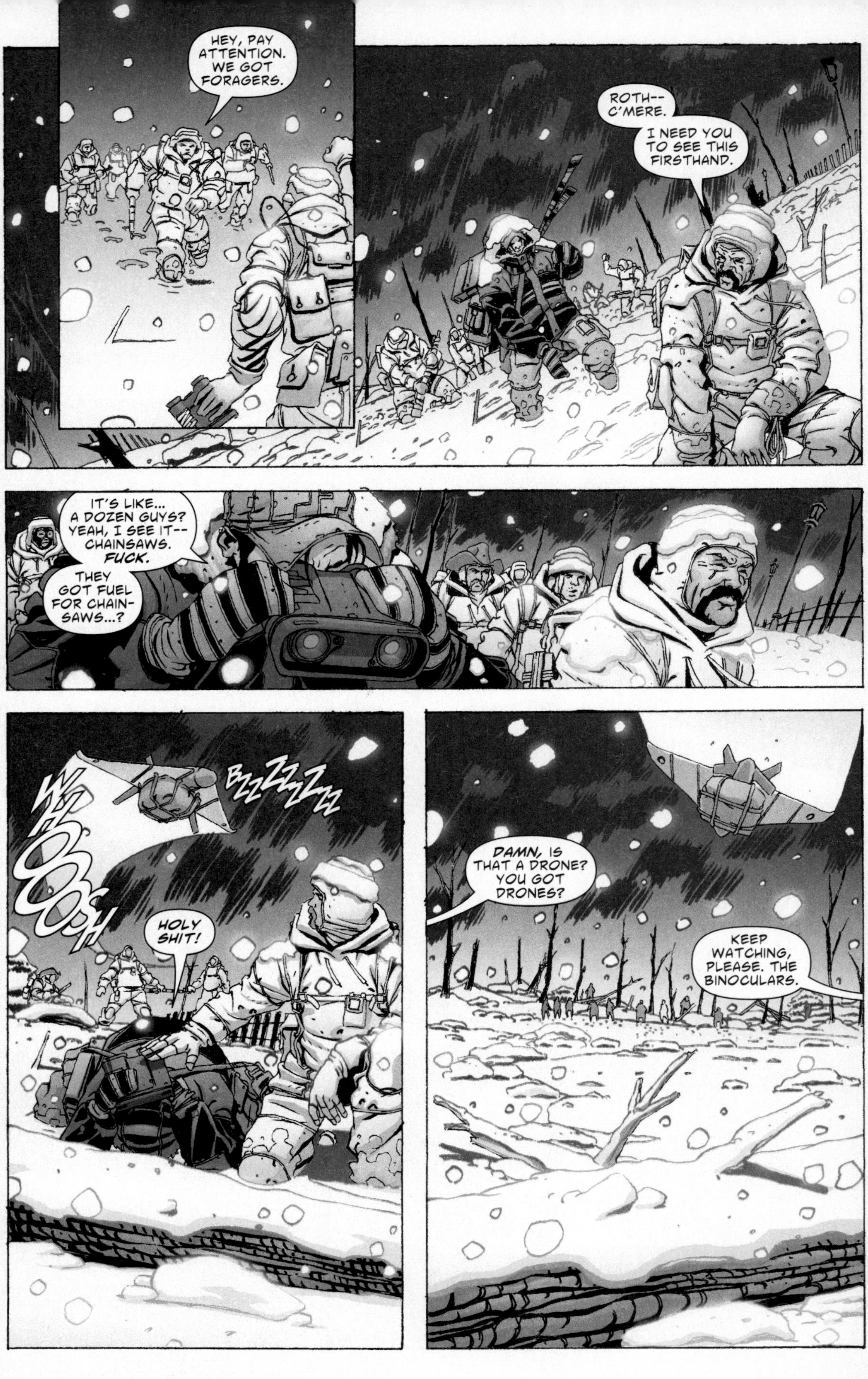
HEY, PAY ATTENTION. WE GOT FORAGERS.
ROTH-- C'MERE.
I NEED YOU TO SEE THIS FIRSTHAND.
IT'S LIKE... A DOZEN GUYS? YEAH, I SEE IT-- CHAINSAWS. FUCK.
THEY GOT FUEL FOR CHAIN-SAWS...?
WHOOOOSH
BZZZZZZZ
HOLY SHIT!
DAMN, IS THAT A DRONE? YOU GOT DRONES?
KEEP WATCHING, PLEASE. THE BINOCULARS.

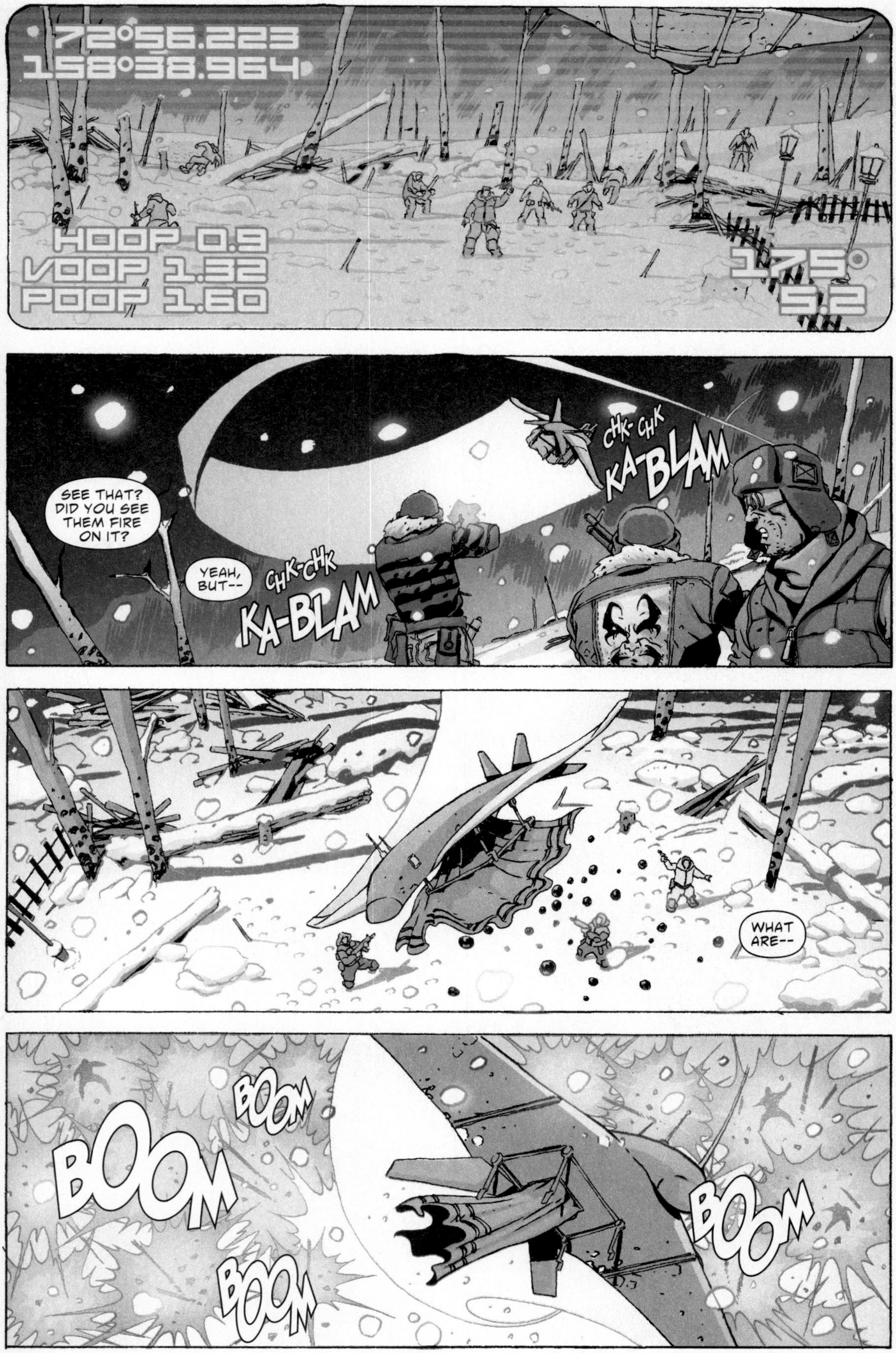

72°56.223
158°38.964
HOOP 0.9
VOOP 1.32
POOP 1.60
175°
5.2
SEE THAT? DID YOU SEE THEM FIRE ON IT?
YEAH, BUT--
CHK-CHK
KA-BLAM
CHK-CHK
KA-BLAM
WHAT ARE--
BOOM
BOOM
BOOM
BOOM

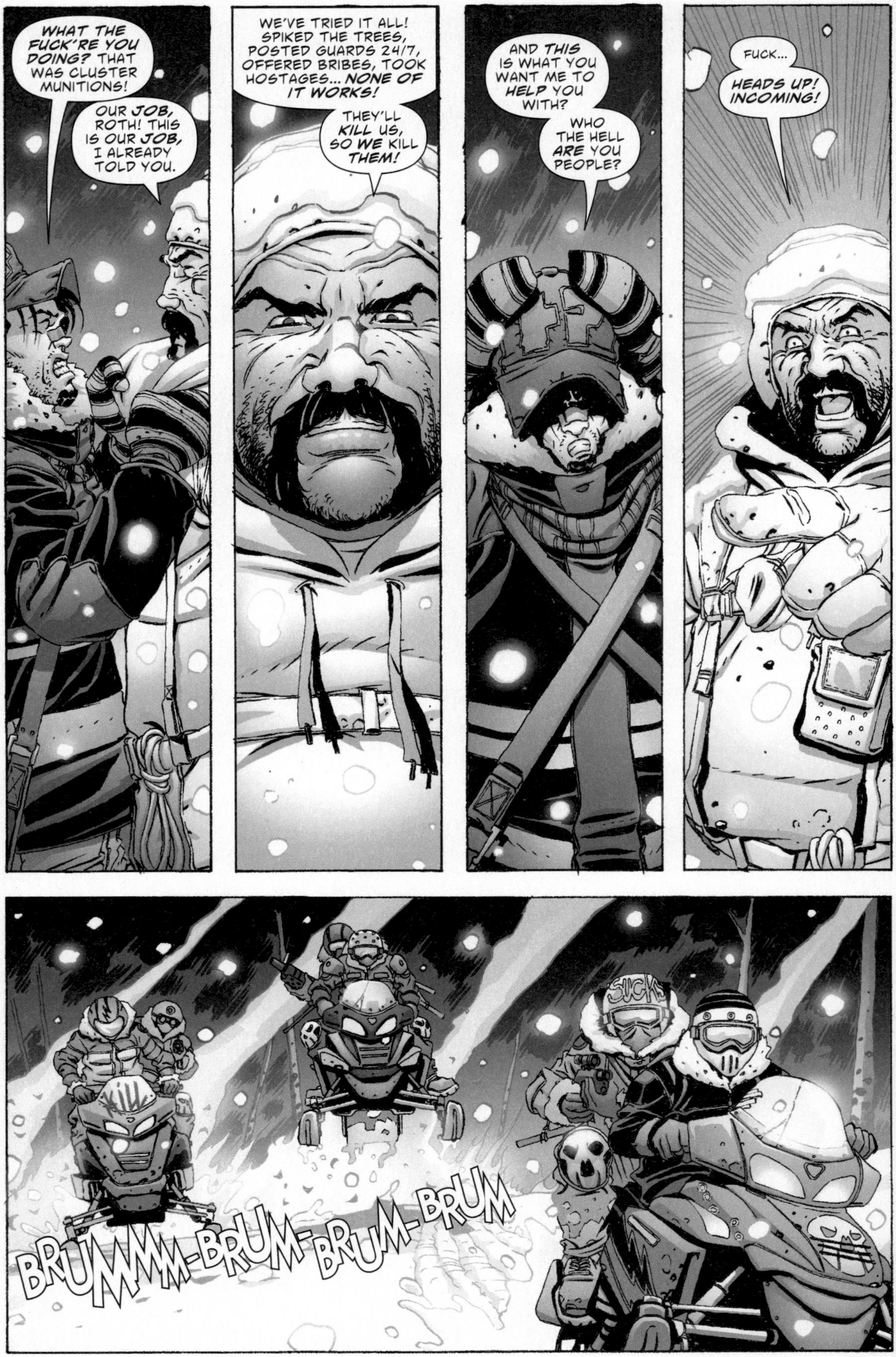

WHAT THE FUCK'RE YOU DOING? THAT WAS CLUSTER MUNITIONS!
OUR JOB, ROTH! THIS IS OUR JOB, I ALREADY TOLD YOU.
WE'VE TRIED IT ALL! SPIKED THE TREES, POSTED GUARDS 24/7, OFFERED BRIBES, TOOK HOSTAGES... NONE OF IT WORKS!
THEY'LL KILL US, SO WE KILL THEM!
AND THIS IS WHAT YOU WANT ME TO HELP YOU WITH?
WHO THE HELL ARE YOU PEOPLE?
FUCK...
HEADS UP! INCOMING!
BRUMMM-BRUM-BRUM-BRUM

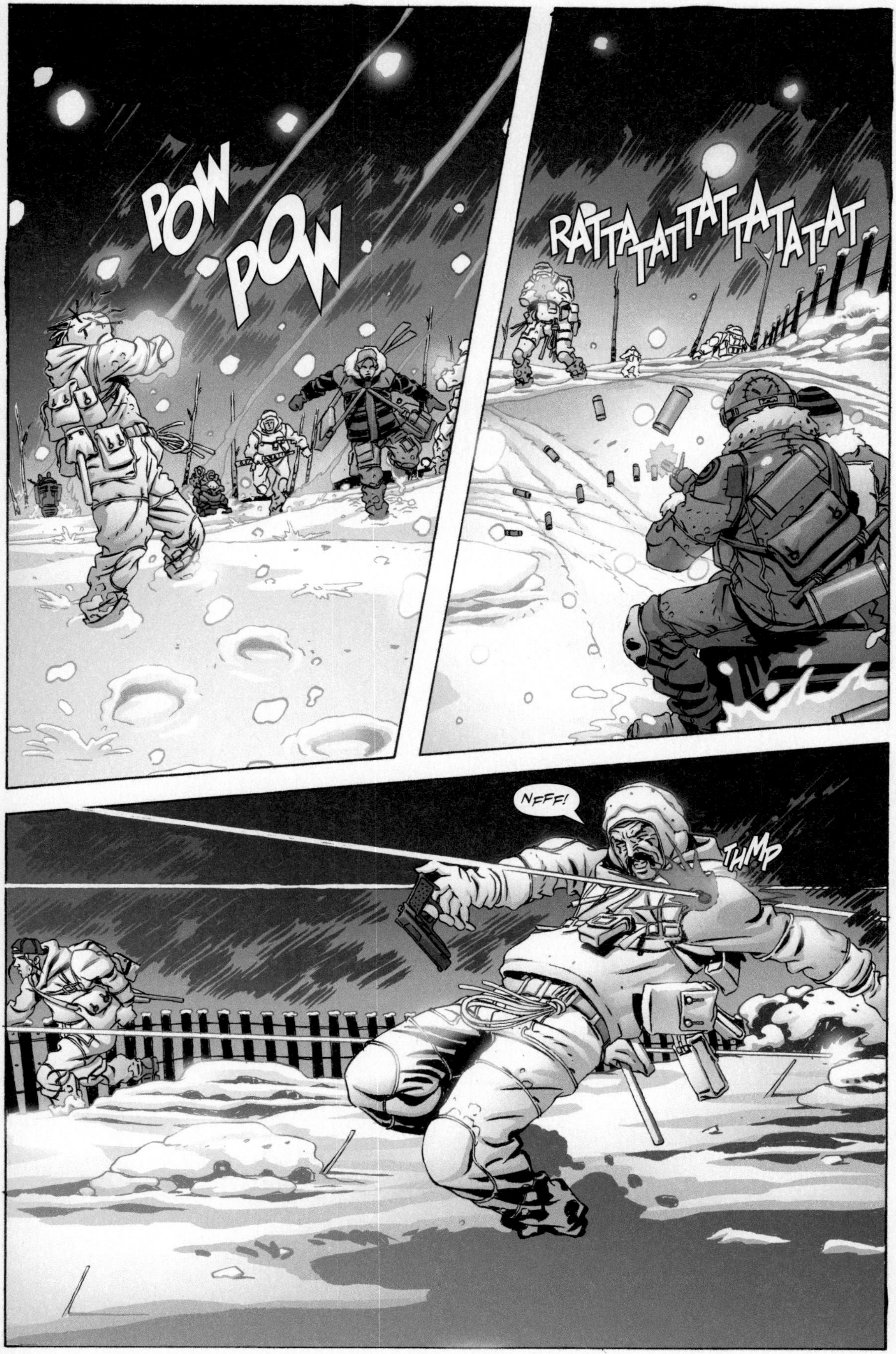
POW
POW
RATTATATTATTATATATAT
NFFF!
THMP

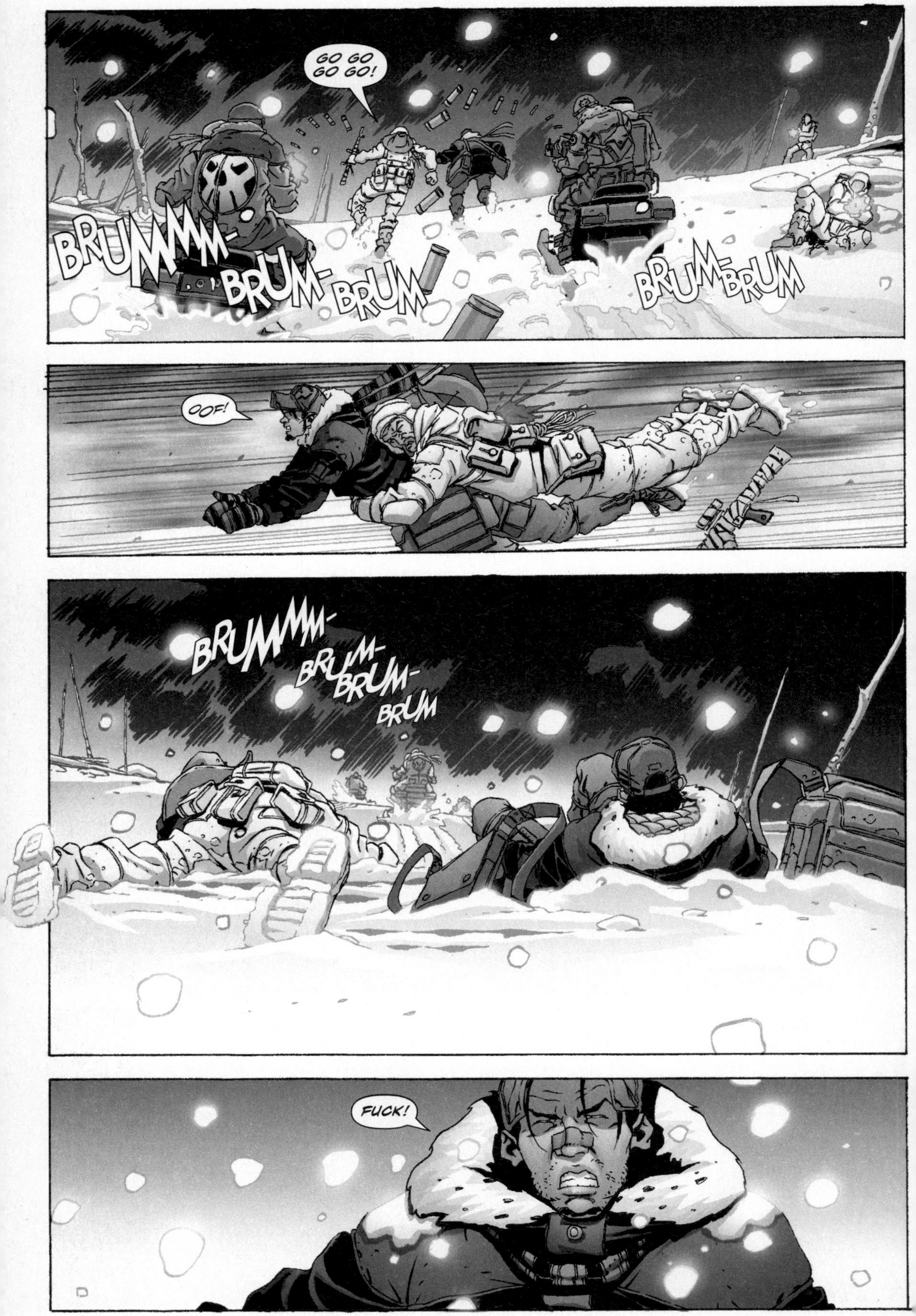
GO GO GO GO!
BRUMMM-BRUM-BRUM
BRUM-BRUM
OOF!
BRUMMM-BRUM-BRUM-BRUM
FUCK!

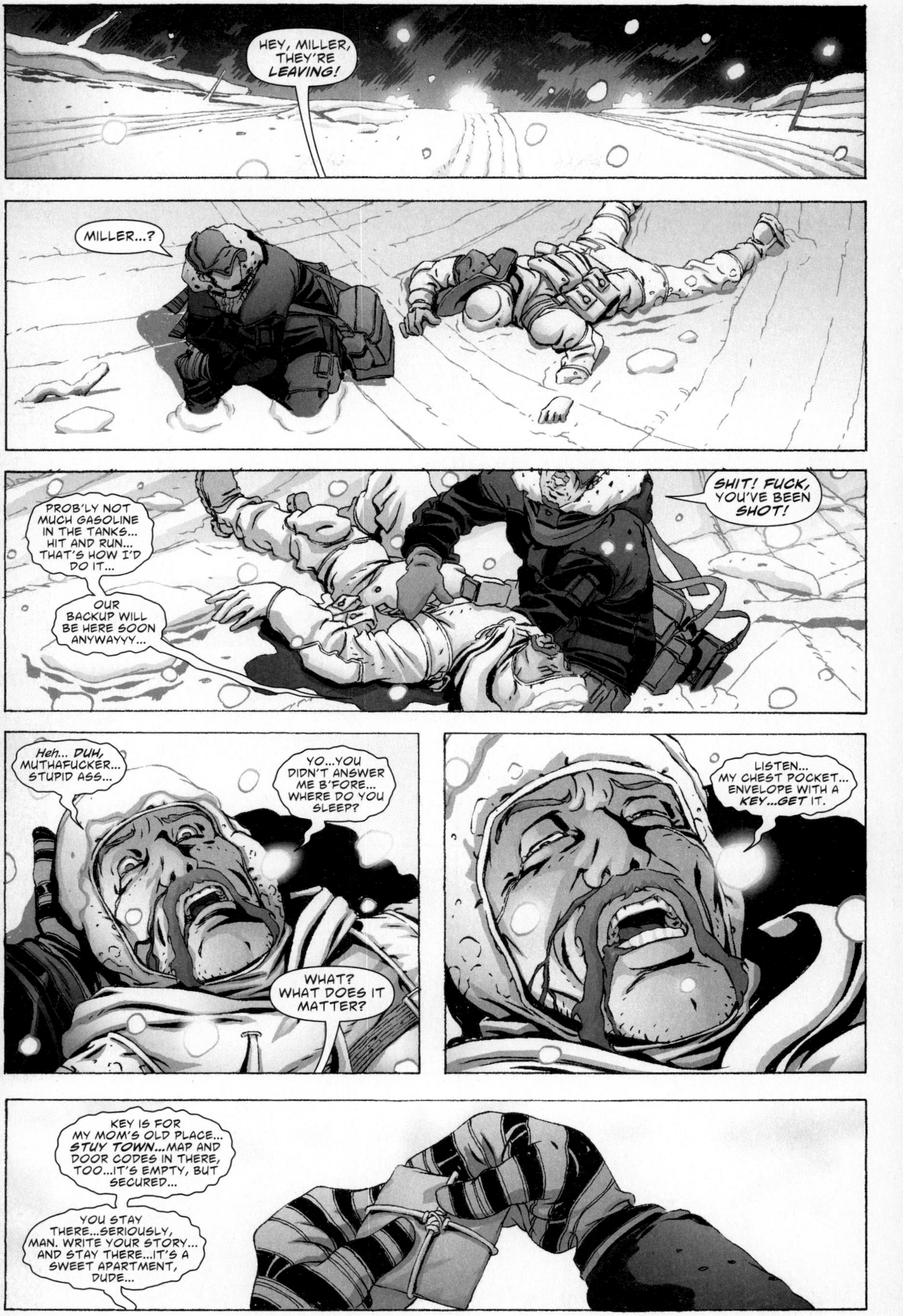
HEY, MILLER, THEY'RE *LEAVING!*
MILLER...?
PROB'LY NOT MUCH GASOLINE IN THE TANKS... HIT AND RUN... THAT'S HOW I'D DO IT...
OUR BACKUP WILL BE HERE SOON ANYWAYYY...
SHIT! FUCK, YOU'VE BEEN *SHOT!*
Heh... DUH, MUTHAFUCKER... STUPID ASS...
YO...YOU DIDN'T ANSWER ME B'FORE... WHERE DO YOU SLEEP?
WHAT? WHAT DOES IT MATTER?
LISTEN... MY CHEST POCKET... ENVELOPE WITH A *KEY...GET* IT.
KEY IS FOR MY MOM'S OLD PLACE... *STUY TOWN...* MAP AND DOOR CODES IN THERE, TOO...IT'S EMPTY, BUT SECURED...
YOU STAY THERE...SERIOUSLY, MAN. WRITE YOUR STORY... AND STAY THERE...IT'S A SWEET APARTMENT, DUDE...

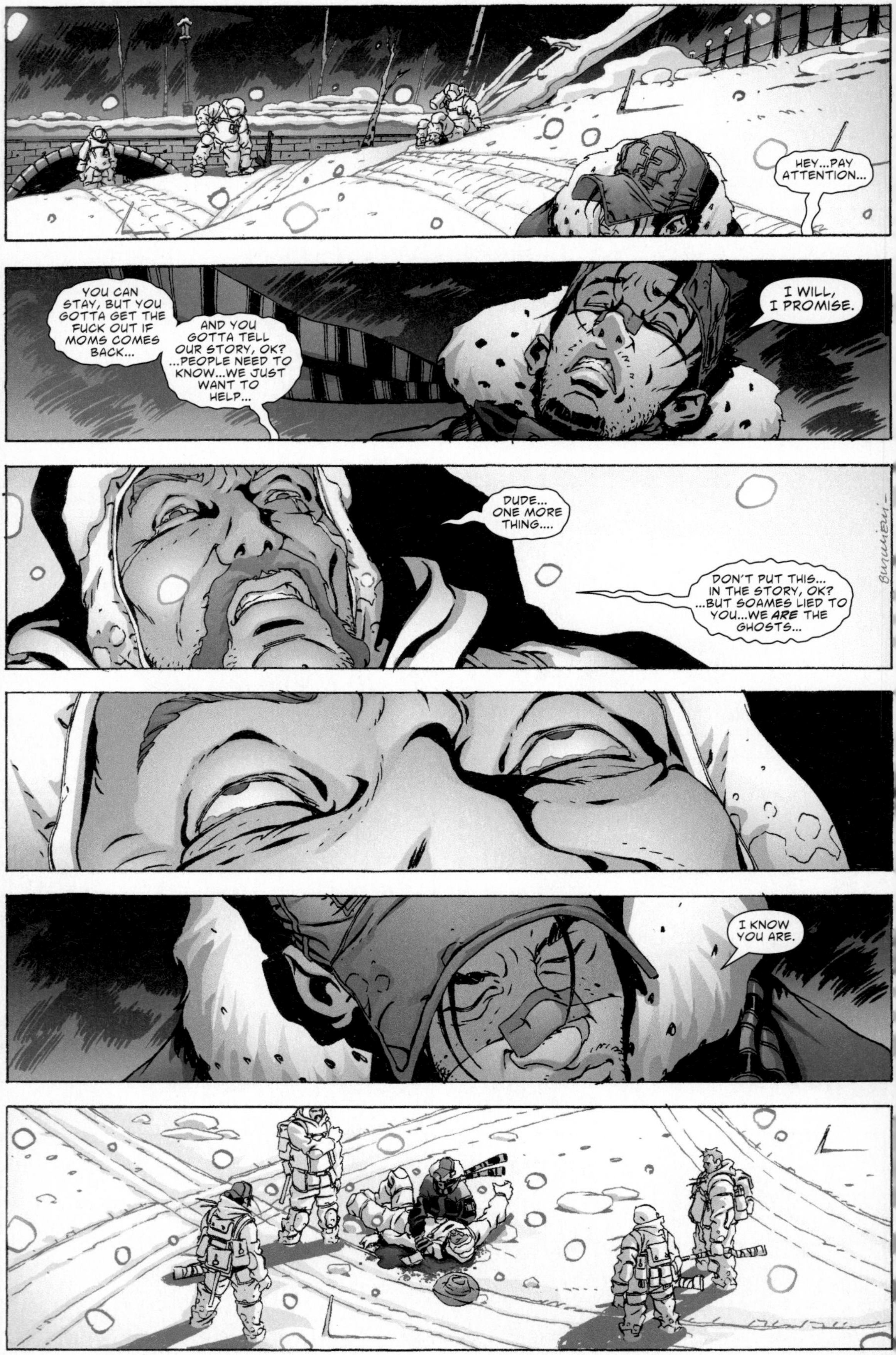
HEY...PAY ATTENTION...
YOU CAN STAY, BUT YOU GOTTA GET THE FUCK OUT IF MOMS COMES BACK...
AND YOU GOTTA TELL OUR STORY, OK? ...PEOPLE NEED TO KNOW...WE JUST WANT TO HELP...
I WILL, I PROMISE.
DUDE... ONE MORE THING....
DON'T PUT THIS... IN THE STORY, OK? ...BUT SOAMES LIED TO YOU...WE *ARE* THE GHOSTS...
I KNOW YOU ARE.

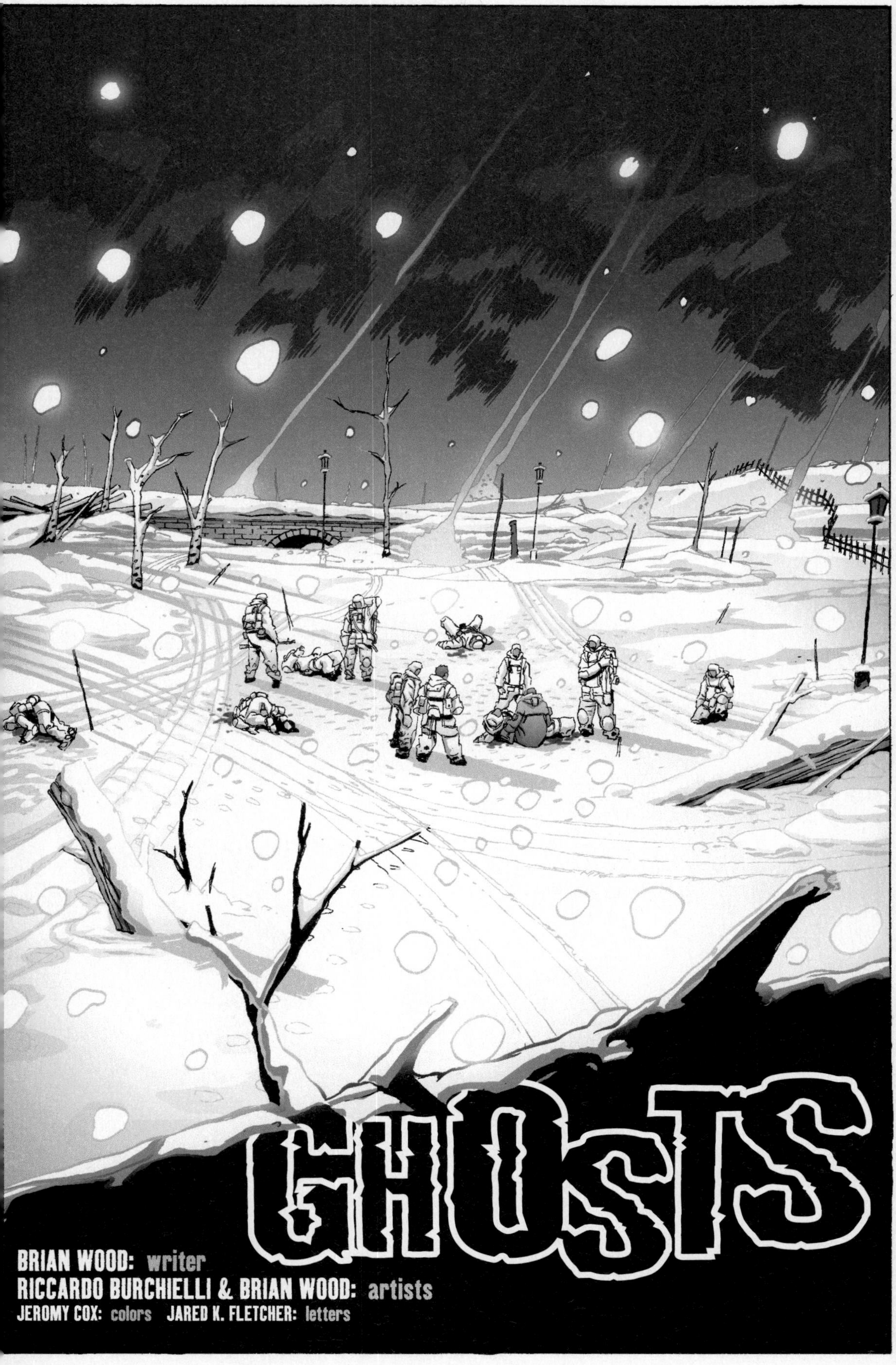
GHOSTS
BRIAN WOOD: writer
RICCARDO BURCHIELLI & BRIAN WOOD: artists
JEROMY COX: colors JARED K. FLETCHER: letters

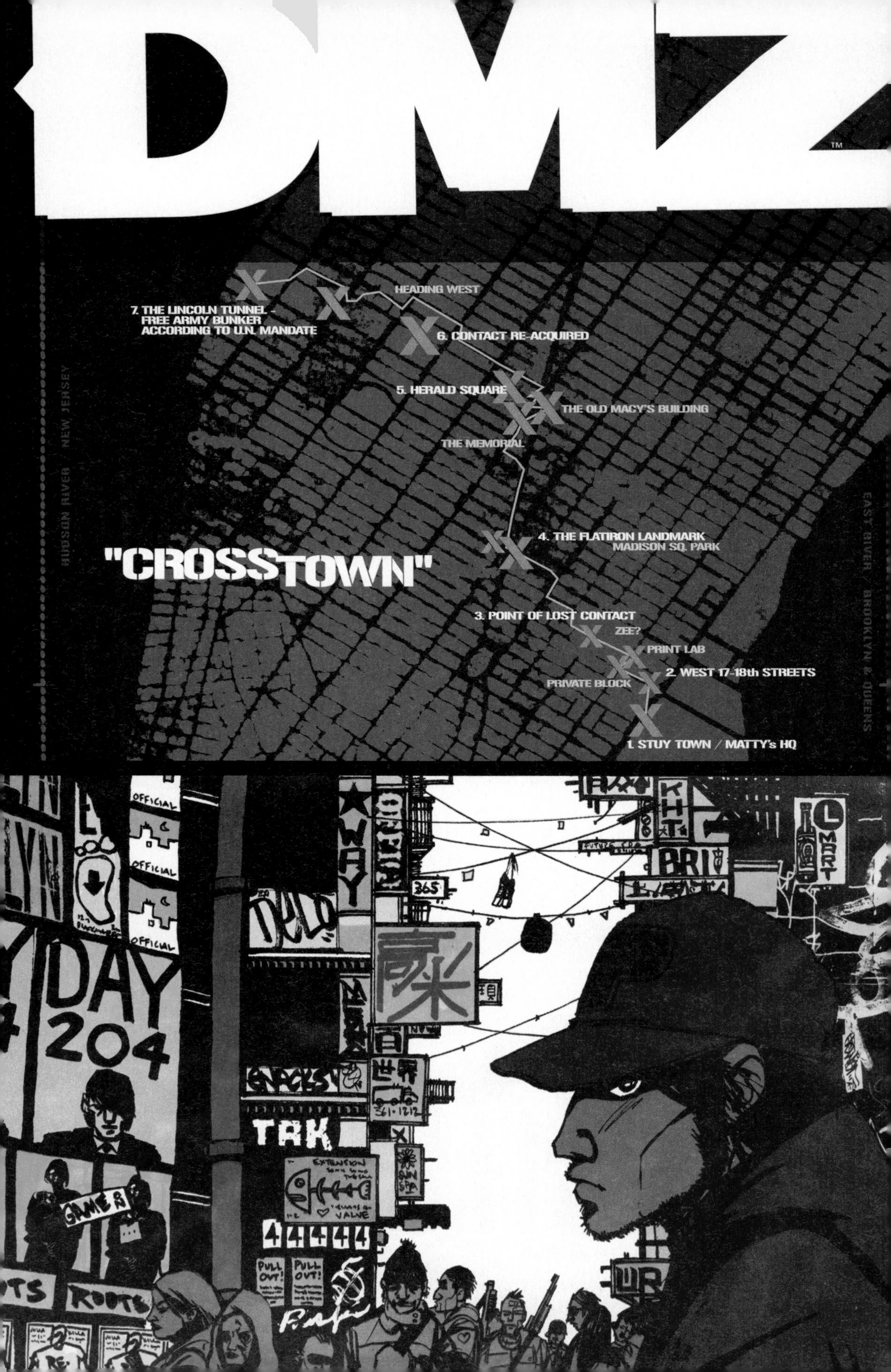
DMZ™
7. THE LINCOLN TUNNEL - FREE ARMY BUNKER ACCORDING TO U.N. MANDATE
HEADING WEST
6. CONTACT RE-ACQUIRED
5. HERALD SQUARE
THE OLD MACY'S BUILDING
THE MEMORIAL
HUDSON RIVER / NEW JERSEY
EAST RIVER / BROOKLYN & QUEENS
"CROSSTOWN"
4. THE FLATIRON LANDMARK
MADISON SQ. PARK
3. POINT OF LOST CONTACT
ZEE?
PRINT LAB
2. WEST 17-18th STREETS
PRIVATE BLOCK
1. STUY TOWN / MATTY's HQ
OFFICIAL
DAY 204
WAY
365
TRK
4 4 4 4 4
PULL OUT!
PULL OUT!
ROOTS

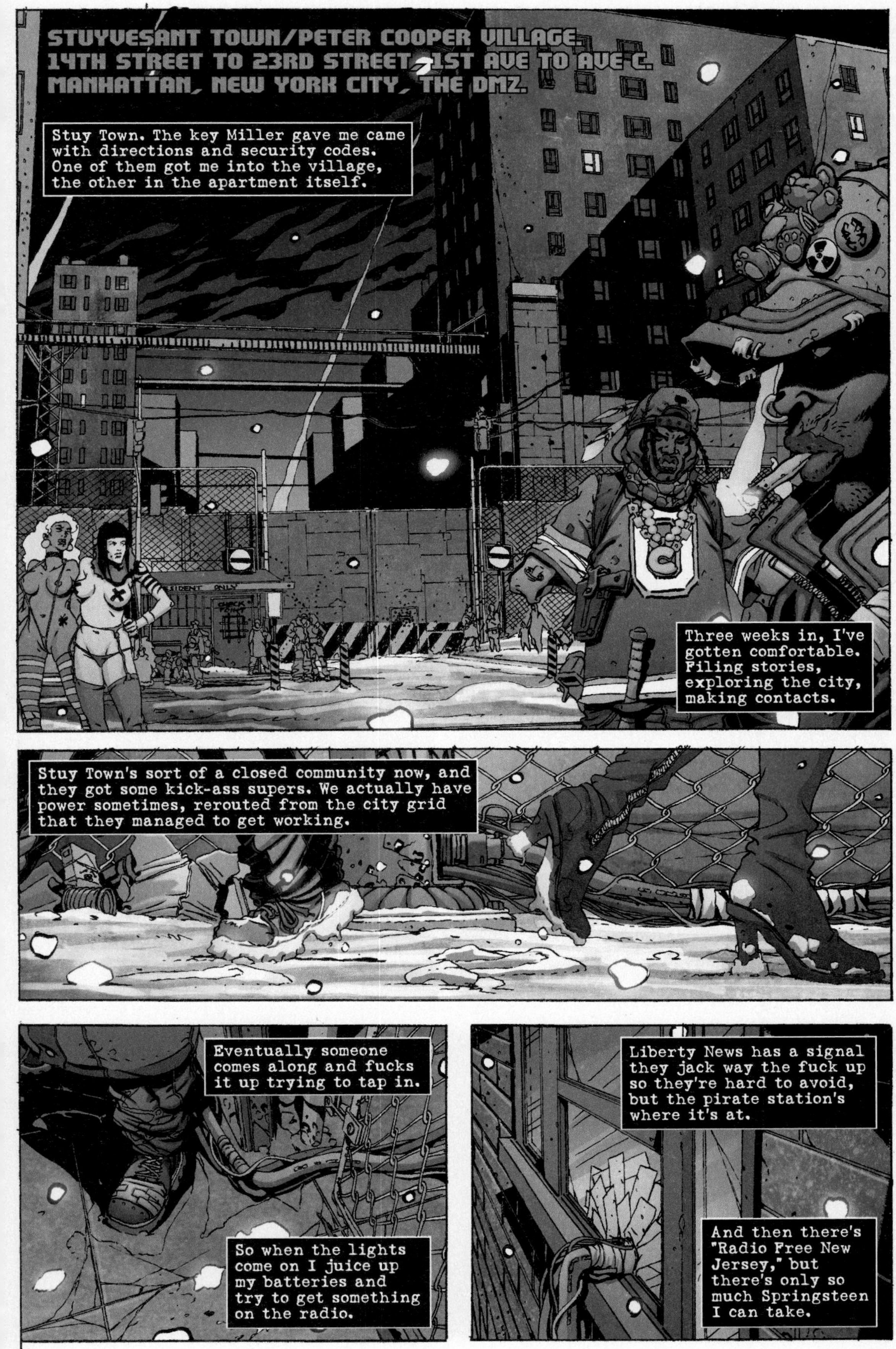
STUYVESANT TOWN/PETER COOPER VILLAGE.
14TH STREET TO 23RD STREET, 1ST AVE TO AVE C.
MANHATTAN, NEW YORK CITY, THE DMZ.
Stuy Town. The key Miller gave me came with directions and security codes. One of them got me into the village, the other in the apartment itself.
Three weeks in, I've gotten comfortable. Filing stories, exploring the city, making contacts.
Stuy Town's sort of a closed community now, and they got some kick-ass supers. We actually have power sometimes, rerouted from the city grid that they managed to get working.
Eventually someone comes along and fucks it up trying to tap in.
So when the lights come on I juice up my batteries and try to get something on the radio.
Liberty News has a signal they jack way the fuck up so they're hard to avoid, but the pirate station's where it's at.
And then there's "Radio Free New Jersey," but there's only so much Springsteen I can take.

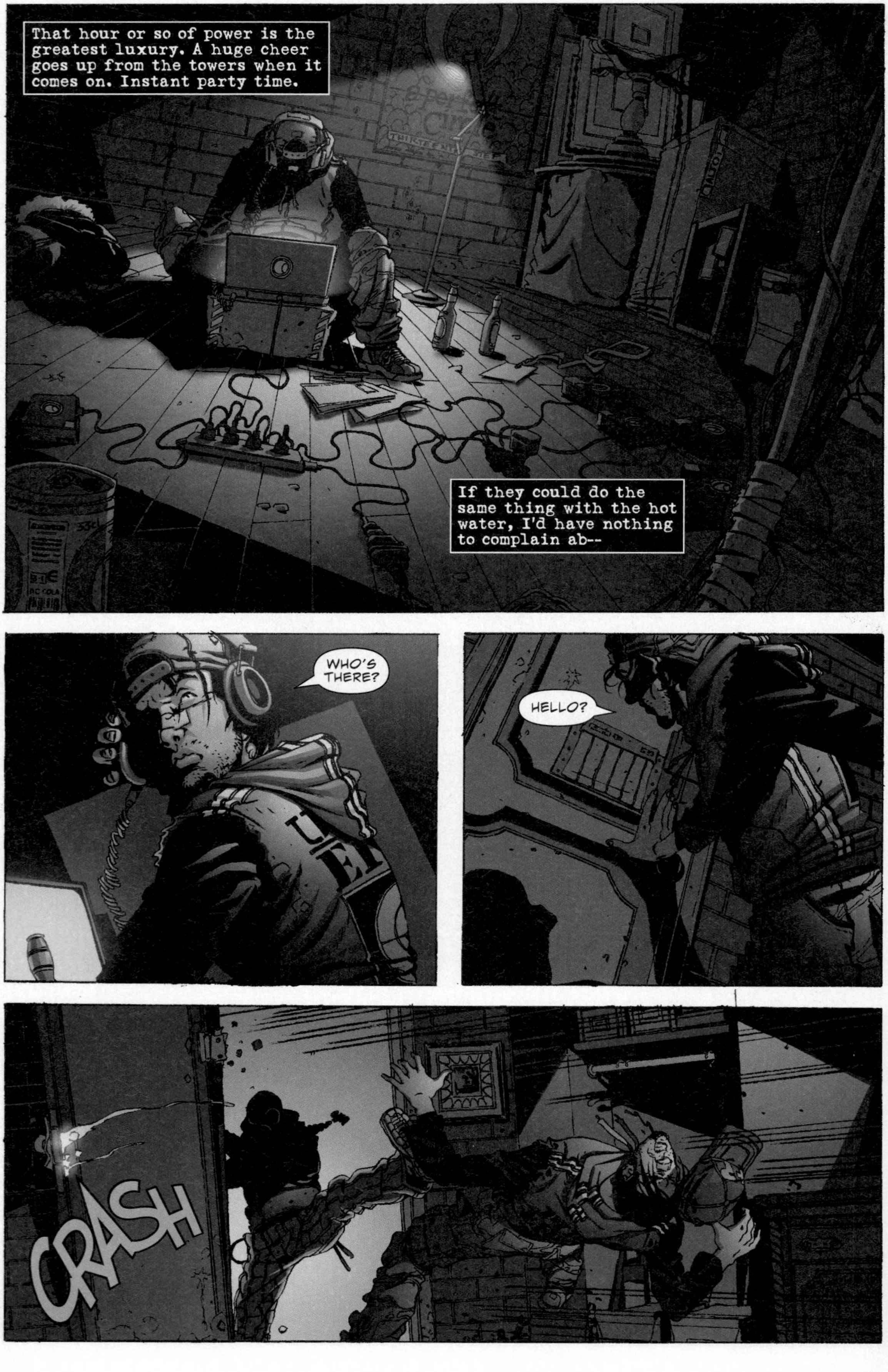
That hour or so of power is the greatest luxury. A huge cheer goes up from the towers when it comes on. Instant party time.
If they could do the same thing with the hot water, I'd have nothing to complain ab--
WHO'S THERE?
HELLO?
CRASH

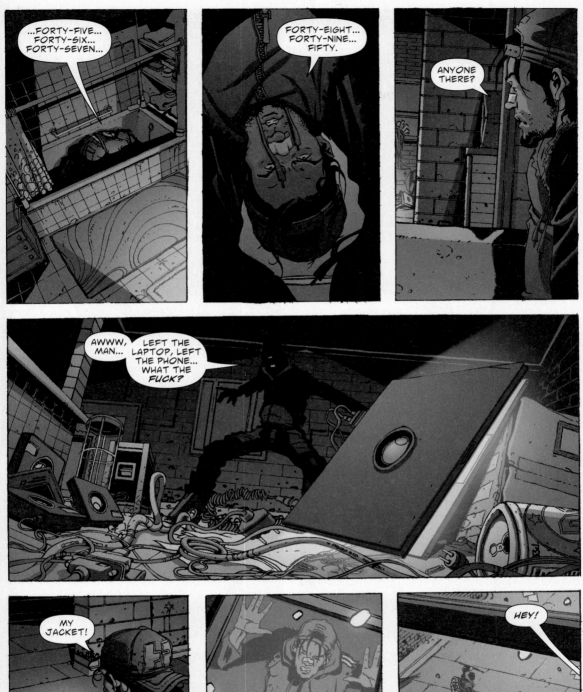

...FORTY-FIVE... FORTY-SIX... FORTY-SEVEN...

FORTY-EIGHT... FORTY-NINE... FIFTY.

ANYONE THERE?

AWWW, MAN... LEFT THE LAPTOP, LEFT THE PHONE... WHAT THE *FUCK?*

MY JACKET!

HEY!

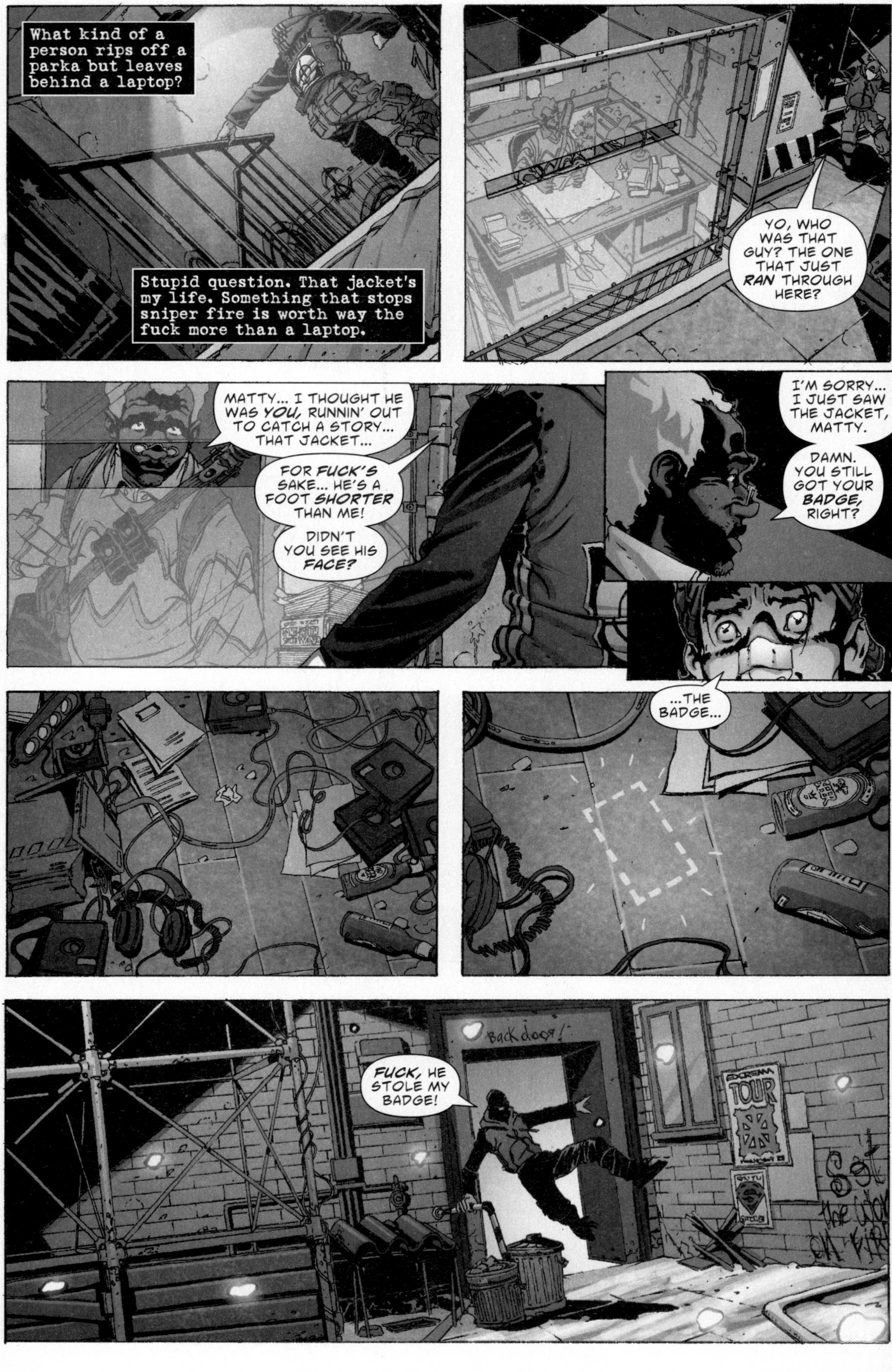
What kind of a person rips off a parka but leaves behind a laptop?
Stupid question. That jacket's my life. Something that stops sniper fire is worth way the fuck more than a laptop.
YO, WHO WAS THAT GUY? THE ONE THAT JUST RAN THROUGH HERE?
MATTY... I THOUGHT HE WAS YOU, RUNNIN' OUT TO CATCH A STORY... THAT JACKET...
FOR FUCK'S SAKE... HE'S A FOOT SHORTER THAN ME!
DIDN'T YOU SEE HIS FACE?
I'M SORRY... I JUST SAW THE JACKET, MATTY.
DAMN. YOU STILL GOT YOUR BADGE, RIGHT?
...THE BADGE...
Back door!
FUCK, HE STOLE MY BADGE!
TOUR

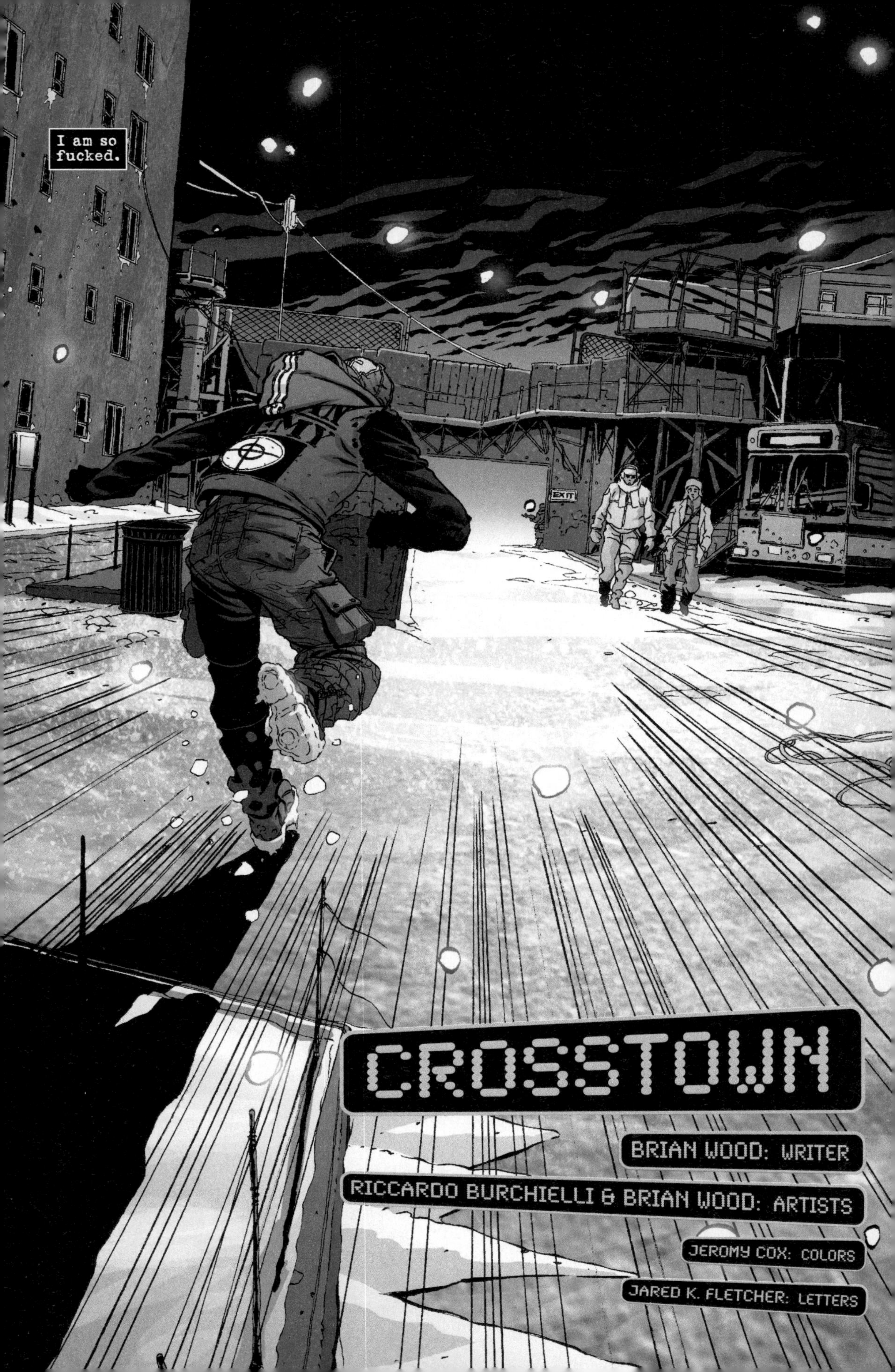
I am so fucked.
EXIT
CROSSTOWN
BRIAN WOOD: WRITER
RICCARDO BURCHIELLI & BRIAN WOOD: ARTISTS
JEROMY COX: COLORS
JARED K. FLETCHER: LETTERS

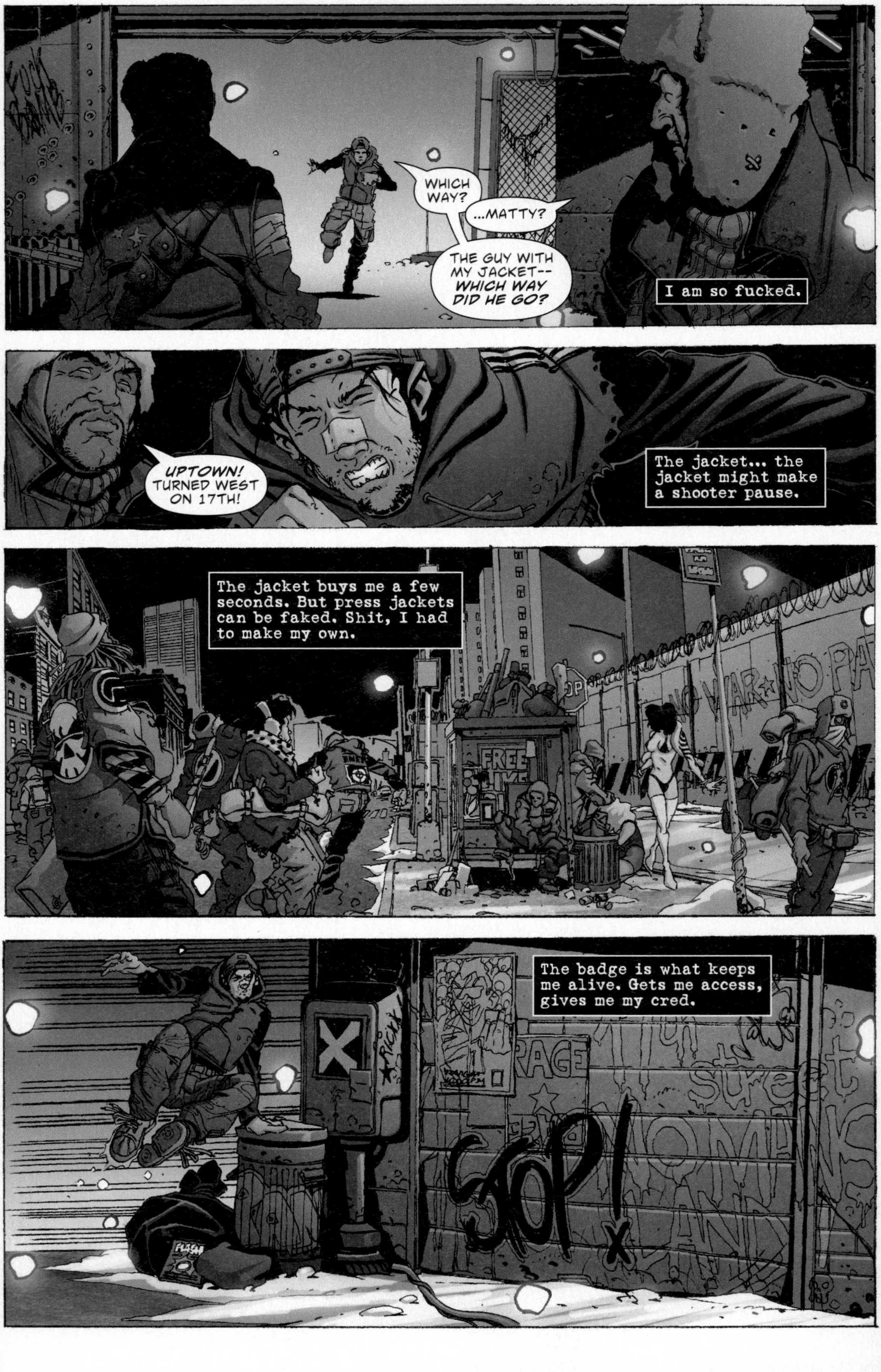
WHICH WAY?
...MATTY?
THE GUY WITH MY JACKET-- *WHICH WAY DID HE GO?*
I am so fucked.
UPTOWN! TURNED WEST ON 17TH!
The jacket... the jacket might make a shooter pause.
The jacket buys me a few seconds. But press jackets can be faked. Shit, I had to make my own.
FREE
RAGE
The badge is what keeps me alive. Gets me access, gives me my cred.

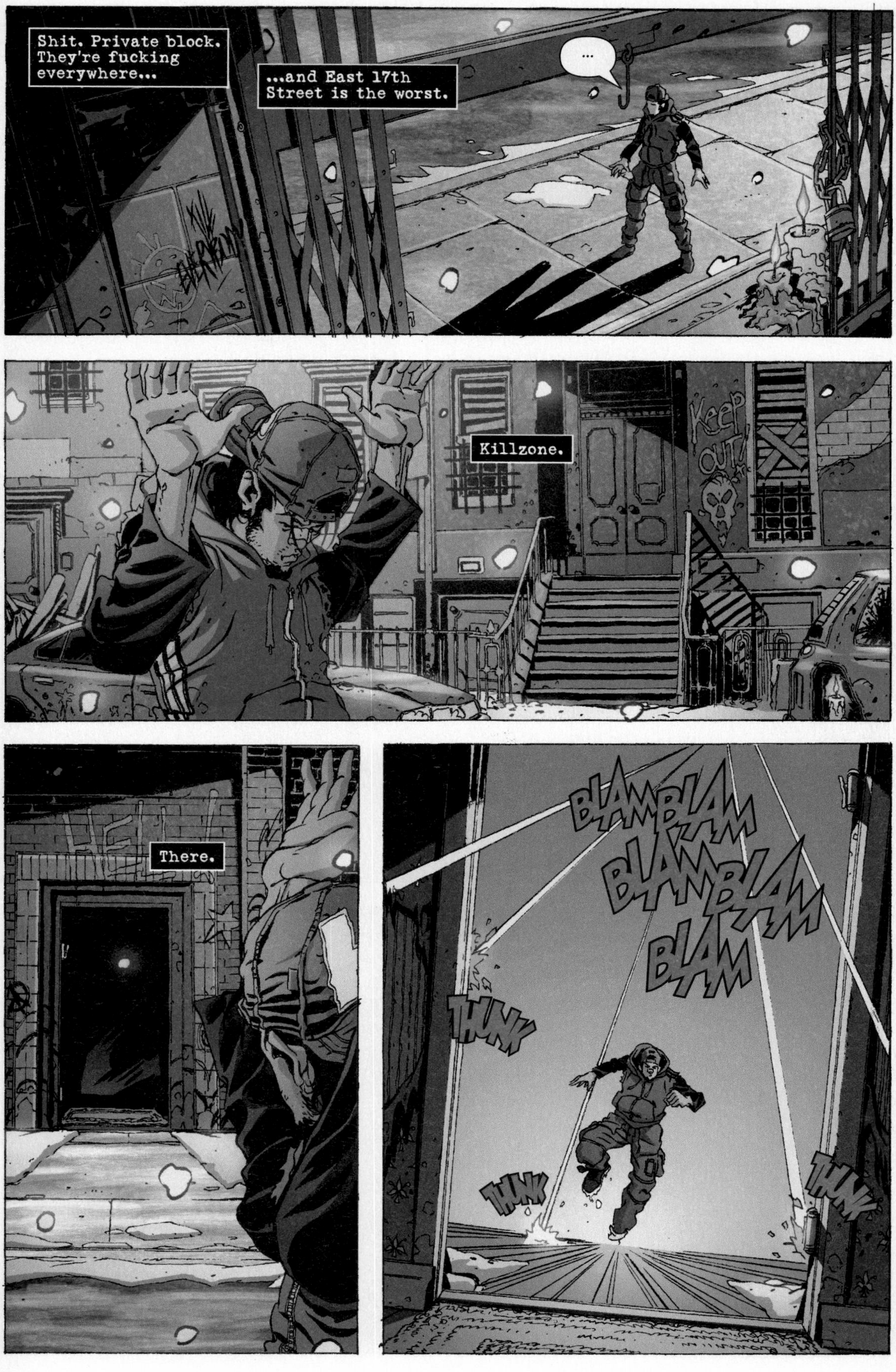
Shit. Private block. They're fucking everywhere...
...and East 17th Street is the worst.
...
Killzone.
Keep OUT!
There.
BLAMBLAM
BLAMBLAM
BLAM
THUNK
THUNK
THUNK

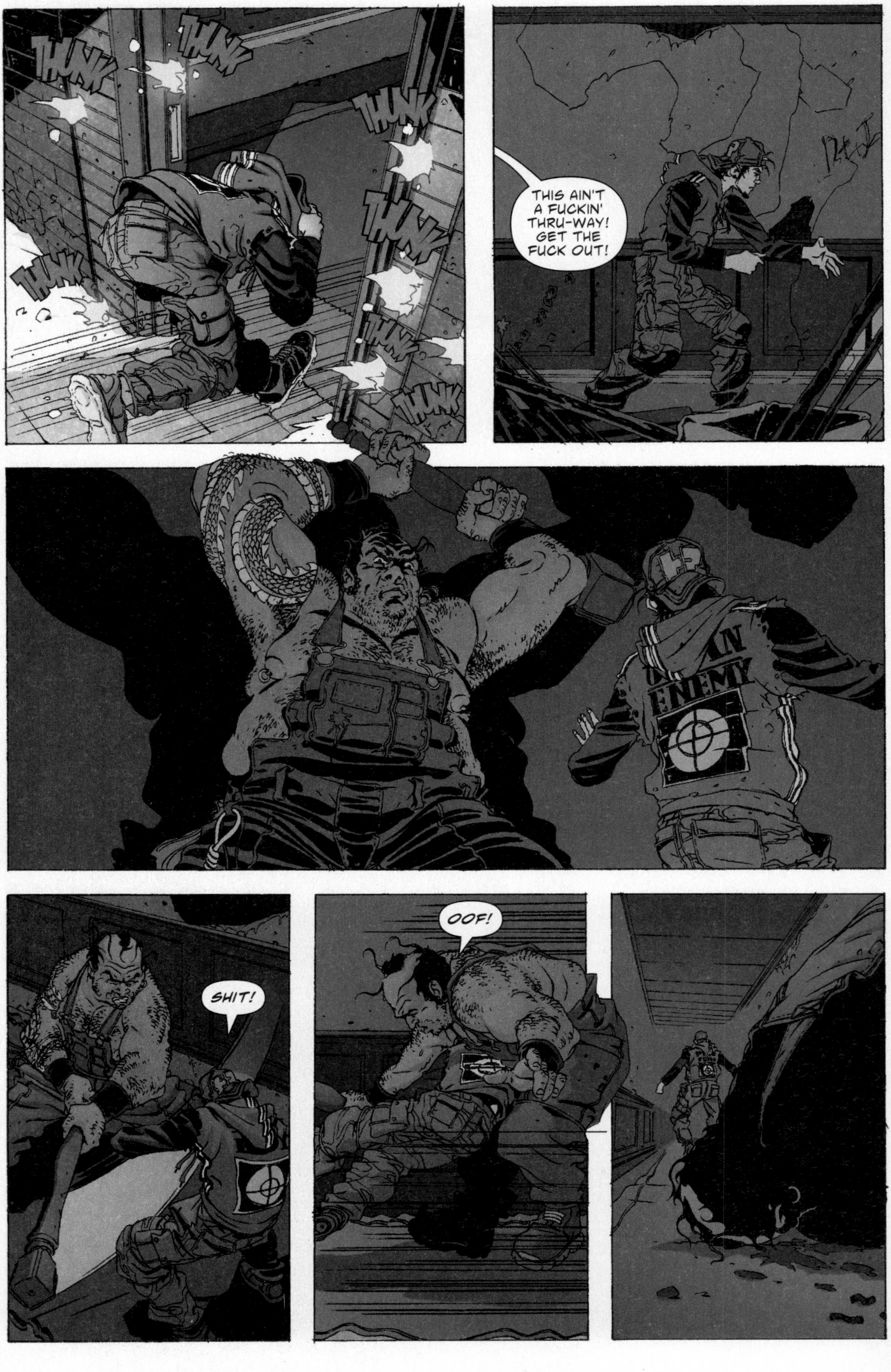
THUNK
THUNK
THUNK
THUNK
THUNK
THUNK
THUNK
THIS AIN'T A FUCKIN' THRU-WAY! GET THE FUCK OUT!
SHIT!
OOF!

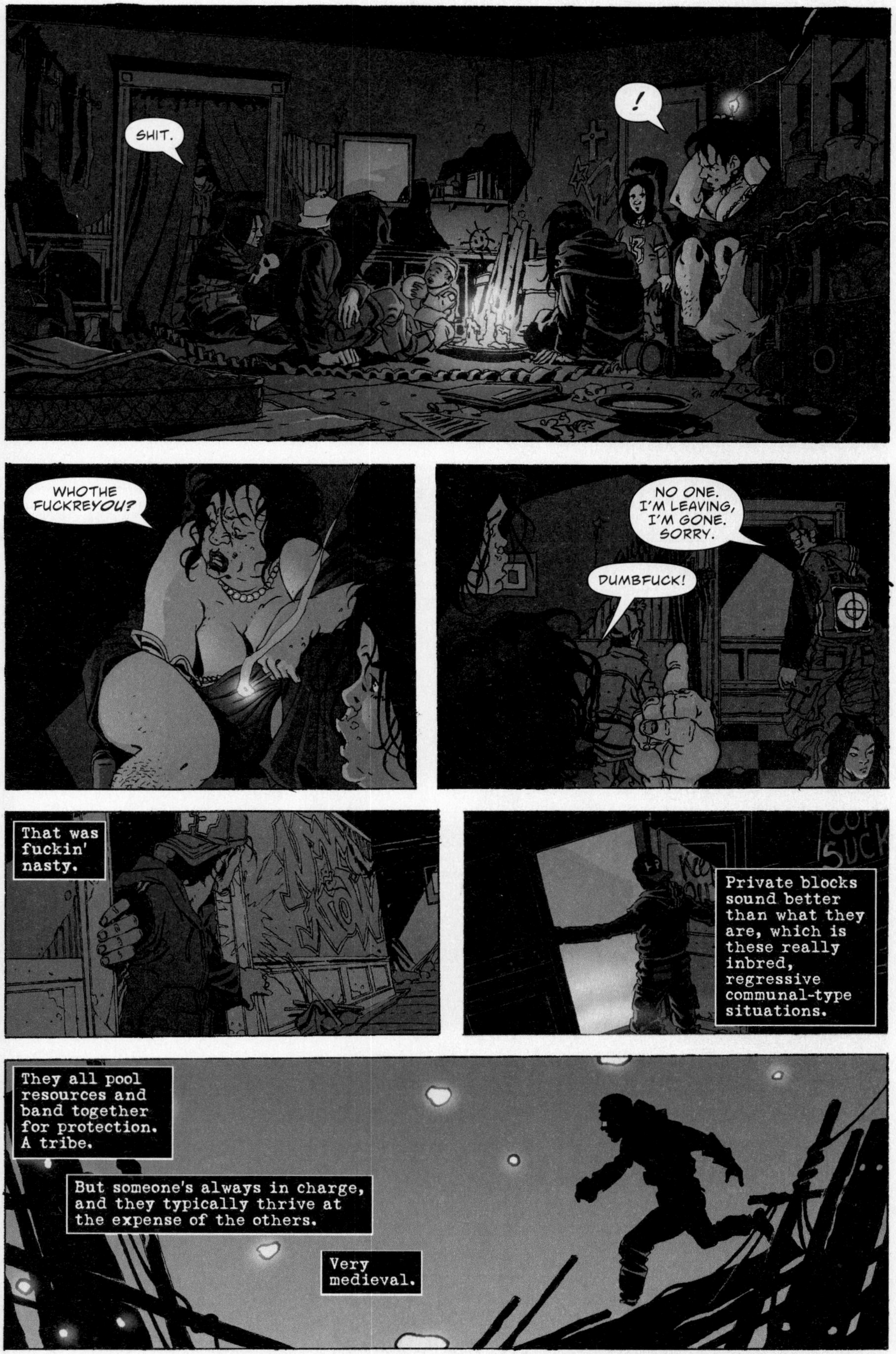
SHIT.
!
WHOTHE FUCKREYOU?
NO ONE. I'M LEAVING, I'M GONE. SORRY.
DUMBFUCK!
That was fuckin' nasty.
Private blocks sound better than what they are, which is these really inbred, regressive communal-type situations.
They all pool resources and band together for protection. A tribe.
But someone's always in charge, and they typically thrive at the expense of the others.
Very medieval.

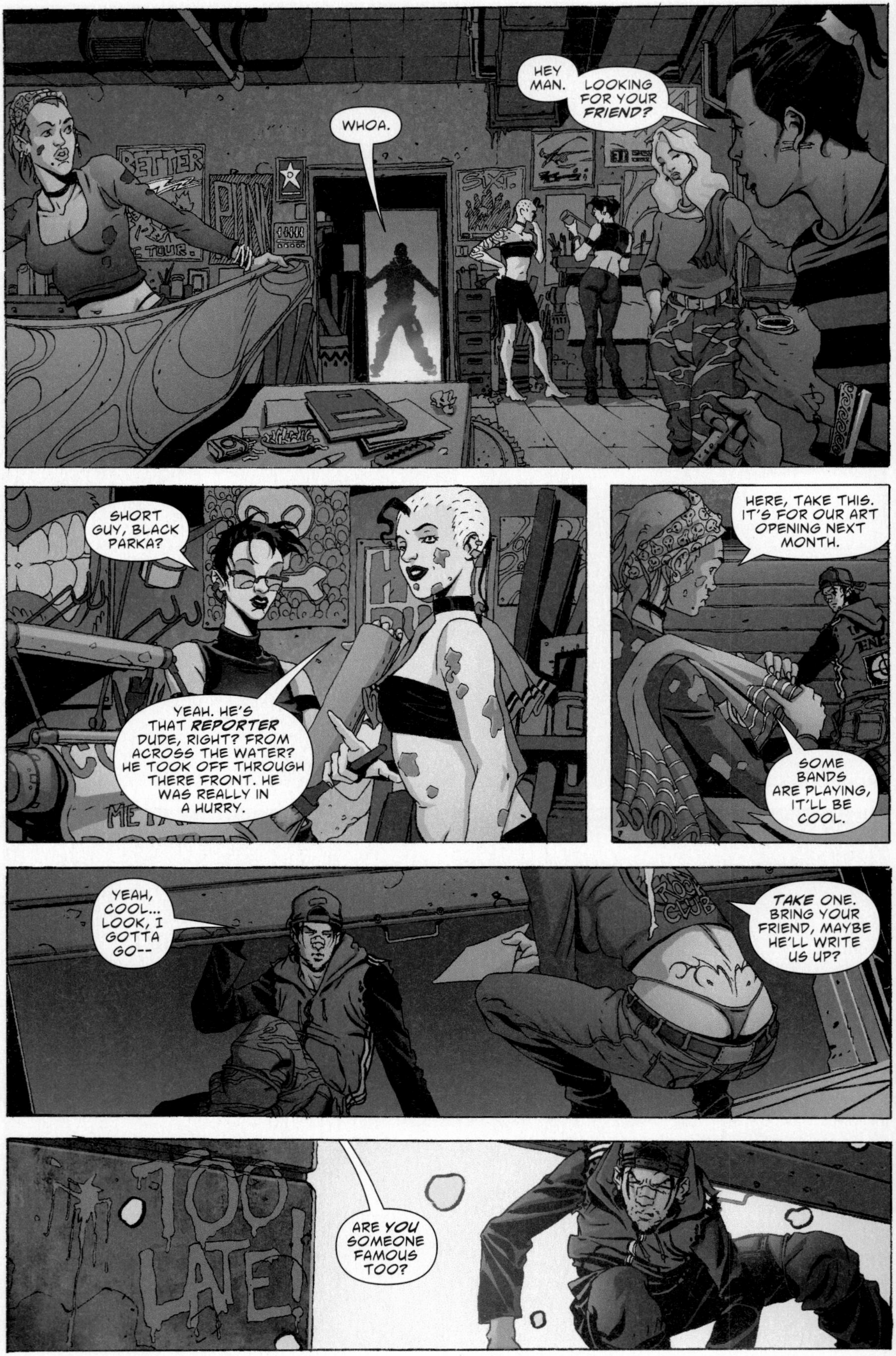
WHOA.
HEY MAN.
LOOKING FOR YOUR *FRIEND?*
SHORT GUY, BLACK PARKA?
YEAH. HE'S THAT *REPORTER* DUDE, RIGHT? FROM ACROSS THE WATER? HE TOOK OFF THROUGH THERE FRONT. HE WAS REALLY IN A HURRY.
HERE, TAKE THIS. IT'S FOR OUR ART OPENING NEXT MONTH.
SOME BANDS ARE PLAYING, IT'LL BE COOL.
YEAH, COOL... LOOK, I GOTTA GO--
TAKE ONE. BRING YOUR FRIEND, MAYBE HE'LL WRITE US UP?
TOO LATE!
ARE *YOU* SOMEONE FAMOUS TOO?

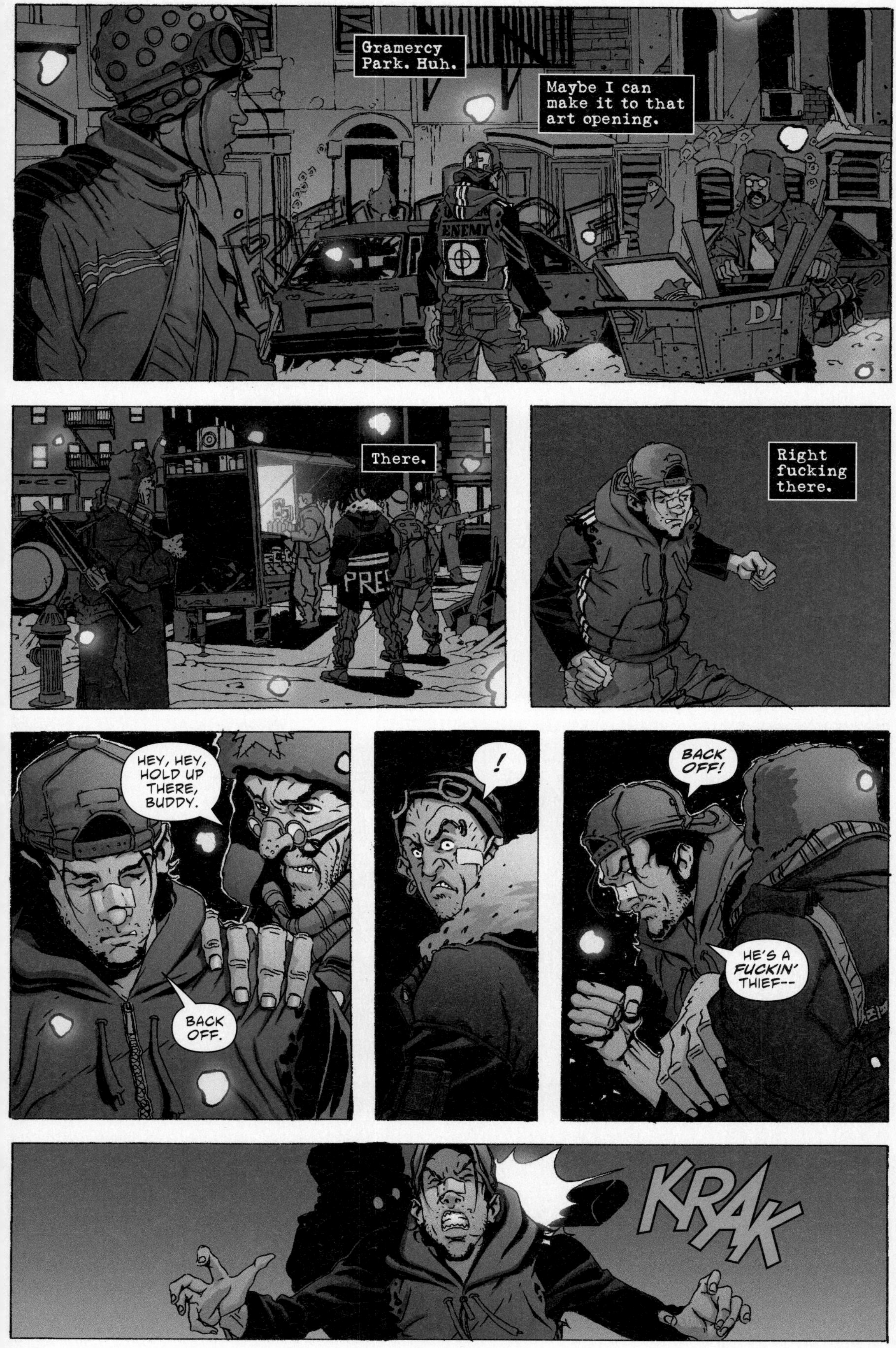
Gramercy Park. Huh.
Maybe I can make it to that art opening.
ENEMY
There.
PRESS
Right fucking there.
HEY, HEY, HOLD UP THERE, BUDDY.
BACK OFF.
!
BACK OFF!
HE'S A FUCKIN' THIEF--
KRAK

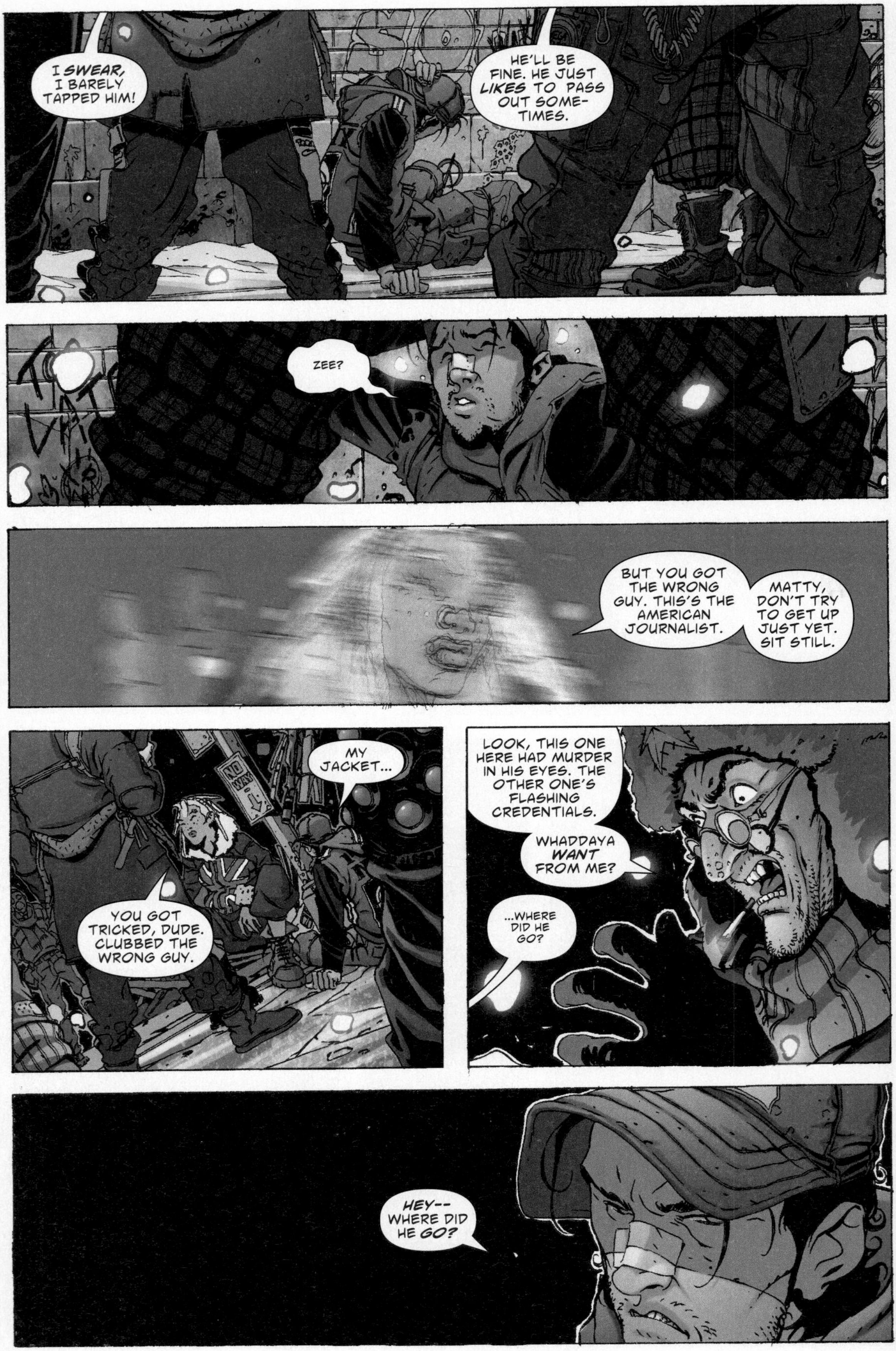
I *SWEAR,* I BARELY TAPPED HIM!
HE'LL BE FINE. HE JUST *LIKES* TO PASS OUT SOME-TIMES.
ZEE?
BUT YOU GOT THE WRONG GUY. THIS'S THE AMERICAN JOURNALIST.
MATTY, DON'T TRY TO GET UP JUST YET. SIT STILL.
MY JACKET...
YOU GOT TRICKED, DUDE. CLUBBED THE WRONG GUY.
LOOK, THIS ONE HERE HAD MURDER IN HIS EYES. THE OTHER ONE'S FLASHING CREDENTIALS.
WHADDAYA *WANT* FROM ME?
...WHERE DID HE GO?
HEY-- WHERE DID HE *GO?*

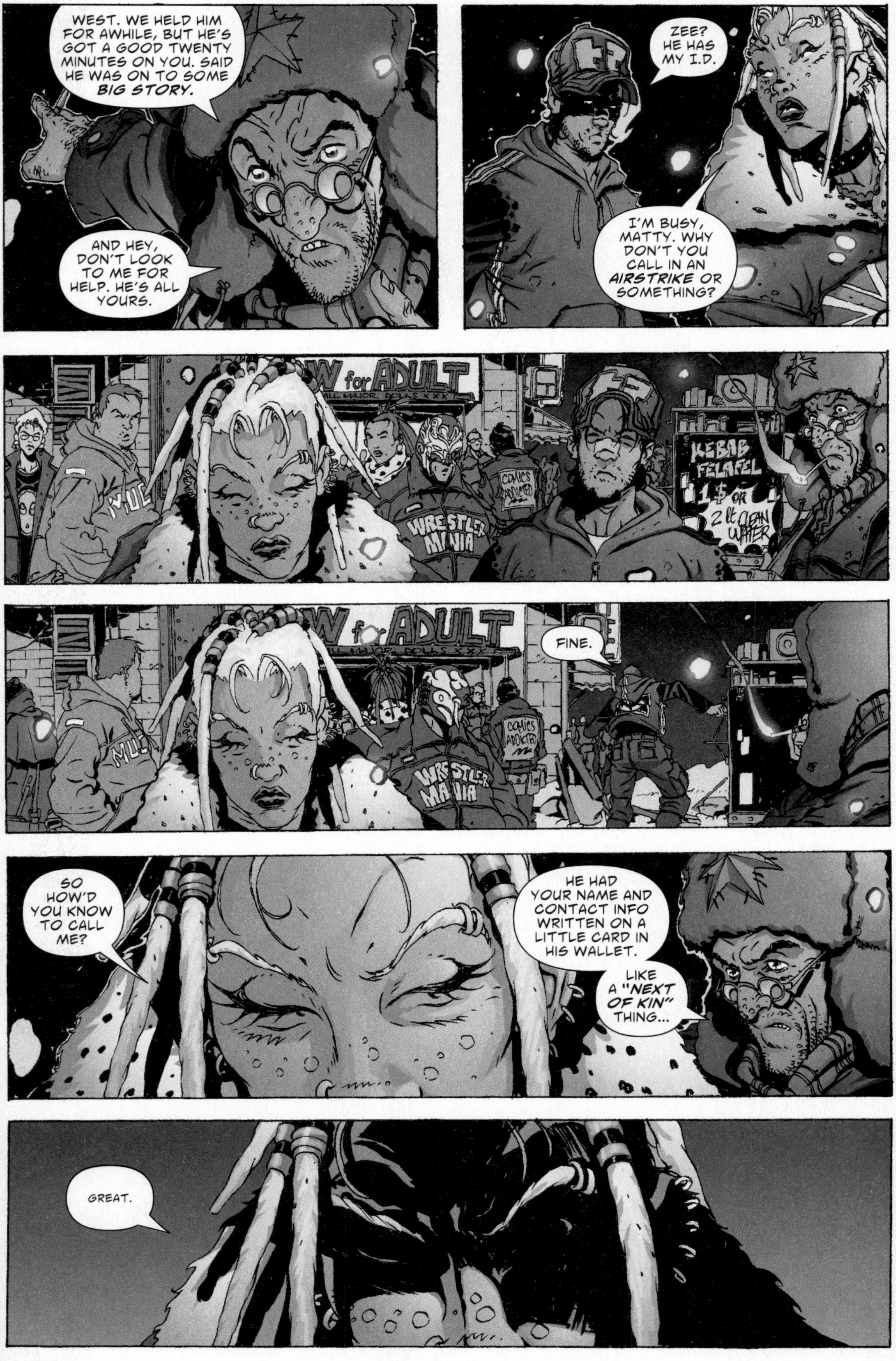

WEST. WE HELD HIM FOR AWHILE, BUT HE'S GOT A GOOD TWENTY MINUTES ON YOU. SAID HE WAS ON TO SOME *BIG STORY.*
AND HEY, DON'T LOOK TO ME FOR HELP. HE'S ALL YOURS.
ZEE? HE HAS MY I.D.
I'M BUSY, MATTY. WHY DON'T YOU CALL IN AN *AIRSTRIKE* OR SOMETHING?
W for ADULT
ALL MAJOR DOLLS XXX
KEBAB FELAFEL 1$ OR 2 lt CLEAN WATER
COMICS ADDICTED
WRESTLER MANIA
FINE.
SO HOW'D YOU KNOW TO CALL ME?
HE HAD YOUR NAME AND CONTACT INFO WRITTEN ON A LITTLE CARD IN HIS WALLET.
LIKE A *"NEXT OF KIN"* THING...
GREAT.

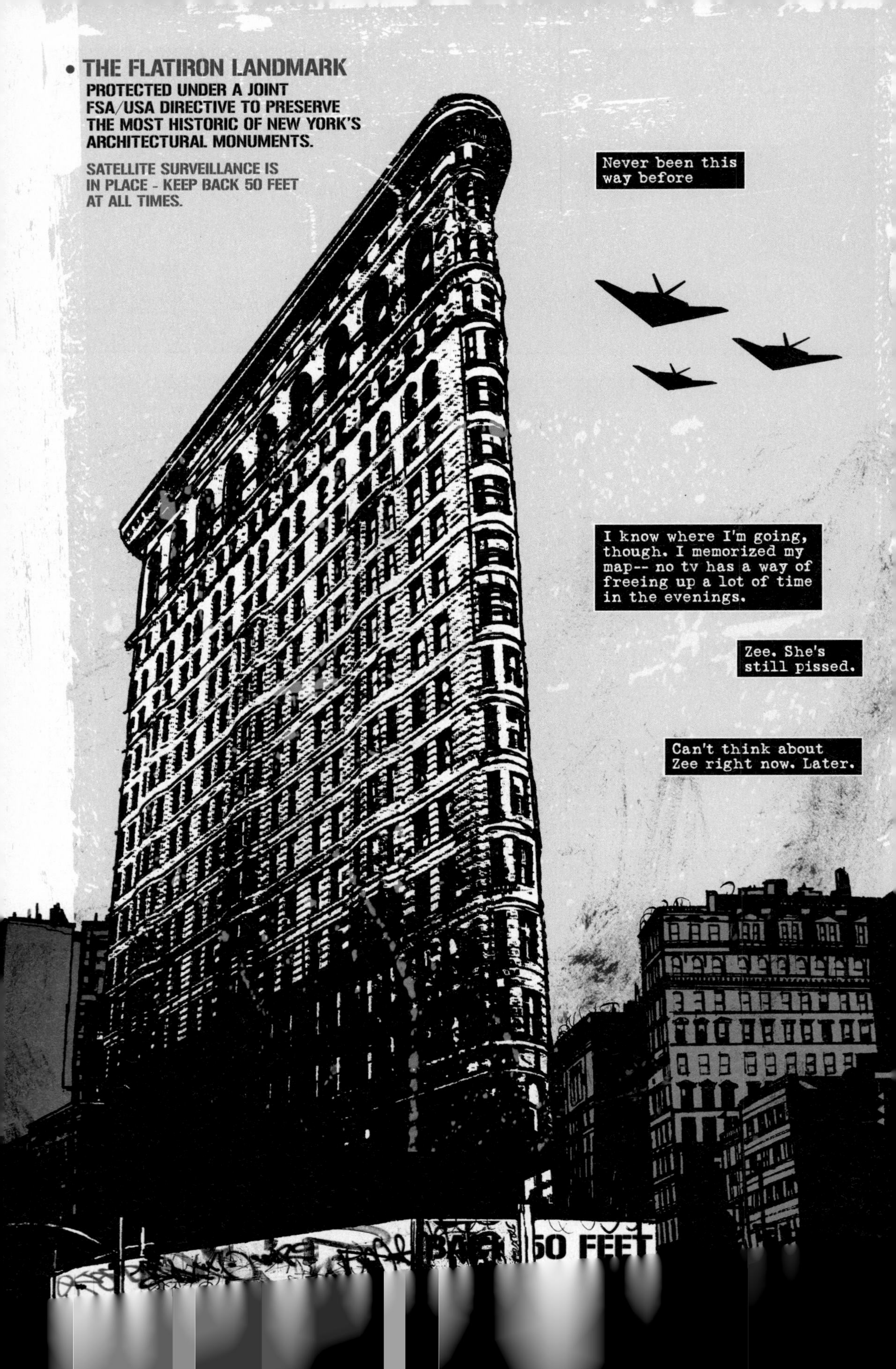
• THE FLATIRON LANDMARK
PROTECTED UNDER A JOINT FSA/USA DIRECTIVE TO PRESERVE THE MOST HISTORIC OF NEW YORK'S ARCHITECTURAL MONUMENTS.
SATELLITE SURVEILLANCE IS IN PLACE - KEEP BACK 50 FEET AT ALL TIMES.
Never been this way before
I know where I'm going, though. I memorized my map-- no tv has a way of freeing up a lot of time in the evenings.
Zee. She's still pissed.
Can't think about Zee right now. Later.
50 FEET

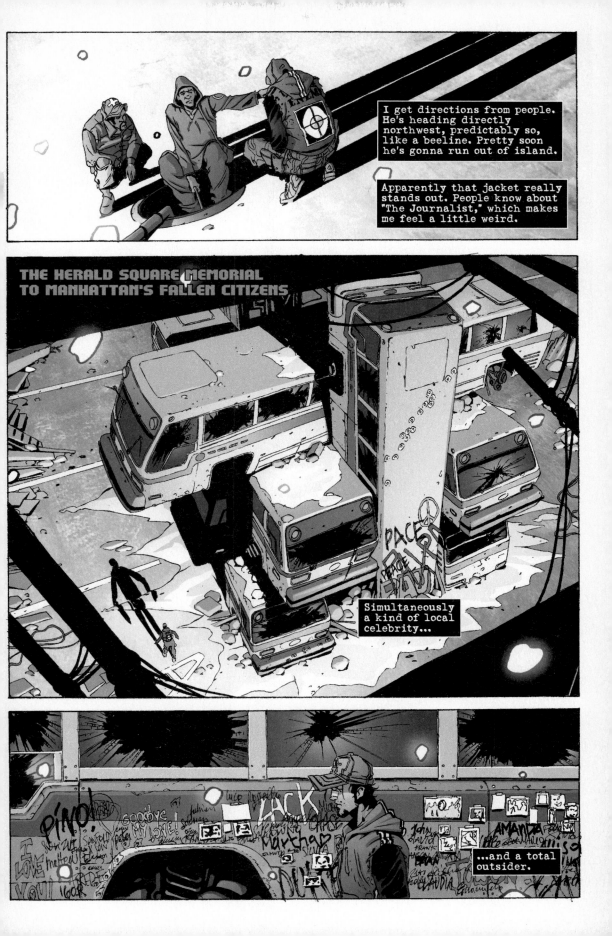

I get directions from people. He's heading directly northwest, predictably so, like a beeline. Pretty soon he's gonna run out of island.

Apparently that jacket really stands out. People know about "The Journalist," which makes me feel a little weird.

THE HERALD SQUARE MEMORIAL TO MANHATTAN'S FALLEN CITIZENS

Simultaneously a kind of local celebrity...

...and a total outsider.

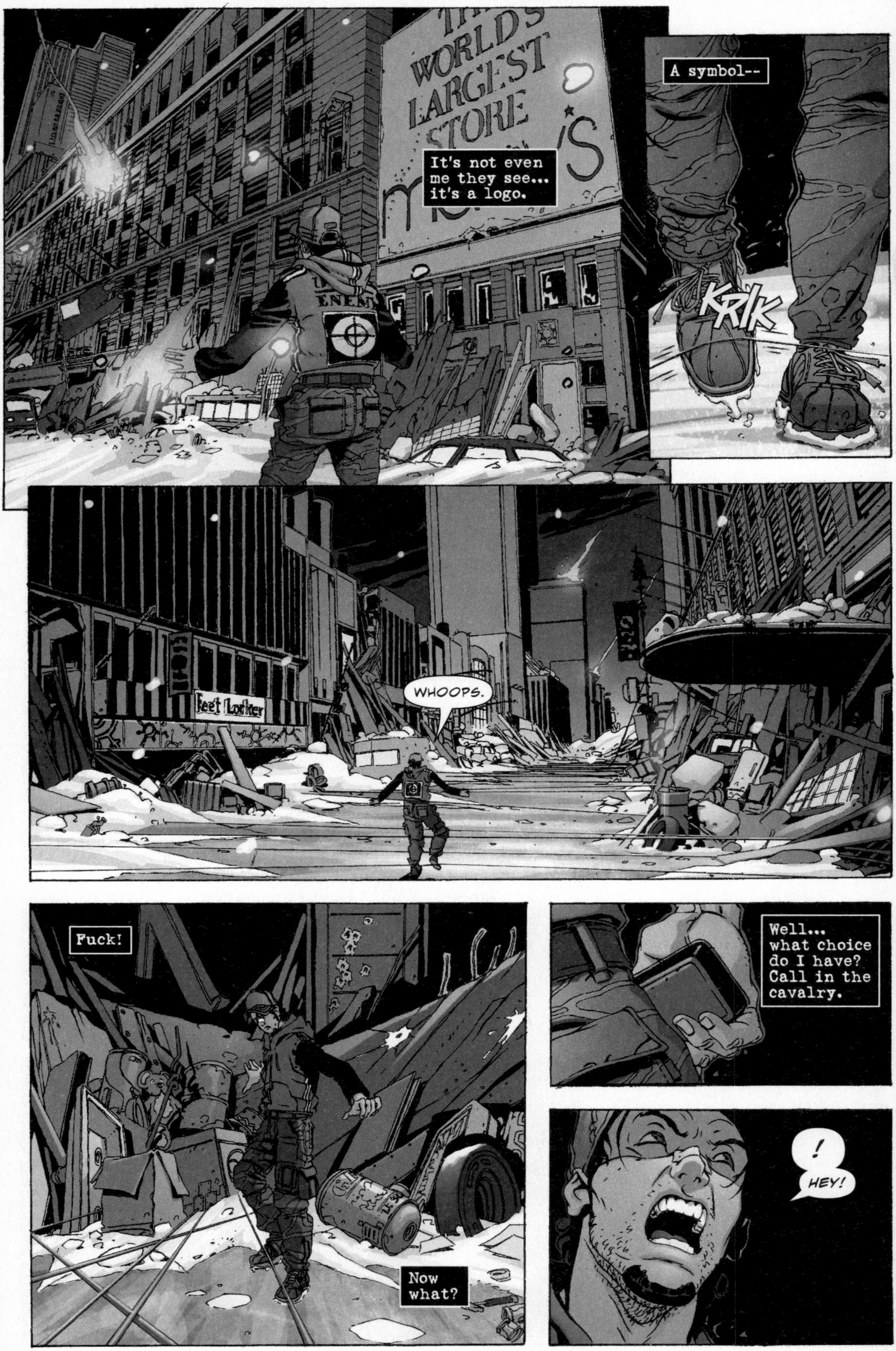
THE WORLD'S LARGEST STORE
It's not even me they see... it's a logo.
A symbol--
KRIK
Feet Locker
WHOOPS.
Fuck!
Now what?
Well... what choice do I have? Call in the cavalry.
!
HEY!

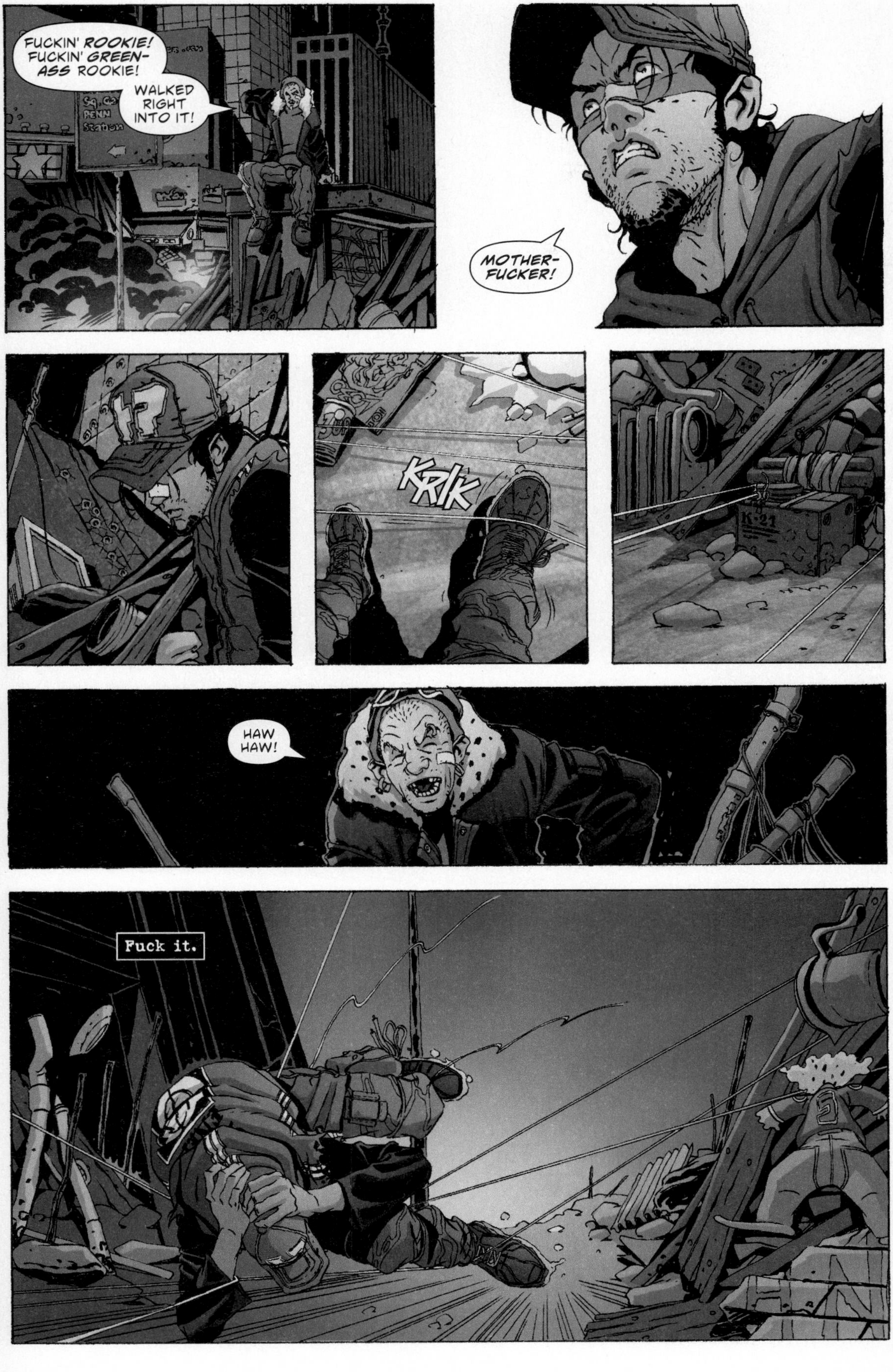

FUCKIN' ROOKIE! FUCKIN' GREEN-ASS ROOKIE!
WALKED RIGHT INTO IT!
MOTHER-FUCKER!
KRIK
HAW HAW!
Fuck it.

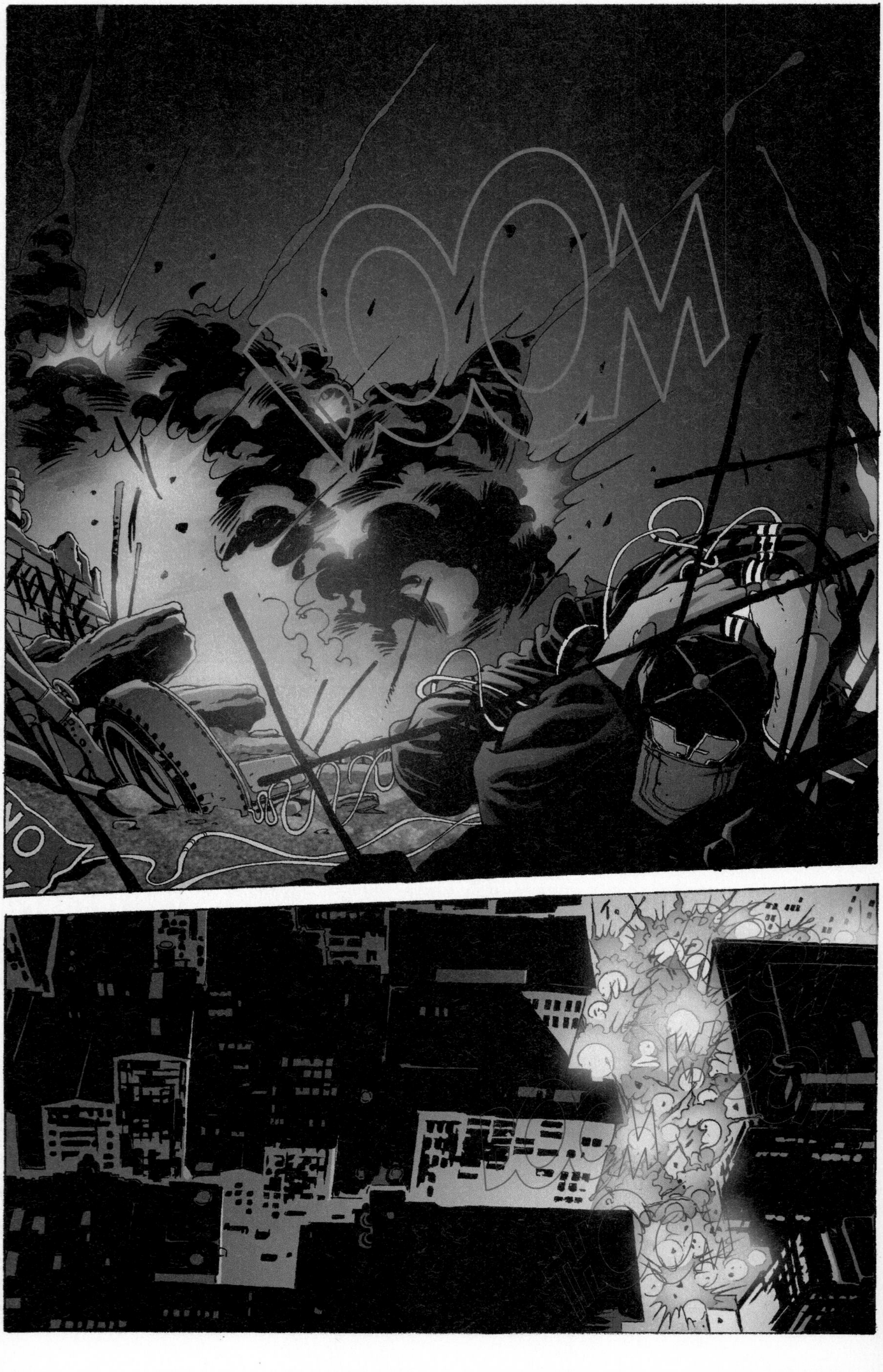
BOOM

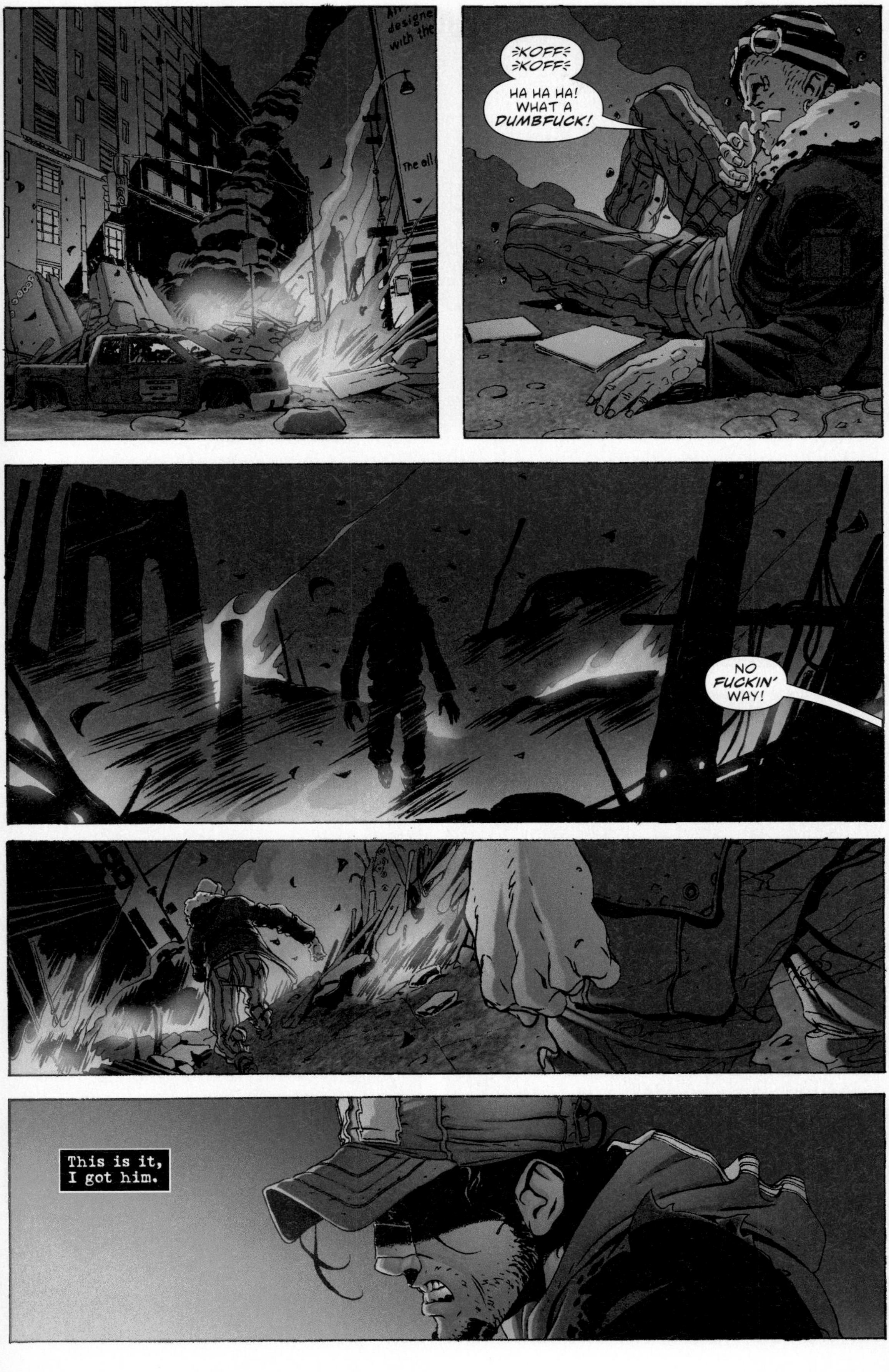

KOFF KOFF
HA HA HA! WHAT A DUMBFUCK!
NO FUCKIN' WAY!
This is it, I got him.

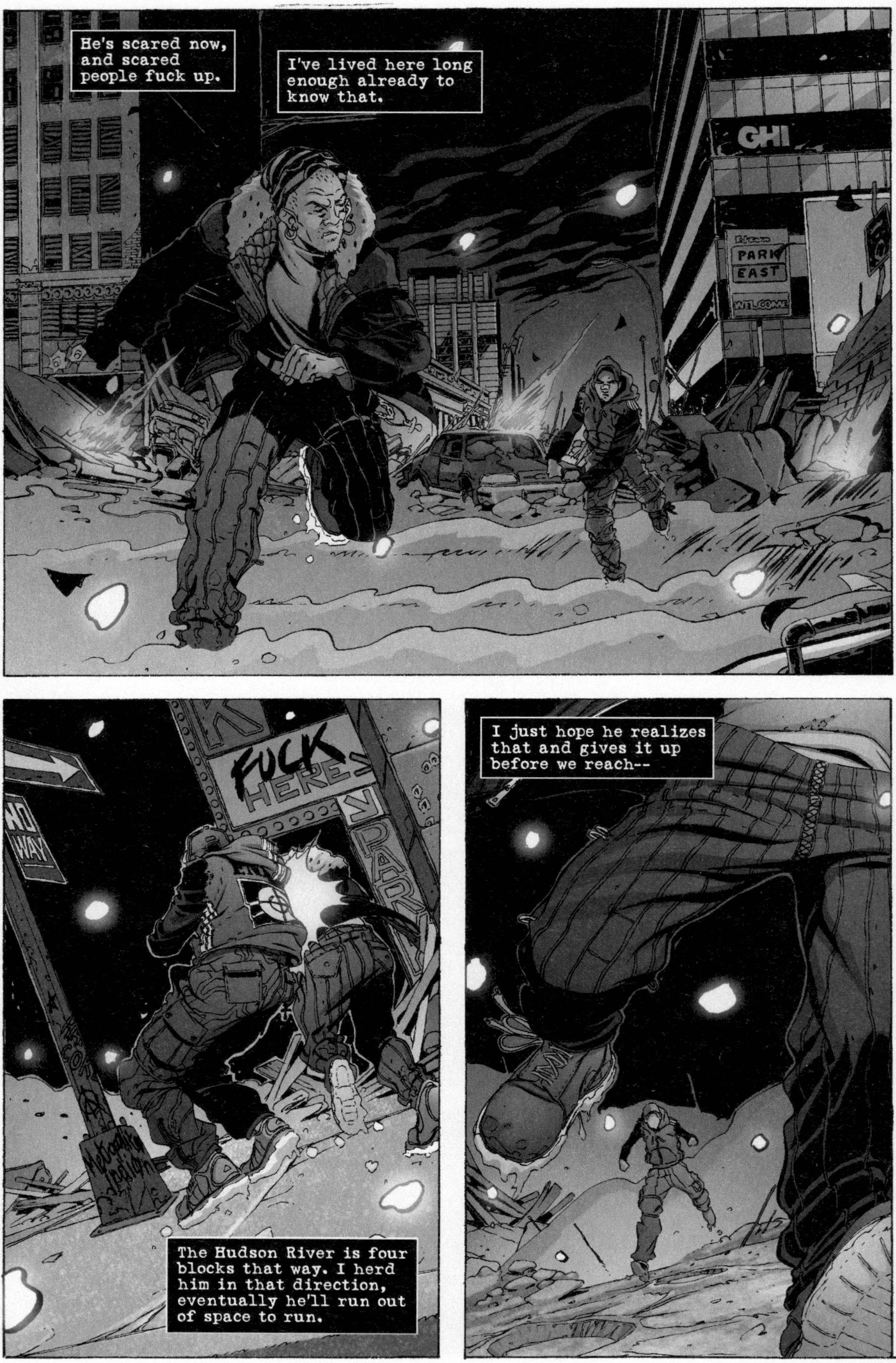
He's scared now, and scared people fuck up.
I've lived here long enough already to know that.
GHI
PARK EAST
WELCOME
FUCK
HERES
NO WAY
The Hudson River is four blocks that way. I herd him in that direction, eventually he'll run out of space to run.
I just hope he realizes that and gives it up before we reach--

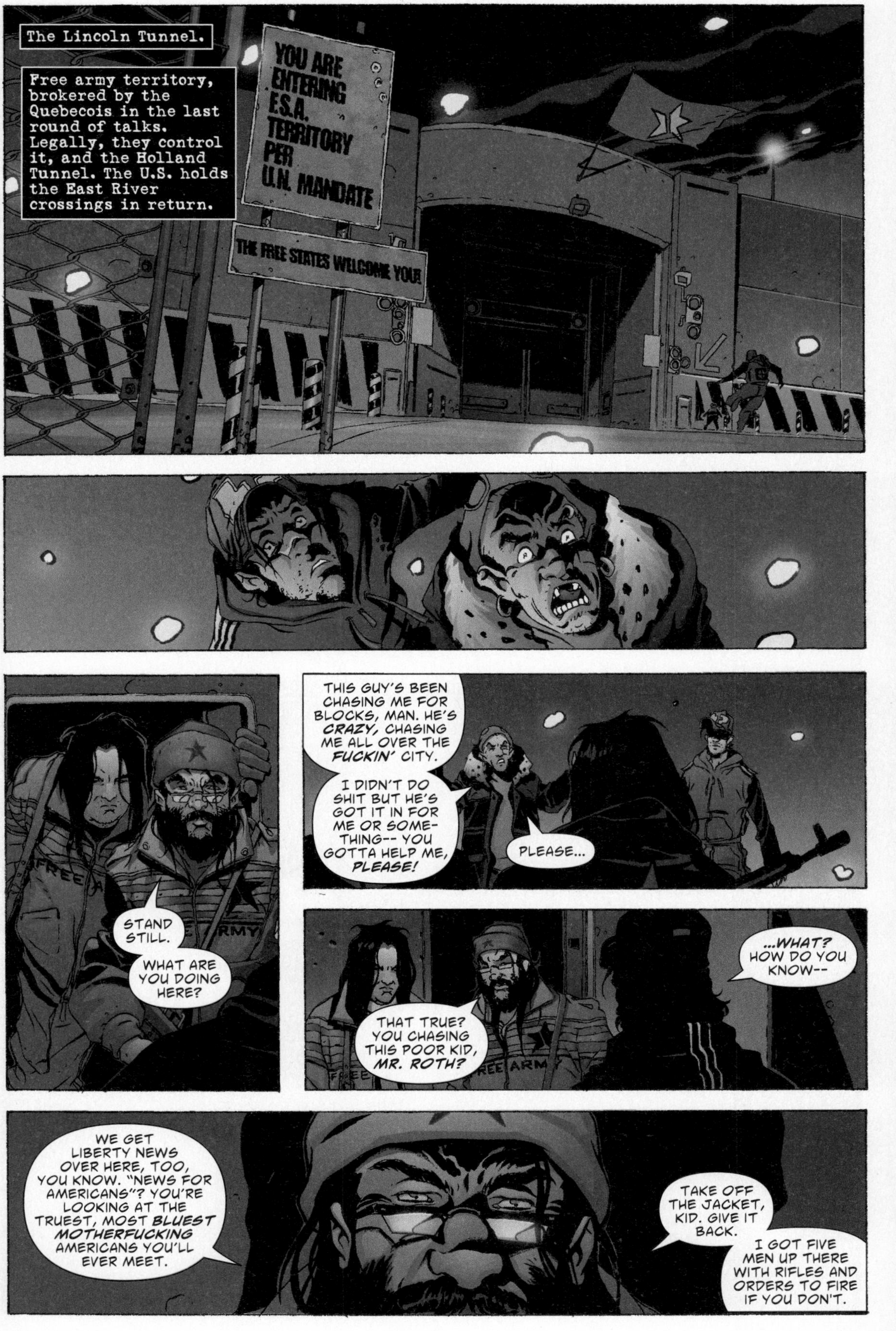
The Lincoln Tunnel.
Free army territory, brokered by the Quebecois in the last round of talks. Legally, they control it, and the Holland Tunnel. The U.S. holds the East River crossings in return.
YOU ARE ENTERING E.S.A. TERRITORY PER U.N. MANDATE
THE FREE STATES WELCOME YOU!
STAND STILL.
WHAT ARE YOU DOING HERE?
THIS GUY'S BEEN CHASING ME FOR BLOCKS, MAN. HE'S CRAZY, CHASING ME ALL OVER THE FUCKIN' CITY.
I DIDN'T DO SHIT BUT HE'S GOT IT IN FOR ME OR SOME-THING-- YOU GOTTA HELP ME, PLEASE!
PLEASE...
THAT TRUE? YOU CHASING THIS POOR KID, MR. ROTH?
...WHAT? HOW DO YOU KNOW--
WE GET LIBERTY NEWS OVER HERE, TOO, YOU KNOW. "NEWS FOR AMERICANS"? YOU'RE LOOKING AT THE TRUEST, MOST BLUEST MOTHERFUCKING AMERICANS YOU'LL EVER MEET.
TAKE OFF THE JACKET, KID. GIVE IT BACK.
I GOT FIVE MEN UP THERE WITH RIFLES AND ORDERS TO FIRE IF YOU DON'T.

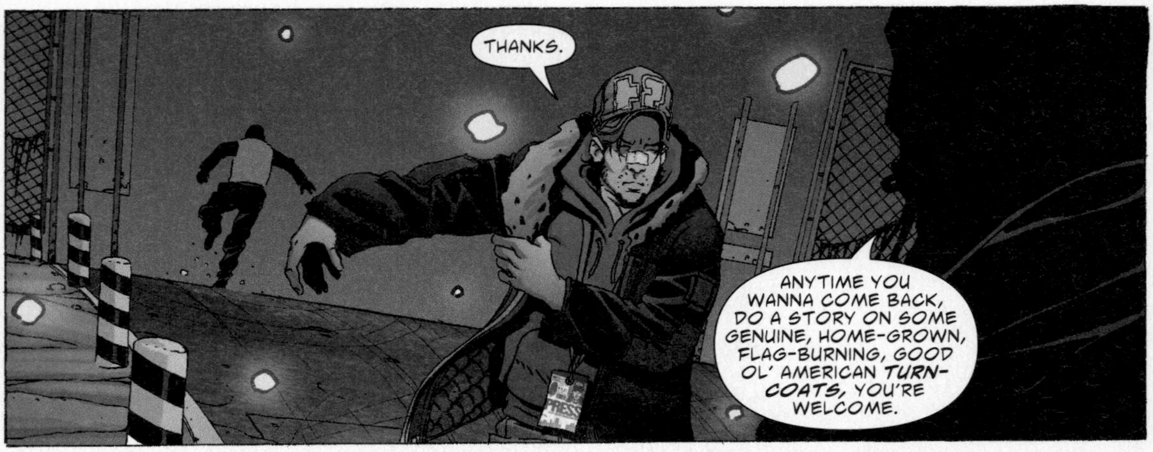
THANKS.
ANYTIME YOU WANNA COME BACK, DO A STORY ON SOME GENUINE, HOME-GROWN, FLAG-BURNING, GOOD OL' AMERICAN *TURN-COATS,* YOU'RE WELCOME.

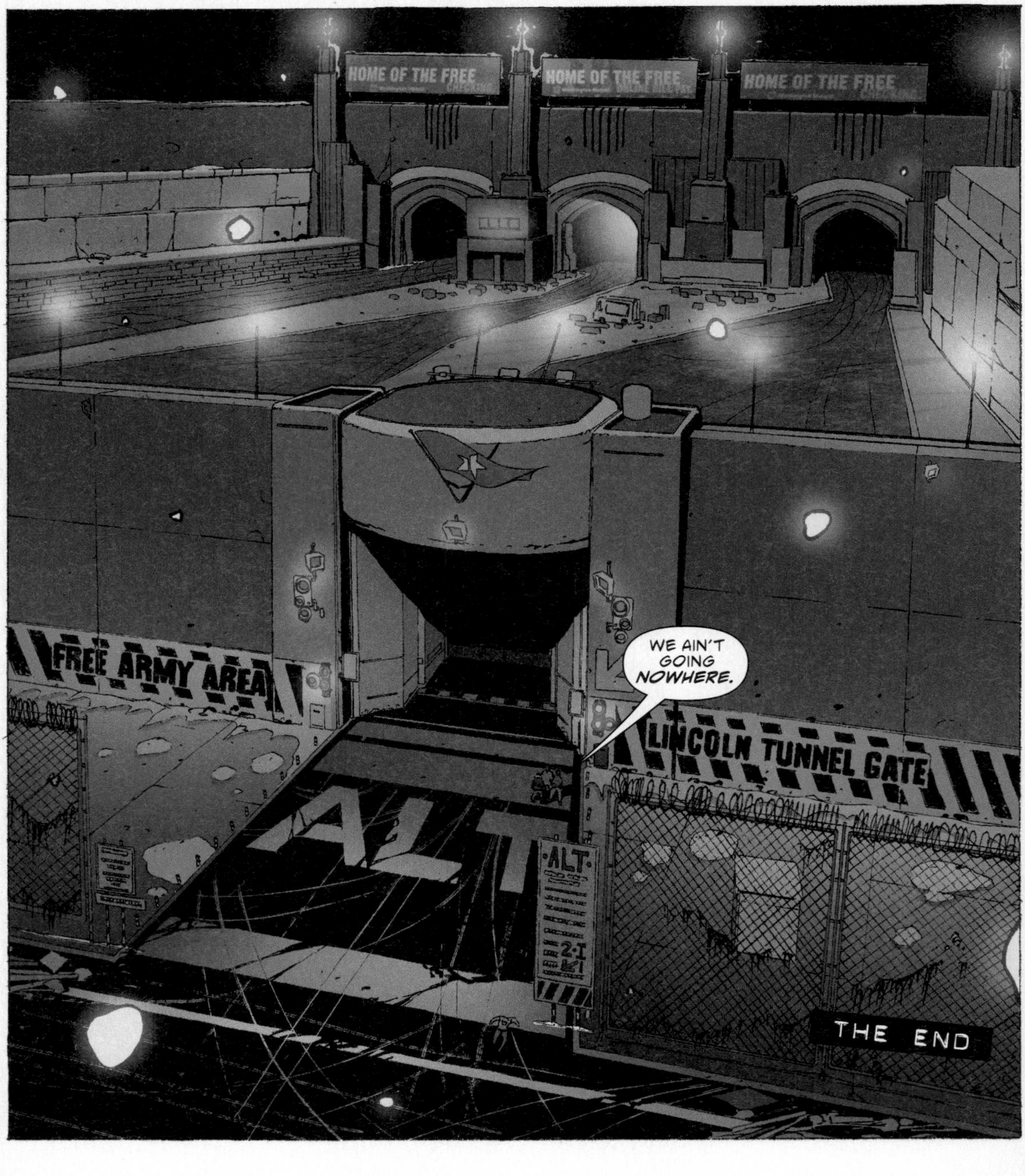
HOME OF THE FREE
HOME OF THE FREE
HOME OF THE FREE
FREE ARMY AREA
WE AIN'T GOING *NOWHERE.*
LINCOLN TUNNEL GATE
ALT
ALT
THE END

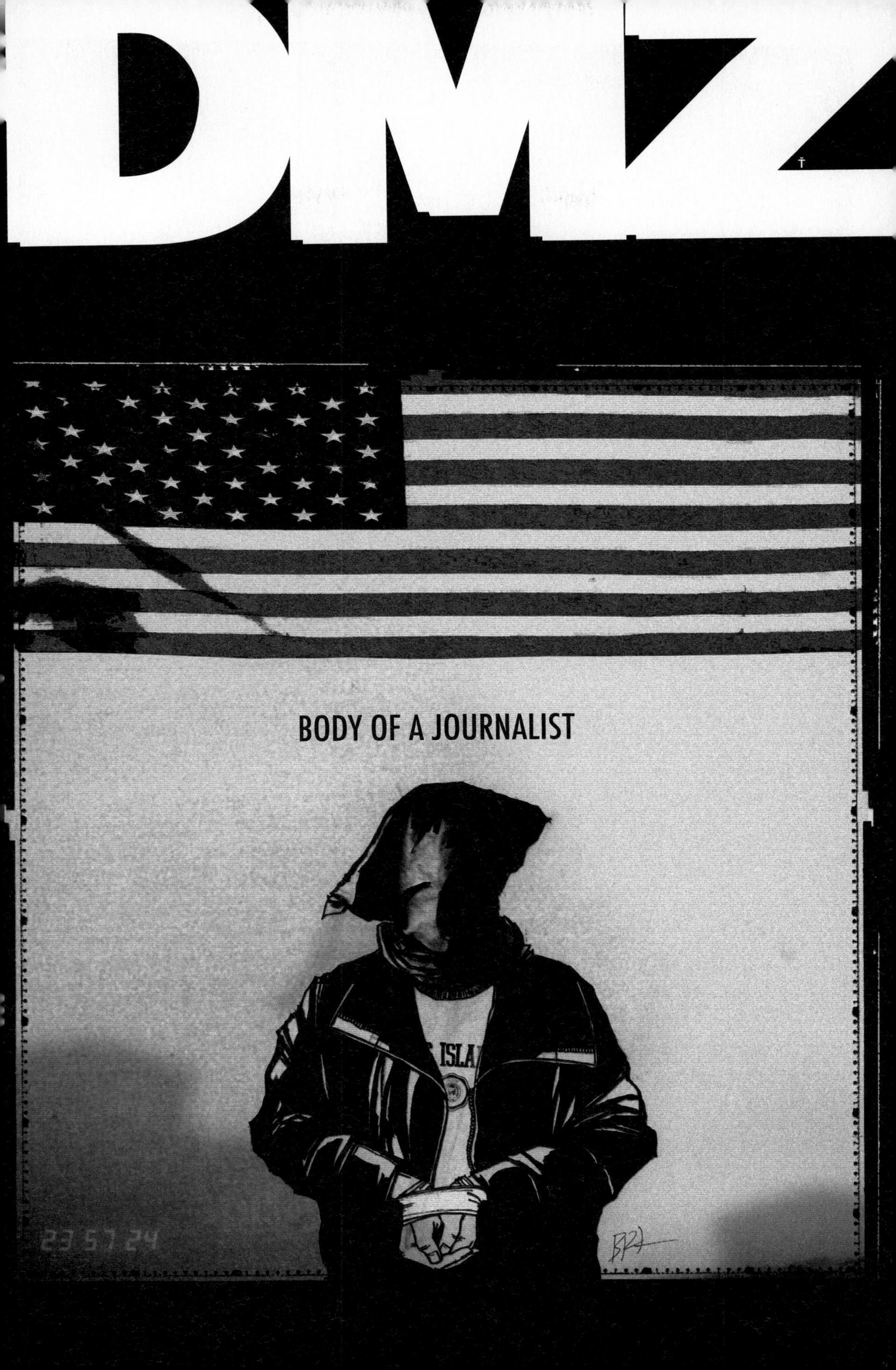
DMZ
BODY OF A JOURNALIST

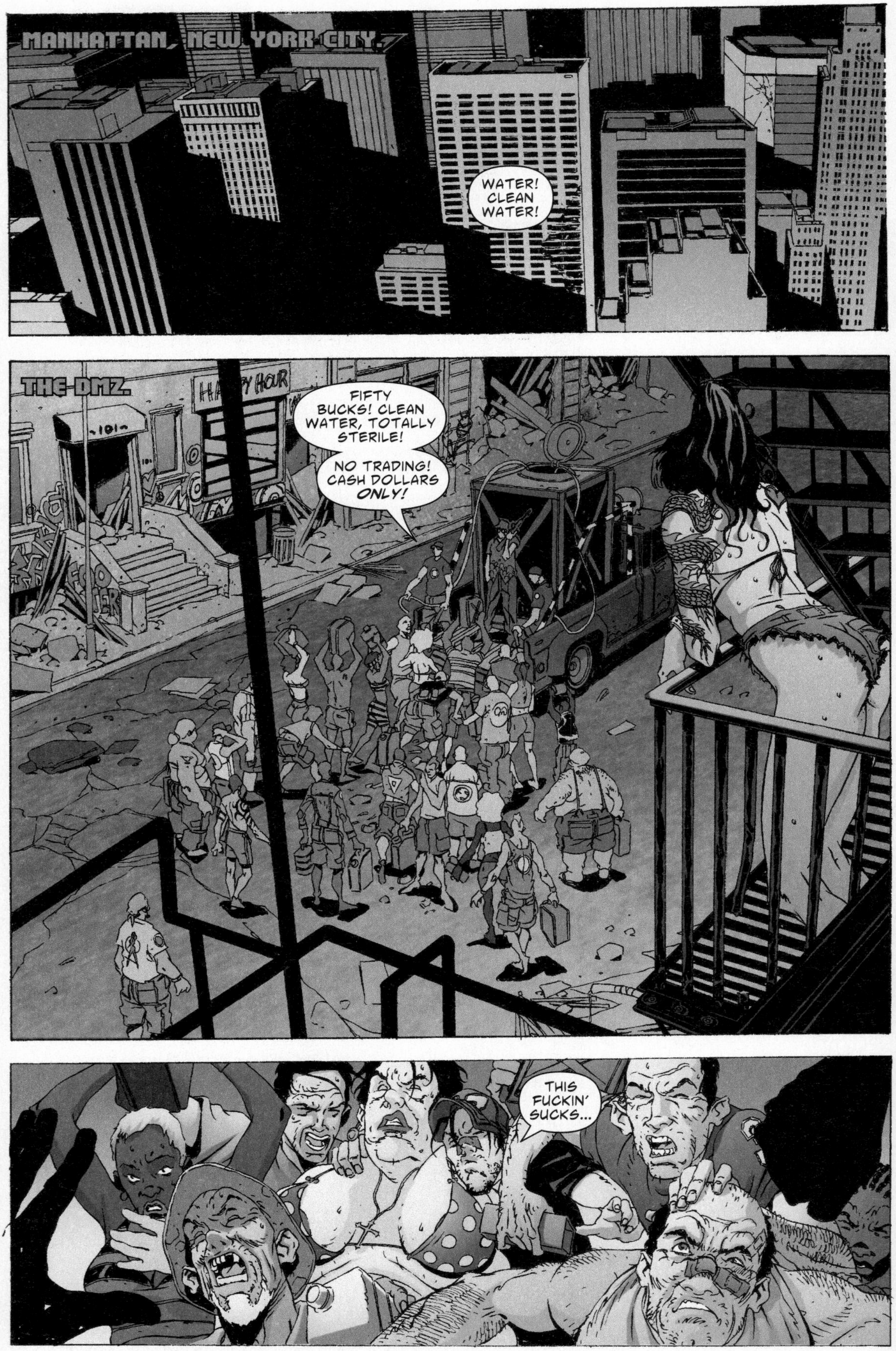
MANHATTAN, NEW YORK CITY.
WATER! CLEAN WATER!
THE DMZ.
FIFTY BUCKS! CLEAN WATER, TOTALLY STERILE!
NO TRADING! CASH DOLLARS *ONLY!*
THIS FUCKIN' SUCKS...

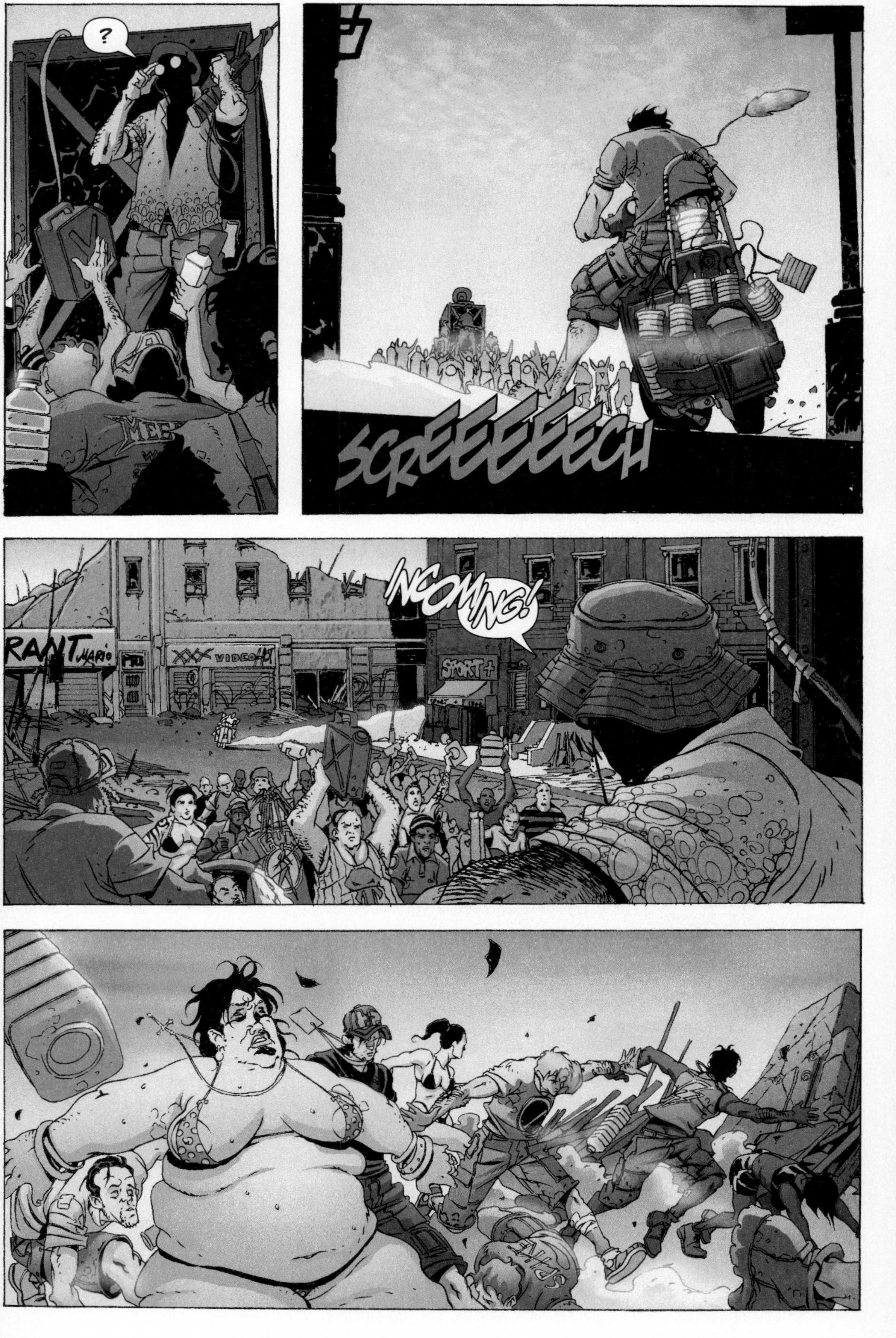
?
SCREEEEEEECH
INCOMING!
RANT MARIO
XXX VIDEO
SPORT +

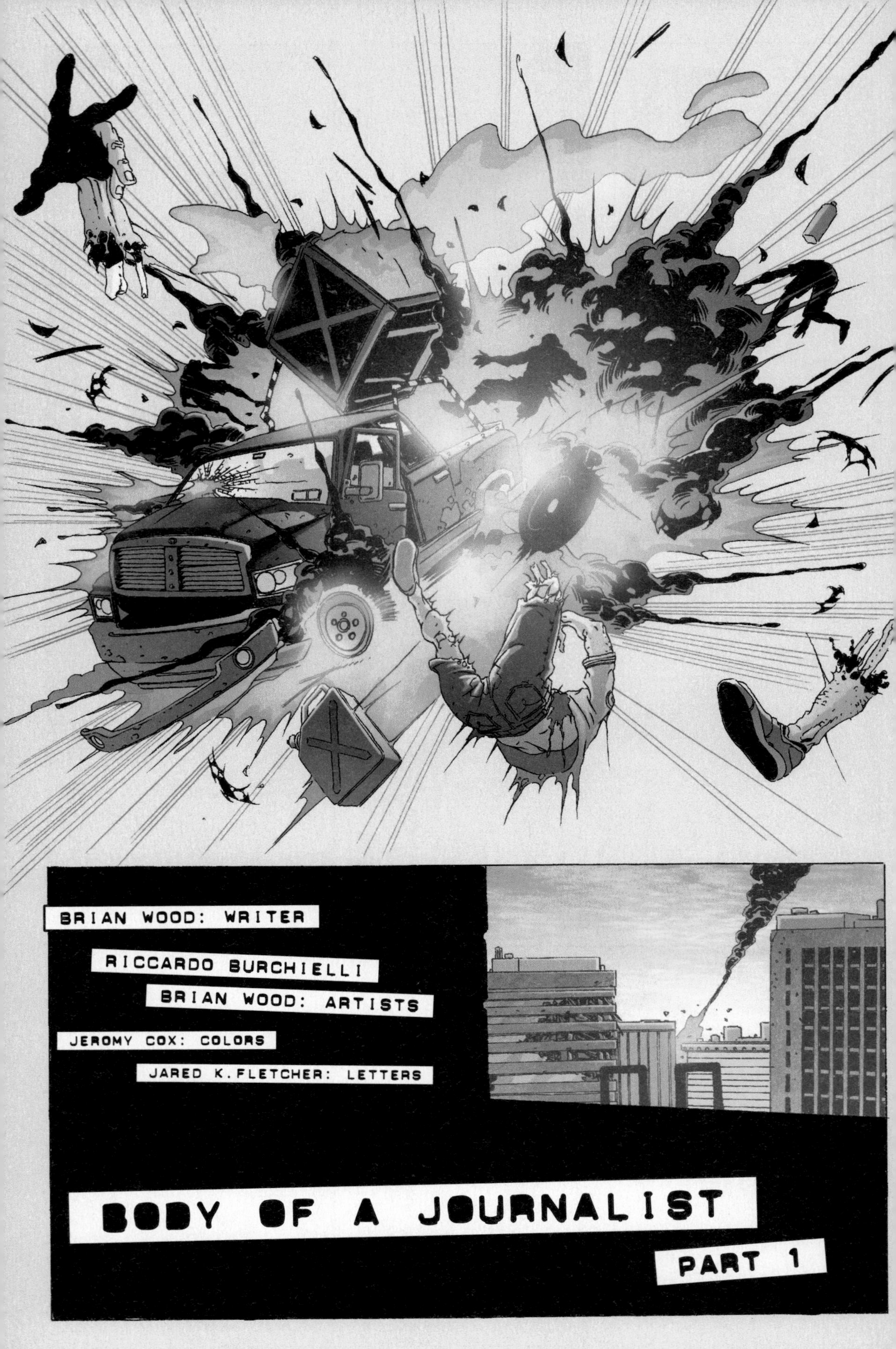
BRIAN WOOD: WRITER
RICCARDO BURCHIELLI
BRIAN WOOD: ARTISTS
JEROMY COX: COLORS
JARED K.FLETCHER: LETTERS
BODY OF A JOURNALIST
PART 1

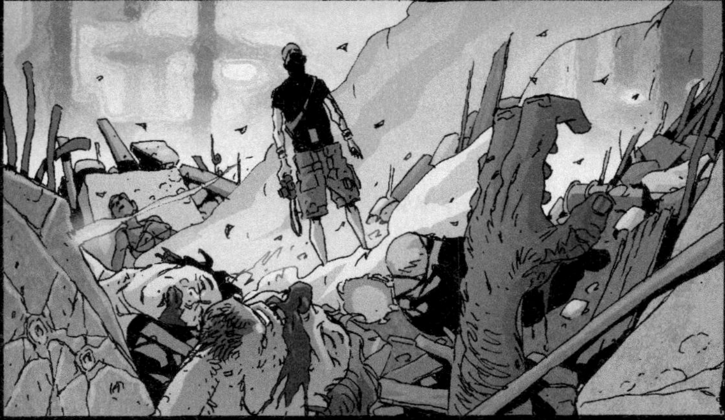

In one of the deadliest days in recent weeks, a suicide-bombing deep in what was once Manhattan's Little Italy claimed the lives of seventeen civilians and three local insurgents, as well as the bomber himself.

Liberty News' Matthew Roth will be providing exclusive images from the scene.

The suspected target was a water delivery truck that was providing drinking water for the area residents. The city's been particularly hard hit by the recent heat wave, with clean, safe water in short supply.

This delivery was not believed to be sanctioned by the tribal bosses who have claimed governance over the area, and the bombing is thought to be retribution.

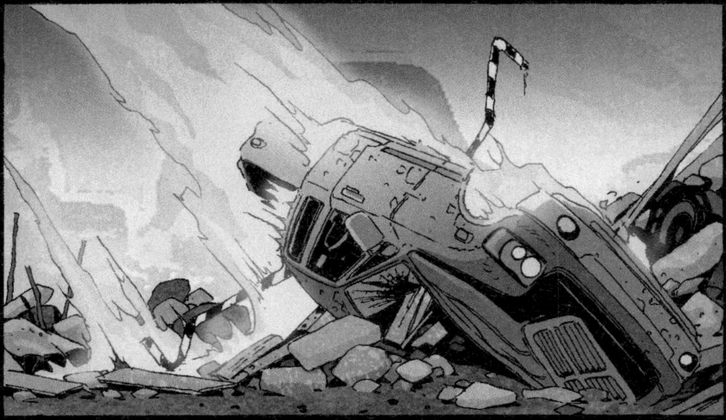

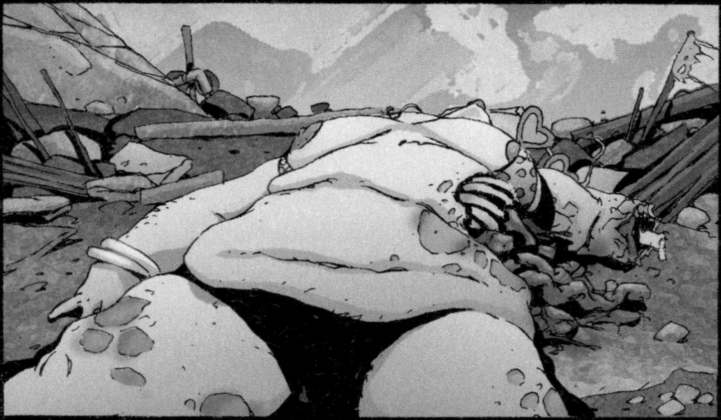

American Military, claiming extraordinary circumstances in the face of increased insurgent violence, have resumed aerial reconnaissance of the city.

This comes despite their having agreed to a mutual no-fly situation with the self-labeled "Free States" earlier this year.

Military spokesmen declined comment.

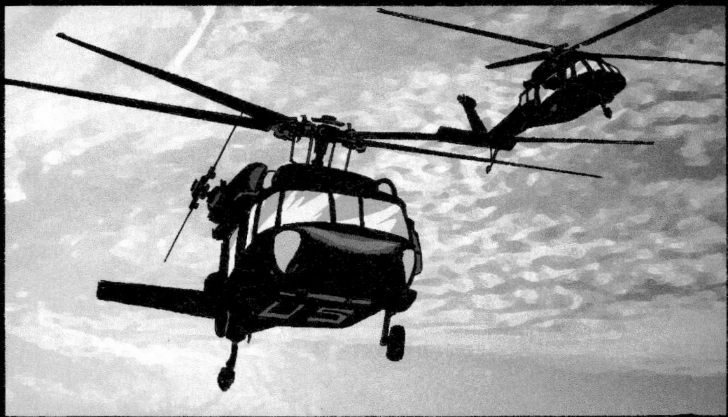

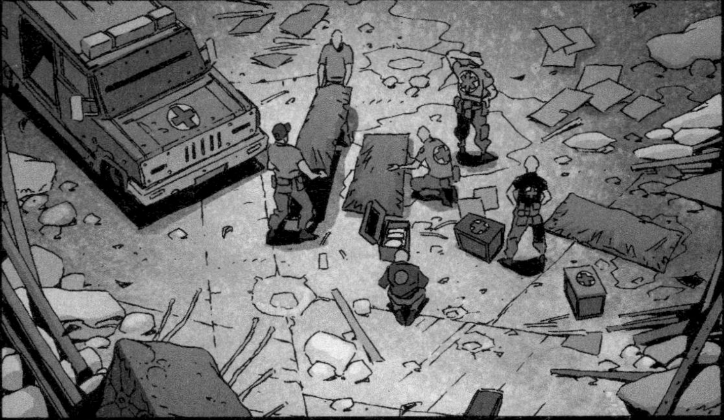

In related news, sniper fire claimed the lives of six American servicemen in Staten Island this morning.

Flatbush Avenue in U.S.-Controlled Brooklyn erupted in violence overnight with a series of drive-by shootings on military housing that eyewitnesses on the scene described as "coordinated."

The high concentration of troops in the heavily residential borough is frequently the subject of intense public debate and protest. "Where the <bleep> do you expect us to go?" an anonymous soldier asked bitterly. "This is all the America we got left."

Seven people were wounded, two fatally.

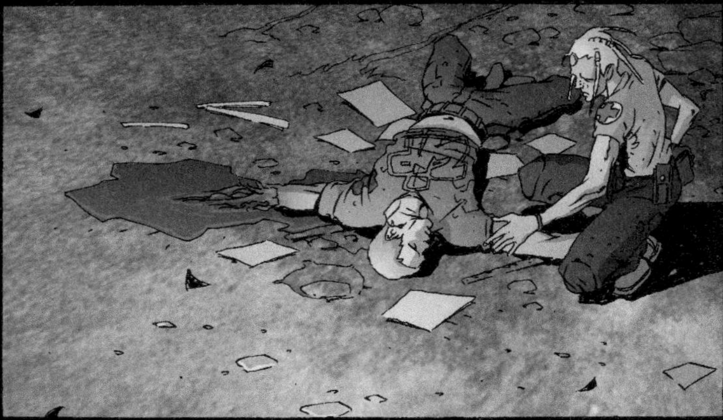

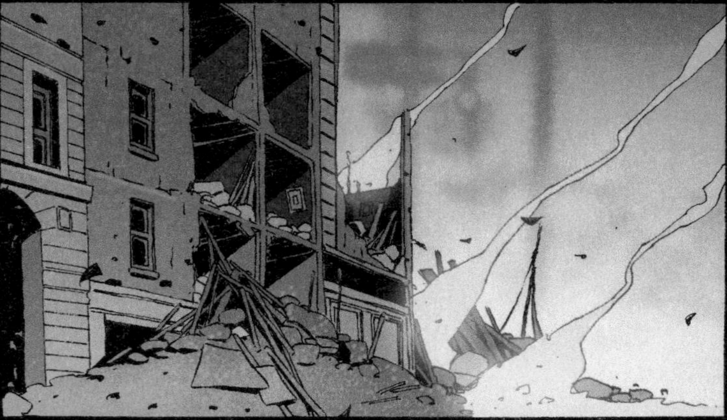

The Pentagon released its official findings concerning a suspected "dirty explosion" recorded in the vicinity of the Statue of Liberty two days ago. Radiation levels came back high, and a general advisory was issued, warning all to avoid the landmark for the next 120-180 days.

Stay tuned for in-depth coverage and analysis of these stories and more.

This has been a Liberty News summary.

News for America, and Americans.

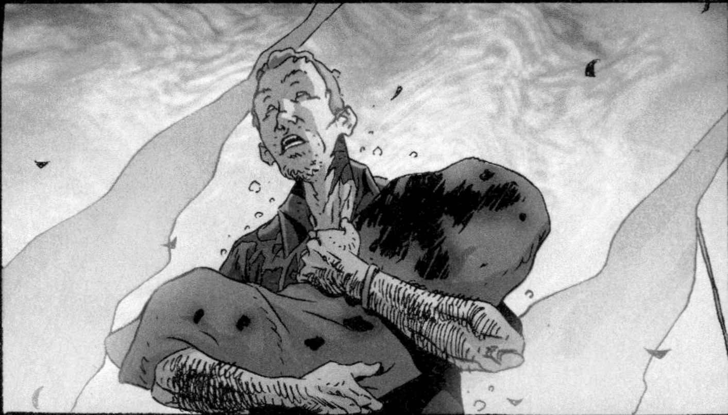

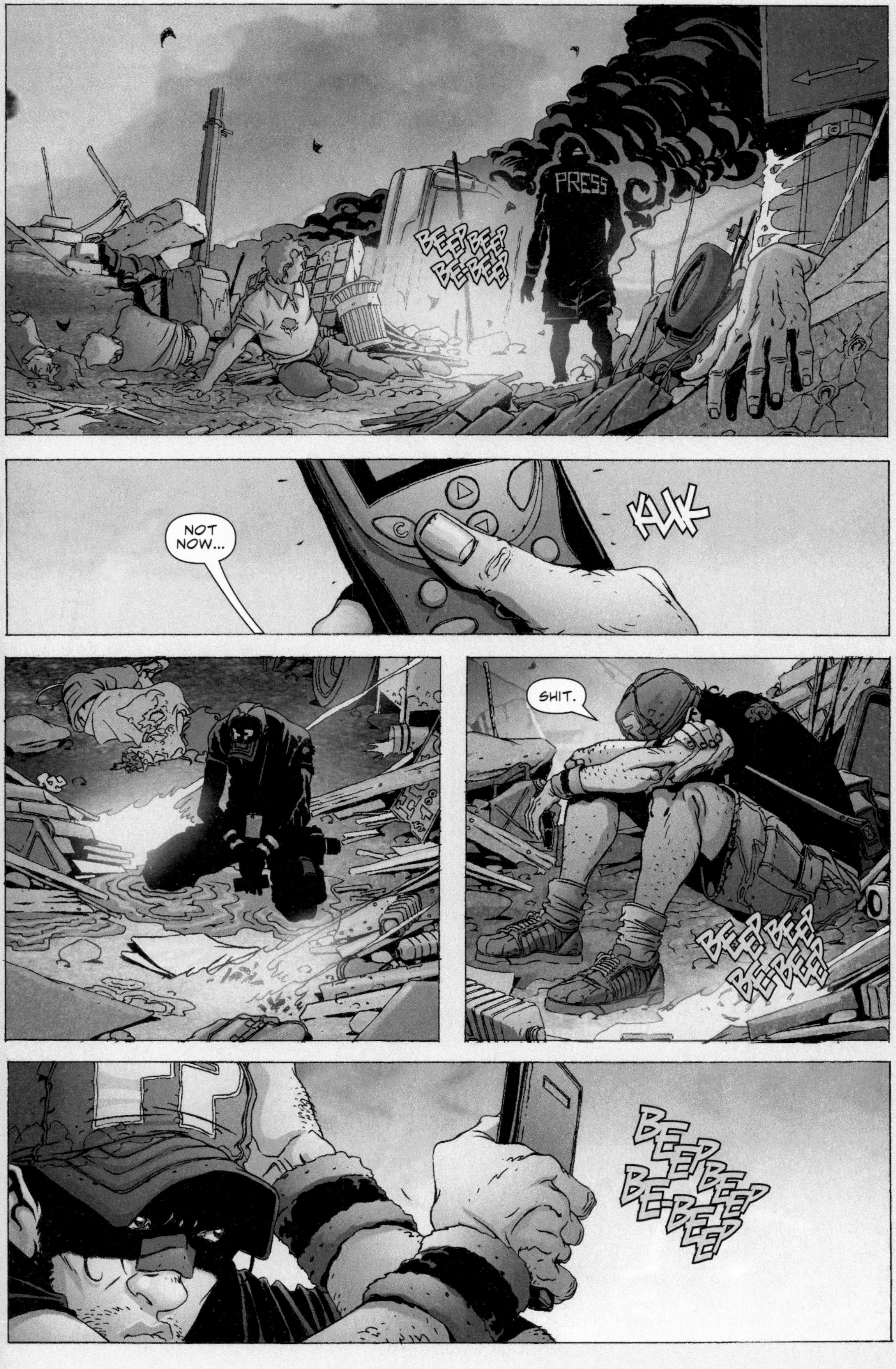
PRESS
BEEP BEEP BE-BEEP
NOT NOW...
KLIK
SHIT.
BEEP BEEP BE-BEEP
BEEP BEEP BE-BEEP

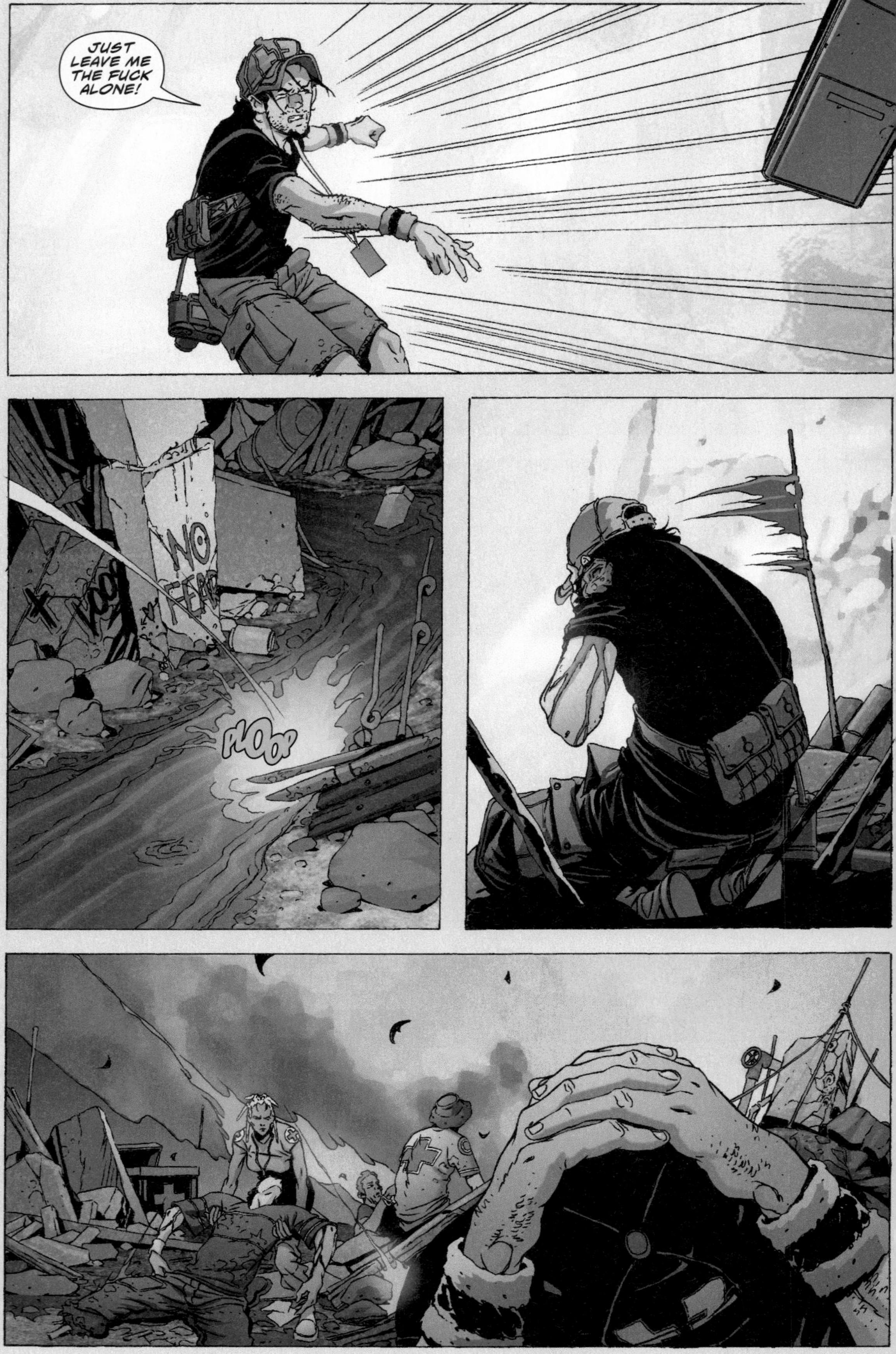
JUST LEAVE ME THE FUCK ALONE!
NO FEAR
PLOOP

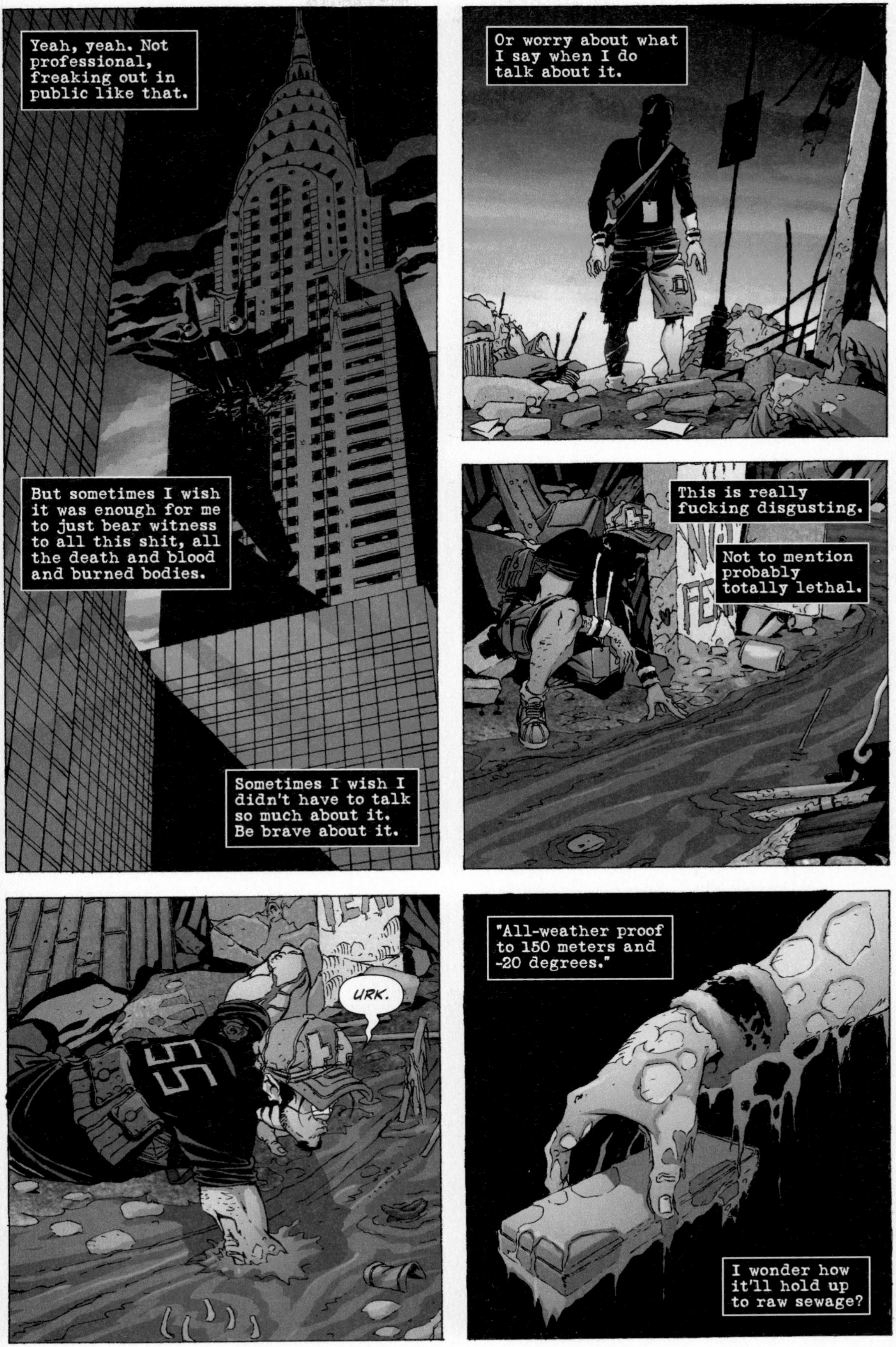
Yeah, yeah. Not professional, freaking out in public like that.
But sometimes I wish it was enough for me to just bear witness to all this shit, all the death and blood and burned bodies.
Sometimes I wish I didn't have to talk so much about it. Be brave about it.
Or worry about what I say when I do talk about it.
This is really fucking disgusting.
Not to mention probably totally lethal.
URK.
"All-weather proof to 150 meters and -20 degrees."
I wonder how it'll hold up to raw sewage?

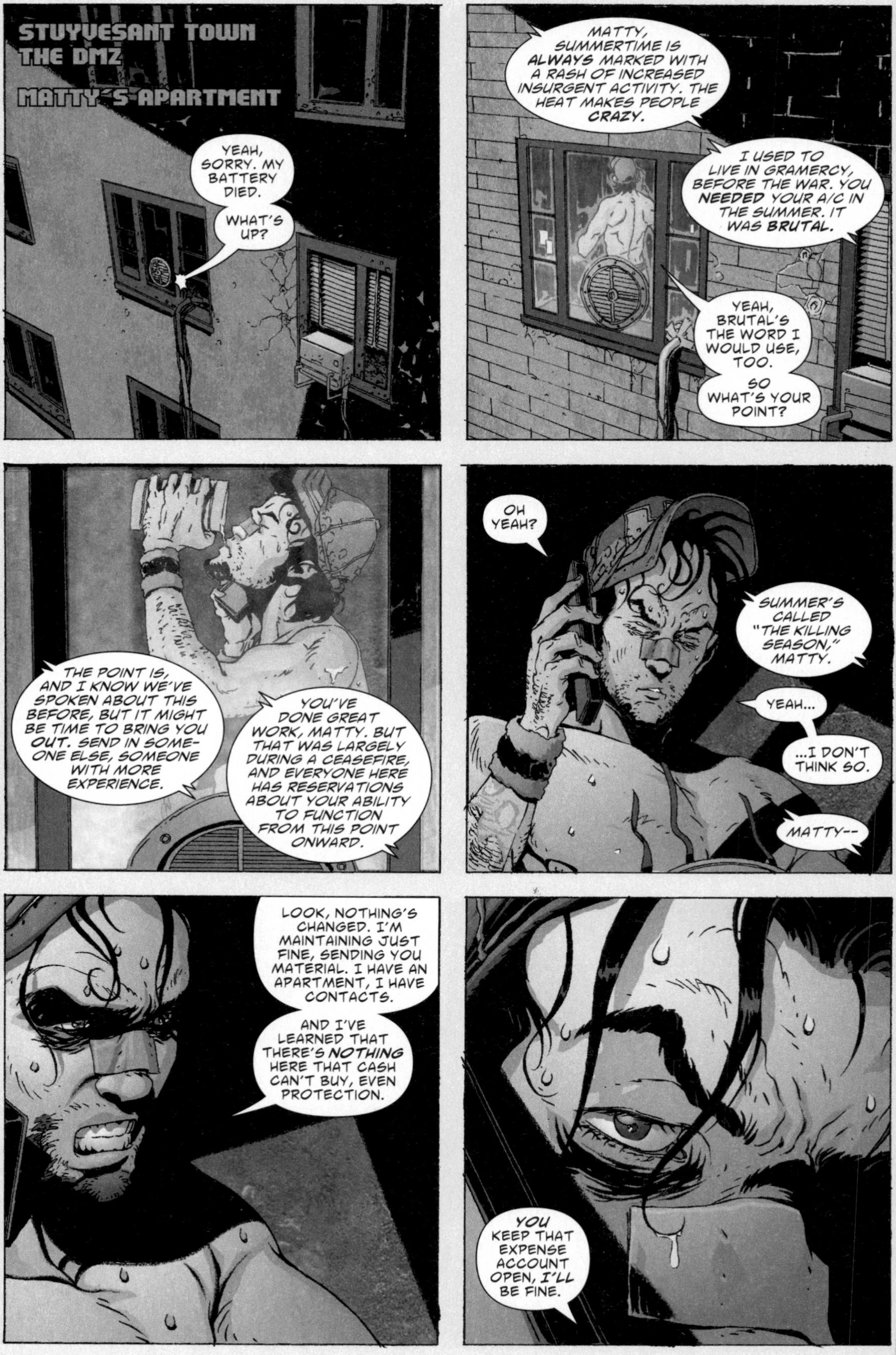
STUYVESANT TOWN
THE DMZ
MATTY'S APARTMENT
YEAH, SORRY. MY BATTERY DIED.
WHAT'S UP?
MATTY, SUMMERTIME IS ALWAYS MARKED WITH A RASH OF INCREASED INSURGENT ACTIVITY. THE HEAT MAKES PEOPLE CRAZY.
I USED TO LIVE IN GRAMERCY, BEFORE THE WAR. YOU NEEDED YOUR A/C IN THE SUMMER. IT WAS BRUTAL.
YEAH, BRUTAL'S THE WORD I WOULD USE, TOO.
SO WHAT'S YOUR POINT?
THE POINT IS, AND I KNOW WE'VE SPOKEN ABOUT THIS BEFORE, BUT IT MIGHT BE TIME TO BRING YOU OUT. SEND IN SOME-ONE ELSE, SOMEONE WITH MORE EXPERIENCE.
YOU'VE DONE GREAT WORK, MATTY. BUT THAT WAS LARGELY DURING A CEASEFIRE, AND EVERYONE HERE HAS RESERVATIONS ABOUT YOUR ABILITY TO FUNCTION FROM THIS POINT ONWARD.
OH YEAH?
SUMMER'S CALLED "THE KILLING SEASON," MATTY.
YEAH...
...I DON'T THINK SO.
MATTY--
LOOK, NOTHING'S CHANGED. I'M MAINTAINING JUST FINE, SENDING YOU MATERIAL. I HAVE AN APARTMENT, I HAVE CONTACTS.
AND I'VE LEARNED THAT THERE'S NOTHING HERE THAT CASH CAN'T BUY, EVEN PROTECTION.
YOU KEEP THAT EXPENSE ACCOUNT OPEN, I'LL BE FINE.

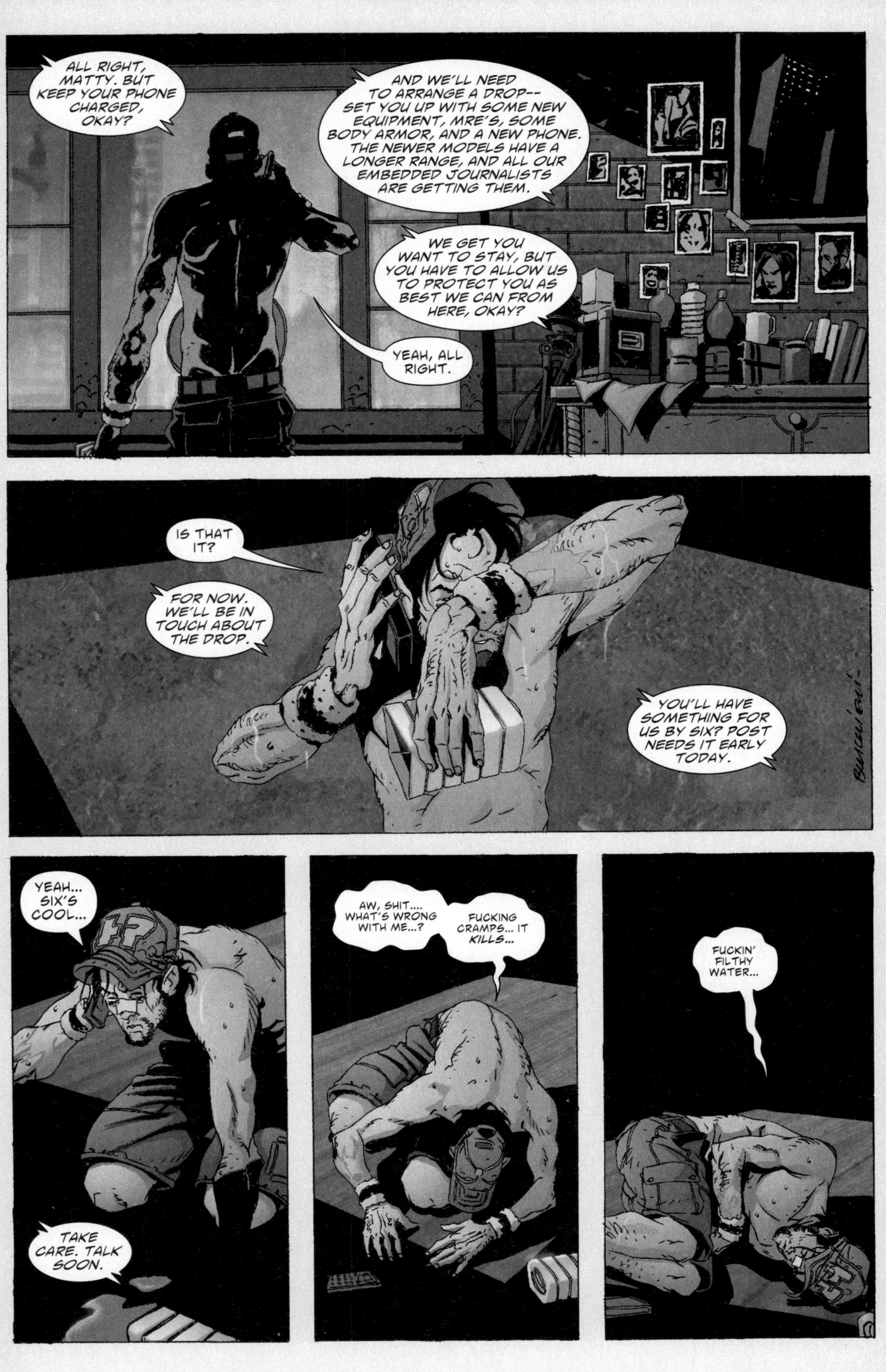
ALL RIGHT, MATTY. BUT KEEP YOUR PHONE CHARGED, OKAY?
AND WE'LL NEED TO ARRANGE A DROP-- SET YOU UP WITH SOME NEW EQUIPMENT, MRE'S, SOME BODY ARMOR, AND A NEW PHONE. THE NEWER MODELS HAVE A LONGER RANGE, AND ALL OUR EMBEDDED JOURNALISTS ARE GETTING THEM.
WE GET YOU WANT TO STAY, BUT YOU HAVE TO ALLOW US TO PROTECT YOU AS BEST WE CAN FROM HERE, OKAY?
YEAH, ALL RIGHT.
IS THAT IT?
FOR NOW. WE'LL BE IN TOUCH ABOUT THE DROP.
YOU'LL HAVE SOMETHING FOR US BY SIX? POST NEEDS IT EARLY TODAY.
YEAH... SIX'S COOL...
TAKE CARE. TALK SOON.
AW, SHIT.... WHAT'S WRONG WITH ME...?
FUCKING CRAMPS... IT KILLS...
FUCKIN' FILTHY WATER...

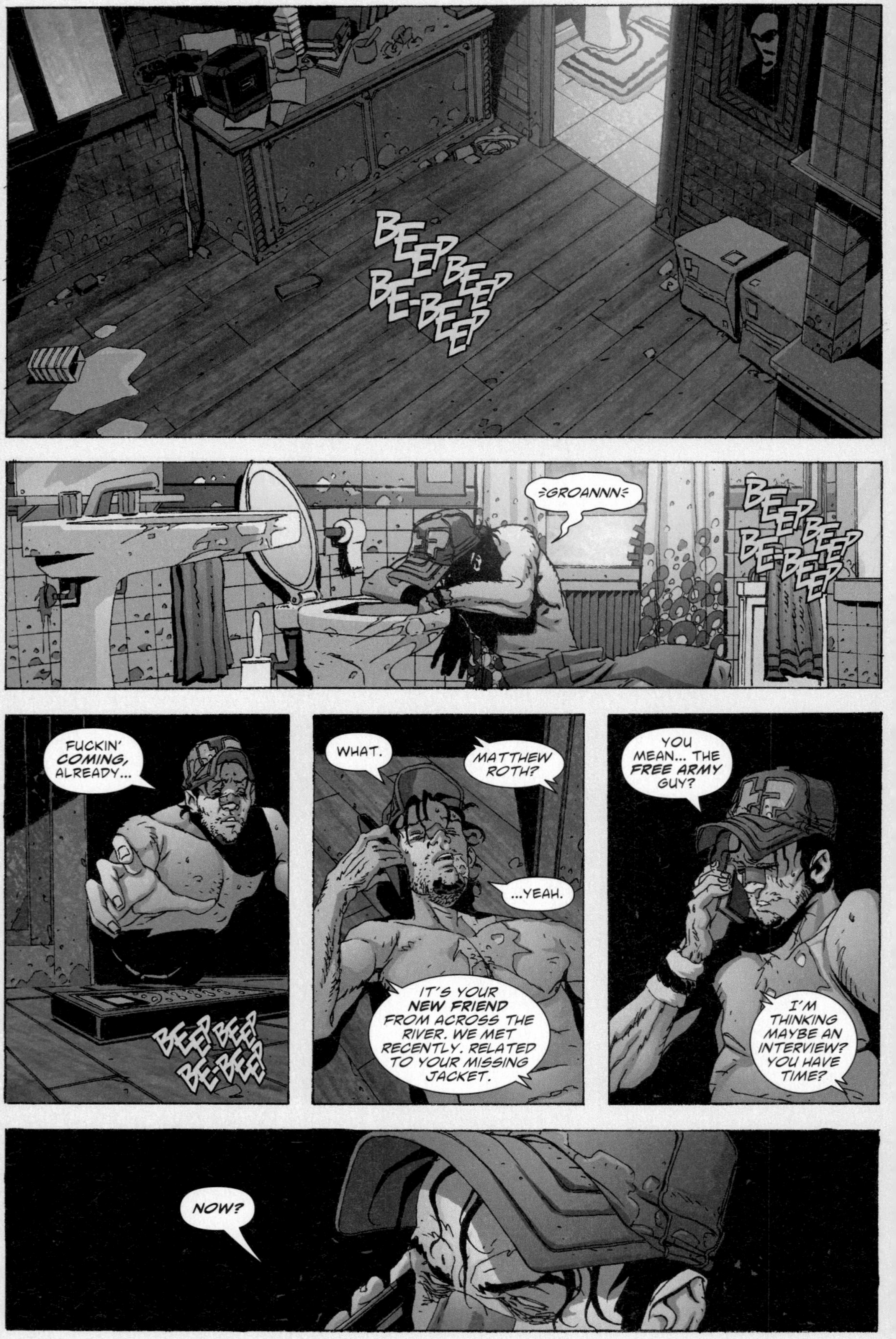
BEEP BEEP BE-BEEP
=GROANNN=
BEEP BEEP BE-BEEP
FUCKIN' COMING, ALREADY...
BEEP BEEP BE-BEEP
WHAT.
MATTHEW ROTH?
...YEAH.
IT'S YOUR NEW FRIEND FROM ACROSS THE RIVER. WE MET RECENTLY. RELATED TO YOUR MISSING JACKET.
YOU MEAN... THE FREE ARMY GUY?
I'M THINKING MAYBE AN INTERVIEW? YOU HAVE TIME?
NOW?

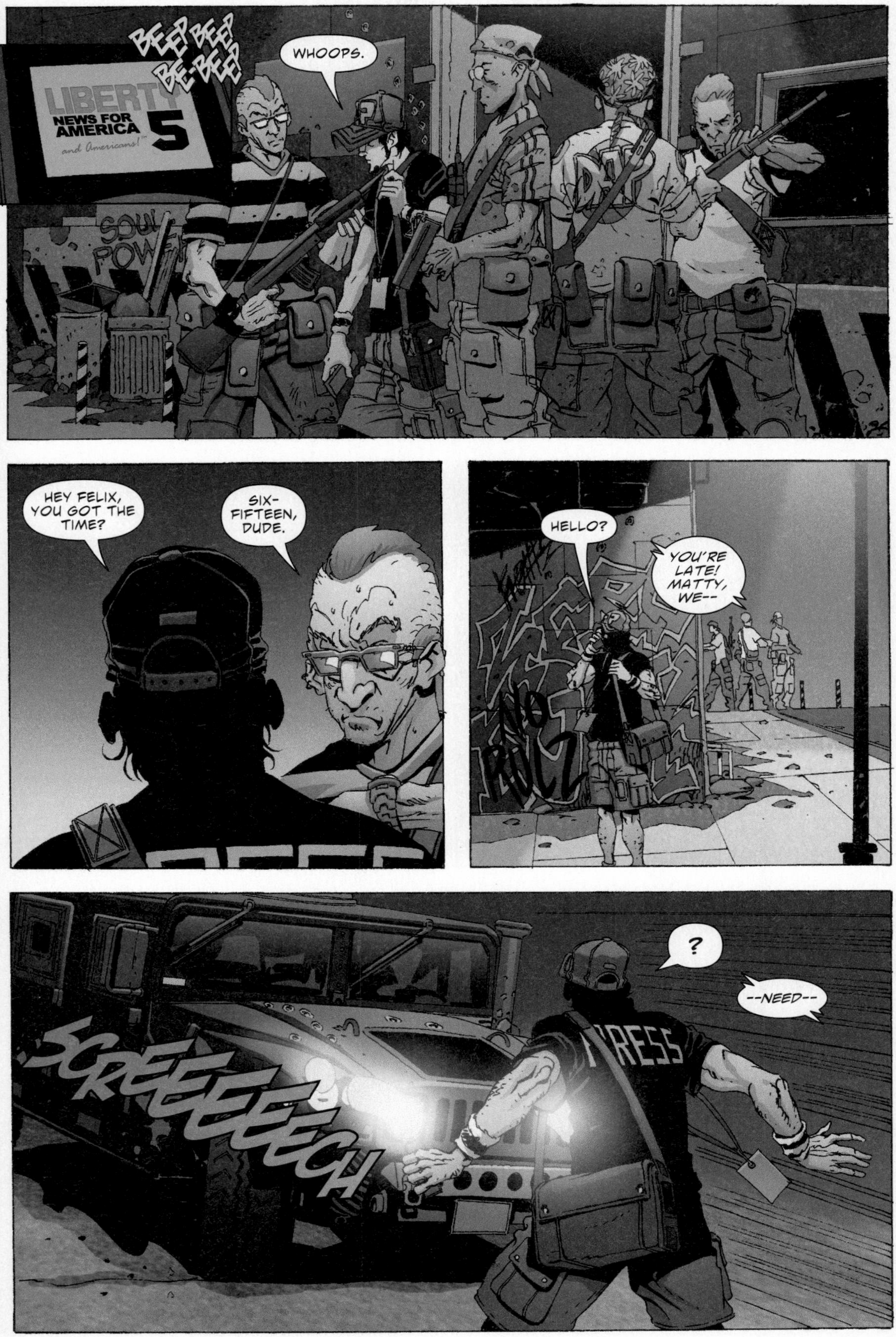
BEEP BEEP BE-BEEP
LIBERTY
NEWS FOR AMERICA
5
and Americans!™
WHOOPS.
SOUL POW
HEY FELIX, YOU GOT THE TIME?
SIX-FIFTEEN, DUDE.
HELLO?
YOU'RE LATE! MATTY, WE--
NO RULZ
?
--NEED--
PRESS
SCREEEEEEECH

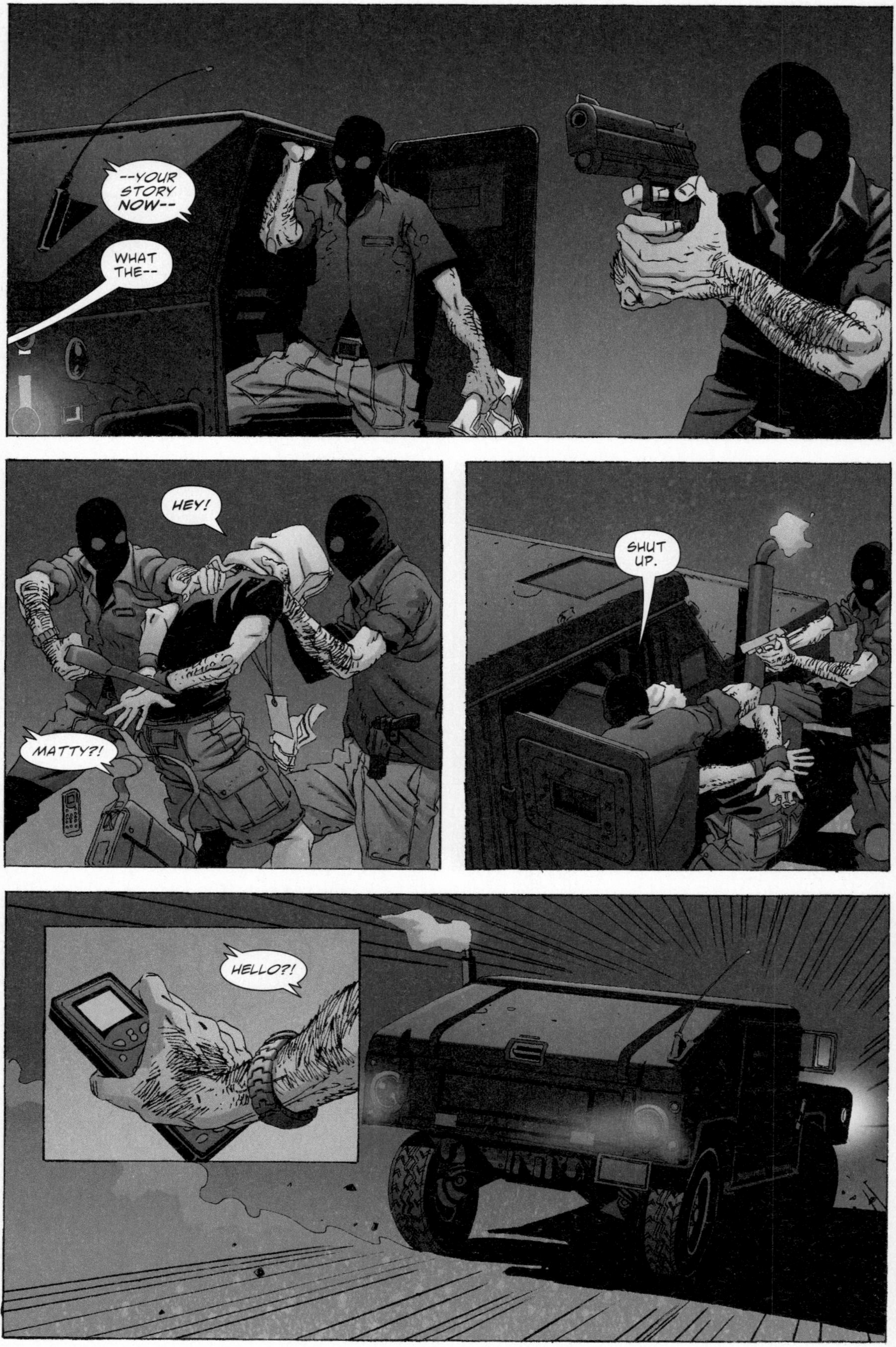
--YOUR STORY NOW--
WHAT THE--
HEY!
MATTY?!
SHUT UP.
HELLO?!

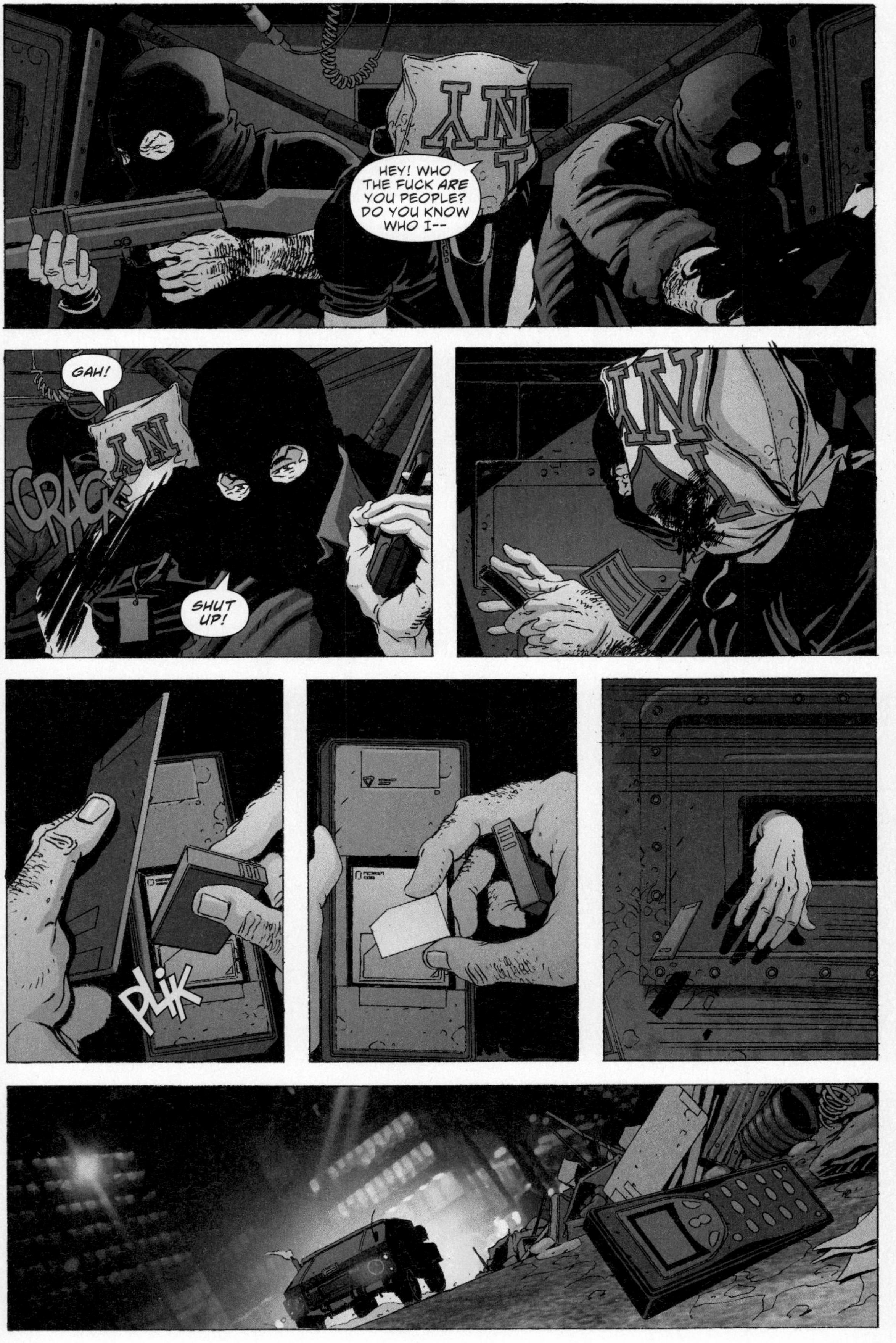
HEY! WHO THE FUCK ARE YOU PEOPLE? DO YOU KNOW WHO I--
GAH!
CRACK
SHUT UP!
PLIK

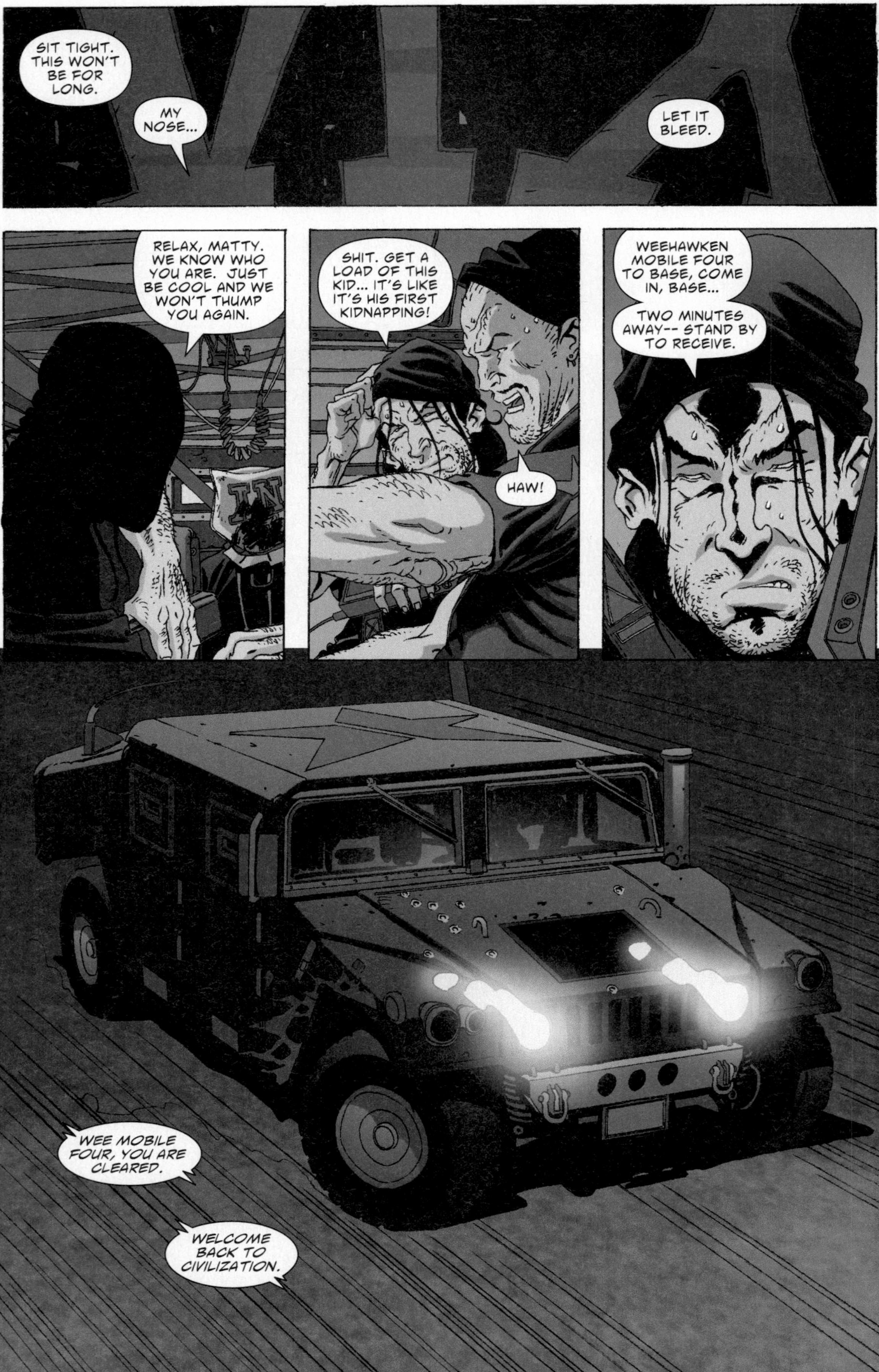
SIT TIGHT. THIS WON'T BE FOR LONG.
MY NOSE...
LET IT BLEED.
RELAX, MATTY. WE KNOW WHO YOU ARE. JUST BE COOL AND WE WON'T THUMP YOU AGAIN.
SHIT. GET A LOAD OF THIS KID... IT'S LIKE IT'S HIS FIRST KIDNAPPING!
HAW!
WEEHAWKEN MOBILE FOUR TO BASE, COME IN, BASE...
TWO MINUTES AWAY-- STAND BY TO RECEIVE.
WEE MOBILE FOUR, YOU ARE CLEARED.
WELCOME BACK TO CIVILIZATION.

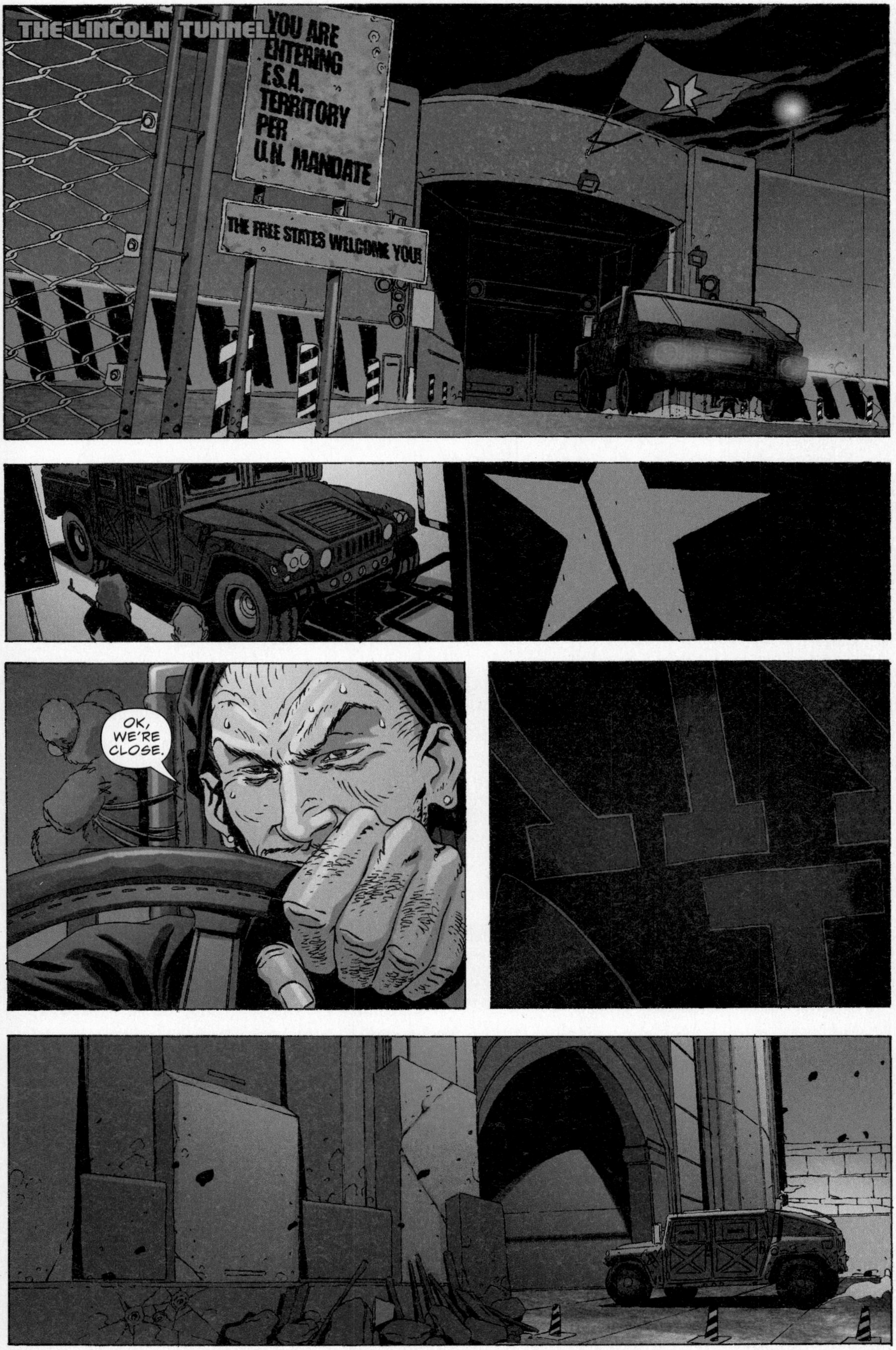
THE LINCOLN TUNNEL.
YOU ARE ENTERING E.S.A. TERRITORY PER U.N. MANDATE
THE FREE STATES WELCOME YOU!
OK, WE'RE CLOSE.

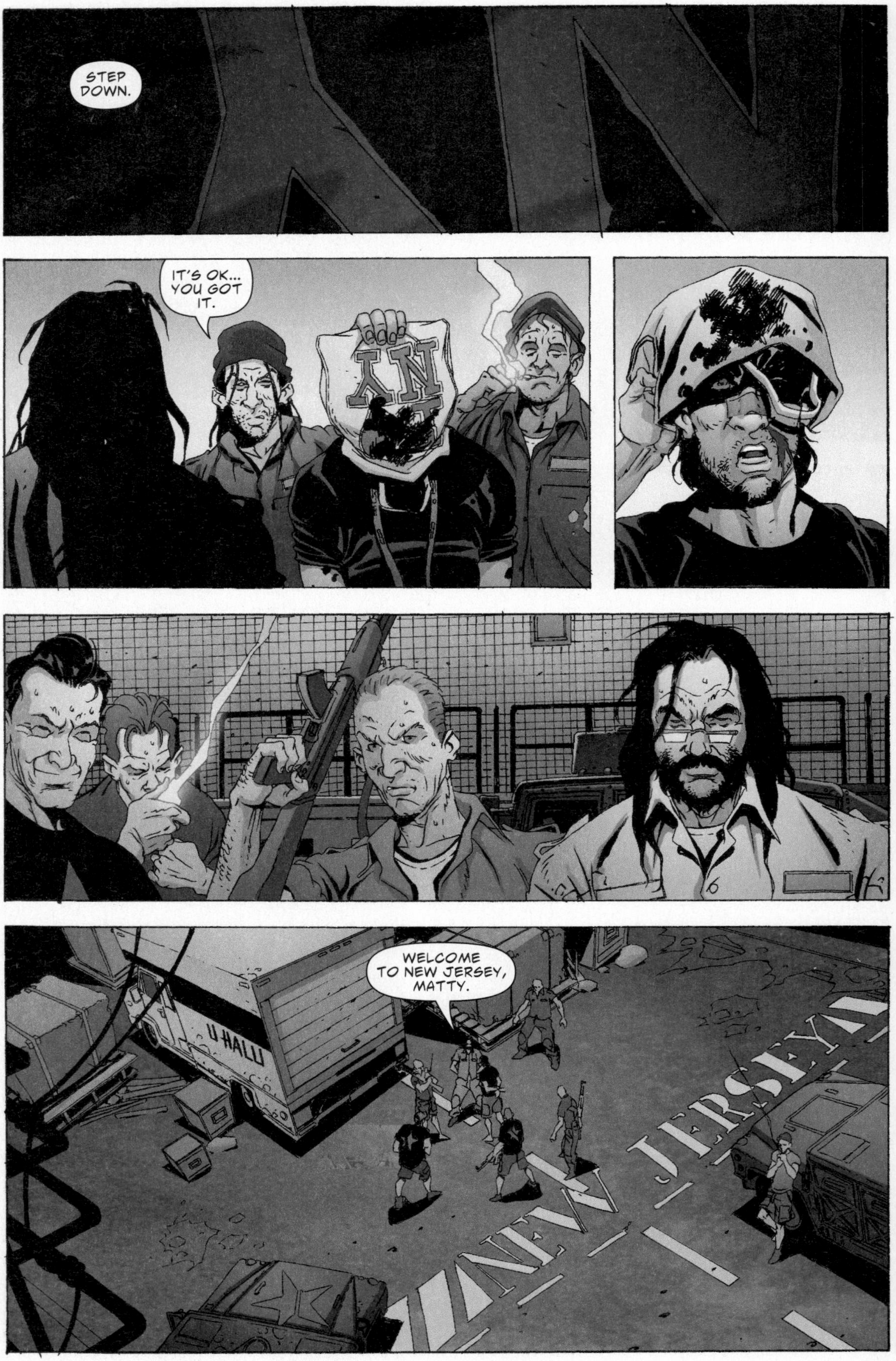
STEP DOWN.
IT'S OK... YOU GOT IT.
NY
WELCOME TO NEW JERSEY, MATTY.
U HALU
NEW JERSEY

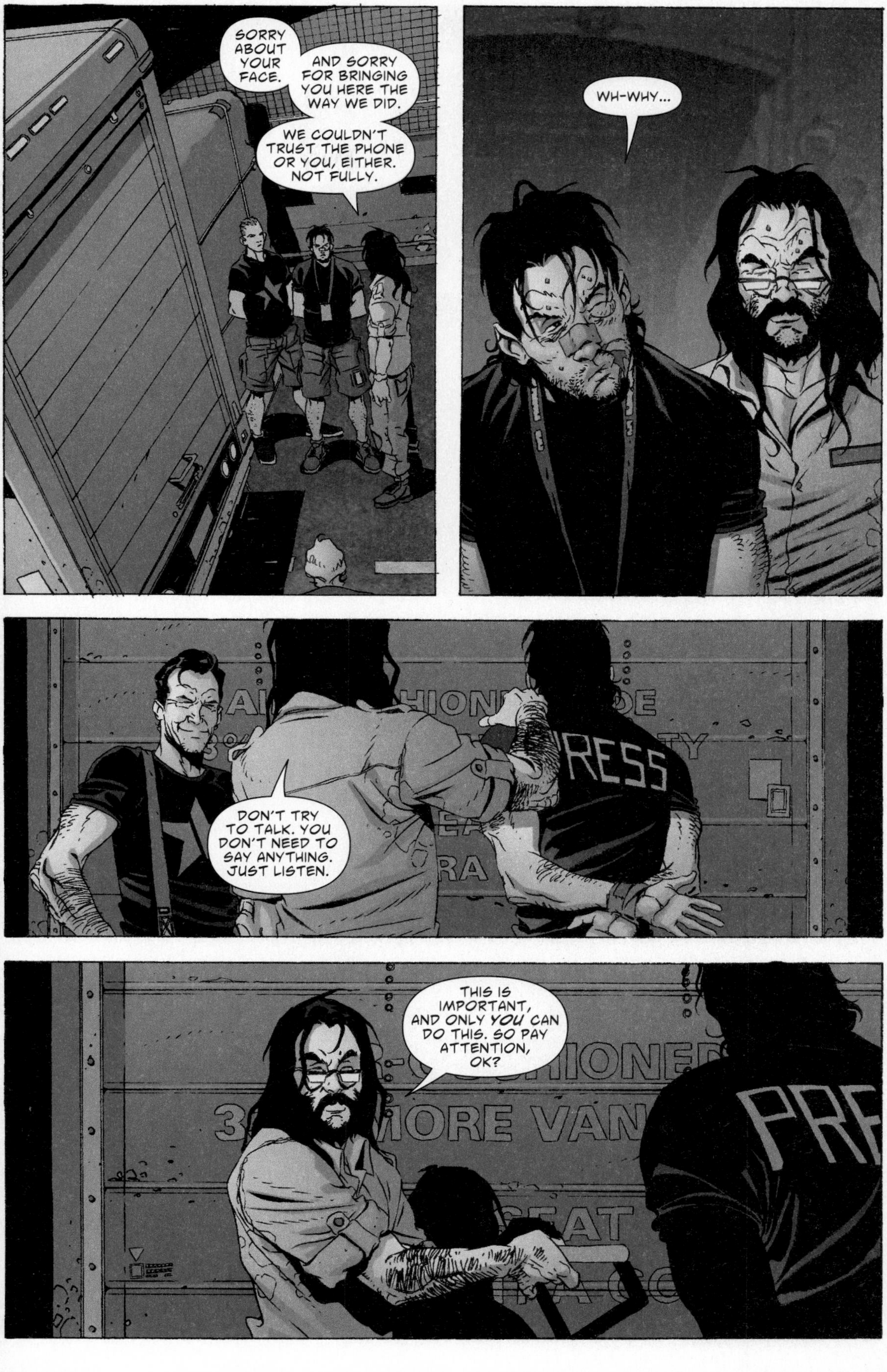
SORRY ABOUT YOUR FACE.
AND SORRY FOR BRINGING YOU HERE THE WAY WE DID.
WE COULDN'T TRUST THE PHONE OR YOU, EITHER. NOT FULLY.
WH-WHY...
PRESS
DON'T TRY TO TALK. YOU DON'T NEED TO SAY ANYTHING. JUST LISTEN.
THIS IS IMPORTANT, AND ONLY *YOU* CAN DO THIS. SO PAY ATTENTION, OK?

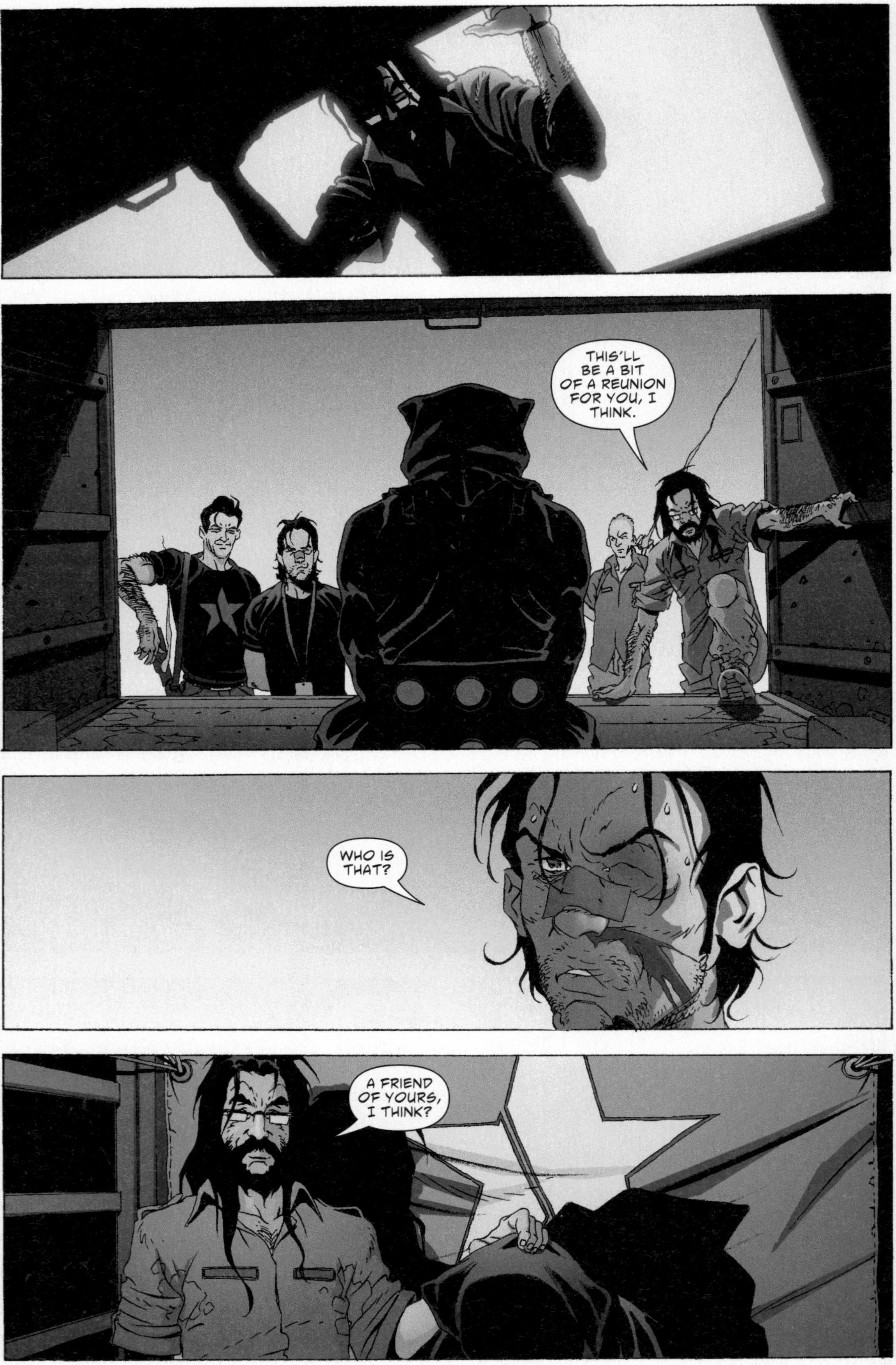
THIS'LL BE A BIT OF A REUNION FOR YOU, I THINK.
WHO IS THAT?
A FRIEND OF YOURS, I THINK?

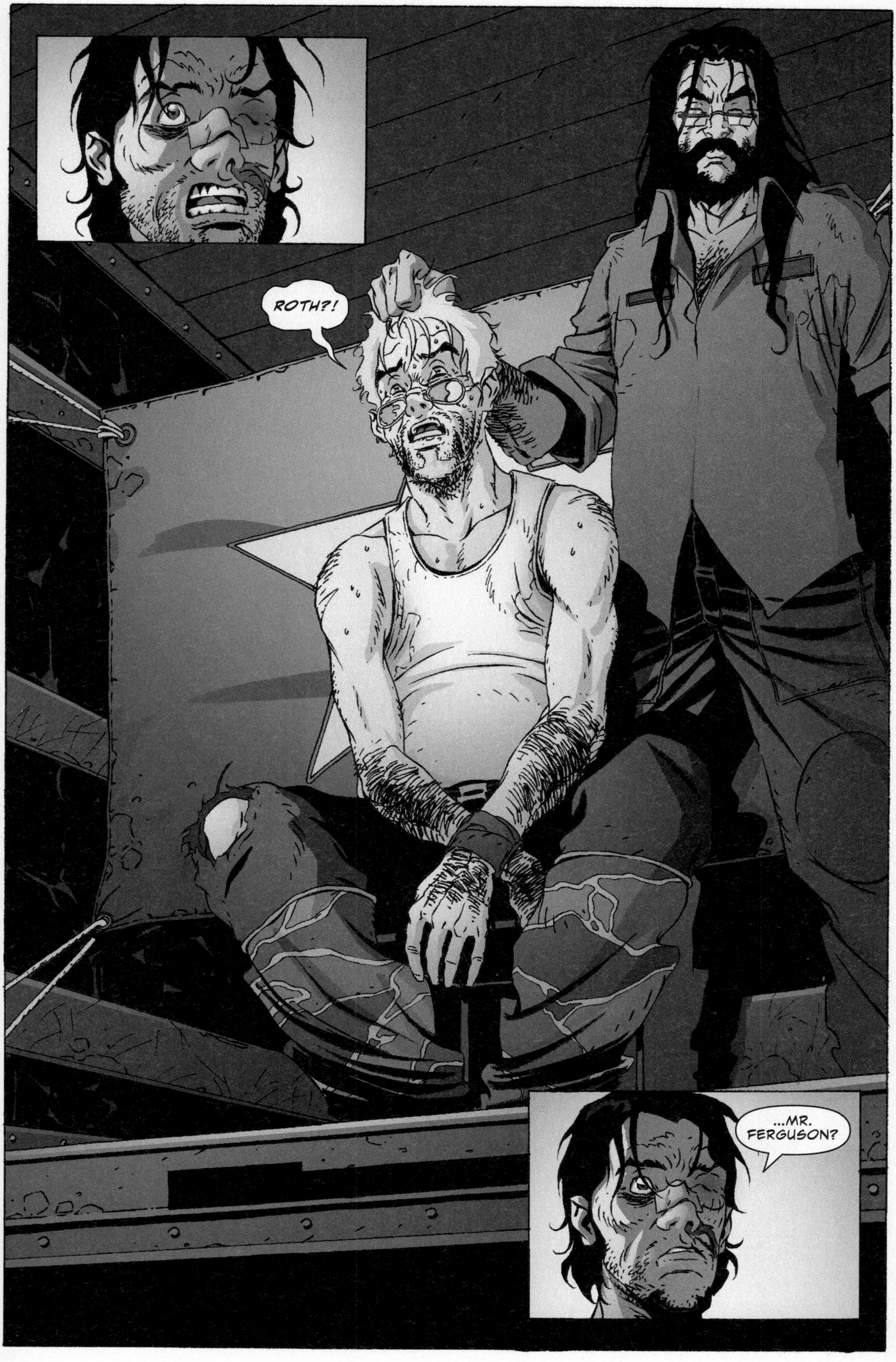
ROTH?!
...MR. FERGUSON?

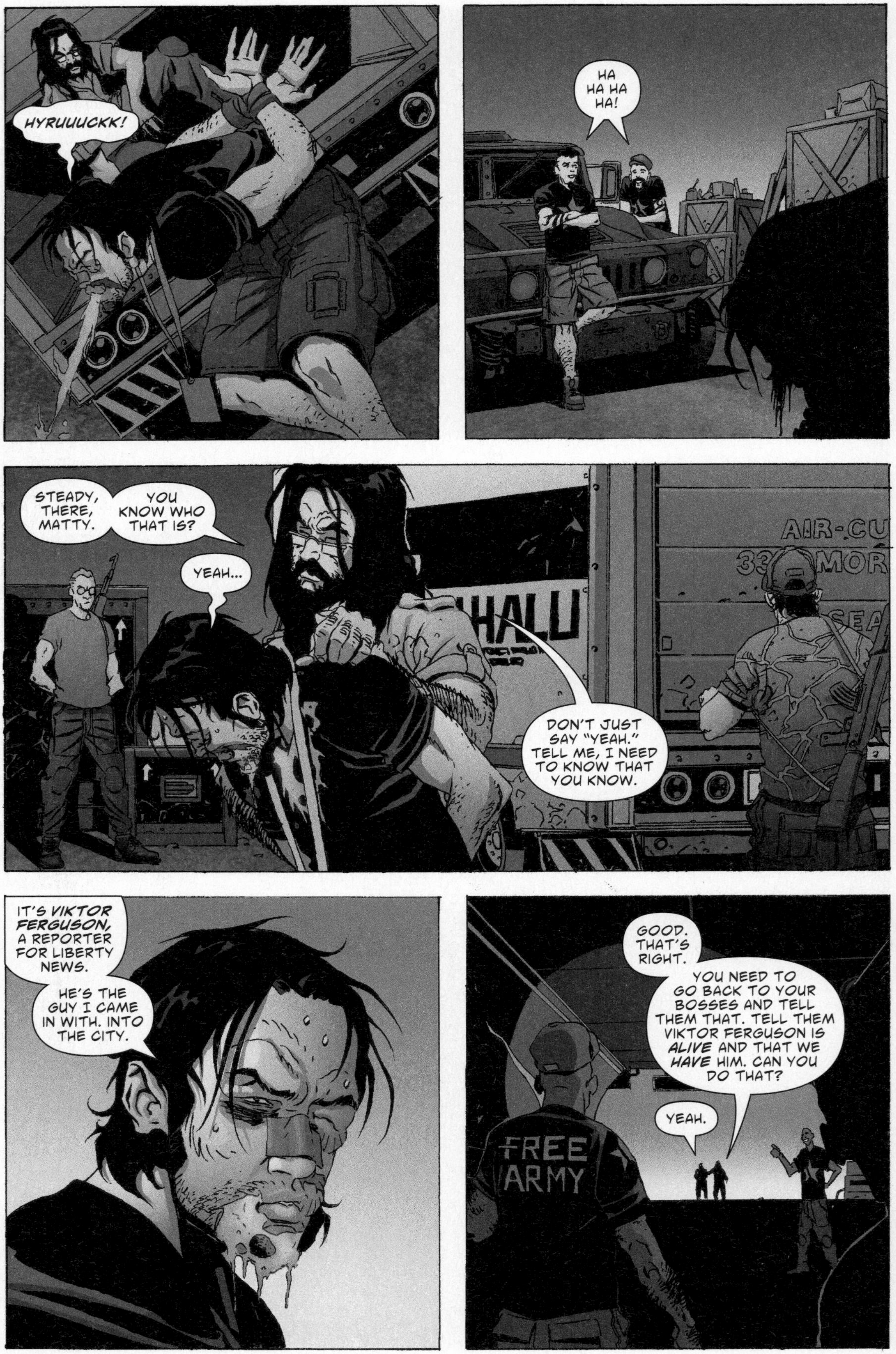
HYRUUUCKK!
HA HA HA HA!
STEADY, THERE, MATTY.
YOU KNOW WHO THAT IS?
YEAH...
DON'T JUST SAY "YEAH." TELL ME, I NEED TO KNOW THAT YOU KNOW.
IT'S VIKTOR FERGUSON, A REPORTER FOR LIBERTY NEWS.
HE'S THE GUY I CAME IN WITH. INTO THE CITY.
GOOD. THAT'S RIGHT.
YOU NEED TO GO BACK TO YOUR BOSSES AND TELL THEM THAT. TELL THEM VIKTOR FERGUSON IS ALIVE AND THAT WE HAVE HIM. CAN YOU DO THAT?
YEAH.
FREE ARMY

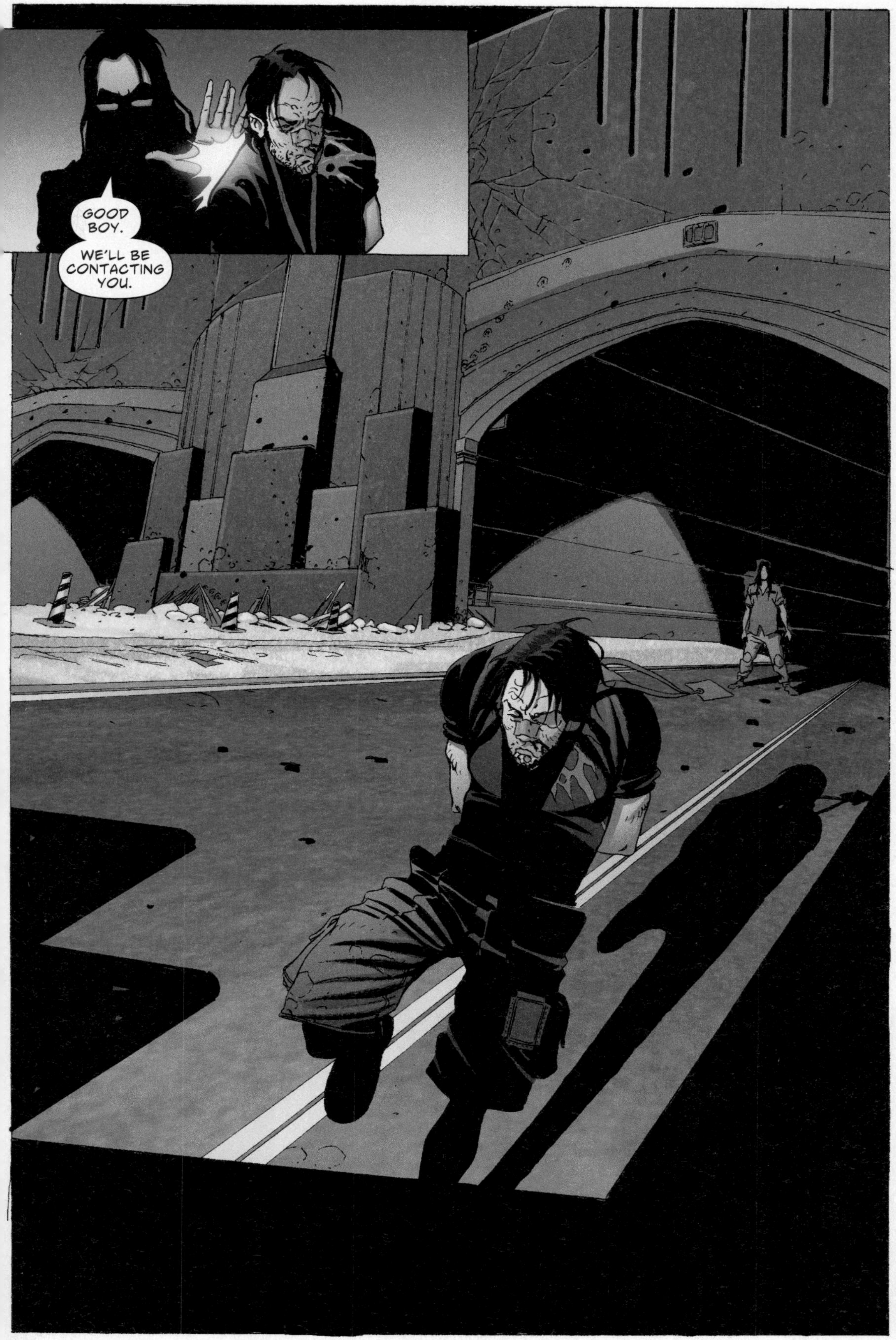
GOOD BOY.
WE'LL BE CONTACTING YOU.

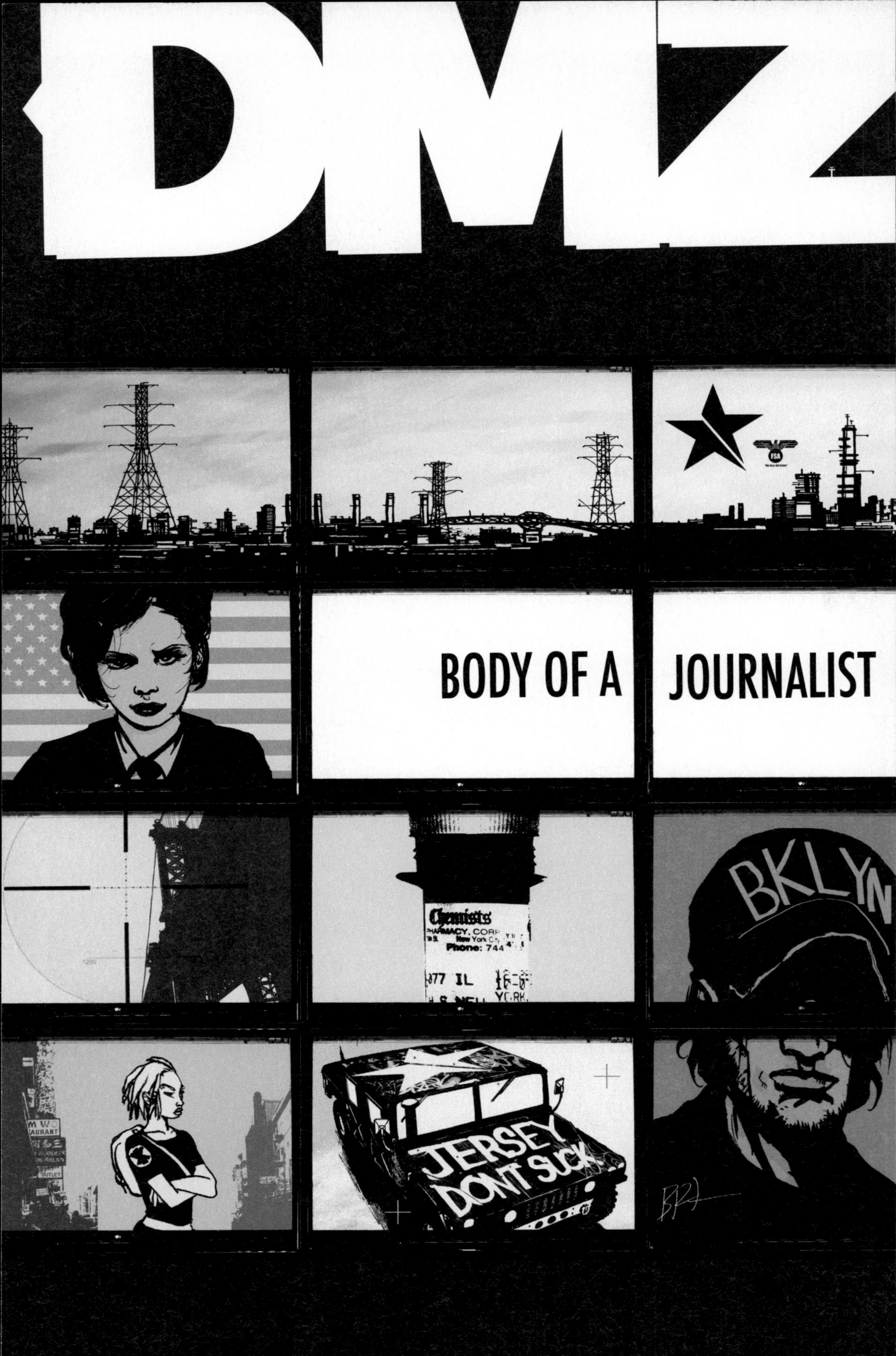
DMZ
BODY OF A JOURNALIST
BKLYN
Chemists
JERSEY
DONT SUCK

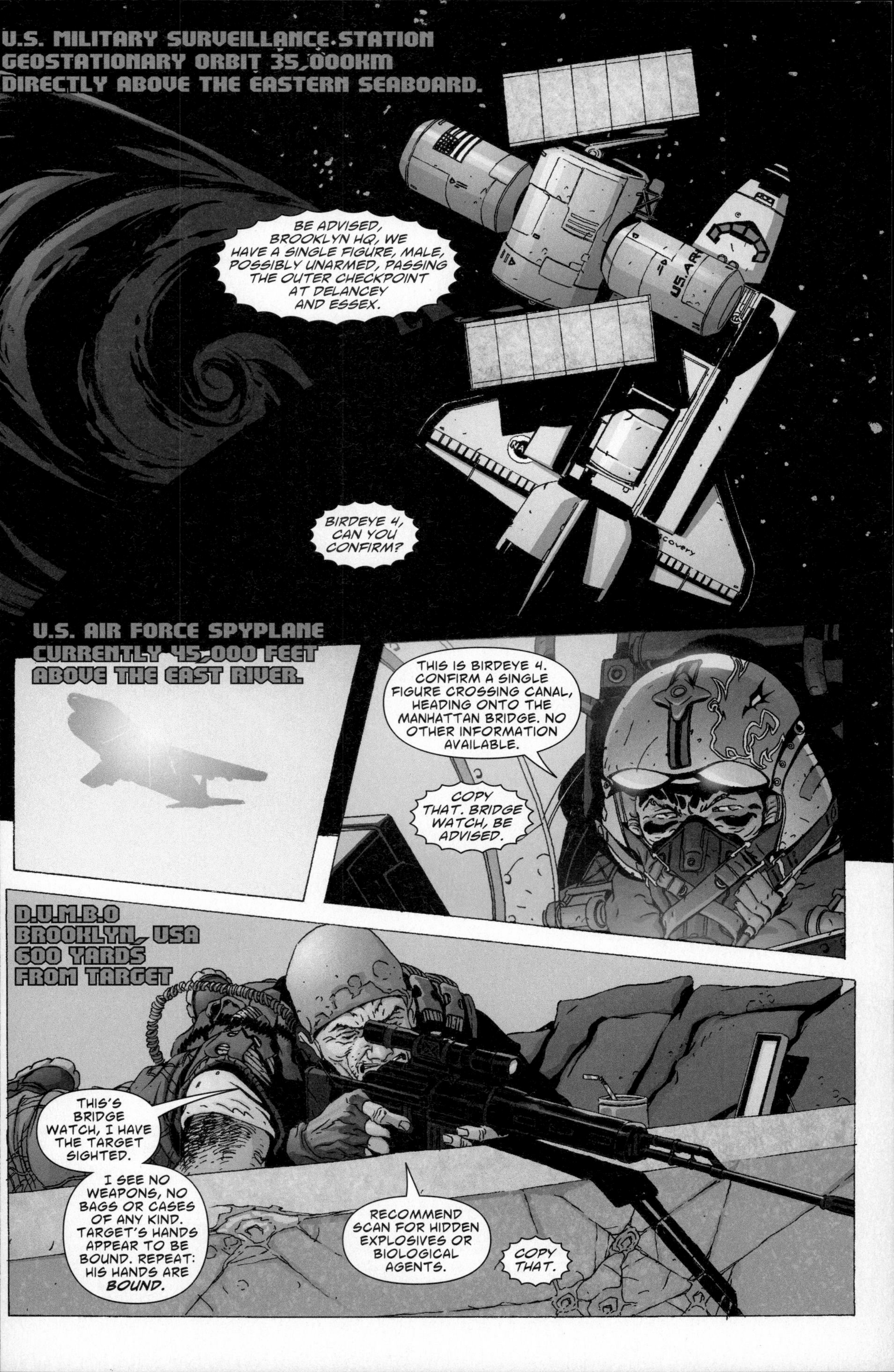
U.S. MILITARY SURVEILLANCE STATION GEOSTATIONARY ORBIT 35,000KM DIRECTLY ABOVE THE EASTERN SEABOARD.
BE ADVISED, BROOKLYN HQ, WE HAVE A SINGLE FIGURE, MALE, POSSIBLY UNARMED, PASSING THE OUTER CHECKPOINT AT DELANCEY AND ESSEX.
BIRDEYE 4, CAN YOU CONFIRM?
U.S. AIR FORCE SPYPLANE CURRENTLY 45,000 FEET ABOVE THE EAST RIVER.
THIS IS BIRDEYE 4. CONFIRM A SINGLE FIGURE CROSSING CANAL, HEADING ONTO THE MANHATTAN BRIDGE. NO OTHER INFORMATION AVAILABLE.
COPY THAT. BRIDGE WATCH, BE ADVISED.
D.U.M.B.O BROOKLYN, USA 600 YARDS FROM TARGET
THIS'S BRIDGE WATCH, I HAVE THE TARGET SIGHTED.
I SEE NO WEAPONS, NO BAGS OR CASES OF ANY KIND. TARGET'S HANDS APPEAR TO BE BOUND. REPEAT: HIS HANDS ARE *BOUND.*
RECOMMEND SCAN FOR HIDDEN EXPLOSIVES OR BIOLOGICAL AGENTS.
COPY THAT.

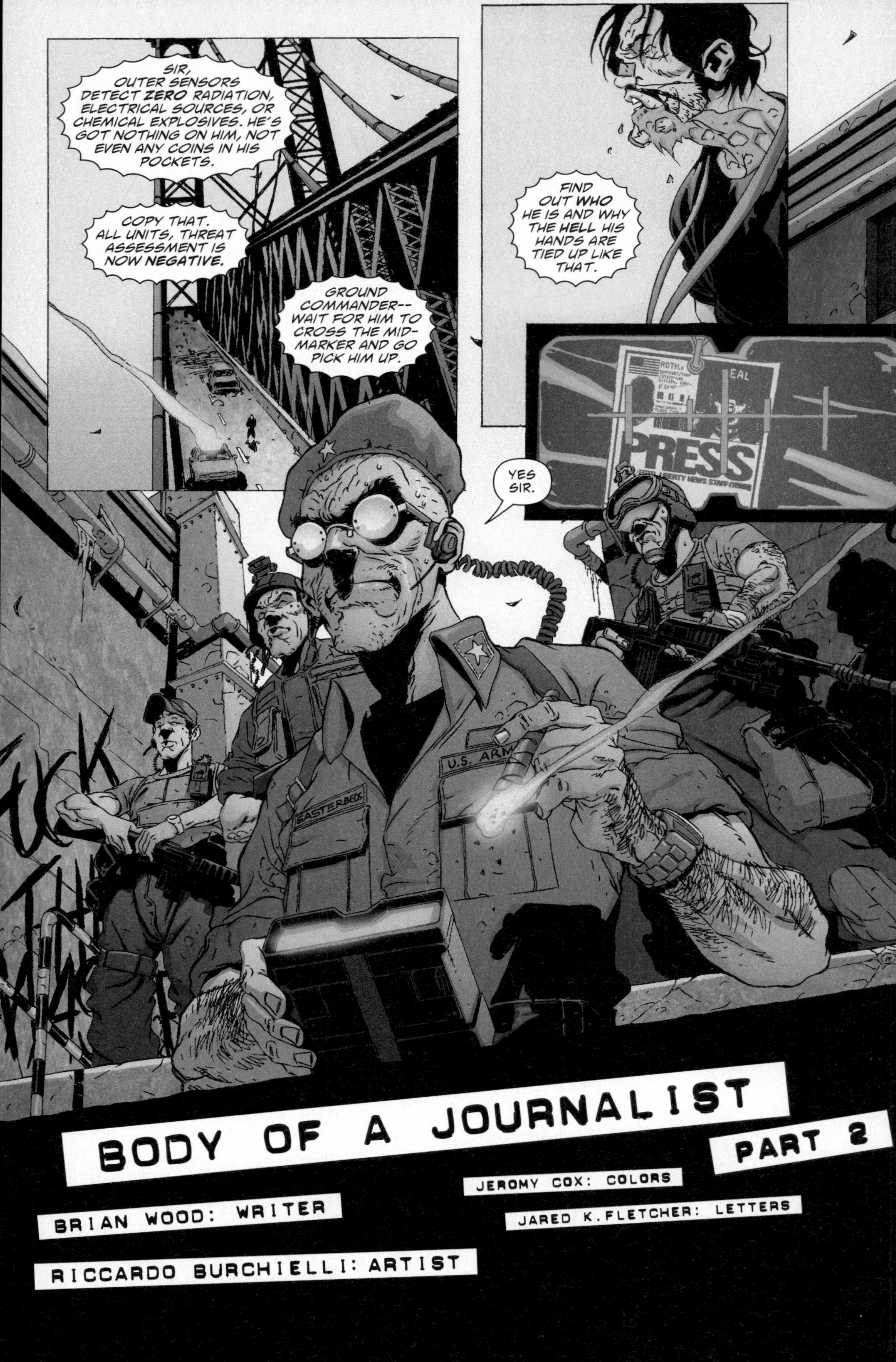
SIR, OUTER SENSORS DETECT ZERO RADIATION, ELECTRICAL SOURCES, OR CHEMICAL EXPLOSIVES. HE'S GOT NOTHING ON HIM, NOT EVEN ANY COINS IN HIS POCKETS.
COPY THAT. ALL UNITS, THREAT ASSESSMENT IS NOW NEGATIVE.
GROUND COMMANDER-- WAIT FOR HIM TO CROSS THE MID-MARKER AND GO PICK HIM UP.
FIND OUT WHO HE IS AND WHY THE HELL HIS HANDS ARE TIED UP LIKE THAT.
PRESS
YES SIR.
BODY OF A JOURNALIST
PART 2
JEROMY COX: COLORS
BRIAN WOOD: WRITER
JARED K.FLETCHER: LETTERS
RICCARDO BURCHIELLI: ARTIST

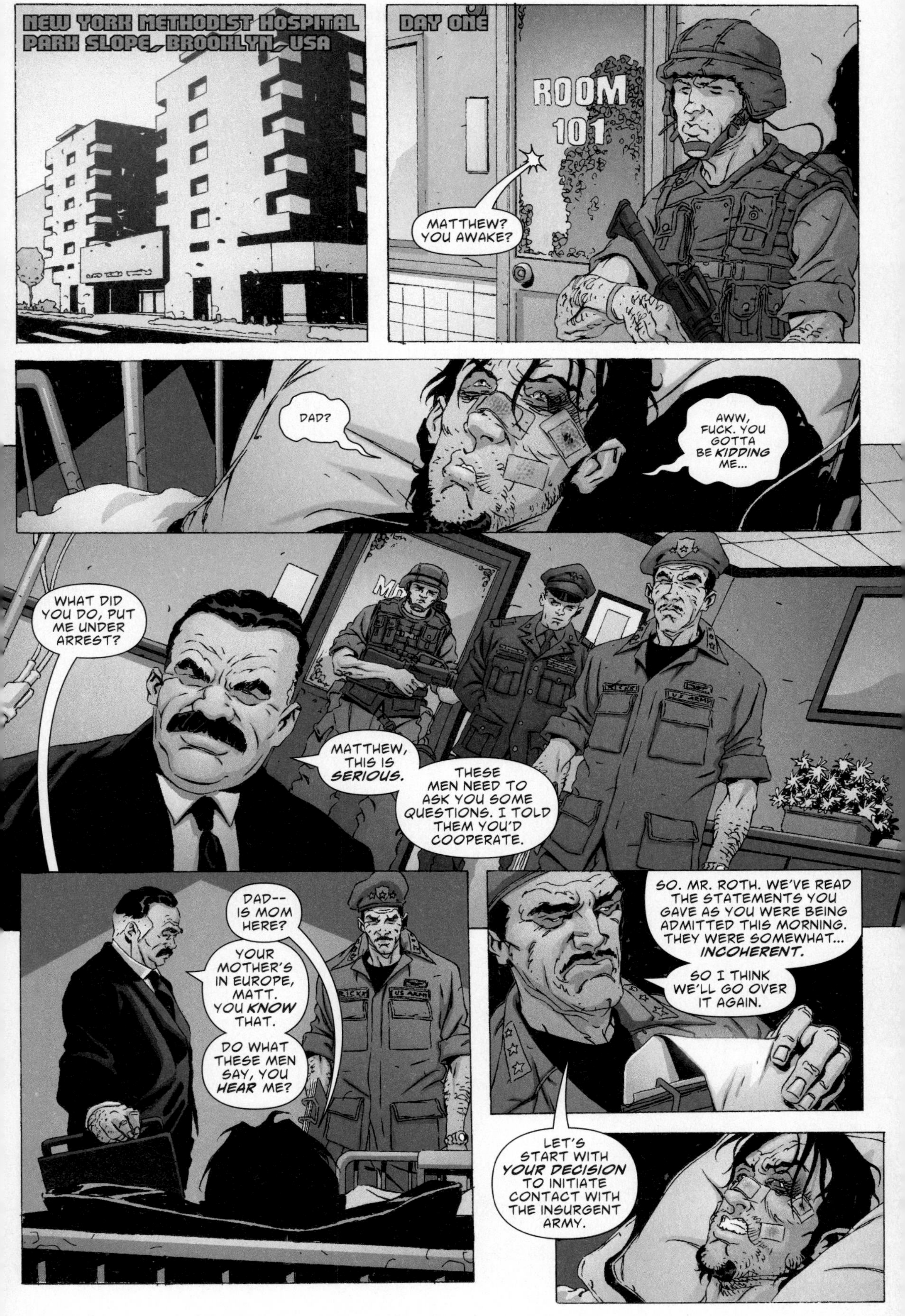
NEW YORK METHODIST HOSPITAL
PARK SLOPE, BROOKLYN, USA
DAY ONE
ROOM 101
MATTHEW? YOU AWAKE?
DAD?
AWW, FUCK. YOU GOTTA BE KIDDING ME...
WHAT DID YOU DO, PUT ME UNDER ARREST?
MATTHEW, THIS IS SERIOUS.
THESE MEN NEED TO ASK YOU SOME QUESTIONS. I TOLD THEM YOU'D COOPERATE.
DAD-- IS MOM HERE?
YOUR MOTHER'S IN EUROPE, MATT. YOU KNOW THAT.
DO WHAT THESE MEN SAY, YOU HEAR ME?
SO. MR. ROTH. WE'VE READ THE STATEMENTS YOU GAVE AS YOU WERE BEING ADMITTED THIS MORNING. THEY WERE SOMEWHAT... INCOHERENT.
SO I THINK WE'LL GO OVER IT AGAIN.
LET'S START WITH YOUR DECISION TO INITIATE CONTACT WITH THE INSURGENT ARMY.

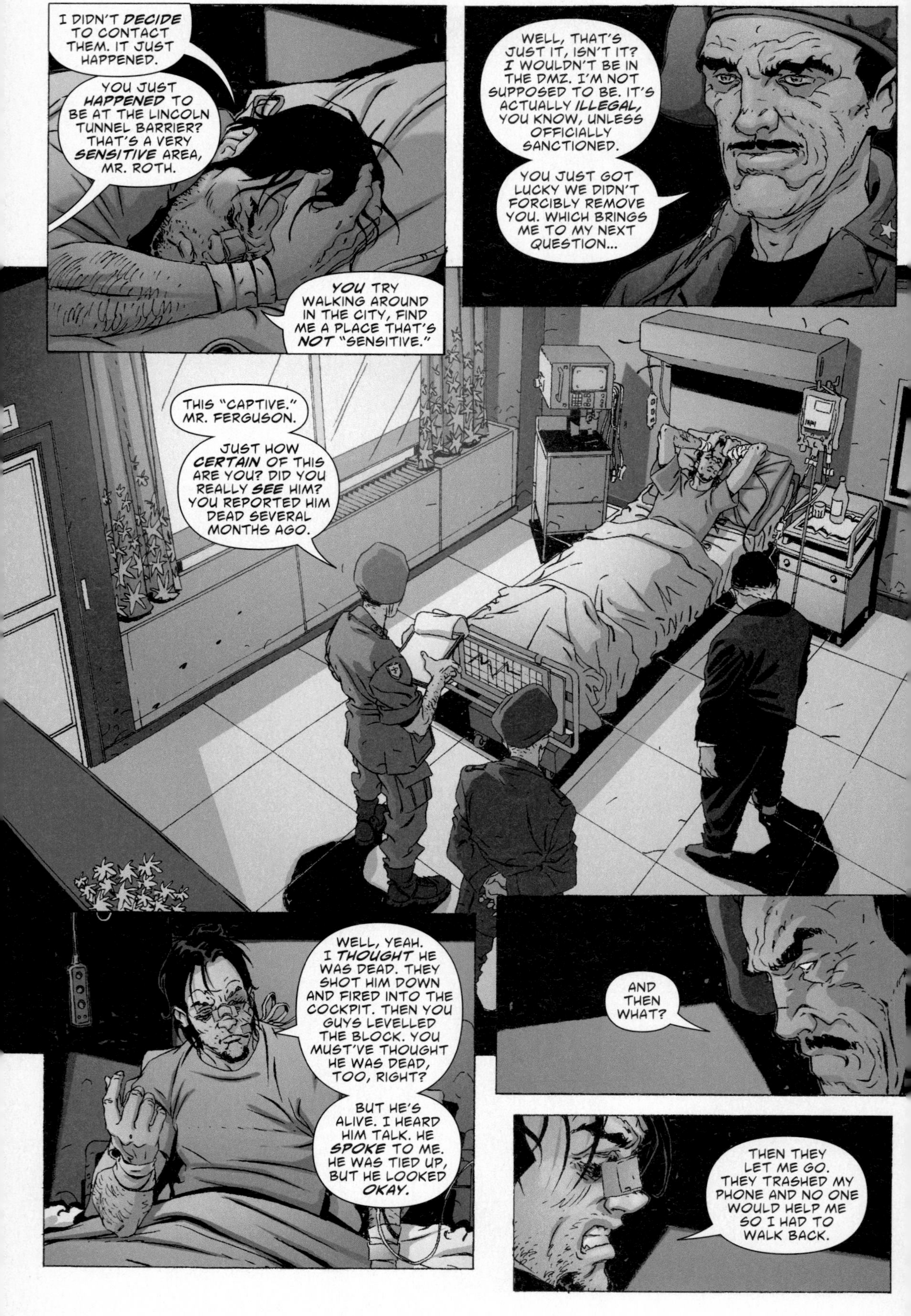
I DIDN'T DECIDE TO CONTACT THEM. IT JUST HAPPENED.
YOU JUST HAPPENED TO BE AT THE LINCOLN TUNNEL BARRIER? THAT'S A VERY SENSITIVE AREA, MR. ROTH.
YOU TRY WALKING AROUND IN THE CITY, FIND ME A PLACE THAT'S NOT "SENSITIVE."
WELL, THAT'S JUST IT, ISN'T IT? I WOULDN'T BE IN THE DMZ. I'M NOT SUPPOSED TO BE. IT'S ACTUALLY ILLEGAL, YOU KNOW, UNLESS OFFICIALLY SANCTIONED.
YOU JUST GOT LUCKY WE DIDN'T FORCIBLY REMOVE YOU. WHICH BRINGS ME TO MY NEXT QUESTION...
THIS "CAPTIVE." MR. FERGUSON.
JUST HOW CERTAIN OF THIS ARE YOU? DID YOU REALLY SEE HIM? YOU REPORTED HIM DEAD SEVERAL MONTHS AGO.
WELL, YEAH. I THOUGHT HE WAS DEAD. THEY SHOT HIM DOWN AND FIRED INTO THE COCKPIT. THEN YOU GUYS LEVELLED THE BLOCK. YOU MUST'VE THOUGHT HE WAS DEAD, TOO, RIGHT?
BUT HE'S ALIVE. I HEARD HIM TALK. HE SPOKE TO ME. HE WAS TIED UP, BUT HE LOOKED OKAY.
AND THEN WHAT?
THEN THEY LET ME GO. THEY TRASHED MY PHONE AND NO ONE WOULD HELP ME SO I HAD TO WALK BACK.

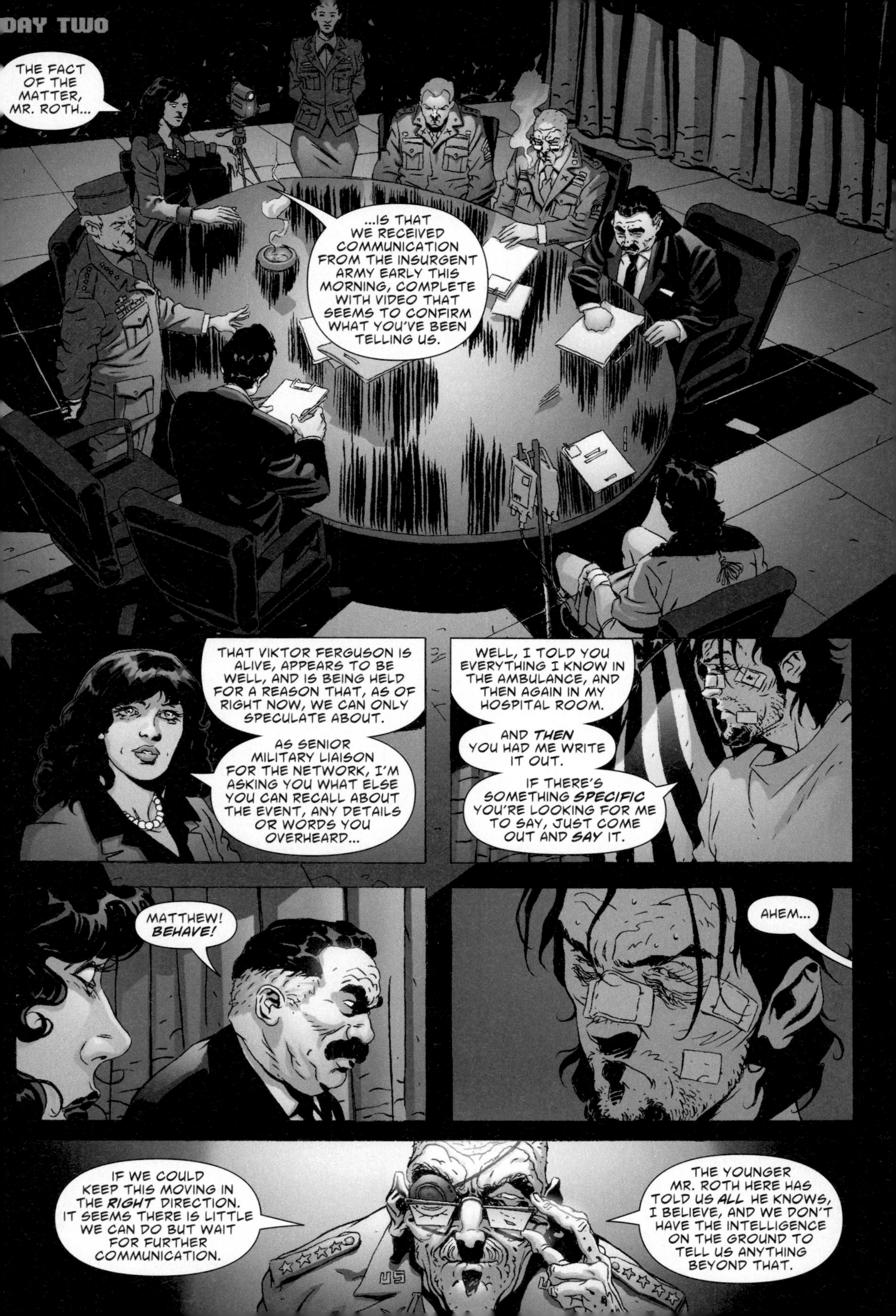
DAY TWO
THE FACT OF THE MATTER, MR. ROTH...
...IS THAT WE RECEIVED COMMUNICATION FROM THE INSURGENT ARMY EARLY THIS MORNING, COMPLETE WITH VIDEO THAT SEEMS TO CONFIRM WHAT YOU'VE BEEN TELLING US.
THAT VIKTOR FERGUSON IS ALIVE, APPEARS TO BE WELL, AND IS BEING HELD FOR A REASON THAT, AS OF RIGHT NOW, WE CAN ONLY SPECULATE ABOUT.
AS SENIOR MILITARY LIAISON FOR THE NETWORK, I'M ASKING YOU WHAT ELSE YOU CAN RECALL ABOUT THE EVENT, ANY DETAILS OR WORDS YOU OVERHEARD...
WELL, I TOLD YOU EVERYTHING I KNOW IN THE AMBULANCE, AND THEN AGAIN IN MY HOSPITAL ROOM.
AND *THEN* YOU HAD ME WRITE IT OUT.
IF THERE'S SOMETHING *SPECIFIC* YOU'RE LOOKING FOR ME TO SAY, JUST COME OUT AND *SAY* IT.
MATTHEW! *BEHAVE!*
AHEM...
IF WE COULD KEEP THIS MOVING IN THE *RIGHT* DIRECTION. IT SEEMS THERE IS LITTLE WE CAN DO BUT WAIT FOR FURTHER COMMUNICATION.
THE YOUNGER MR. ROTH HERE HAS TOLD US *ALL* HE KNOWS, I BELIEVE, AND WE DON'T HAVE THE INTELLIGENCE ON THE GROUND TO TELL US ANYTHING BEYOND THAT.

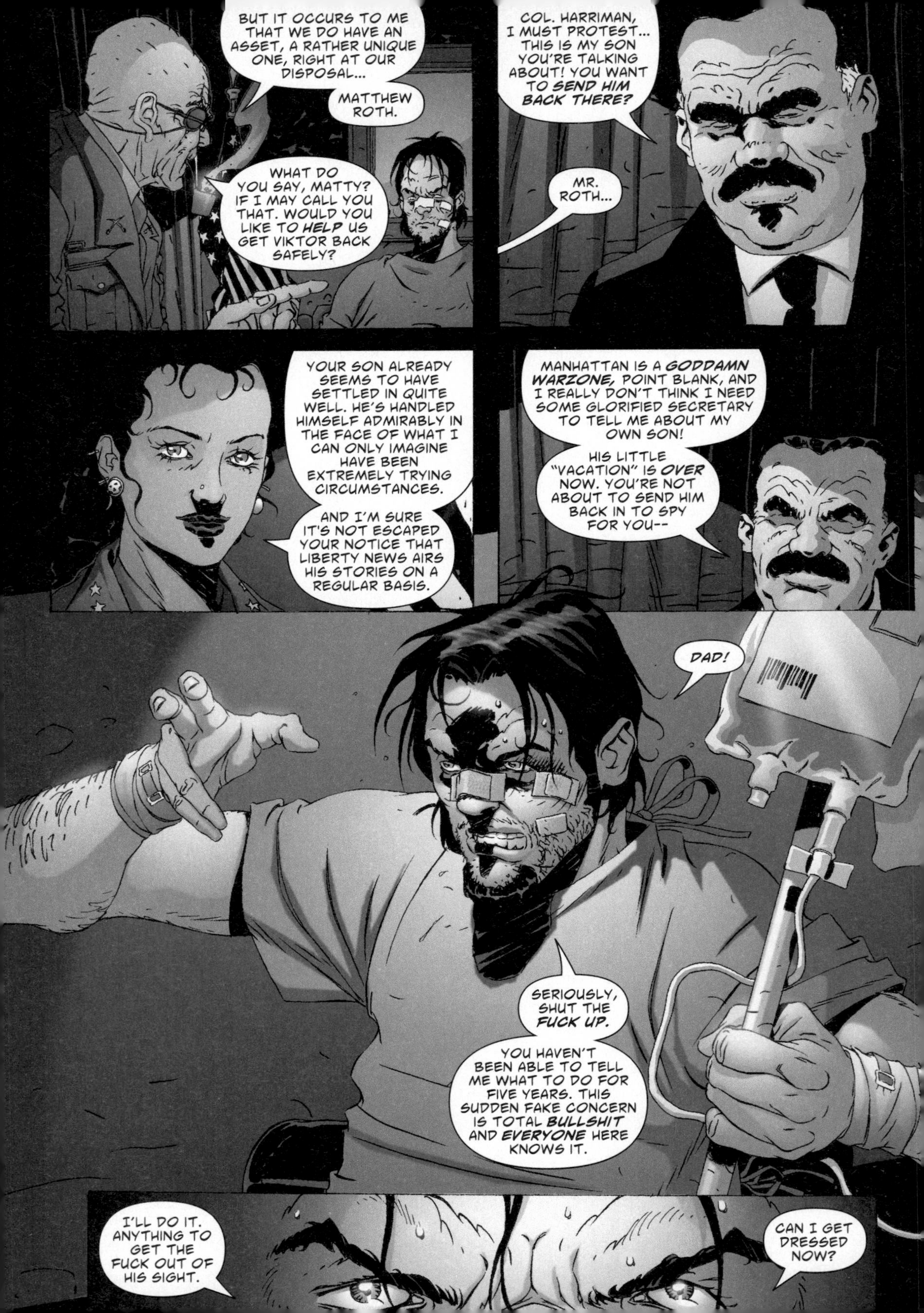

BUT IT OCCURS TO ME THAT WE DO HAVE AN ASSET, A RATHER UNIQUE ONE, RIGHT AT OUR DISPOSAL...
MATTHEW ROTH.
WHAT DO YOU SAY, MATTY? IF I MAY CALL YOU THAT. WOULD YOU LIKE TO HELP US GET VIKTOR BACK SAFELY?
COL. HARRIMAN, I MUST PROTEST... THIS IS MY SON YOU'RE TALKING ABOUT! YOU WANT TO SEND HIM BACK THERE?
MR. ROTH...
YOUR SON ALREADY SEEMS TO HAVE SETTLED IN QUITE WELL. HE'S HANDLED HIMSELF ADMIRABLY IN THE FACE OF WHAT I CAN ONLY IMAGINE HAVE BEEN EXTREMELY TRYING CIRCUMSTANCES.
AND I'M SURE IT'S NOT ESCAPED YOUR NOTICE THAT LIBERTY NEWS AIRS HIS STORIES ON A REGULAR BASIS.
MANHATTAN IS A GODDAMN WARZONE, POINT BLANK, AND I REALLY DON'T THINK I NEED SOME GLORIFIED SECRETARY TO TELL ME ABOUT MY OWN SON!
HIS LITTLE "VACATION" IS OVER NOW. YOU'RE NOT ABOUT TO SEND HIM BACK IN TO SPY FOR YOU--
DAD!
SERIOUSLY, SHUT THE FUCK UP.
YOU HAVEN'T BEEN ABLE TO TELL ME WHAT TO DO FOR FIVE YEARS. THIS SUDDEN FAKE CONCERN IS TOTAL BULLSHIT AND EVERYONE HERE KNOWS IT.
I'LL DO IT. ANYTHING TO GET THE FUCK OUT OF HIS SIGHT.
CAN I GET DRESSED NOW?

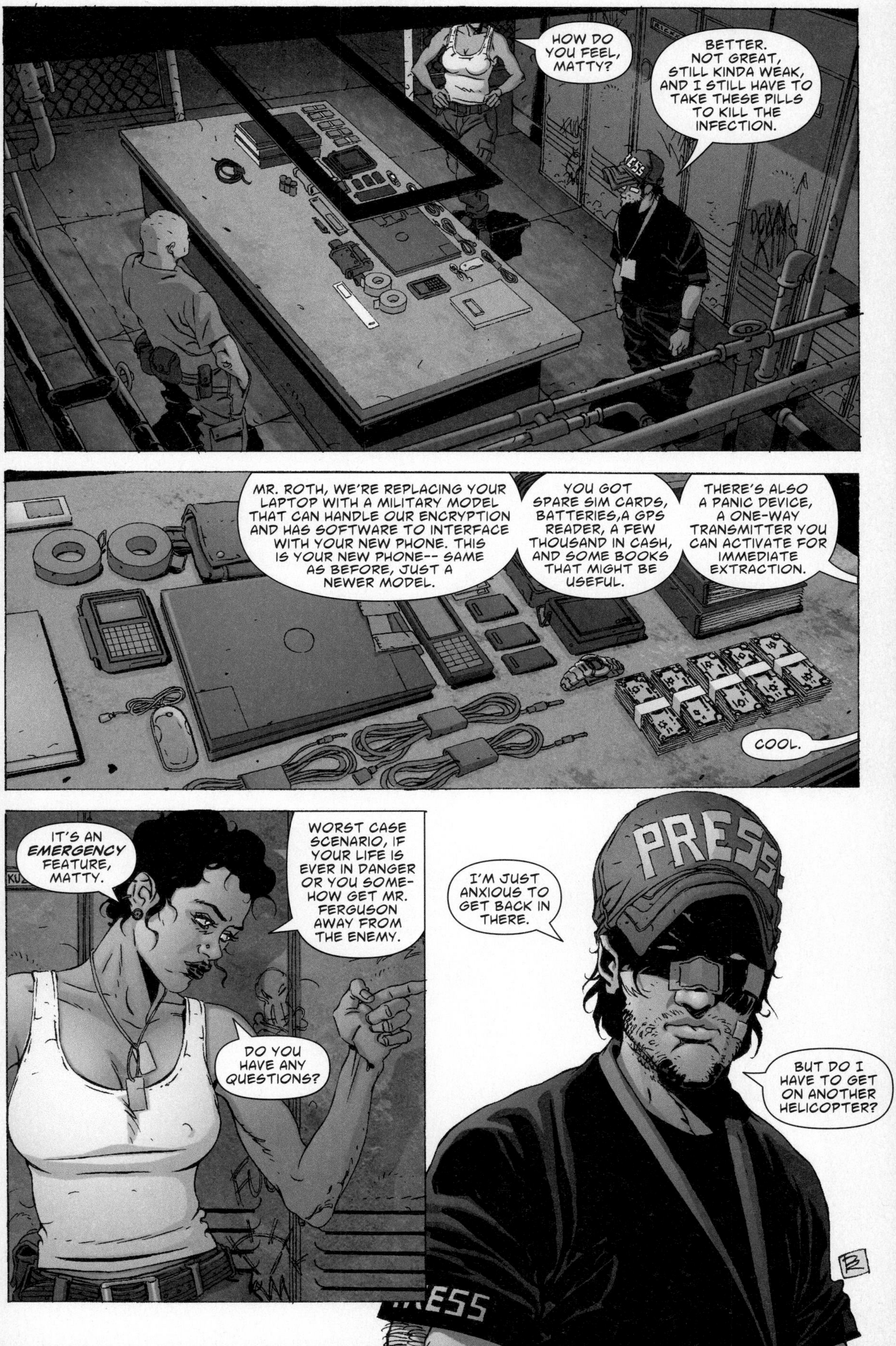
HOW DO YOU FEEL, MATTY?
BETTER. NOT GREAT, STILL KINDA WEAK, AND I STILL HAVE TO TAKE THESE PILLS TO KILL THE INFECTION.
MR. ROTH, WE'RE REPLACING YOUR LAPTOP WITH A MILITARY MODEL THAT CAN HANDLE OUR ENCRYPTION AND HAS SOFTWARE TO INTERFACE WITH YOUR NEW PHONE. THIS IS YOUR NEW PHONE-- SAME AS BEFORE, JUST A NEWER MODEL.
YOU GOT SPARE SIM CARDS, BATTERIES,A GPS READER, A FEW THOUSAND IN CASH, AND SOME BOOKS THAT MIGHT BE USEFUL.
THERE'S ALSO A PANIC DEVICE, A ONE-WAY TRANSMITTER YOU CAN ACTIVATE FOR IMMEDIATE EXTRACTION.
COOL.
IT'S AN *EMERGENCY* FEATURE, MATTY.
WORST CASE SCENARIO, IF YOUR LIFE IS EVER IN DANGER OR YOU SOME-HOW GET MR. FERGUSON AWAY FROM THE ENEMY.
DO YOU HAVE ANY QUESTIONS?
PRESS
I'M JUST ANXIOUS TO GET BACK IN THERE.
BUT DO I HAVE TO GET ON ANOTHER HELICOPTER?

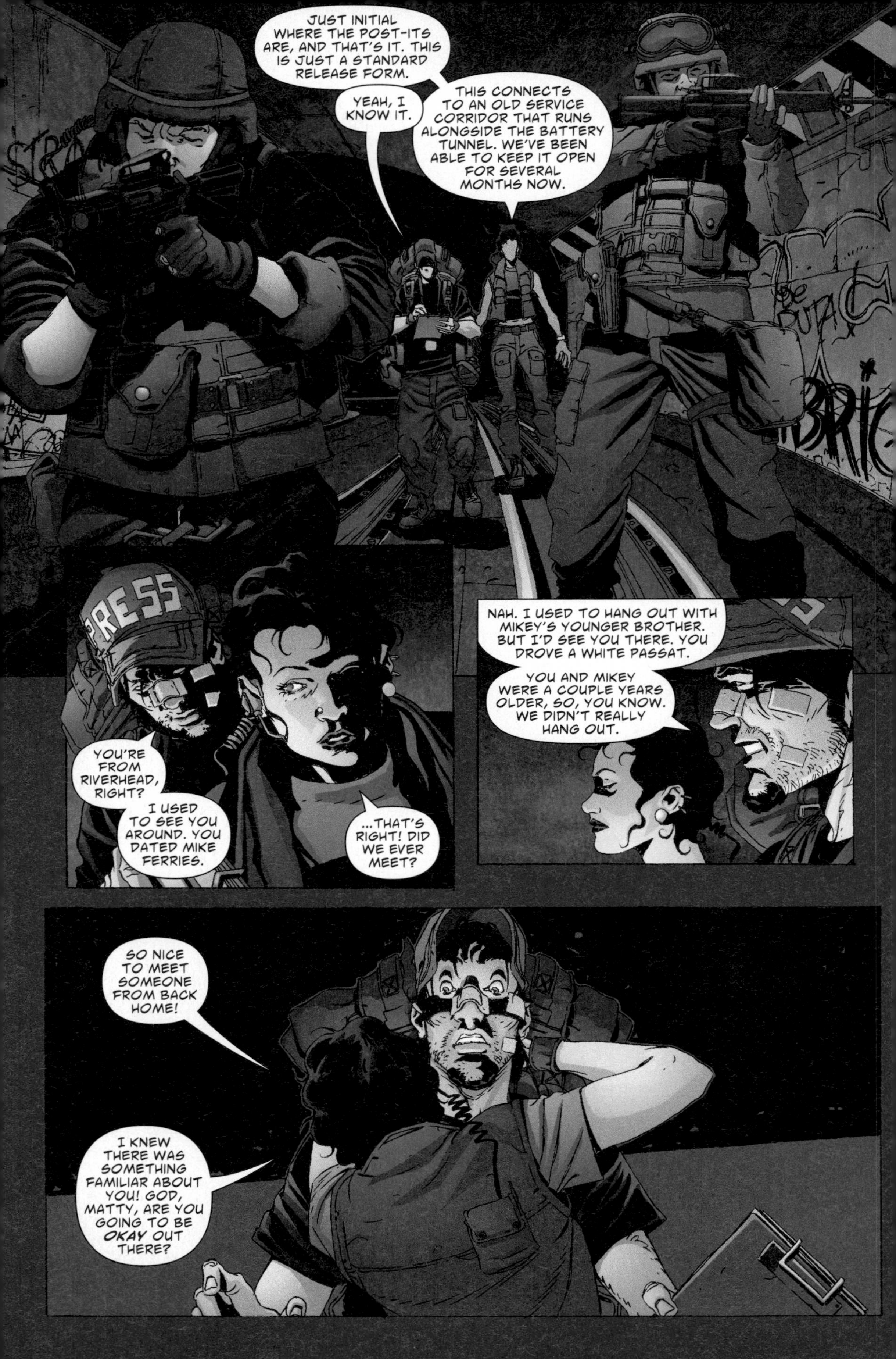
JUST INITIAL WHERE THE POST-ITS ARE, AND THAT'S IT. THIS IS JUST A STANDARD RELEASE FORM.
YEAH, I KNOW IT.
THIS CONNECTS TO AN OLD SERVICE CORRIDOR THAT RUNS ALONGSIDE THE BATTERY TUNNEL. WE'VE BEEN ABLE TO KEEP IT OPEN FOR SEVERAL MONTHS NOW.
PRESS
YOU'RE FROM RIVERHEAD, RIGHT?
I USED TO SEE YOU AROUND. YOU DATED MIKE FERRIES.
...THAT'S RIGHT! DID WE EVER MEET?
NAH. I USED TO HANG OUT WITH MIKEY'S YOUNGER BROTHER. BUT I'D SEE YOU THERE. YOU DROVE A WHITE PASSAT.
YOU AND MIKEY WERE A COUPLE YEARS OLDER, SO, YOU KNOW. WE DIDN'T REALLY HANG OUT.
SO NICE TO MEET SOMEONE FROM BACK HOME!
I KNEW THERE WAS SOMETHING FAMILIAR ABOUT YOU! GOD, MATTY, ARE YOU GOING TO BE *OKAY* OUT THERE?

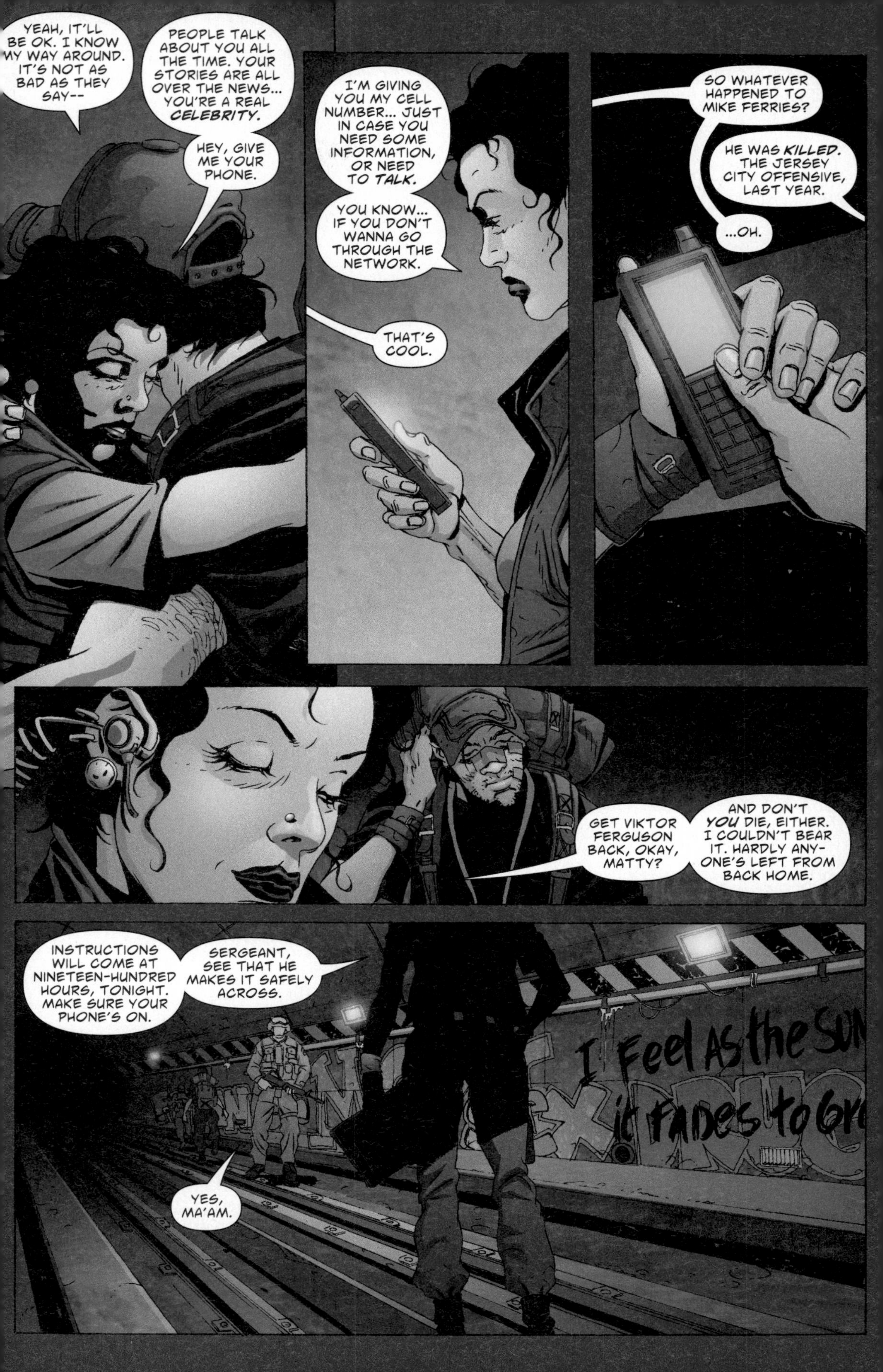
YEAH, IT'LL BE OK. I KNOW MY WAY AROUND. IT'S NOT AS BAD AS THEY SAY--
PEOPLE TALK ABOUT YOU ALL THE TIME. YOUR STORIES ARE ALL OVER THE NEWS... YOU'RE A REAL CELEBRITY.
HEY, GIVE ME YOUR PHONE.
I'M GIVING YOU MY CELL NUMBER... JUST IN CASE YOU NEED SOME INFORMATION, OR NEED TO TALK.
YOU KNOW... IF YOU DON'T WANNA GO THROUGH THE NETWORK.
THAT'S COOL.
SO WHATEVER HAPPENED TO MIKE FERRIES?
HE WAS KILLED. THE JERSEY CITY OFFENSIVE, LAST YEAR.
...OH.
GET VIKTOR FERGUSON BACK, OKAY, MATTY?
AND DON'T YOU DIE, EITHER. I COULDN'T BEAR IT. HARDLY ANYONE'S LEFT FROM BACK HOME.
INSTRUCTIONS WILL COME AT NINETEEN-HUNDRED HOURS, TONIGHT. MAKE SURE YOUR PHONE'S ON.
SERGEANT, SEE THAT HE MAKES IT SAFELY ACROSS.
I Feel As the Su
it Fades to Gre
YES, MA'AM.

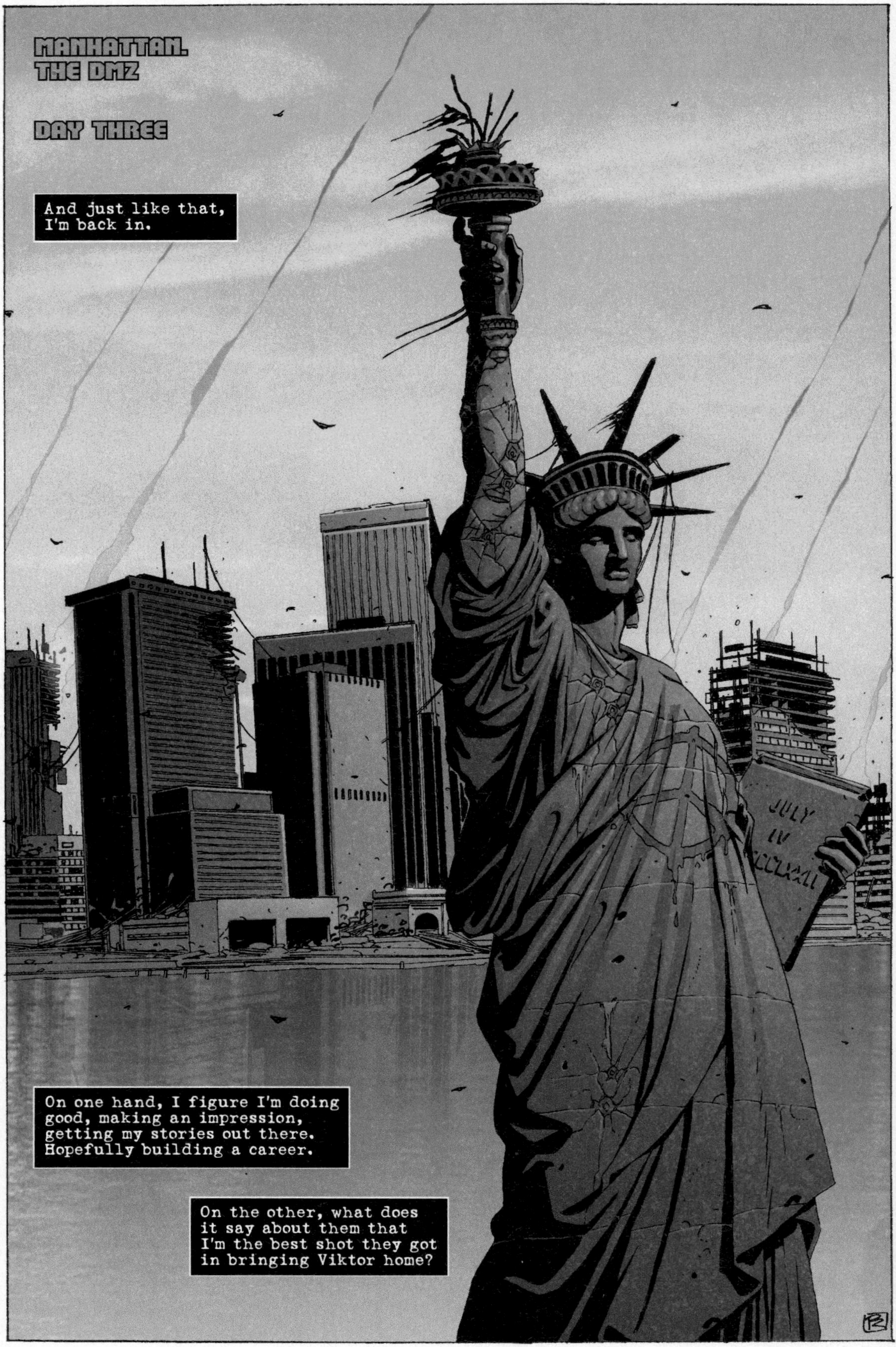
MANHATTAN.
THE DMZ
DAY THREE
And just like that,
I'm back in.
JULY
IV
On one hand, I figure I'm doing
good, making an impression,
getting my stories out there.
Hopefully building a career.
On the other, what does
it say about them that
I'm the best shot they got
in bringing Viktor home?

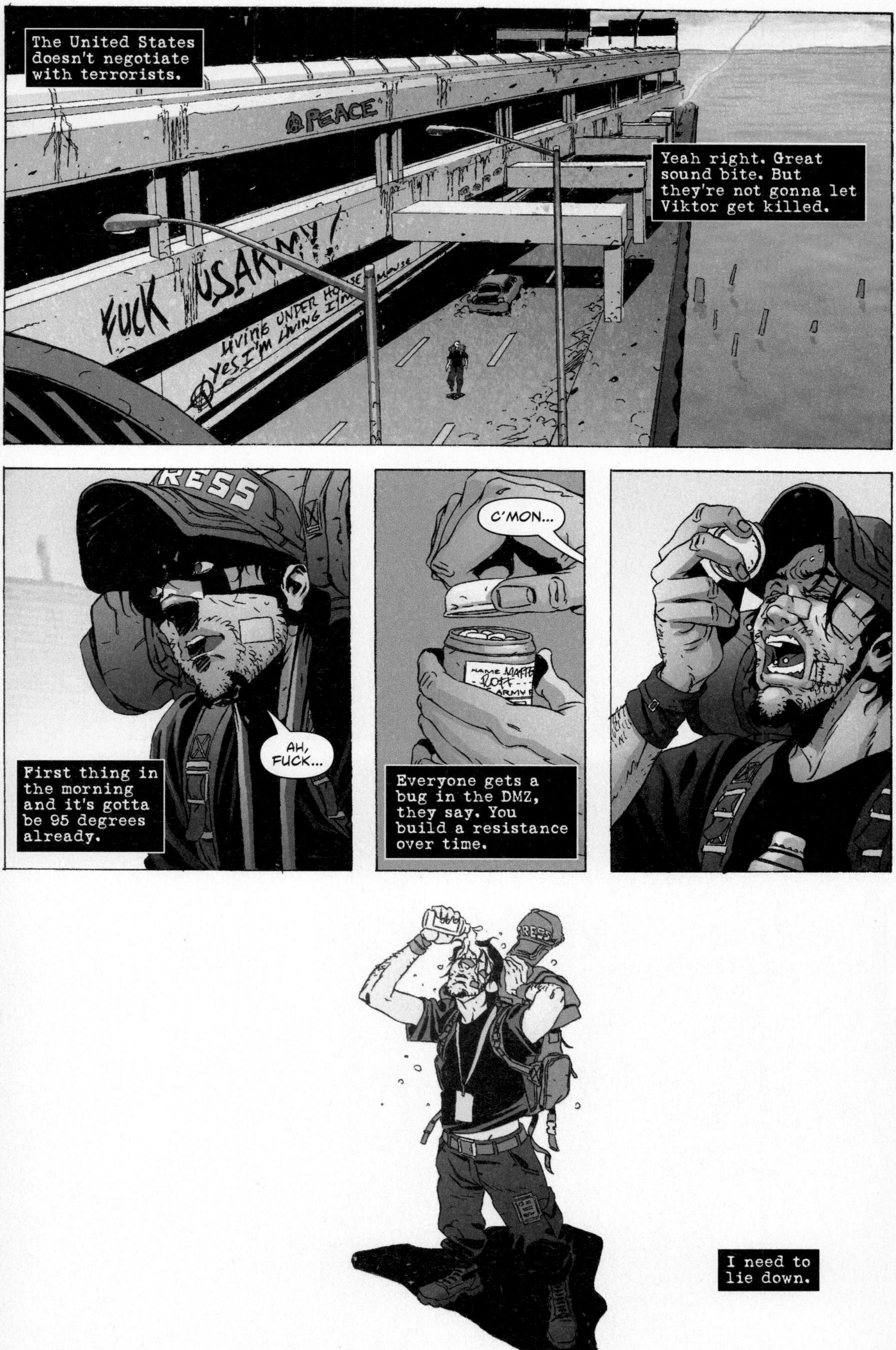
The United States doesn't negotiate with terrorists.
PEACE
FUCK USARMY!
Yeah right. Great sound bite. But they're not gonna let Viktor get killed.
RESS
AH, FUCK...
First thing in the morning and it's gotta be 95 degrees already.
C'MON...
Everyone gets a bug in the DMZ, they say. You build a resistance over time.
I need to lie down.

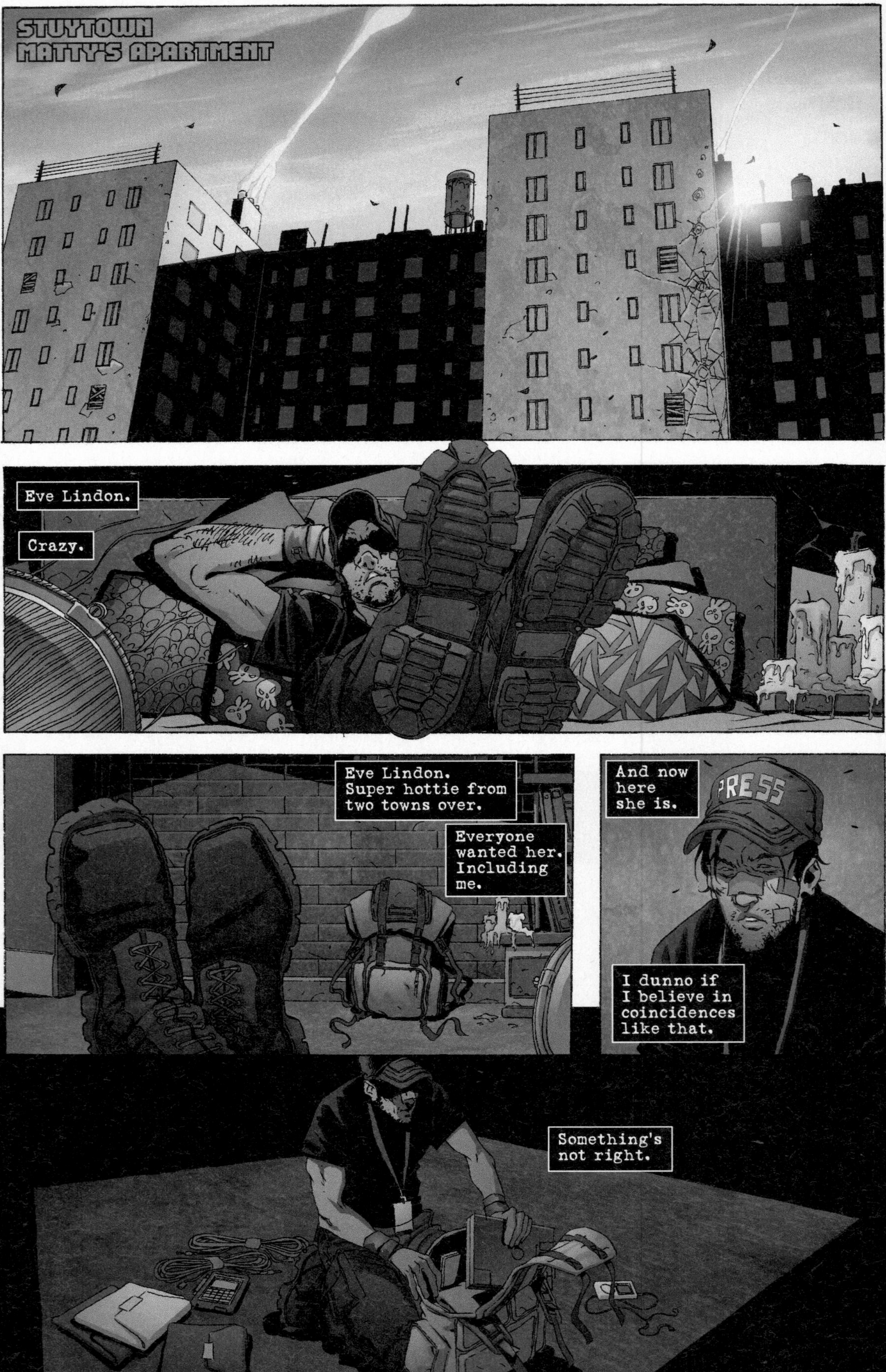
STUYTOWN
MATTY'S APARTMENT
Eve Lindon.
Crazy.
Eve Lindon. Super hottie from two towns over.
Everyone wanted her. Including me.
And now here she is.
PRESS
I dunno if I believe in coincidences like that.
Something's not right.

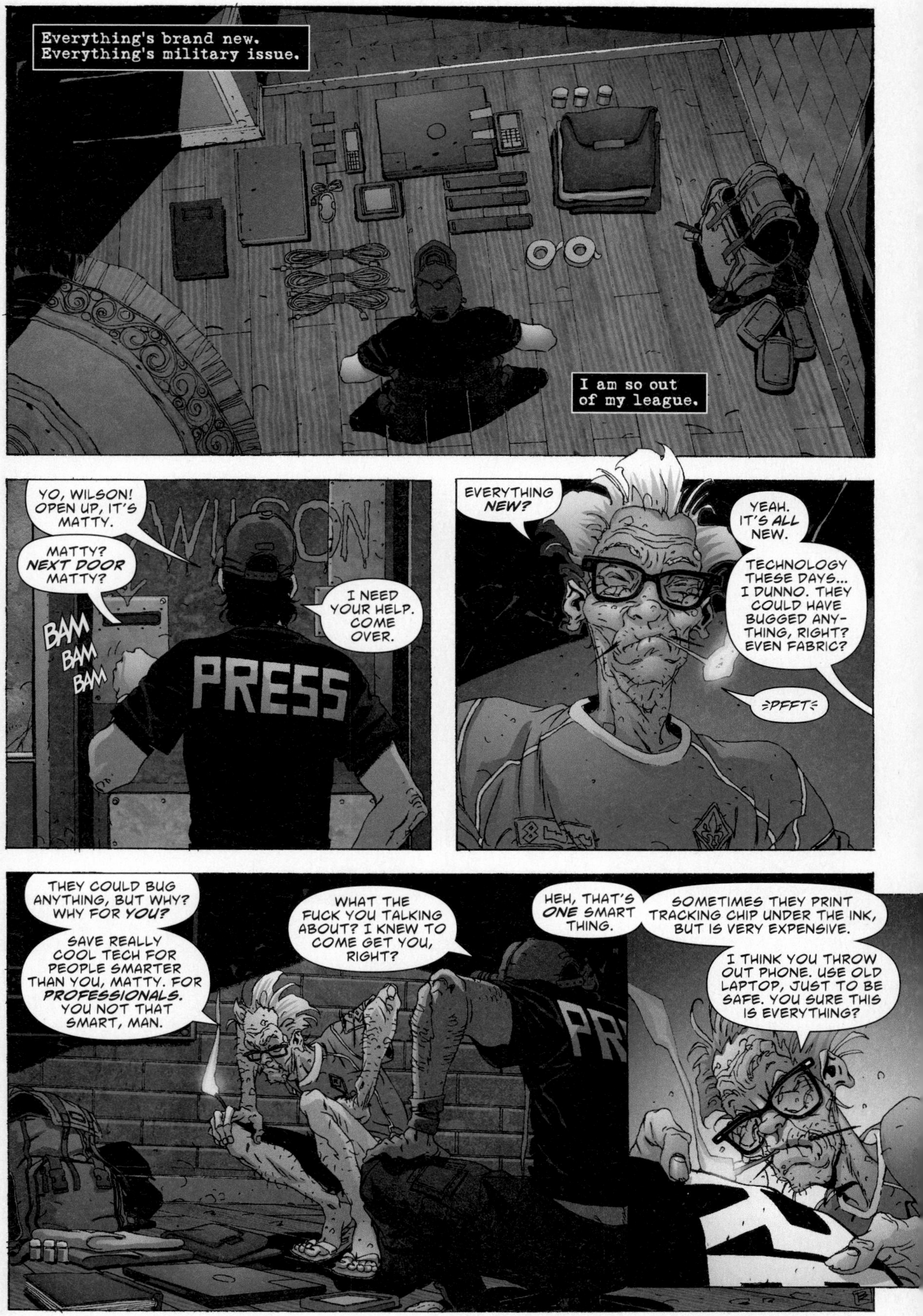
Everything's brand new.
Everything's military issue.
I am so out of my league.
YO, WILSON! OPEN UP, IT'S MATTY.
MATTY? NEXT DOOR MATTY?
BAM BAM BAM
I NEED YOUR HELP. COME OVER.
WILSON
PRESS
EVERYTHING NEW?
YEAH. IT'S ALL NEW.
TECHNOLOGY THESE DAYS... I DUNNO. THEY COULD HAVE BUGGED ANYTHING, RIGHT? EVEN FABRIC?
PFFT
THEY COULD BUG ANYTHING, BUT WHY? WHY FOR YOU?
SAVE REALLY COOL TECH FOR PEOPLE SMARTER THAN YOU, MATTY. FOR PROFESSIONALS. YOU NOT THAT SMART, MAN.
WHAT THE FUCK YOU TALKING ABOUT? I KNEW TO COME GET YOU, RIGHT?
HEH, THAT'S ONE SMART THING.
SOMETIMES THEY PRINT TRACKING CHIP UNDER THE INK, BUT IS VERY EXPENSIVE.
I THINK YOU THROW OUT PHONE. USE OLD LAPTOP, JUST TO BE SAFE. YOU SURE THIS IS EVERYTHING?

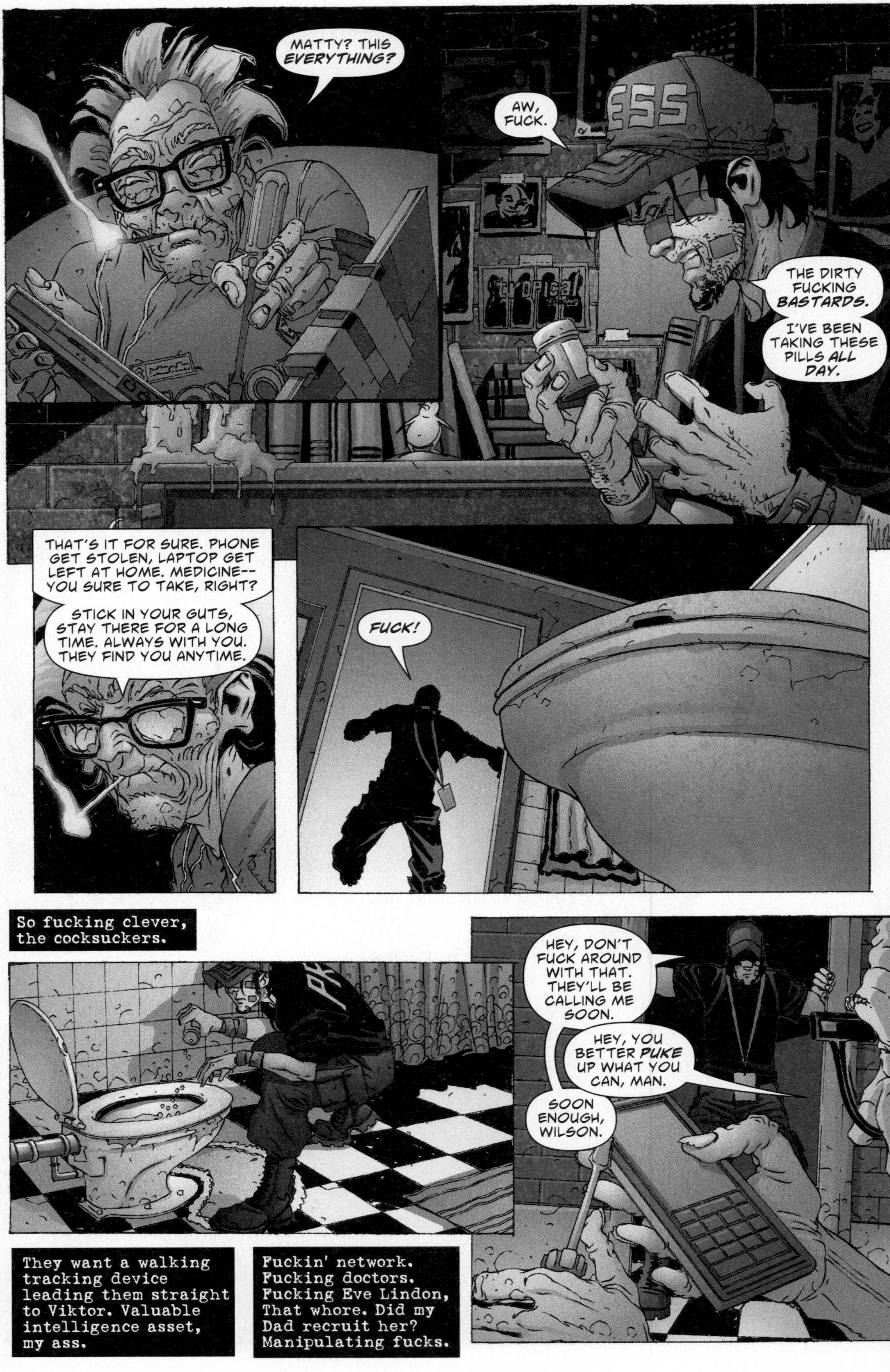
MATTY? THIS EVERYTHING?
AW, FUCK.
THE DIRTY FUCKING BASTARDS.
I'VE BEEN TAKING THESE PILLS ALL DAY.
THAT'S IT FOR SURE. PHONE GET STOLEN, LAPTOP GET LEFT AT HOME. MEDICINE-- YOU SURE TO TAKE, RIGHT?
STICK IN YOUR GUTS, STAY THERE FOR A LONG TIME. ALWAYS WITH YOU. THEY FIND YOU ANYTIME.
FUCK!
So fucking clever, the cocksuckers.
HEY, DON'T FUCK AROUND WITH THAT. THEY'LL BE CALLING ME SOON.
HEY, YOU BETTER PUKE UP WHAT YOU CAN, MAN.
SOON ENOUGH, WILSON.
They want a walking tracking device leading them straight to Viktor. Valuable intelligence asset, my ass.
Fuckin' network. Fucking doctors. Fucking Eve Lindon, That whore. Did my Dad recruit her? Manipulating fucks.

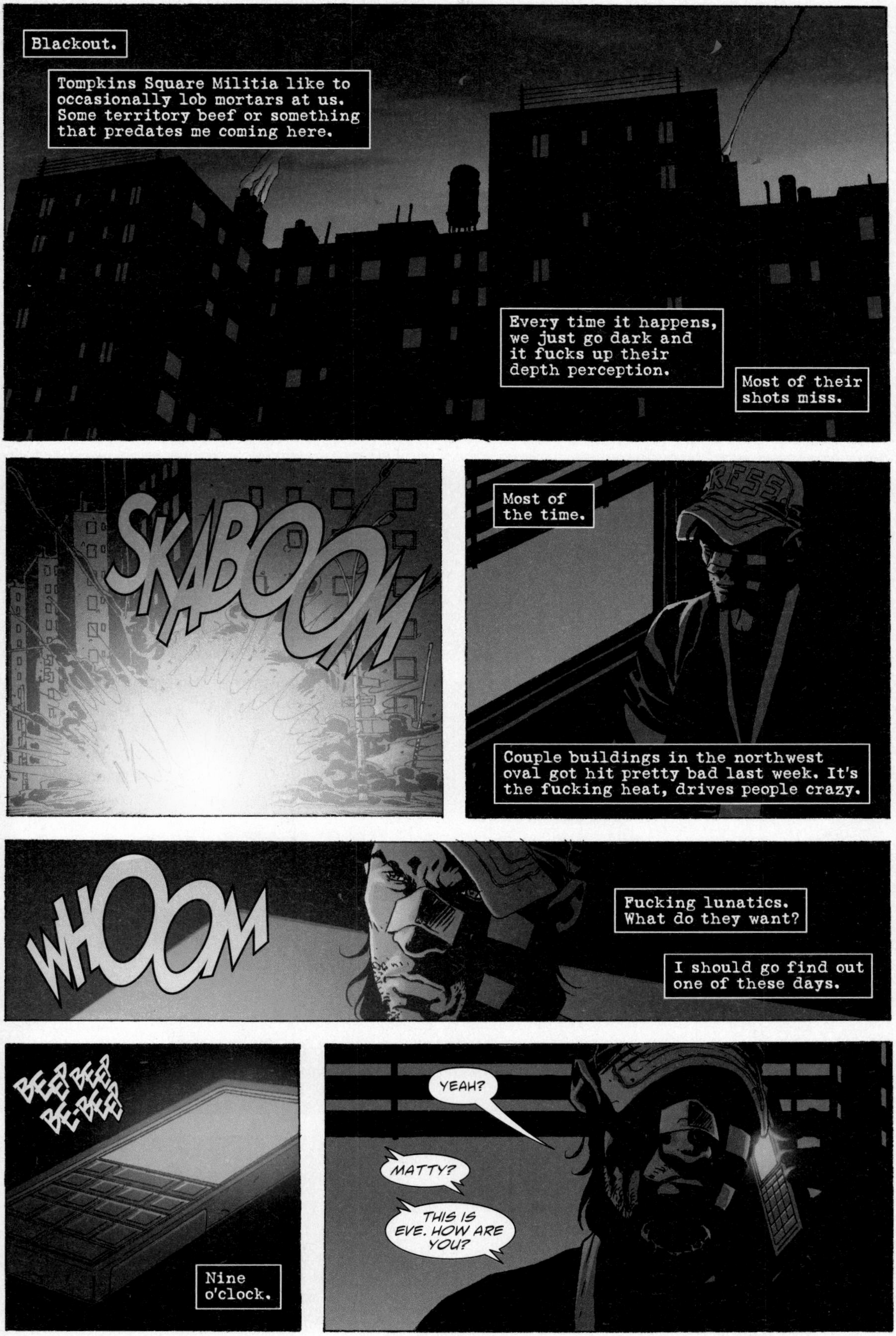
Blackout.
Tompkins Square Militia like to occasionally lob mortars at us. Some territory beef or something that predates me coming here.
Every time it happens, we just go dark and it fucks up their depth perception.
Most of their shots miss.
SKABOOM
Most of the time.
Couple buildings in the northwest oval got hit pretty bad last week. It's the fucking heat, drives people crazy.
WHOOM
Fucking lunatics. What do they want?
I should go find out one of these days.
BEEP BEEP BE-BEEP
Nine o'clock.
YEAH?
MATTY?
THIS IS EVE. HOW ARE YOU?

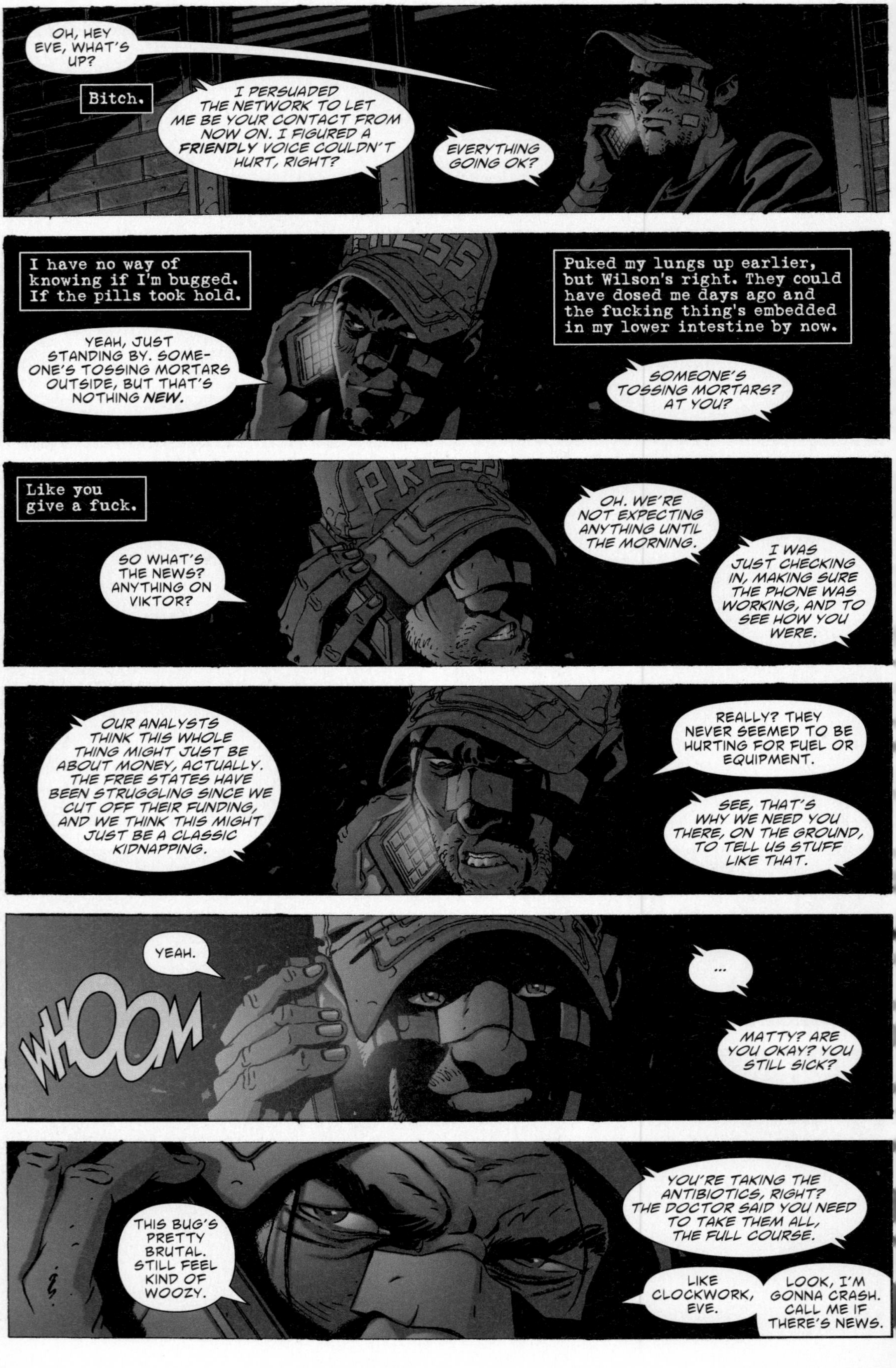
OH, HEY EVE, WHAT'S UP?
Bitch.
I PERSUADED THE NETWORK TO LET ME BE YOUR CONTACT FROM NOW ON. I FIGURED A FRIENDLY VOICE COULDN'T HURT, RIGHT?
EVERYTHING GOING OK?
I have no way of knowing if I'm bugged. If the pills took hold.
Puked my lungs up earlier, but Wilson's right. They could have dosed me days ago and the fucking thing's embedded in my lower intestine by now.
YEAH, JUST STANDING BY. SOMEONE'S TOSSING MORTARS OUTSIDE, BUT THAT'S NOTHING NEW.
SOMEONE'S TOSSING MORTARS? AT YOU?
Like you give a fuck.
OH. WE'RE NOT EXPECTING ANYTHING UNTIL THE MORNING.
I WAS JUST CHECKING IN, MAKING SURE THE PHONE WAS WORKING, AND TO SEE HOW YOU WERE.
SO WHAT'S THE NEWS? ANYTHING ON VIKTOR?
OUR ANALYSTS THINK THIS WHOLE THING MIGHT JUST BE ABOUT MONEY, ACTUALLY. THE FREE STATES HAVE BEEN STRUGGLING SINCE WE CUT OFF THEIR FUNDING, AND WE THINK THIS MIGHT JUST BE A CLASSIC KIDNAPPING.
REALLY? THEY NEVER SEEMED TO BE HURTING FOR FUEL OR EQUIPMENT.
SEE, THAT'S WHY WE NEED YOU THERE, ON THE GROUND, TO TELL US STUFF LIKE THAT.
YEAH.
WHOOM
...
MATTY? ARE YOU OKAY? YOU STILL SICK?
THIS BUG'S PRETTY BRUTAL. STILL FEEL KIND OF WOOZY.
YOU'RE TAKING THE ANTIBIOTICS, RIGHT? THE DOCTOR SAID YOU NEED TO TAKE THEM ALL, THE FULL COURSE.
LIKE CLOCKWORK, EVE.
LOOK, I'M GONNA CRASH. CALL ME IF THERE'S NEWS.

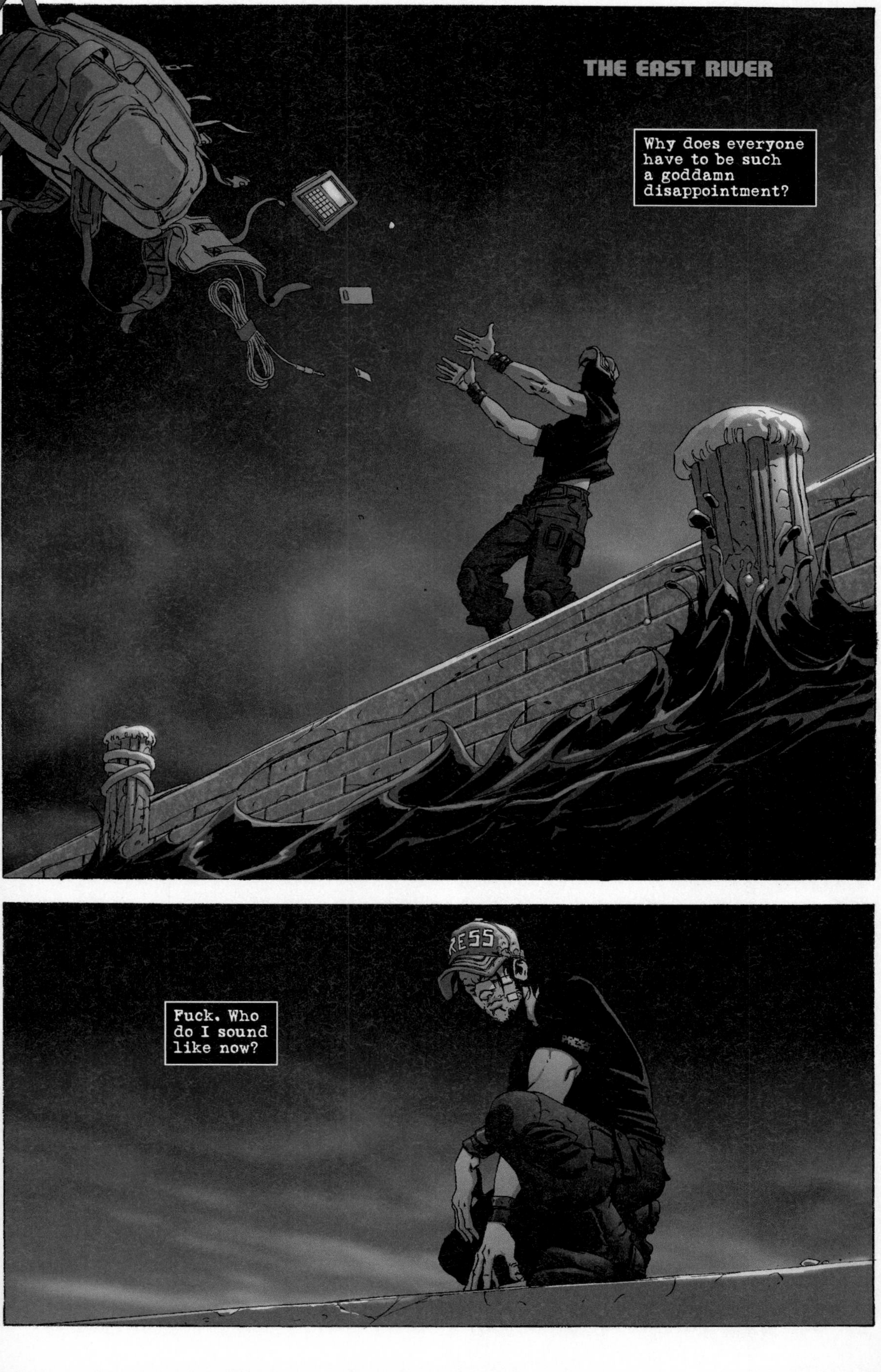
THE EAST RIVER
Why does everyone have to be such a goddamn disappointment?
Fuck. Who do I sound like now?

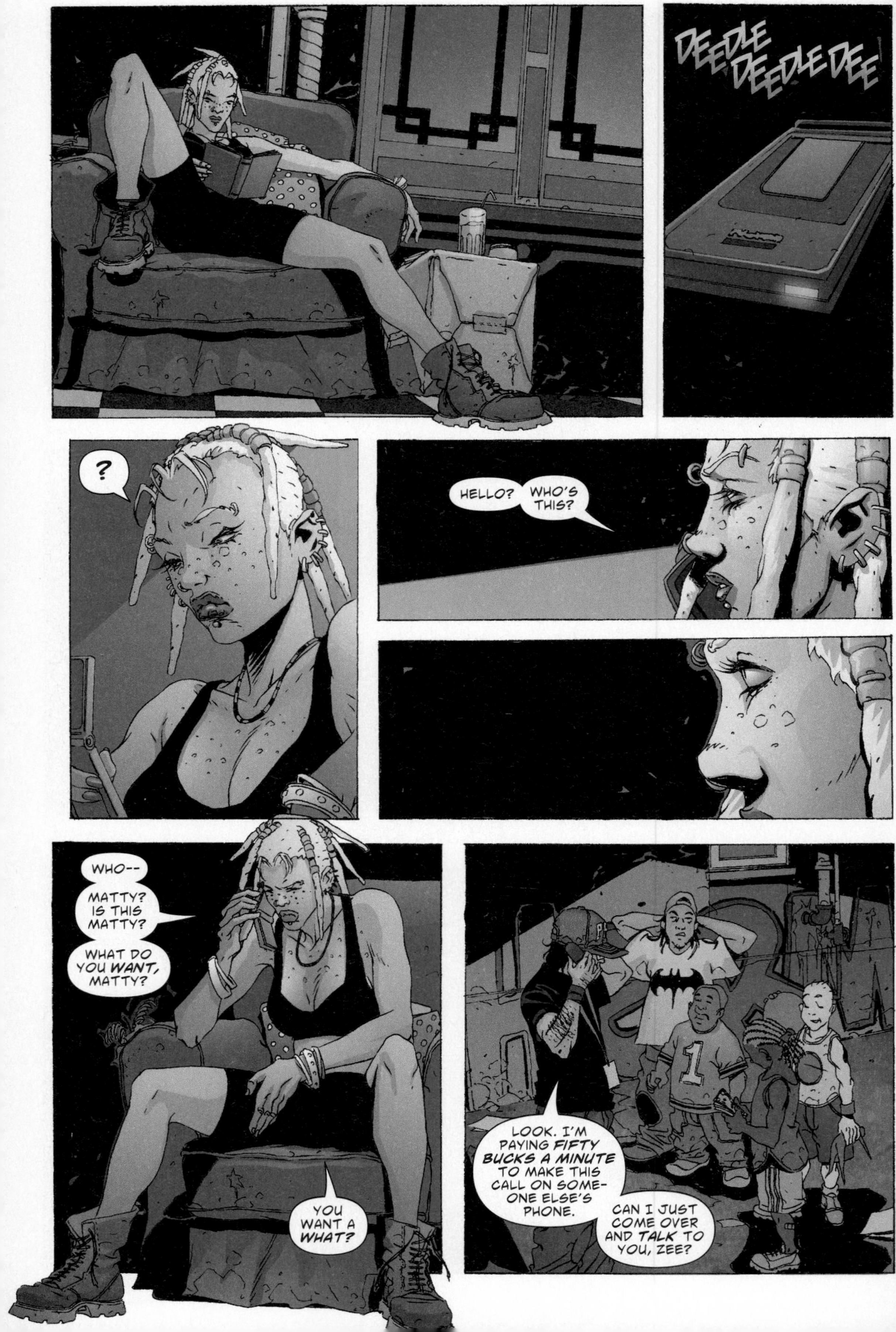
DEEDLE DEEDLE DEEDLE DEE
?
HELLO? WHO'S THIS?
WHO--
MATTY? IS THIS MATTY?
WHAT DO YOU WANT, MATTY?
YOU WANT A WHAT?
LOOK. I'M PAYING FIFTY BUCKS A MINUTE TO MAKE THIS CALL ON SOME-ONE ELSE'S PHONE.
CAN I JUST COME OVER AND TALK TO YOU, ZEE?

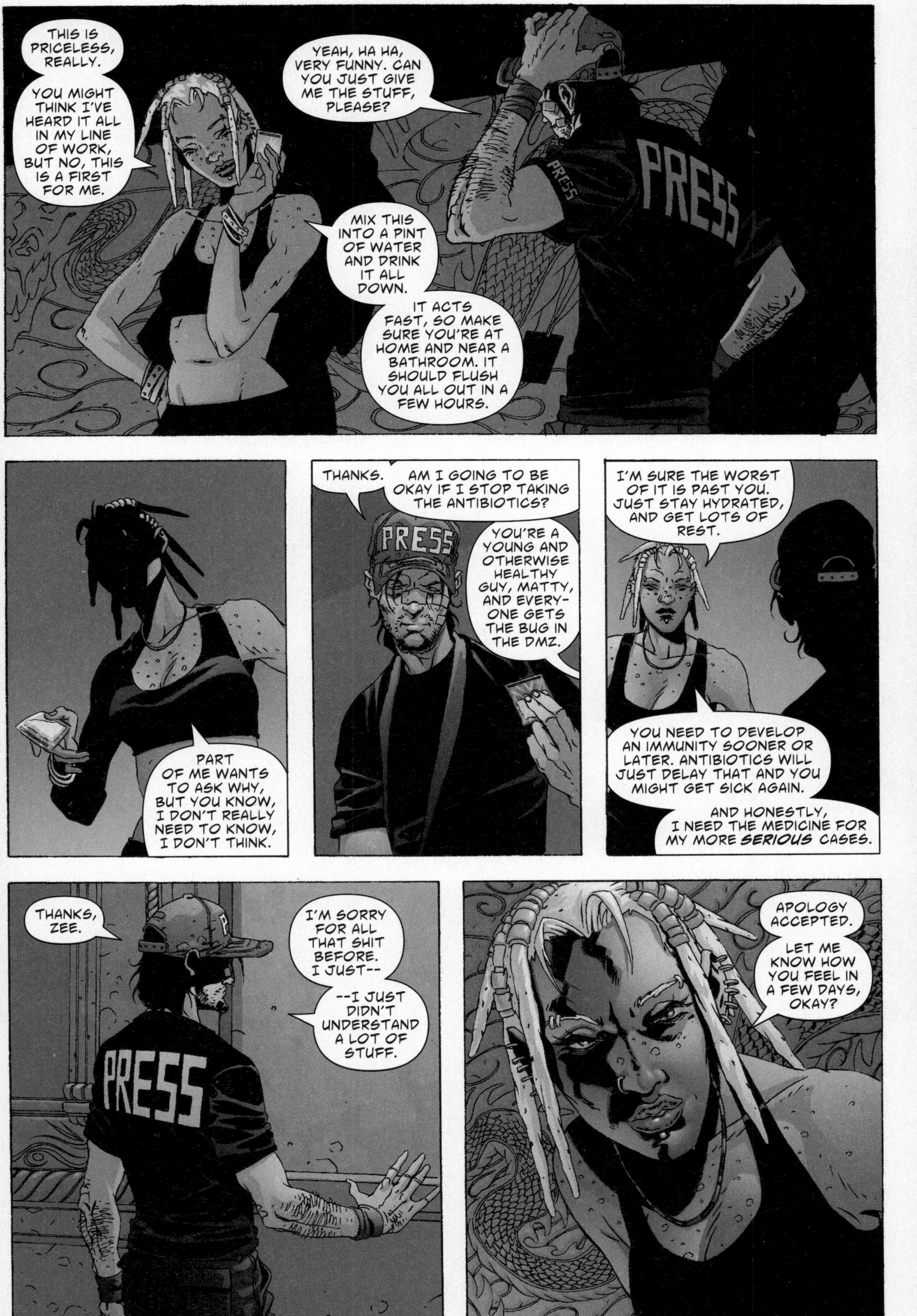
THIS IS PRICELESS, REALLY.
YOU MIGHT THINK I'VE HEARD IT ALL IN MY LINE OF WORK, BUT NO, THIS IS A FIRST FOR ME.
YEAH, HA HA, VERY FUNNY. CAN YOU JUST GIVE ME THE STUFF, PLEASE?
MIX THIS INTO A PINT OF WATER AND DRINK IT ALL DOWN.
IT ACTS FAST, SO MAKE SURE YOU'RE AT HOME AND NEAR A BATHROOM. IT SHOULD FLUSH YOU ALL OUT IN A FEW HOURS.
PRESS
PART OF ME WANTS TO ASK WHY, BUT YOU KNOW, I DON'T REALLY NEED TO KNOW, I DON'T THINK.
THANKS.
AM I GOING TO BE OKAY IF I STOP TAKING THE ANTIBIOTICS?
PRESS
YOU'RE A YOUNG AND OTHERWISE HEALTHY GUY, MATTY, AND EVERY-ONE GETS THE BUG IN THE DMZ.
I'M SURE THE WORST OF IT IS PAST YOU. JUST STAY HYDRATED, AND GET LOTS OF REST.
YOU NEED TO DEVELOP AN IMMUNITY SOONER OR LATER. ANTIBIOTICS WILL JUST DELAY THAT AND YOU MIGHT GET SICK AGAIN.
AND HONESTLY, I NEED THE MEDICINE FOR MY MORE *SERIOUS* CASES.
THANKS, ZEE.
I'M SORRY FOR ALL THAT SHIT BEFORE. I JUST--
--I JUST DIDN'T UNDERSTAND A LOT OF STUFF.
PRESS
APOLOGY ACCEPTED.
LET ME KNOW HOW YOU FEEL IN A FEW DAYS, OKAY?

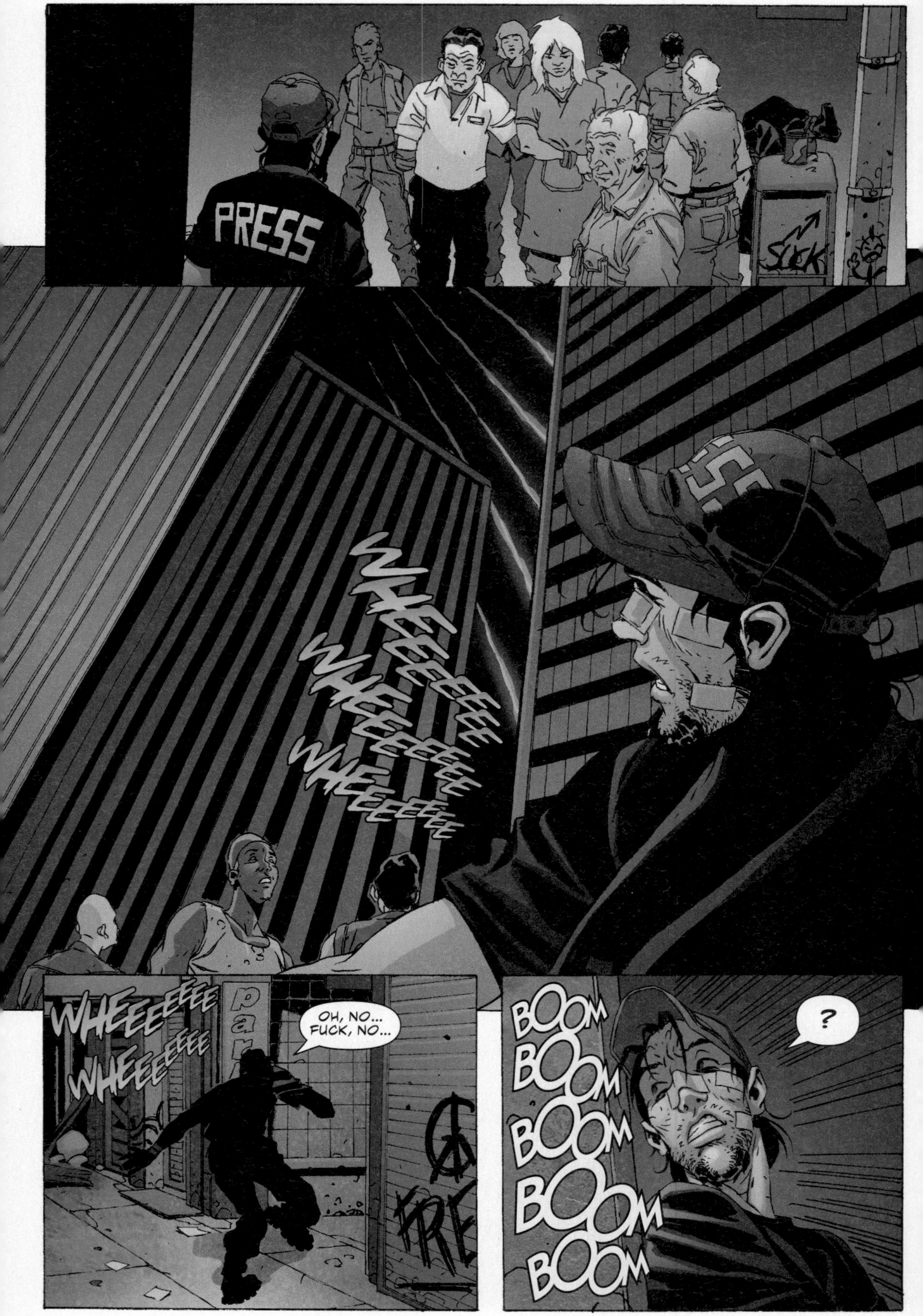
PRESS
SICK
WHEEEEEEEE
WHEEEEEEEEE
WHEEEEEEEE
WHEEEEEEEE
WHEEEEEEEE
OH, NO... FUCK, NO...
BOOM
BOOM
BOOM
BOOM
BOOM
?

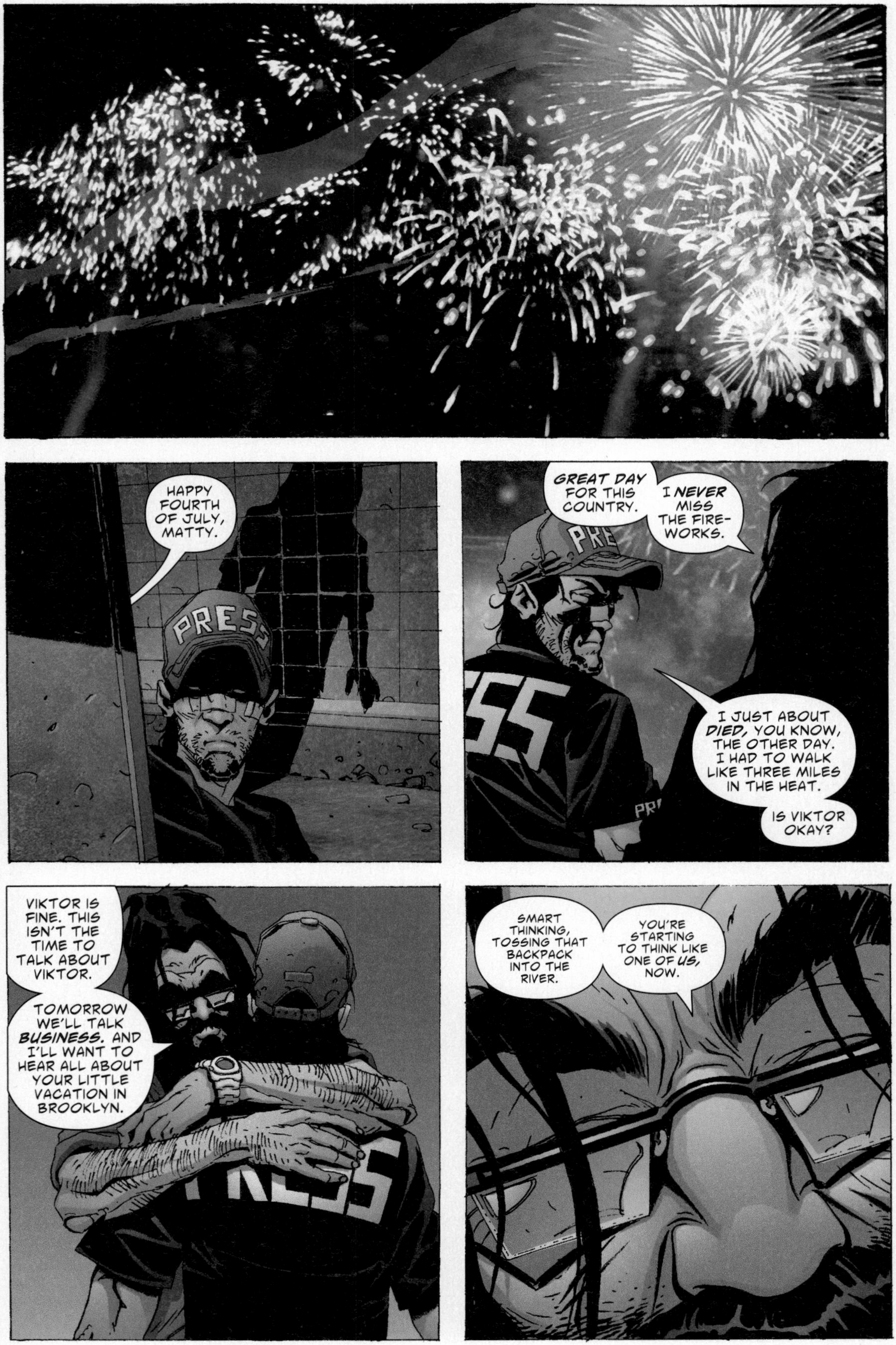

HAPPY FOURTH OF JULY, MATTY.
GREAT DAY FOR THIS COUNTRY.
I NEVER MISS THE FIRE-WORKS.
PRESS
I JUST ABOUT DIED, YOU KNOW, THE OTHER DAY. I HAD TO WALK LIKE THREE MILES IN THE HEAT.
IS VIKTOR OKAY?
VIKTOR IS FINE. THIS ISN'T THE TIME TO TALK ABOUT VIKTOR.
TOMORROW WE'LL TALK BUSINESS. AND I'LL WANT TO HEAR ALL ABOUT YOUR LITTLE VACATION IN BROOKLYN.
SMART THINKING, TOSSING THAT BACKPACK INTO THE RIVER.
YOU'RE STARTING TO THINK LIKE ONE OF US, NOW.

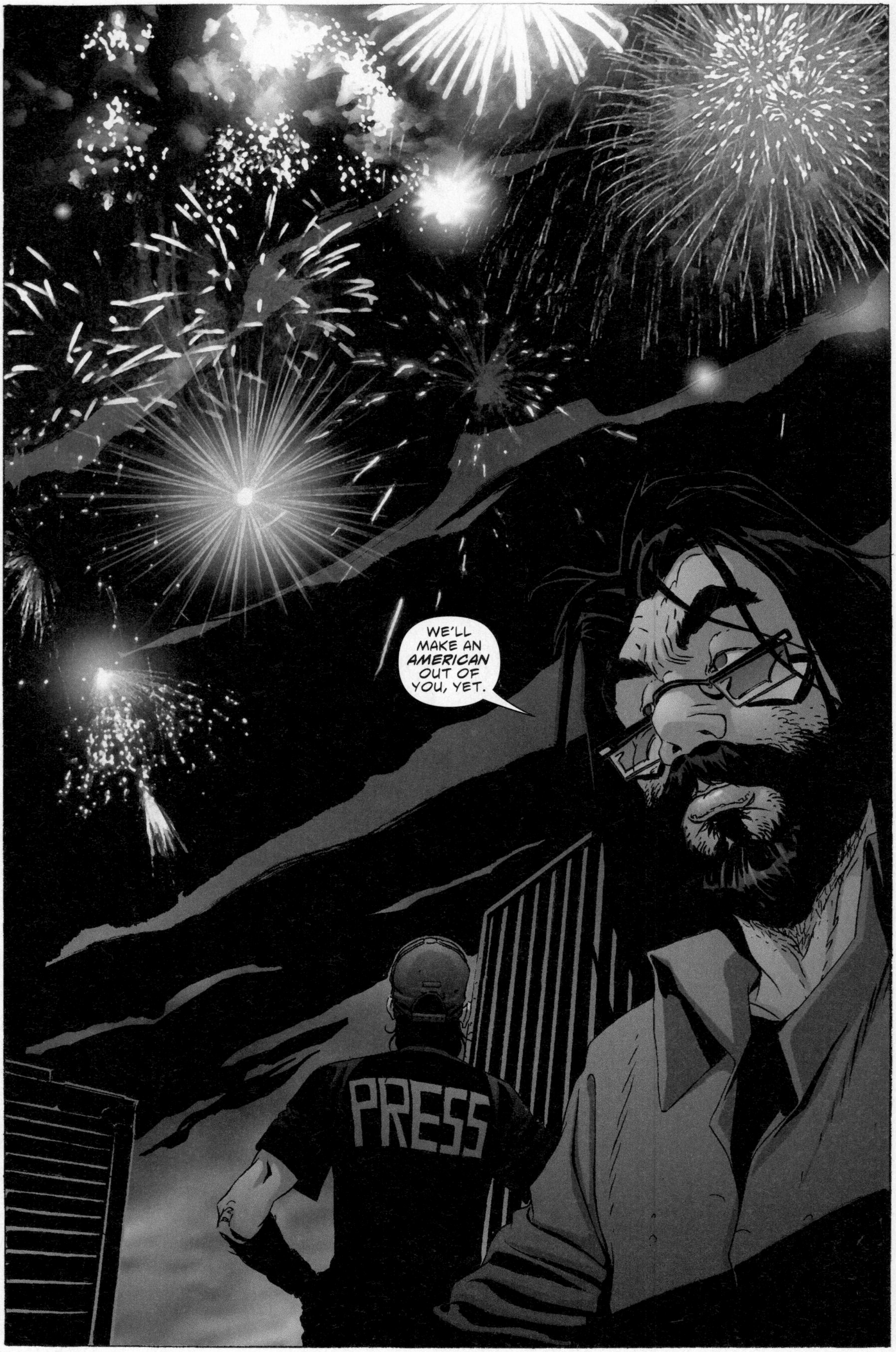
WE'LL MAKE AN AMERICAN OUT OF YOU, YET.
PRESS

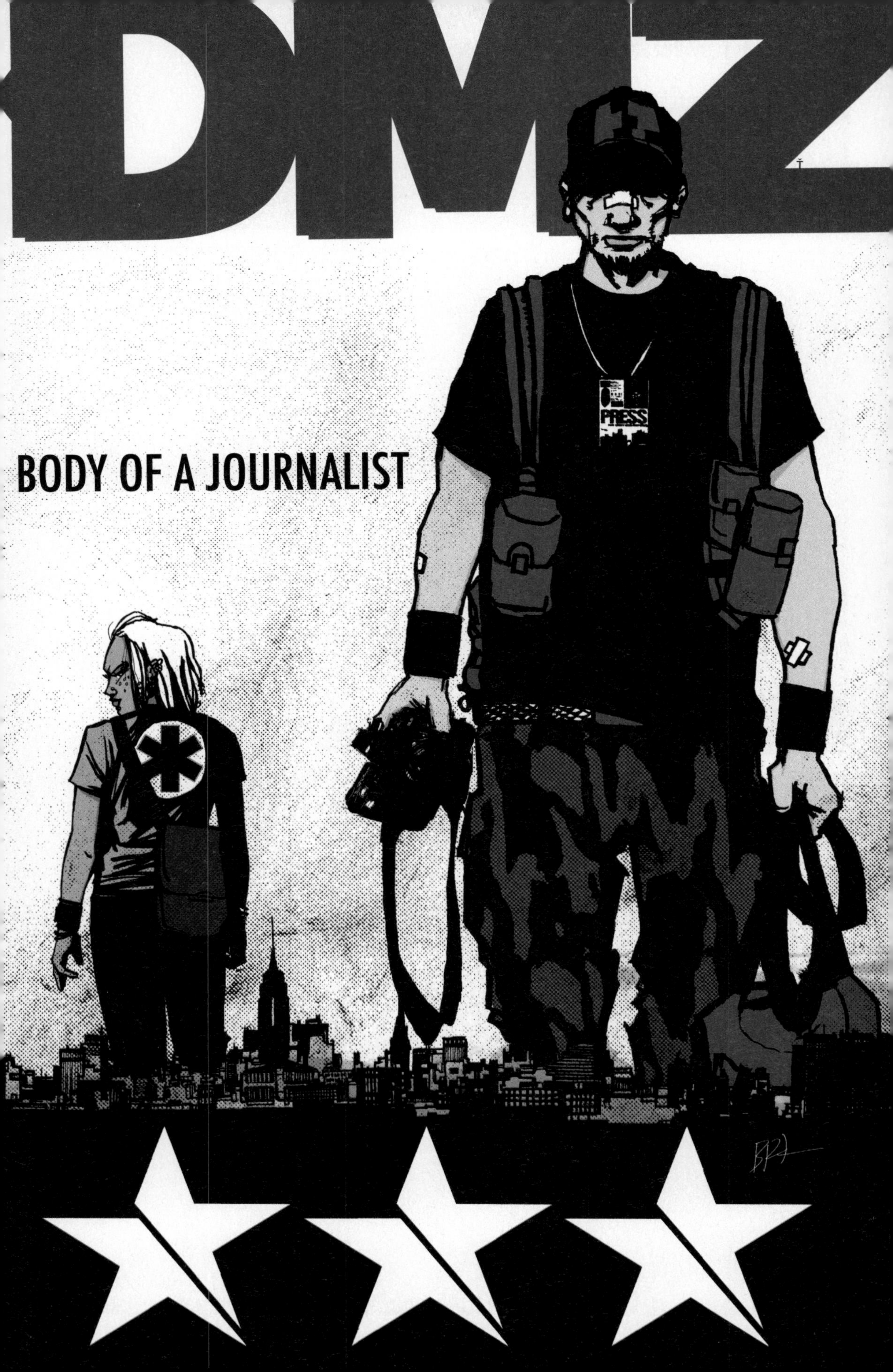
DMZ
BODY OF A JOURNALIST
PRESS

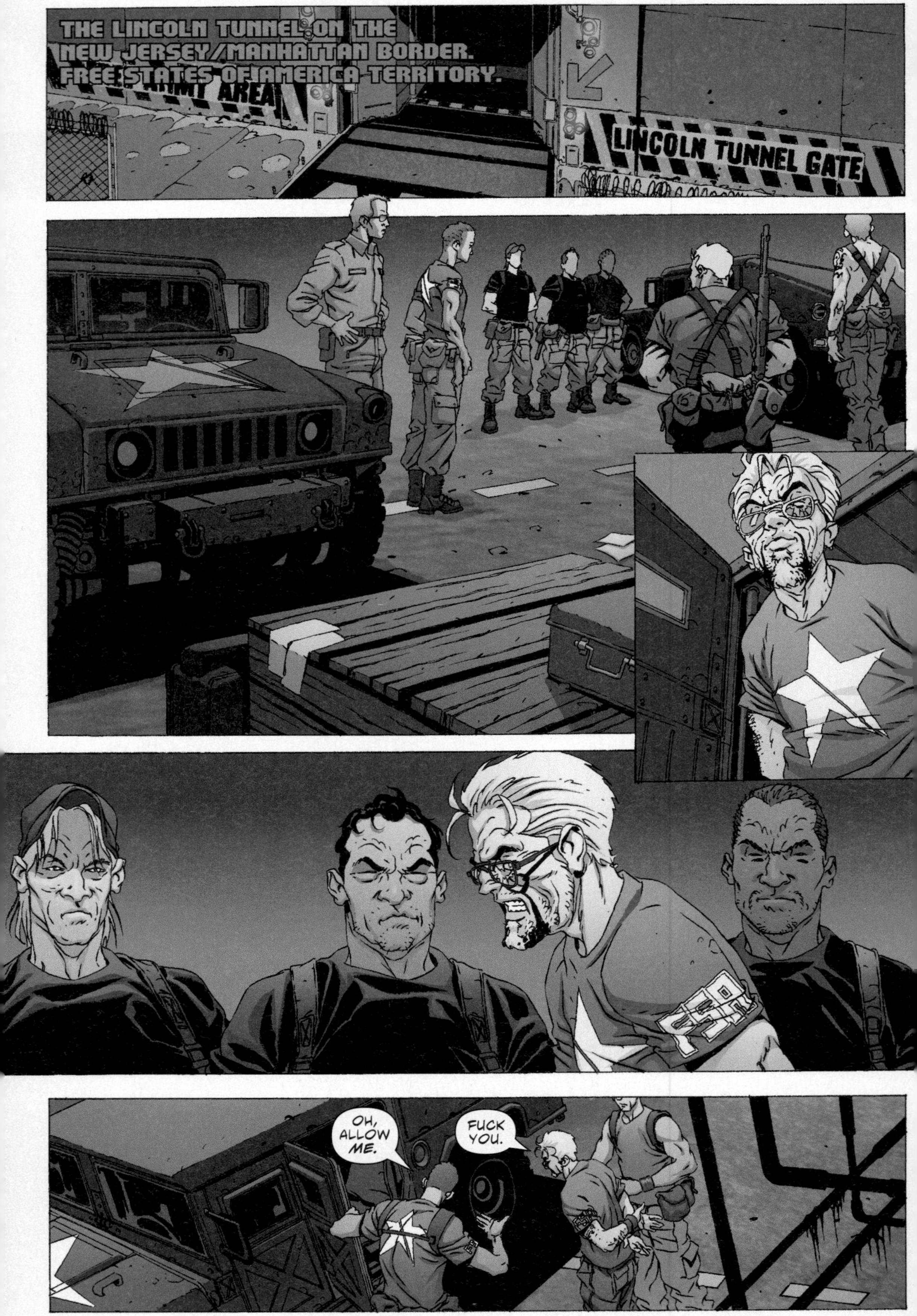
THE LINCOLN TUNNEL ON THE NEW JERSEY/MANHATTAN BORDER. FREE STATES OF AMERICA TERRITORY.
ARMY AREA
LINCOLN TUNNEL GATE
OH, ALLOW ME.
FUCK YOU.

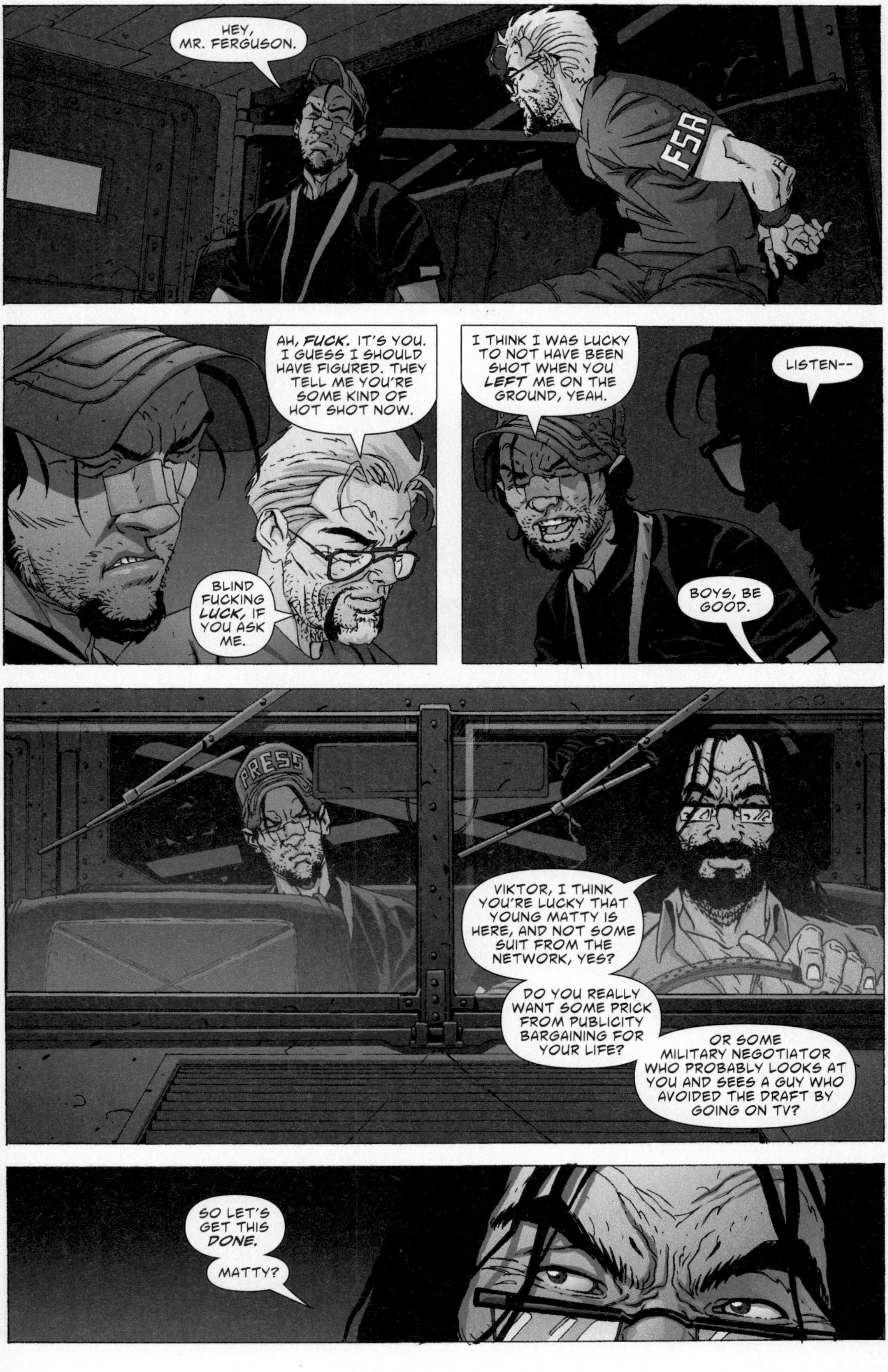

HEY, MR. FERGUSON.
AH, FUCK. IT'S YOU. I GUESS I SHOULD HAVE FIGURED. THEY TELL ME YOU'RE SOME KIND OF HOT SHOT NOW.
BLIND FUCKING LUCK, IF YOU ASK ME.
I THINK I WAS LUCKY TO NOT HAVE BEEN SHOT WHEN YOU LEFT ME ON THE GROUND, YEAH.
LISTEN--
BOYS, BE GOOD.
PRESS
VIKTOR, I THINK YOU'RE LUCKY THAT YOUNG MATTY IS HERE, AND NOT SOME SUIT FROM THE NETWORK, YES?
DO YOU REALLY WANT SOME PRICK FROM PUBLICITY BARGAINING FOR YOUR LIFE?
OR SOME MILITARY NEGOTIATOR WHO PROBABLY LOOKS AT YOU AND SEES A GUY WHO AVOIDED THE DRAFT BY GOING ON TV?
SO LET'S GET THIS DONE.
MATTY?

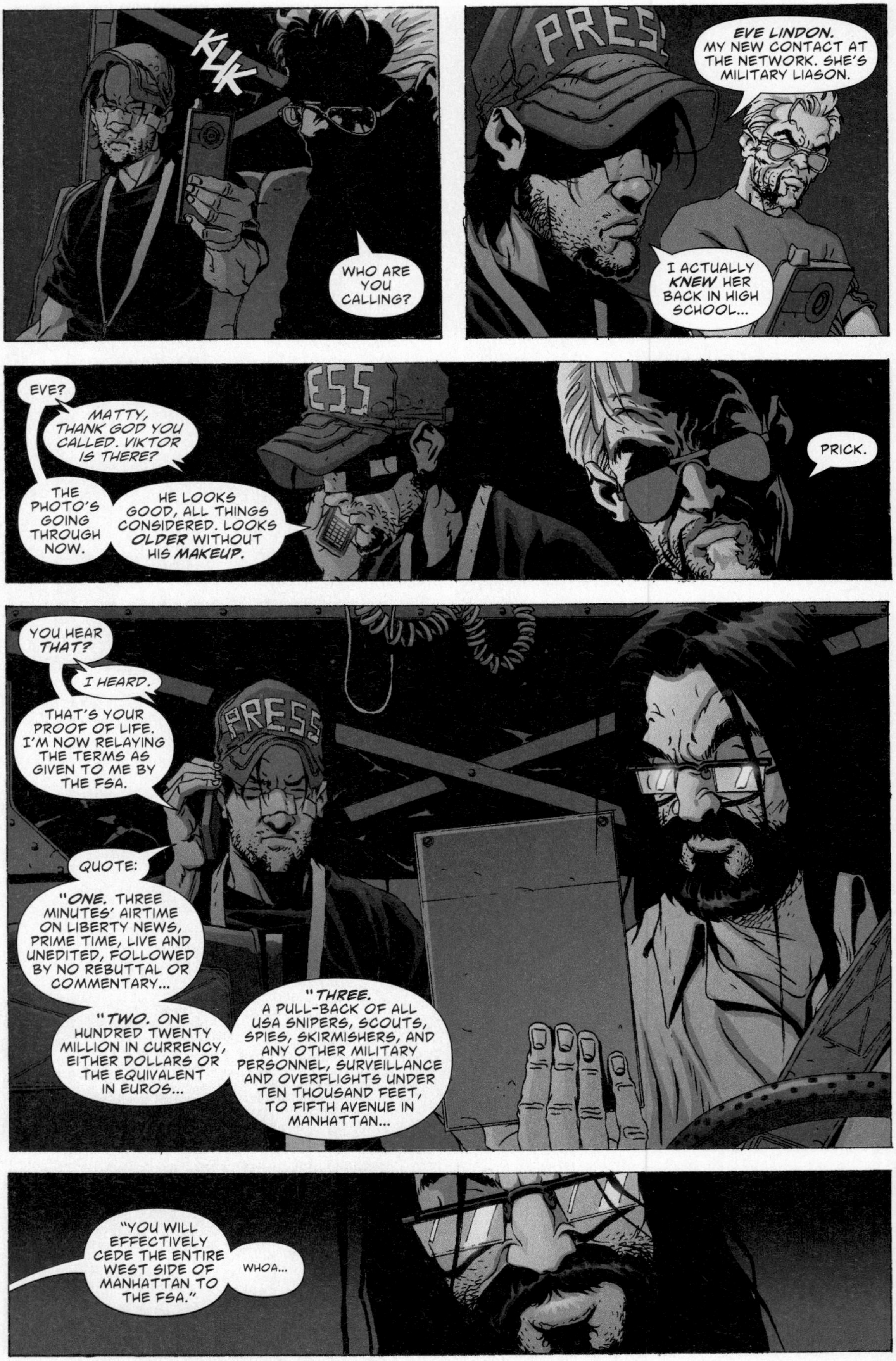
KLIK
WHO ARE YOU CALLING?
EVE LINDON. MY NEW CONTACT AT THE NETWORK. SHE'S MILITARY LIASON.
I ACTUALLY KNEW HER BACK IN HIGH SCHOOL...
EVE?
MATTY, THANK GOD YOU CALLED. VIKTOR IS THERE?
THE PHOTO'S GOING THROUGH NOW.
HE LOOKS GOOD, ALL THINGS CONSIDERED. LOOKS OLDER WITHOUT HIS MAKEUP.
PRICK.
YOU HEAR THAT?
I HEARD.
THAT'S YOUR PROOF OF LIFE. I'M NOW RELAYING THE TERMS AS GIVEN TO ME BY THE FSA.
QUOTE:
"ONE. THREE MINUTES' AIRTIME ON LIBERTY NEWS, PRIME TIME, LIVE AND UNEDITED, FOLLOWED BY NO REBUTTAL OR COMMENTARY...
"TWO. ONE HUNDRED TWENTY MILLION IN CURRENCY, EITHER DOLLARS OR THE EQUIVALENT IN EUROS...
"THREE. A PULL-BACK OF ALL USA SNIPERS, SCOUTS, SPIES, SKIRMISHERS, AND ANY OTHER MILITARY PERSONNEL, SURVEILLANCE AND OVERFLIGHTS UNDER TEN THOUSAND FEET, TO FIFTH AVENUE IN MANHATTAN...
"YOU WILL EFFECTIVELY CEDE THE ENTIRE WEST SIDE OF MANHATTAN TO THE FSA."
WHOA...

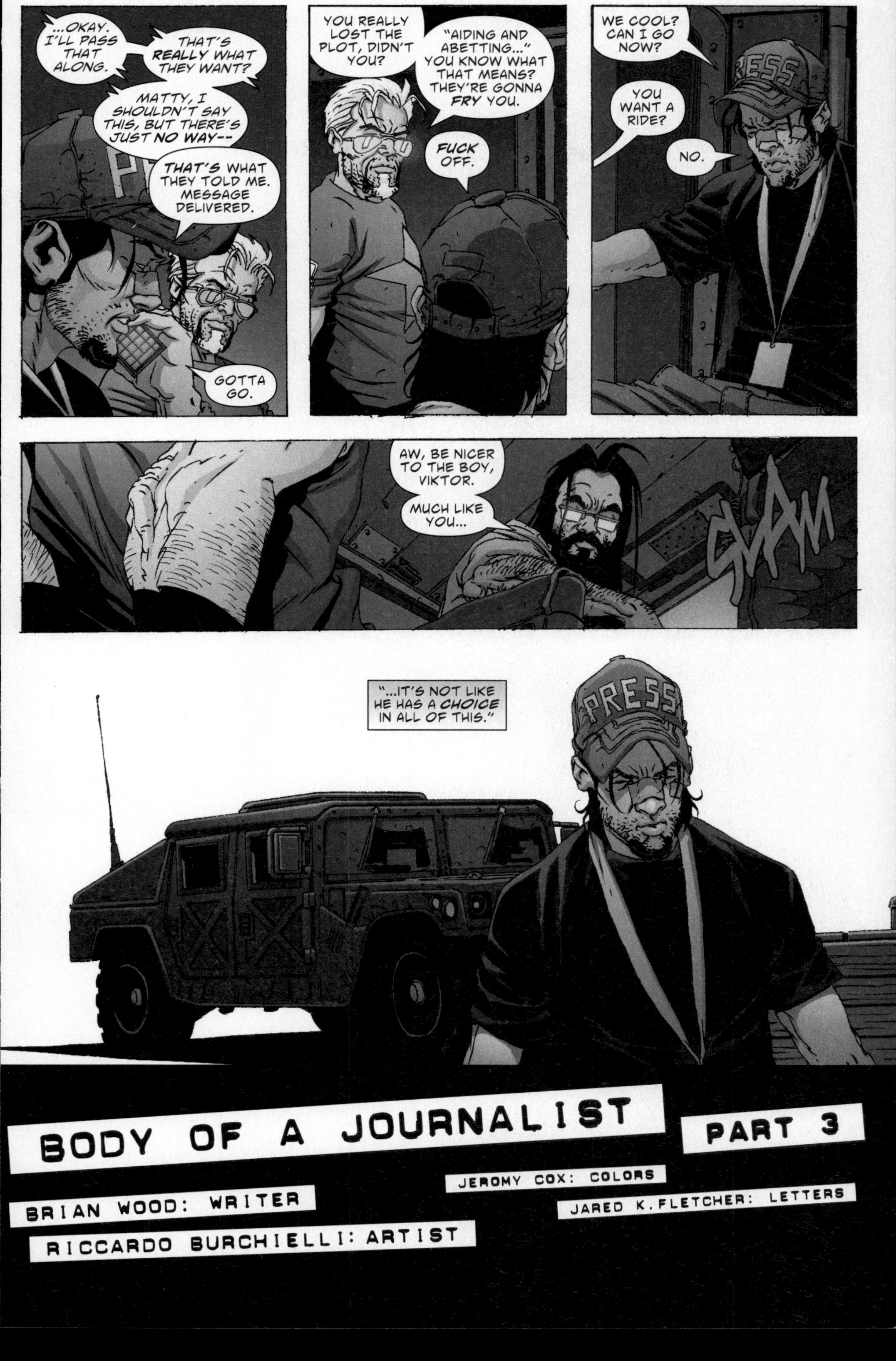
...OKAY. I'LL PASS THAT ALONG.
THAT'S REALLY WHAT THEY WANT?
MATTY, I SHOULDN'T SAY THIS, BUT THERE'S JUST NO WAY--
THAT'S WHAT THEY TOLD ME. MESSAGE DELIVERED.
GOTTA GO.
YOU REALLY LOST THE PLOT, DIDN'T YOU?
"AIDING AND ABETTING..." YOU KNOW WHAT THAT MEANS? THEY'RE GONNA FRY YOU.
FUCK OFF.
WE COOL? CAN I GO NOW?
YOU WANT A RIDE?
NO.
AW, BE NICER TO THE BOY, VIKTOR.
MUCH LIKE YOU...
GVAM
"...IT'S NOT LIKE HE HAS A CHOICE IN ALL OF THIS."
BODY OF A JOURNALIST
PART 3
BRIAN WOOD: WRITER
RICCARDO BURCHIELLI: ARTIST
JEROMY COX: COLORS
JARED K.FLETCHER: LETTERS

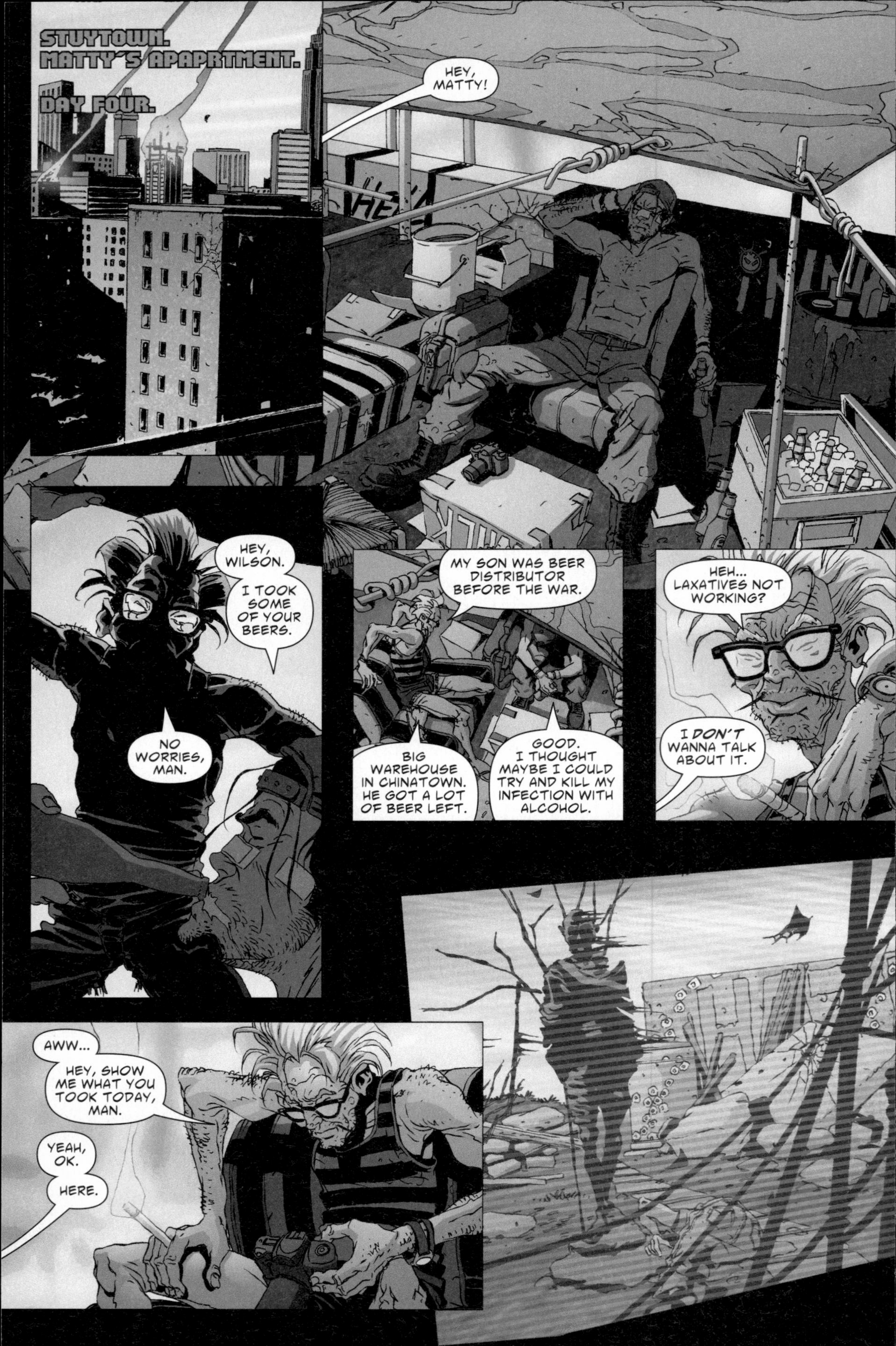
STUYTOWN. MATTY'S APAPRTMENT.
DAY FOUR.
HEY, MATTY!
HEY, WILSON.
I TOOK SOME OF YOUR BEERS.
NO WORRIES, MAN.
MY SON WAS BEER DISTRIBUTOR BEFORE THE WAR.
BIG WAREHOUSE IN CHINATOWN. HE GOT A LOT OF BEER LEFT.
GOOD. I THOUGHT MAYBE I COULD TRY AND KILL MY INFECTION WITH ALCOHOL.
HEH... LAXATIVES NOT WORKING?
I DON'T WANNA TALK ABOUT IT.
AWW...
HEY, SHOW ME WHAT YOU TOOK TODAY, MAN.
YEAH, OK.
HERE.

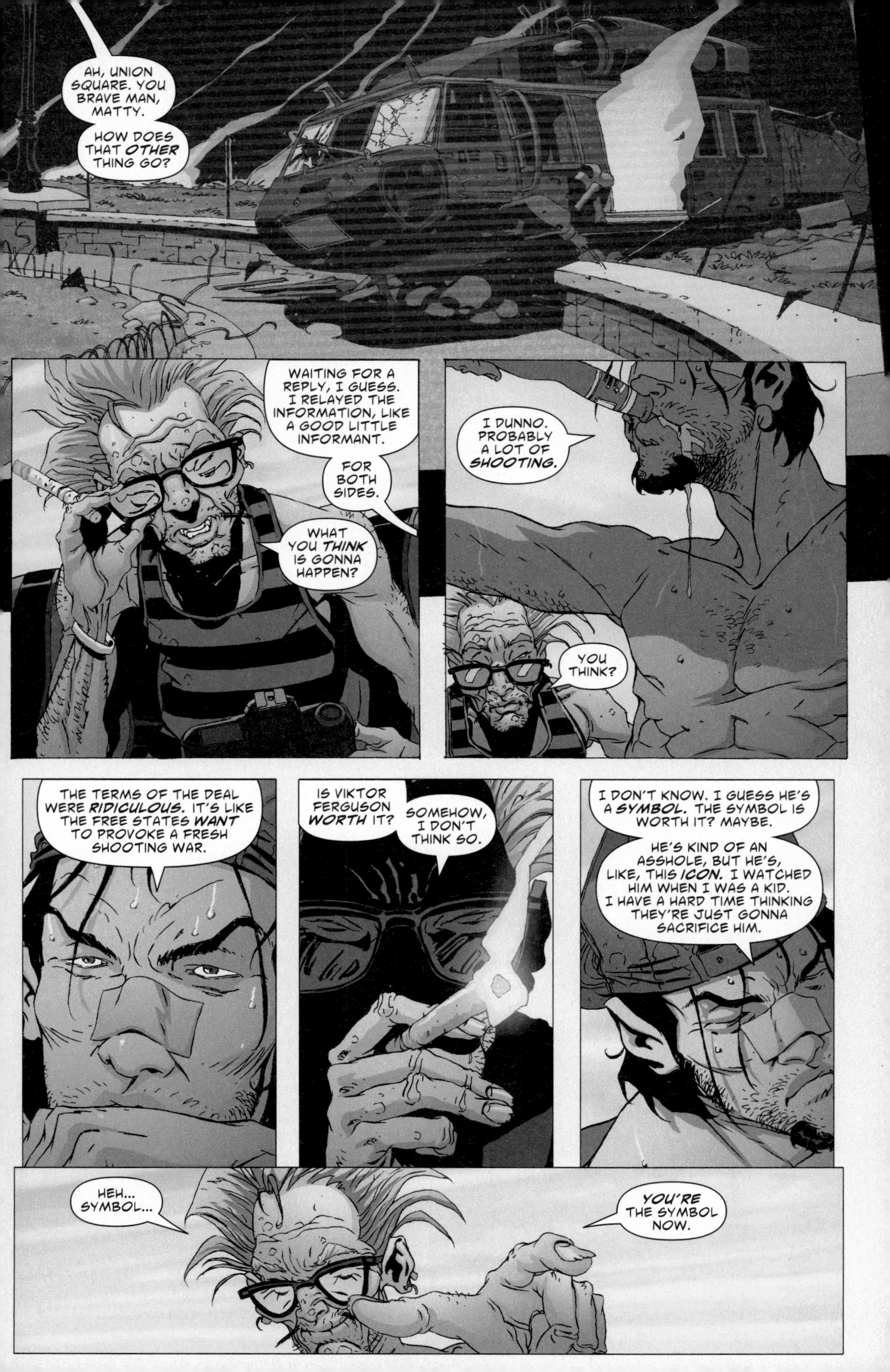

AH, UNION SQUARE. YOU BRAVE MAN, MATTY.
HOW DOES THAT OTHER THING GO?
WAITING FOR A REPLY, I GUESS. I RELAYED THE INFORMATION, LIKE A GOOD LITTLE INFORMANT.
FOR BOTH SIDES.
WHAT YOU THINK IS GONNA HAPPEN?
I DUNNO. PROBABLY A LOT OF SHOOTING.
YOU THINK?
THE TERMS OF THE DEAL WERE RIDICULOUS. IT'S LIKE THE FREE STATES WANT TO PROVOKE A FRESH SHOOTING WAR.
IS VIKTOR FERGUSON WORTH IT?
SOMEHOW, I DON'T THINK SO.
I DON'T KNOW. I GUESS HE'S A SYMBOL. THE SYMBOL IS WORTH IT? MAYBE.
HE'S KIND OF AN ASSHOLE, BUT HE'S, LIKE, THIS ICON. I WATCHED HIM WHEN I WAS A KID. I HAVE A HARD TIME THINKING THEY'RE JUST GONNA SACRIFICE HIM.
HEH... SYMBOL...
YOU'RE THE SYMBOL NOW.

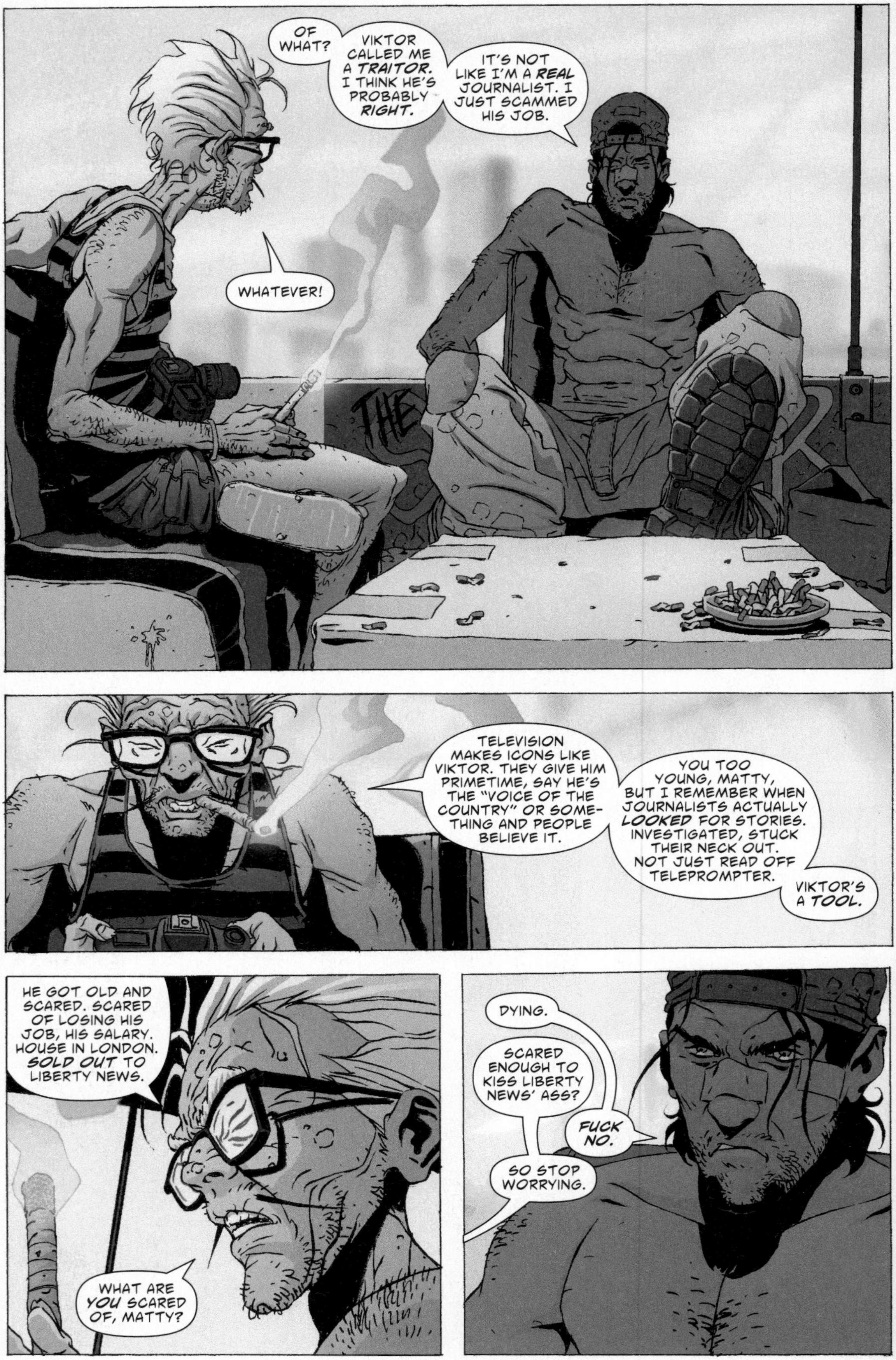
OF WHAT?
VIKTOR CALLED ME A TRAITOR. I THINK HE'S PROBABLY RIGHT.
IT'S NOT LIKE I'M A REAL JOURNALIST. I JUST SCAMMED HIS JOB.
WHATEVER!
THE
TELEVISION MAKES ICONS LIKE VIKTOR. THEY GIVE HIM PRIMETIME, SAY HE'S THE "VOICE OF THE COUNTRY" OR SOMETHING AND PEOPLE BELIEVE IT.
YOU TOO YOUNG, MATTY, BUT I REMEMBER WHEN JOURNALISTS ACTUALLY LOOKED FOR STORIES. INVESTIGATED, STUCK THEIR NECK OUT. NOT JUST READ OFF TELEPROMPTER.
VIKTOR'S A TOOL.
HE GOT OLD AND SCARED. SCARED OF LOSING HIS JOB, HIS SALARY. HOUSE IN LONDON. SOLD OUT TO LIBERTY NEWS.
WHAT ARE YOU SCARED OF, MATTY?
DYING.
SCARED ENOUGH TO KISS LIBERTY NEWS' ASS?
FUCK NO.
SO STOP WORRYING.

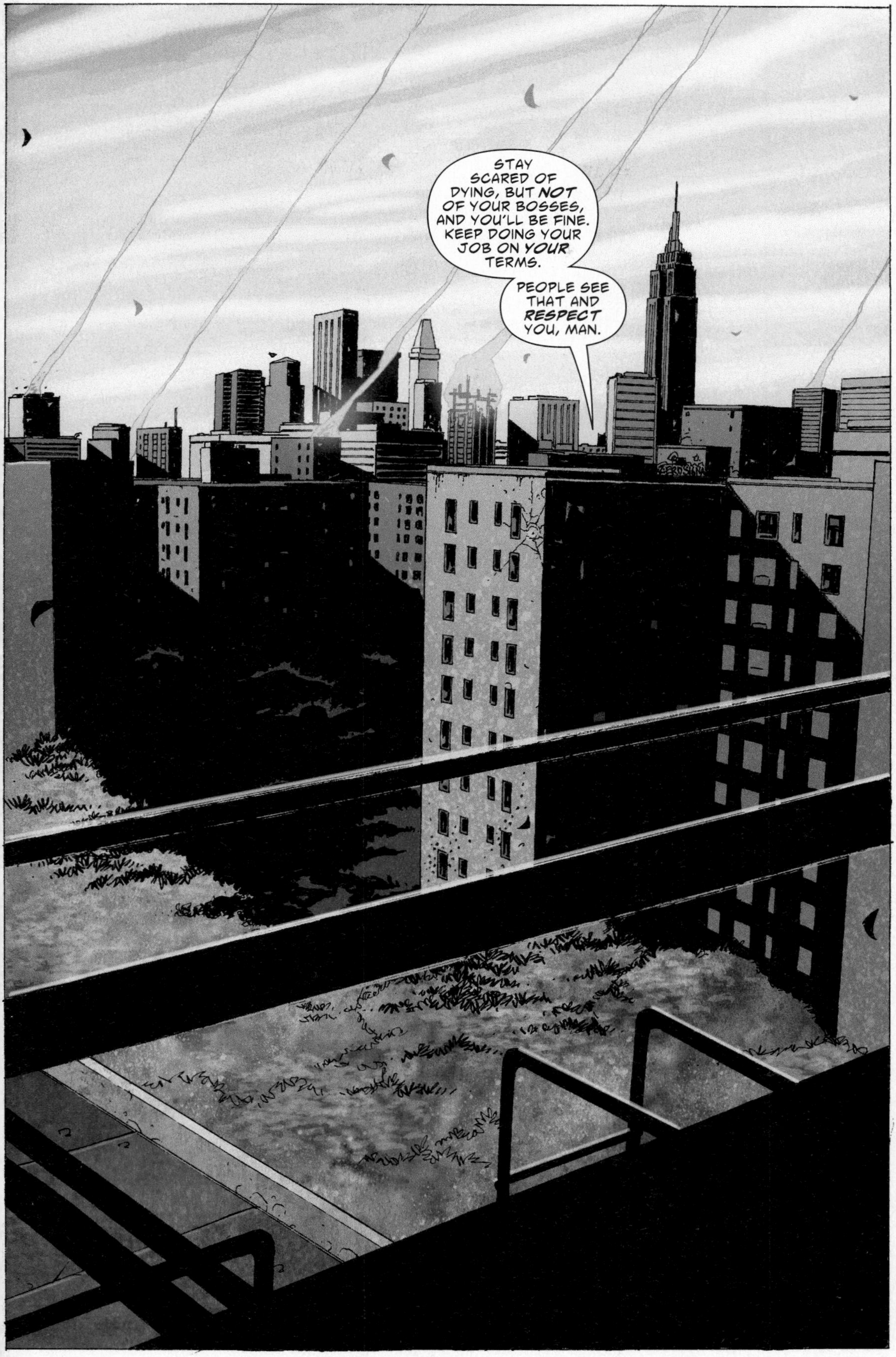
STAY SCARED OF DYING, BUT NOT OF YOUR BOSSES, AND YOU'LL BE FINE. KEEP DOING YOUR JOB ON YOUR TERMS.
PEOPLE SEE THAT AND RESPECT YOU, MAN.

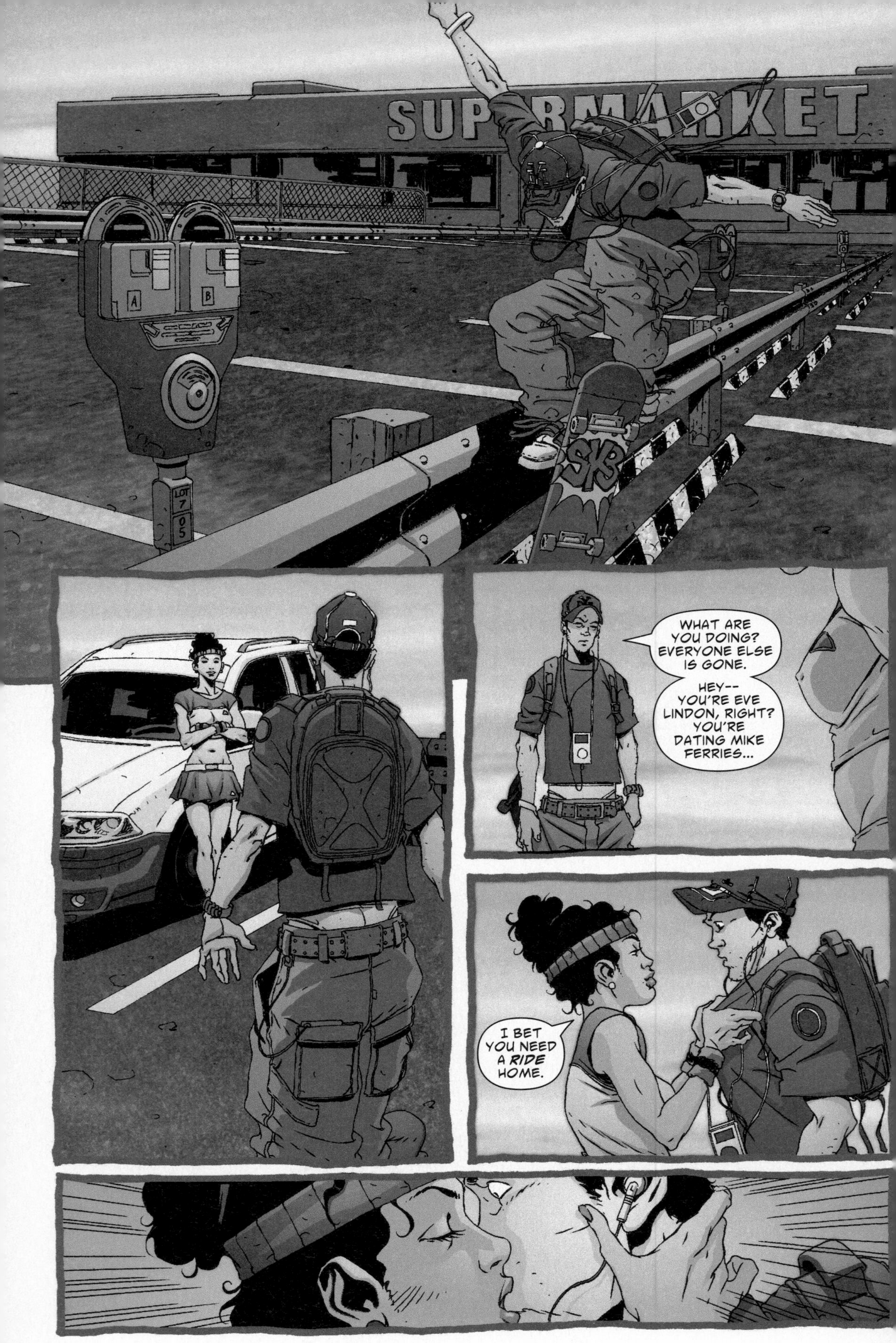
SUPERMARKET
A
B
LOT 7 05
WHAT ARE YOU DOING? EVERYONE ELSE IS GONE.
HEY-- YOU'RE EVE LINDON, RIGHT? YOU'RE DATING MIKE FERRIES...
I BET YOU NEED A *RIDE* HOME.

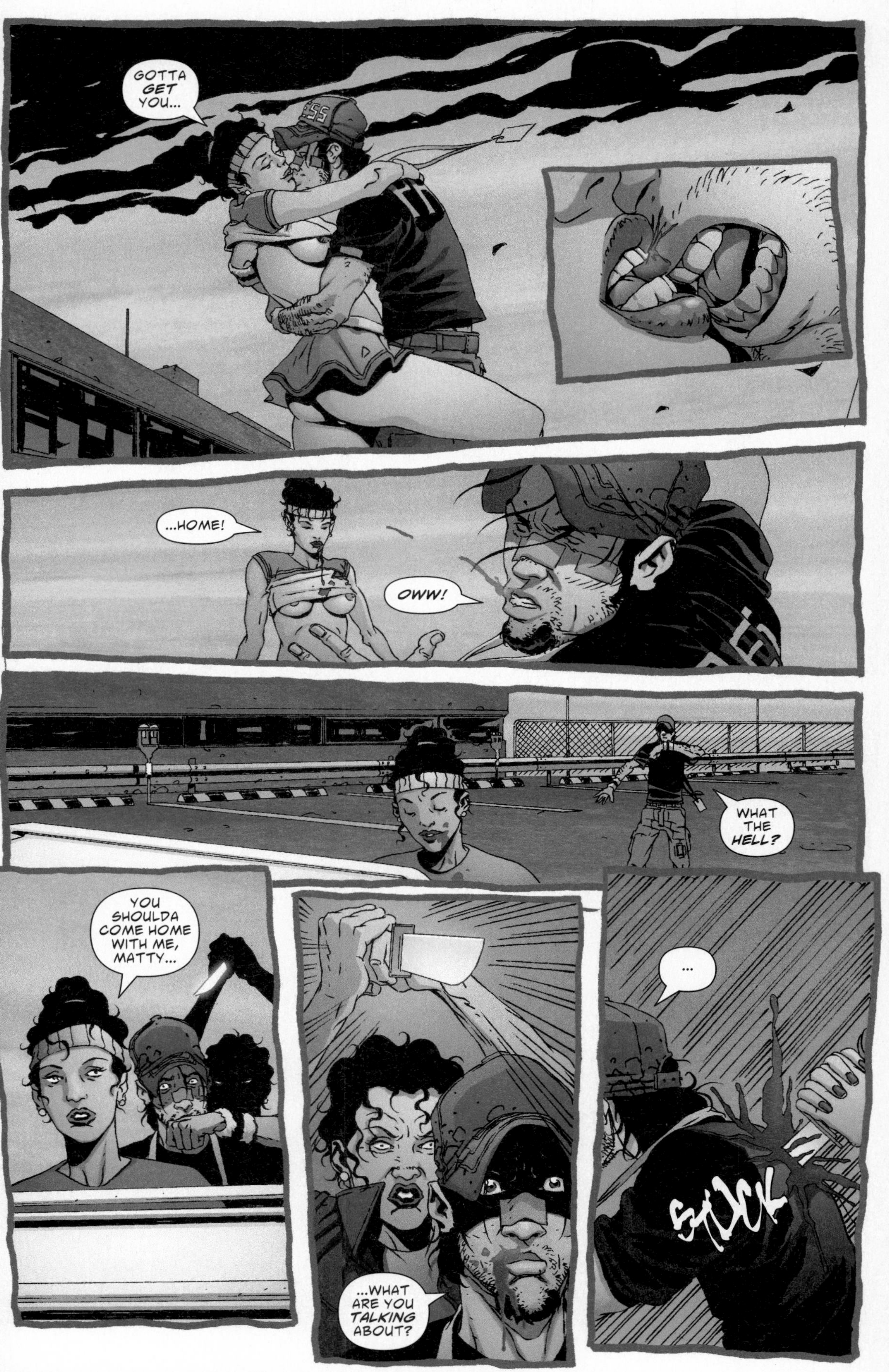
GOTTA GET YOU...
...HOME!
OWW!
WHAT THE HELL?
YOU SHOULDA COME HOME WITH ME, MATTY...
...WHAT ARE YOU TALKING ABOUT?
...
SHUCK

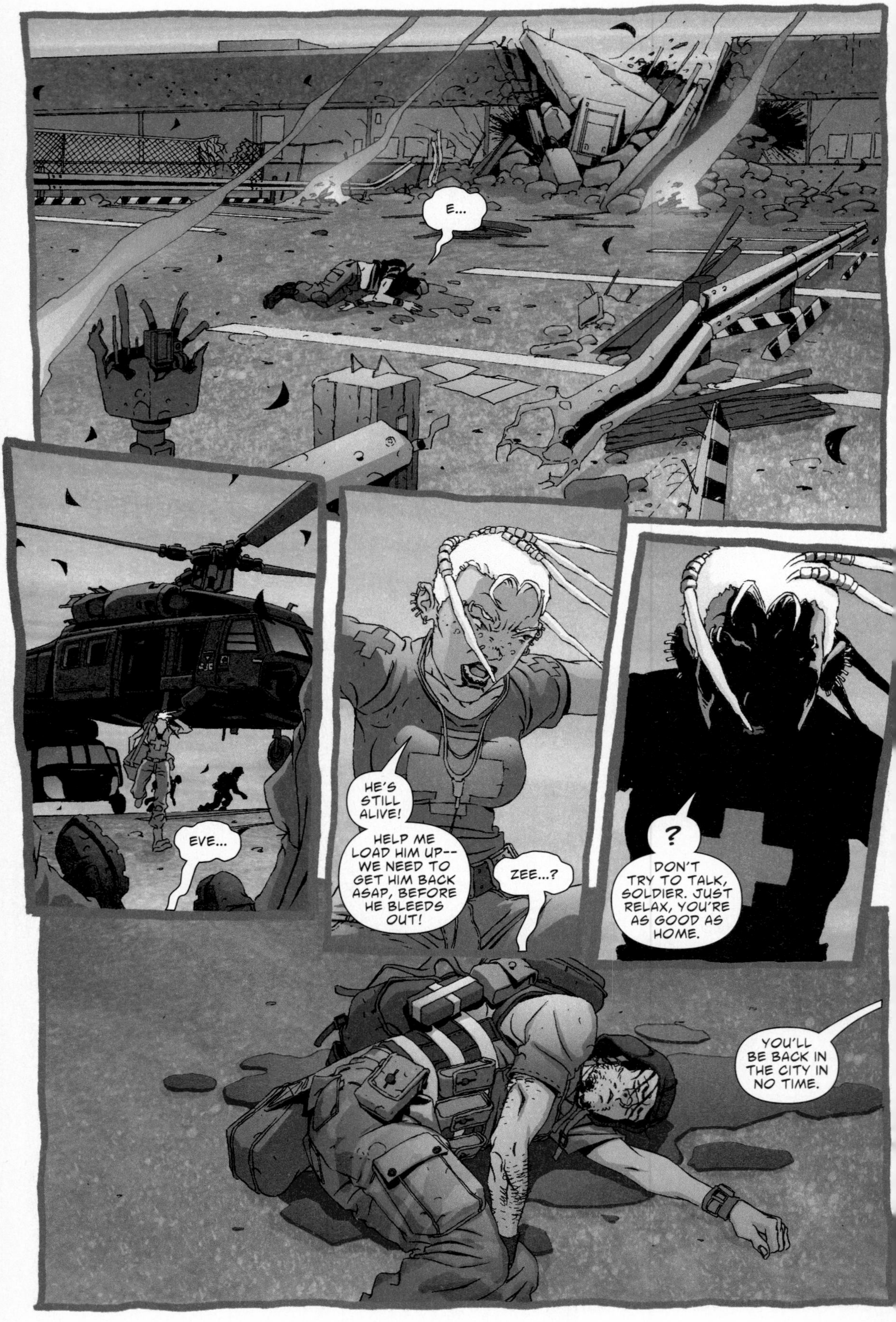
E...
EVE...
HE'S STILL ALIVE!
HELP ME LOAD HIM UP-- WE NEED TO GET HIM BACK ASAP, BEFORE HE BLEEDS OUT!
ZEE...?
?
DON'T TRY TO TALK, SOLDIER. JUST RELAX, YOU'RE AS GOOD AS HOME.
YOU'LL BE BACK IN THE CITY IN NO TIME.

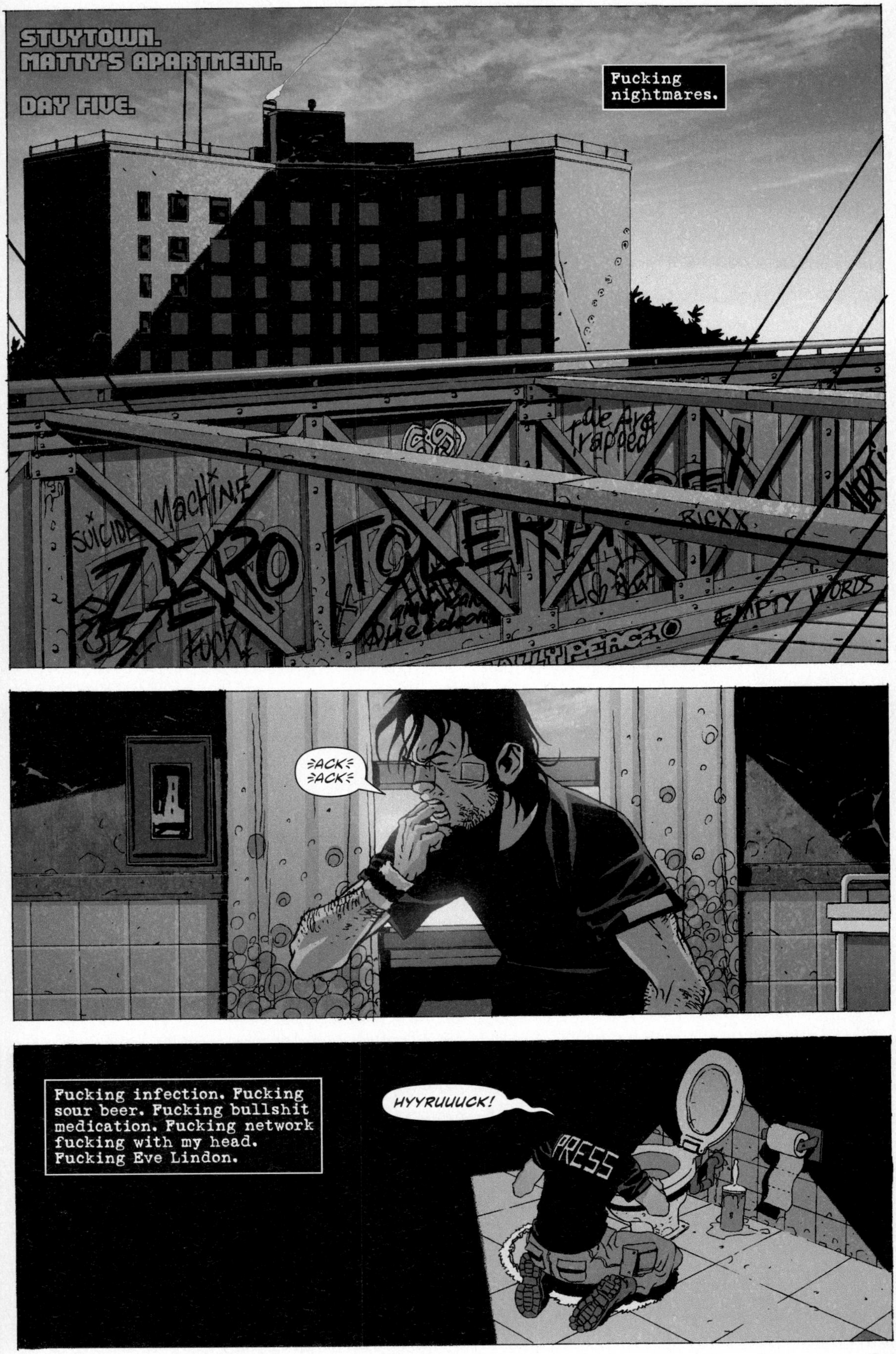
STUYTOWN.
MATTY'S APARTMENT.
DAY FIVE.
Fucking nightmares.
ACK ACK
Fucking infection. Fucking sour beer. Fucking bullshit medication. Fucking network fucking with my head. Fucking Eve Lindon.
HYYRUUUCK!
PRESS

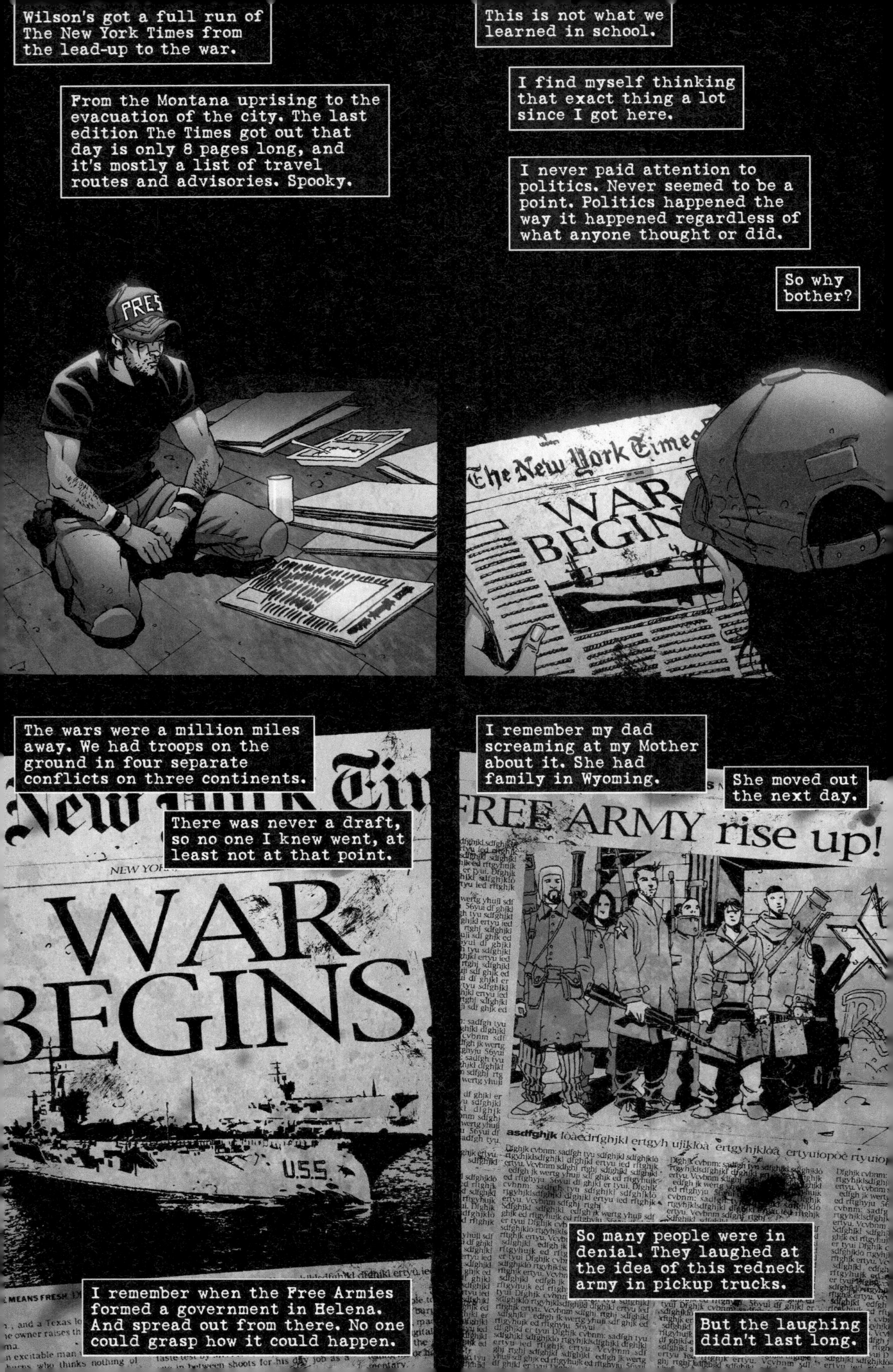

Wilson's got a full run of The New York Times from the lead-up to the war.
From the Montana uprising to the evacuation of the city. The last edition The Times got out that day is only 8 pages long, and it's mostly a list of travel routes and advisories. Spooky.
PRES
This is not what we learned in school.
I find myself thinking that exact thing a lot since I got here.
I never paid attention to politics. Never seemed to be a point. Politics happened the way it happened regardless of what anyone thought or did.
So why bother?
The New York Times
WAR BEGINS
The wars were a million miles away. We had troops on the ground in four separate conflicts on three continents.
There was never a draft, so no one I knew went, at least not at that point.
WAR BEGINS
U.S.S
I remember when the Free Armies formed a government in Helena. And spread out from there. No one could grasp how it could happen.
I remember my dad screaming at my Mother about it. She had family in Wyoming.
She moved out the next day.
FREE ARMY rise up!
So many people were in denial. They laughed at the idea of this redneck army in pickup trucks.
But the laughing didn't last long.

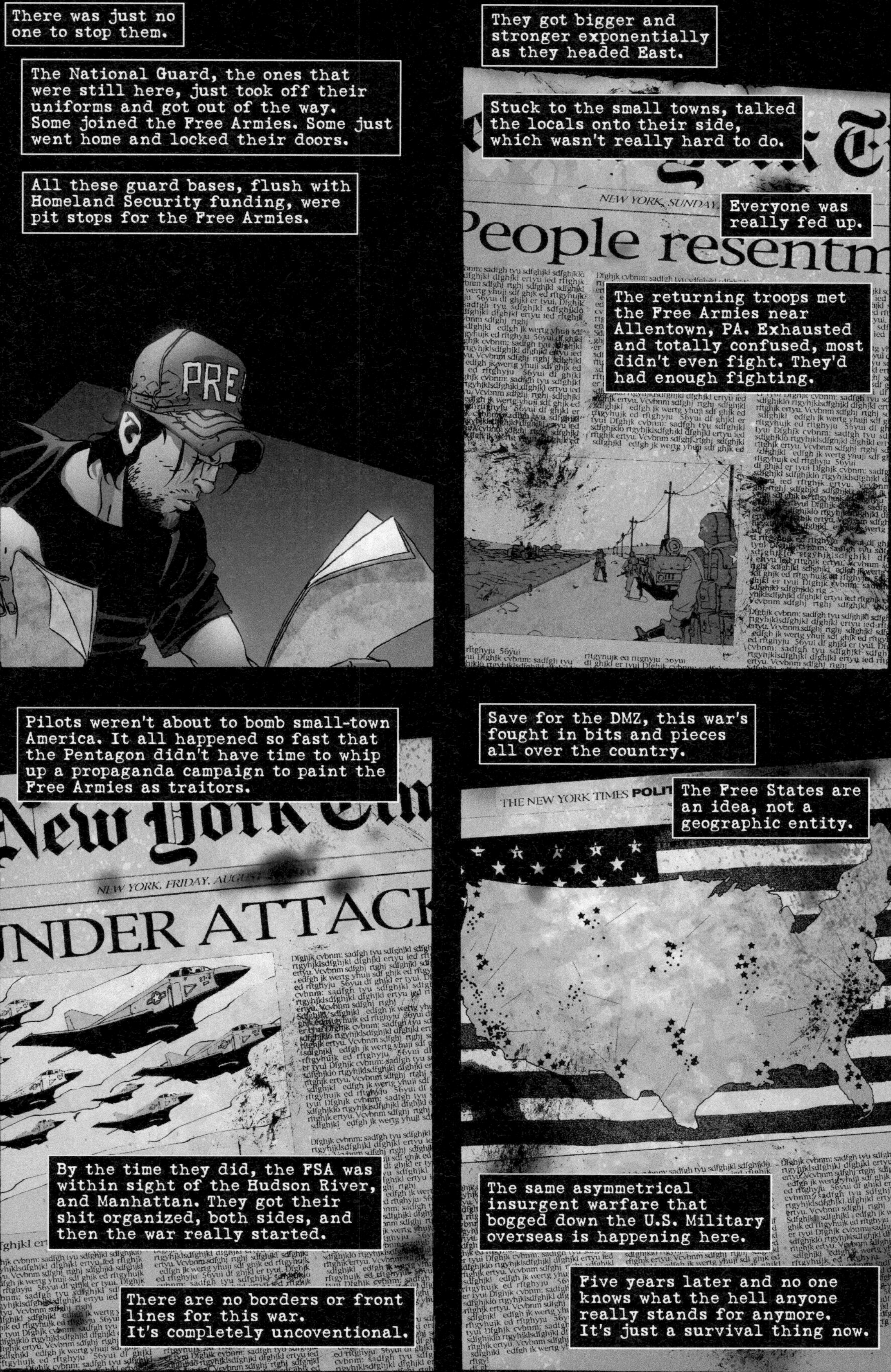
There was just no one to stop them.
The National Guard, the ones that were still here, just took off their uniforms and got out of the way. Some joined the Free Armies. Some just went home and locked their doors.
All these guard bases, flush with Homeland Security funding, were pit stops for the Free Armies.
PRE
They got bigger and stronger exponentially as they headed East.
Stuck to the small towns, talked the locals onto their side, which wasn't really hard to do.
NEW YORK, SUNDAY,
Everyone was really fed up.
People resentm
The returning troops met the Free Armies near Allentown, PA. Exhausted and totally confused, most didn't even fight. They'd had enough fighting.
Pilots weren't about to bomb small-town America. It all happened so fast that the Pentagon didn't have time to whip up a propaganda campaign to paint the Free Armies as traitors.
New York Tim
NEW YORK, FRIDAY, AUGU
UNDER ATTACK
By the time they did, the FSA was within sight of the Hudson River, and Manhattan. They got their shit organized, both sides, and then the war really started.
There are no borders or front lines for this war.
It's completely uncoventional.
Save for the DMZ, this war's fought in bits and pieces all over the country.
THE NEW YORK TIMES POLIT
The Free States are an idea, not a geographic entity.
The same asymmetrical insurgent warfare that bogged down the U.S. Military overseas is happening here.
Five years later and no one knows what the hell anyone really stands for anymore. It's just a survival thing now.

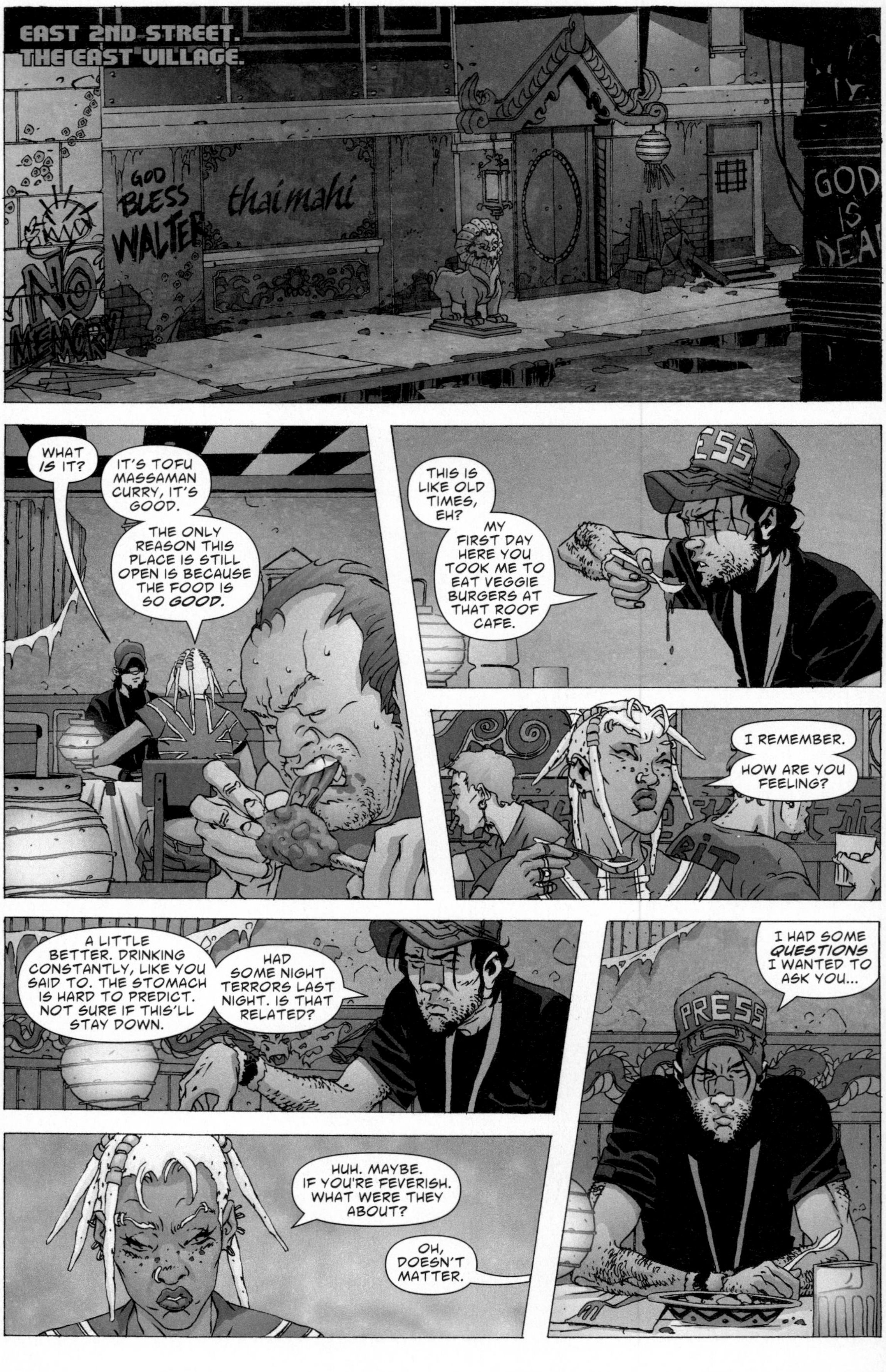
EAST 2ND STREET. THE EAST VILLAGE.
GOD BLESS WALTER
thaimahi
GOD IS DEAD
NO MEMORY
WHAT IS IT?
IT'S TOFU MASSAMAN CURRY, IT'S GOOD.
THE ONLY REASON THIS PLACE IS STILL OPEN IS BECAUSE THE FOOD IS SO GOOD.
THIS IS LIKE OLD TIMES, EH?
MY FIRST DAY HERE YOU TOOK ME TO EAT VEGGIE BURGERS AT THAT ROOF CAFE.
I REMEMBER.
HOW ARE YOU FEELING?
A LITTLE BETTER. DRINKING CONSTANTLY, LIKE YOU SAID TO. THE STOMACH IS HARD TO PREDICT. NOT SURE IF THIS'LL STAY DOWN.
HAD SOME NIGHT TERRORS LAST NIGHT. IS THAT RELATED?
I HAD SOME QUESTIONS I WANTED TO ASK YOU...
PRESS
HUH. MAYBE. IF YOU'RE FEVERISH. WHAT WERE THEY ABOUT?
OH, DOESN'T MATTER.

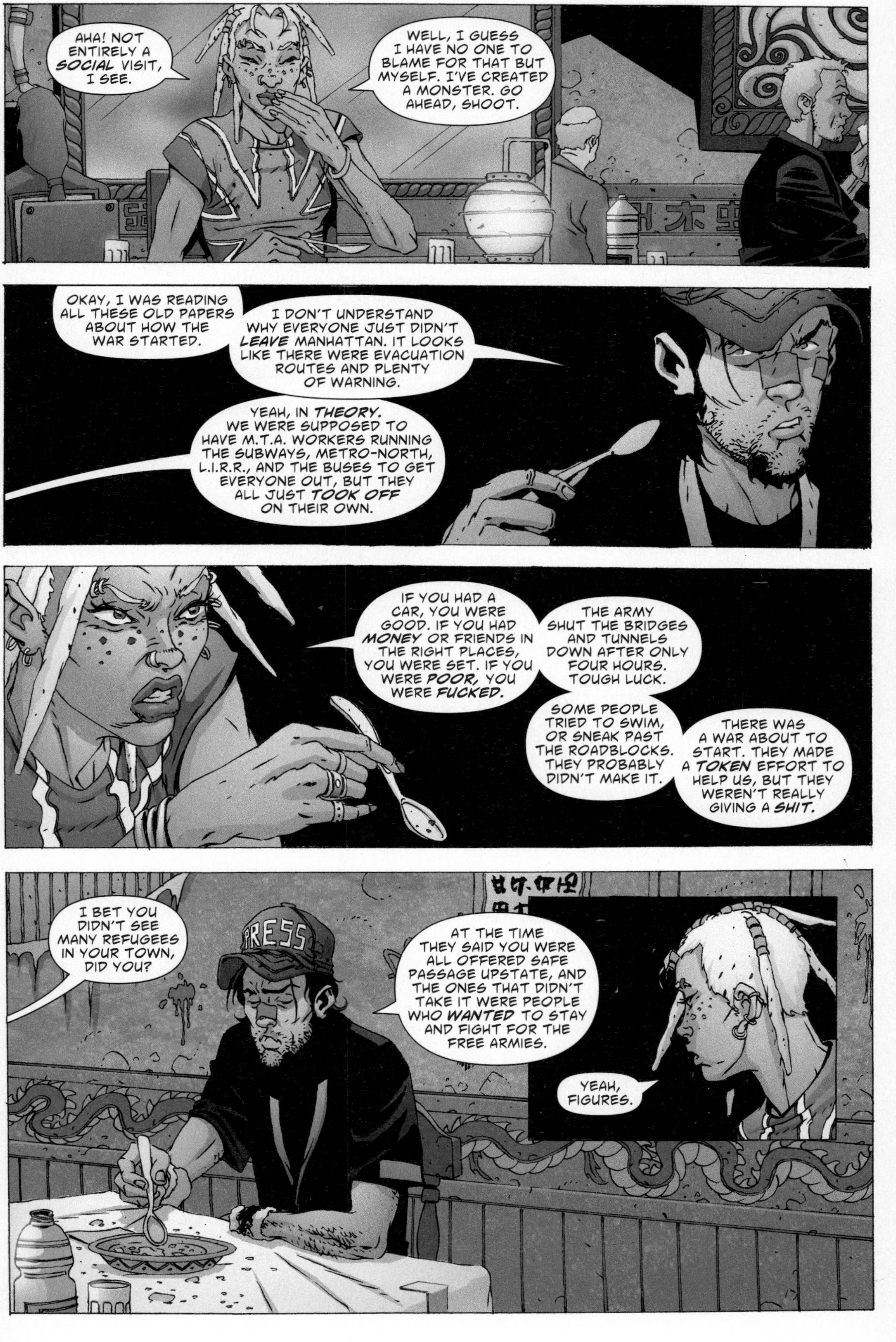
AHA! NOT ENTIRELY A *SOCIAL* VISIT, I SEE.
WELL, I GUESS I HAVE NO ONE TO BLAME FOR THAT BUT MYSELF. I'VE CREATED A MONSTER. GO AHEAD, SHOOT.
OKAY, I WAS READING ALL THESE OLD PAPERS ABOUT HOW THE WAR STARTED.
I DON'T UNDERSTAND WHY EVERYONE JUST DIDN'T *LEAVE* MANHATTAN. IT LOOKS LIKE THERE WERE EVACUATION ROUTES AND PLENTY OF WARNING.
YEAH, IN *THEORY.* WE WERE SUPPOSED TO HAVE M.T.A. WORKERS RUNNING THE SUBWAYS, METRO-NORTH, L.I.R.R., AND THE BUSES TO GET EVERYONE OUT, BUT THEY ALL JUST *TOOK OFF* ON THEIR OWN.
IF YOU HAD A CAR, YOU WERE GOOD. IF YOU HAD *MONEY* OR FRIENDS IN THE RIGHT PLACES, YOU WERE SET. IF YOU WERE *POOR,* YOU WERE *FUCKED.*
THE ARMY SHUT THE BRIDGES AND TUNNELS DOWN AFTER ONLY FOUR HOURS. TOUGH LUCK.
SOME PEOPLE TRIED TO SWIM, OR SNEAK PAST THE ROADBLOCKS. THEY PROBABLY DIDN'T MAKE IT.
THERE WAS A WAR ABOUT TO START. THEY MADE A *TOKEN* EFFORT TO HELP US, BUT THEY WEREN'T REALLY GIVING A *SHIT.*
I BET YOU DIDN'T SEE MANY REFUGEES IN YOUR TOWN, DID YOU?
PRESS
AT THE TIME THEY SAID YOU WERE ALL OFFERED SAFE PASSAGE UPSTATE, AND THE ONES THAT DIDN'T TAKE IT WERE PEOPLE WHO *WANTED* TO STAY AND FIGHT FOR THE FREE ARMIES.
YEAH, FIGURES.

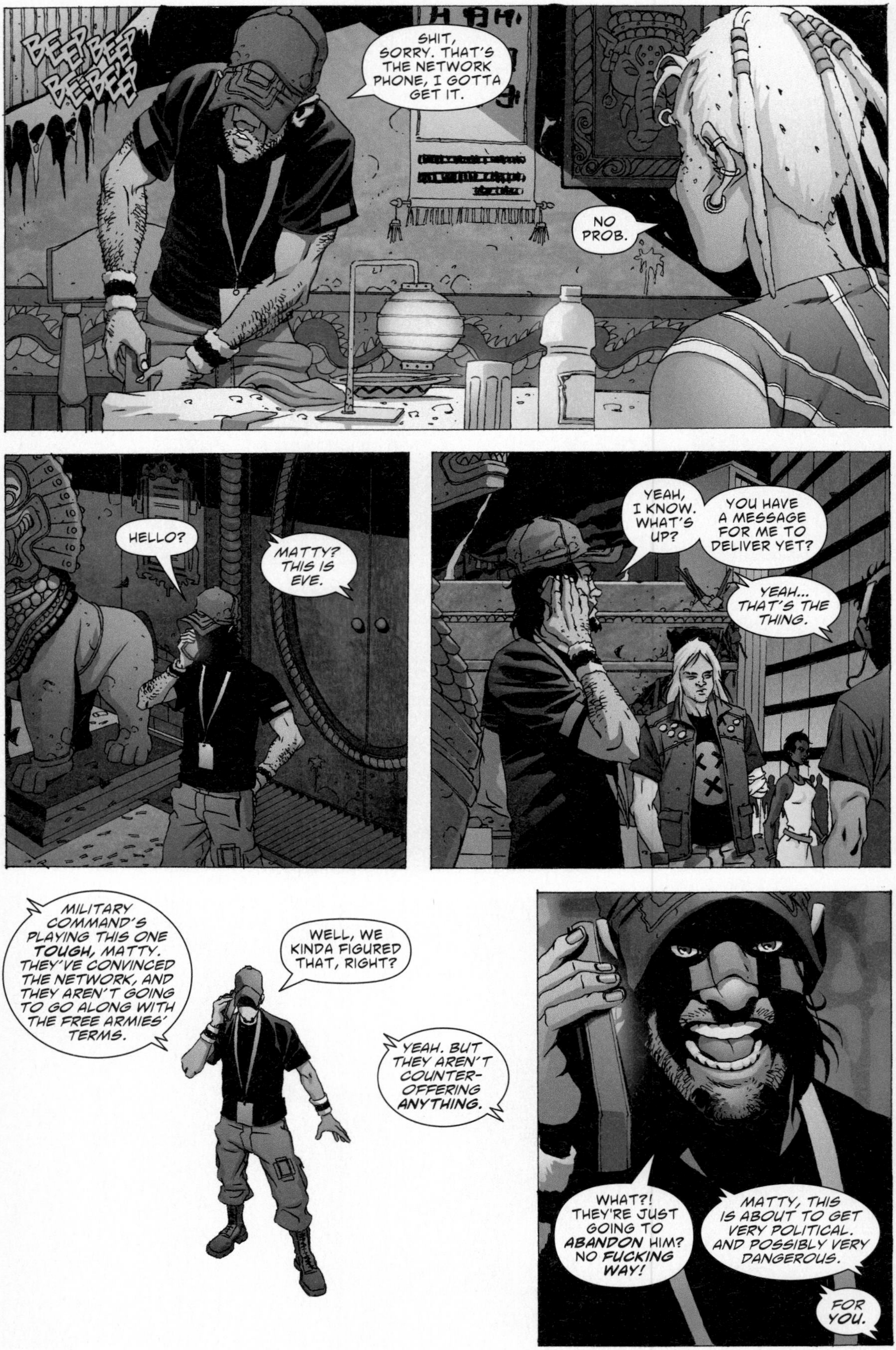
BEEP BEEP BE-BEEP
SHIT, SORRY. THAT'S THE NETWORK PHONE, I GOTTA GET IT.
NO PROB.
HELLO?
MATTY? THIS IS EVE.
YEAH, I KNOW. WHAT'S UP?
YOU HAVE A MESSAGE FOR ME TO DELIVER YET?
YEAH... THAT'S THE THING.
MILITARY COMMAND'S PLAYING THIS ONE TOUGH, MATTY. THEY'VE CONVINCED THE NETWORK, AND THEY AREN'T GOING TO GO ALONG WITH THE FREE ARMIES' TERMS.
WELL, WE KINDA FIGURED THAT, RIGHT?
YEAH. BUT THEY AREN'T COUNTER-OFFERING ANYTHING.
WHAT?! THEY'RE JUST GOING TO ABANDON HIM? NO FUCKING WAY!
MATTY, THIS IS ABOUT TO GET VERY POLITICAL. AND POSSIBLY VERY DANGEROUS.
FOR YOU.

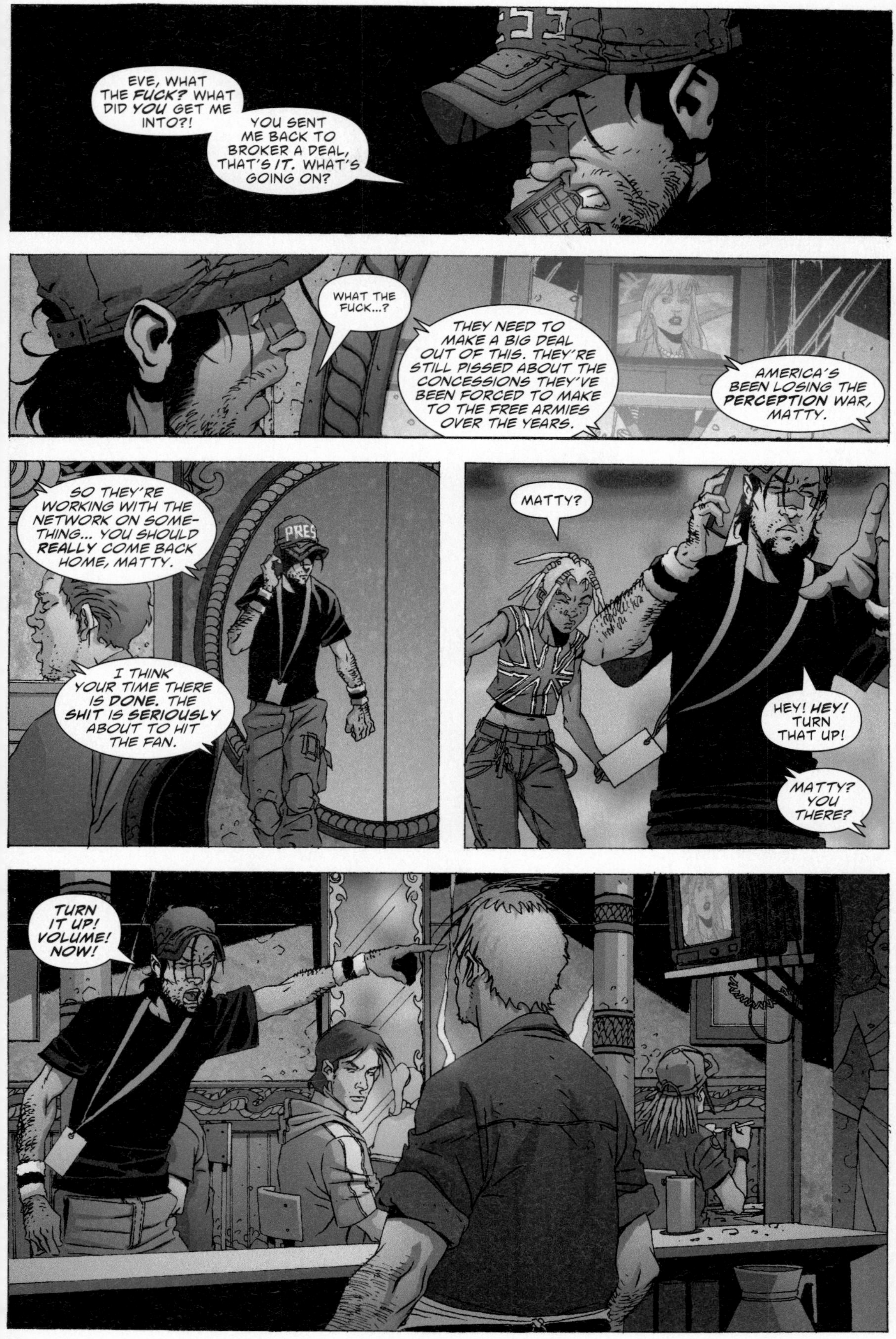

EVE, WHAT THE FUCK? WHAT DID YOU GET ME INTO?!
YOU SENT ME BACK TO BROKER A DEAL, THAT'S IT. WHAT'S GOING ON?
WHAT THE FUCK...?
THEY NEED TO MAKE A BIG DEAL OUT OF THIS. THEY'RE STILL PISSED ABOUT THE CONCESSIONS THEY'VE BEEN FORCED TO MAKE TO THE FREE ARMIES OVER THE YEARS.
AMERICA'S BEEN LOSING THE PERCEPTION WAR, MATTY.
SO THEY'RE WORKING WITH THE NETWORK ON SOME-THING... YOU SHOULD REALLY COME BACK HOME, MATTY.
I THINK YOUR TIME THERE IS DONE. THE SHIT IS SERIOUSLY ABOUT TO HIT THE FAN.
MATTY?
HEY! HEY! TURN THAT UP!
MATTY? YOU THERE?
TURN IT UP! VOLUME! NOW!

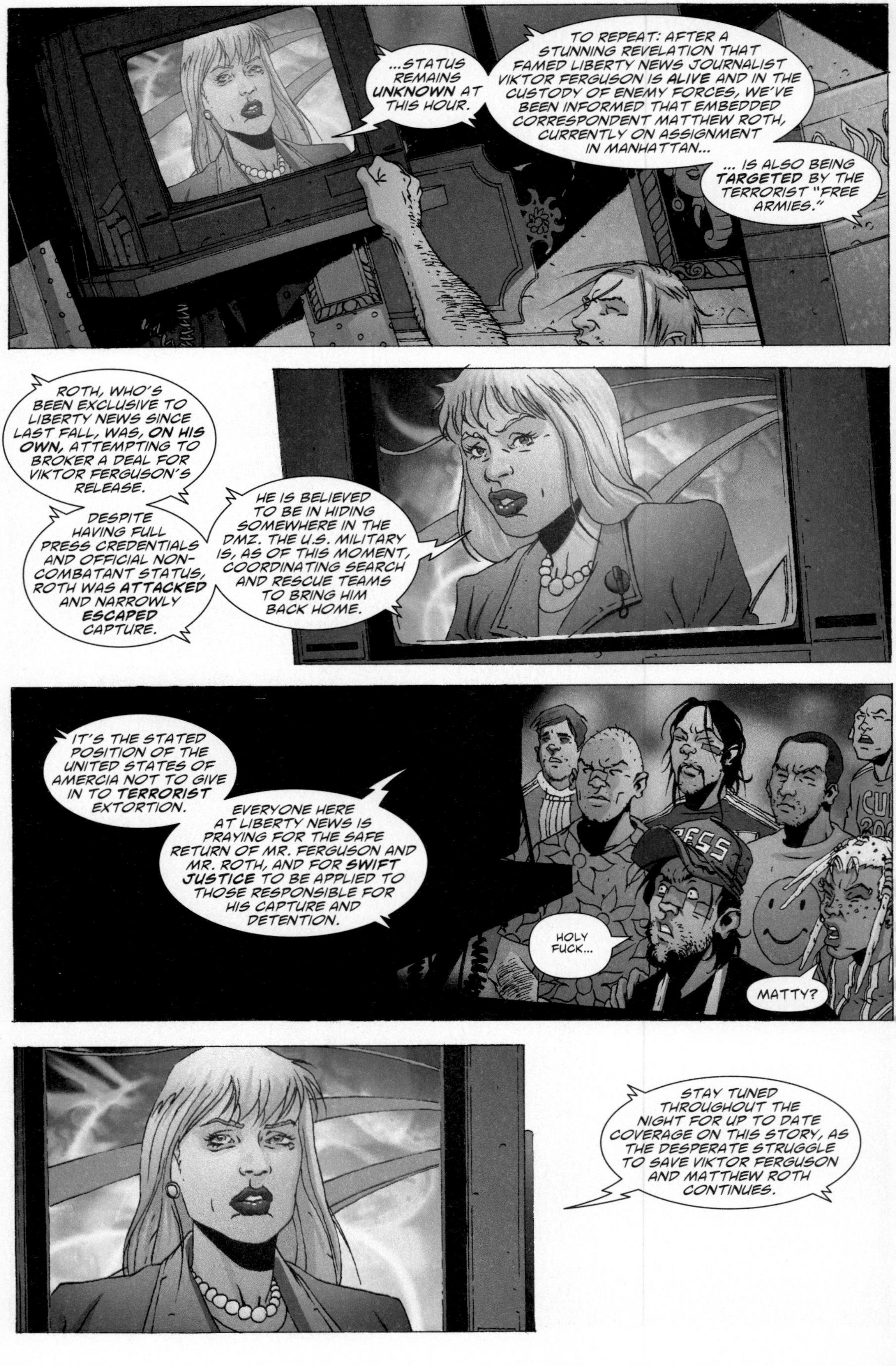
...STATUS REMAINS UNKNOWN AT THIS HOUR.
TO REPEAT: AFTER A STUNNING REVELATION THAT FAMED LIBERTY NEWS JOURNALIST VIKTOR FERGUSON IS ALIVE AND IN THE CUSTODY OF ENEMY FORCES, WE'VE BEEN INFORMED THAT EMBEDDED CORRESPONDENT MATTHEW ROTH, CURRENTLY ON ASSIGNMENT IN MANHATTAN...
... IS ALSO BEING TARGETED BY THE TERRORIST "FREE ARMIES."
ROTH, WHO'S BEEN EXCLUSIVE TO LIBERTY NEWS SINCE LAST FALL, WAS, ON HIS OWN, ATTEMPTING TO BROKER A DEAL FOR VIKTOR FERGUSON'S RELEASE.
DESPITE HAVING FULL PRESS CREDENTIALS AND OFFICIAL NON-COMBATANT STATUS, ROTH WAS ATTACKED AND NARROWLY ESCAPED CAPTURE.
HE IS BELIEVED TO BE IN HIDING SOMEWHERE IN THE DMZ. THE U.S. MILITARY IS, AS OF THIS MOMENT, COORDINATING SEARCH AND RESCUE TEAMS TO BRING HIM BACK HOME.
IT'S THE STATED POSITION OF THE UNITED STATES OF AMERCIA NOT TO GIVE IN TO TERRORIST EXTORTION.
EVERYONE HERE AT LIBERTY NEWS IS PRAYING FOR THE SAFE RETURN OF MR. FERGUSON AND MR. ROTH, AND FOR SWIFT JUSTICE TO BE APPLIED TO THOSE RESPONSIBLE FOR HIS CAPTURE AND DETENTION.
HOLY FUCK...
MATTY?
STAY TUNED THROUGHOUT THE NIGHT FOR UP TO DATE COVERAGE ON THIS STORY, AS THE DESPERATE STRUGGLE TO SAVE VIKTOR FERGUSON AND MATTHEW ROTH CONTINUES.

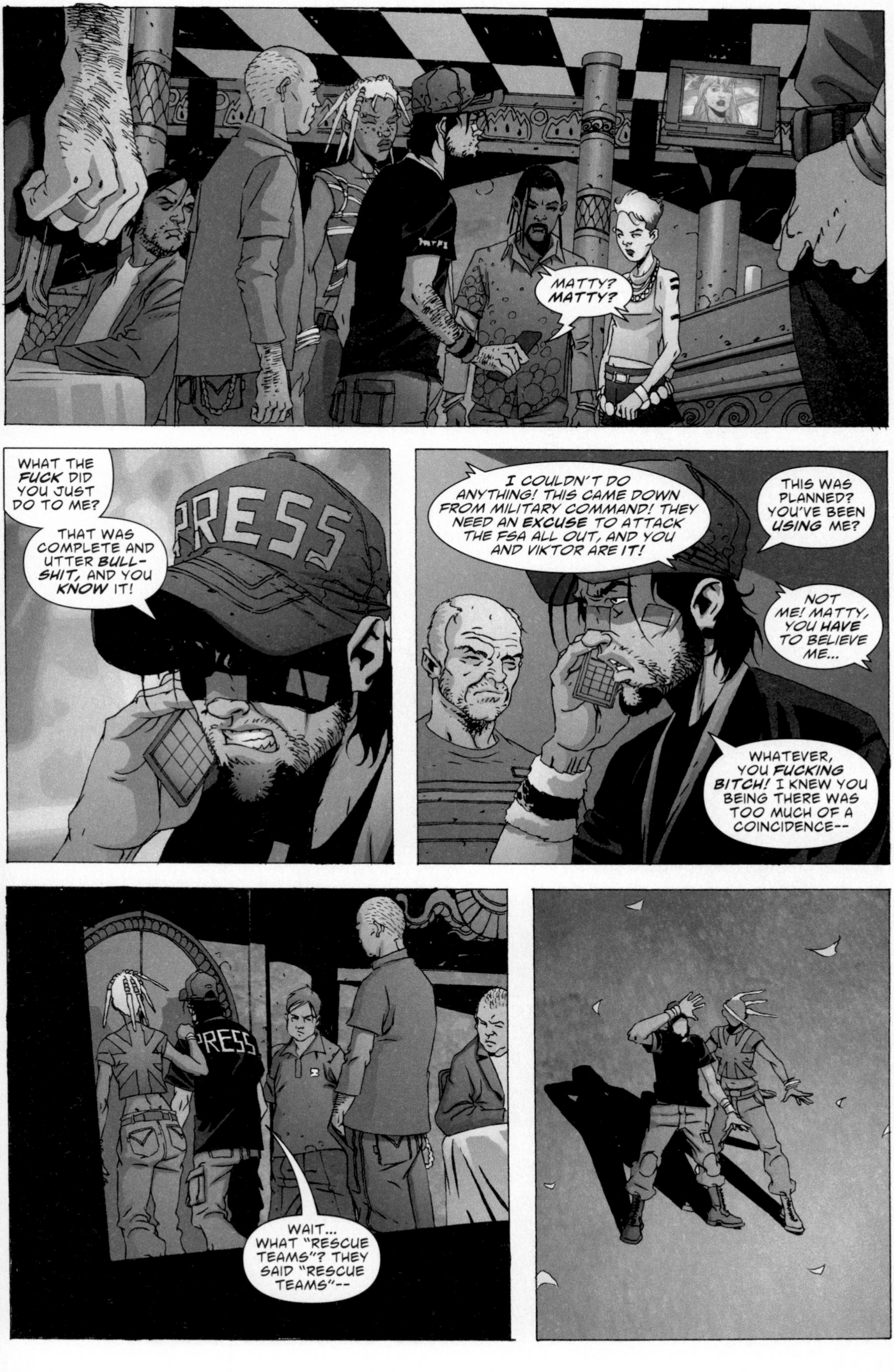
MATTY? MATTY?
WHAT THE FUCK DID YOU JUST DO TO ME?
THAT WAS COMPLETE AND UTTER BULL-SHIT, AND YOU KNOW IT!
I COULDN'T DO ANYTHING! THIS CAME DOWN FROM MILITARY COMMAND! THEY NEED AN EXCUSE TO ATTACK THE FSA ALL OUT, AND YOU AND VIKTOR ARE IT!
THIS WAS PLANNED? YOU'VE BEEN USING ME?
NOT ME! MATTY, YOU HAVE TO BELIEVE ME...
WHATEVER, YOU FUCKING BITCH! I KNEW YOU BEING THERE WAS TOO MUCH OF A COINCIDENCE--
PRESS
WAIT... WHAT "RESCUE TEAMS"? THEY SAID "RESCUE TEAMS"--

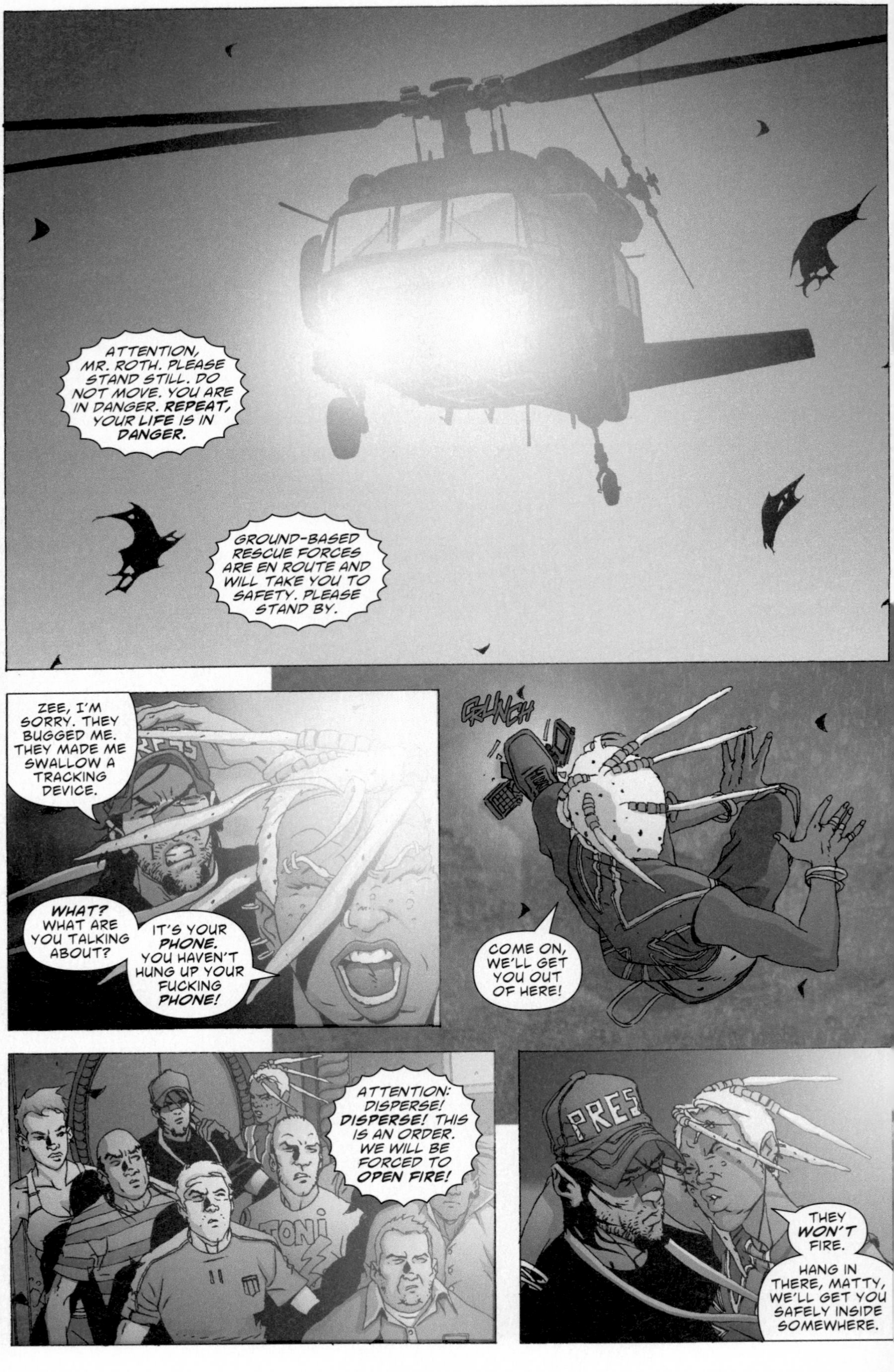
ATTENTION, MR. ROTH. PLEASE STAND STILL. DO NOT MOVE. YOU ARE IN DANGER. REPEAT, YOUR LIFE IS IN DANGER.
GROUND-BASED RESCUE FORCES ARE EN ROUTE AND WILL TAKE YOU TO SAFETY. PLEASE STAND BY.
ZEE, I'M SORRY. THEY BUGGED ME. THEY MADE ME SWALLOW A TRACKING DEVICE.
WHAT? WHAT ARE YOU TALKING ABOUT?
IT'S YOUR PHONE. YOU HAVEN'T HUNG UP YOUR FUCKING PHONE!
CRUNCH
COME ON, WE'LL GET YOU OUT OF HERE!
ATTENTION: DISPERSE! DISPERSE! THIS IS AN ORDER. WE WILL BE FORCED TO OPEN FIRE!
THEY WON'T FIRE.
HANG IN THERE, MATTY, WE'LL GET YOU SAFELY INSIDE SOMEWHERE.

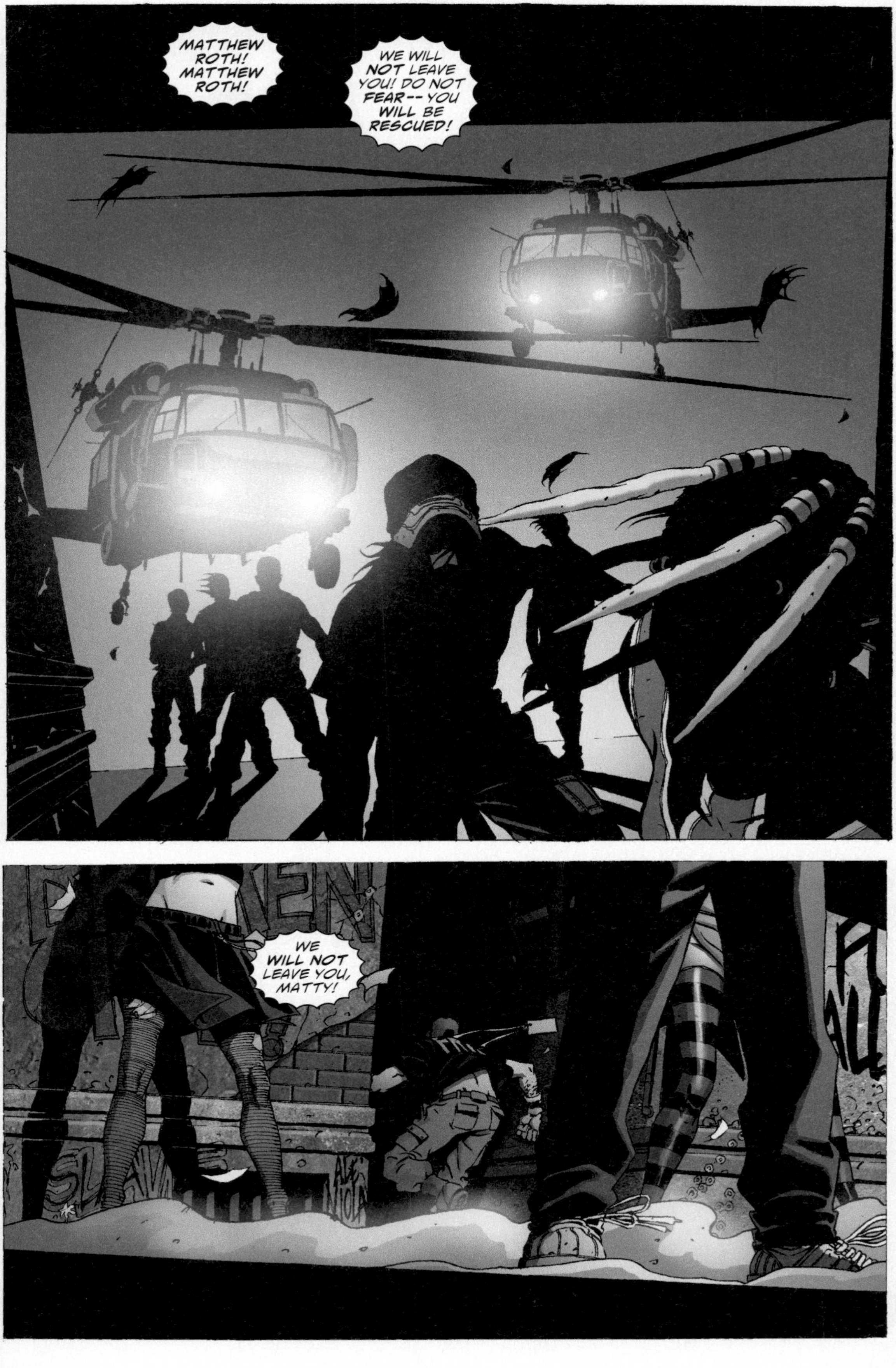
MATTHEW ROTH! MATTHEW ROTH!
WE WILL NOT LEAVE YOU! DO NOT FEAR-- YOU WILL BE RESCUED!
WE WILL NOT LEAVE YOU, MATTY!

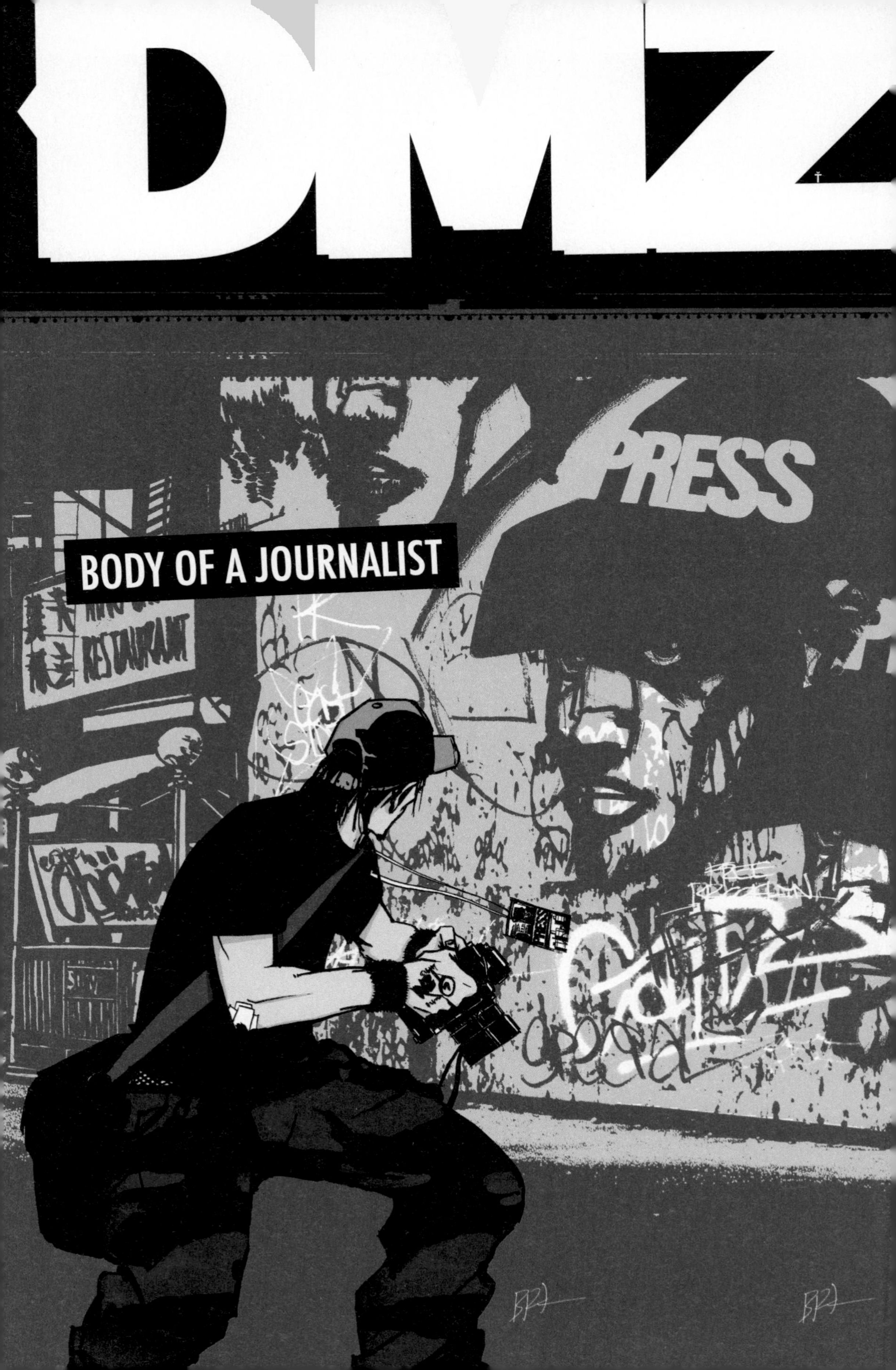
DMZ
BODY OF A JOURNALIST
PRESS
RESTAURANT

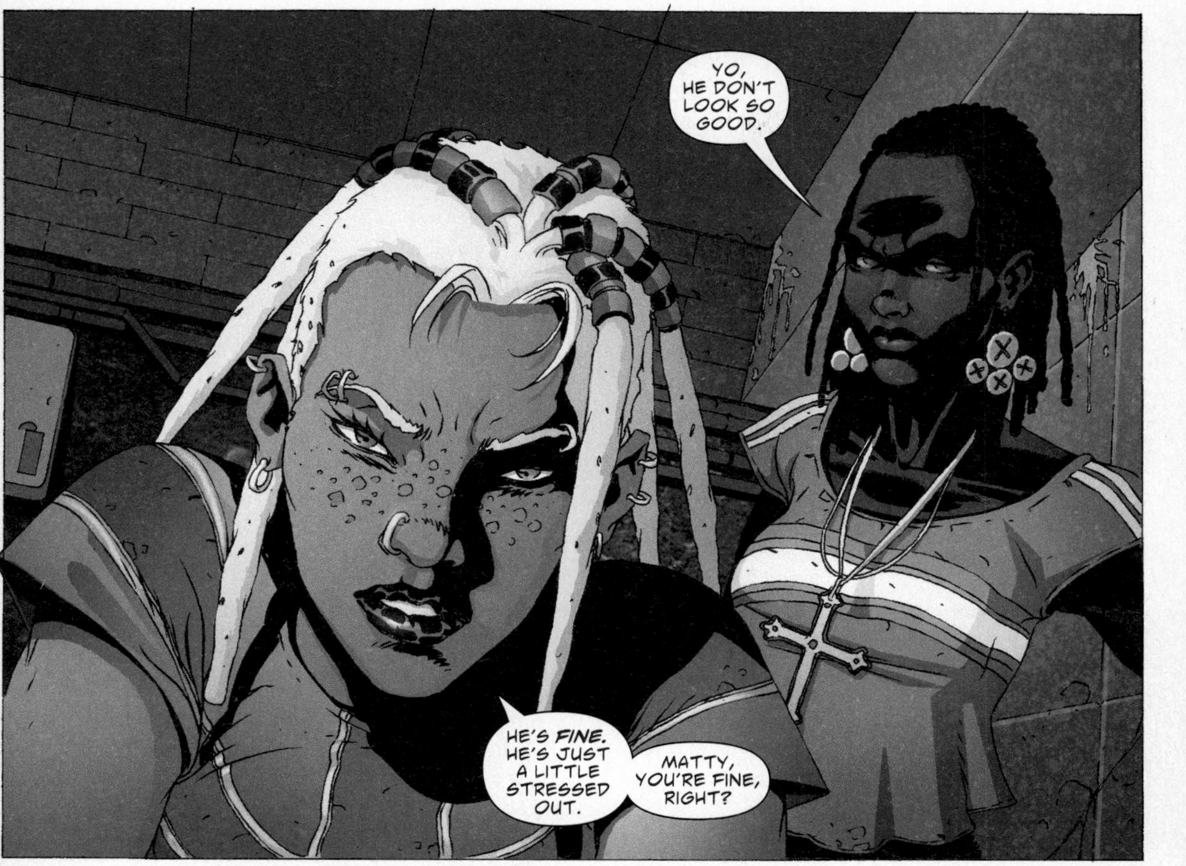
YO, HE DON'T LOOK SO GOOD.
HE'S *FINE*. HE'S JUST A LITTLE STRESSED OUT.
MATTY, YOU'RE FINE, RIGHT?

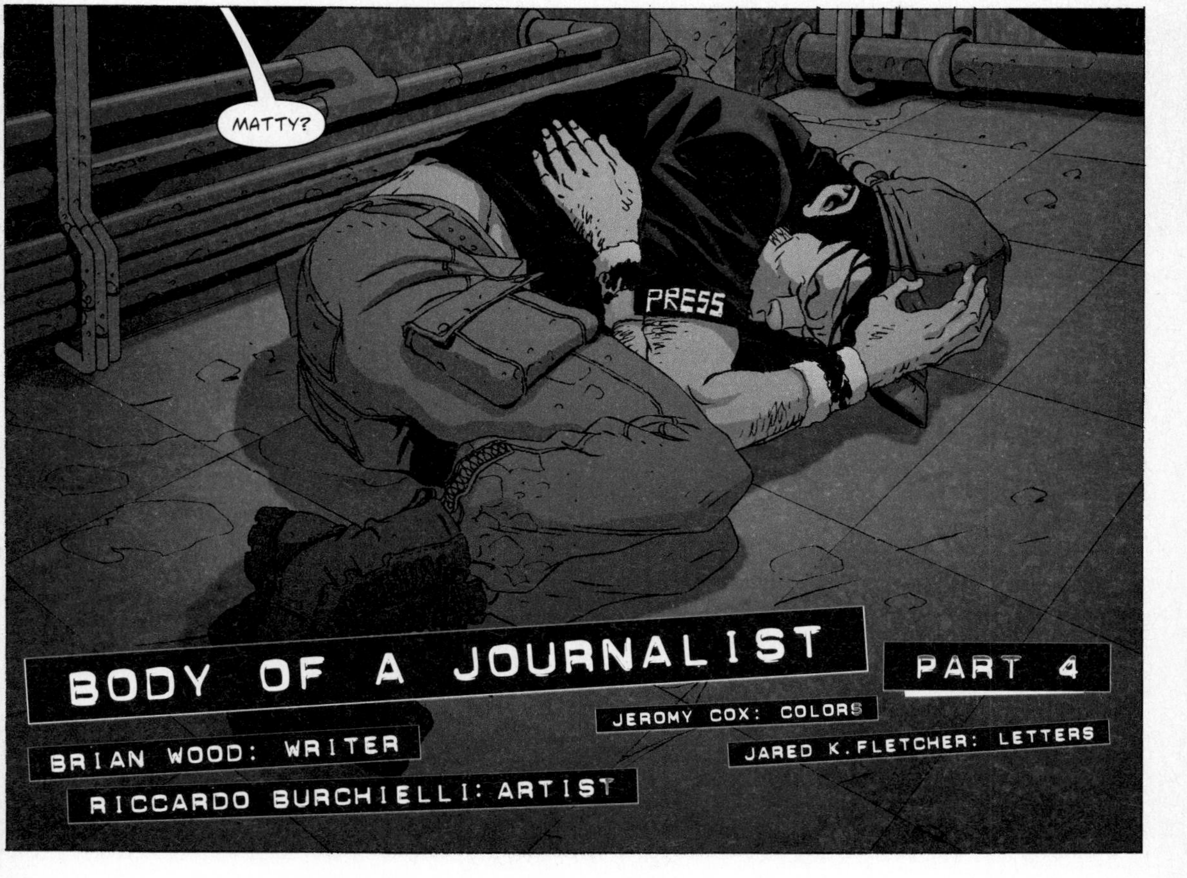
MATTY?
PRESS
BODY OF A JOURNALIST
PART 4
JEROMY COX: COLORS
BRIAN WOOD: WRITER
JARED K.FLETCHER: LETTERS
RICCARDO BURCHIELLI: ARTIST

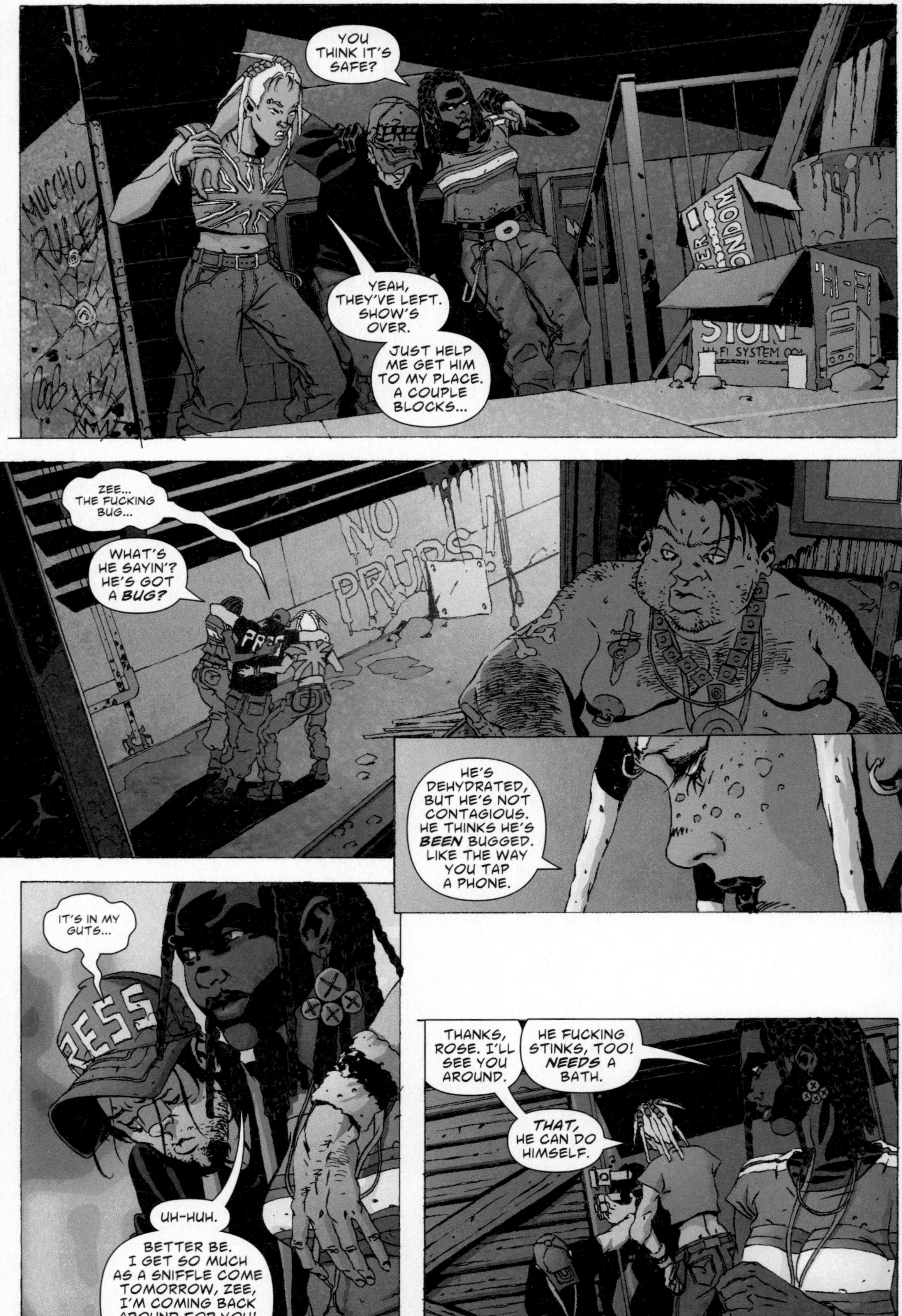
YOU THINK IT'S SAFE?
YEAH, THEY'VE LEFT. SHOW'S OVER.
JUST HELP ME GET HIM TO MY PLACE. A COUPLE BLOCKS...
MUCCHIO RULEZ
CONDOM
HI-FI
SION
HI-FI SYSTEM
ZEE... THE FUCKING BUG...
WHAT'S HE SAYIN'? HE'S GOT A *BUG?*
NO PRUPS
HE'S DEHYDRATED, BUT HE'S NOT CONTAGIOUS. HE THINKS HE'S *BEEN* BUGGED. LIKE THE WAY YOU TAP A PHONE.
IT'S IN MY GUTS...
RESS
UH-HUH.
BETTER BE. I GET SO MUCH AS A SNIFFLE COME TOMORROW, ZEE, I'M COMING BACK AROUND FOR YOU!
THANKS, ROSE. I'LL SEE YOU AROUND.
HE FUCKING STINKS, TOO! *NEEDS* A BATH.
THAT, HE CAN DO HIMSELF.

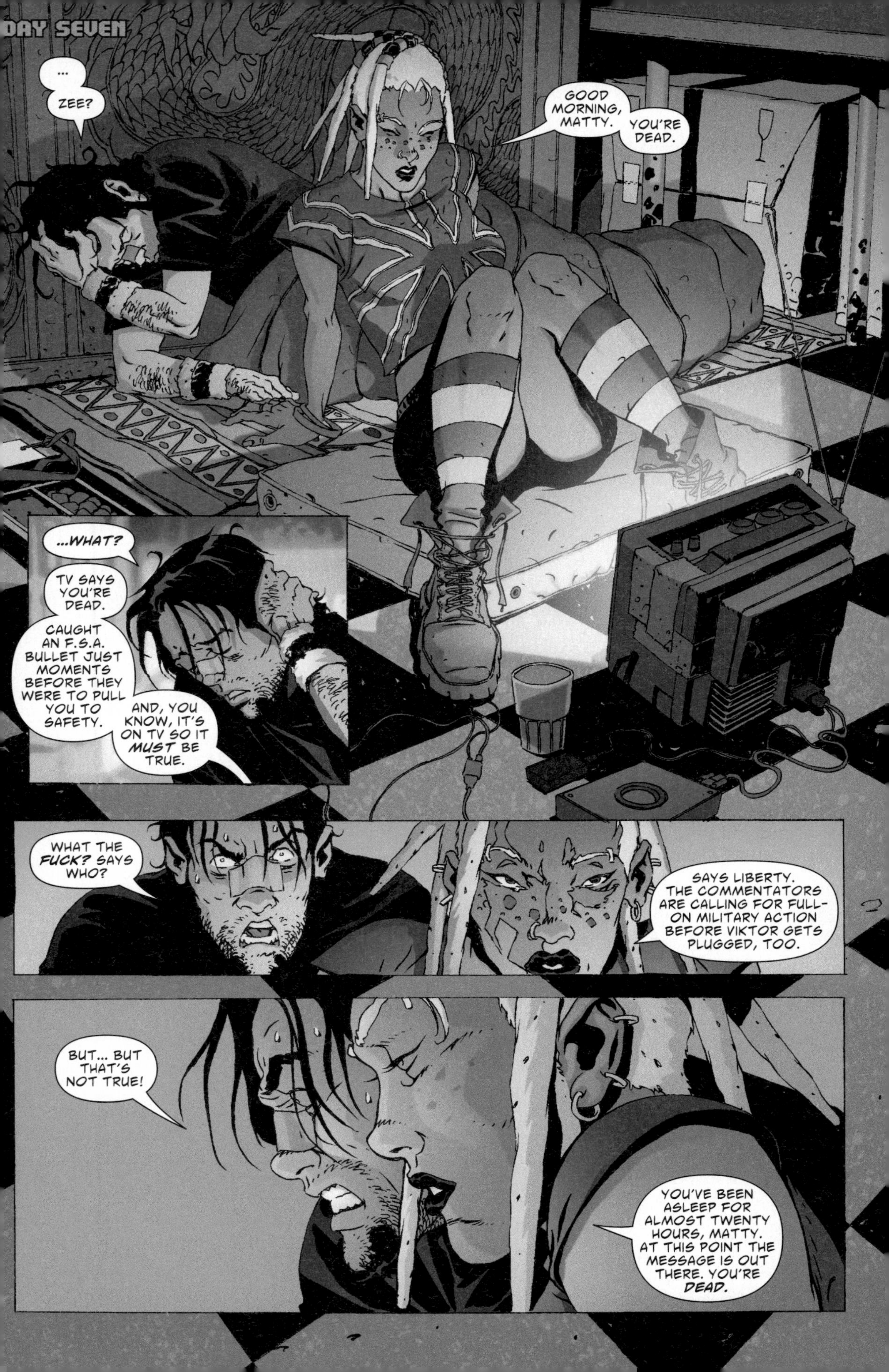
DAY SEVEN
... ZEE?
GOOD MORNING, MATTY.
YOU'RE DEAD.
...WHAT?
TV SAYS YOU'RE DEAD.
CAUGHT AN F.S.A. BULLET JUST MOMENTS BEFORE THEY WERE TO PULL YOU TO SAFETY.
AND, YOU KNOW, IT'S ON TV SO IT *MUST* BE TRUE.
WHAT THE *FUCK?* SAYS WHO?
SAYS LIBERTY. THE COMMENTATORS ARE CALLING FOR FULL-ON MILITARY ACTION BEFORE VIKTOR GETS PLUGGED, TOO.
BUT... BUT THAT'S NOT TRUE!
YOU'VE BEEN ASLEEP FOR ALMOST TWENTY HOURS, MATTY. AT THIS POINT THE MESSAGE IS OUT THERE. YOU'RE *DEAD.*

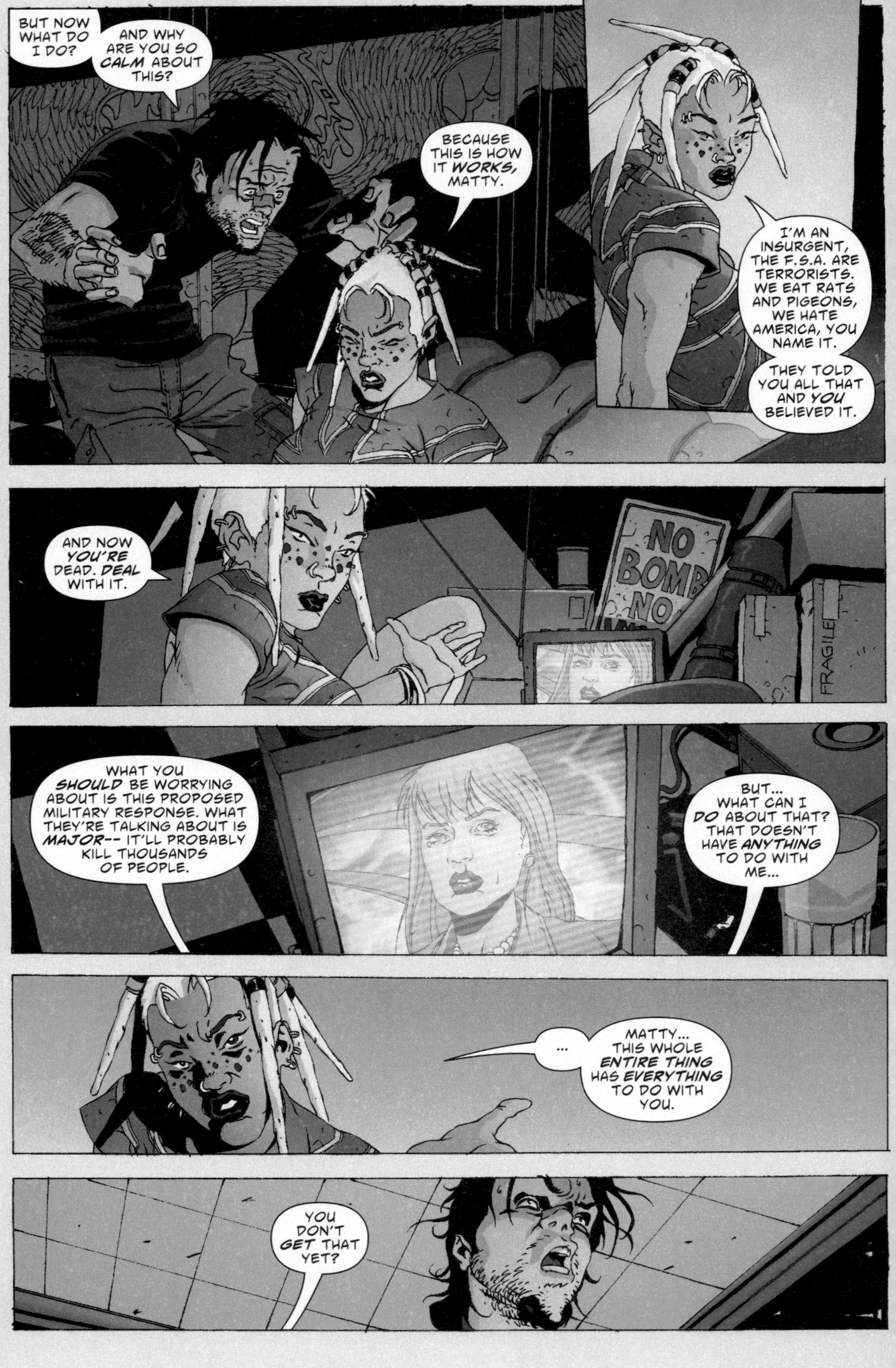
BUT NOW WHAT DO I DO?
AND WHY ARE YOU SO *CALM* ABOUT THIS?
BECAUSE THIS IS HOW IT *WORKS,* MATTY.
I'M AN INSURGENT, THE F.S.A. ARE TERRORISTS. WE EAT RATS AND PIGEONS, WE HATE AMERICA, YOU NAME IT.
THEY TOLD YOU ALL THAT AND *YOU* BELIEVED IT.
AND NOW *YOU'RE* DEAD. *DEAL* WITH IT.
NO BOMB NO
FRAGILE
WHAT YOU *SHOULD* BE WORRYING ABOUT IS THIS PROPOSED MILITARY RESPONSE. WHAT THEY'RE TALKING ABOUT IS *MAJOR--* IT'LL PROBABLY KILL THOUSANDS OF PEOPLE.
BUT... WHAT CAN I *DO* ABOUT THAT? THAT DOESN'T HAVE *ANYTHING* TO DO WITH ME...
...
MATTY... THIS WHOLE *ENTIRE THING* HAS *EVERYTHING* TO DO WITH YOU.
YOU DON'T *GET* THAT YET?

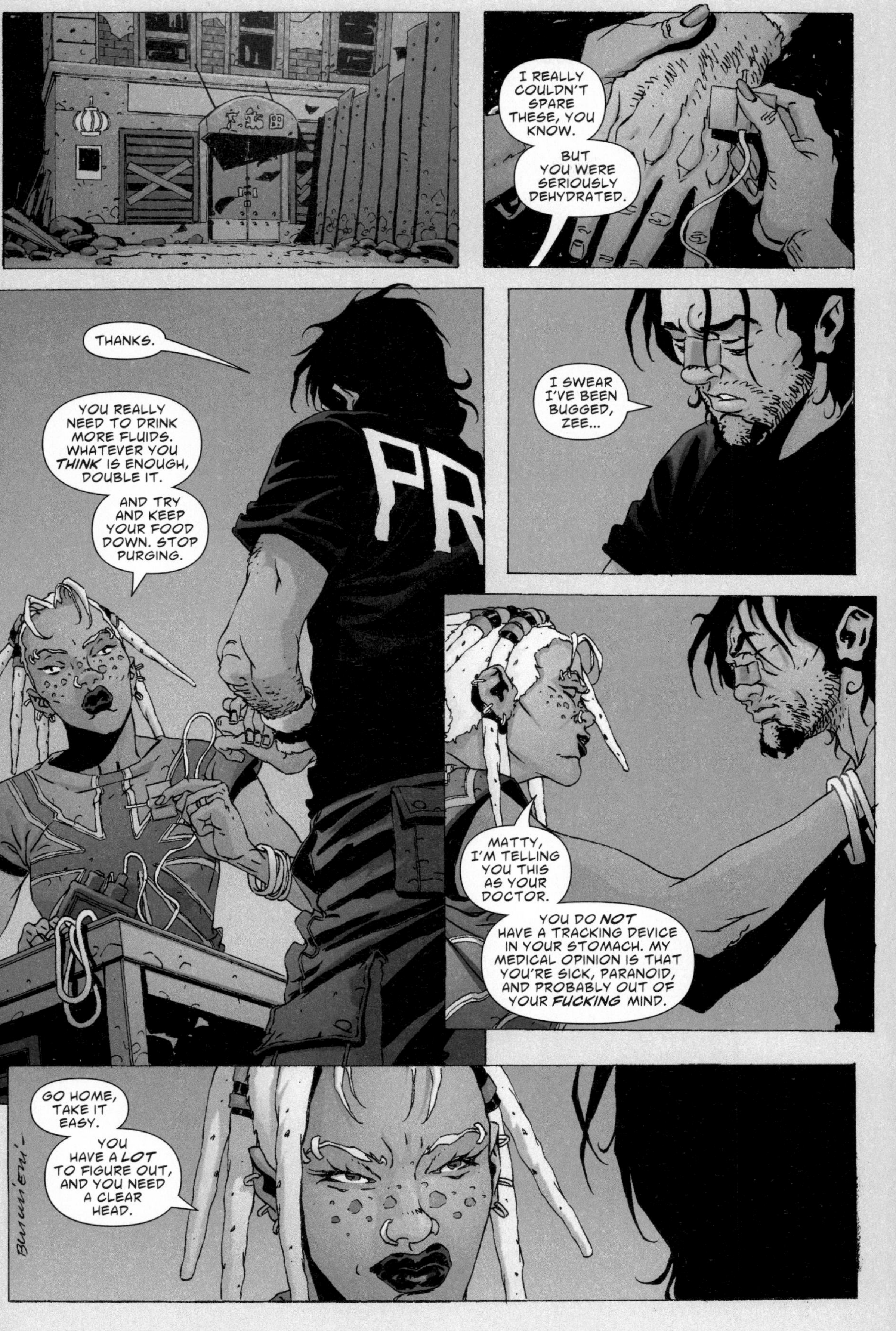
I REALLY COULDN'T SPARE THESE, YOU KNOW.
BUT YOU WERE SERIOUSLY DEHYDRATED.
THANKS.
YOU REALLY NEED TO DRINK MORE FLUIDS. WHATEVER YOU *THINK* IS ENOUGH, DOUBLE IT.
AND TRY AND KEEP YOUR FOOD DOWN. STOP PURGING.
I SWEAR I'VE BEEN BUGGED, ZEE...
MATTY, I'M TELLING YOU THIS AS YOUR DOCTOR.
YOU DO **NOT** HAVE A TRACKING DEVICE IN YOUR STOMACH. MY MEDICAL OPINION IS THAT YOU'RE SICK, PARANOID, AND PROBABLY OUT OF YOUR ***FUCKING*** MIND.
GO HOME, TAKE IT EASY.
YOU HAVE A ***LOT*** TO FIGURE OUT, AND YOU NEED A CLEAR HEAD.

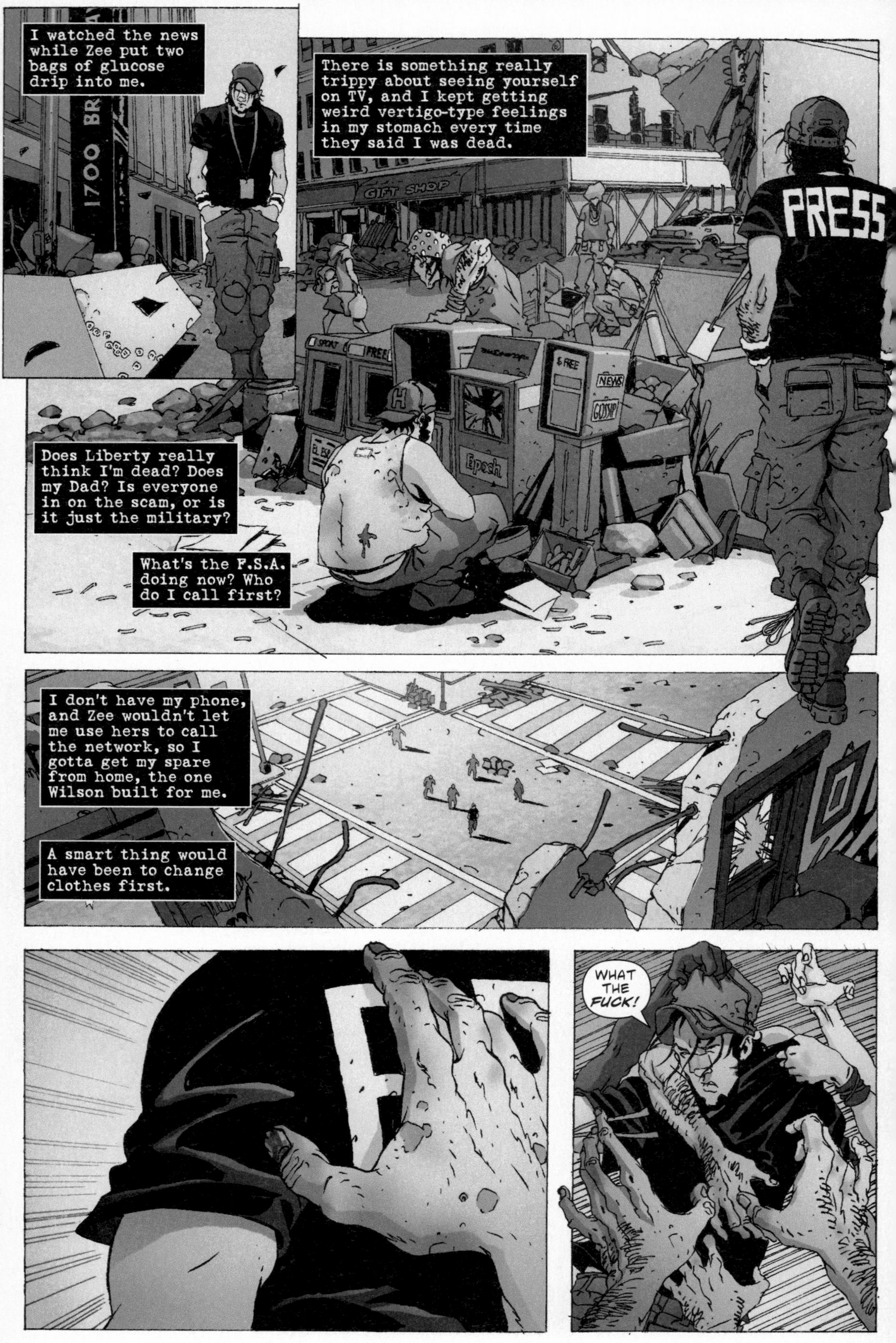
I watched the news while Zee put two bags of glucose drip into me.
1700 BR
There is something really trippy about seeing yourself on TV, and I kept getting weird vertigo-type feelings in my stomach every time they said I was dead.
GIFT SHOP
PRESS
SPORT
FREE
$ FREE
NEWS
GOSSIP
Epoch
Does Liberty really think I'm dead? Does my Dad? Is everyone in on the scam, or is it just the military?
What's the F.S.A. doing now? Who do I call first?
I don't have my phone, and Zee wouldn't let me use hers to call the network, so I gotta get my spare from home, the one Wilson built for me.
A smart thing would have been to change clothes first.
WHAT THE FUCK!

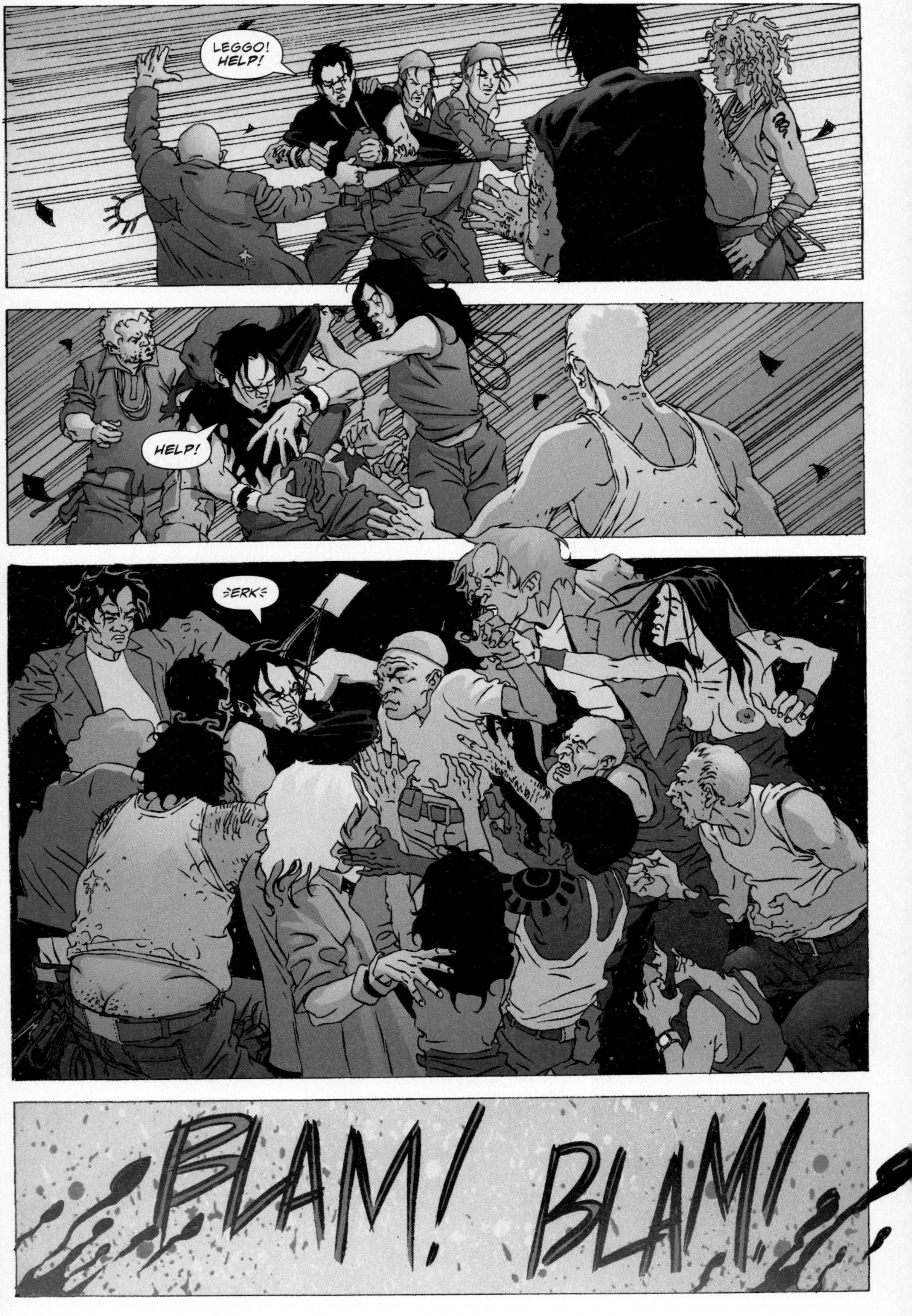
LEGGO! HELP!
HELP!
ERK
BLAM! BLAM!

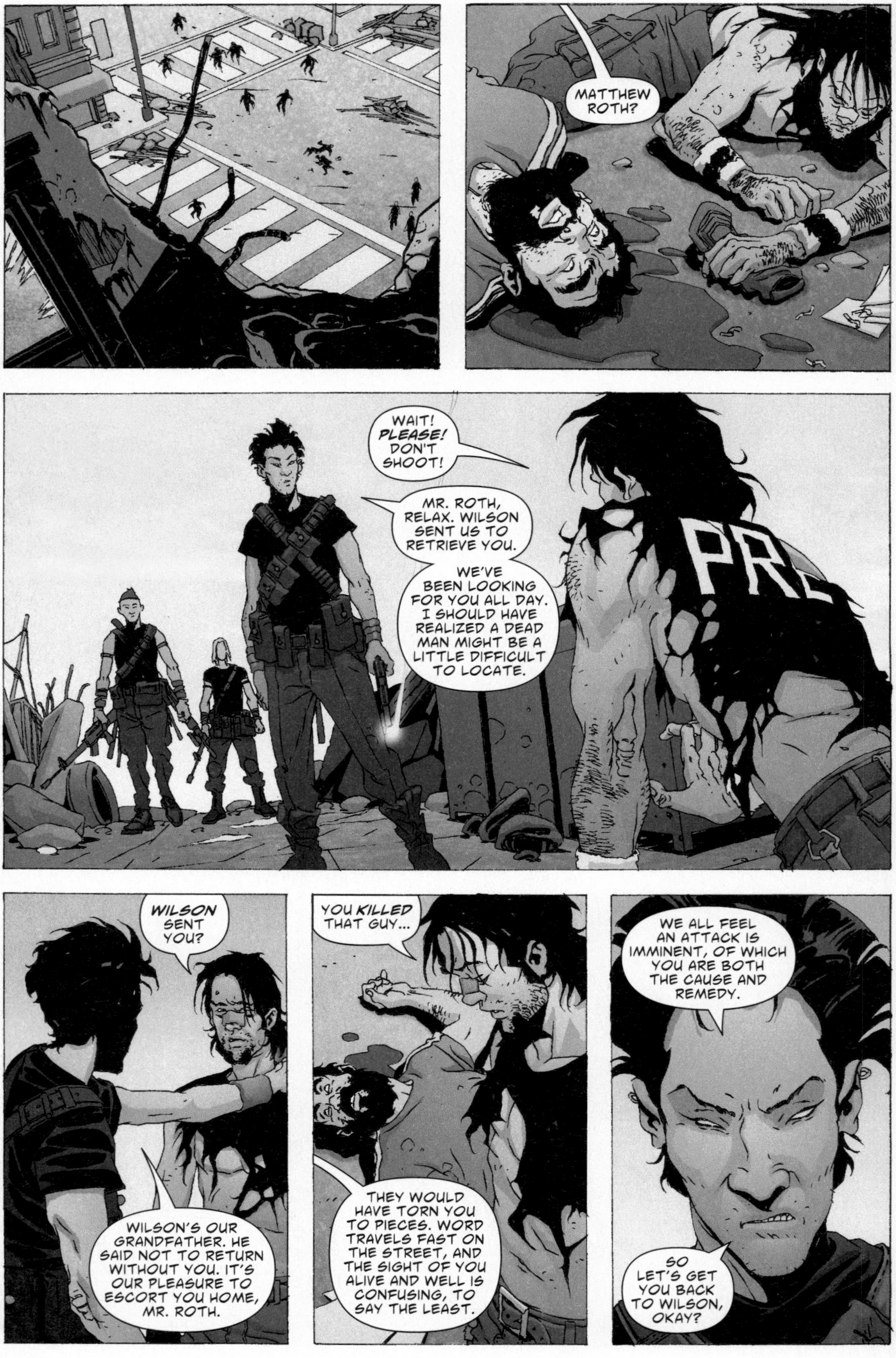
MATTHEW ROTH?
WAIT! *PLEASE!* DON'T SHOOT!
MR. ROTH, RELAX. WILSON SENT US TO RETRIEVE YOU.
WE'VE BEEN LOOKING FOR YOU ALL DAY. I SHOULD HAVE REALIZED A DEAD MAN MIGHT BE A LITTLE DIFFICULT TO LOCATE.
PRE
WILSON SENT YOU?
WILSON'S OUR GRANDFATHER. HE SAID NOT TO RETURN WITHOUT YOU. IT'S OUR PLEASURE TO ESCORT YOU HOME, MR. ROTH.
YOU *KILLED* THAT GUY...
THEY WOULD HAVE TORN YOU TO PIECES. WORD TRAVELS FAST ON THE STREET, AND THE SIGHT OF YOU ALIVE AND WELL IS CONFUSING, TO SAY THE LEAST.
WE ALL FEEL AN ATTACK IS IMMINENT, OF WHICH YOU ARE BOTH THE CAUSE AND REMEDY.
SO LET'S GET YOU BACK TO WILSON, OKAY?

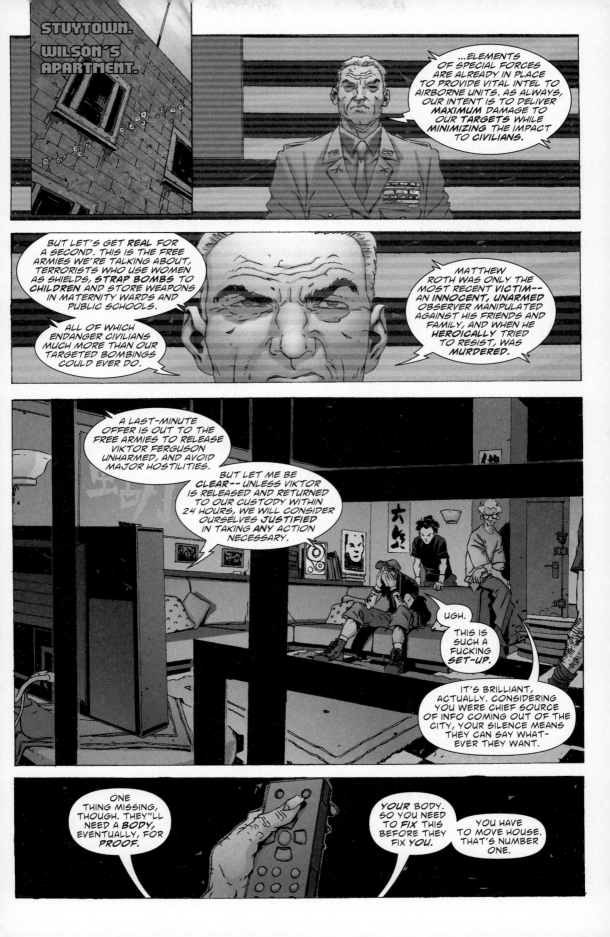

STUYTOWN.
WILSON'S
APARTMENT.

...ELEMENTS OF SPECIAL FORCES ARE ALREADY IN PLACE TO PROVIDE VITAL INTEL TO AIRBORNE UNITS. AS ALWAYS, OUR INTENT IS TO DELIVER MAXIMUM DAMAGE TO OUR TARGETS WHILE MINIMIZING THE IMPACT TO CIVILIANS.

BUT LET'S GET REAL FOR A SECOND. THIS IS THE FREE ARMIES WE'RE TALKING ABOUT, TERRORISTS WHO USE WOMEN AS SHIELDS, STRAP BOMBS TO CHILDREN AND STORE WEAPONS IN MATERNITY WARDS AND PUBLIC SCHOOLS.

ALL OF WHICH ENDANGER CIVILIANS MUCH MORE THAN OUR TARGETED BOMBINGS COULD EVER DO.

MATTHEW ROTH WAS ONLY THE MOST RECENT VICTIM-- AN INNOCENT, UNARMED OBSERVER MANIPULATED AGAINST HIS FRIENDS AND FAMILY, AND WHEN HE HEROICALLY TRIED TO RESIST, WAS MURDERED.

A LAST-MINUTE OFFER IS OUT TO THE FREE ARMIES TO RELEASE VIKTOR FERGUSON UNHARMED, AND AVOID MAJOR HOSTILITIES.

BUT LET ME BE CLEAR-- UNLESS VIKTOR IS RELEASED AND RETURNED TO OUR CUSTODY WITHIN 24 HOURS, WE WILL CONSIDER OURSELVES JUSTIFIED IN TAKING ANY ACTION NECESSARY.

UGH.

THIS IS SUCH A FUCKING SET-UP.

IT'S BRILLIANT, ACTUALLY. CONSIDERING YOU WERE CHIEF SOURCE OF INFO COMING OUT OF THE CITY, YOUR SILENCE MEANS THEY CAN SAY WHAT-EVER THEY WANT.

ONE THING MISSING, THOUGH. THEY'LL NEED A BODY, EVENTUALLY, FOR PROOF.

YOUR BODY. SO YOU NEED TO FIX THIS BEFORE THEY FIX YOU.

YOU HAVE TO MOVE HOUSE. THAT'S NUMBER ONE.

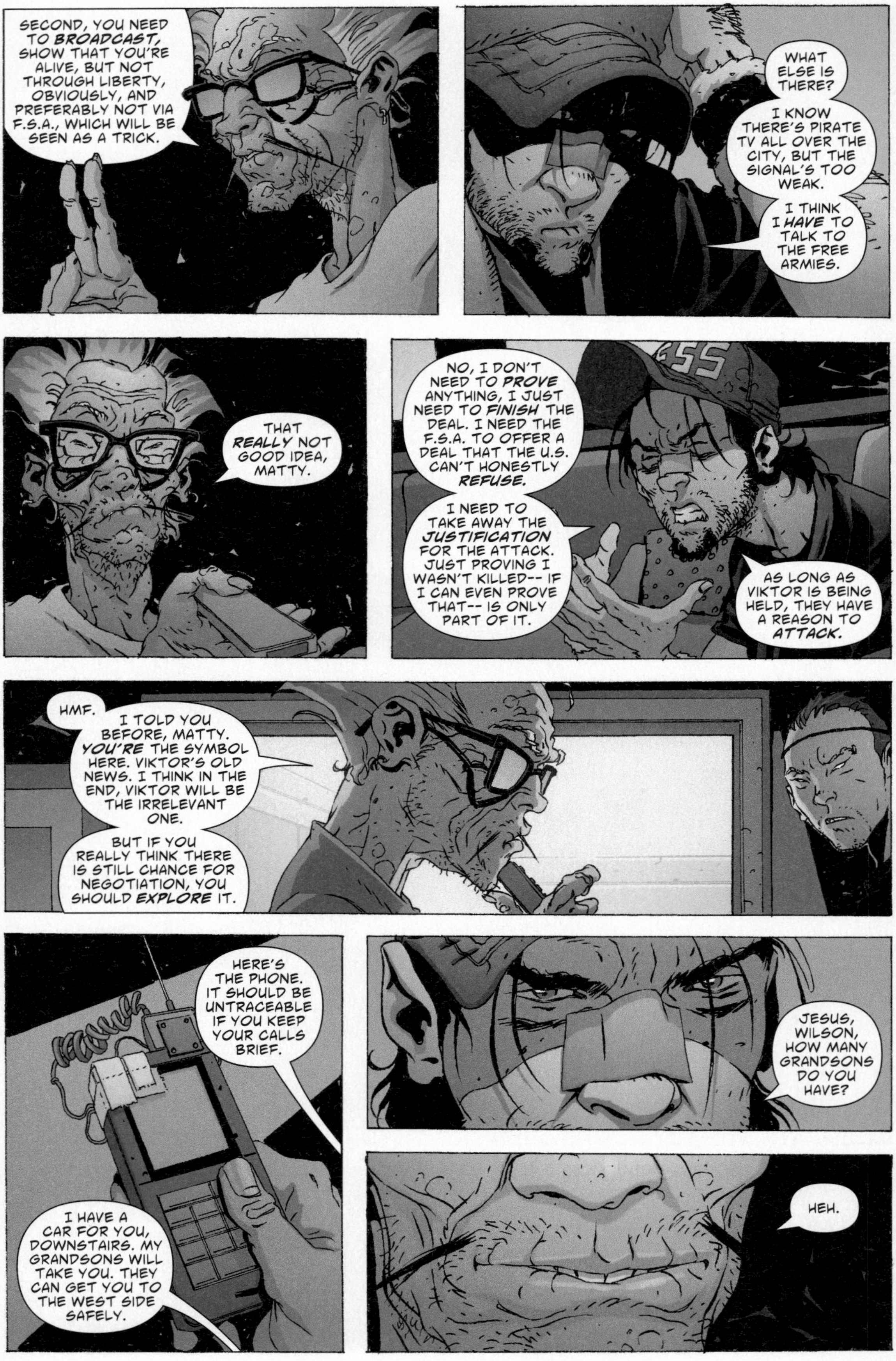
SECOND, YOU NEED TO BROADCAST, SHOW THAT YOU'RE ALIVE, BUT NOT THROUGH LIBERTY, OBVIOUSLY, AND PREFERABLY NOT VIA F.S.A., WHICH WILL BE SEEN AS A TRICK.
WHAT ELSE IS THERE?
I KNOW THERE'S PIRATE TV ALL OVER THE CITY, BUT THE SIGNAL'S TOO WEAK.
I THINK I HAVE TO TALK TO THE FREE ARMIES.
THAT REALLY NOT GOOD IDEA, MATTY.
NO, I DON'T NEED TO PROVE ANYTHING, I JUST NEED TO FINISH THE DEAL. I NEED THE F.S.A. TO OFFER A DEAL THAT THE U.S. CAN'T HONESTLY REFUSE.
I NEED TO TAKE AWAY THE JUSTIFICATION FOR THE ATTACK. JUST PROVING I WASN'T KILLED-- IF I CAN EVEN PROVE THAT-- IS ONLY PART OF IT.
AS LONG AS VIKTOR IS BEING HELD, THEY HAVE A REASON TO ATTACK.
HMF.
I TOLD YOU BEFORE, MATTY. YOU'RE THE SYMBOL HERE. VIKTOR'S OLD NEWS. I THINK IN THE END, VIKTOR WILL BE THE IRRELEVANT ONE.
BUT IF YOU REALLY THINK THERE IS STILL CHANCE FOR NEGOTIATION, YOU SHOULD EXPLORE IT.
HERE'S THE PHONE. IT SHOULD BE UNTRACEABLE IF YOU KEEP YOUR CALLS BRIEF.
I HAVE A CAR FOR YOU, DOWNSTAIRS. MY GRANDSONS WILL TAKE YOU. THEY CAN GET YOU TO THE WEST SIDE SAFELY.
JESUS, WILSON, HOW MANY GRANDSONS DO YOU HAVE?
HEH.

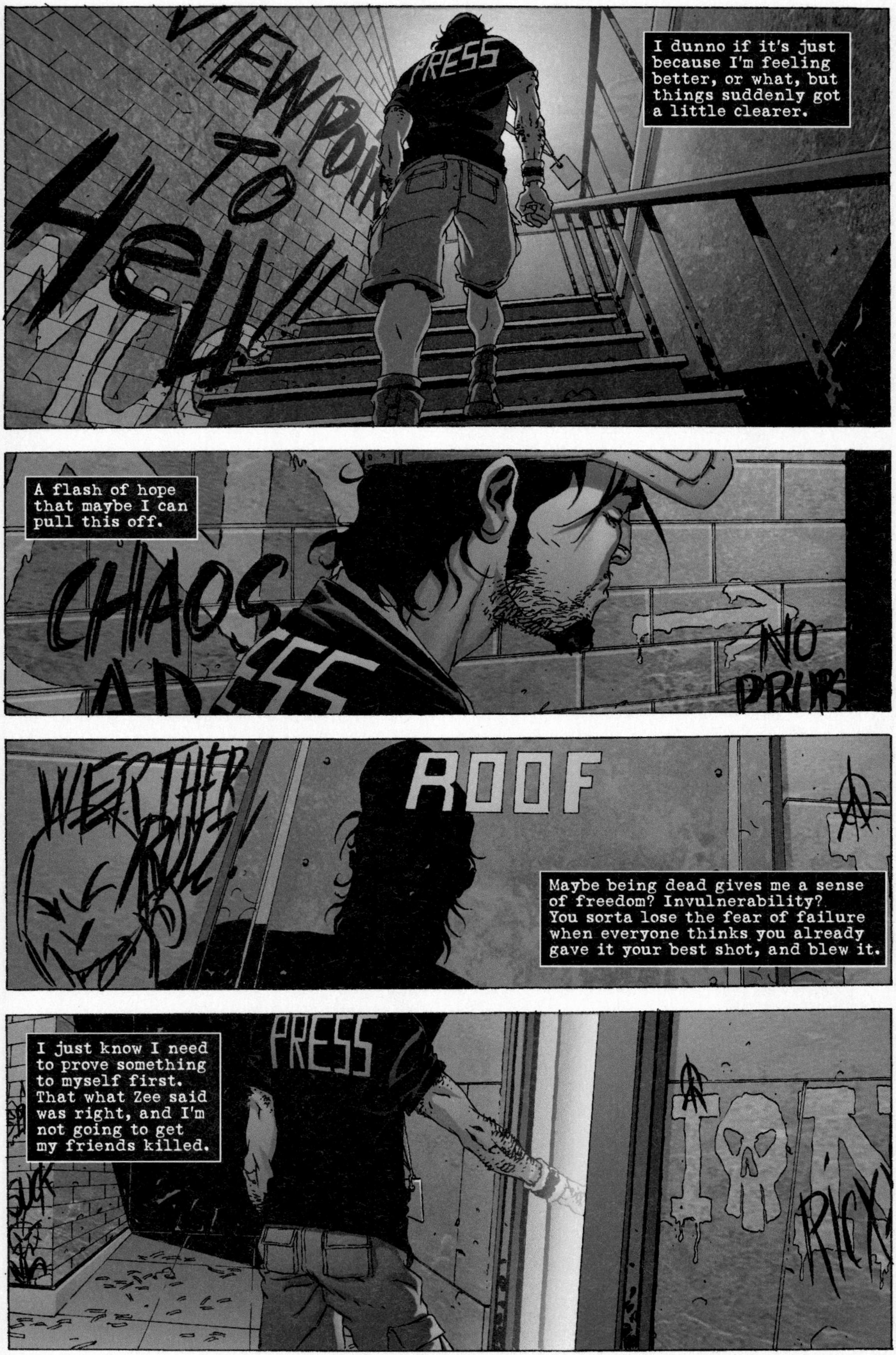
PRESS
I dunno if it's just because I'm feeling better, or what, but things suddenly got a little clearer.
A flash of hope that maybe I can pull this off.
CHAOS
ROOF
Maybe being dead gives me a sense of freedom? Invulnerability? You sorta lose the fear of failure when everyone thinks you already gave it your best shot, and blew it.
PRESS
I just know I need to prove something to myself first. That what Zee said was right, and I'm not going to get my friends killed.

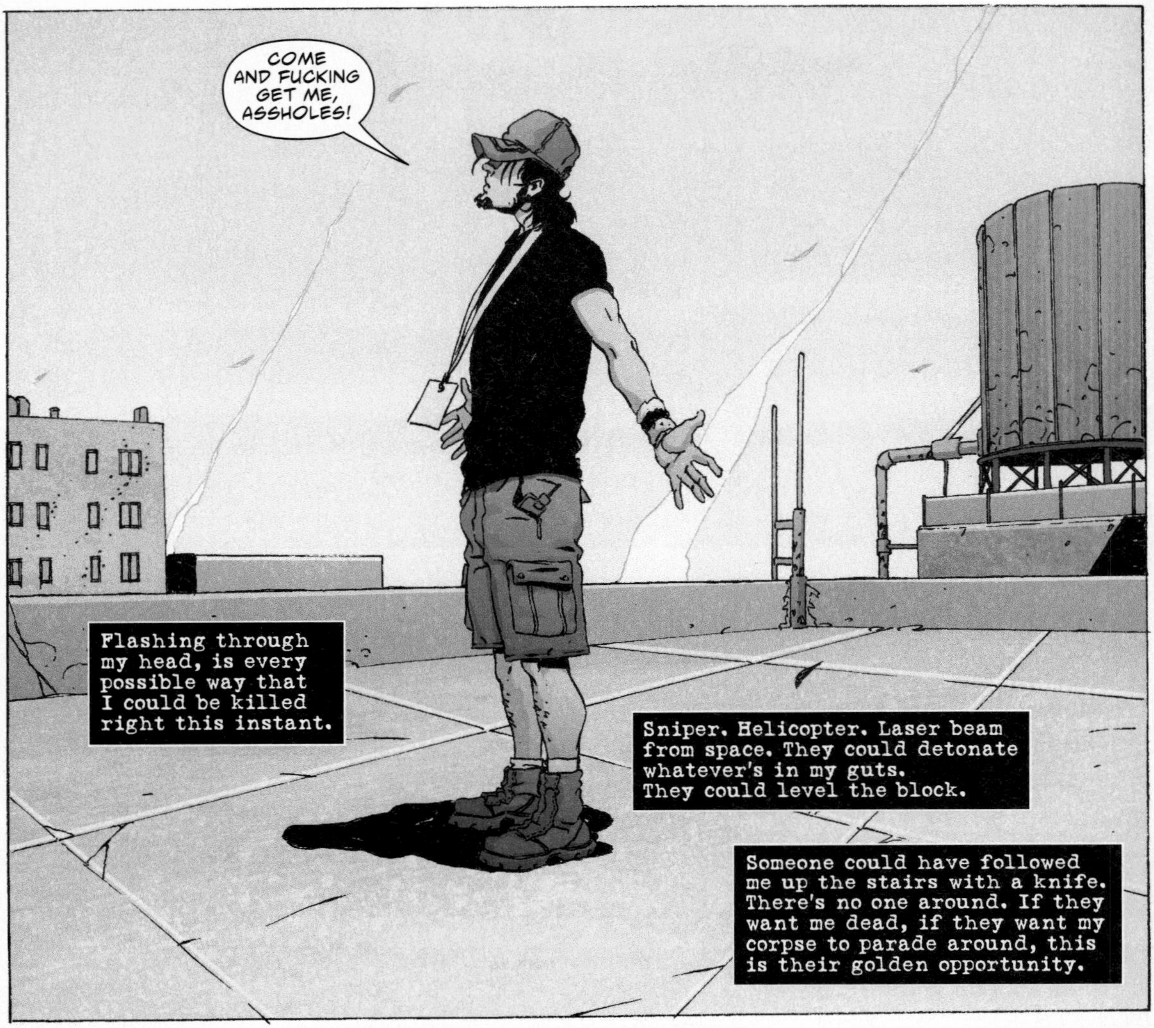
COME AND FUCKING GET ME, ASSHOLES!
Flashing through my head, is every possible way that I could be killed right this instant.
Sniper. Helicopter. Laser beam from space. They could detonate whatever's in my guts. They could level the block.
Someone could have followed me up the stairs with a knife. There's no one around. If they want me dead, if they want my corpse to parade around, this is their golden opportunity.

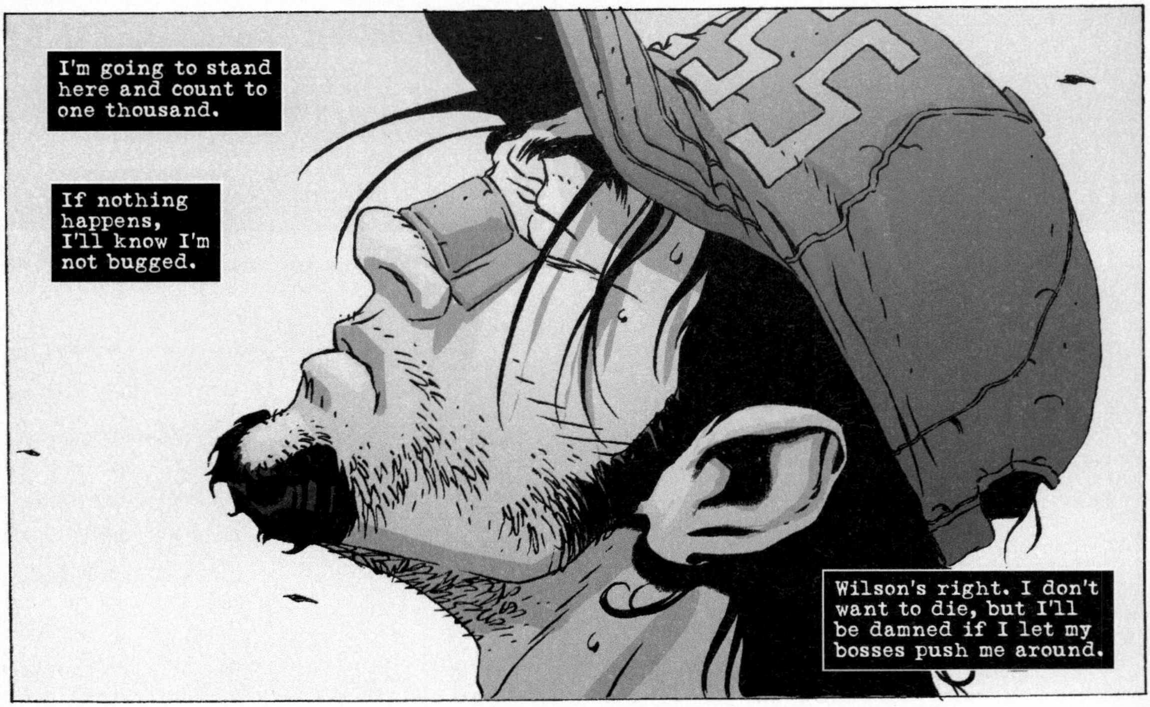
I'm going to stand here and count to one thousand.
If nothing happens, I'll know I'm not bugged.
Wilson's right. I don't want to die, but I'll be damned if I let my bosses push me around.

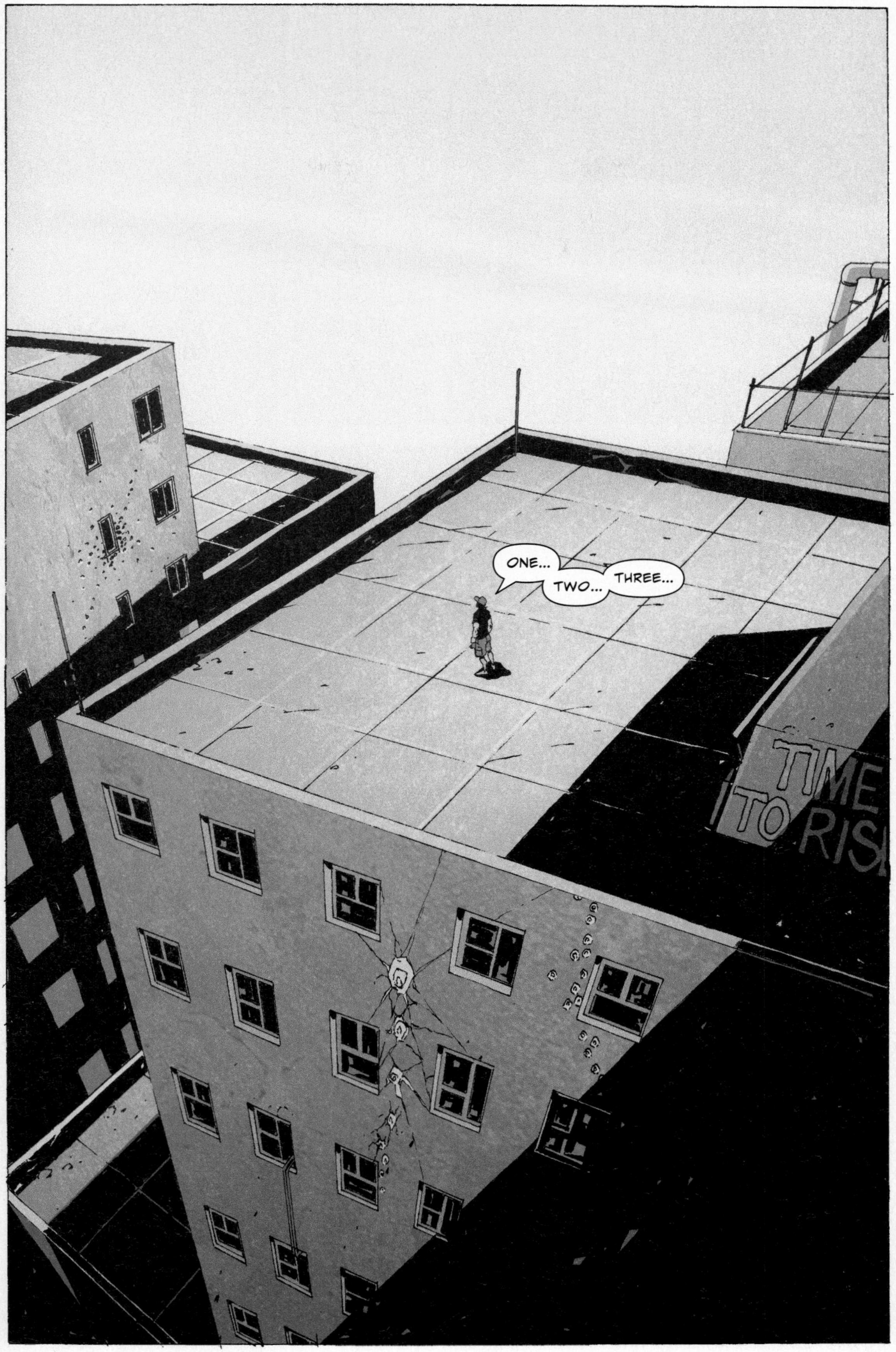
ONE...
TWO...
THREE...
TIME
TO RIS

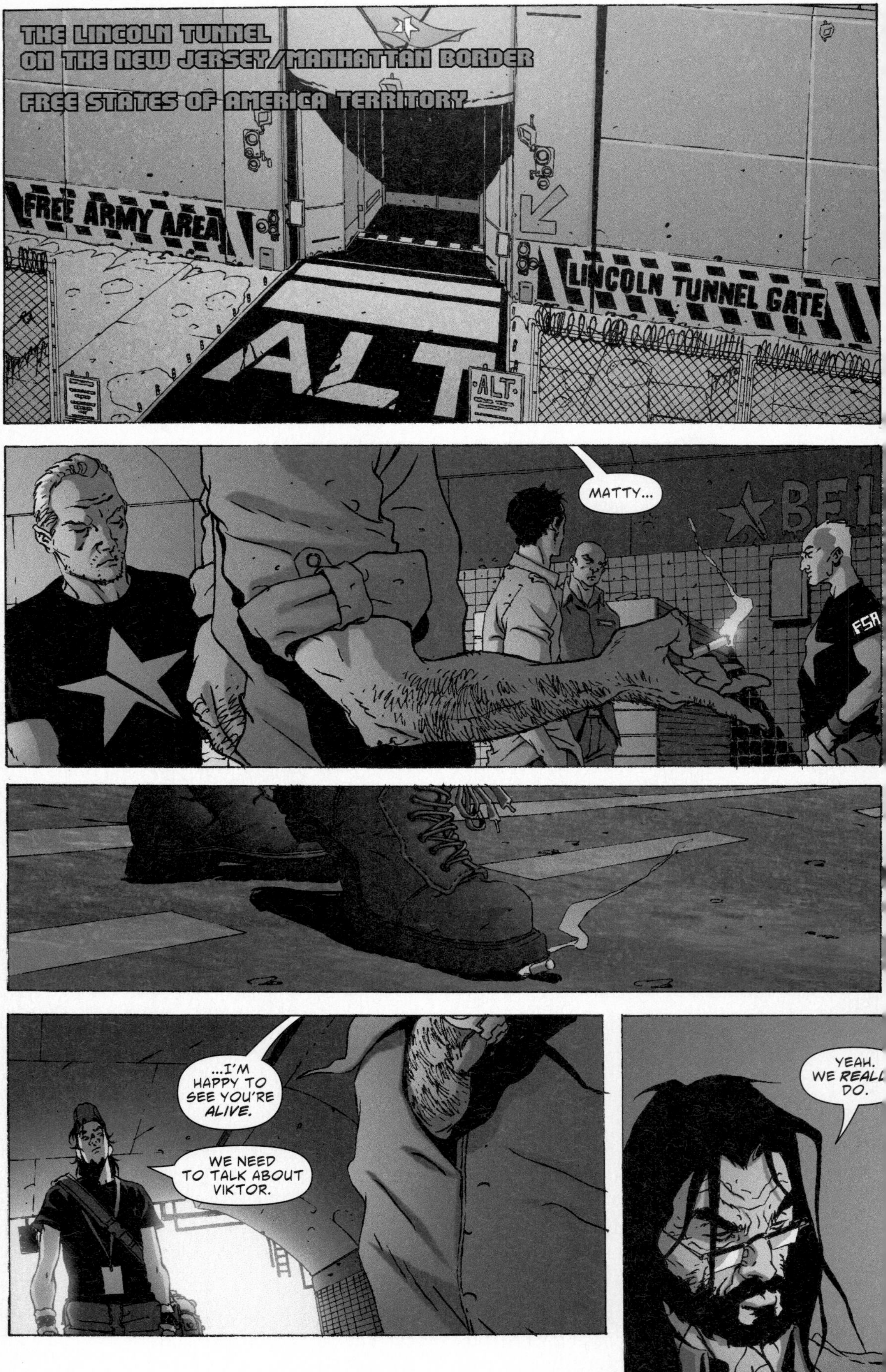
THE LINCOLN TUNNEL
ON THE NEW JERSEY/MANHATTAN BORDER
FREE STATES OF AMERICA TERRITORY
FREE ARMY AREA
LINCOLN TUNNEL GATE
ALT
ALT
MATTY...
FSA
...I'M HAPPY TO SEE YOU'RE *ALIVE.*
WE NEED TO TALK ABOUT VIKTOR.
YEAH. WE *REALL* DO.

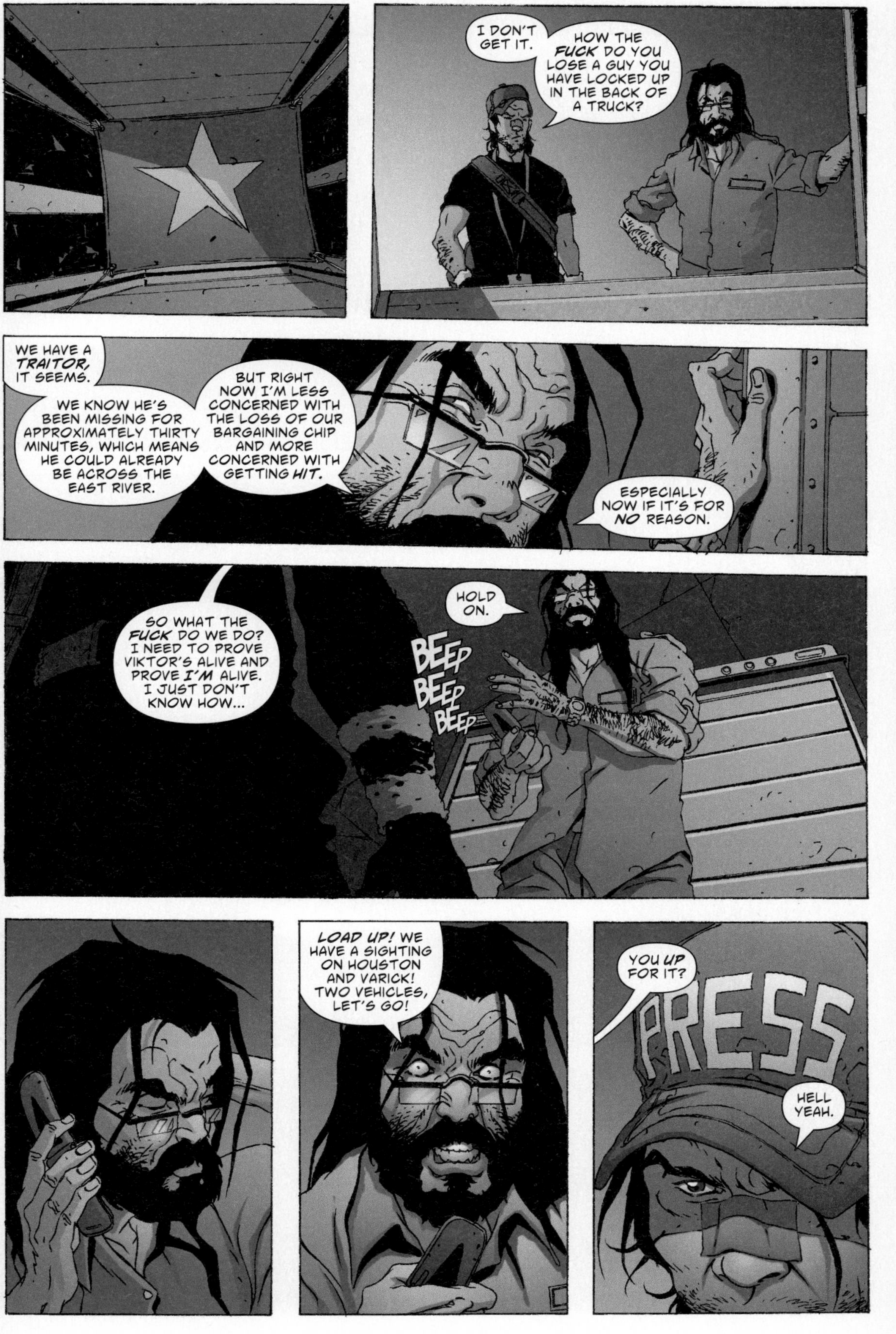

I DON'T GET IT.
HOW THE *FUCK* DO YOU LOSE A GUY YOU HAVE LOCKED UP IN THE BACK OF A TRUCK?
WE HAVE A *TRAITOR,* IT SEEMS.
WE KNOW HE'S BEEN MISSING FOR APPROXIMATELY THIRTY MINUTES, WHICH MEANS HE COULD ALREADY BE ACROSS THE EAST RIVER.
BUT RIGHT NOW I'M LESS CONCERNED WITH THE LOSS OF OUR BARGAINING CHIP AND MORE CONCERNED WITH GETTING *HIT.*
ESPECIALLY NOW IF IT'S FOR *NO* REASON.
SO WHAT THE *FUCK* DO WE DO? I NEED TO PROVE VIKTOR'S ALIVE AND PROVE *I'M* ALIVE. I JUST DON'T KNOW HOW...
HOLD ON.
BEEP BEEP BEEP
LOAD UP! WE HAVE A SIGHTING ON HOUSTON AND VARICK! TWO VEHICLES, LET'S GO!
YOU *UP* FOR IT?
PRESS
HELL YEAH.

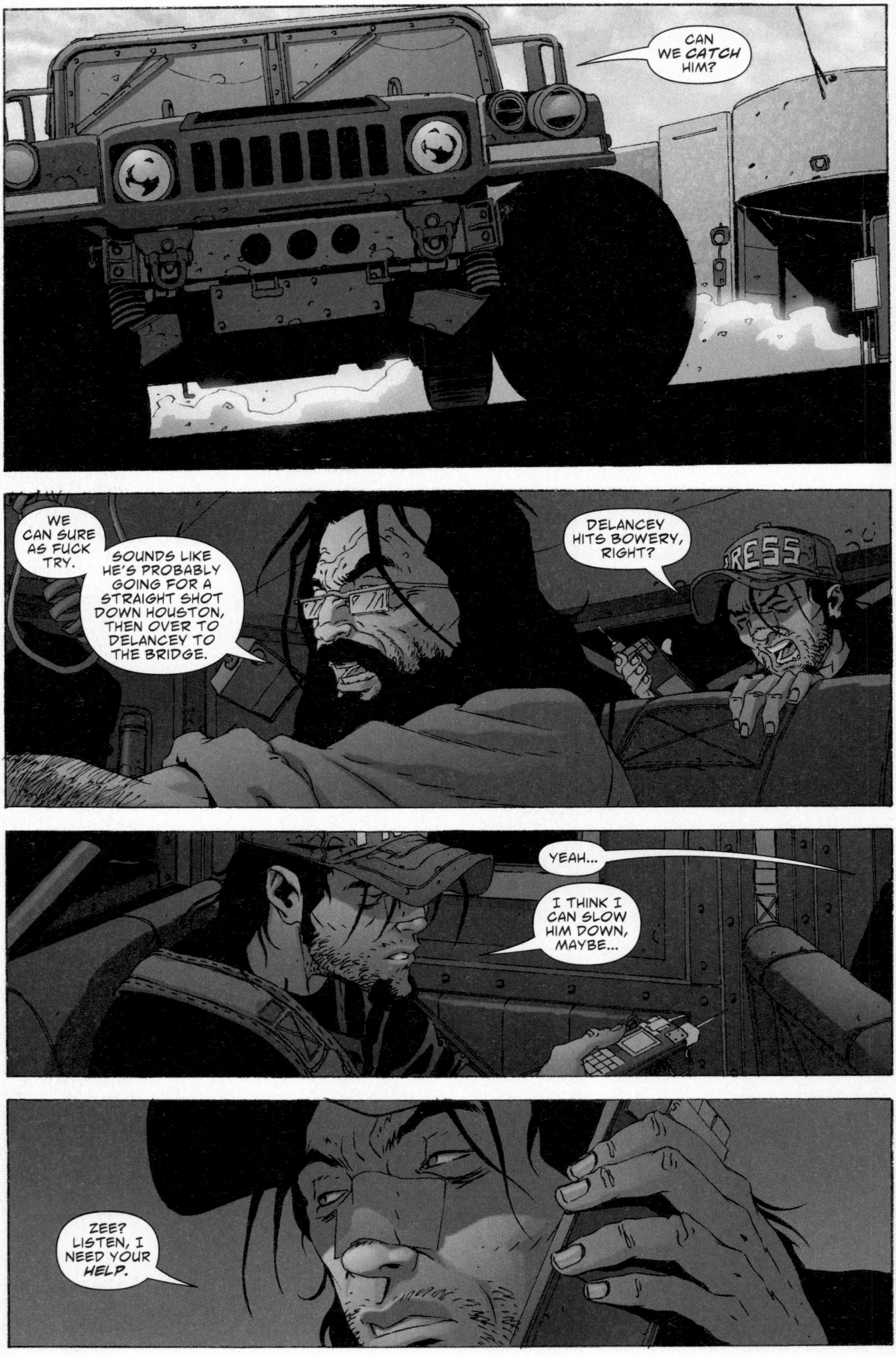
CAN WE CATCH HIM?
WE CAN SURE AS FUCK TRY.
SOUNDS LIKE HE'S PROBABLY GOING FOR A STRAIGHT SHOT DOWN HOUSTON, THEN OVER TO DELANCEY TO THE BRIDGE.
DELANCEY HITS BOWERY, RIGHT?
PRESS
YEAH...
I THINK I CAN SLOW HIM DOWN, MAYBE...
ZEE? LISTEN, I NEED YOUR HELP.

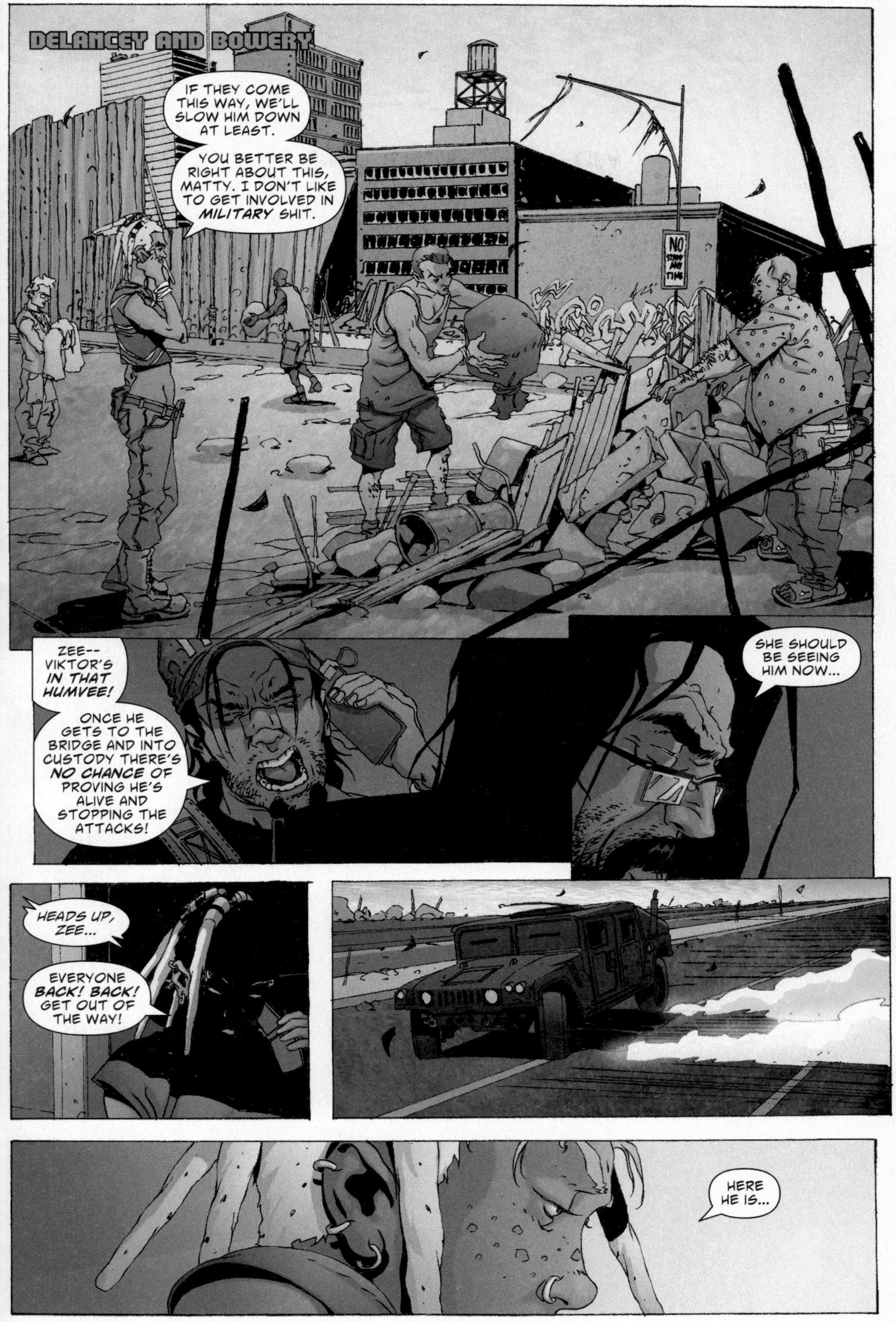
DELANCEY AND BOWERY
IF THEY COME THIS WAY, WE'LL SLOW HIM DOWN AT LEAST.
YOU BETTER BE RIGHT ABOUT THIS, MATTY. I DON'T LIKE TO GET INVOLVED IN MILITARY SHIT.
ZEE-- VIKTOR'S IN THAT HUMVEE!
ONCE HE GETS TO THE BRIDGE AND INTO CUSTODY THERE'S NO CHANCE OF PROVING HE'S ALIVE AND STOPPING THE ATTACKS!
SHE SHOULD BE SEEING HIM NOW...
HEADS UP, ZEE...
EVERYONE BACK! BACK! GET OUT OF THE WAY!
HERE HE IS...

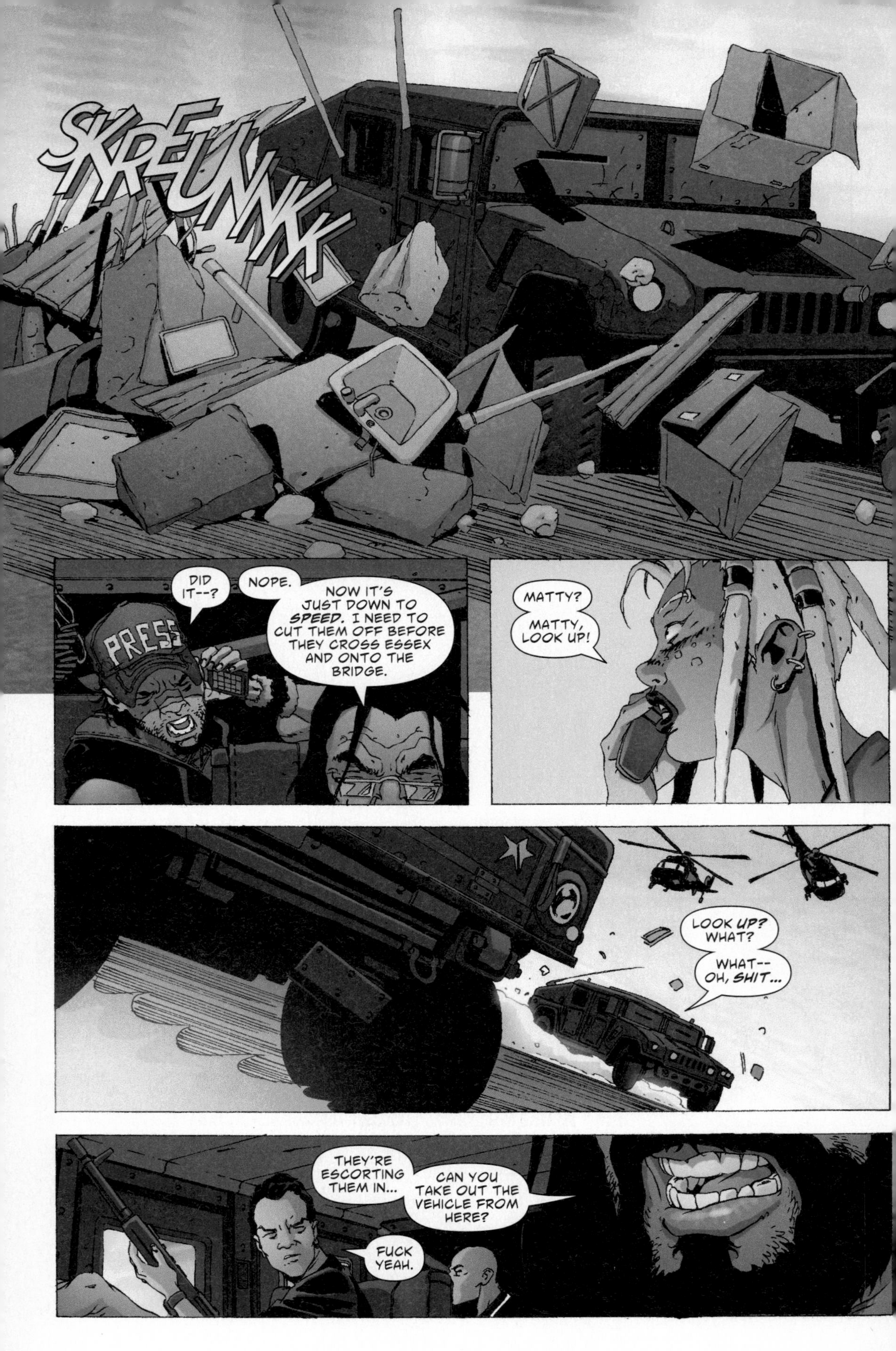
SKREUNKK
DID IT--?
NOPE.
NOW IT'S JUST DOWN TO SPEED. I NEED TO CUT THEM OFF BEFORE THEY CROSS ESSEX AND ONTO THE BRIDGE.
PRESS
MATTY?
MATTY, LOOK UP!
LOOK UP? WHAT?
WHAT-- OH, SHIT...
THEY'RE ESCORTING THEM IN...
CAN YOU TAKE OUT THE VEHICLE FROM HERE?
FUCK YEAH.

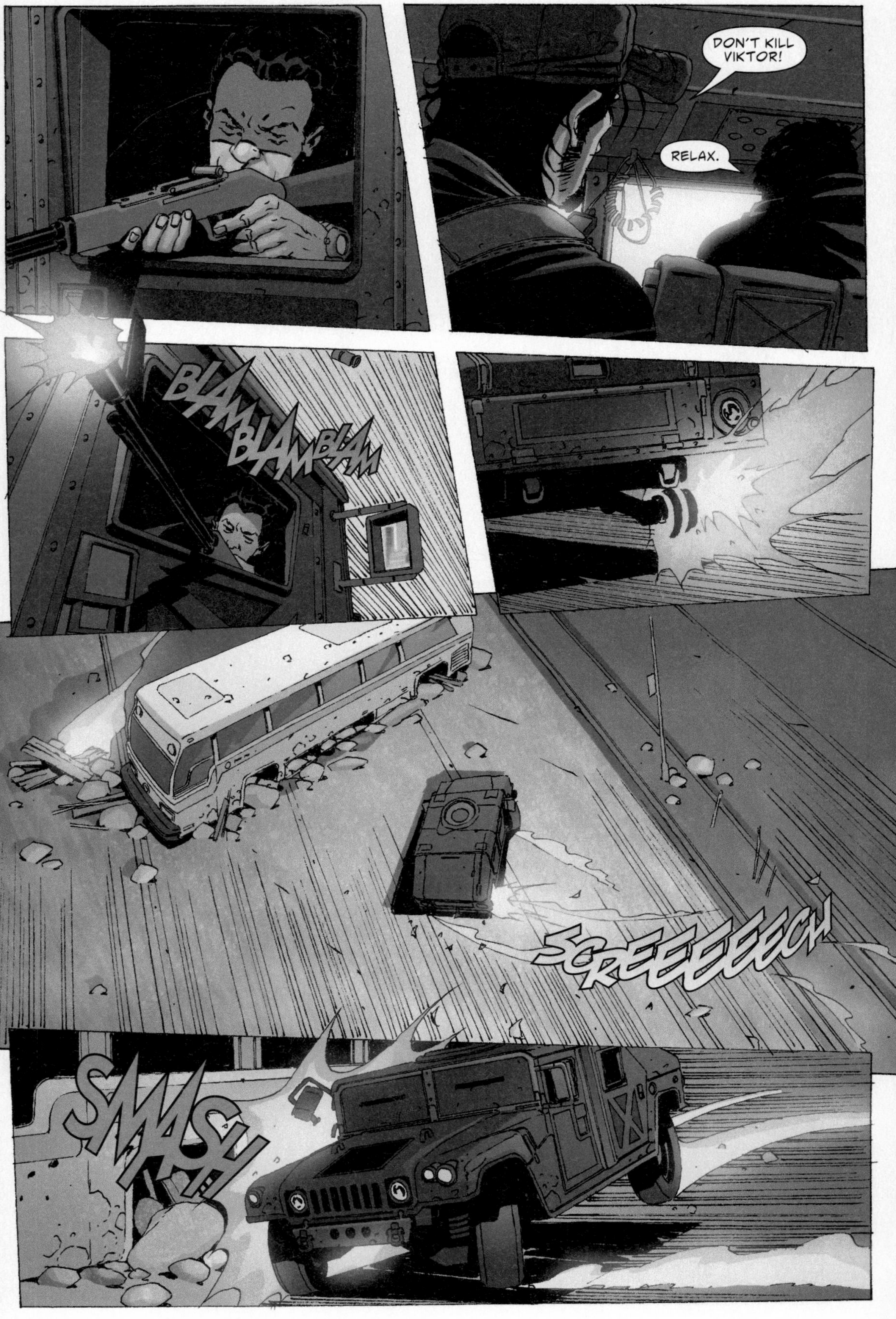
DON'T KILL VIKTOR!
RELAX.
BLAM BLAM BLAM BLAM
SCREEEEEECH
SMASH

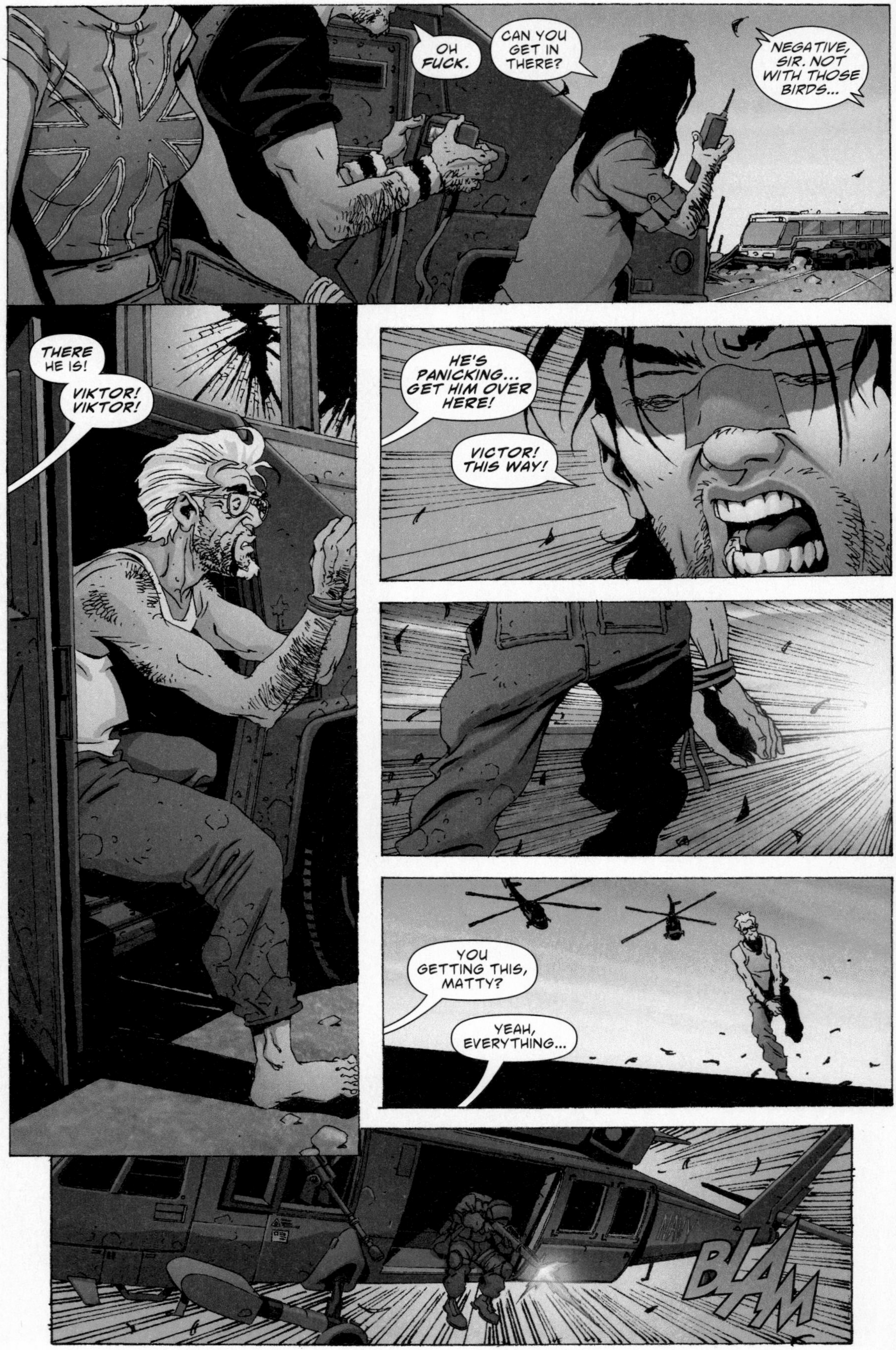
OH FUCK.
CAN YOU GET IN THERE?
NEGATIVE, SIR. NOT WITH THOSE BIRDS...
THERE HE IS!
VIKTOR! VIKTOR!
HE'S PANICKING... GET HIM OVER HERE!
VICTOR! THIS WAY!
YOU GETTING THIS, MATTY?
YEAH, EVERYTHING...
BLAM

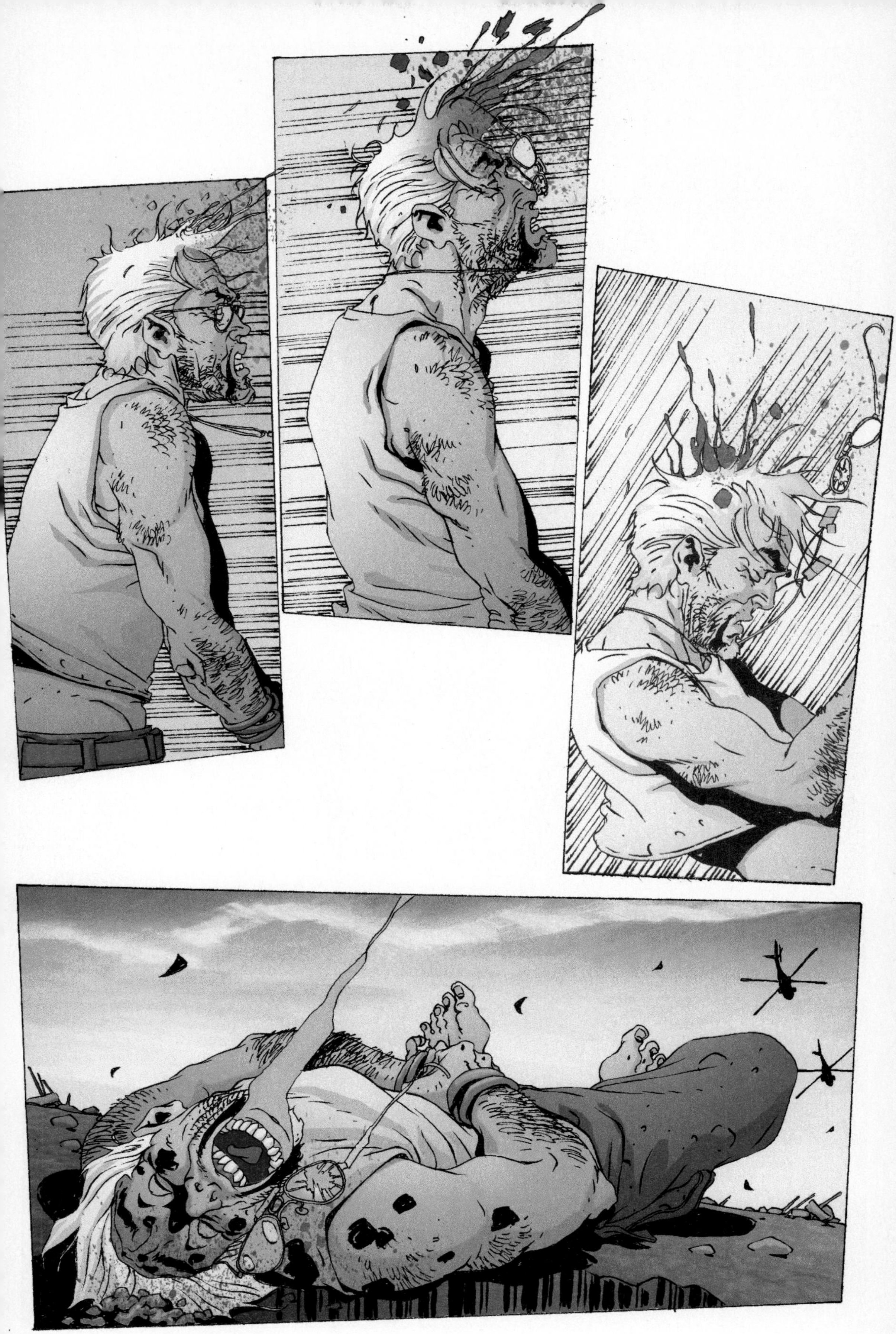

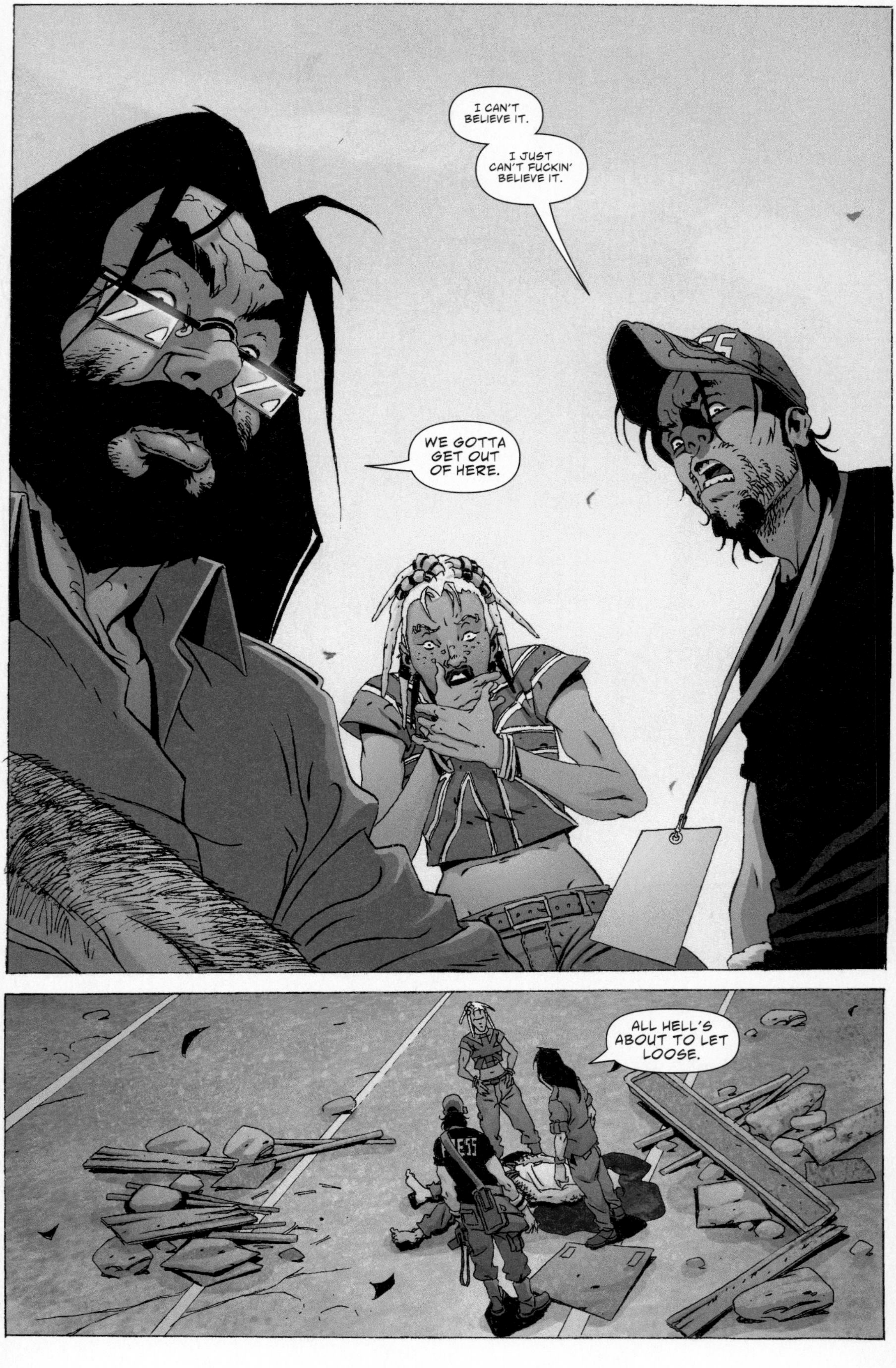
I CAN'T BELIEVE IT.
I JUST CAN'T FUCKIN' BELIEVE IT.
WE GOTTA GET OUT OF HERE.
ALL HELL'S ABOUT TO LET LOOSE.

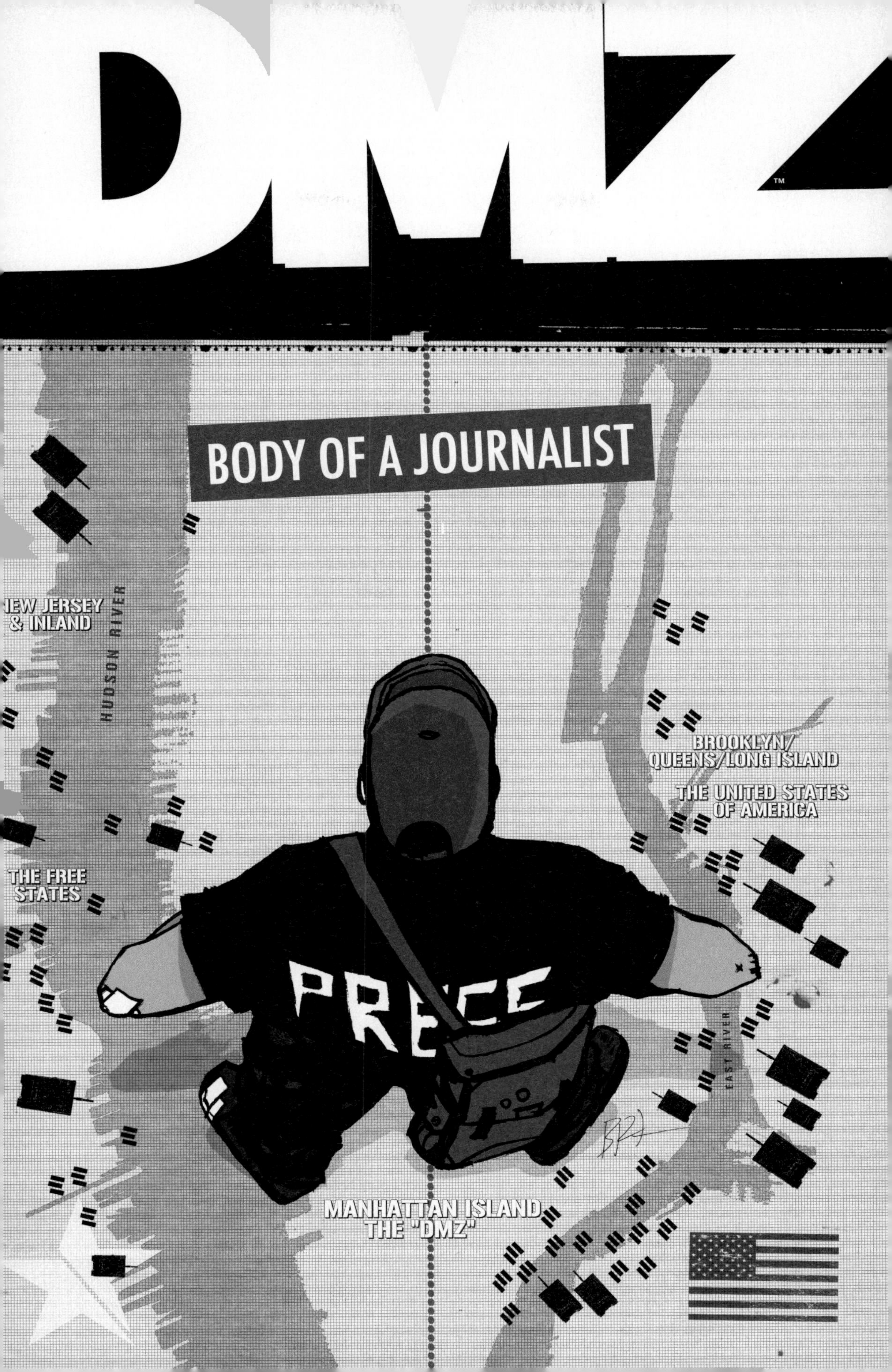
DMZ™
BODY OF A JOURNALIST
EW JERSEY & INLAND
HUDSON RIVER
THE FREE STATES
BROOKLYN/ QUEENS/LONG ISLAND
THE UNITED STATES OF AMERICA
EAST RIVER
MANHATTAN ISLAND THE "DMZ"

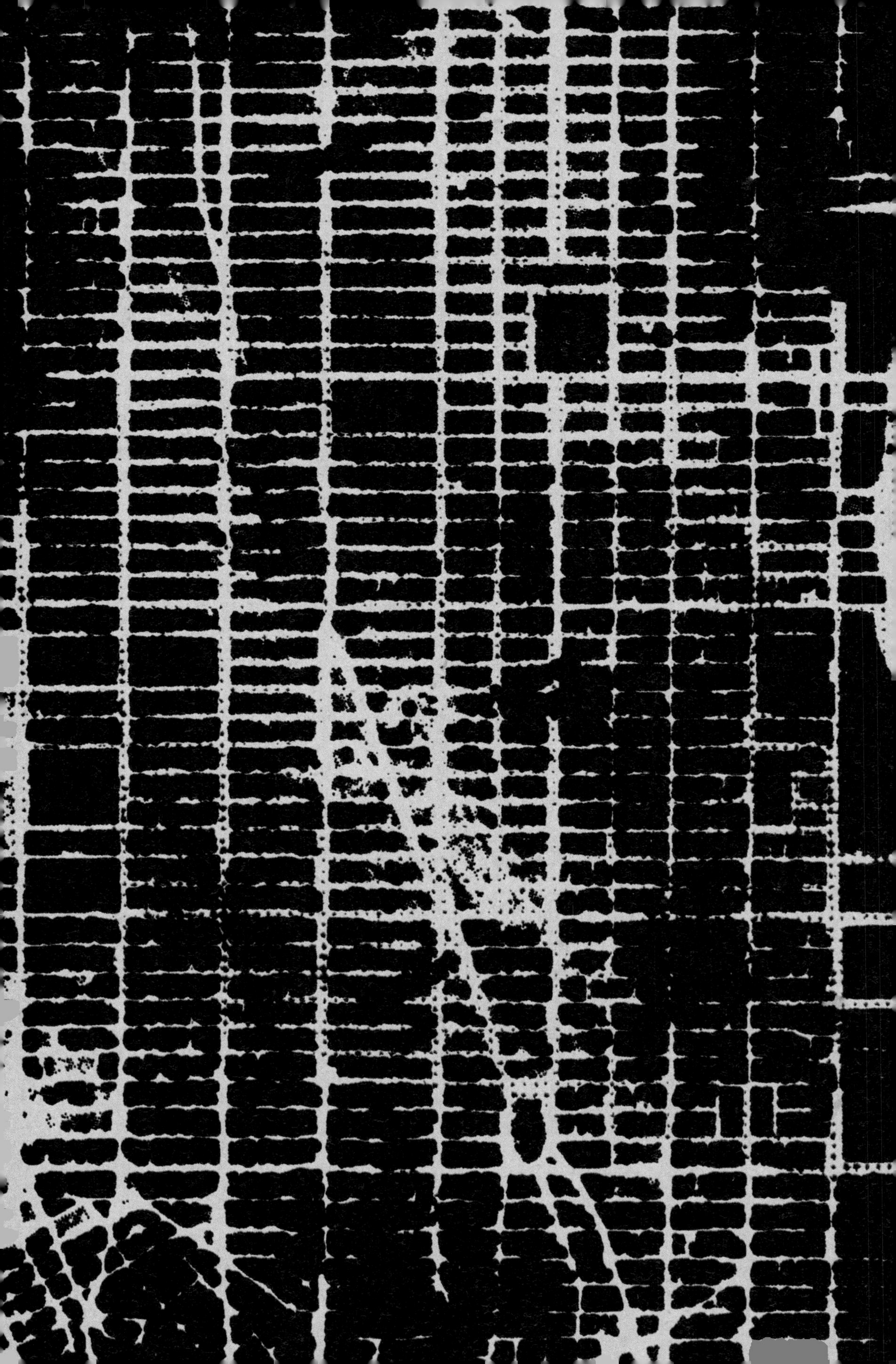

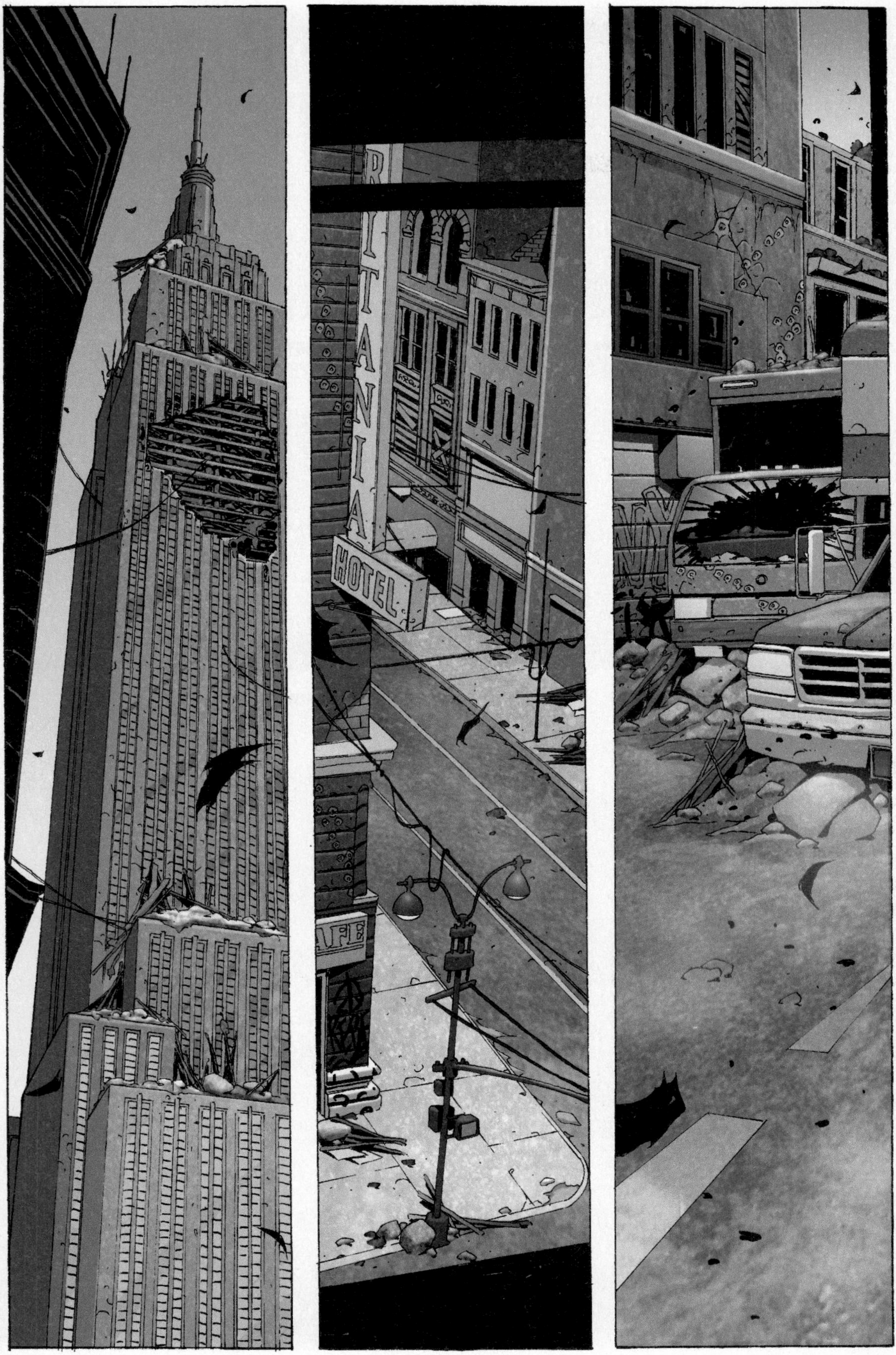
RITANIA
HOTEL
AFE

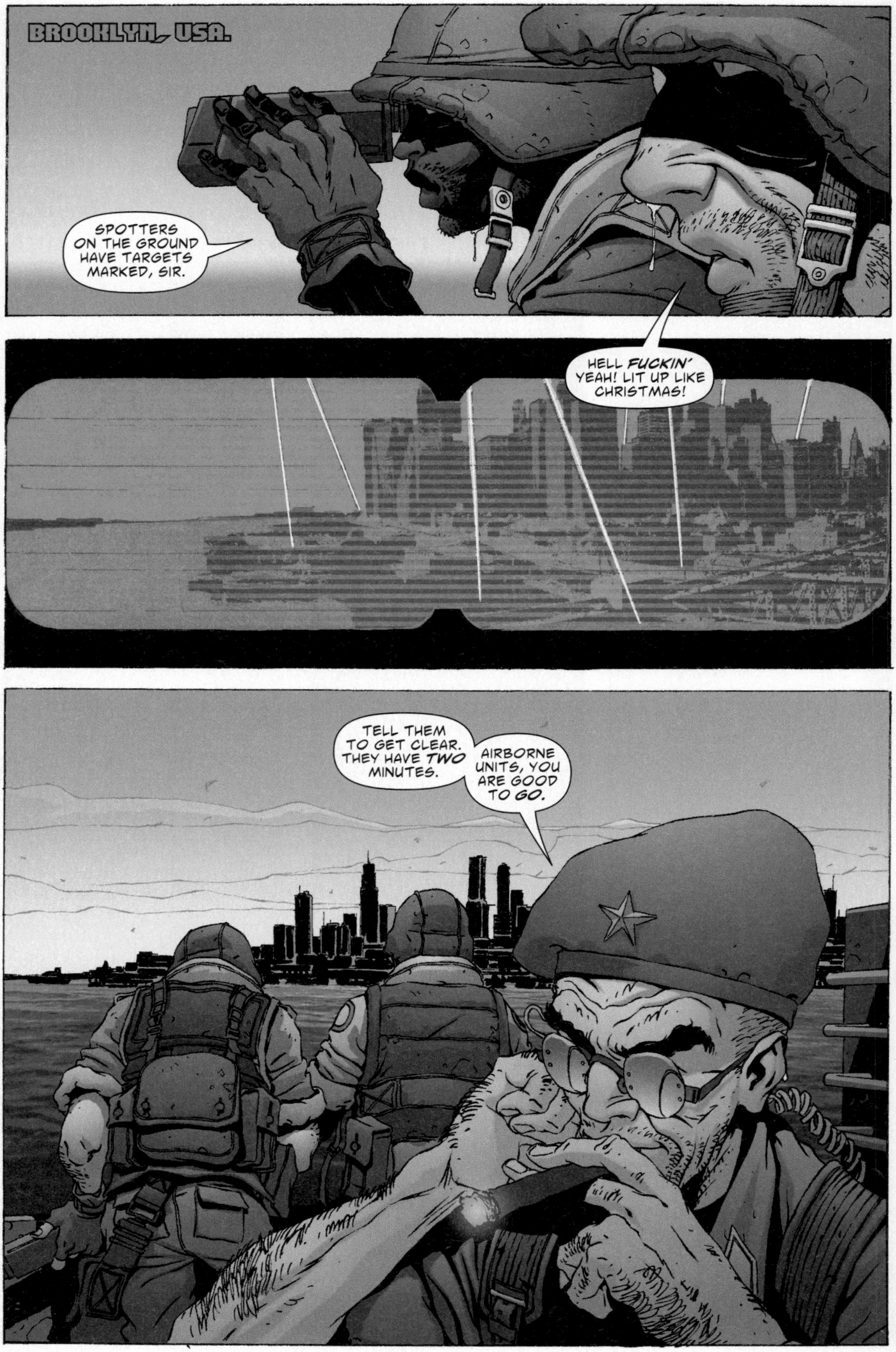
BROOKLYN, USA.
SPOTTERS ON THE GROUND HAVE TARGETS MARKED, SIR.
HELL FUCKIN' YEAH! LIT UP LIKE CHRISTMAS!
TELL THEM TO GET CLEAR. THEY HAVE TWO MINUTES.
AIRBORNE UNITS, YOU ARE GOOD TO GO.

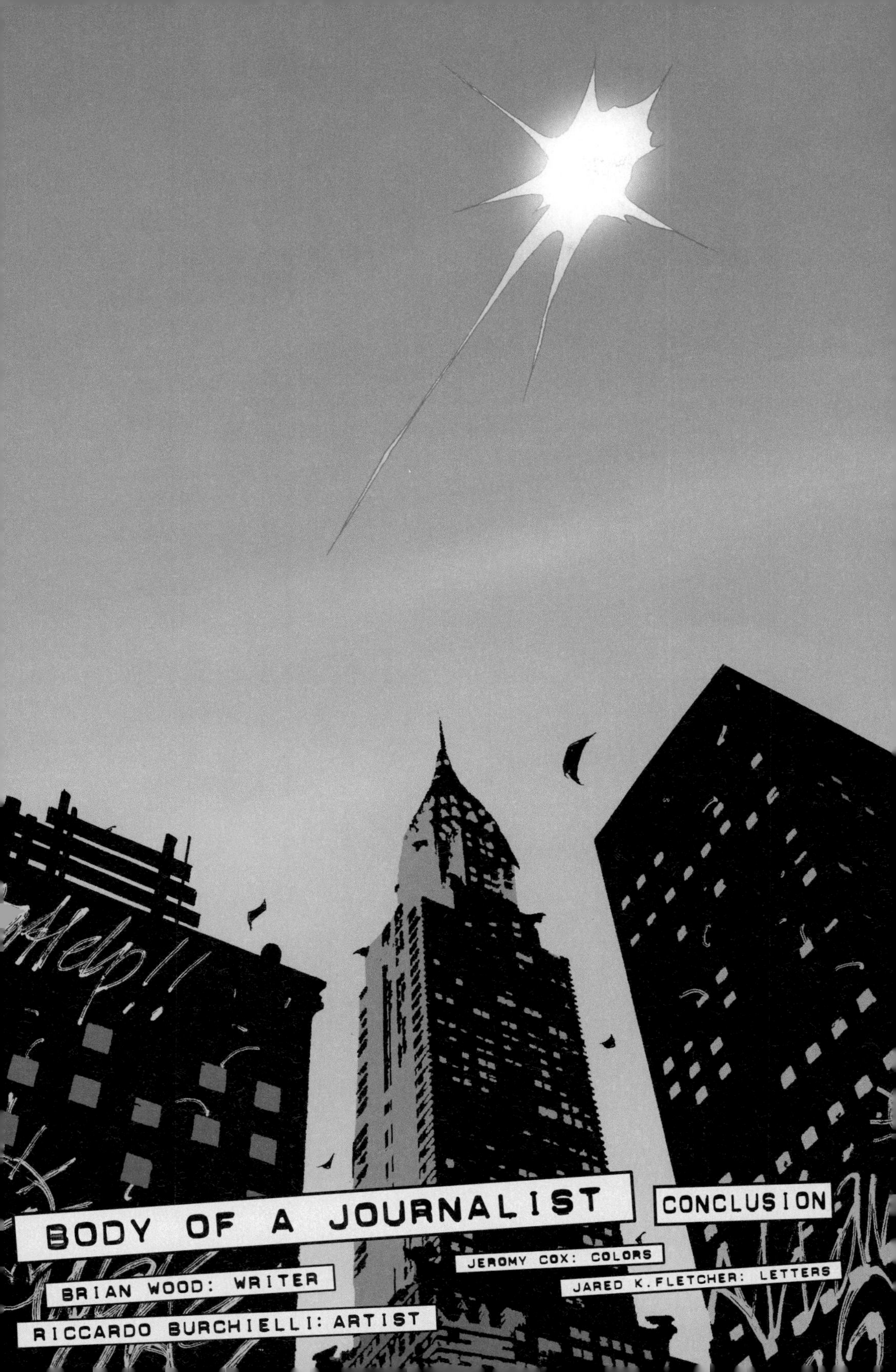

HELP!!
BODY OF A JOURNALIST
CONCLUSION
BRIAN WOOD: WRITER
RICCARDO BURCHIELLI: ARTIST
JEROMY COX: COLORS
JARED K. FLETCHER: LETTERS

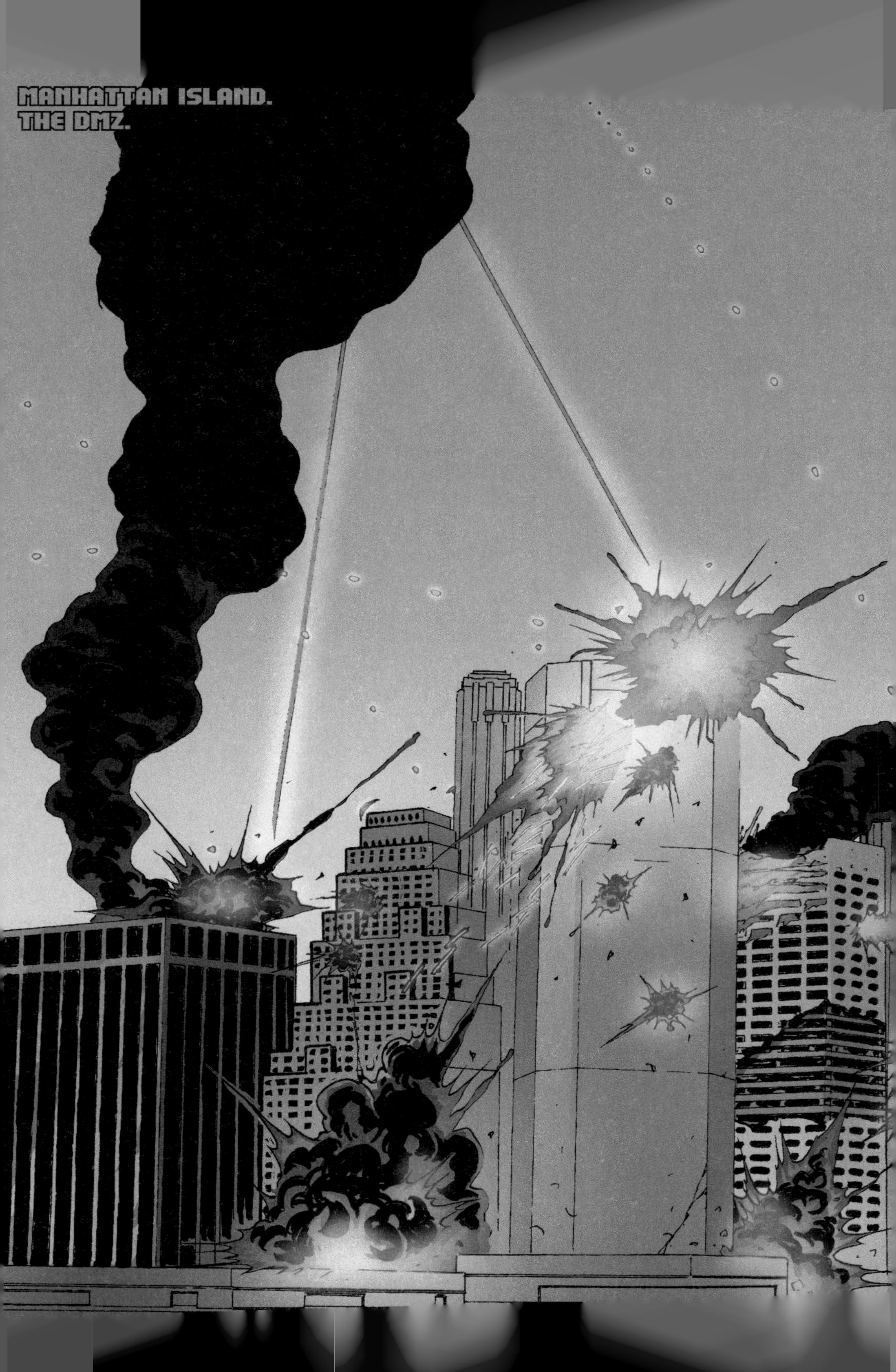
MANHATTAN ISLAND.
THE DMZ.

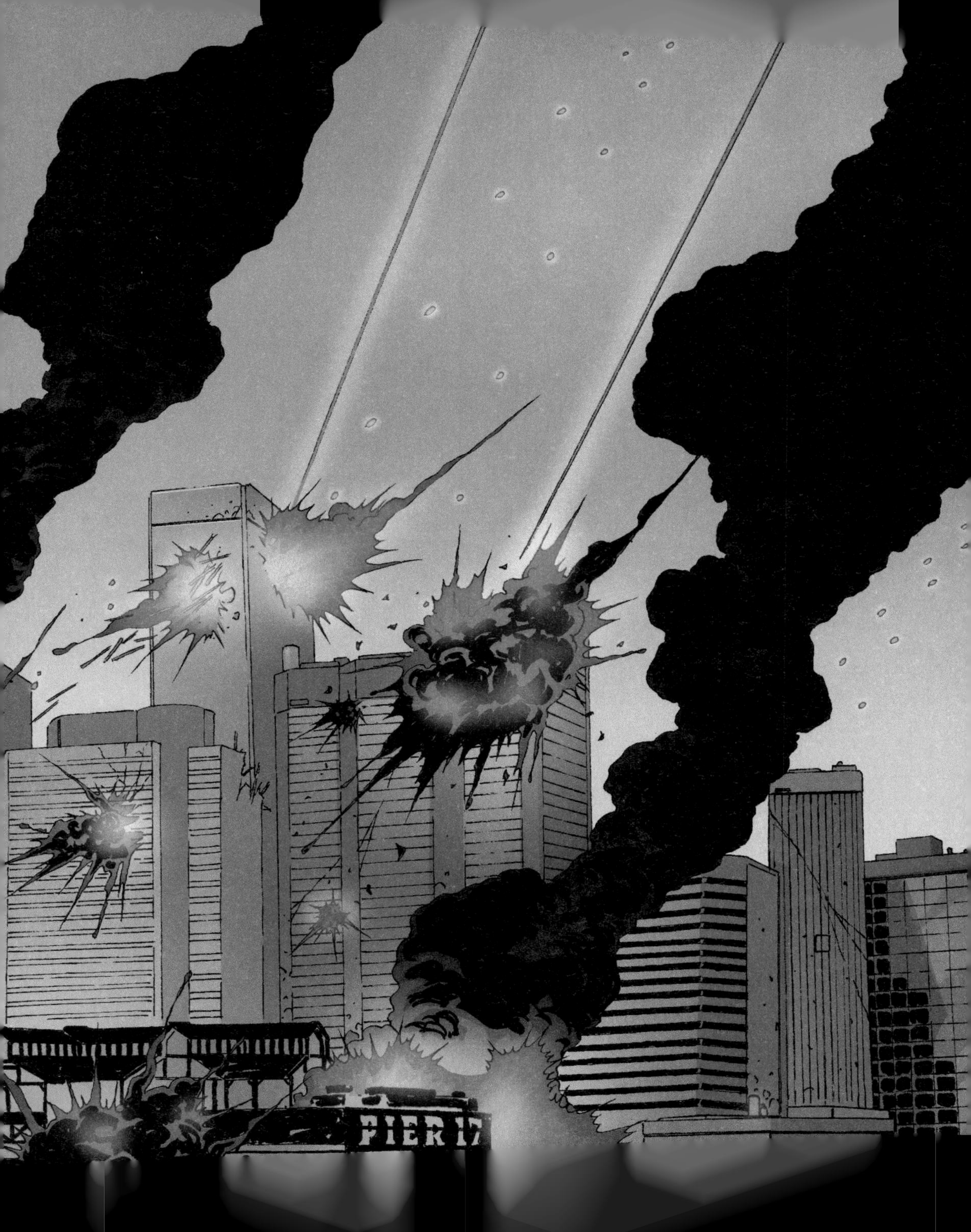
PIER 17

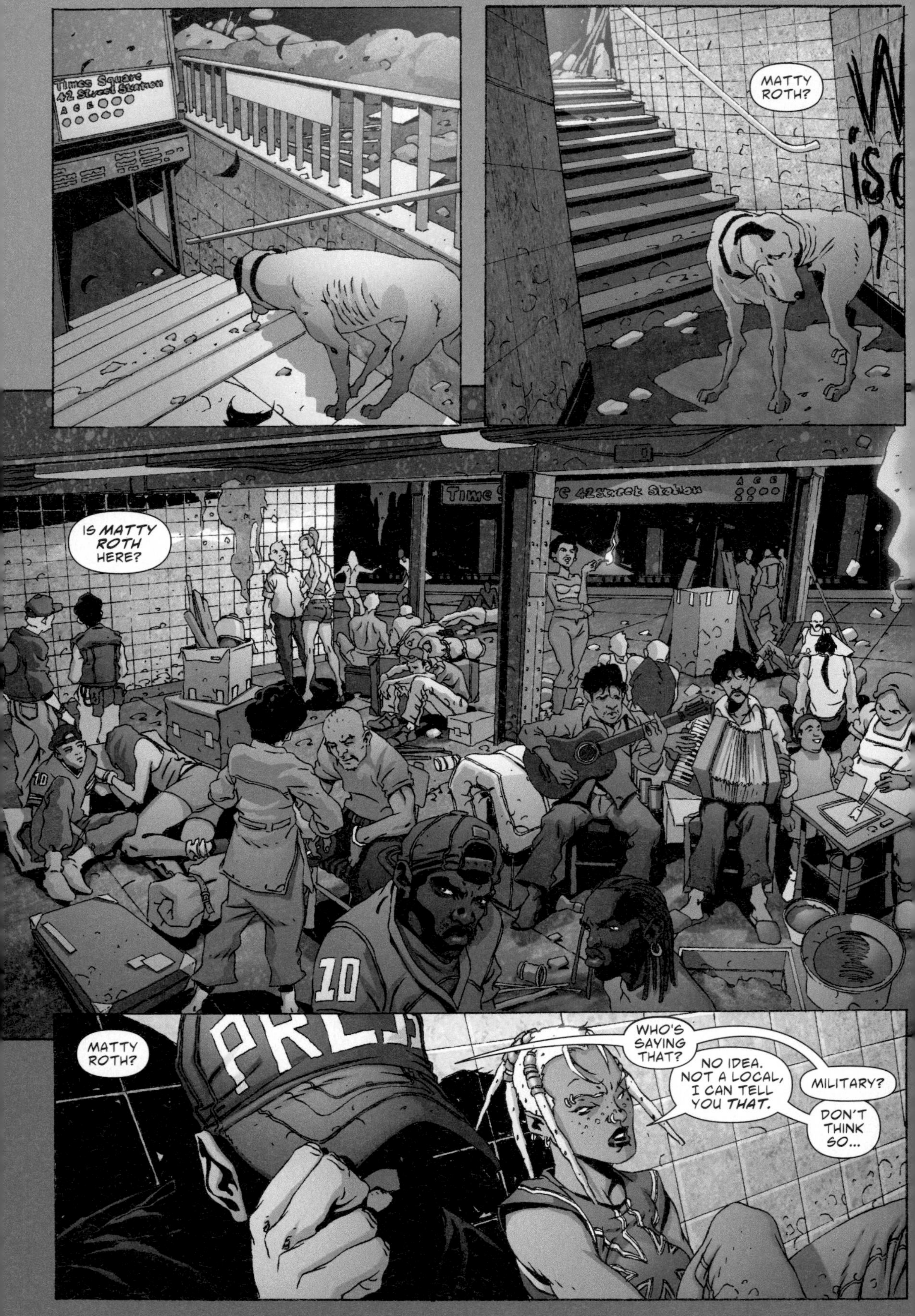
Times Square
42 Street Station
A C E
MATTY ROTH?
IS MATTY ROTH HERE?
MATTY ROTH?
WHO'S SAYING THAT?
NO IDEA. NOT A LOCAL, I CAN TELL YOU THAT.
MILITARY?
DON'T THINK SO...

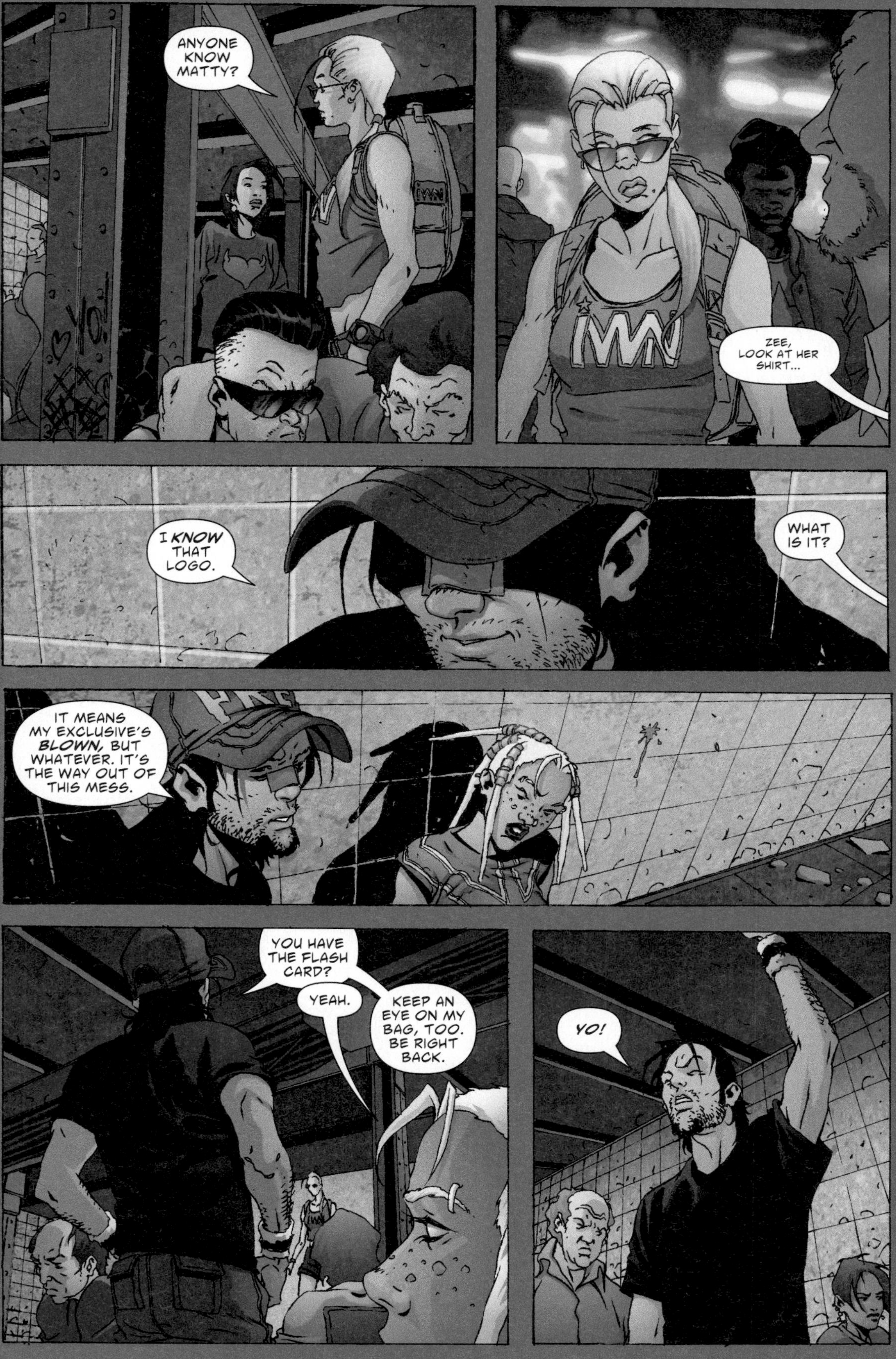
ANYONE KNOW MATTY?
ZEE, LOOK AT HER SHIRT...
I *KNOW* THAT LOGO.
WHAT IS IT?
IT MEANS MY EXCLUSIVE'S ***BLOWN,*** BUT WHATEVER. IT'S THE WAY OUT OF THIS MESS.
YOU HAVE THE FLASH CARD?
YEAH.
KEEP AN EYE ON MY BAG, TOO. BE RIGHT BACK.
YO!

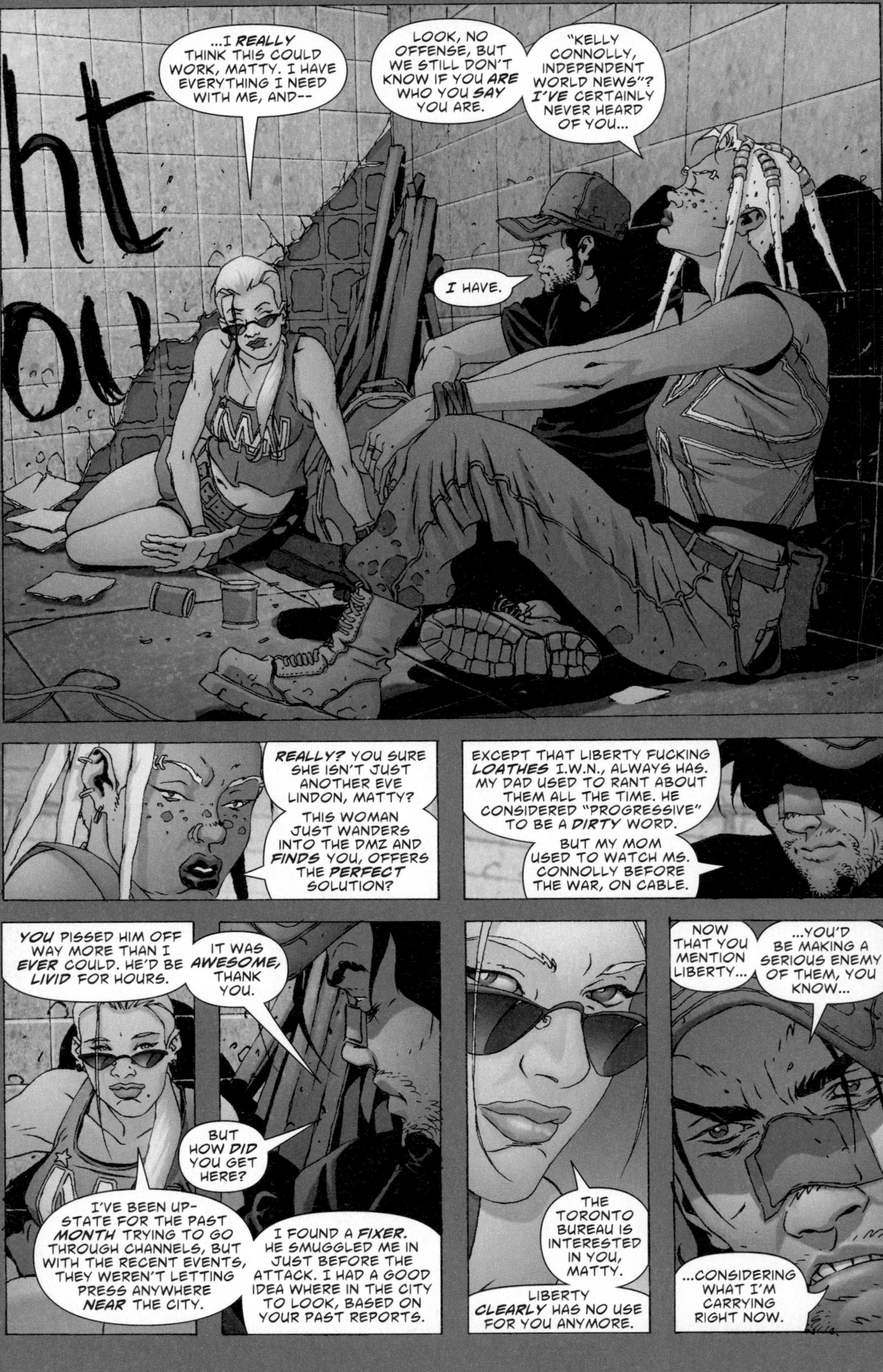
...I REALLY THINK THIS COULD WORK, MATTY. I HAVE EVERYTHING I NEED WITH ME, AND--
LOOK, NO OFFENSE, BUT WE STILL DON'T KNOW IF YOU ARE WHO YOU SAY YOU ARE.
"KELLY CONNOLLY, INDEPENDENT WORLD NEWS"? I'VE CERTAINLY NEVER HEARD OF YOU...
I HAVE.
REALLY? YOU SURE SHE ISN'T JUST ANOTHER EVE LINDON, MATTY?
THIS WOMAN JUST WANDERS INTO THE DMZ AND FINDS YOU, OFFERS THE PERFECT SOLUTION?
EXCEPT THAT LIBERTY FUCKING LOATHES I.W.N., ALWAYS HAS. MY DAD USED TO RANT ABOUT THEM ALL THE TIME. HE CONSIDERED "PROGRESSIVE" TO BE A DIRTY WORD.
BUT MY MOM USED TO WATCH MS. CONNOLLY BEFORE THE WAR, ON CABLE.
YOU PISSED HIM OFF WAY MORE THAN I EVER COULD. HE'D BE LIVID FOR HOURS.
IT WAS AWESOME, THANK YOU.
BUT HOW DID YOU GET HERE?
I'VE BEEN UP-STATE FOR THE PAST MONTH TRYING TO GO THROUGH CHANNELS, BUT WITH THE RECENT EVENTS, THEY WEREN'T LETTING PRESS ANYWHERE NEAR THE CITY.
I FOUND A FIXER. HE SMUGGLED ME IN JUST BEFORE THE ATTACK. I HAD A GOOD IDEA WHERE IN THE CITY TO LOOK, BASED ON YOUR PAST REPORTS.
THE TORONTO BUREAU IS INTERESTED IN YOU, MATTY.
LIBERTY CLEARLY HAS NO USE FOR YOU ANYMORE.
NOW THAT YOU MENTION LIBERTY...
...YOU'D BE MAKING A SERIOUS ENEMY OF THEM, YOU KNOW...
...CONSIDERING WHAT I'M CARRYING RIGHT NOW.

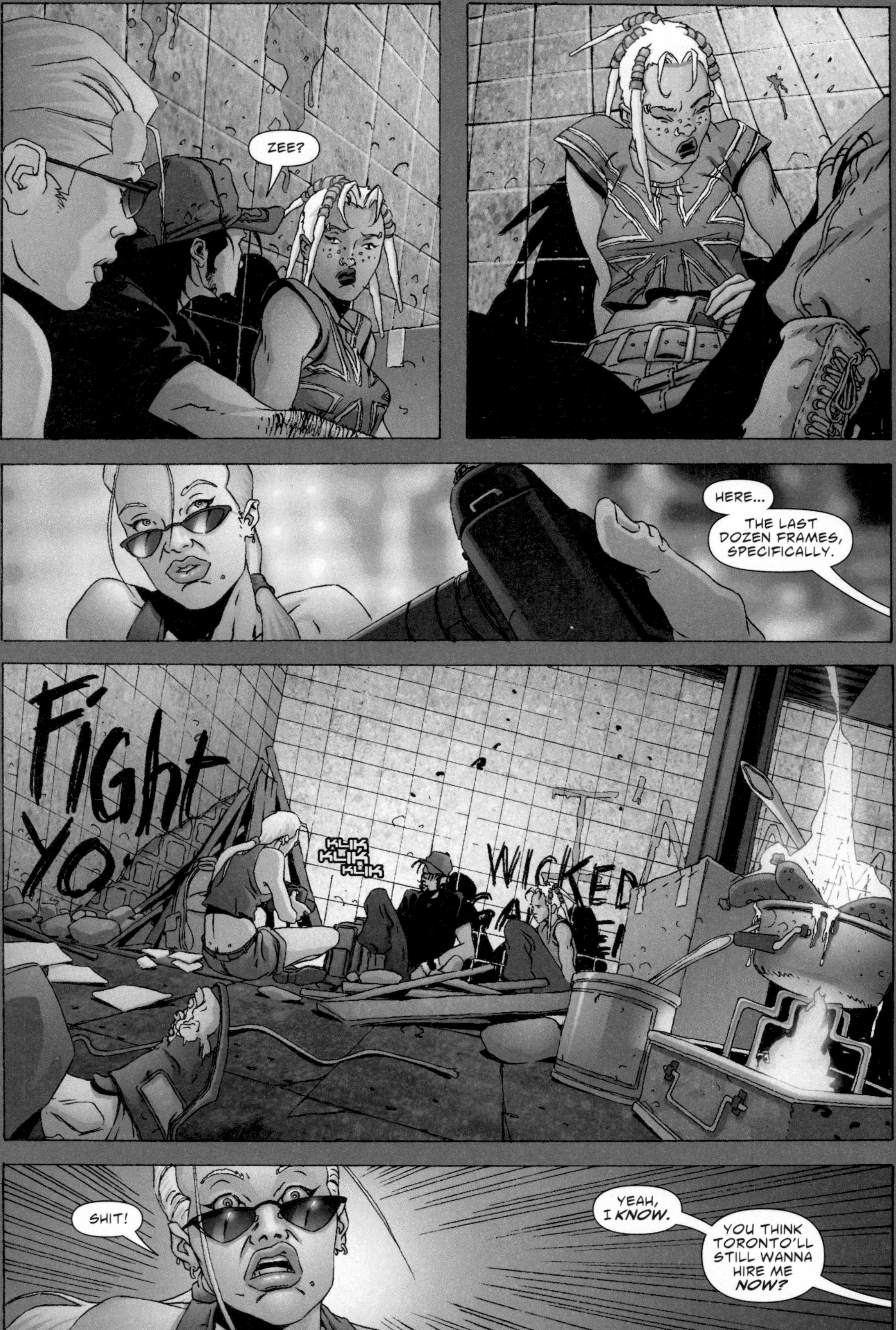
ZEE?
HERE... THE LAST DOZEN FRAMES, SPECIFICALLY.
FIGHT YO
KLIK KLIK KLIK
WICKED
SHIT!
YEAH, I KNOW.
YOU THINK TORONTO'LL STILL WANNA HIRE ME NOW?

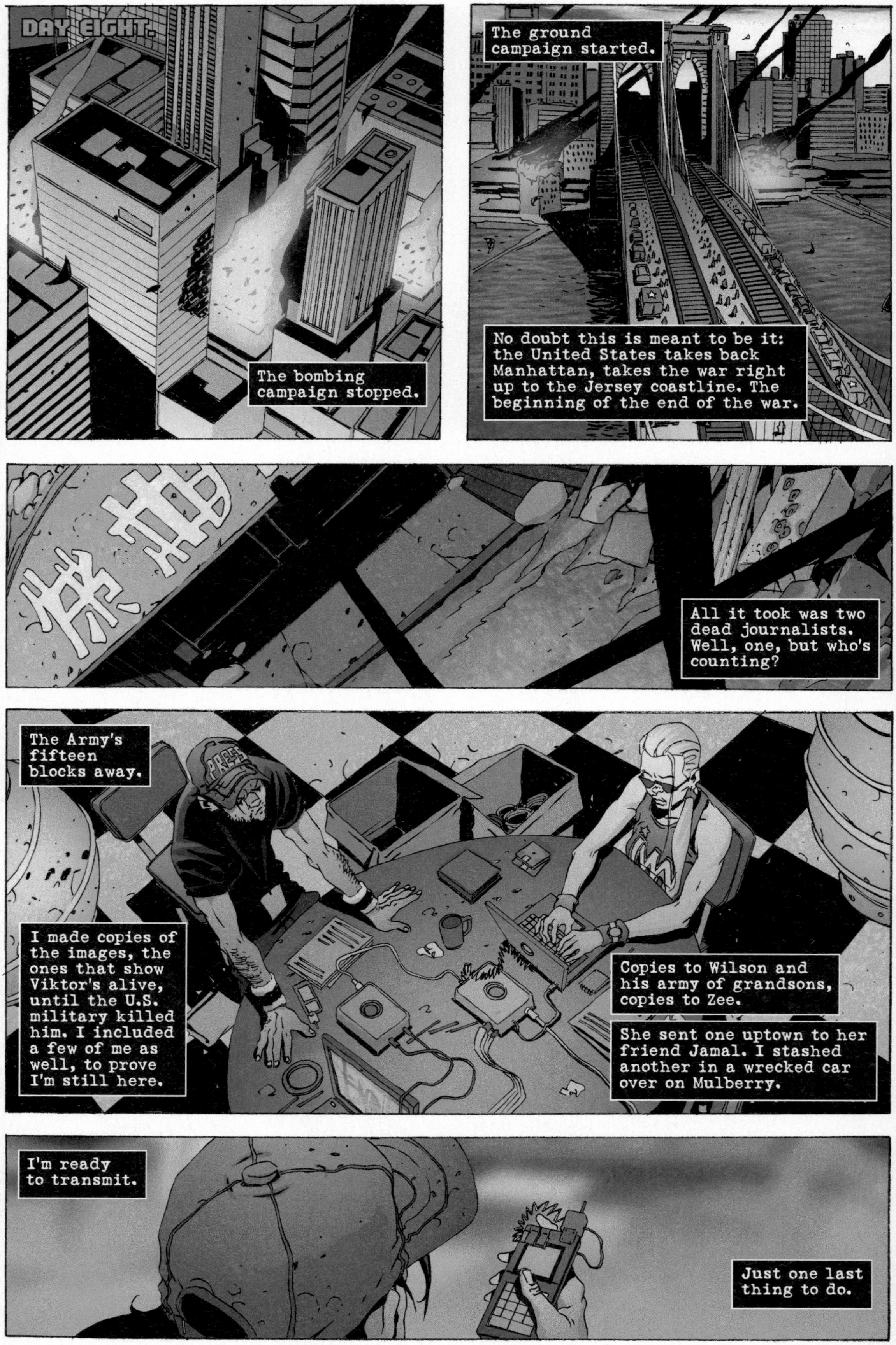
DAY EIGHT.
The bombing campaign stopped.
The ground campaign started.
No doubt this is meant to be it: the United States takes back Manhattan, takes the war right up to the Jersey coastline. The beginning of the end of the war.
All it took was two dead journalists. Well, one, but who's counting?
The Army's fifteen blocks away.
I made copies of the images, the ones that show Viktor's alive, until the U.S. military killed him. I included a few of me as well, to prove I'm still here.
Copies to Wilson and his army of grandsons, copies to Zee.
She sent one uptown to her friend Jamal. I stashed another in a wrecked car over on Mulberry.
I'm ready to transmit.
Just one last thing to do.

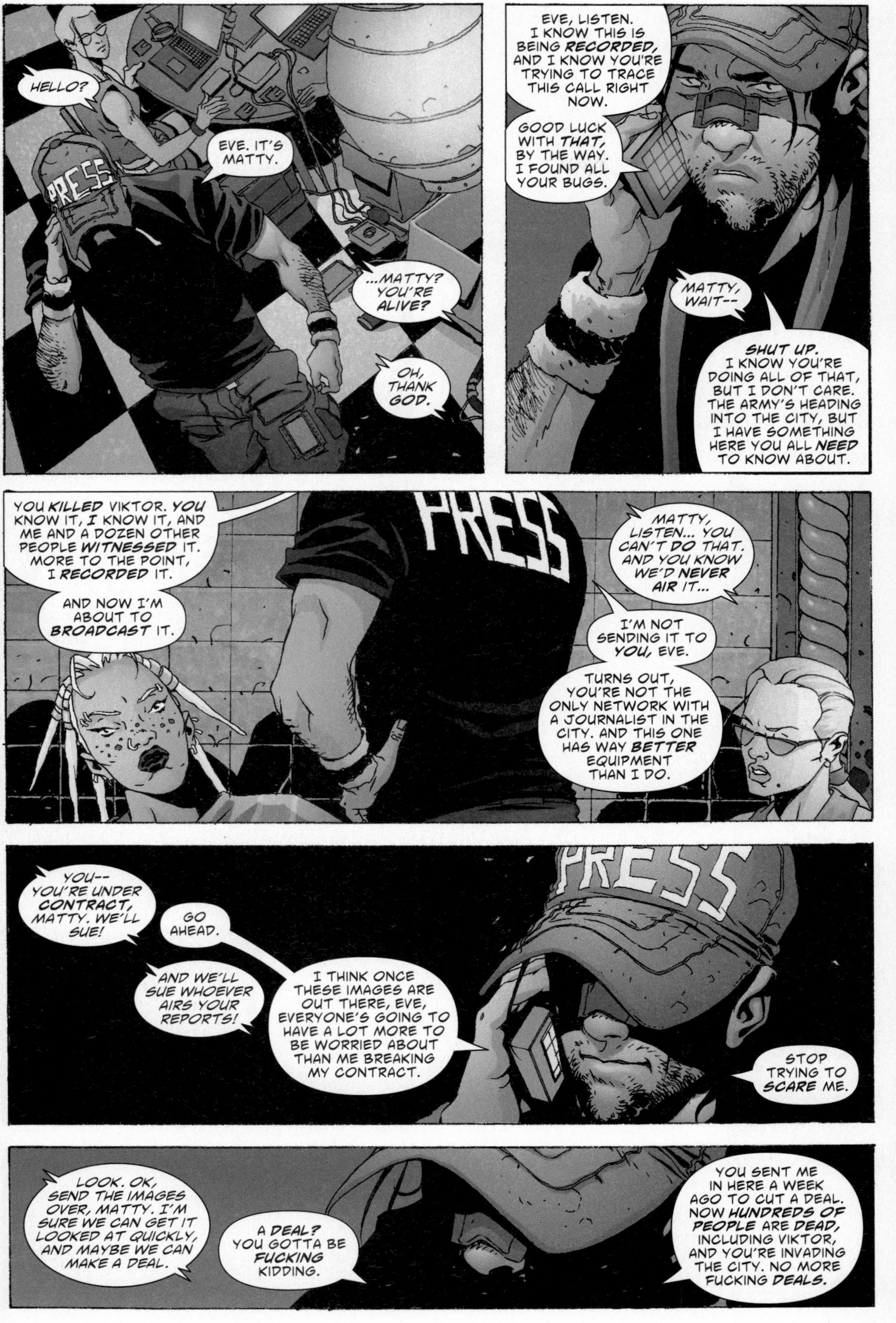
HELLO?
EVE. IT'S MATTY.
...MATTY? YOU'RE ALIVE?
OH, THANK GOD.
EVE, LISTEN. I KNOW THIS IS BEING RECORDED, AND I KNOW YOU'RE TRYING TO TRACE THIS CALL RIGHT NOW.
GOOD LUCK WITH THAT, BY THE WAY. I FOUND ALL YOUR BUGS.
MATTY, WAIT--
SHUT UP. I KNOW YOU'RE DOING ALL OF THAT, BUT I DON'T CARE. THE ARMY'S HEADING INTO THE CITY, BUT I HAVE SOMETHING HERE YOU ALL NEED TO KNOW ABOUT.
YOU KILLED VIKTOR. YOU KNOW IT, I KNOW IT, AND ME AND A DOZEN OTHER PEOPLE WITNESSED IT. MORE TO THE POINT, I RECORDED IT.
AND NOW I'M ABOUT TO BROADCAST IT.
PRESS
MATTY, LISTEN... YOU CAN'T DO THAT. AND YOU KNOW WE'D NEVER AIR IT...
I'M NOT SENDING IT TO YOU, EVE.
TURNS OUT, YOU'RE NOT THE ONLY NETWORK WITH A JOURNALIST IN THE CITY. AND THIS ONE HAS WAY BETTER EQUIPMENT THAN I DO.
YOU-- YOU'RE UNDER CONTRACT, MATTY. WE'LL SUE!
GO AHEAD.
AND WE'LL SUE WHOEVER AIRS YOUR REPORTS!
I THINK ONCE THESE IMAGES ARE OUT THERE, EVE, EVERYONE'S GOING TO HAVE A LOT MORE TO BE WORRIED ABOUT THAN ME BREAKING MY CONTRACT.
STOP TRYING TO SCARE ME.
LOOK. OK, SEND THE IMAGES OVER, MATTY. I'M SURE WE CAN GET IT LOOKED AT QUICKLY, AND MAYBE WE CAN MAKE A DEAL.
A DEAL? YOU GOTTA BE FUCKING KIDDING.
YOU SENT ME IN HERE A WEEK AGO TO CUT A DEAL. NOW HUNDREDS OF PEOPLE ARE DEAD, INCLUDING VIKTOR, AND YOU'RE INVADING THE CITY. NO MORE FUCKING DEALS.

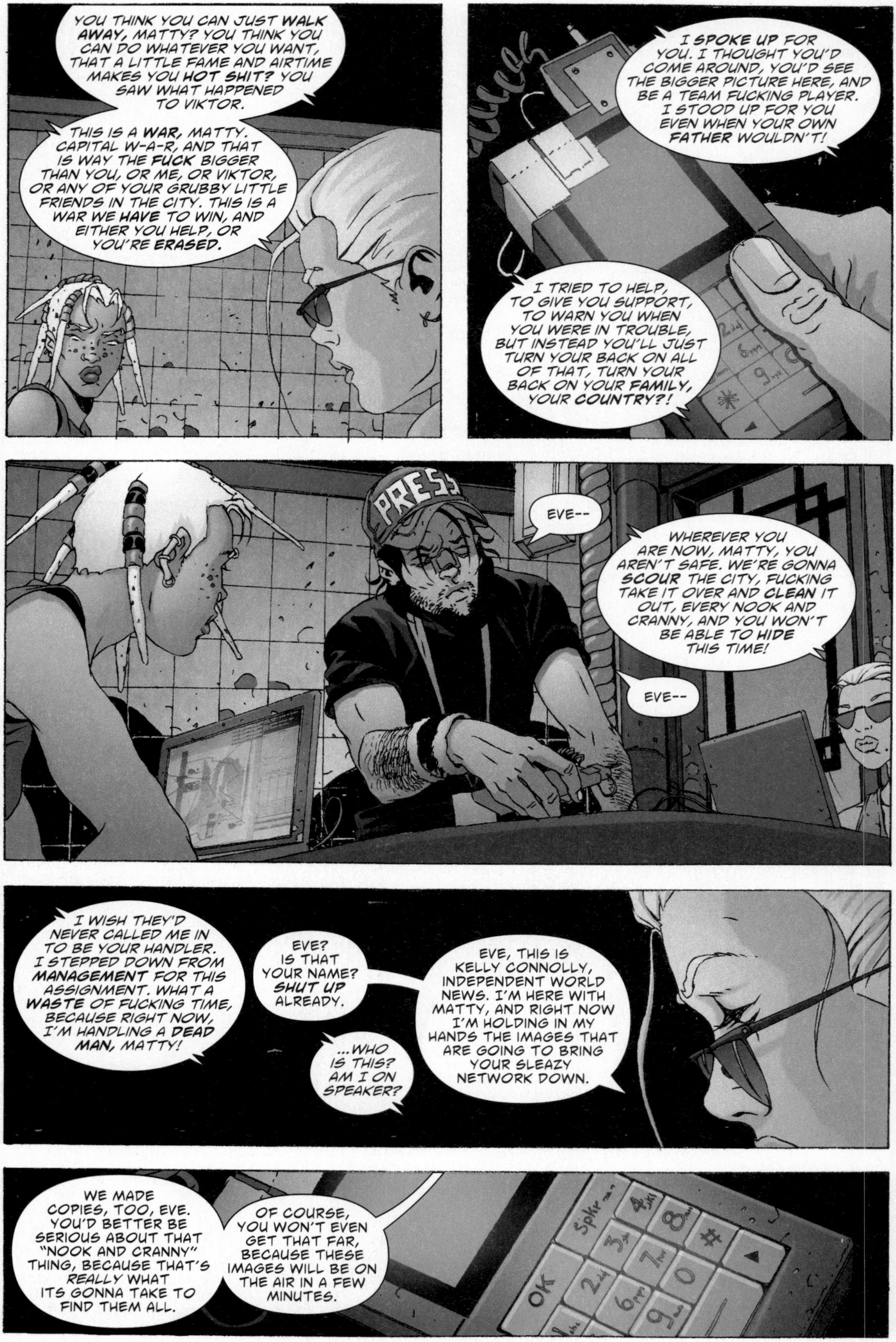

YOU THINK YOU CAN JUST WALK AWAY, MATTY? YOU THINK YOU CAN DO WHATEVER YOU WANT, THAT A LITTLE FAME AND AIRTIME MAKES YOU HOT SHIT? YOU SAW WHAT HAPPENED TO VIKTOR.
THIS IS A WAR, MATTY. CAPITAL W-A-R, AND THAT IS WAY THE FUCK BIGGER THAN YOU, OR ME, OR VIKTOR, OR ANY OF YOUR GRUBBY LITTLE FRIENDS IN THE CITY. THIS IS A WAR WE HAVE TO WIN, AND EITHER YOU HELP, OR YOU'RE ERASED.
I SPOKE UP FOR YOU. I THOUGHT YOU'D COME AROUND, YOU'D SEE THE BIGGER PICTURE HERE, AND BE A TEAM FUCKING PLAYER. I STOOD UP FOR YOU EVEN WHEN YOUR OWN FATHER WOULDN'T!
I TRIED TO HELP, TO GIVE YOU SUPPORT, TO WARN YOU WHEN YOU WERE IN TROUBLE, BUT INSTEAD YOU'LL JUST TURN YOUR BACK ON ALL OF THAT, TURN YOUR BACK ON YOUR FAMILY, YOUR COUNTRY?!
PRESS
EVE--
WHEREVER YOU ARE NOW, MATTY, YOU AREN'T SAFE. WE'RE GONNA SCOUR THE CITY, FUCKING TAKE IT OVER AND CLEAN IT OUT, EVERY NOOK AND CRANNY, AND YOU WON'T BE ABLE TO HIDE THIS TIME!
EVE--
I WISH THEY'D NEVER CALLED ME IN TO BE YOUR HANDLER. I STEPPED DOWN FROM MANAGEMENT FOR THIS ASSIGNMENT. WHAT A WASTE OF FUCKING TIME, BECAUSE RIGHT NOW, I'M HANDLING A DEAD MAN, MATTY!
EVE? IS THAT YOUR NAME? SHUT UP ALREADY.
...WHO IS THIS? AM I ON SPEAKER?
EVE, THIS IS KELLY CONNOLLY, INDEPENDENT WORLD NEWS. I'M HERE WITH MATTY, AND RIGHT NOW I'M HOLDING IN MY HANDS THE IMAGES THAT ARE GOING TO BRING YOUR SLEAZY NETWORK DOWN.
WE MADE COPIES, TOO, EVE. YOU'D BETTER BE SERIOUS ABOUT THAT "NOOK AND CRANNY" THING, BECAUSE THAT'S REALLY WHAT ITS GONNA TAKE TO FIND THEM ALL.
OF COURSE, YOU WON'T EVEN GET THAT FAR, BECAUSE THESE IMAGES WILL BE ON THE AIR IN A FEW MINUTES.

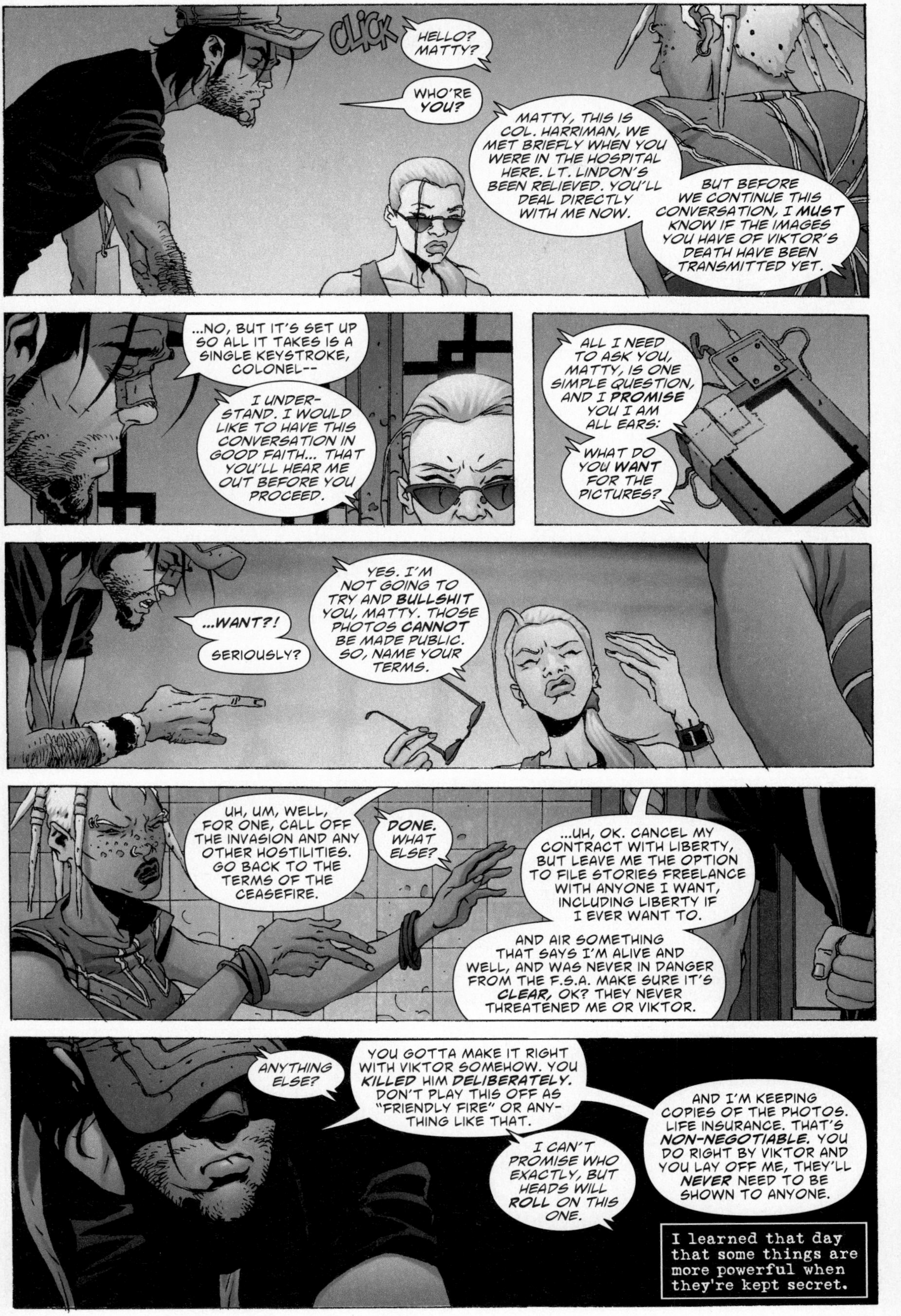
CLICK
HELLO? MATTY?
WHO'RE YOU?
MATTY, THIS IS COL. HARRIMAN, WE MET BRIEFLY WHEN YOU WERE IN THE HOSPITAL HERE. LT. LINDON'S BEEN RELIEVED. YOU'LL DEAL DIRECTLY WITH ME NOW.
BUT BEFORE WE CONTINUE THIS CONVERSATION, I MUST KNOW IF THE IMAGES YOU HAVE OF VIKTOR'S DEATH HAVE BEEN TRANSMITTED YET.
...NO, BUT IT'S SET UP SO ALL IT TAKES IS A SINGLE KEYSTROKE, COLONEL--
I UNDERSTAND. I WOULD LIKE TO HAVE THIS CONVERSATION IN GOOD FAITH... THAT YOU'LL HEAR ME OUT BEFORE YOU PROCEED.
ALL I NEED TO ASK YOU, MATTY, IS ONE SIMPLE QUESTION, AND I PROMISE YOU I AM ALL EARS:
WHAT DO YOU WANT FOR THE PICTURES?
...WANT?!
SERIOUSLY?
YES. I'M NOT GOING TO TRY AND BULLSHIT YOU, MATTY. THOSE PHOTOS CANNOT BE MADE PUBLIC. SO, NAME YOUR TERMS.
UH, UM, WELL, FOR ONE, CALL OFF THE INVASION AND ANY OTHER HOSTILITIES. GO BACK TO THE TERMS OF THE CEASEFIRE.
DONE. WHAT ELSE?
...UH, OK. CANCEL MY CONTRACT WITH LIBERTY, BUT LEAVE ME THE OPTION TO FILE STORIES FREELANCE WITH ANYONE I WANT, INCLUDING LIBERTY IF I EVER WANT TO.
AND AIR SOMETHING THAT SAYS I'M ALIVE AND WELL, AND WAS NEVER IN DANGER FROM THE F.S.A. MAKE SURE IT'S CLEAR, OK? THEY NEVER THREATENED ME OR VIKTOR.
ANYTHING ELSE?
YOU GOTTA MAKE IT RIGHT WITH VIKTOR SOMEHOW. YOU KILLED HIM DELIBERATELY. DON'T PLAY THIS OFF AS "FRIENDLY FIRE" OR ANYTHING LIKE THAT.
I CAN'T PROMISE WHO EXACTLY, BUT HEADS WILL ROLL ON THIS ONE.
AND I'M KEEPING COPIES OF THE PHOTOS. LIFE INSURANCE. THAT'S NON-NEGOTIABLE. YOU DO RIGHT BY VIKTOR AND YOU LAY OFF ME, THEY'LL NEVER NEED TO BE SHOWN TO ANYONE.
I learned that day that some things are more powerful when they're kept secret.

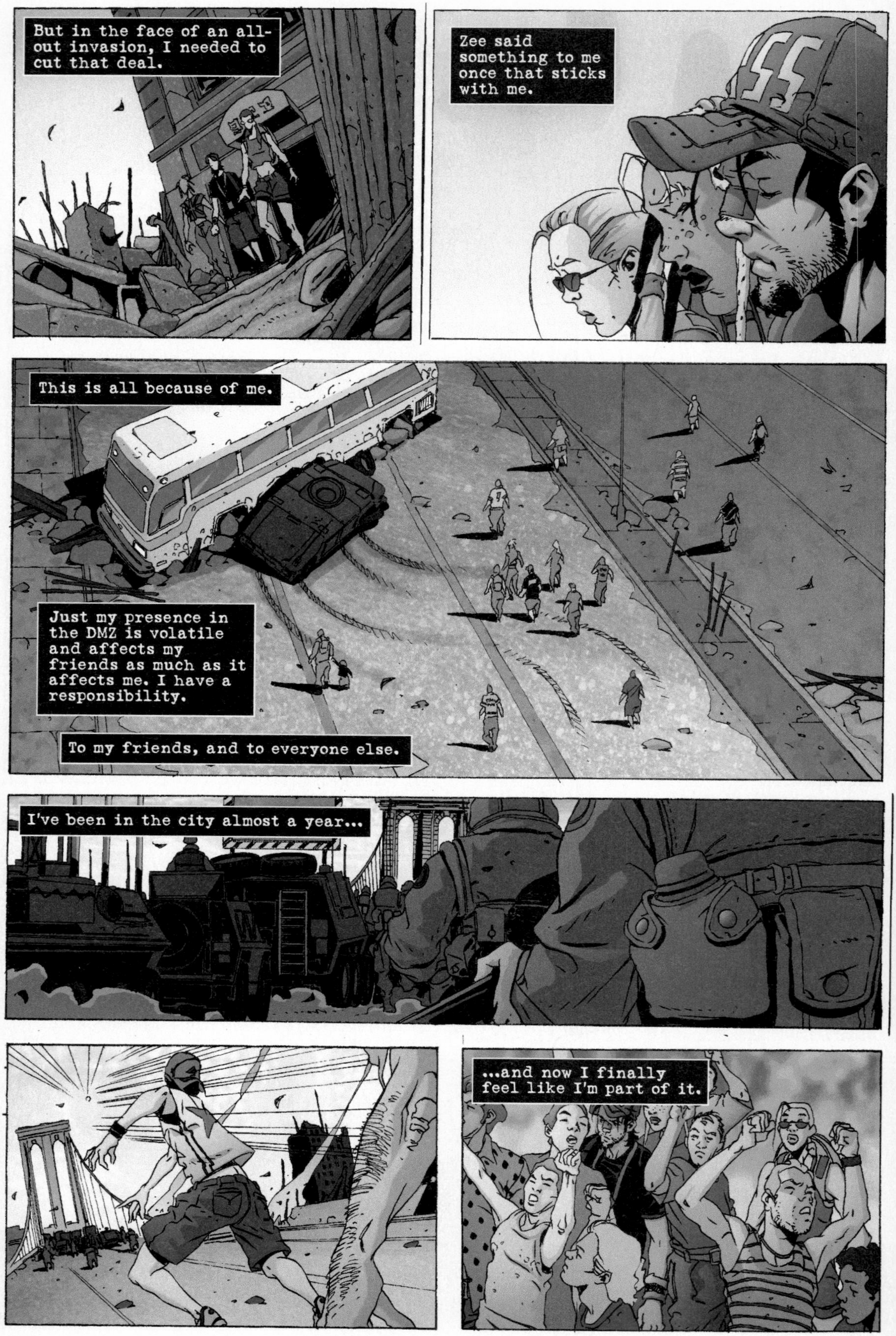
But in the face of an all-out invasion, I needed to cut that deal.
Zee said something to me once that sticks with me.
This is all because of me.
Just my presence in the DMZ is volatile and affects my friends as much as it affects me. I have a responsibility.
To my friends, and to everyone else.
I've been in the city almost a year...
...and now I finally feel like I'm part of it.

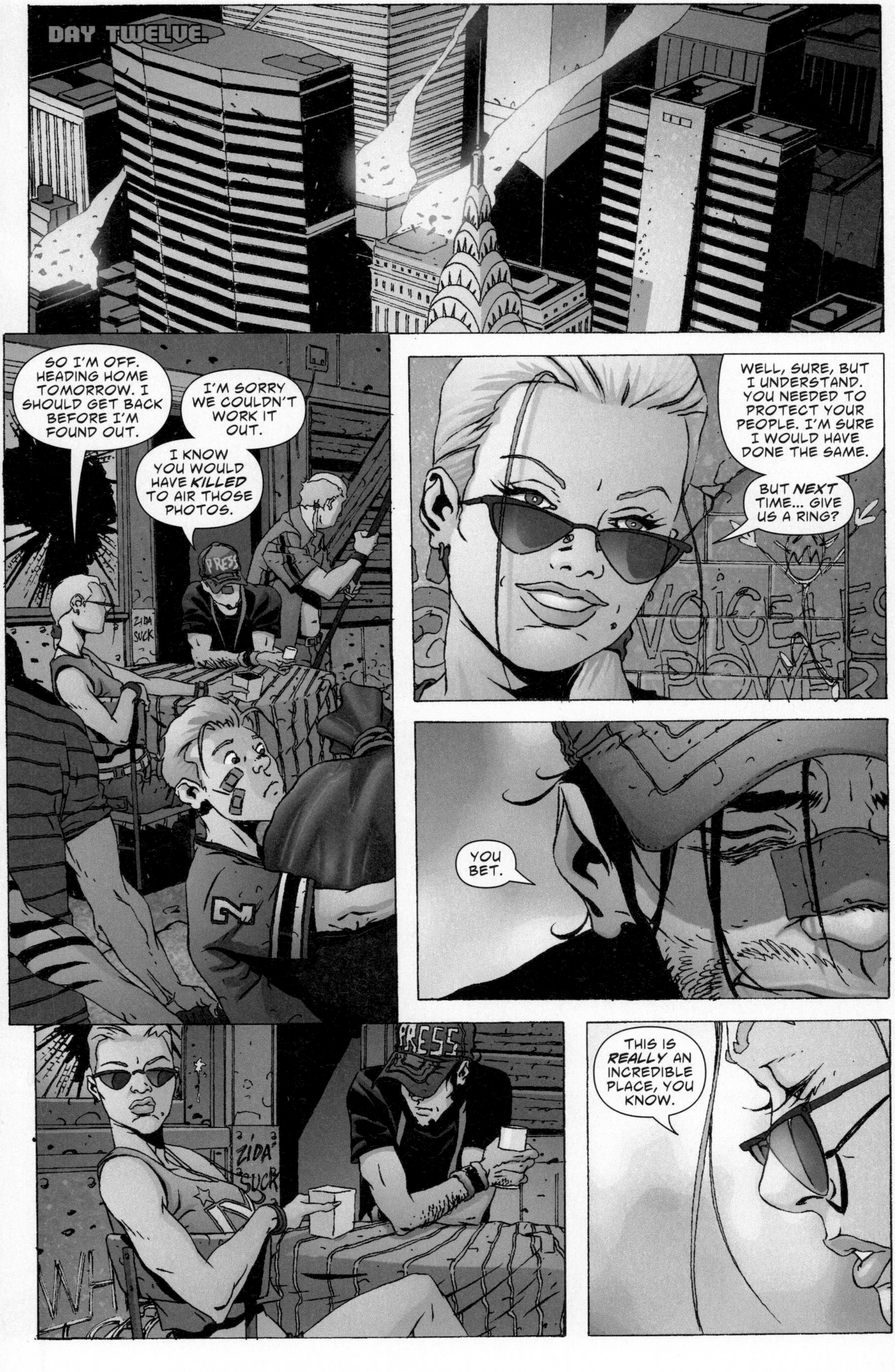
DAY TWELVE.
SO I'M OFF. HEADING HOME TOMORROW. I SHOULD GET BACK BEFORE I'M FOUND OUT.
I'M SORRY WE COULDN'T WORK IT OUT.
I KNOW YOU WOULD HAVE KILLED TO AIR THOSE PHOTOS.
PRESS
ZIDA SUCK
WELL, SURE, BUT I UNDERSTAND. YOU NEEDED TO PROTECT YOUR PEOPLE. I'M SURE I WOULD HAVE DONE THE SAME.
BUT NEXT TIME... GIVE US A RING?
VOICELESS POWER
YOU BET.
PRESS
ZIDA SUCK
THIS IS REALLY AN INCREDIBLE PLACE, YOU KNOW.

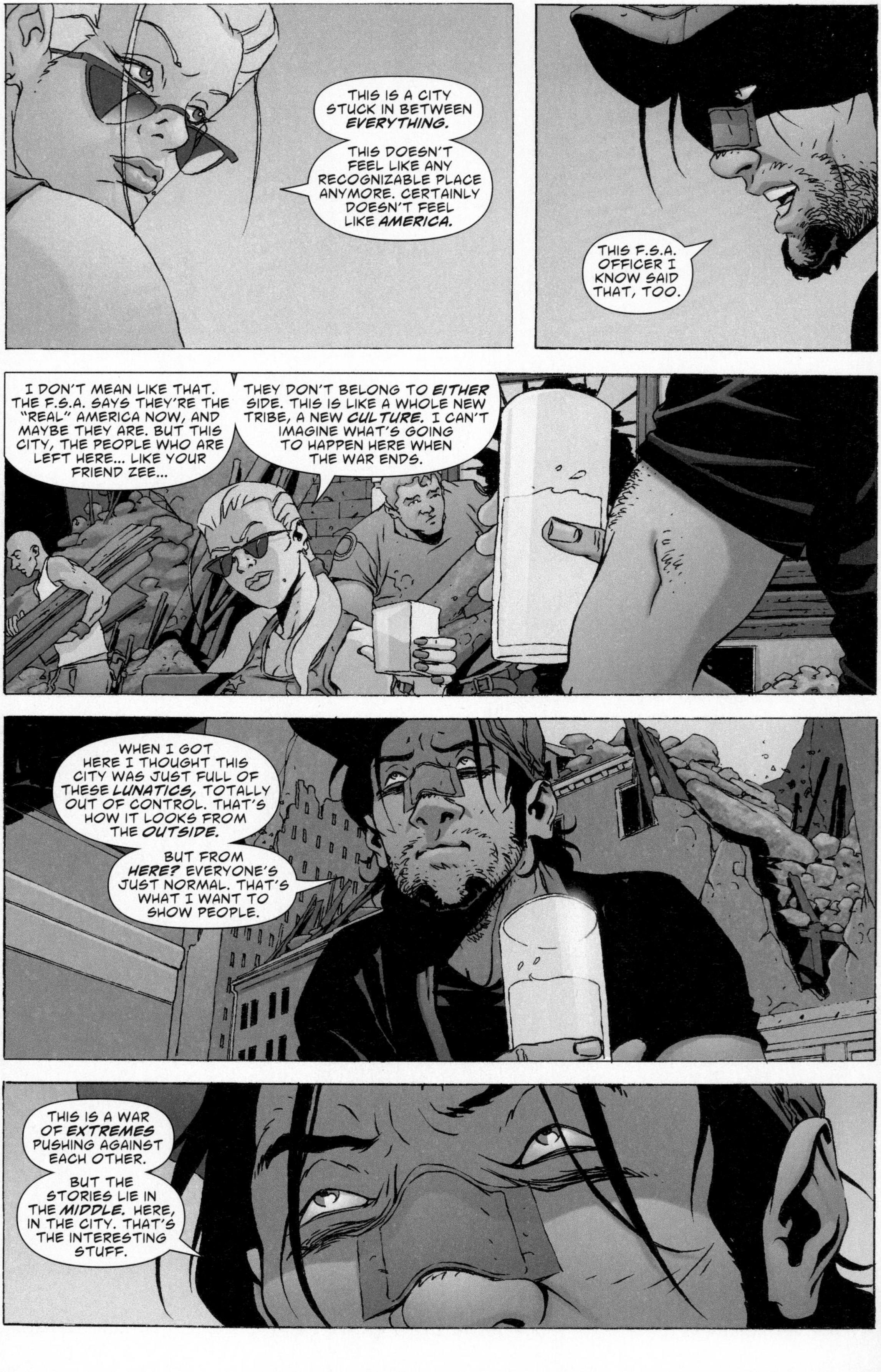
THIS IS A CITY STUCK IN BETWEEN *EVERYTHING.*
THIS DOESN'T FEEL LIKE ANY RECOGNIZABLE PLACE ANYMORE. CERTAINLY DOESN'T FEEL LIKE *AMERICA.*
THIS F.S.A. OFFICER I KNOW SAID THAT, TOO.
I DON'T MEAN LIKE THAT. THE F.S.A. SAYS THEY'RE THE "REAL" AMERICA NOW, AND MAYBE THEY ARE. BUT THIS CITY, THE PEOPLE WHO ARE LEFT HERE... LIKE YOUR FRIEND ZEE...
THEY DON'T BELONG TO *EITHER* SIDE. THIS IS LIKE A WHOLE NEW TRIBE, A NEW *CULTURE.* I CAN'T IMAGINE WHAT'S GOING TO HAPPEN HERE WHEN THE WAR ENDS.
WHEN I GOT HERE I THOUGHT THIS CITY WAS JUST FULL OF THESE *LUNATICS,* TOTALLY OUT OF CONTROL. THAT'S HOW IT LOOKS FROM THE *OUTSIDE.*
BUT FROM *HERE?* EVERYONE'S JUST NORMAL. THAT'S WHAT I WANT TO SHOW PEOPLE.
THIS IS A WAR OF *EXTREMES* PUSHING AGAINST EACH OTHER.
BUT THE STORIES LIE IN THE *MIDDLE.* HERE, IN THE CITY. THAT'S THE INTERESTING STUFF.

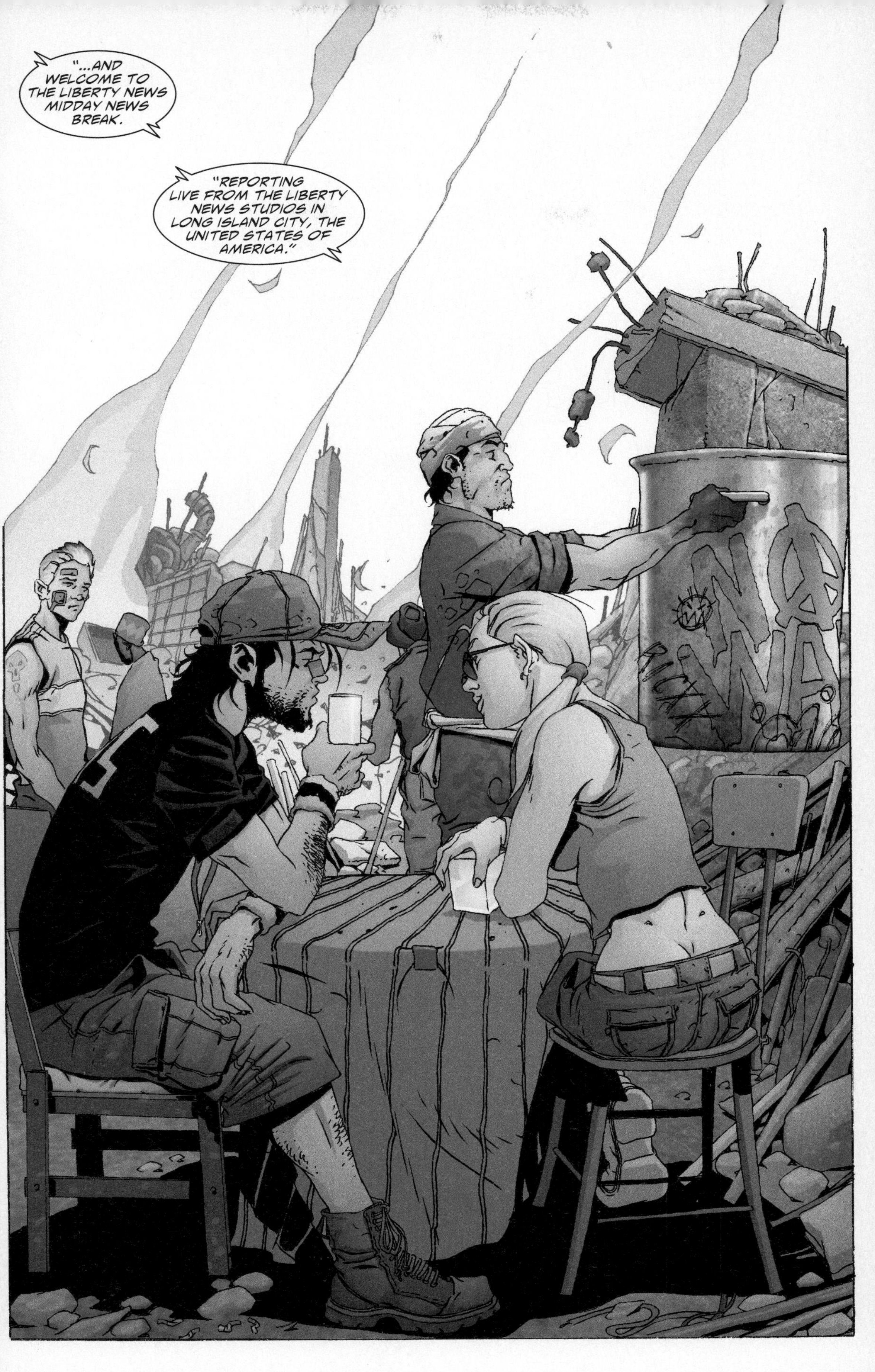
"...AND WELCOME TO THE LIBERTY NEWS MIDDAY NEWS BREAK.
"REPORTING LIVE FROM THE LIBERTY NEWS STUDIOS IN LONG ISLAND CITY, THE UNITED STATES OF AMERICA."

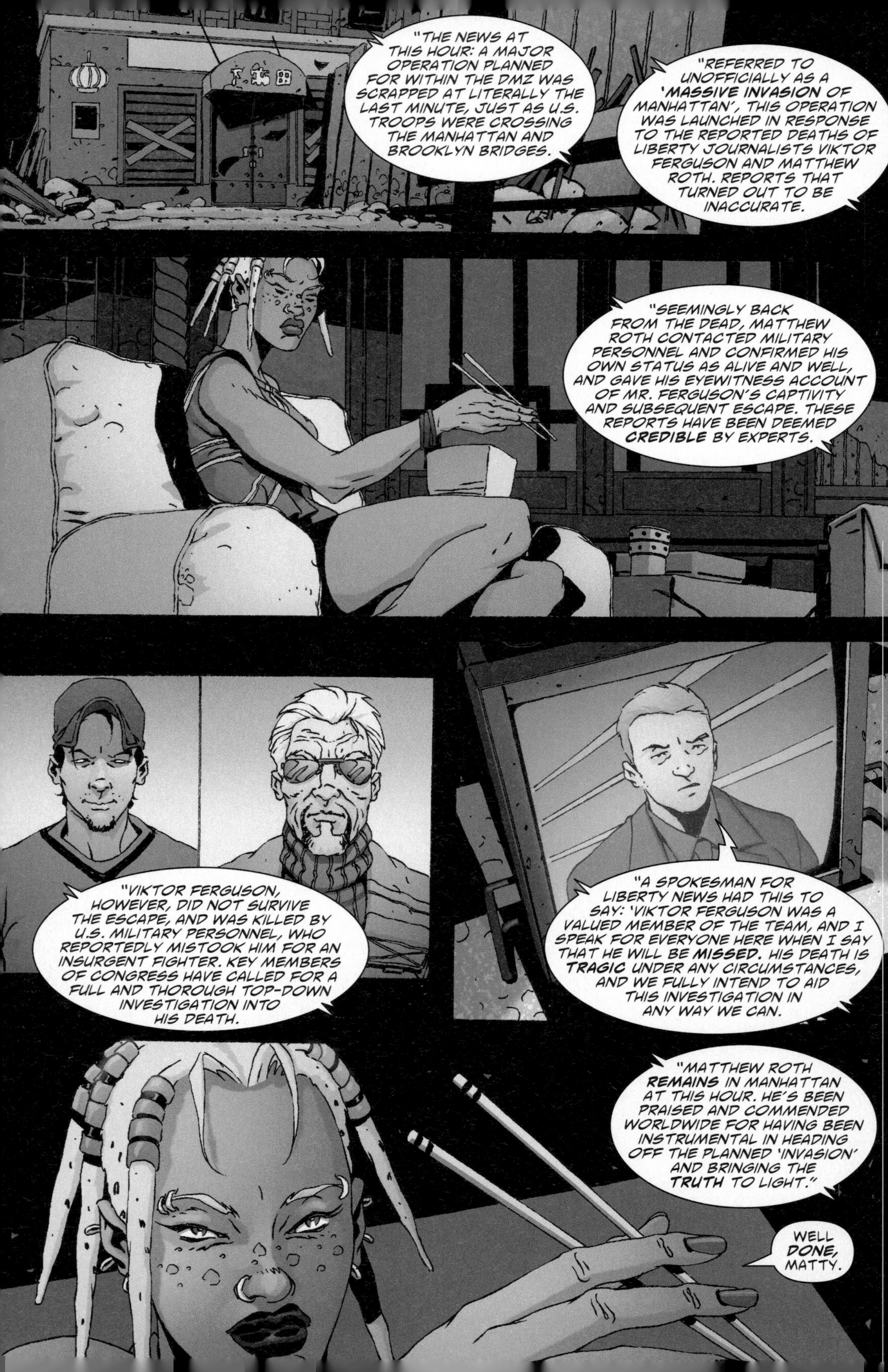
"THE NEWS AT THIS HOUR: A MAJOR OPERATION PLANNED FOR WITHIN THE DMZ WAS SCRAPPED AT LITERALLY THE LAST MINUTE, JUST AS U.S. TROOPS WERE CROSSING THE MANHATTAN AND BROOKLYN BRIDGES.
"REFERRED TO UNOFFICIALLY AS A 'MASSIVE INVASION OF MANHATTAN', THIS OPERATION WAS LAUNCHED IN RESPONSE TO THE REPORTED DEATHS OF LIBERTY JOURNALISTS VIKTOR FERGUSON AND MATTHEW ROTH. REPORTS THAT TURNED OUT TO BE INACCURATE.
"SEEMINGLY BACK FROM THE DEAD, MATTHEW ROTH CONTACTED MILITARY PERSONNEL AND CONFIRMED HIS OWN STATUS AS ALIVE AND WELL, AND GAVE HIS EYEWITNESS ACCOUNT OF MR. FERGUSON'S CAPTIVITY AND SUBSEQUENT ESCAPE. THESE REPORTS HAVE BEEN DEEMED CREDIBLE BY EXPERTS.
"VIKTOR FERGUSON, HOWEVER, DID NOT SURVIVE THE ESCAPE, AND WAS KILLED BY U.S. MILITARY PERSONNEL, WHO REPORTEDLY MISTOOK HIM FOR AN INSURGENT FIGHTER. KEY MEMBERS OF CONGRESS HAVE CALLED FOR A FULL AND THOROUGH TOP-DOWN INVESTIGATION INTO HIS DEATH.
"A SPOKESMAN FOR LIBERTY NEWS HAD THIS TO SAY: 'VIKTOR FERGUSON WAS A VALUED MEMBER OF THE TEAM, AND I SPEAK FOR EVERYONE HERE WHEN I SAY THAT HE WILL BE MISSED. HIS DEATH IS TRAGIC UNDER ANY CIRCUMSTANCES, AND WE FULLY INTEND TO AID THIS INVESTIGATION IN ANY WAY WE CAN.
"MATTHEW ROTH REMAINS IN MANHATTAN AT THIS HOUR. HE'S BEEN PRAISED AND COMMENDED WORLDWIDE FOR HAVING BEEN INSTRUMENTAL IN HEADING OFF THE PLANNED 'INVASION' AND BRINGING THE TRUTH TO LIGHT."
WELL DONE, MATTY.

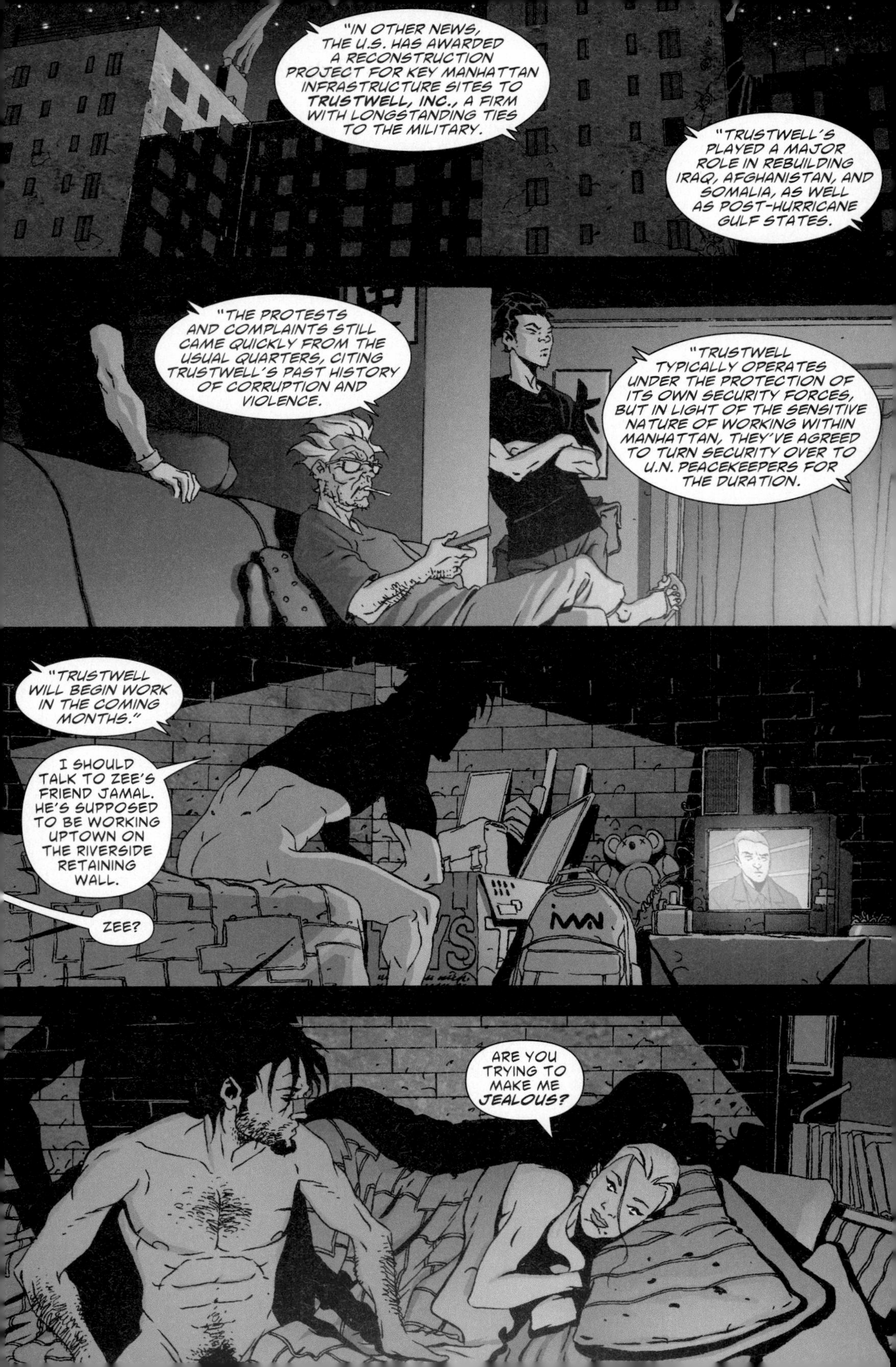
"IN OTHER NEWS, THE U.S. HAS AWARDED A RECONSTRUCTION PROJECT FOR KEY MANHATTAN INFRASTRUCTURE SITES TO TRUSTWELL, INC., A FIRM WITH LONGSTANDING TIES TO THE MILITARY.
"TRUSTWELL'S PLAYED A MAJOR ROLE IN REBUILDING IRAQ, AFGHANISTAN, AND SOMALIA, AS WELL AS POST-HURRICANE GULF STATES.
"THE PROTESTS AND COMPLAINTS STILL CAME QUICKLY FROM THE USUAL QUARTERS, CITING TRUSTWELL'S PAST HISTORY OF CORRUPTION AND VIOLENCE.
"TRUSTWELL TYPICALLY OPERATES UNDER THE PROTECTION OF ITS OWN SECURITY FORCES, BUT IN LIGHT OF THE SENSITIVE NATURE OF WORKING WITHIN MANHATTAN, THEY'VE AGREED TO TURN SECURITY OVER TO U.N. PEACEKEEPERS FOR THE DURATION.
"TRUSTWELL WILL BEGIN WORK IN THE COMING MONTHS."
I SHOULD TALK TO ZEE'S FRIEND JAMAL. HE'S SUPPOSED TO BE WORKING UPTOWN ON THE RIVERSIDE RETAINING WALL.
ZEE?
ARE YOU TRYING TO MAKE ME JEALOUS?

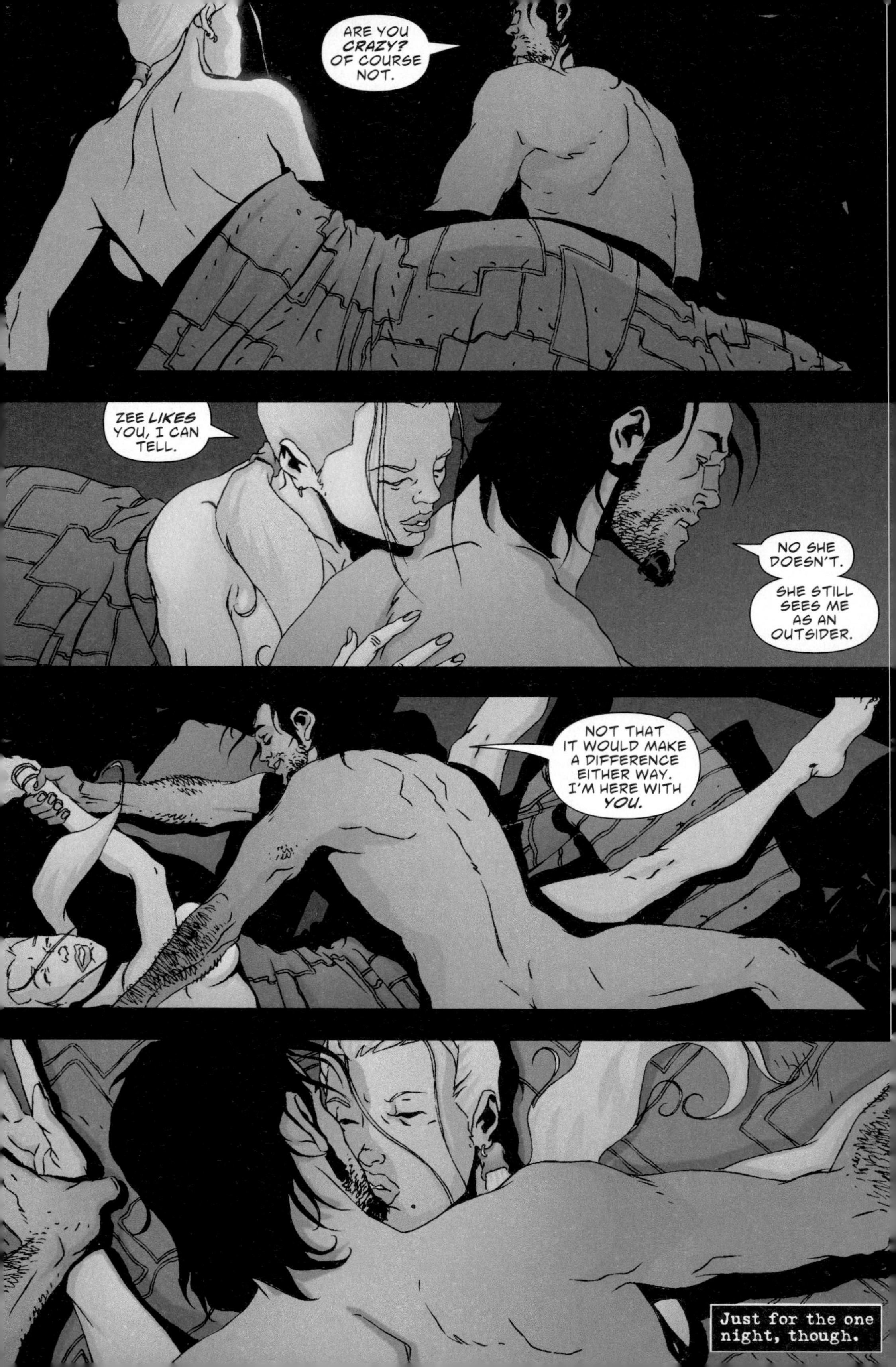
ARE YOU CRAZY? OF COURSE NOT.
ZEE LIKES YOU, I CAN TELL.
NO SHE DOESN'T.
SHE STILL SEES ME AS AN OUTSIDER.
NOT THAT IT WOULD MAKE A DIFFERENCE EITHER WAY. I'M HERE WITH YOU.
Just for the one night, though.

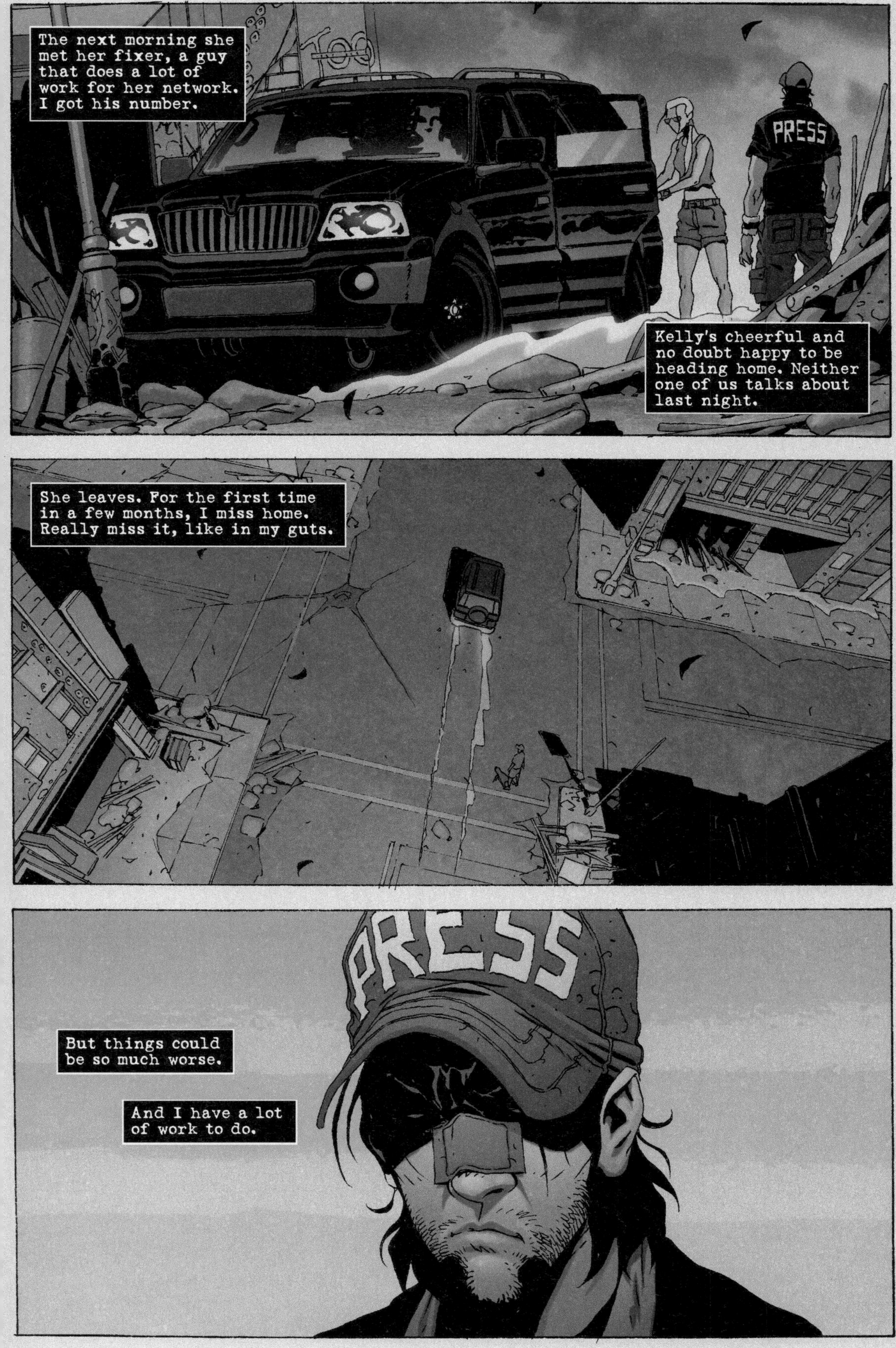
The next morning she met her fixer, a guy that does a lot of work for her network. I got his number.
PRESS
Kelly's cheerful and no doubt happy to be heading home. Neither one of us talks about last night.
She leaves. For the first time in a few months, I miss home. Really miss it, like in my guts.
PRESS
But things could be so much worse.
And I have a lot of work to do.

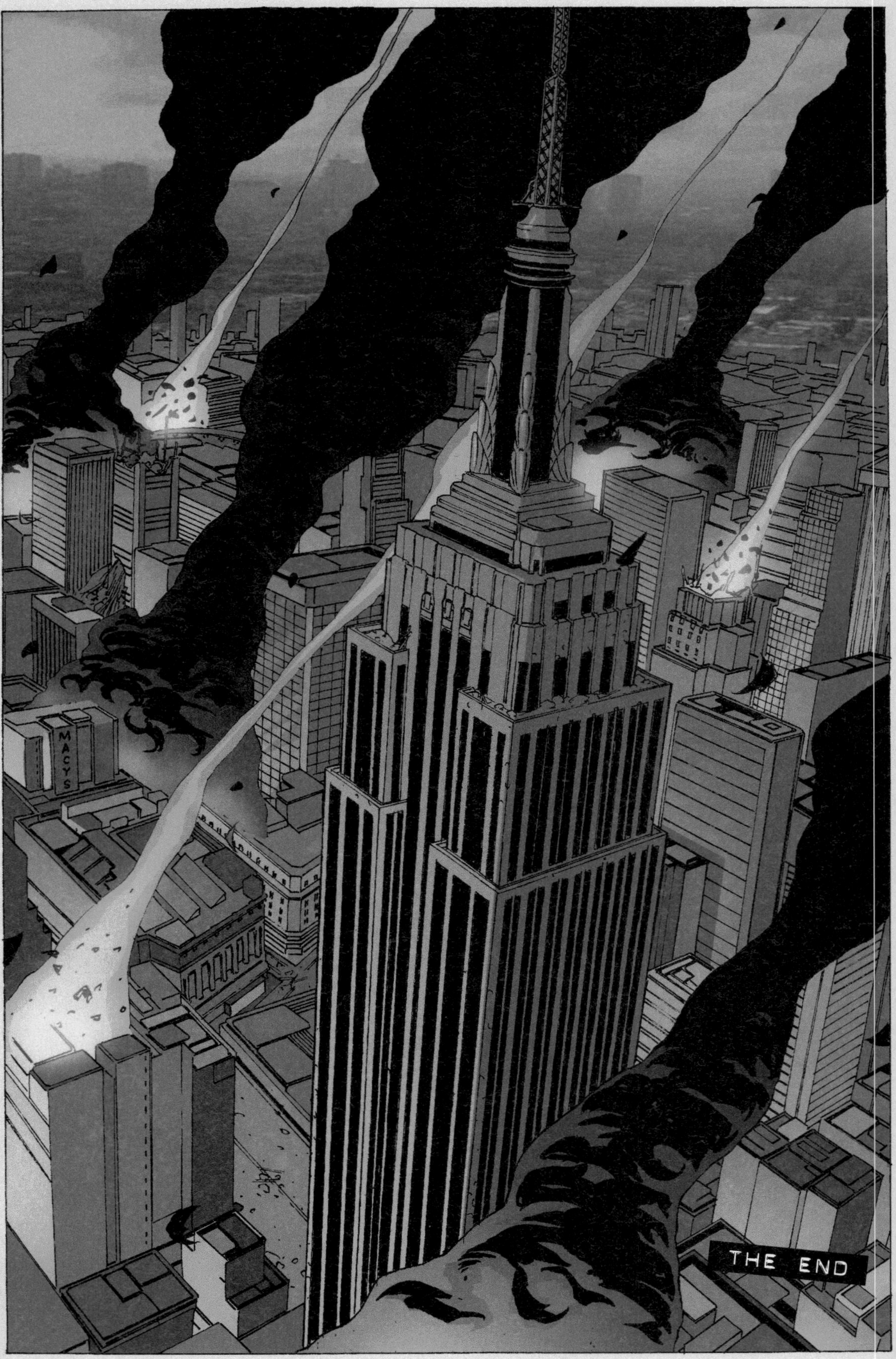
MACYS
THE END

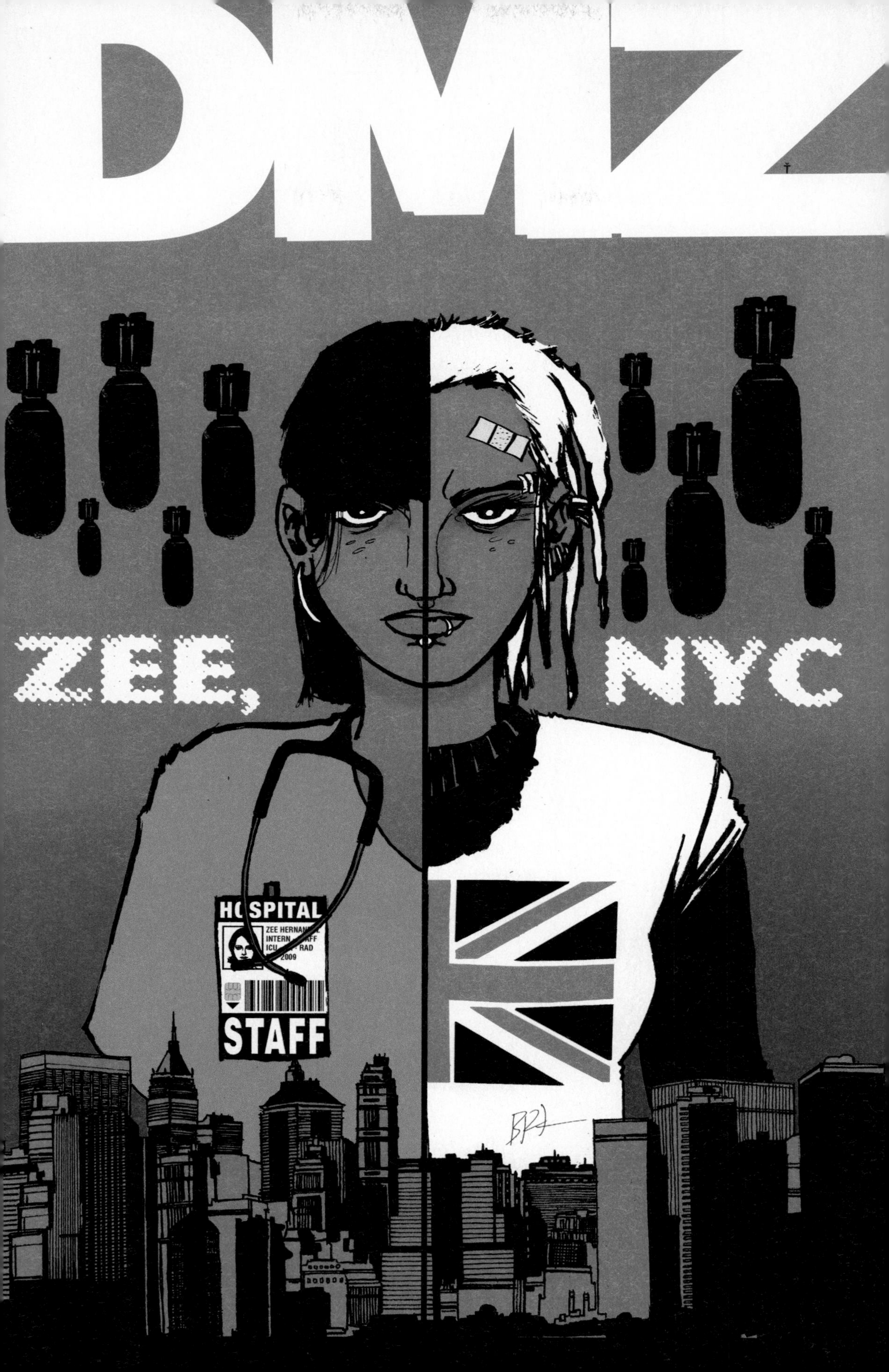
DMZ
ZEE, NYC
HOSPITAL
ZEE HERNAN
INTERN
ICU
RAD
2009
STAFF

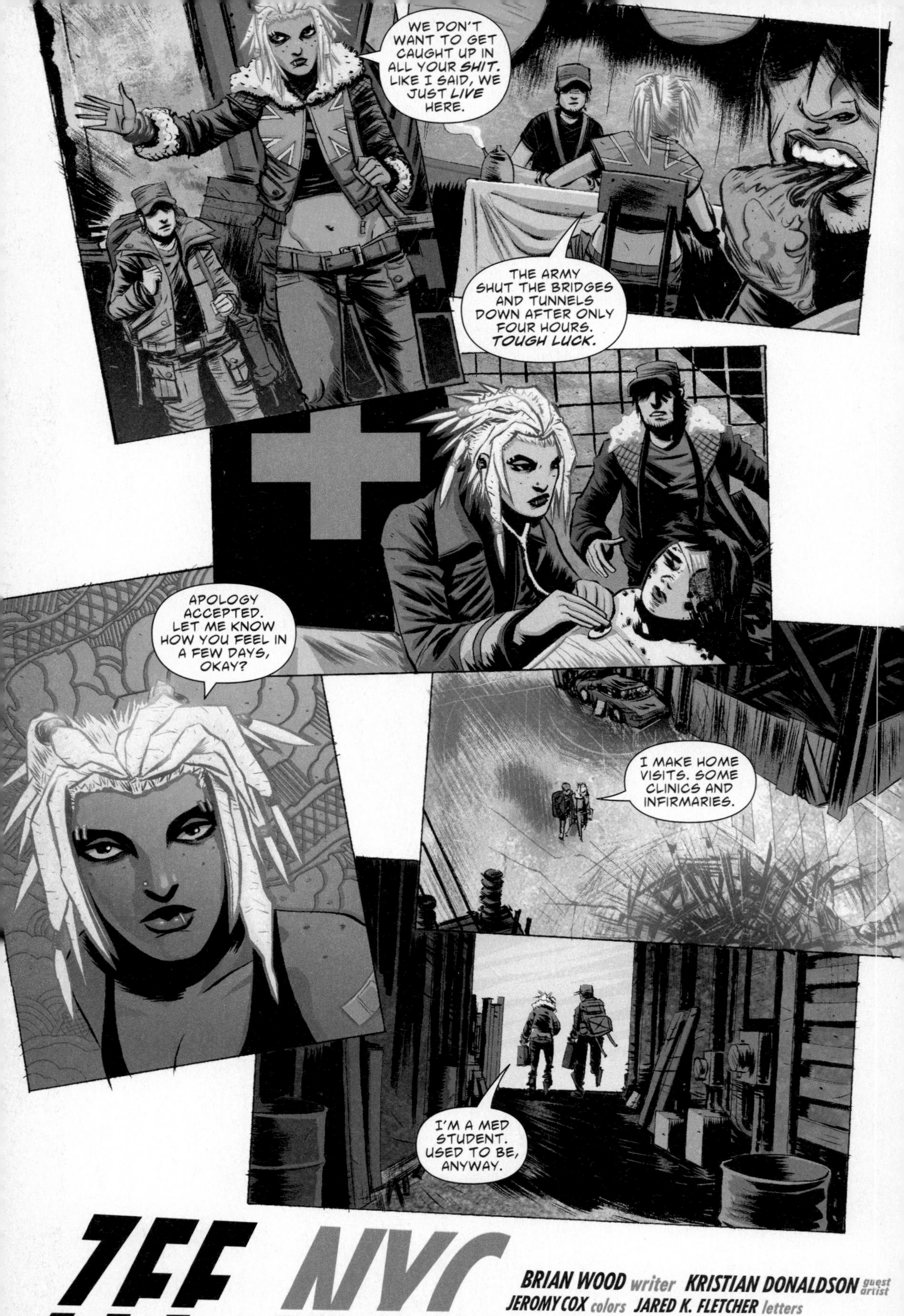
WE DON'T WANT TO GET CAUGHT UP IN ALL YOUR *SHIT*. LIKE I SAID, WE JUST *LIVE* HERE.
THE ARMY SHUT THE BRIDGES AND TUNNELS DOWN AFTER ONLY FOUR HOURS. *TOUGH LUCK.*
APOLOGY ACCEPTED. LET ME KNOW HOW YOU FEEL IN A FEW DAYS, OKAY?
I MAKE HOME VISITS. SOME CLINICS AND INFIRMARIES.
I'M A MED STUDENT. USED TO BE, ANYWAY.

ZEE, NYC

BRIAN WOOD writer **KRISTIAN DONALDSON** guest artist
JEROMY COX colors **JARED K. FLETCHER** letters

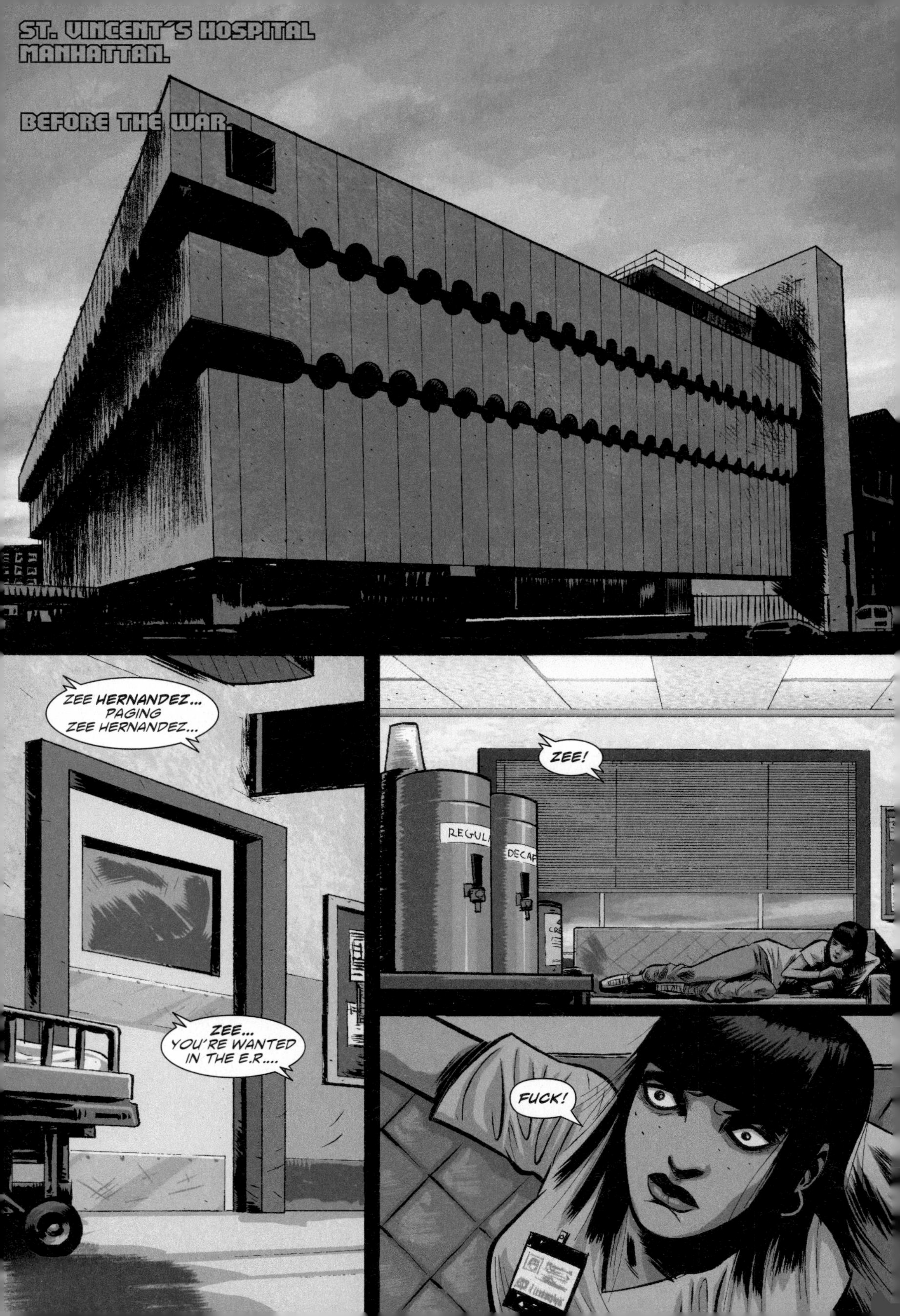
ST. VINCENT'S HOSPITAL
MANHATTAN.
BEFORE THE WAR.
ZEE HERNANDEZ... PAGING ZEE HERNANDEZ...
ZEE... YOU'RE WANTED IN THE E.R....
ZEE!
REGUL
DECAF
FUCK!

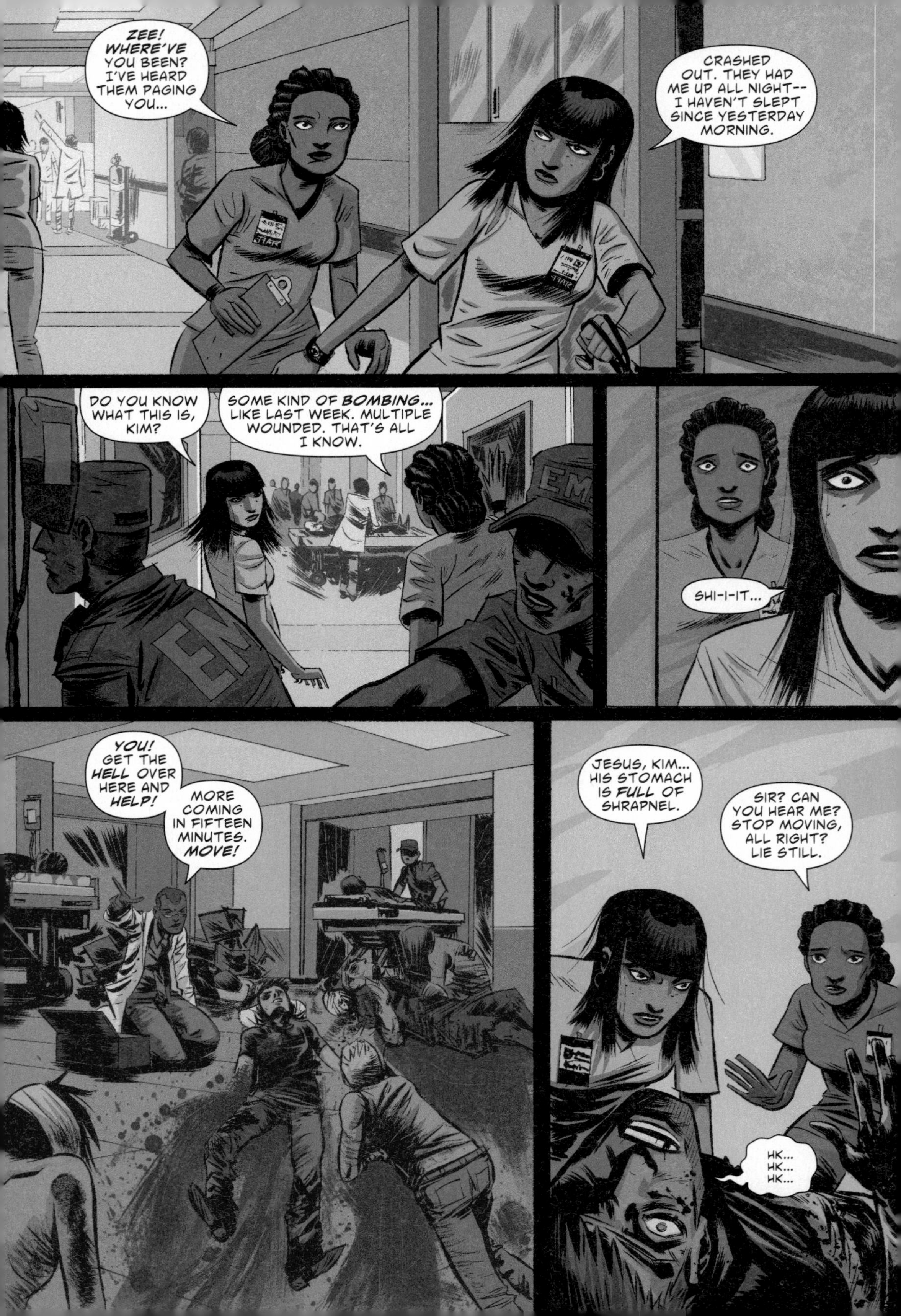
ZEE! WHERE'VE YOU BEEN? I'VE HEARD THEM PAGING YOU...
CRASHED OUT. THEY HAD ME UP ALL NIGHT-- I HAVEN'T SLEPT SINCE YESTERDAY MORNING.
DO YOU KNOW WHAT THIS IS, KIM?
SOME KIND OF BOMBING... LIKE LAST WEEK. MULTIPLE WOUNDED. THAT'S ALL I KNOW.
SHI-I-IT...
YOU! GET THE HELL OVER HERE AND HELP!
MORE COMING IN FIFTEEN MINUTES. MOVE!
JESUS, KIM... HIS STOMACH IS FULL OF SHRAPNEL.
SIR? CAN YOU HEAR ME? STOP MOVING, ALL RIGHT? LIE STILL.
HK... HK... HK...

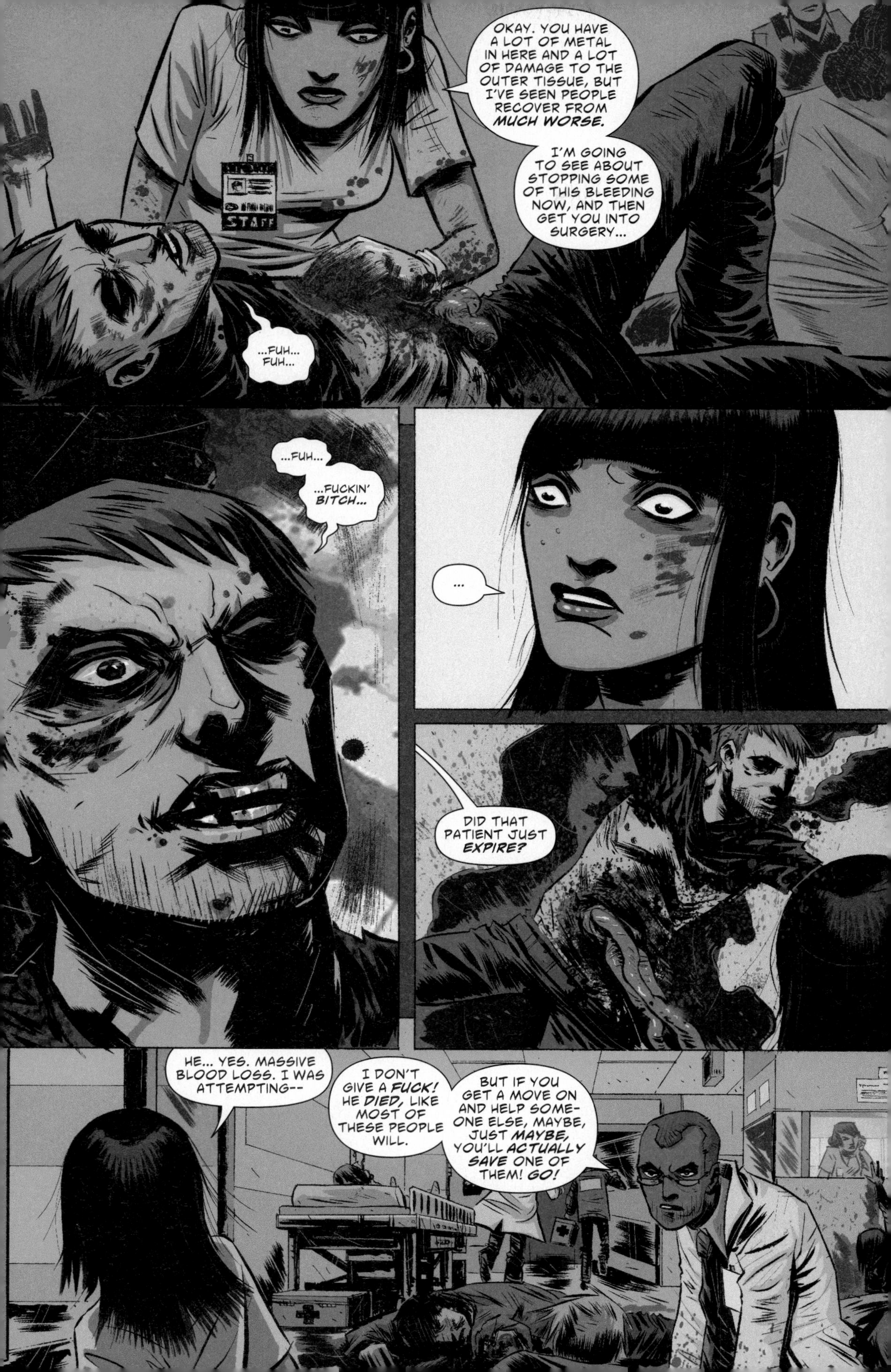
OKAY. YOU HAVE A LOT OF METAL IN HERE AND A LOT OF DAMAGE TO THE OUTER TISSUE, BUT I'VE SEEN PEOPLE RECOVER FROM MUCH WORSE.
I'M GOING TO SEE ABOUT STOPPING SOME OF THIS BLEEDING NOW, AND THEN GET YOU INTO SURGERY...
STAFF
...FUH... FUH...
...FUH...
...FUCKIN' BITCH...
...
DID THAT PATIENT JUST EXPIRE?
HE... YES. MASSIVE BLOOD LOSS. I WAS ATTEMPTING--
I DON'T GIVE A FUCK! HE DIED, LIKE MOST OF THESE PEOPLE WILL.
BUT IF YOU GET A MOVE ON AND HELP SOME-ONE ELSE, MAYBE, JUST MAYBE, YOU'LL ACTUALLY SAVE ONE OF THEM! GO!

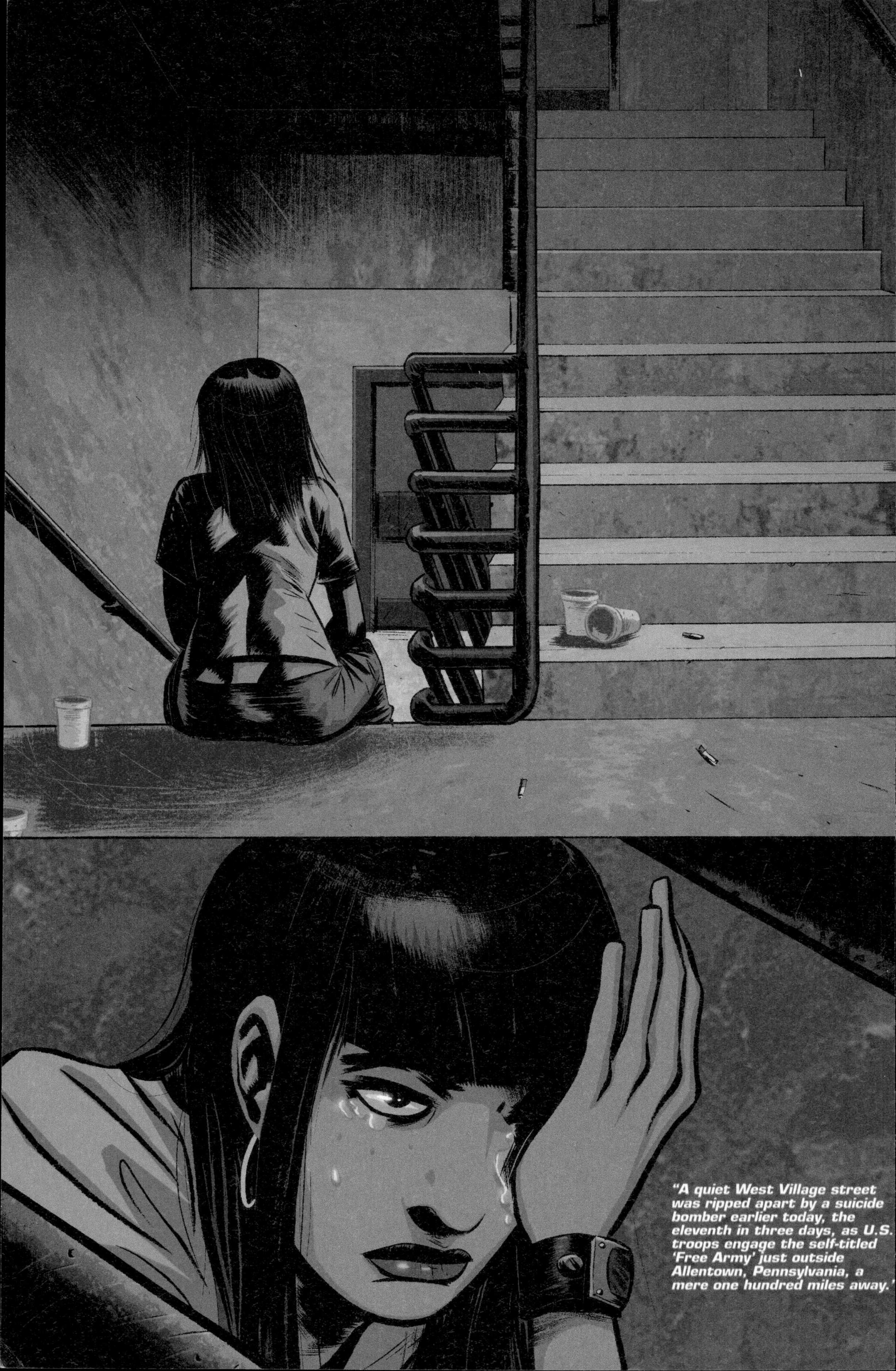
"A quiet West Village street was ripped apart by a suicide bomber earlier today, the eleventh in three days, as U.S. troops engage the self-titled 'Free Army' just outside Allentown, Pennsylvania, a mere one hundred miles away.'

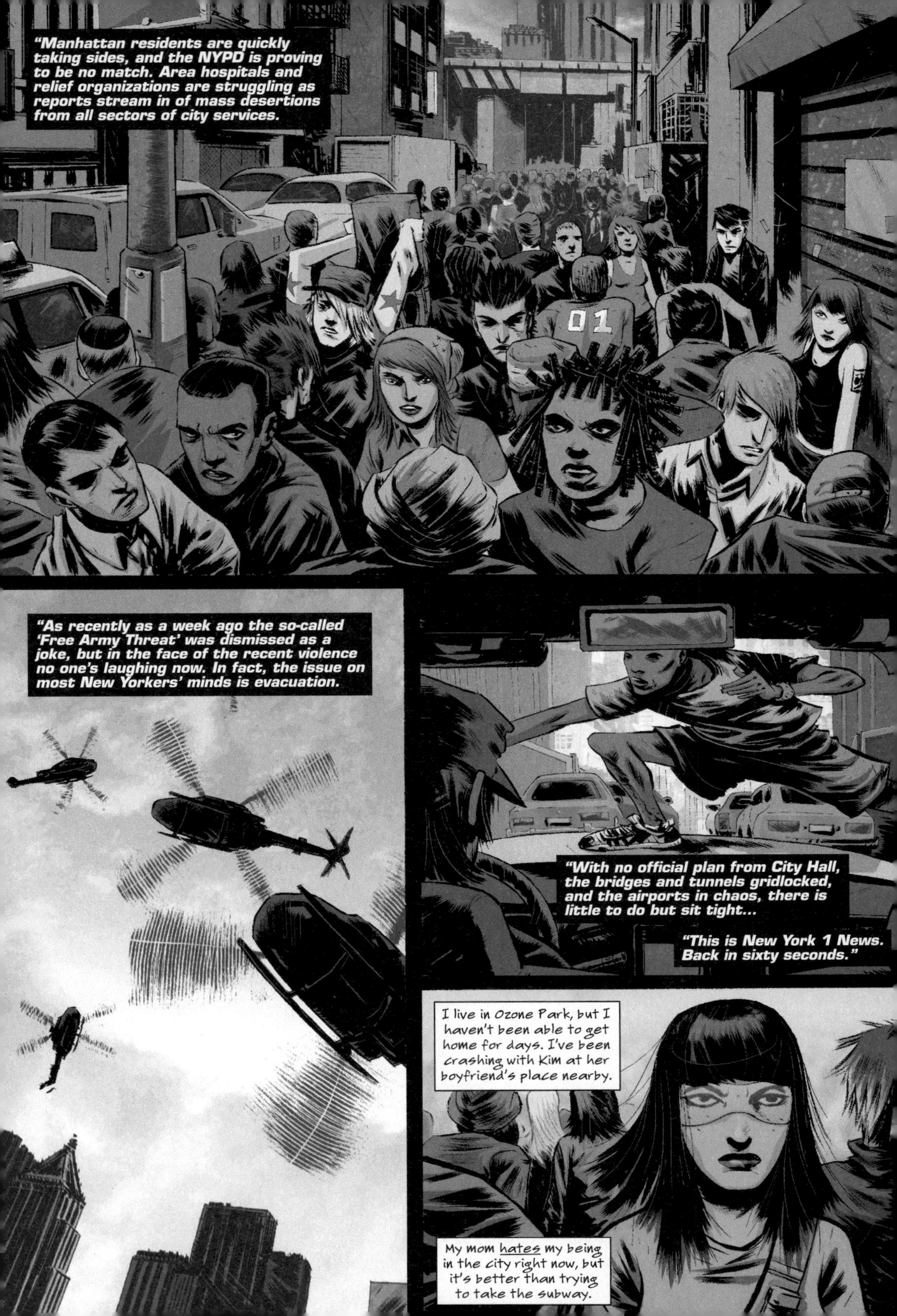
"Manhattan residents are quickly taking sides, and the NYPD is proving to be no match. Area hospitals and relief organizations are struggling as reports stream in of mass desertions from all sectors of city services.
01
"As recently as a week ago the so-called 'Free Army Threat' was dismissed as a joke, but in the face of the recent violence no one's laughing now. In fact, the issue on most New Yorkers' minds is evacuation.
"With no official plan from City Hall, the bridges and tunnels gridlocked, and the airports in chaos, there is little to do but sit tight...
"This is New York 1 News. Back in sixty seconds."
I live in Ozone Park, but I haven't been able to get home for days. I've been crashing with Kim at her boyfriend's place nearby.
My mom hates my being in the city right now, but it's better than trying to take the subway.

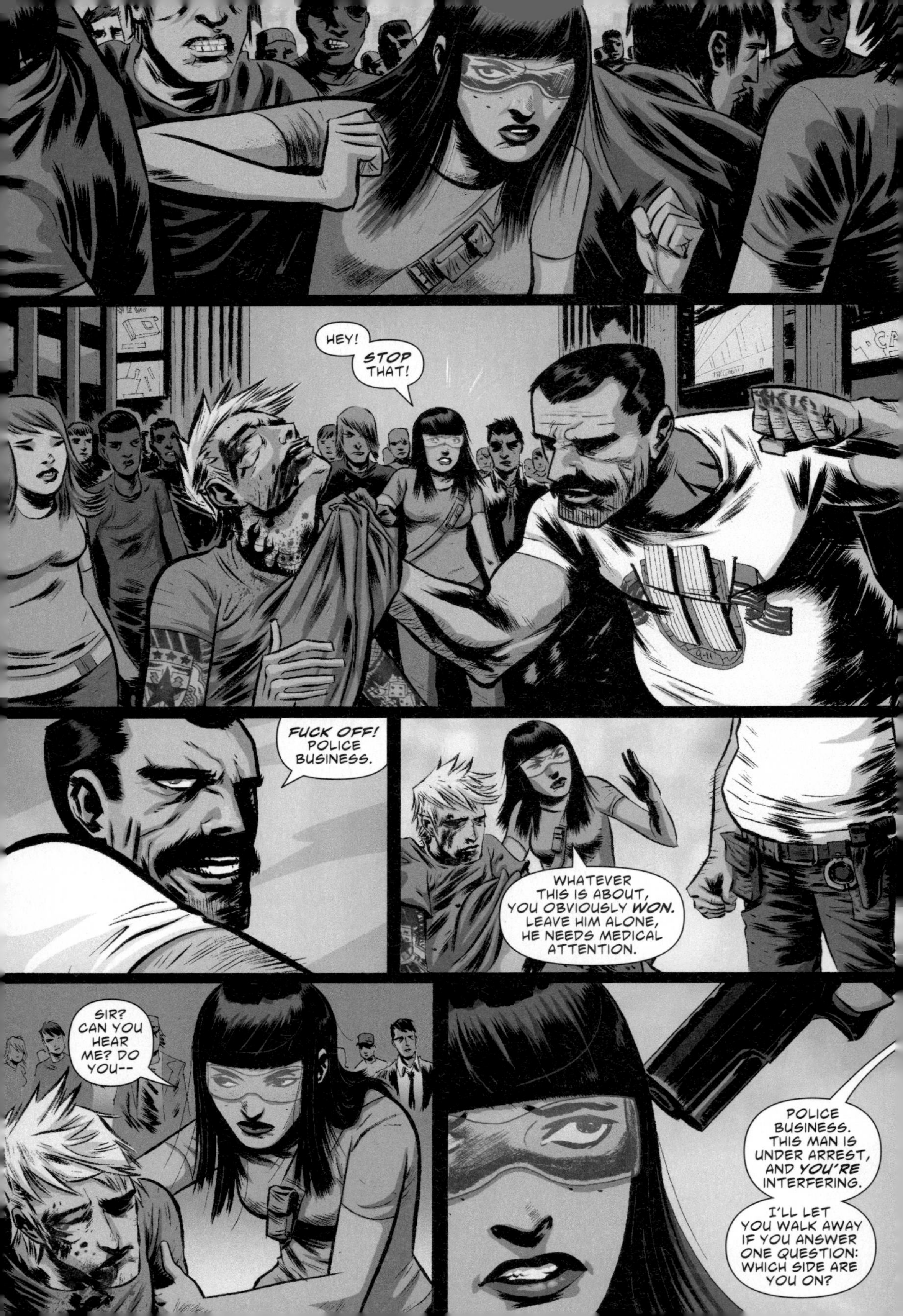

HEY! STOP THAT!
FUCK OFF! POLICE BUSINESS.
WHATEVER THIS IS ABOUT, YOU OBVIOUSLY WON. LEAVE HIM ALONE, HE NEEDS MEDICAL ATTENTION.
SIR? CAN YOU HEAR ME? DO YOU--
POLICE BUSINESS. THIS MAN IS UNDER ARREST, AND YOU'RE INTERFERING.
I'LL LET YOU WALK AWAY IF YOU ANSWER ONE QUESTION: WHICH SIDE ARE YOU ON?

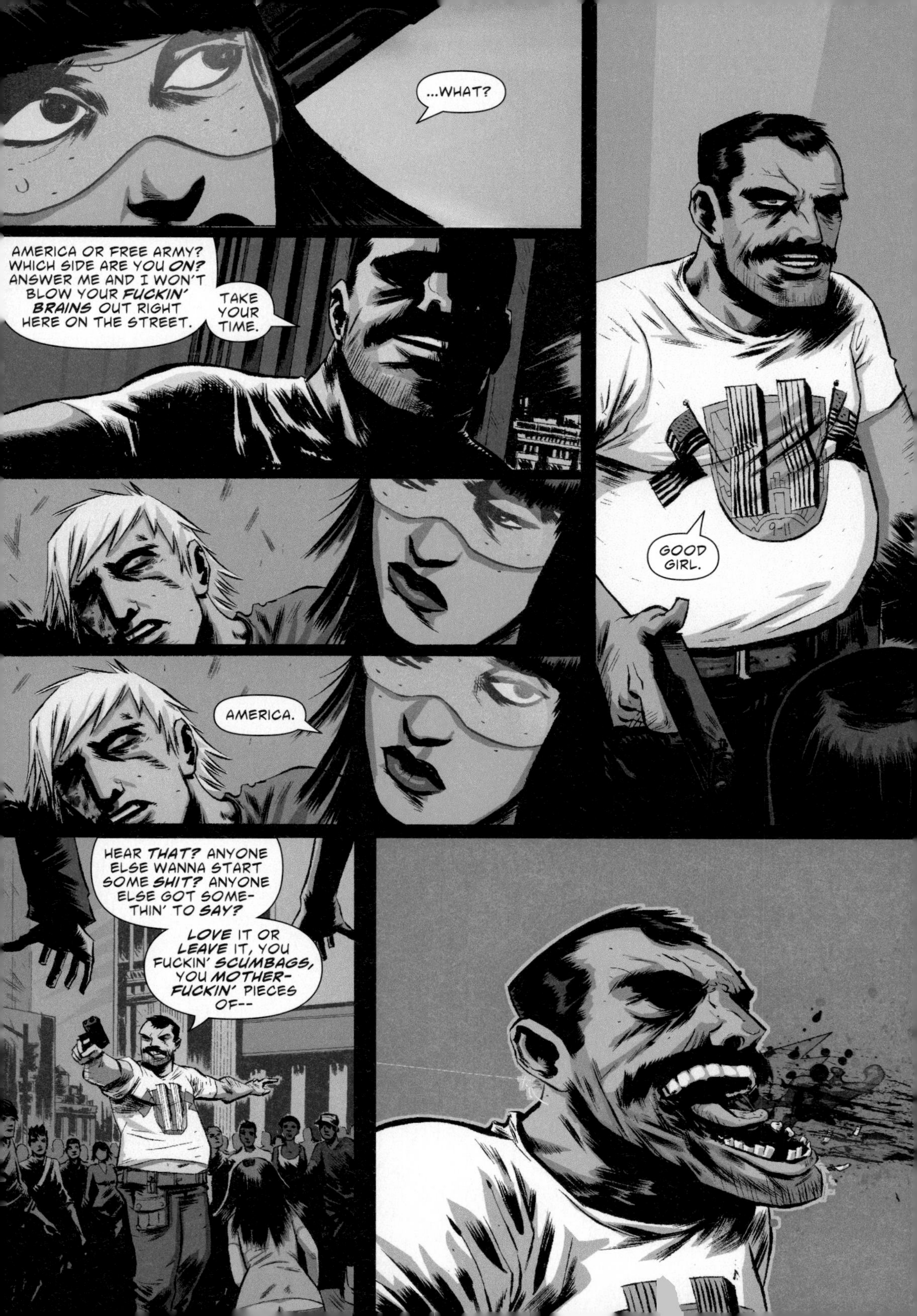
...WHAT?
AMERICA OR FREE ARMY? WHICH SIDE ARE YOU ON? ANSWER ME AND I WON'T BLOW YOUR FUCKIN' BRAINS OUT RIGHT HERE ON THE STREET.
TAKE YOUR TIME.
AMERICA.
GOOD GIRL.
HEAR THAT? ANYONE ELSE WANNA START SOME SHIT? ANYONE ELSE GOT SOME-THIN' TO SAY?
LOVE IT OR LEAVE IT, YOU FUCKIN' SCUMBAGS, YOU MOTHER-FUCKIN' PIECES OF--

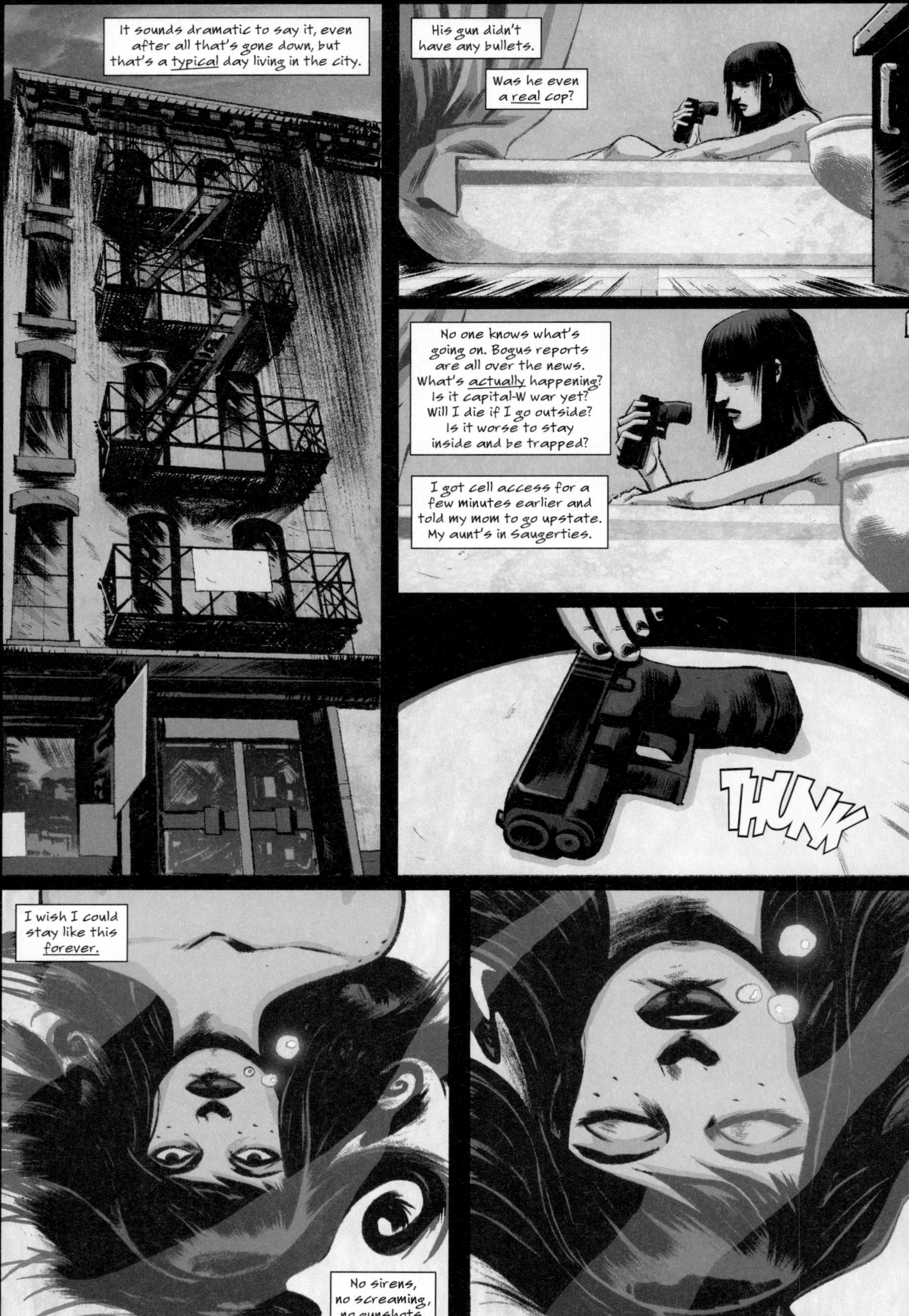
It sounds dramatic to say it, even after all that's gone down, but that's a typical day living in the city.
His gun didn't have any bullets.
Was he even a real cop?
No one knows what's going on. Bogus reports are all over the news. What's actually happening? Is it capital-W war yet? Will I die if I go outside? Is it worse to stay inside and be trapped?
I got cell access for a few minutes earlier and told my mom to go upstate. My aunt's in Saugerties.
THUNK
I wish I could stay like this forever.
No sirens, no screaming, no gunshots.

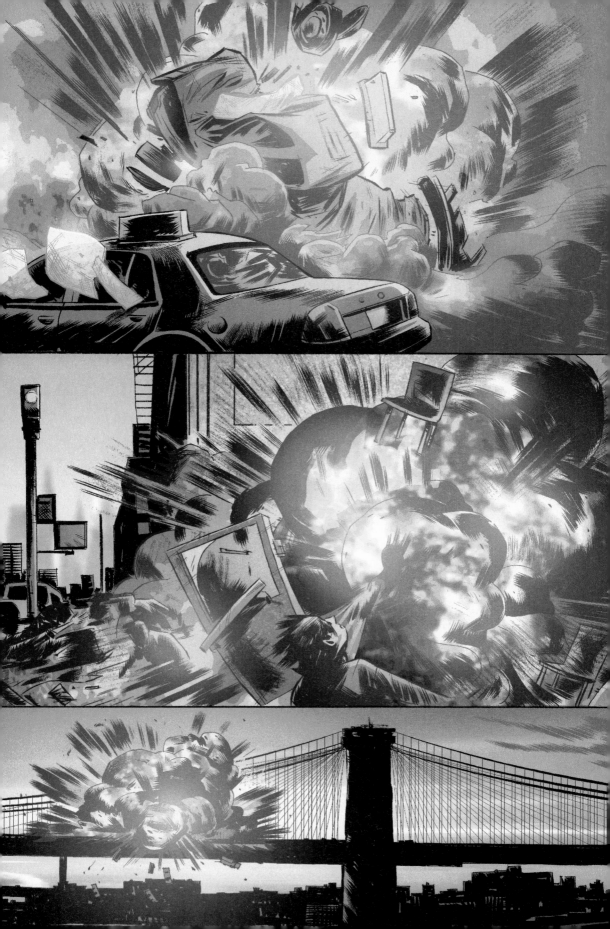

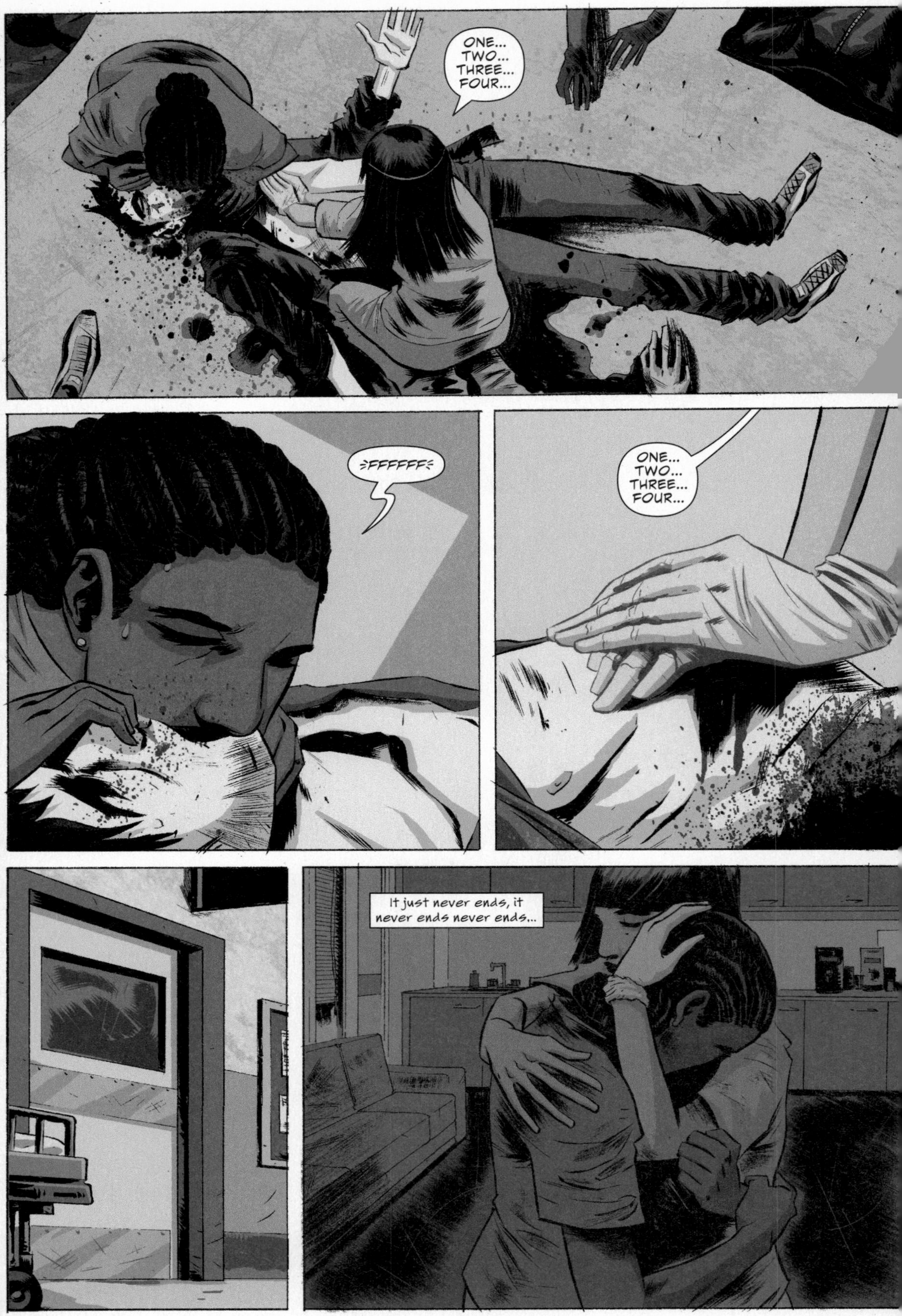
ONE... TWO... THREE... FOUR...
≈FFFFFF≈
ONE... TWO... THREE... FOUR...
It just never ends, it never ends never ends...

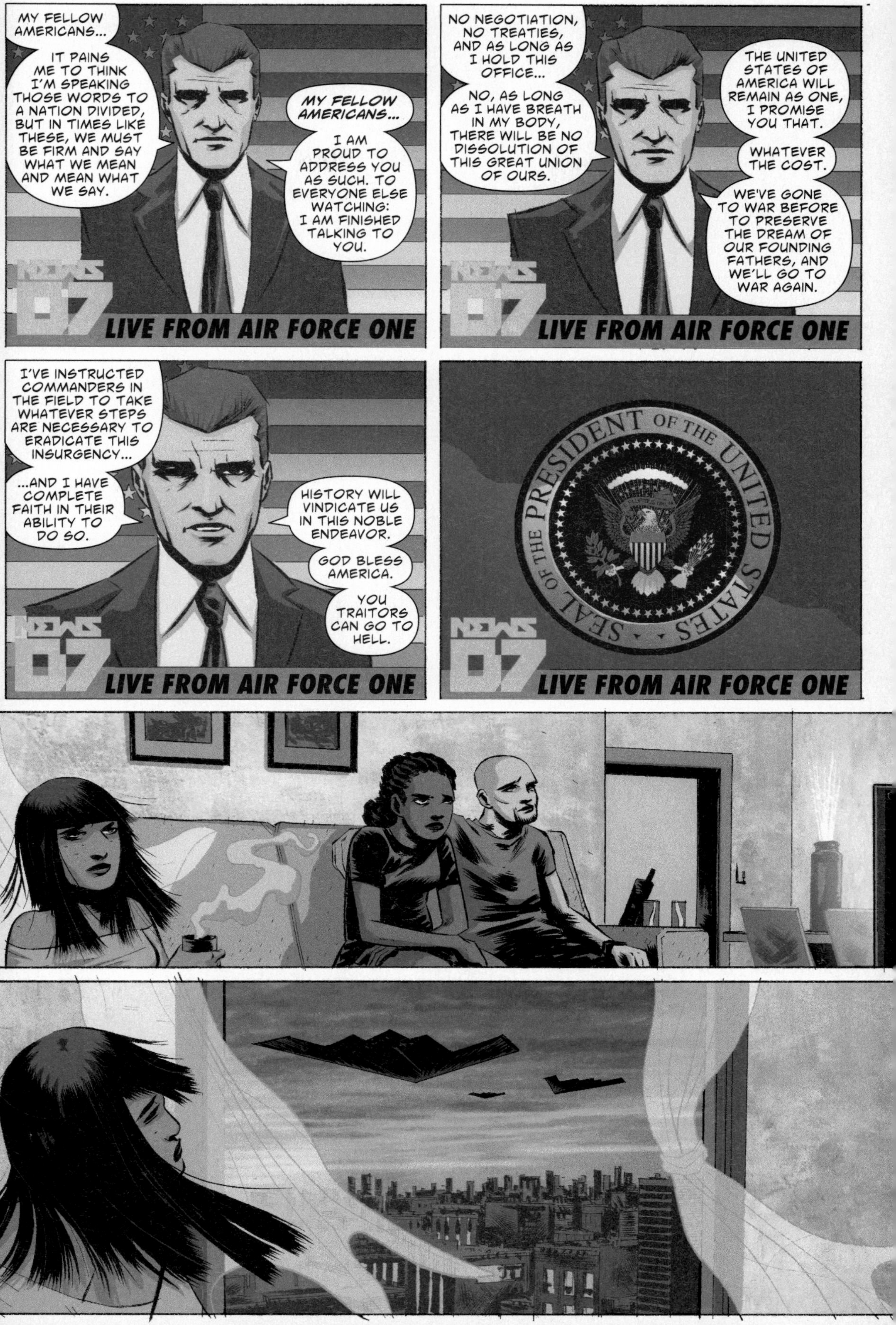

MY FELLOW AMERICANS...
IT PAINS ME TO THINK I'M SPEAKING THOSE WORDS TO A NATION DIVIDED, BUT IN TIMES LIKE THESE, WE MUST BE FIRM AND SAY WHAT WE MEAN AND MEAN WHAT WE SAY.
MY FELLOW AMERICANS...
I AM PROUD TO ADDRESS YOU AS SUCH. TO EVERYONE ELSE WATCHING: I AM FINISHED TALKING TO YOU.
NEWS 07
LIVE FROM AIR FORCE ONE
NO NEGOTIATION, NO TREATIES, AND AS LONG AS I HOLD THIS OFFICE...
NO, AS LONG AS I HAVE BREATH IN MY BODY, THERE WILL BE NO DISSOLUTION OF THIS GREAT UNION OF OURS.
THE UNITED STATES OF AMERICA WILL REMAIN AS ONE, I PROMISE YOU THAT.
WHATEVER THE COST.
WE'VE GONE TO WAR BEFORE TO PRESERVE THE DREAM OF OUR FOUNDING FATHERS, AND WE'LL GO TO WAR AGAIN.
NEWS 07
LIVE FROM AIR FORCE ONE
I'VE INSTRUCTED COMMANDERS IN THE FIELD TO TAKE WHATEVER STEPS ARE NECESSARY TO ERADICATE THIS INSURGENCY...
...AND I HAVE COMPLETE FAITH IN THEIR ABILITY TO DO SO.
HISTORY WILL VINDICATE US IN THIS NOBLE ENDEAVOR.
GOD BLESS AMERICA.
YOU TRAITORS CAN GO TO HELL.
NEWS 07
LIVE FROM AIR FORCE ONE
SEAL OF THE PRESIDENT OF THE UNITED STATES
NEWS 07
LIVE FROM AIR FORCE ONE

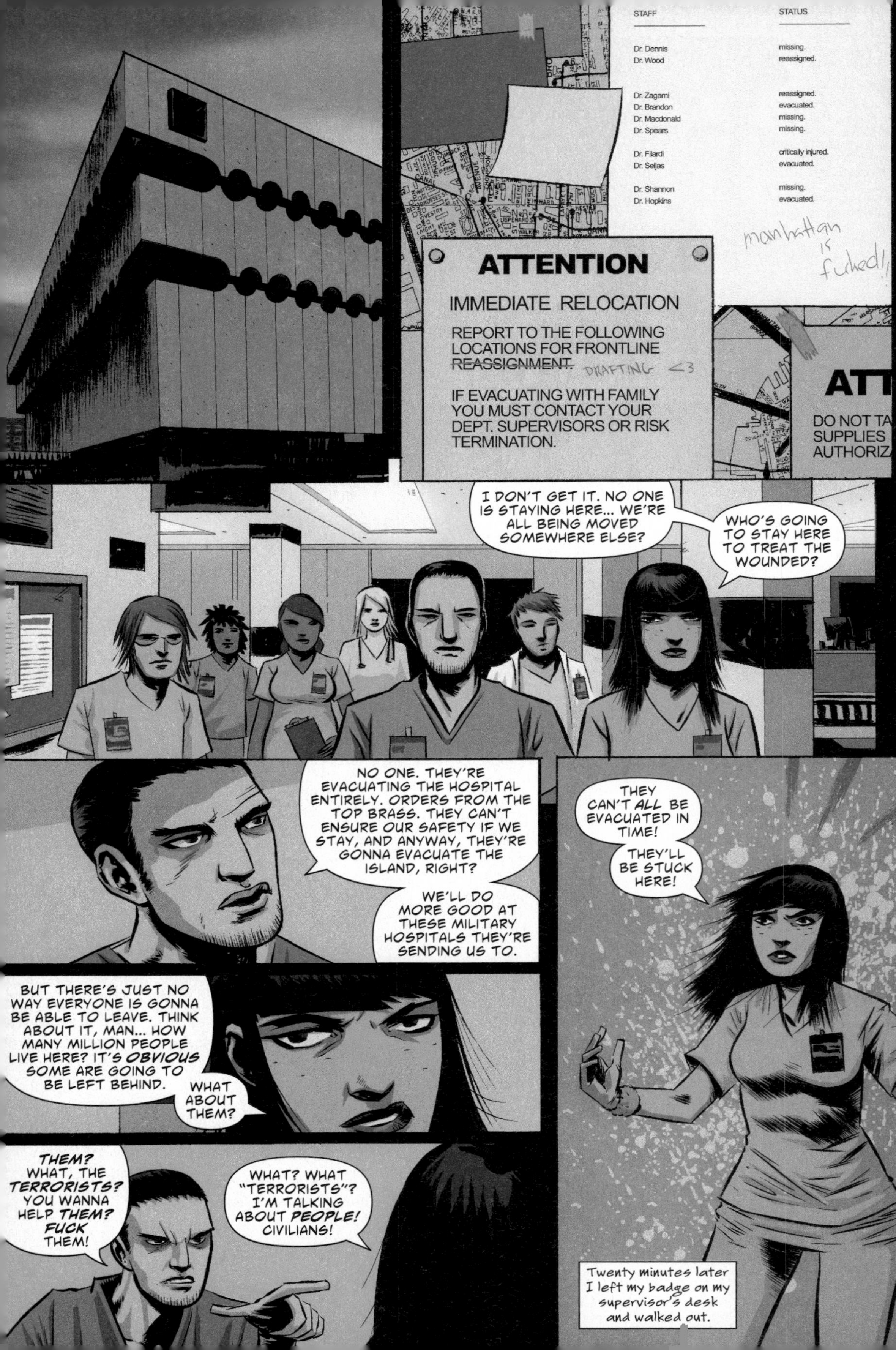
STAFF
STATUS
Dr. Dennis missing.
Dr. Wood reassigned.
Dr. Zagami reassigned.
Dr. Brandon evacuated.
Dr. Macdonald missing.
Dr. Spears missing.
Dr. Filardi critically injured.
Dr. Seijas evacuated.
Dr. Shannon missing.
Dr. Hopkins evacuated.
manhattan is fucked!!
ATTENTION
IMMEDIATE RELOCATION
REPORT TO THE FOLLOWING LOCATIONS FOR FRONTLINE ~~REASSIGNMENT.~~ DRAFTING <3
IF EVACUATING WITH FAMILY YOU MUST CONTACT YOUR DEPT. SUPERVISORS OR RISK TERMINATION.
ATT
DO NOT TA
SUPPLIES
AUTHORIZ
I DON'T GET IT. NO ONE IS STAYING HERE... WE'RE ALL BEING MOVED SOMEWHERE ELSE?
WHO'S GOING TO STAY HERE TO TREAT THE WOUNDED?
NO ONE. THEY'RE EVACUATING THE HOSPITAL ENTIRELY. ORDERS FROM THE TOP BRASS. THEY CAN'T ENSURE OUR SAFETY IF WE STAY, AND ANYWAY, THEY'RE GONNA EVACUATE THE ISLAND, RIGHT?
WE'LL DO MORE GOOD AT THESE MILITARY HOSPITALS THEY'RE SENDING US TO.
BUT THERE'S JUST NO WAY EVERYONE IS GONNA BE ABLE TO LEAVE. THINK ABOUT IT, MAN... HOW MANY MILLION PEOPLE LIVE HERE? IT'S *OBVIOUS* SOME ARE GOING TO BE LEFT BEHIND.
WHAT ABOUT THEM?
THEM? WHAT, THE *TERRORISTS?* YOU WANNA HELP *THEM? FUCK* THEM!
WHAT? WHAT "TERRORISTS"? I'M TALKING ABOUT *PEOPLE!* CIVILIANS!
THEY CAN'T *ALL* BE EVACUATED IN TIME!
THEY'LL BE STUCK HERE!
Twenty minutes later I left my badge on my supervisor's desk and walked out.

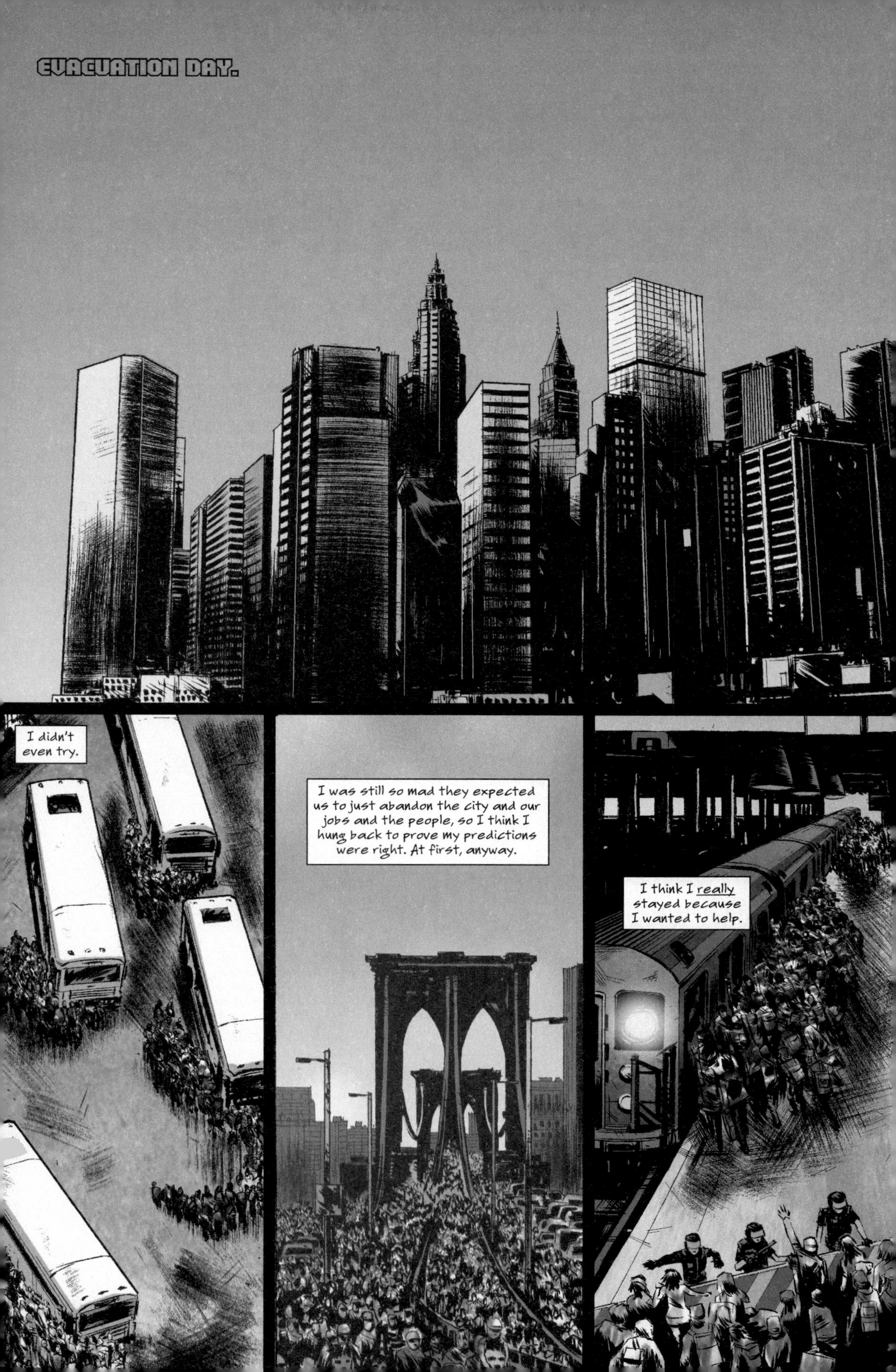
EVACUATION DAY.
I didn't even try.
I was still so mad they expected us to just abandon the city and our jobs and the people, so I think I hung back to prove my predictions were right. At first, anyway.
I think I really stayed because I wanted to help.

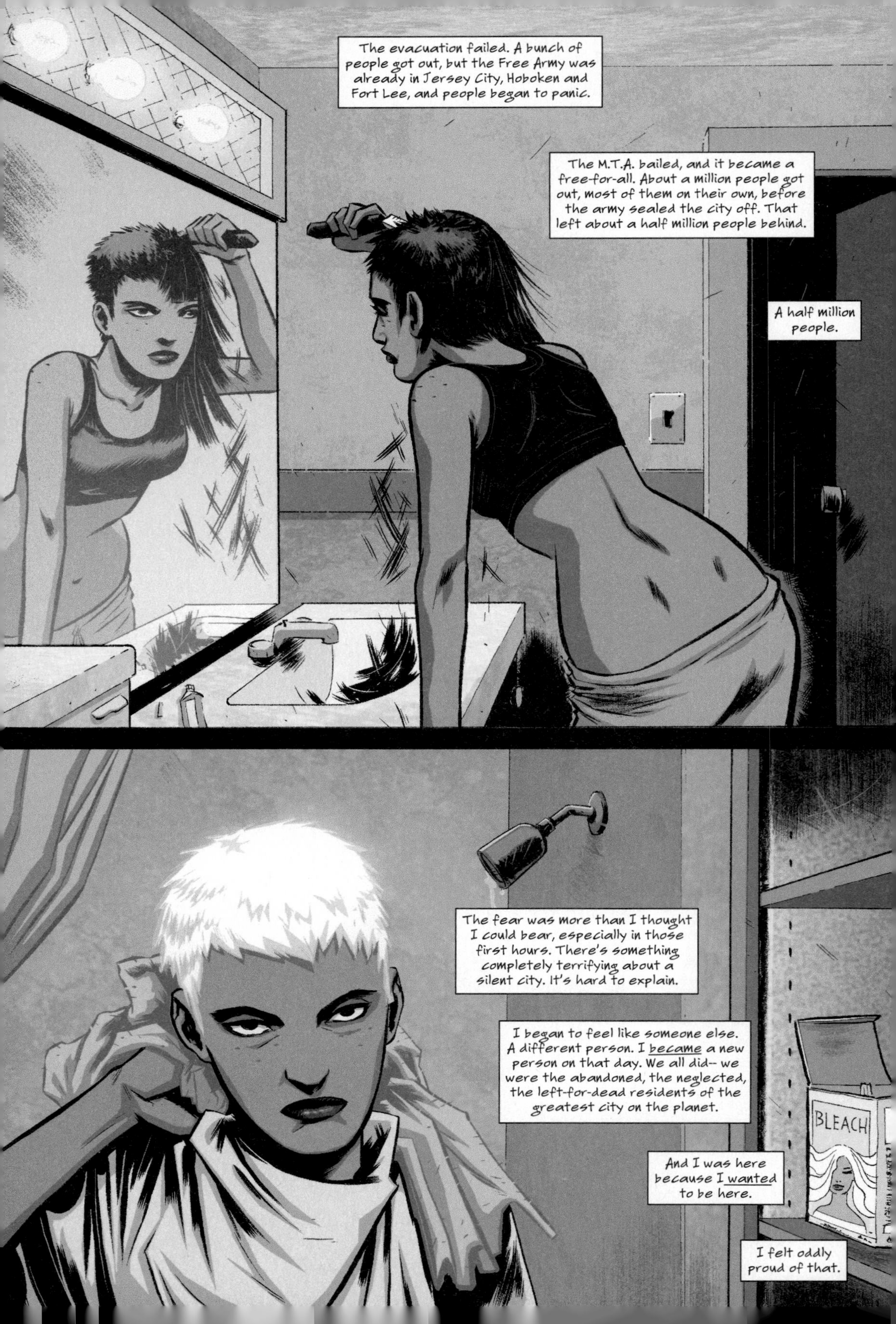
The evacuation failed. A bunch of people got out, but the Free Army was already in Jersey City, Hoboken and Fort Lee, and people began to panic.
The M.T.A. bailed, and it became a free-for-all. About a million people got out, most of them on their own, before the army sealed the city off. That left about a half million people behind.
A half million people.
The fear was more than I thought I could bear, especially in those first hours. There's something completely terrifying about a silent city. It's hard to explain.
I began to feel like someone else. A different person. I became a new person on that day. We all did-- we were the abandoned, the neglected, the left-for-dead residents of the greatest city on the planet.
And I was here because I wanted to be here.
I felt oddly proud of that.
BLEACH

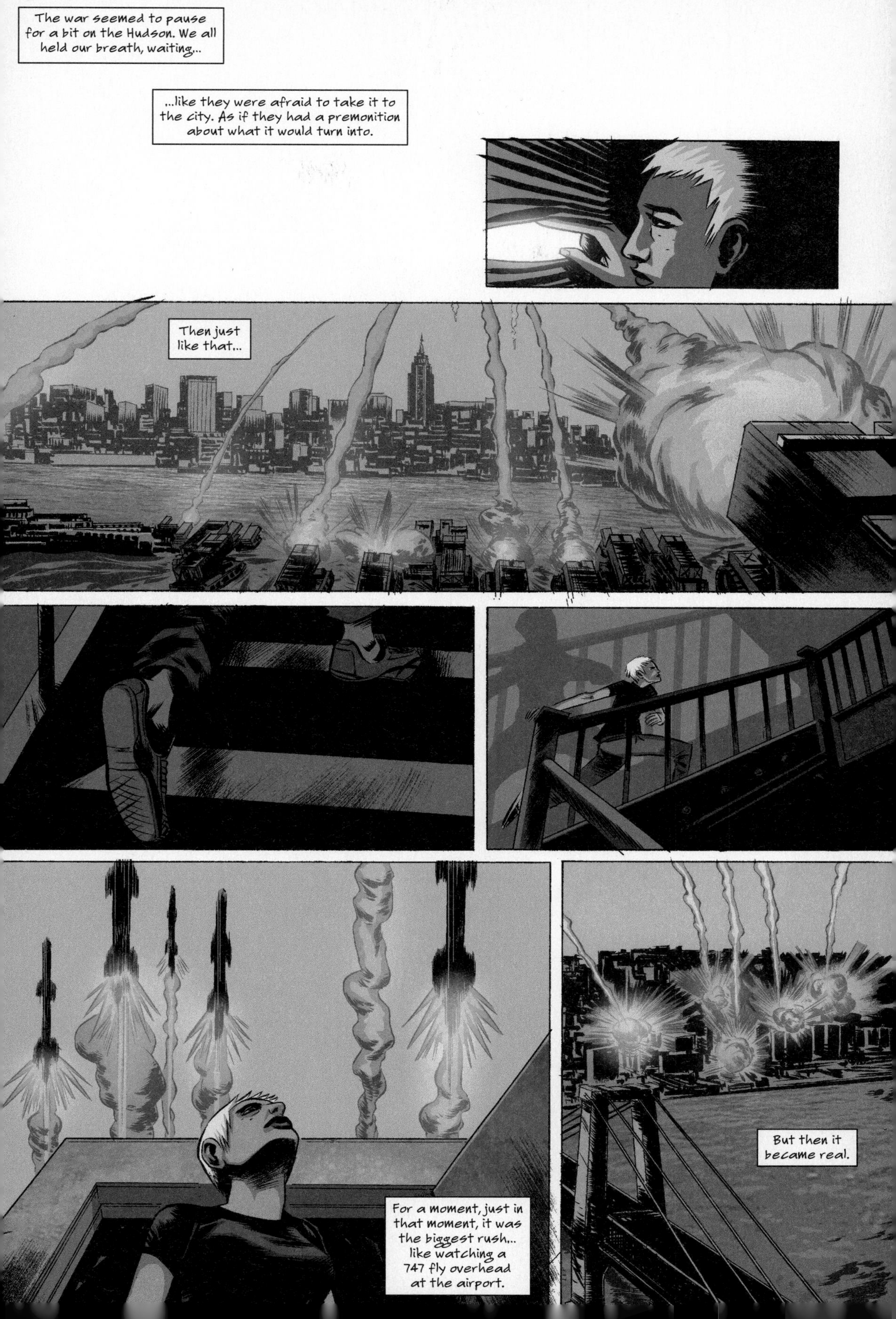
The war seemed to pause for a bit on the Hudson. We all held our breath, waiting...
...like they were afraid to take it to the city. As if they had a premonition about what it would turn into.
Then just like that...
For a moment, just in that moment, it was the biggest rush... like watching a 747 fly overhead at the airport.
But then it became real.

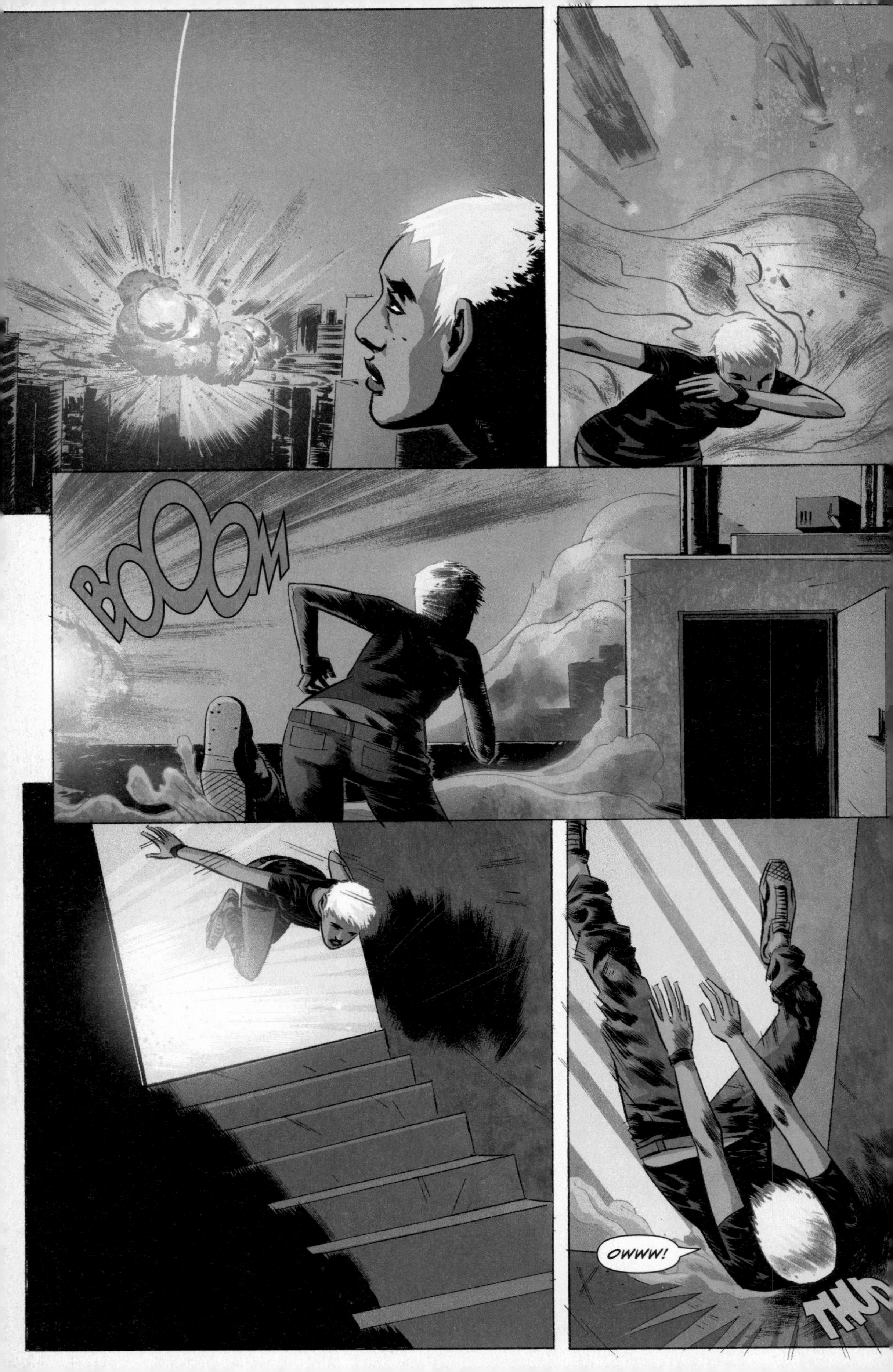
BOOOM
OWWW!
THUD

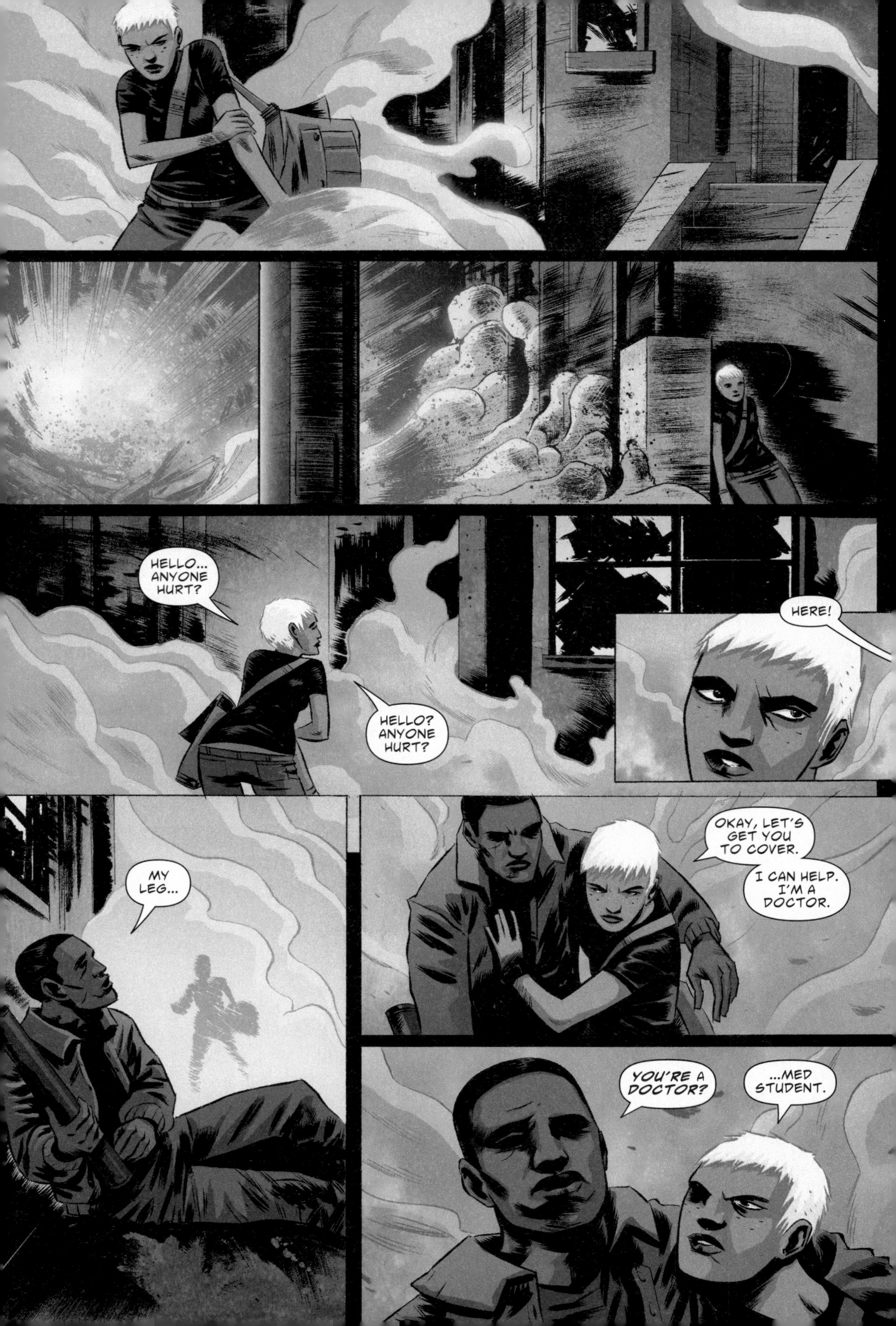

HELLO... ANYONE HURT?
HELLO? ANYONE HURT?
HERE!
MY LEG...
OKAY, LET'S GET YOU TO COVER.
I CAN HELP. I'M A DOCTOR.
YOU'RE A DOCTOR?
...MED STUDENT.

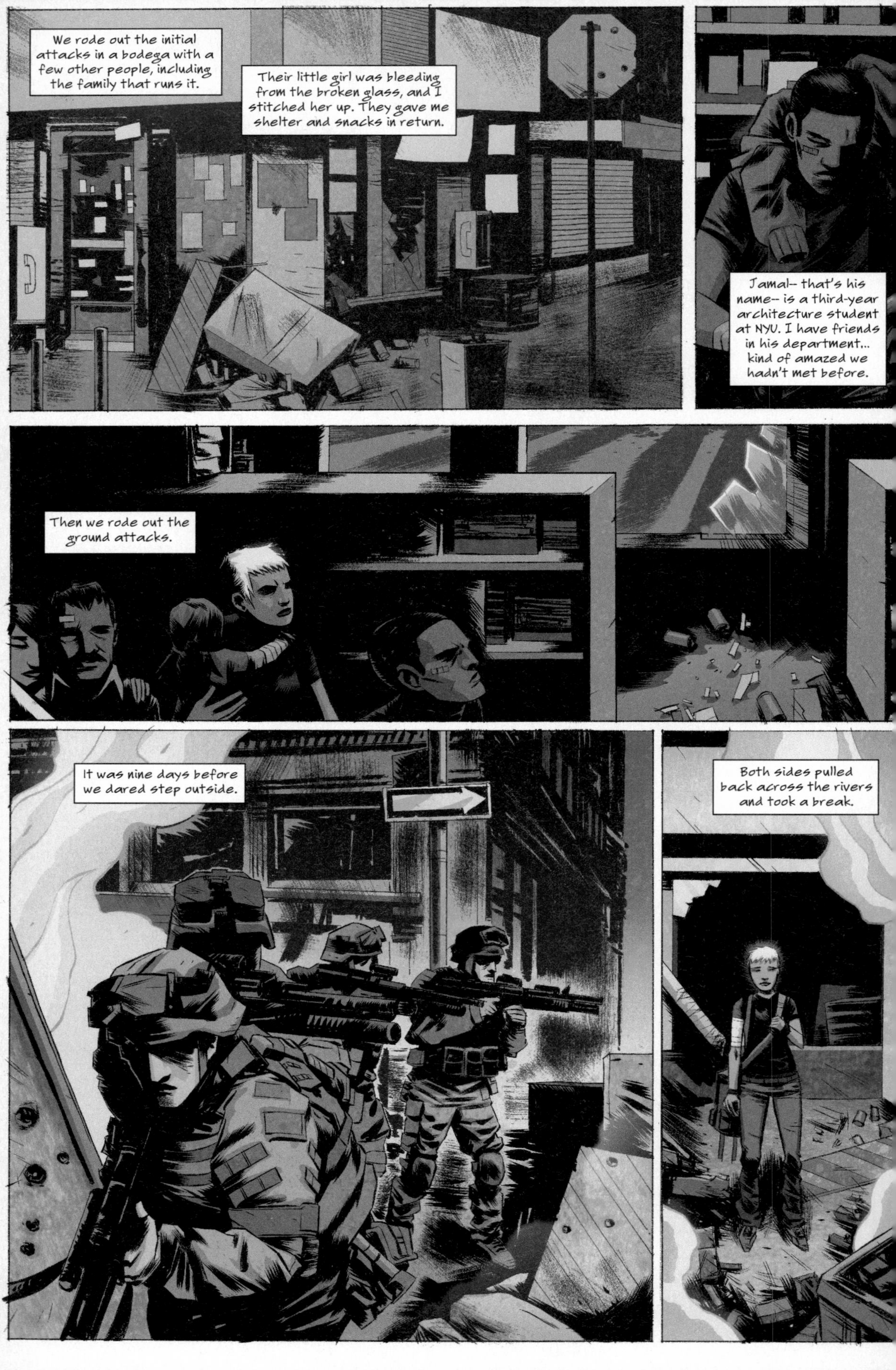
We rode out the initial attacks in a bodega with a few other people, including the family that runs it.
Their little girl was bleeding from the broken glass, and I stitched her up. They gave me shelter and snacks in return.
Jamal-- that's his name-- is a third-year architecture student at NYU. I have friends in his department... kind of amazed we hadn't met before.
Then we rode out the ground attacks.
It was nine days before we dared step outside.
Both sides pulled back across the rivers and took a break.

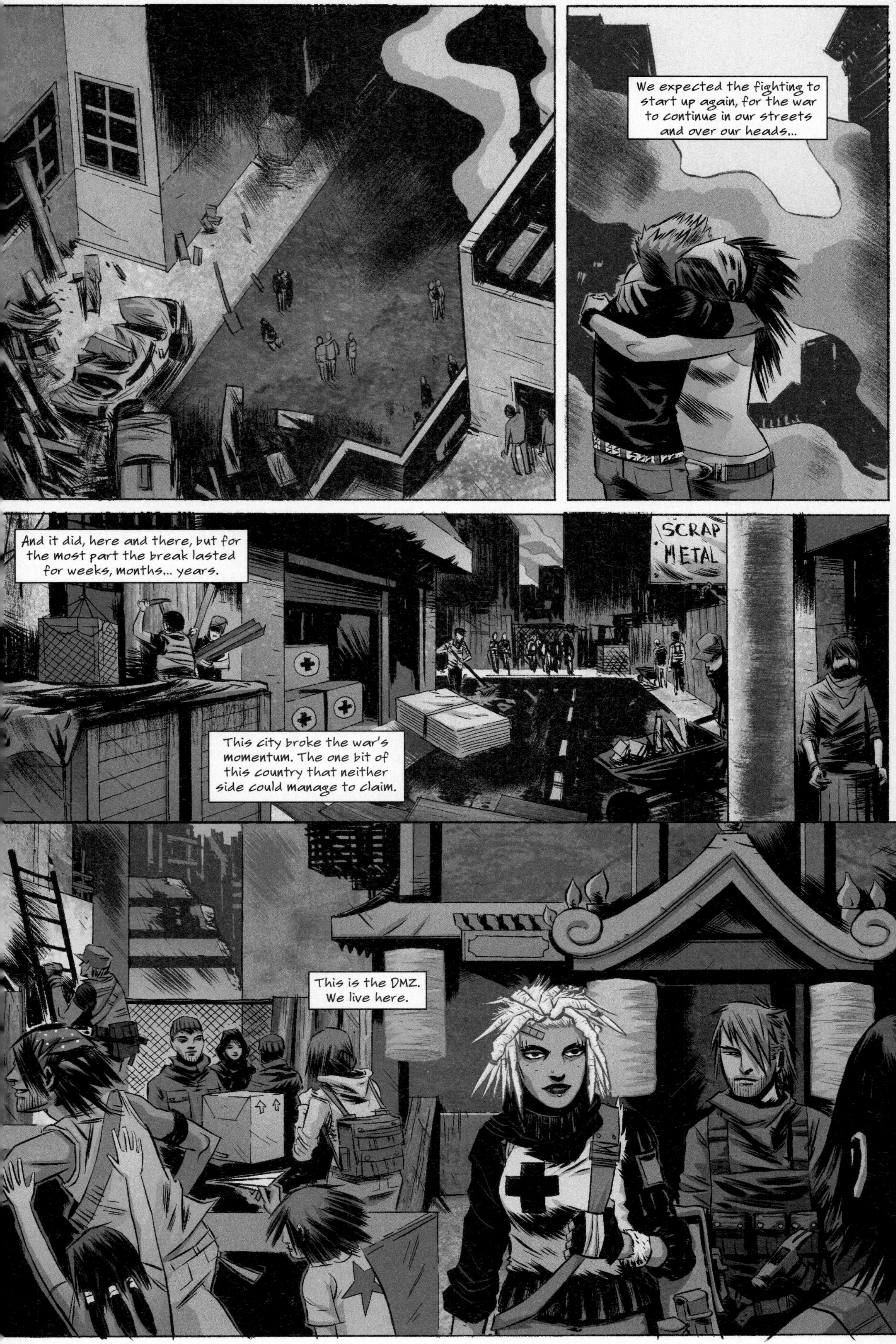
We expected the fighting to start up again, for the war to continue in our streets and over our heads...
And it did, here and there, but for the most part the break lasted for weeks, months... years.
SCRAP METAL
This city broke the war's momentum. The one bit of this country that neither side could manage to claim.
This is the DMZ. We live here.

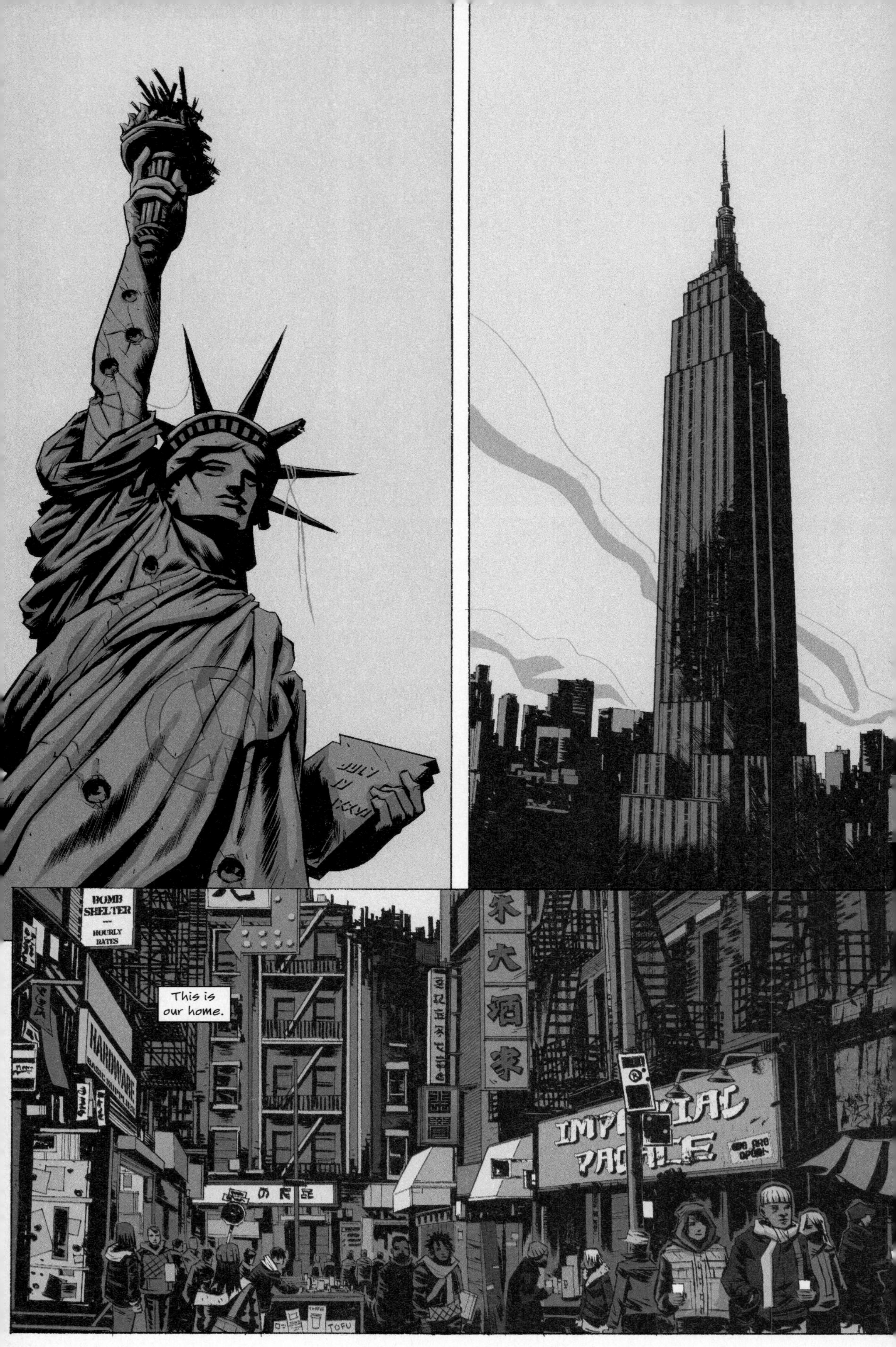
BOMB SHELTER
HOURLY RATES
This is our home.
HARDWARE
TOFU

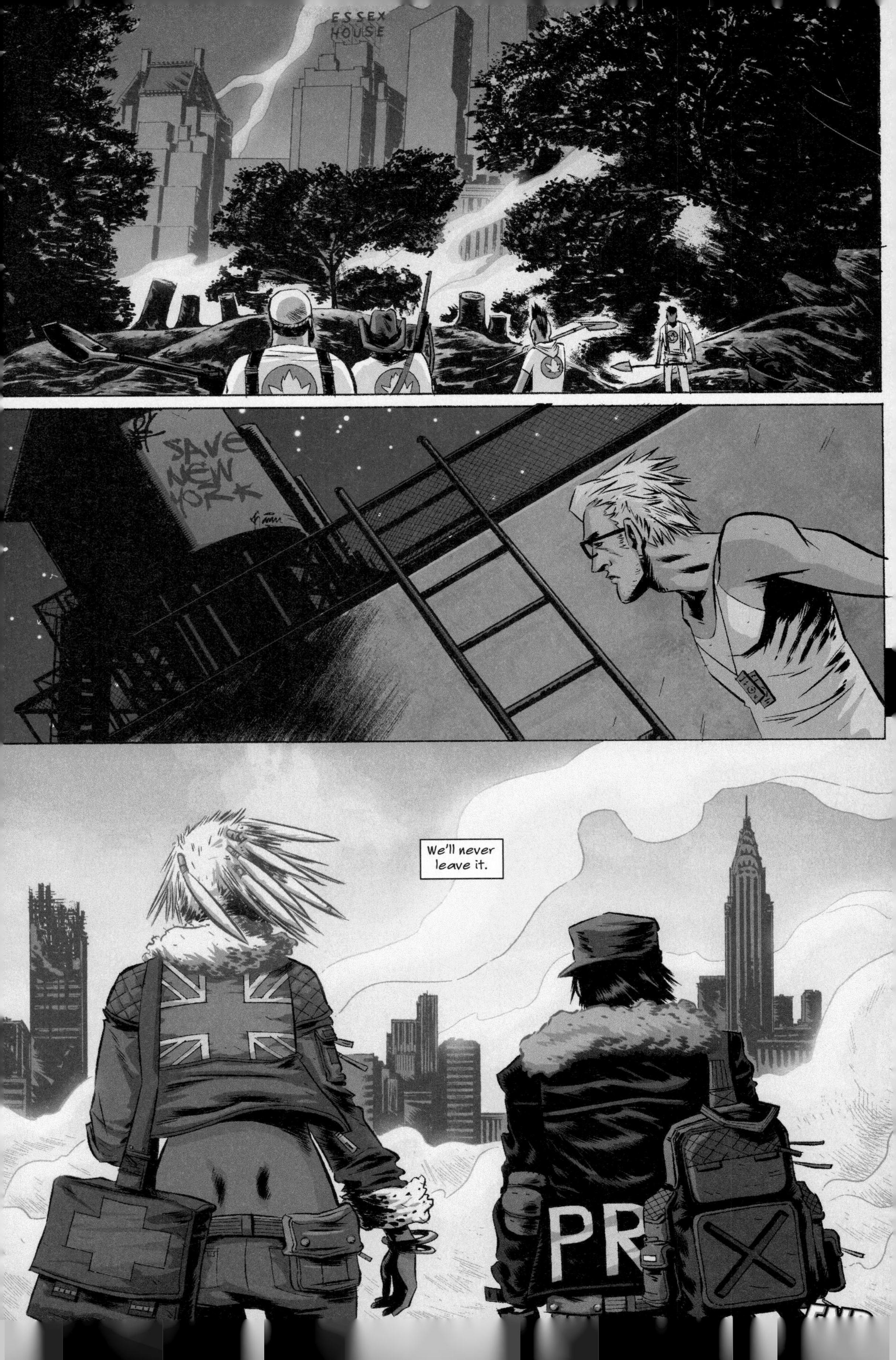
ESSEX HOUSE
SAVE NEW YORK
We'll never leave it.
PR

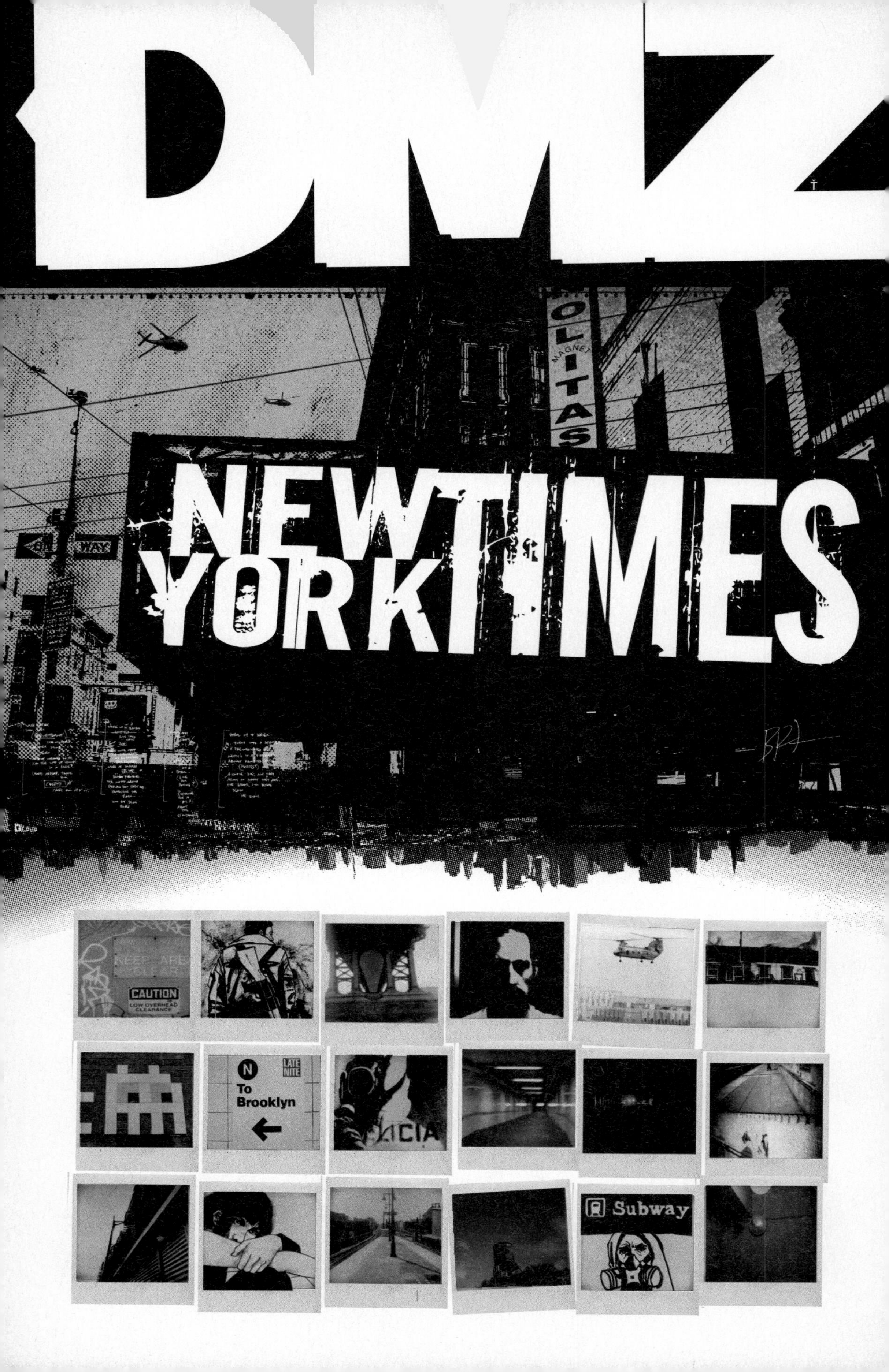
DMZ
NEW YORK TIMES
WAY
KEEP AREA CLEAR
CAUTION
LOW OVERHEAD CLEARANCE
N
LATE NITE
To Brooklyn
Subway

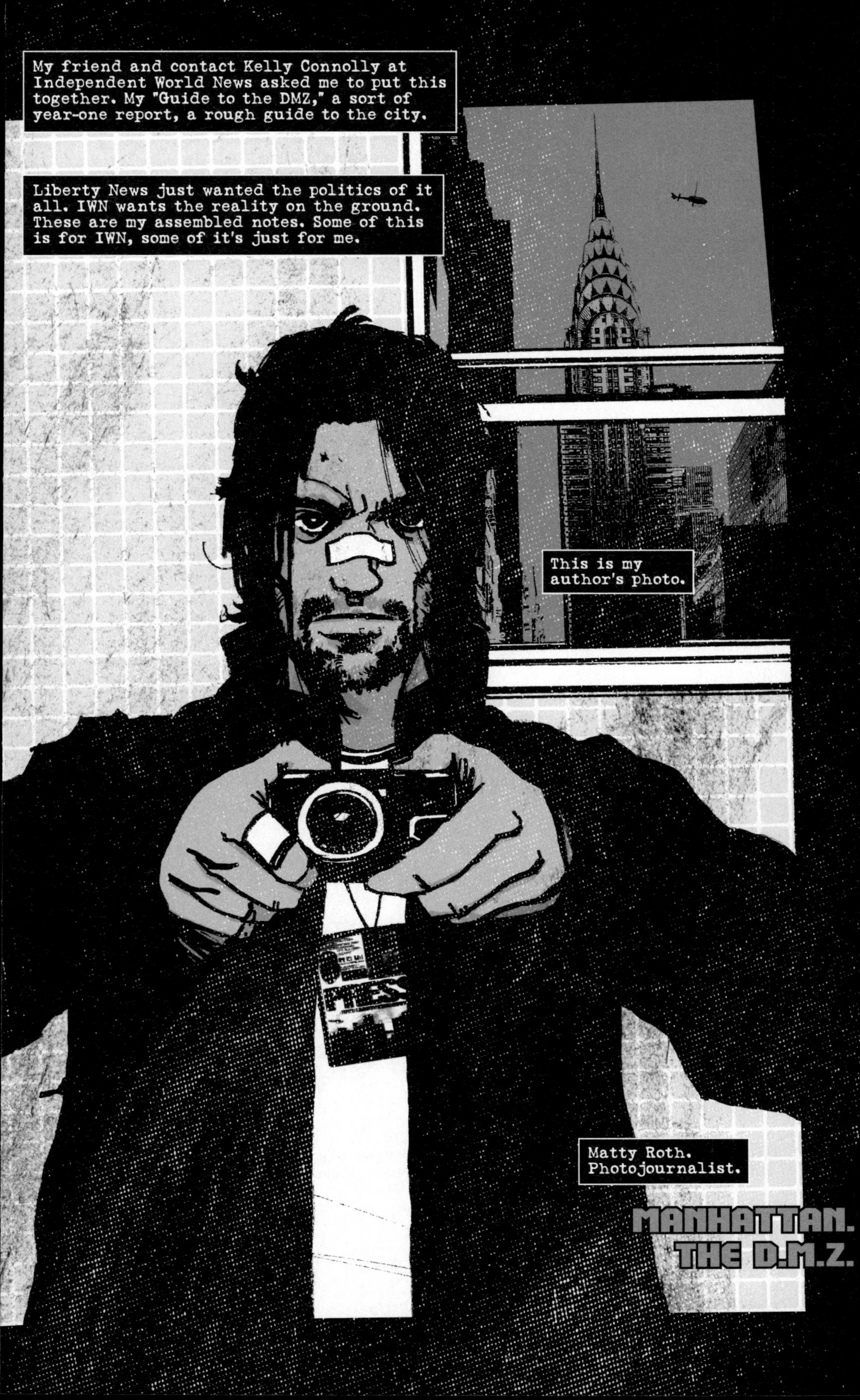
My friend and contact Kelly Connolly at Independent World News asked me to put this together. My "Guide to the DMZ," a sort of year-one report, a rough guide to the city.
Liberty News just wanted the politics of it all. IWN wants the reality on the ground. These are my assembled notes. Some of this is for IWN, some of it's just for me.
This is my author's photo.
Matty Roth. Photojournalist.
MANHATTAN. THE D.M.Z.

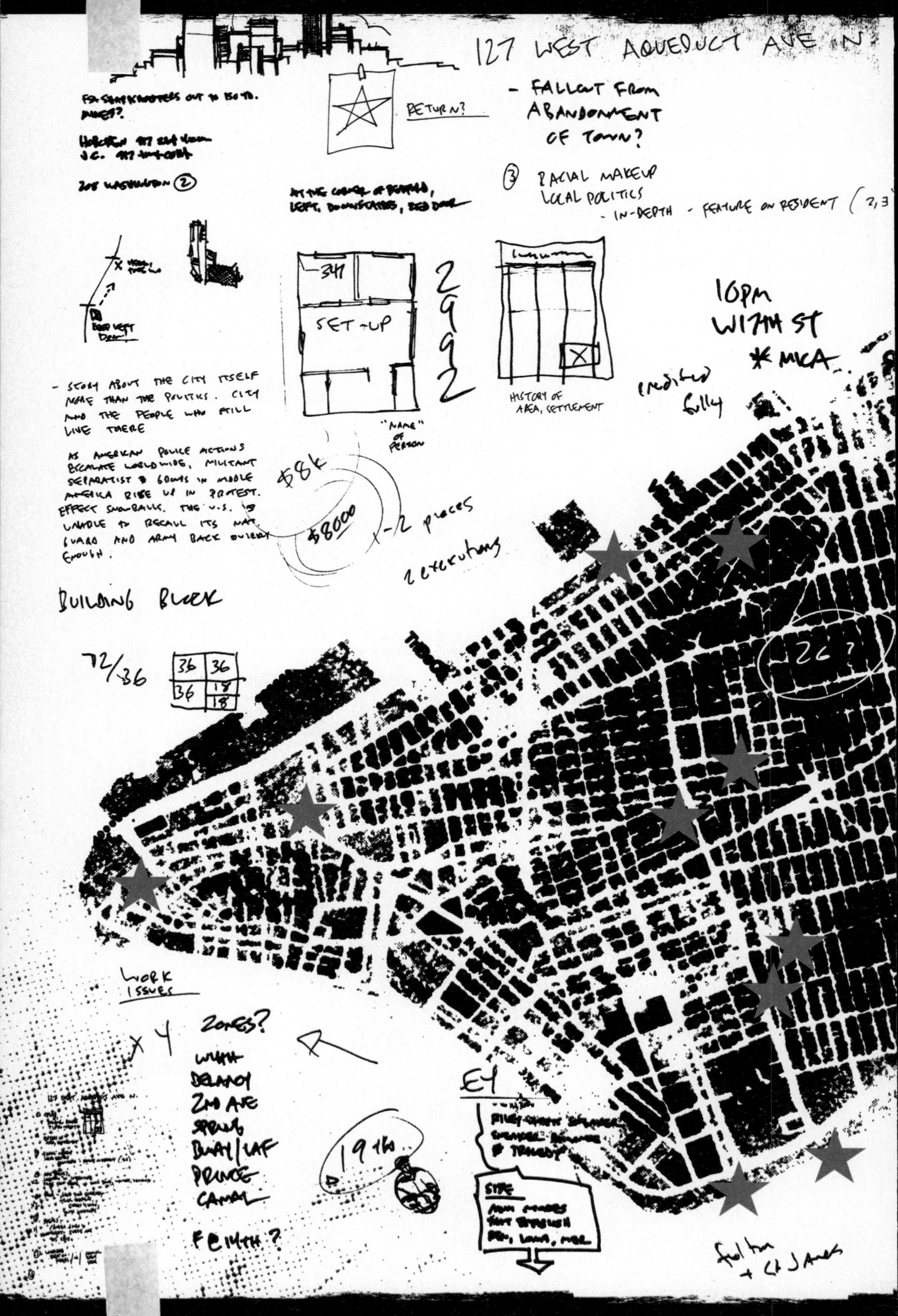
127 WEST AQUEDUCT AVE N
RETURN?
- FALLOUT FROM ABANDONMENT OF TOWN?
③ RACIAL MAKEUP
LOCAL POLITICS
- IN-DEPTH - FEATURE ON RESIDENT (2,3
208 WASHINGTON ②
LEFT, DOWNSTAIRS, RED DOOR
SET-UP
2992
HISTORY OF AREA, SETTLEMENT
"NAME" OF PERSON
10PM
- STORY ABOUT THE CITY ITSELF MORE THAN THE POLITICS. CITY AND THE PEOPLE WHO STILL LIVE THERE
AS AMERICAN POLICE ACTIONS ESCALATE WORLDWIDE, MILITANT SEPARATIST GROUPS IN MIDDLE AMERICA RISE UP IN PROTEST. EFFECT SNOWBALLS. THE U.S. IS UNABLE TO RECALL ITS NAT. GUARD AND ARMY BACK QUICKLY ENOUGH.
$8k
$8000
x-2 places
2 executions
BUILDING BLOCK
72/36
36 36
36 18
18
26?
WORK ISSUES
x4
ZONES?
DELANCY
2ND AVE
SPRING
PRINCE
CANAL
1916
SITE

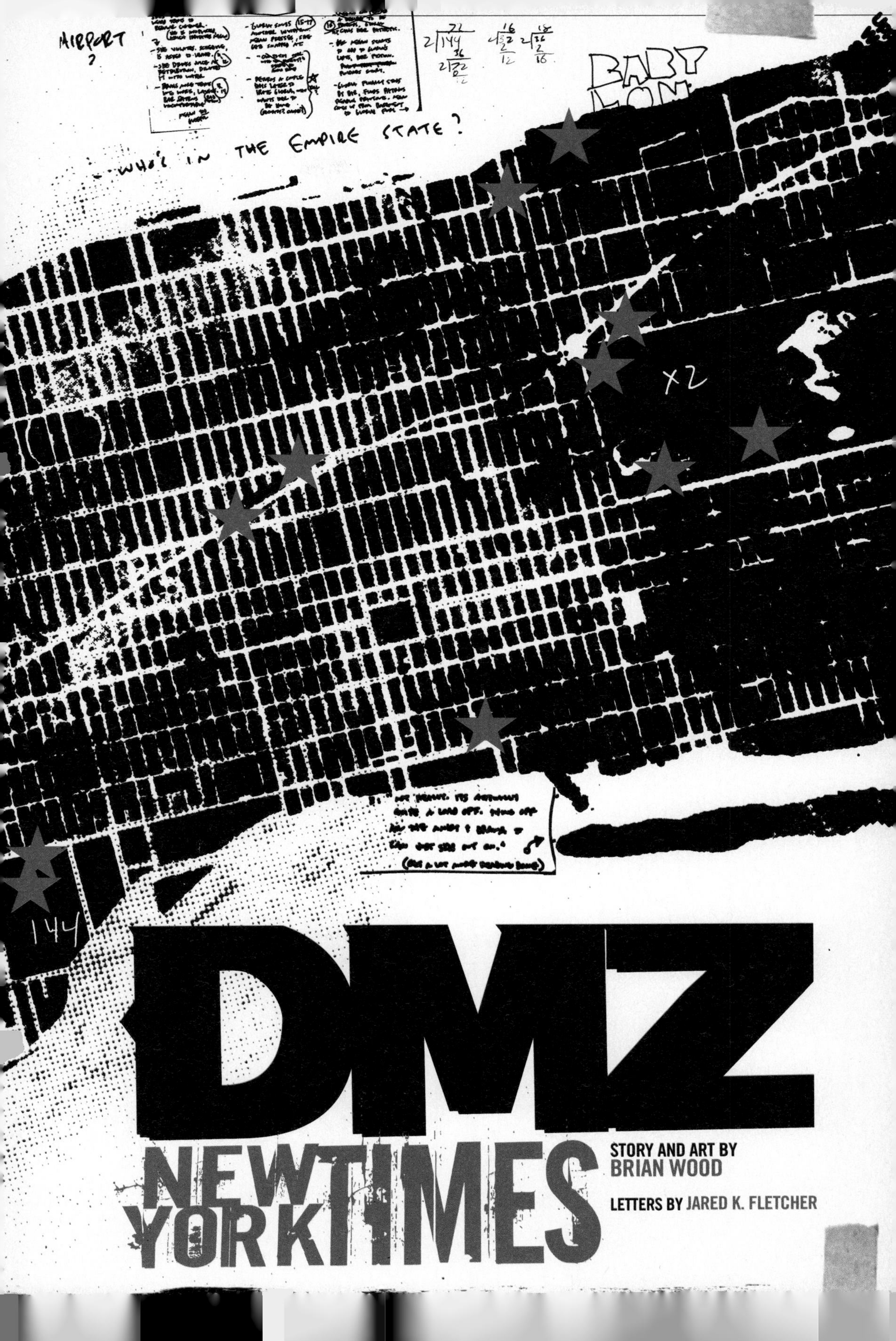
AIRPORT ?
WHO'S IN THE EMPIRE STATE?
BABY MOM
x2
144

DMZ

NEW YORK TIMES

STORY AND ART BY
BRIAN WOOD

LETTERS BY JARED K. FLETCHER

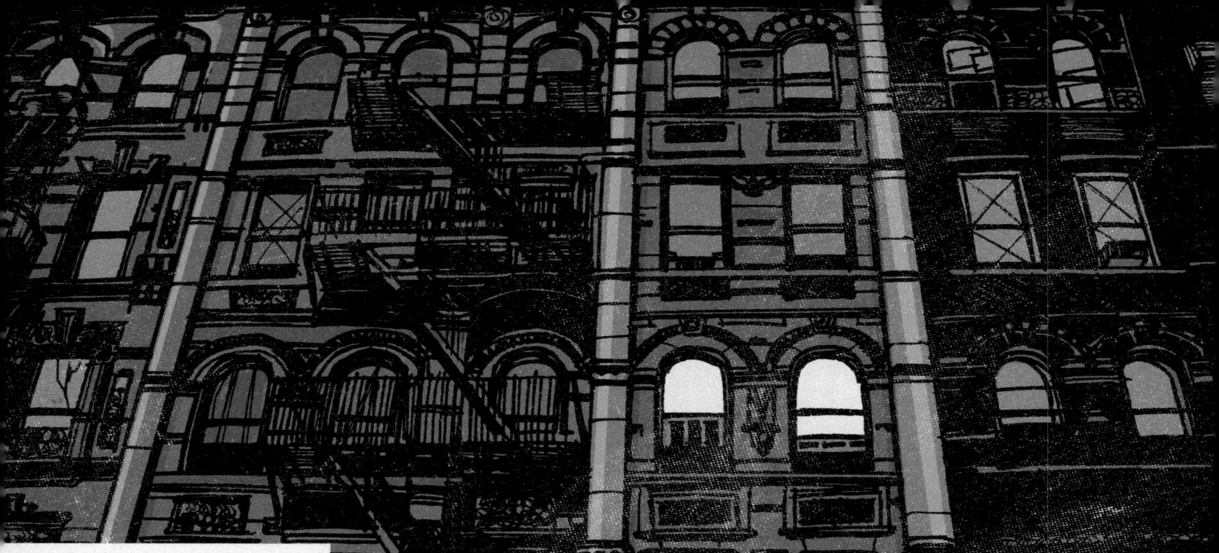

NEIGHBORHOODS

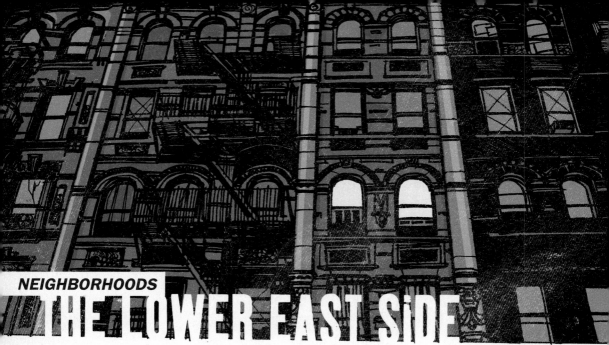

THE LOWER EAST SiDE

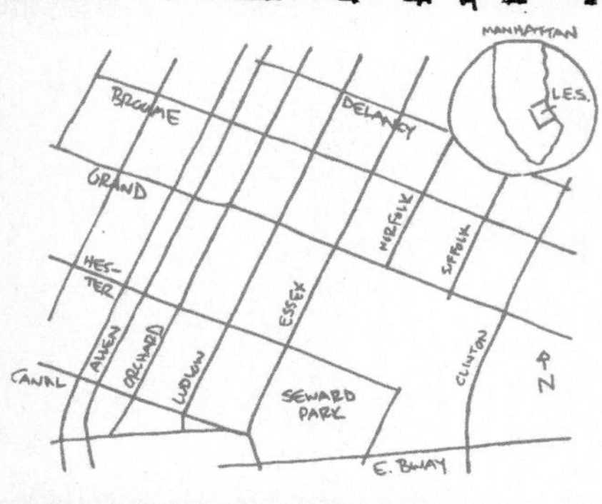

MANHATTAN
L.E.S.
BROOME
DELANCY
GRAND
NORFOLK
SUFFOLK
HES-TER
ESSEX
ALLEN
ORCHARD
LUDLOW
CLINTON
CANAL
SEWARD PARK
E. BWAY
N

Location/Boundaries: South of Houston to Canal, Bowery to the river. Sort of a mix of hipsters and the immigrant working class, based on existing signage and the people who hang around. Ruined museum on Orchard protected by extremist local types suggests tenement culture in the past, and the recreated old-style immigrant tenement building they've preserved becomes an ironic statement... I can think of several families now who wish they had it that good.

Zee lives near here. Neighborhood milita is a circus... by my count, close to twenty groups have carved up this area, some only occupying a block or two. Bizarre, Trotsky-esque lunatics have the lockdown on Zee's block. They're the assholes who took out the helicopter I came in on, and they won't talk to me. Zee says to leave them alone. They don't talk to anyone.

Trouble spots: Norfolk down to Grand. Suffolk just below Houston. Hester any time of day or night. Militias keep Seward Park stable, but all I ever see going on there are Chinese doing tai-chi in the morning. Grand belongs to Wilson's Grandsons. The playgrounds that run along Allen St. are fucking deathzones.

U.S. Military's got good line-of-sight on a lot of this neighborhood, and the proximity to the bridges can be tricky. I've documented seventeen cases of random killings from U.S. sniper fire... bored river guards? People learn to keep a building between them and the water. Leaves streets like Houston and Delancey and Canal pretty empty.

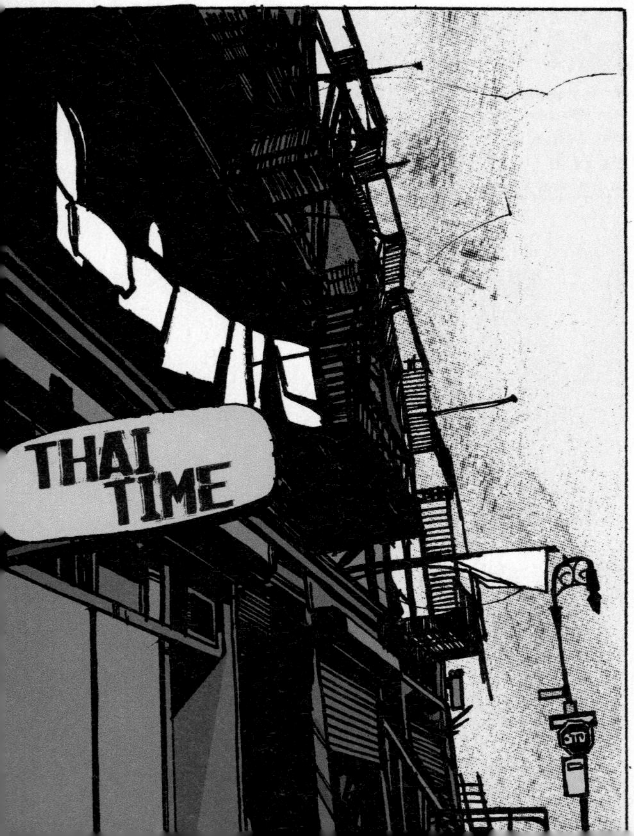

THAI TIME

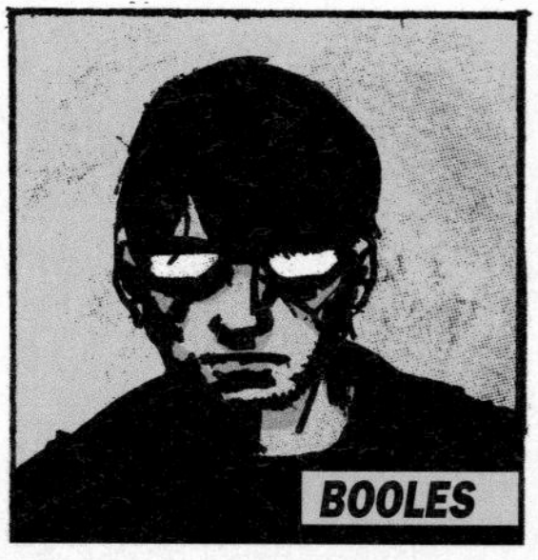

BOOLES

(Ageless, raceless hipster somehow claiming an entire building on lower Eldridge. Filthy black denim everything, looks like he might have been a roadie for The Ramones. Everyone leaves him alone, except me, it seems. –Matty)

Name: Booles ***Age:*** Pre-War

X Factor: Live and let live, man.

Personality: What? I don't know.

Days Spent: Walking my block, picking up shit, looking for valuables. Staying out of the way, in bed by 9 p.m. before the nighttime shit starts up.

On the War: Trashed my city, shrunk my world. Now my world's my home, my roof garden, my two hands. Before, I had rent to worry about, ConEd, late fees, asshole bar-hopping pretty boys and smoking bans. So who knows? Could be worse.

Anything Else? Watch what you breathe, man. Air's poisoned.

NOTES

THAI TIME: Where the old Pink Pony was (I'm told). Zee takes me there. They open in the morning. Soy roti made on the premises, back garden devoted to growing fresh produce. Vegan, but cool.

PIANOS: Music venue. Weirdly closed scene – you gotta know people. I get in as "Press" most of the time.

HESTER MILITIA: Unstable crew, but a Colombian cat named Parco gets me through if necessary. Prefer to take the long way around. Parco's shifty, one of those lazy-looking guys who's already worked out a few ways to kill you five mins after meeting you.

SUBWAYS: Not worth it. Army nutbags walk the F tracks from the York stop in DUMBO into the city, start shit for laughs. Plus you never know what third rails are live.

BARS: A lot of booze flows in the L.E.S. How? No one knows, no one cares. Safe spots: Welcome to the Johnsons, Arlene's, Fat Baby, Verlaine.

OVERALL VIBE: Lot of nooks and quiet blocks, militias too distracted to bother civilians most of the time. Apartments are hard to come by – this place is dense with people, but close to the river you can find unclaimed spots if you're desperate and crazy enough. You can find better spots uptown, but this is where civilization's happening, where the culture is.

EIGHBORHOODS

CENTRAL PARK

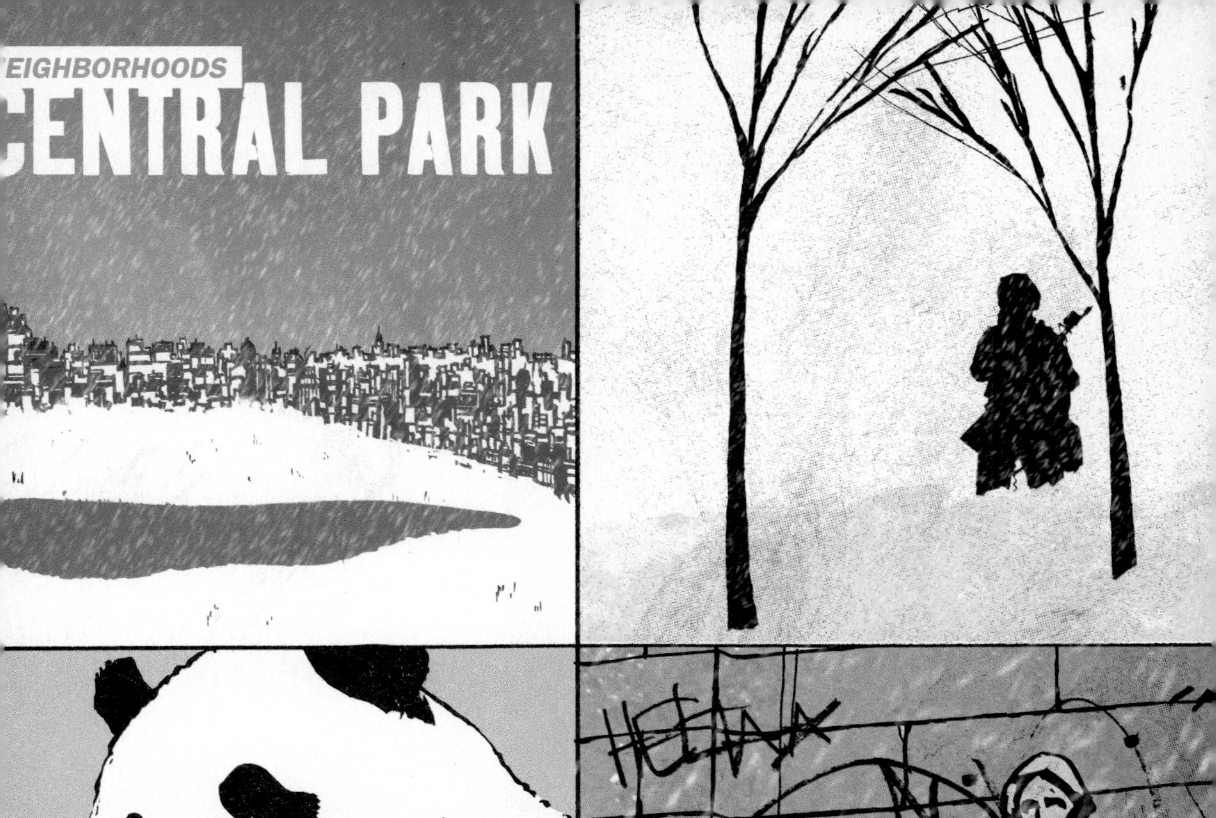

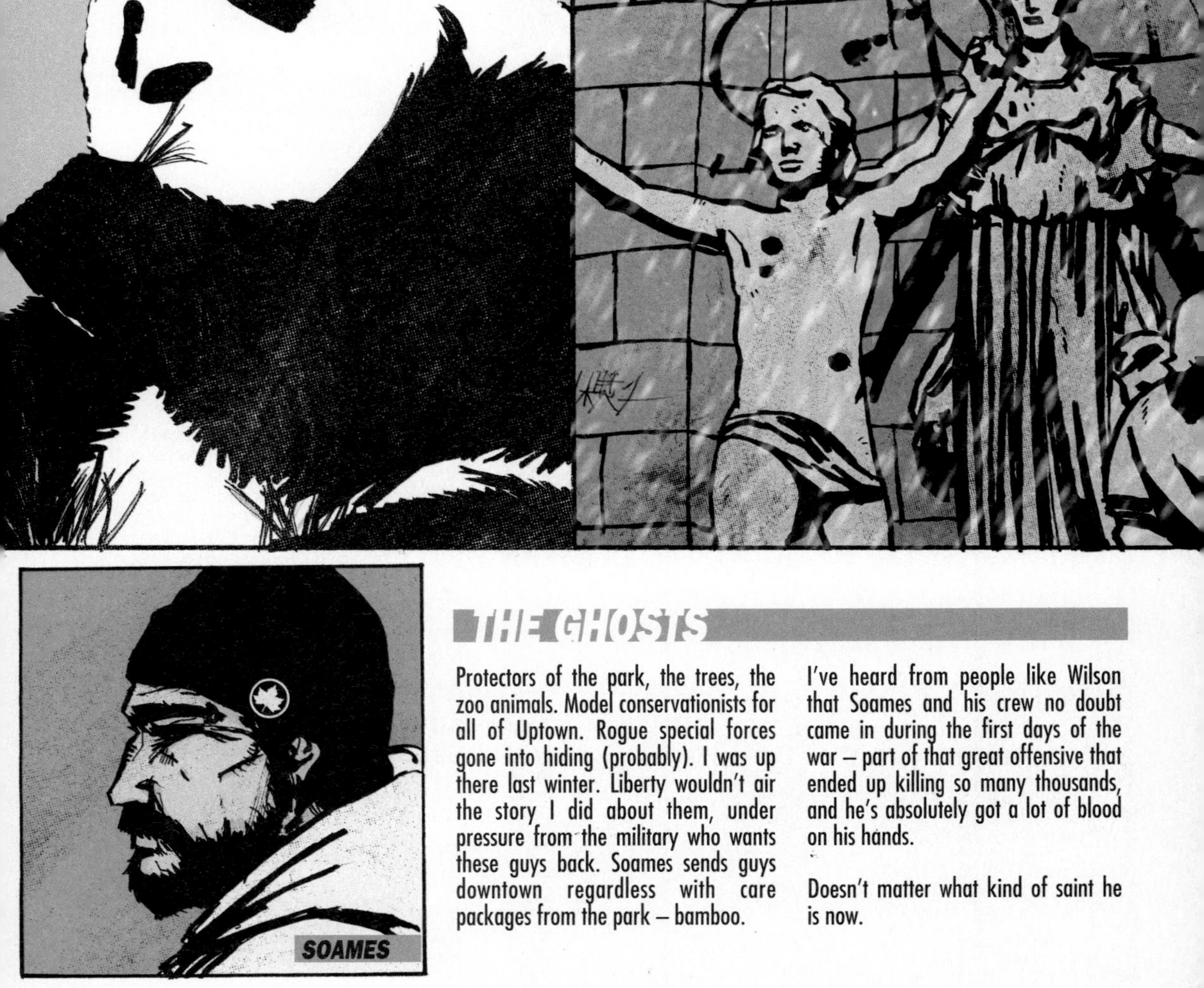
SOAMES

THE GHOSTS

Protectors of the park, the trees, the zoo animals. Model conservationists for all of Uptown. Rogue special forces gone into hiding (probably). I was up there last winter. Liberty wouldn't air the story I did about them, under pressure from the military who wants these guys back. Soames sends guys downtown regardless with care packages from the park – bamboo.

I've heard from people like Wilson that Soames and his crew no doubt came in during the first days of the war – part of that great offensive that ended up killing so many thousands, and he's absolutely got a lot of blood on his hands.

Doesn't matter what kind of saint he is now.

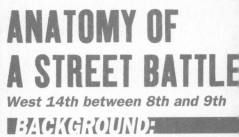

ANATOMY OF A STREET BATTLE

West 14th between 8th and 9th

BACKGROUND:

Free States Army (FSA)-backed militants pretty much control that weste edge of the city, from about 9th or 10th Ave to the river, with support fro snipers and artillery from Jersey. They made some moves a few months ag to extend further, moving closer to 8th Ave. The Union Square West (USW crew moved to intercept.

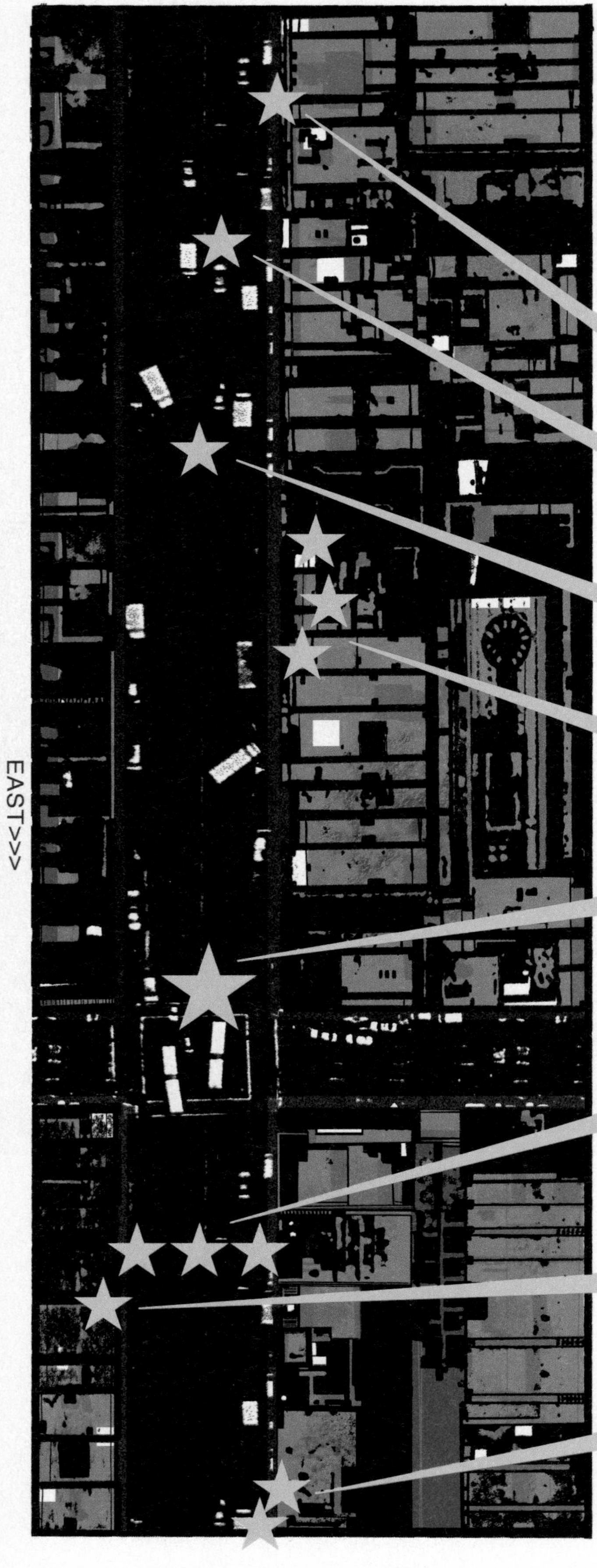

EAST>>>

• Storefront explosion here. No one knows who caused it or how, but it provided some confusion and smoke cover for the FSA elements to make their way east.

• Vehicles provide additional cover. Some of these aren't wrecks but fresh trucks that the FSA drove in just prior to the explosion. Lends support to the notion that the storefront explosion was all part of a plan.

• Snipers seem to have the block covered to about here. Oddly, they didn't continue to move forward as the ground units did. Once those units got beyond the sphere of protection the snipers afforded, they were in trouble.

• Additional FSA-backed fighters appeared over these rooftops.

• The intersection. Torched buses block the way, and the fighting gets bogged down. Random street crazies engage the FSA fighters here and slow them up enough for the USW fighters to reach 8th Ave. Corners and intersections are the worst possible place to linger in the DMZ, anywhere... too many angles, too many crazies, too much strategic value.

• USW fighters start to appear in larger numbers. FSA snipers still not moving forward. The FSA fighters control the intersection, thanks to the buses, but have zero flank support and cannot continue eastward. USW has probably sent men the long way around, back to 7th Ave and west on 13th and 15th to come around on the sides, but they never show up in time.

• A second storefront explosion here. The USW fighters scatter, probably thinking the blast came from above, even drone aircraft. More likely a bullet clipped a gasline, or a boobytrap was triggered.

• USW moves back to this point. FSA stays put in the buses. Some shots fired from north and south along the avenue, but nothing coordinated. FSA retreats after dark, probably laying traps. In the morning locals rope off the buses and post warnings for the block. No one moves in to occupy.

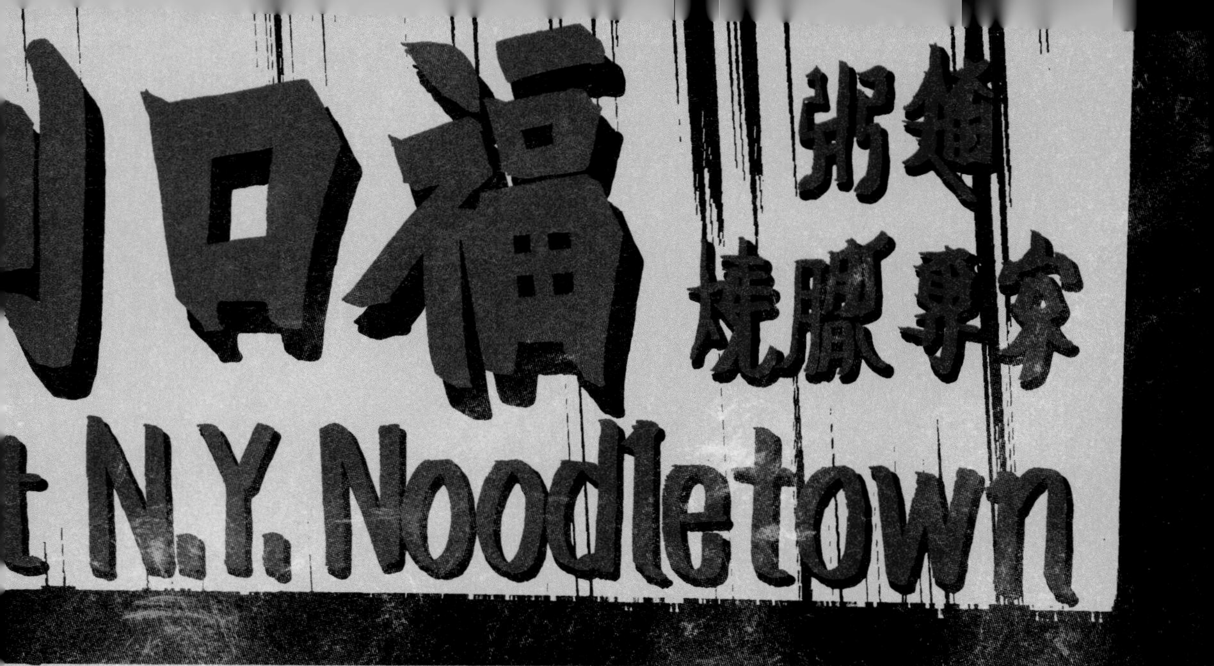
t N.Y. Noodletown

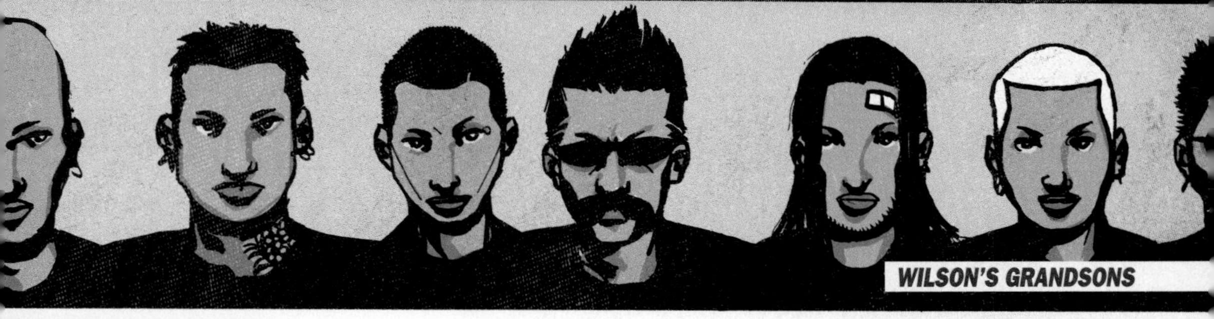

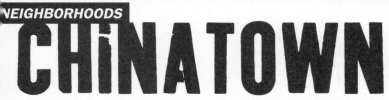

WILSON'S GRANDSONS

NEIGHBORHOODS

CHINATOWN

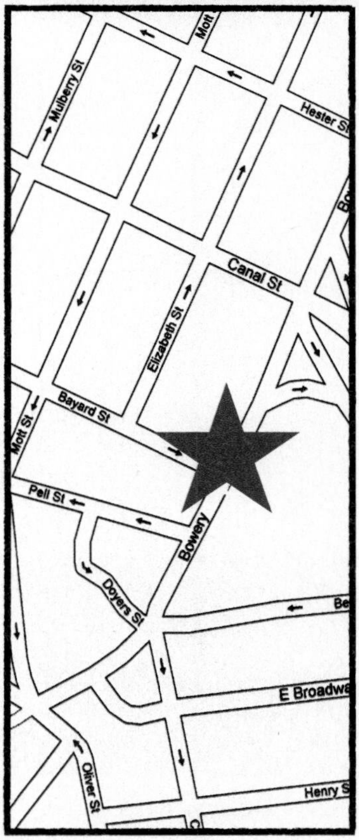
Mott
Mulberry St
Hester St
Canal St
Elizabeth St
Bayard St
Mott St
Pell St
Bowery
Doyers St
E Broadwa
Oliver St
Henry S

ASIANS – Probably the largest ethnic group ignored during the evacuations. Now they completely occupy their neighborhood and pretty much shut the doors behind them. Tourists (assuming there would be some) can no longer score Prada knockoffs on Canal, yuppies can't get bubble tea, hipsters can't find bootlegs of HK flicks, and I can't get noodles from N.Y. Noodle Town whenever I want.

The U.S. military's reach extends into parts of Chinatown ust like it does the Lower East Side, but for some reason it's less of a danger down here. Canal is still left pretty vacant, but the entrance to the Manhattan Bridge is *right there,* and the Bowery is a busy street. The U.S. leaves Chinatown alone.

I'd ask Wilson why, but I'm a little afraid of what the answer might be.

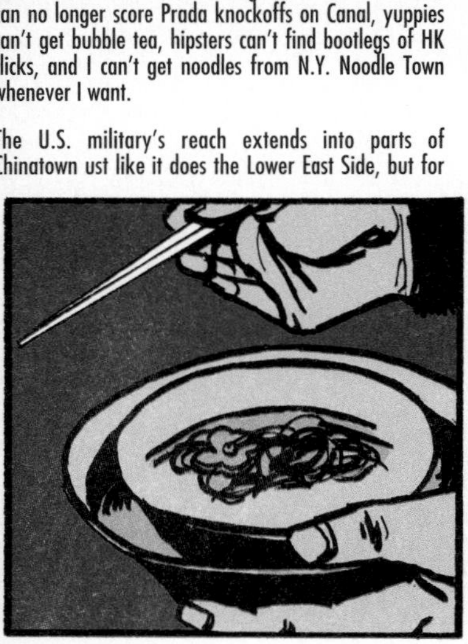

NOTES

Wilson threw some kind of old-style wedding party for one of his granddaughters (don't ask), and I was invited. Total token white guy, but with camera. Here I am, well-known photojournalist working for two networks, and I'm reduced to being Wilson's wedding photographer.

CONSUMED WHILE ON THE JOB:

Roast Pork and Noodle Soup
Ha Moon Mai Fun
Salt Fish and Chicken Rice
Chinese Vegetables with Oyster Sauce
A dozen Heineken

A Grandson brought me home. I was lit. Felt good – first time in a year I could let my guard down and know people were looking out for me.

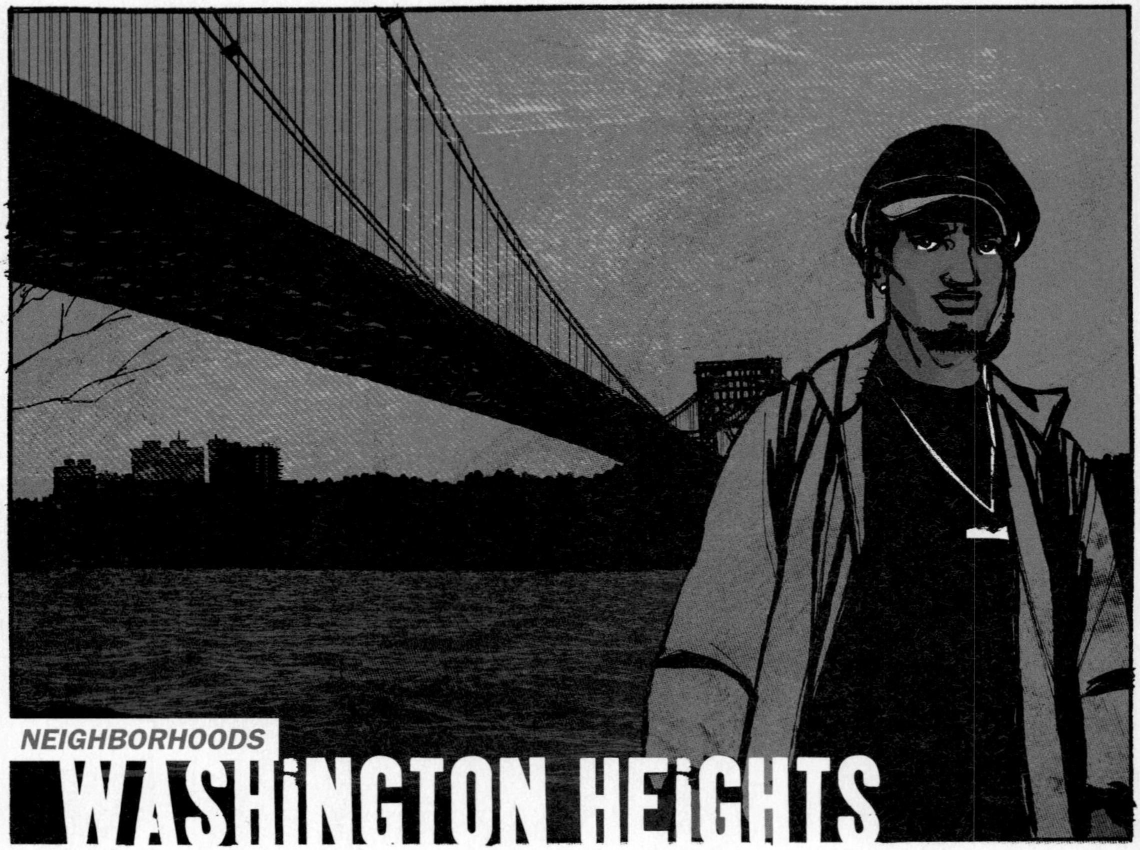

NEIGHBORHOODS

WASHiNGTON HEiGHTS

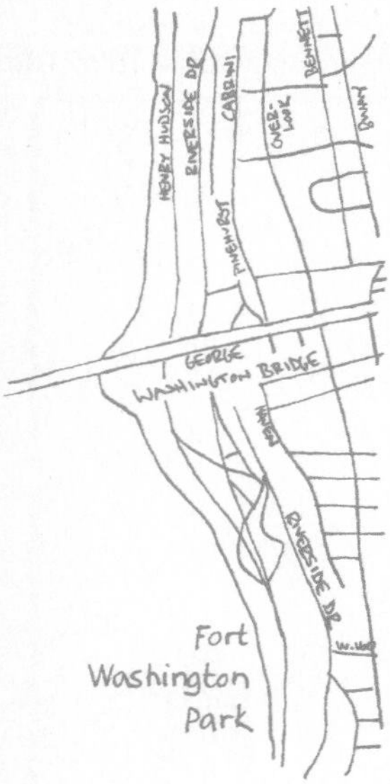
HENRY HUDSON
RIVERSIDE DR
CABRINI
OVER-LOOK
BENNETT
BWAY
PINEHURST
GEORGE WASHINGTON BRIDGE
Fort Washington Park

Massive residential neighborhood uptown, north of Harlem. Strange to see hundreds, if not thousands, of beautiful pre-war buildings sitting vacant. Faces peer at you from windows here and there, but most people who stayed behind moved downtown. I don't blame them, it's spooky as hell up here. And I think there is something inside us, on an instinctual, animal level, to seek the protection of groups. The people are all downtown, as is most of the food and power and culture.

Uptown is the realm of animals, shut-ins, looters, and mass graves.

Zee's friend Jamal, along with his crew of engineers and architects, have been working on the retaining walls that run along the Henry Hudson. They're crumbling, and it's not really the sort of problem that can be ignored if anyone is ever going to want to live along Riverside Drive ever again. They're fixing them for free, but rumor has it this is one of the sites that Trustwell is being paid to take care of when they move in next month.

JAMAL

Name: Jamal Greene

Age: 23

X Factor: Skill and pride in my work.

Where's Home? Born and raised on Bennett Ave and 186th.

Days Spent: I live in a tent in Riverside Park, but it's nicer than it sounds. Some of the buildings along Riverside still have working plumbing, pulling water from the roof towers, so I can shower and flush a toilet.

On the War: Am I an asshole for seeing a bright side? I'm a 23-yo ex-student with no degree, and here I am working on these walls. This is the sort of work I dreamed about when I was young: designing and building something that'll make a real difference to my city. I wouldn't be doing this right now if the war hadn't happened, I bet.

Anything Else? Take good care of each other. We're family.

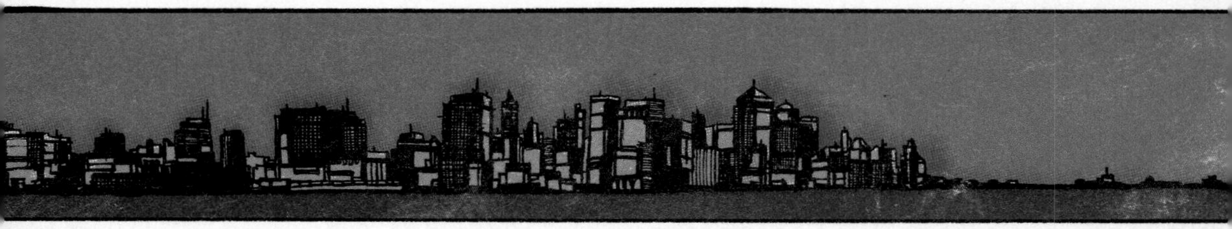

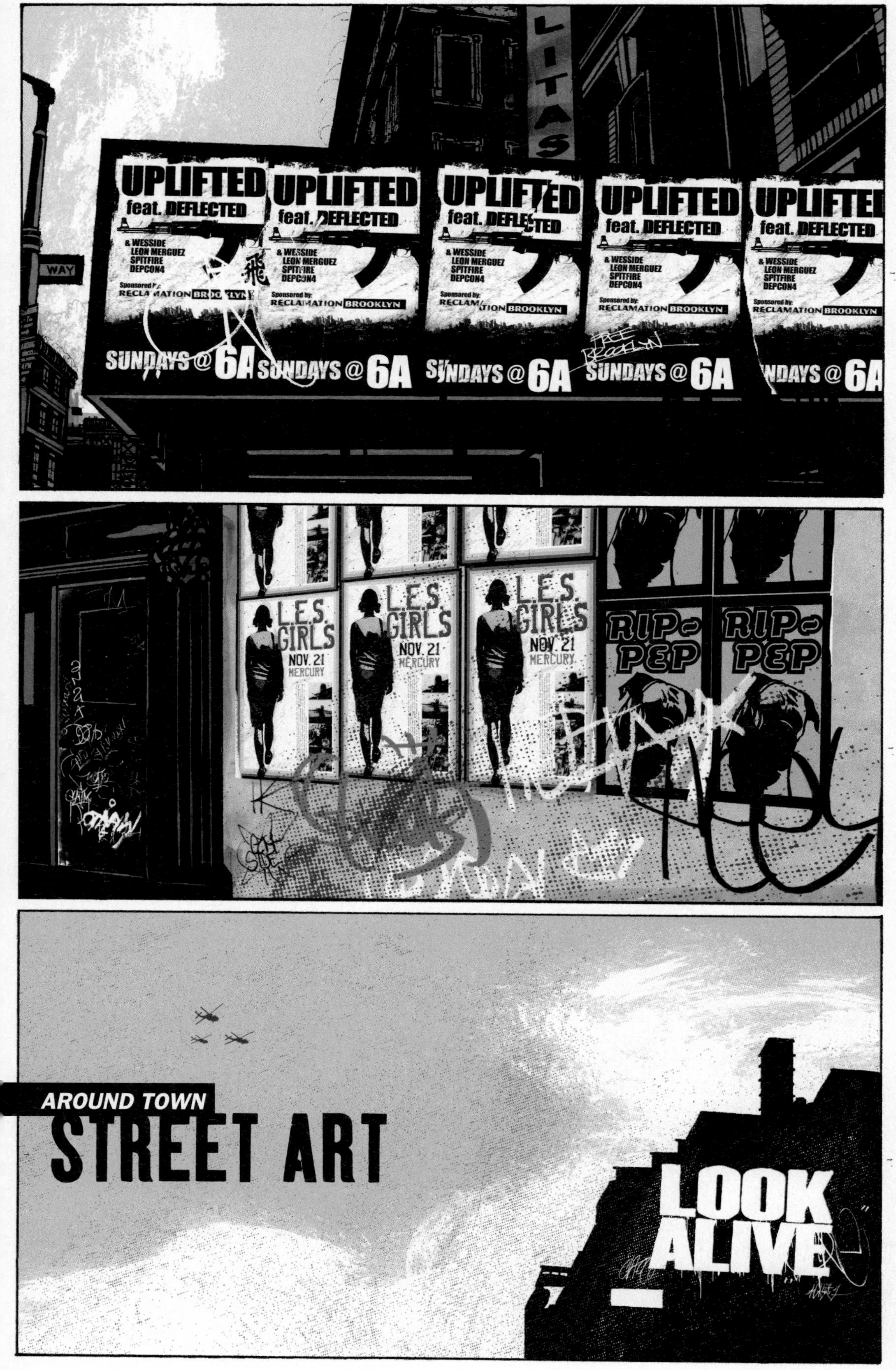
LITAS
WAY
UPLIFTED
feat. DEFLECTED
& WESSIDE
LEON MERGUEZ
SPITFIRE
DEPCON4
Sponsored by:
RECLAMATION BROOKLYN
SUNDAYS @ 6A
FREE BROOKLYN
L.E.S. GIRLS
NOV. 21
MERCURY
RIP-PEP
AROUND TOWN
STREET ART
LOOK ALIVE

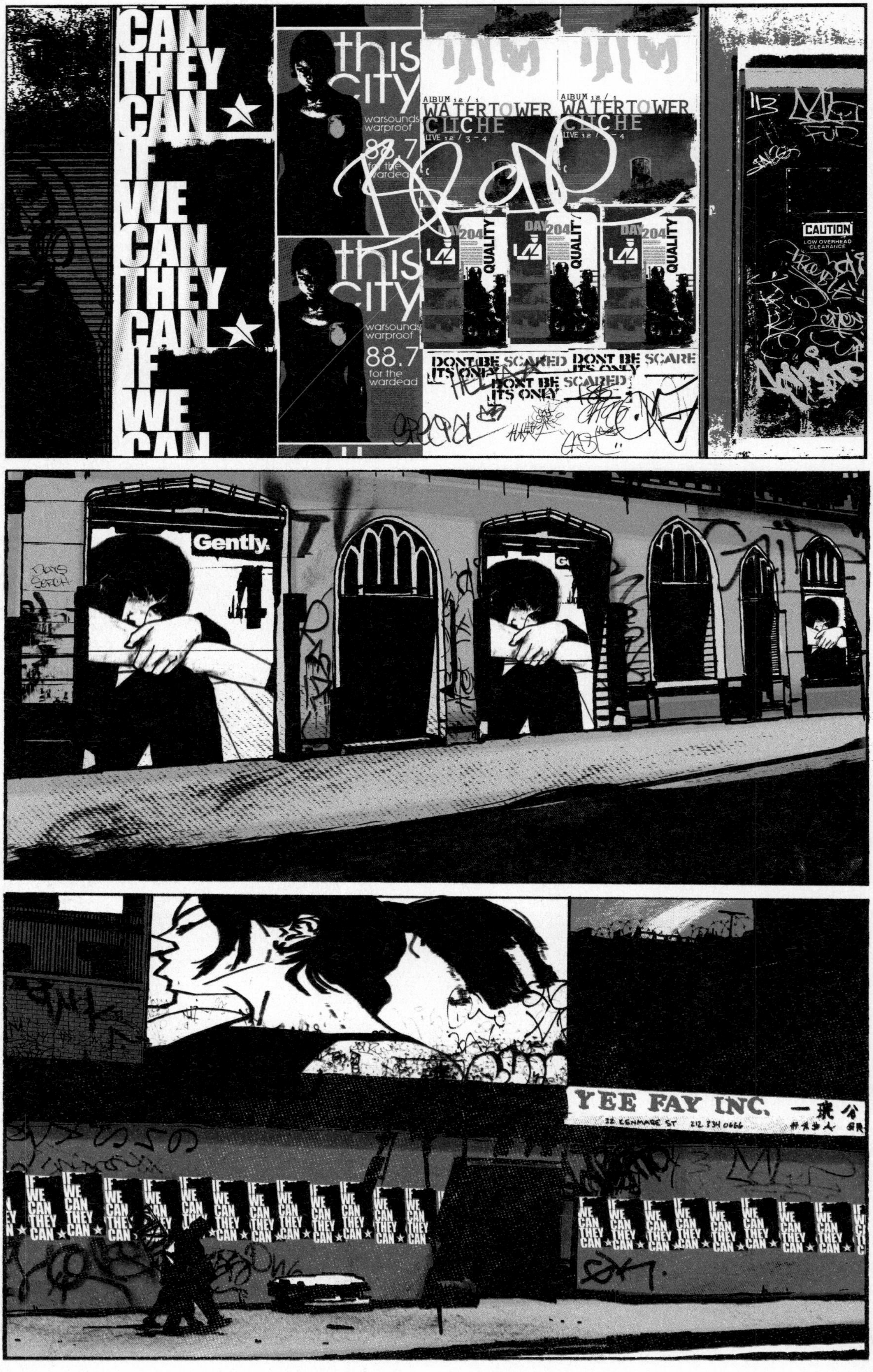
CAN THEY CAN IF WE CAN THEY CAN IF WE CAN
this city
warsounds warproof
88.7
for the wardead
this city
warsounds warproof
88.7
for the wardead
ALBUM 12 / 1
WATERTOWER CLICHE
LIVE 12 / 3-4
ALBUM 12 / 1
WATERTOWER CLICHE
LIVE 12 / 3-4
DAY 204
QUALITY
DONT BE SCARED ITS ONLY
CAUTION
LOW OVERHEAD CLEARANCE
Gently.
4
YEE FAY INC.
32 KENMARE ST 212 334 0666
IF WE CAN THEY CAN

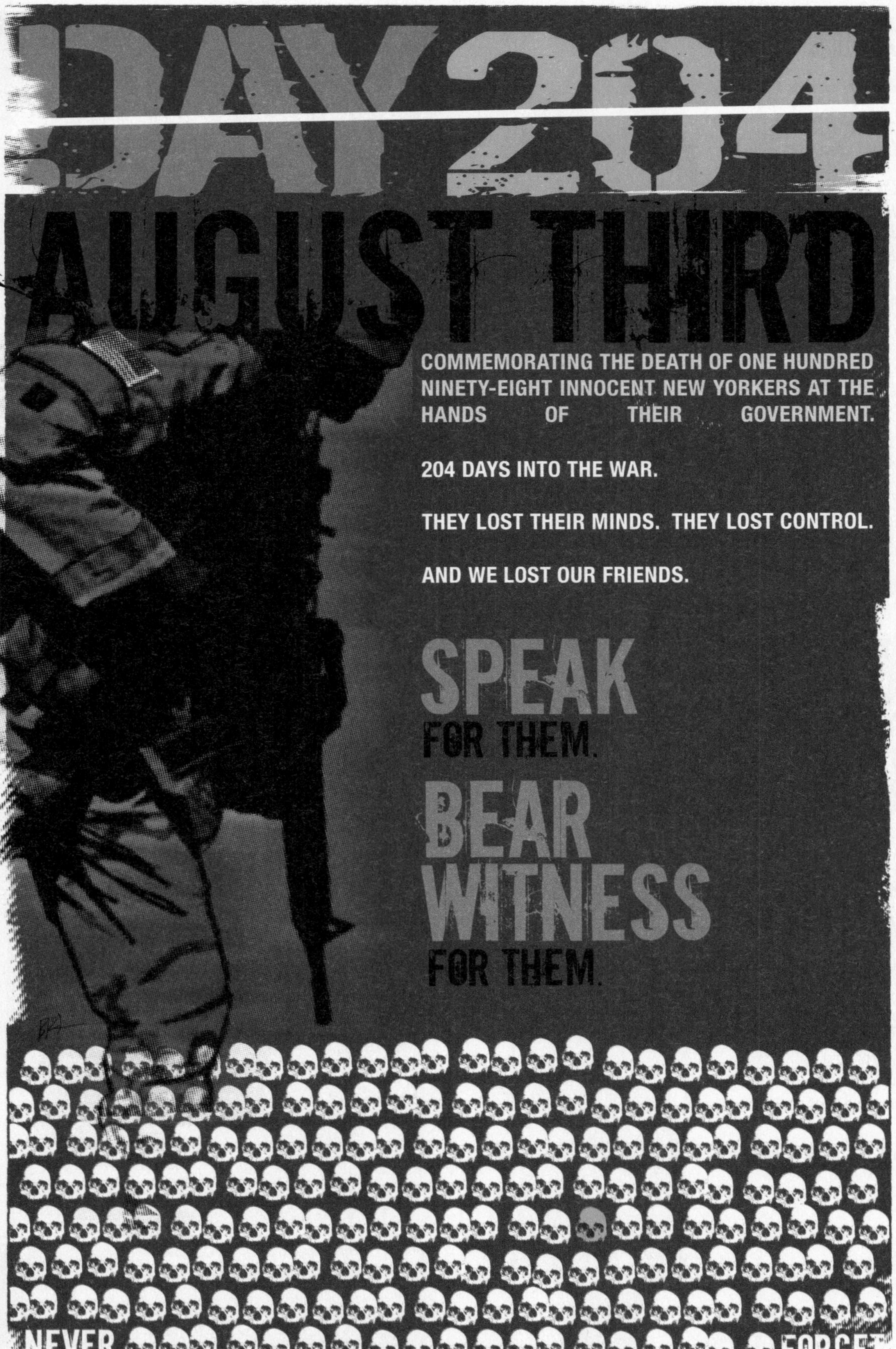

DAY 204
AUGUST THIRD
COMMEMORATING THE DEATH OF ONE HUNDRED NINETY-EIGHT INNOCENT NEW YORKERS AT THE HANDS OF THEIR GOVERNMENT.
204 DAYS INTO THE WAR.
THEY LOST THEIR MINDS. THEY LOST CONTROL.
AND WE LOST OUR FRIENDS.
SPEAK
FOR THEM.
BEAR WITNESS
FOR THEM.
NEVER
FORGET

MUCH WAS DECIDED BEFORE YOU WERE BORN

Name: Delo

Age: 27

Where's Home?
Washington Square Park

On the War: "You do what it takes to get by, whatever the situation. War, no war, not much seemed to change for me day-to-day."

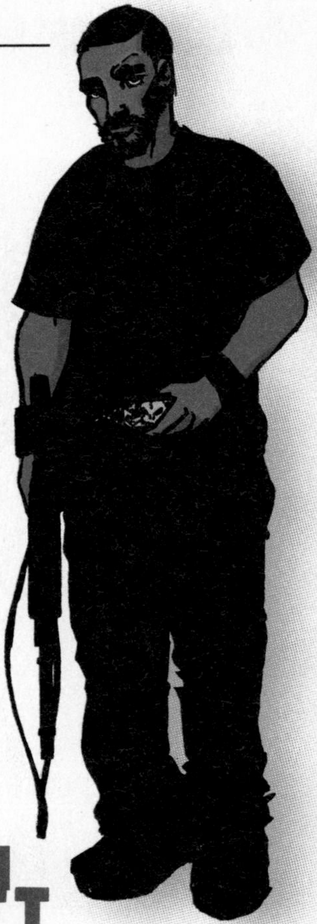

AROUND TOWN

STREET CULTURE

Name: Annie

Age: 32

What Do You Do?
"Vegetarian chef for my own restaurant, Risen. We built a small greenhouse in the back and can grow everything we need year-round."

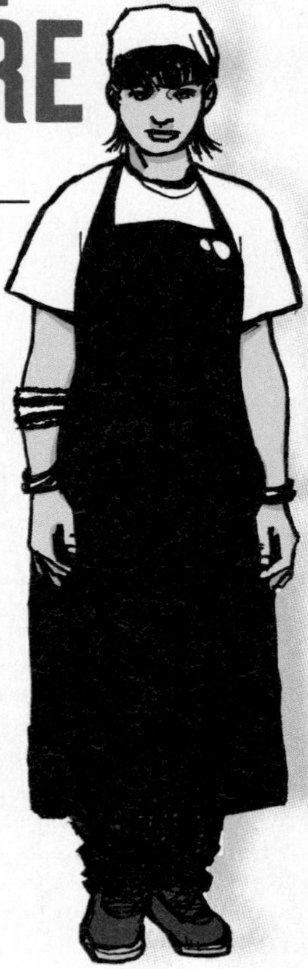

Name: Rosa ***Age:*** 39 ***Occupation:*** Artist

How Do You Deal? "You can't be a recluse. You can't stay inside and hide from the war. It's been so many years now and you learn what to wear, where to walk, who to trust. I love my life. In many ways I feel freer than I did before the war."

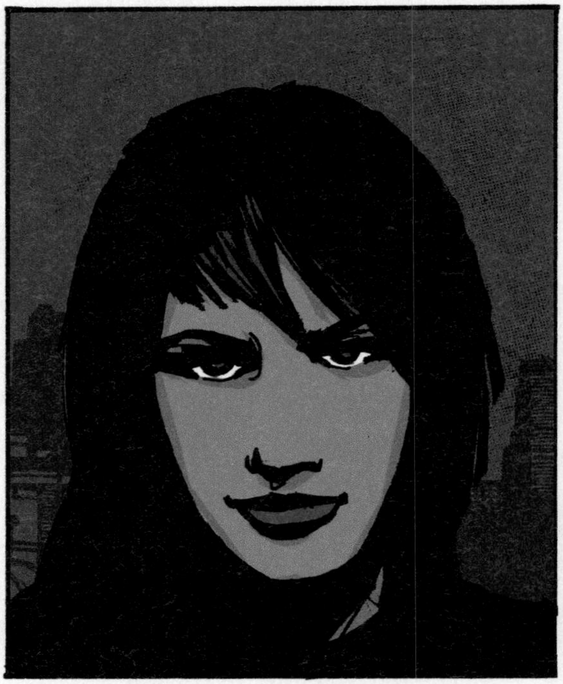

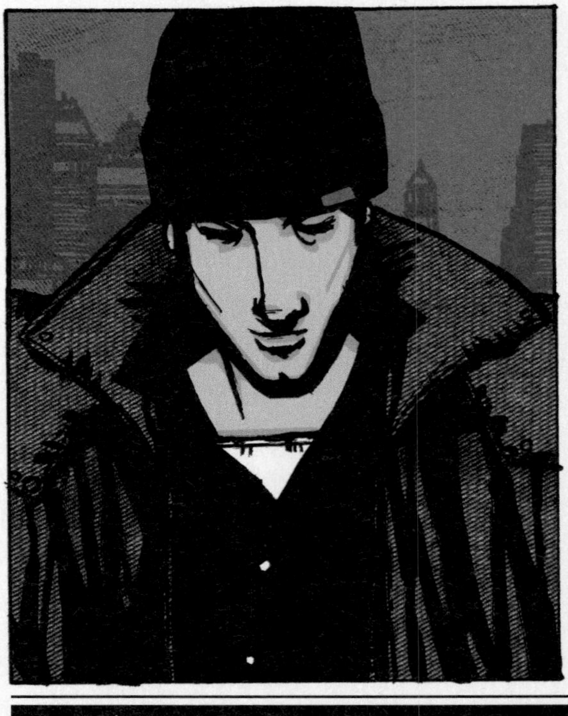

Name: Random Fire ***Age:*** 19 ***Occupation:*** DJ

On the War: "Everything's underground now, music, fashion, culture. Block by block, everyone does their thing. We're all fueled by innovation and style, not money, so it's pure, it's all pure now."

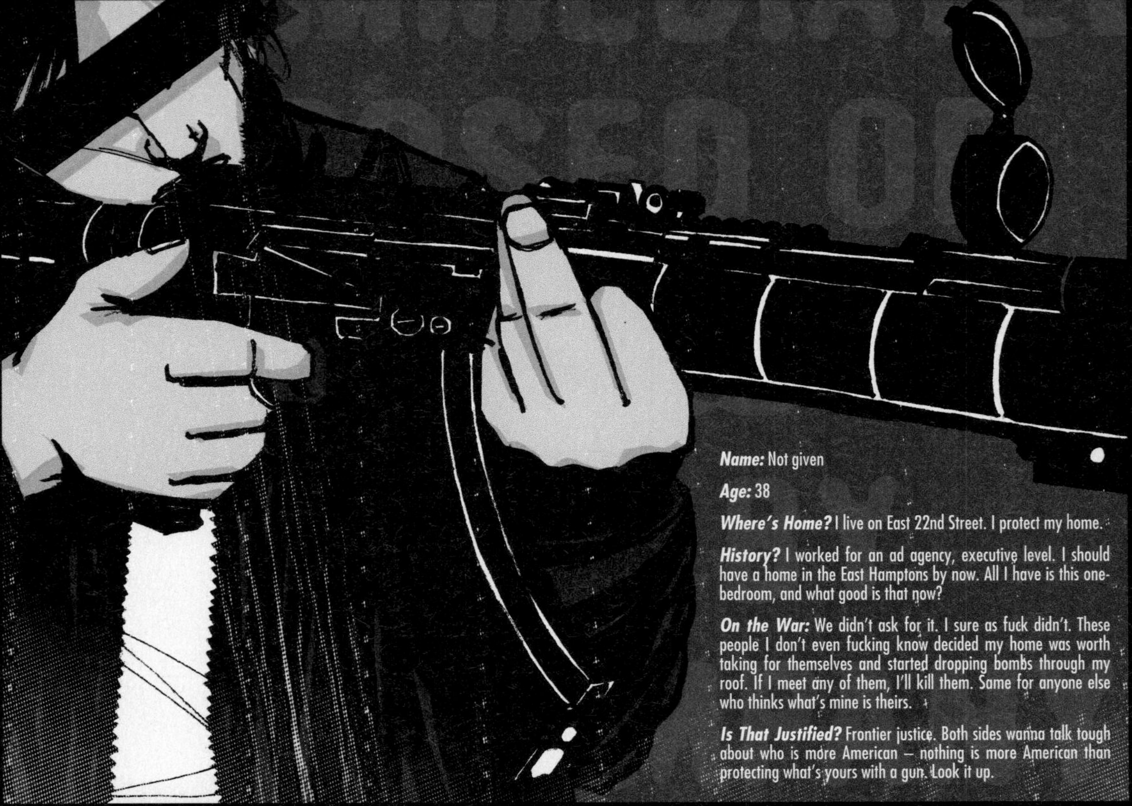

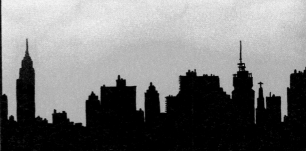

Name: Not given

Age: 38

Where's Home? I live on East 22nd Street. I protect my home.

History? I worked for an ad agency, executive level. I should have a home in the East Hamptons by now. All I have is this one-bedroom, and what good is that now?

On the War: We didn't ask for it. I sure as fuck didn't. These people I don't even fucking know decided my home was worth taking for themselves and started dropping bombs through my roof. If I meet any of them, I'll kill them. Same for anyone else who thinks what's mine is theirs.

Is That Justified? Frontier justice. Both sides wanna talk tough about who is more American – nothing is more American than protecting what's yours with a gun. Look it up.

Name: Jenny

Age: 20

Where's Home? East 9th St.

What Do You Do? I sell vintage clothes from a storefront near me.

Vintage Clothes? Clothes don't have to be that old now to be vintage. My boyfriend finds entire wardrobes in apartments in the Upper East Side, just sitting there in these huge walk-ins. I have an entire rack of Gucci.

On the War: I'm from Parsippany, here as a student. I don't know where my family is, but my boyfriend and I take care of each other.

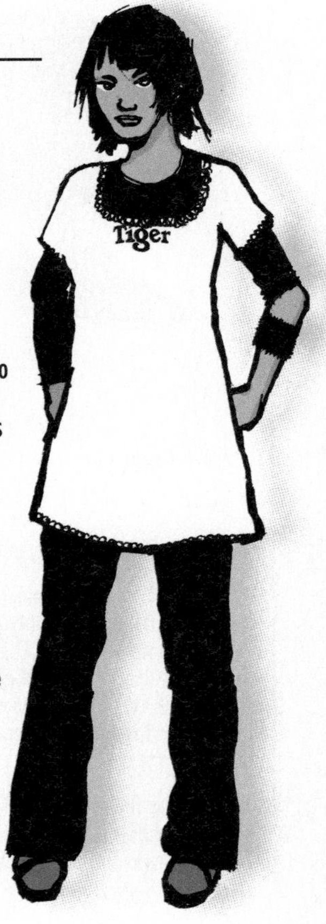
Tiger

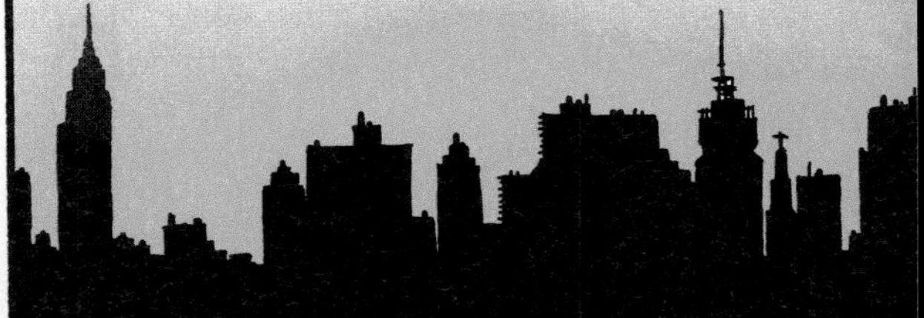

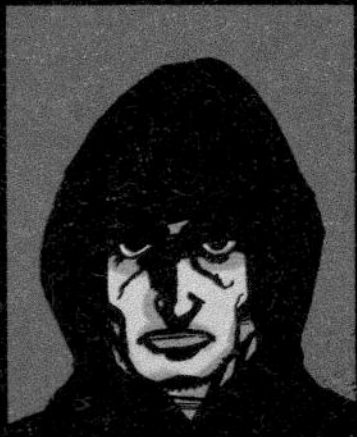

Name: César

Age: 29

"I grew up in Bay Ridge. My fucking bad luck to be in the city when the bombing started. Haven't been able to get home since."

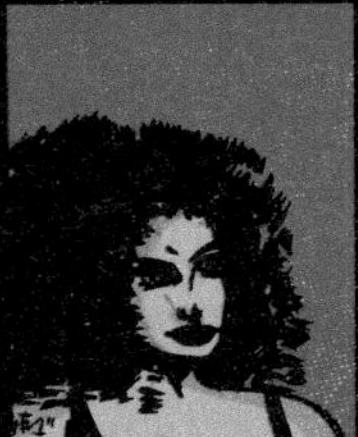

Name: Angie

Age: 25

"I'm not political, but this war is all about politics. I don't know what to say, except that if everyone was just cool with each other..."

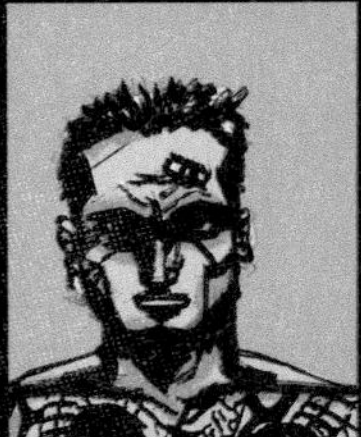

Name: Jin

Age: 24

"Life is better, definitely. Everything is easier to do and to get. I love the war."

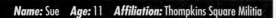

Name: Sue ***Age:*** 11 ***Affiliation:*** Thompkins Square Militia

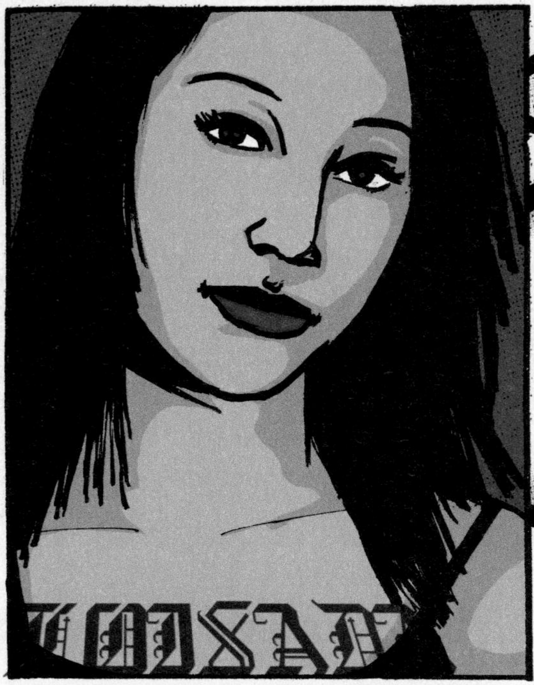

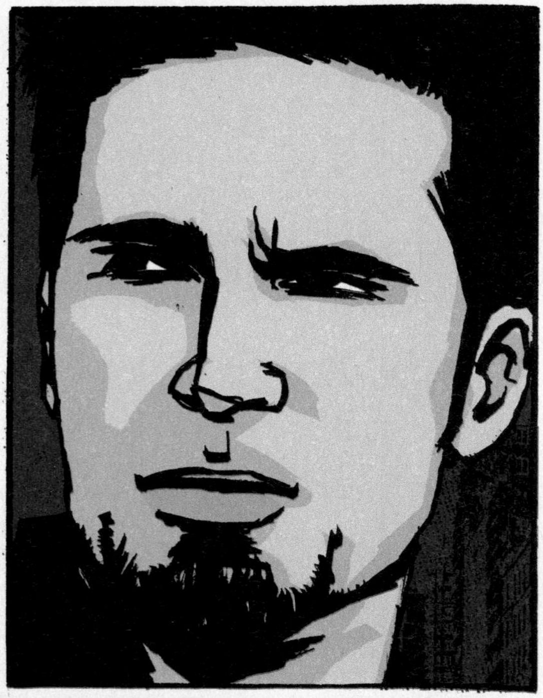

Name: Mike ***Age:*** 36 ***Affiliation:*** The Nation of Fearghus

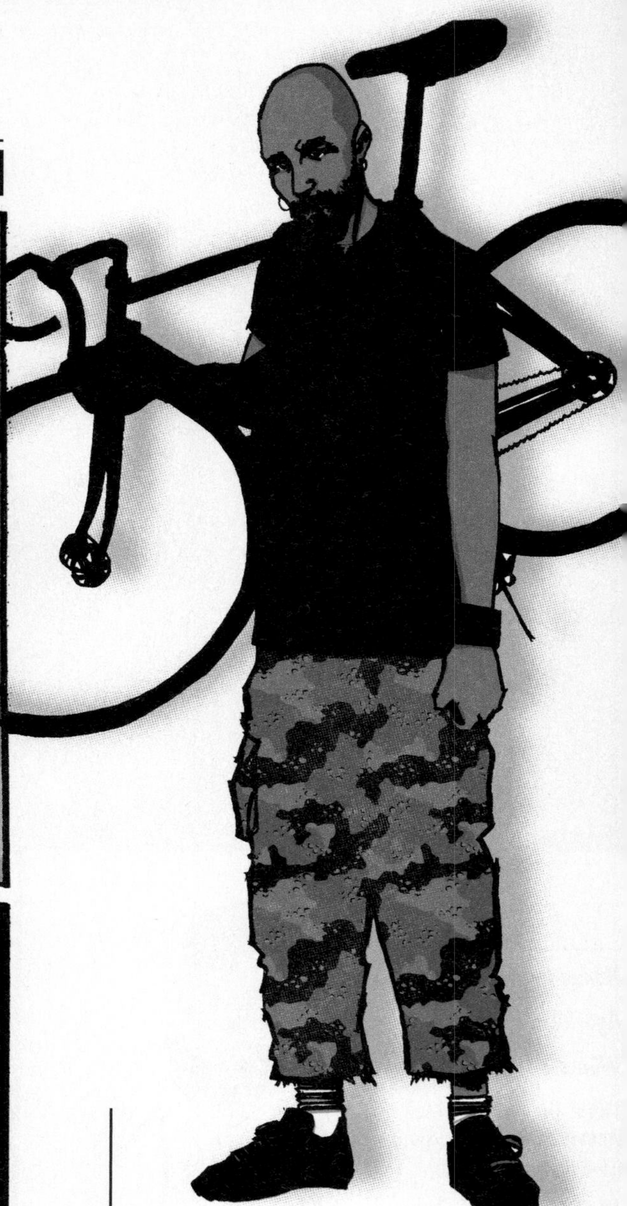

Name: Magnus

Age: 42

Where's Home? Varick, just below Houston

What Do You Do? Freelance bike messenger. I've been a messenger for twenty years. I predate this war. I've always ridden a bike. They can crater the streets, they can embargo the oil, they can ban traffic, but nothing will ever beat the bike for efficiency and practicality. I can go anywhere in this city. No one shoots the messenger!

Affiliation: None. Myself. I'll deliver for anyone who pays. I've seen every corner of this city, and as far as I can tell, everyone's fucking bonkers. So who cares? I work for everyone.

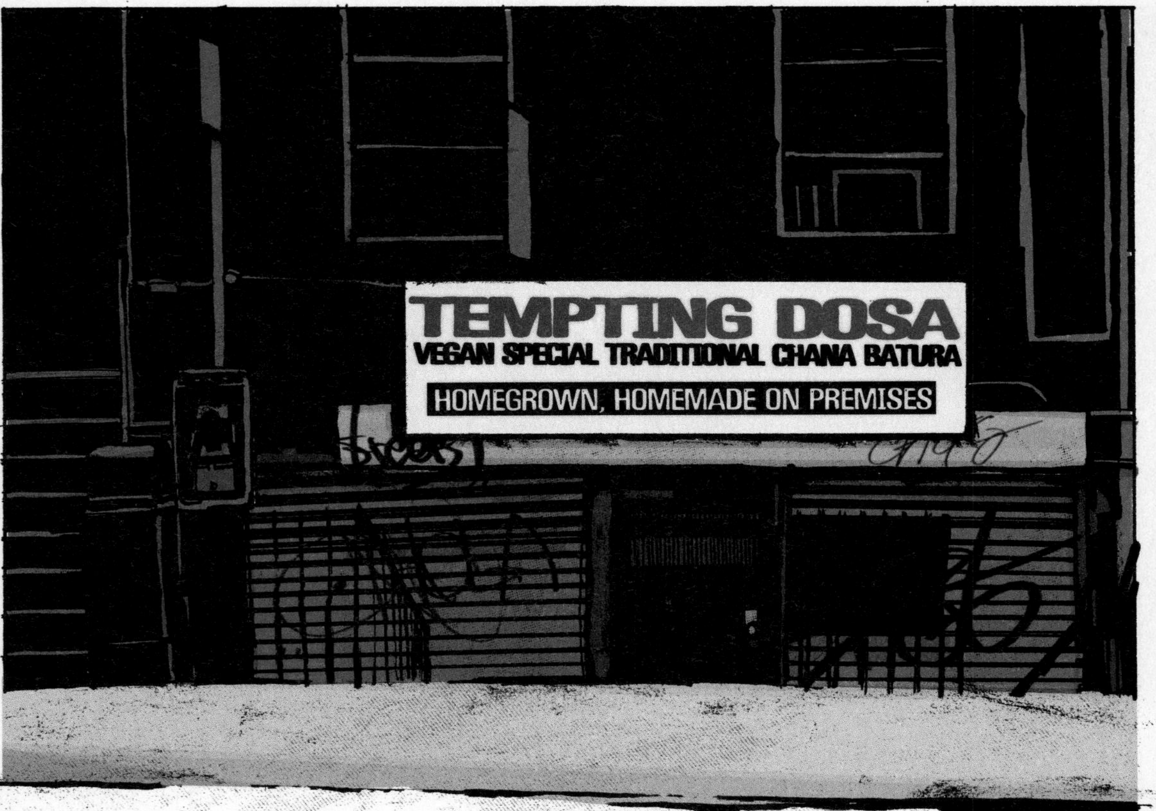
TEMPTING DOSA
VEGAN SPECIAL TRADITIONAL CHANA BATURA
HOMEGROWN, HOMEMADE ON PREMISES

DiNiNG OUT

I ate here once with Zee – her culinary instincts have never let me down – and what the hell do I know about vegan food or dosas? Nothing, and I was ready to revolt when this thing came out as big as a football. Huge goddamn dosas! is what I was told. Amen.

Like a lot of places around here, they grow their own food out back, in the basements (sprouts grow well in the dark, who knew?) and on the roofs. And also like many places, you don't need any money. They'll accept any sort of beneficial trade. I used to pay in cash when Liberty was funding me, but now I pay with all sorts of crap: working lightbulbs, extension cords I find, broken furniture they can mend, other food, beer stolen from Wilson, bamboo... or a press review or even some manual labor in the gardens. Money's not super-valuable to the average person here. It's about the day-to-day, living off the grid, getting by and being happy. The people who try and hoard money and stash goods are the ones living only for the day when the war ends, but who knows when that'll happen? In the meantime they're the miserable ones.

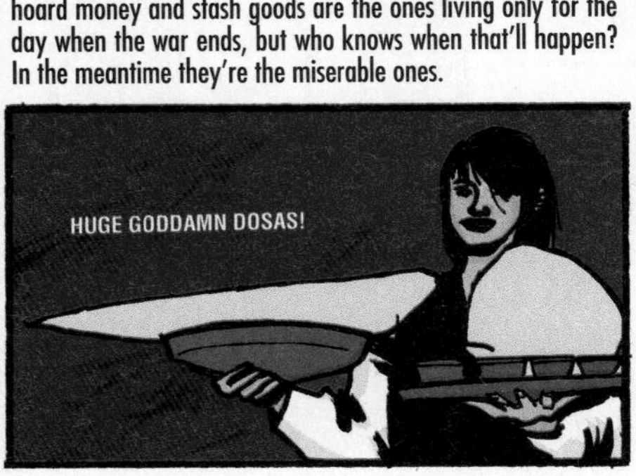
HUGE GODDAMN DOSAS!

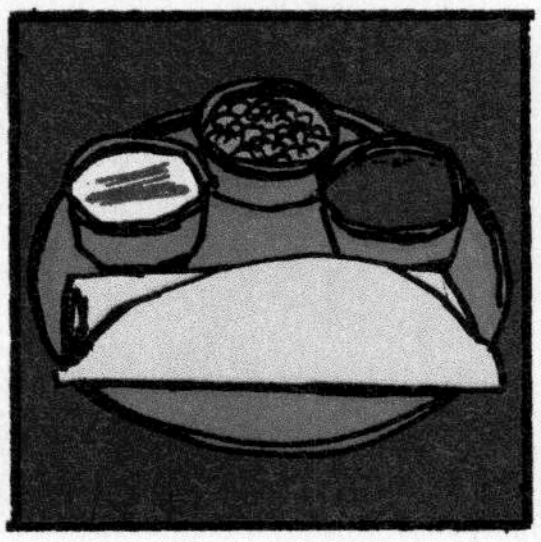

Tempting Dosa... I eat here a few days a week. They make a real effort, and it shows. It's on Grand Street, technically part of Wilson's territory, but they make an exception and let anyone come eat. They get respect for the food and their cool attitude, and it pays off. It's a safe block.

I usually order dosa and cold tea, but I'd recommend the Medu Wada, the rice and lentil pancakes, and in the winter either of the soups.

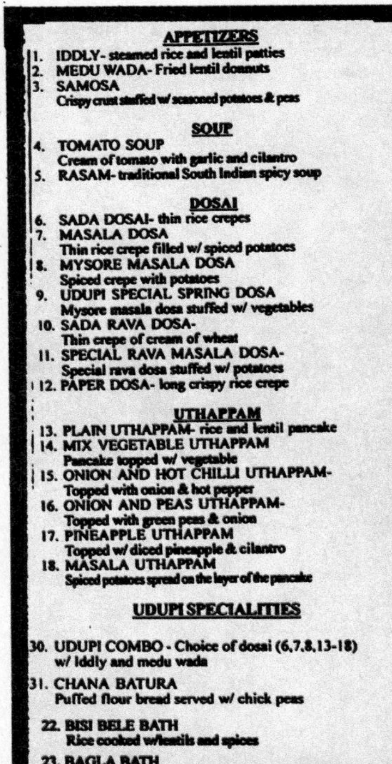

APPETIZERS

1. IDDLY- steamed rice and lentil patties
2. MEDU WADA- Fried lentil donnuts
3. SAMOSA
Crispy crust stuffed w/ seasoned potatoes & peas

SOUP

4. TOMATO SOUP
Cream of tomato with garlic and cilantro
5. RASAM- traditional South Indian spicy soup

DOSAI

6. SADA DOSAI- thin rice crepes
7. MASALA DOSA
Thin rice crepe filled w/ spiced potatoes
8. MYSORE MASALA DOSA
Spiced crepe with potatoes
9. UDUPI SPECIAL SPRING DOSA
Mysore masala dosa stuffed w/ vegetables
10. SADA RAVA DOSA-
Thin crepe of cream of wheat
11. SPECIAL RAVA MASALA DOSA-
Special rava dosa stuffed w/ potatoes
12. PAPER DOSA- long crispy rice crepe

UTHAPPAM

13. PLAIN UTHAPPAM- rice and lentil pancake
14. MIX VEGETABLE UTHAPPAM
Pancake topped w/ vegetable
15. ONION AND HOT CHILLI UTHAPPAM-
Topped with onion & hot pepper
16. ONION AND PEAS UTHAPPAM-
Topped with green peas & onion
17. PINEAPPLE UTHAPPAM
Topped w/ diced pineapple & cilantro
18. MASALA UTHAPPAM
Spiced potatoes spread on the layer of the pancake

UDUPI SPECIALITIES

30. UDUPI COMBO - Choice of dosai (6,7,8,13-18)
w/ Iddly and medu wada
31. CHANA BATURA
Puffed flour bread served w/ chick peas
22. BISI BELE BATH
Rice cooked w/lentils and spices
23. BAGLA BATH

MUSIC

One of the biggest surprises I got when I came here was that the arts scene is fucking booming. I guess it's always booming here, but I dunno... I didn't think people would be in the mood because of the war. That sounds stupid, but that's how I thought back then.

VENUES

These are the places you can hear music most nights. It's informal – you show up and see who's playing each night. No such thing as a schedule.

DELANCY'S KITCHEN: Delancey is an iffy street in terms of security, and that fucking subway entrance is right in front. Never queue up in front of this place if you can help it. If snipers don't take shots at you from the bridge, the subway lunatics will. But this is one of the best places to see bands, so if you can get in safely, do it.

N.S.F.W.'s: Still around. There is a sense of pride about this place, and pride always leads to violence. The Nation of Fearghus used to control it, but they got ousted by some unknown set, so avoid N.S.F.W.'s until that settles down.

ANNIE'S BODEGA: I love Annie's. Great place.

STEREO LOUNGE: Same security risk as Delancy's. Worth it most nights.

TRAILERPARK: Avoid. Too close to the river.

INTERCONTINENTAL: Right in the middle of one of the busiest areas of the city, especially at night. Makes me a little nervous because of the proximity to Little Tokyo and the Polish sector, and this place has a weird vibe, this smelly black box of a club with horrible bands.

Simon Strong's not a real rock star, but he plays one in the DMZ. Weekly fixture at Trailerpark. Not recommended.

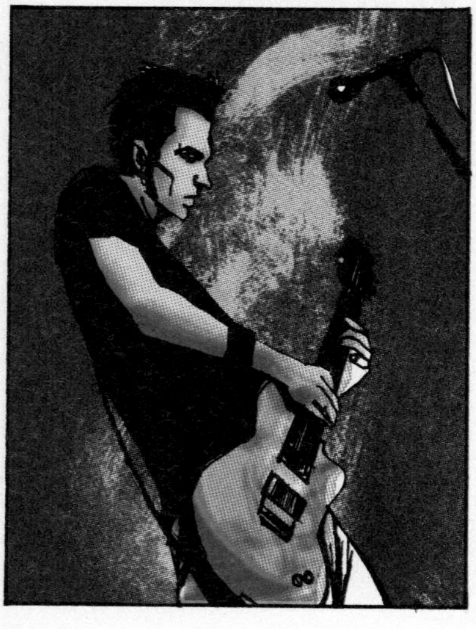

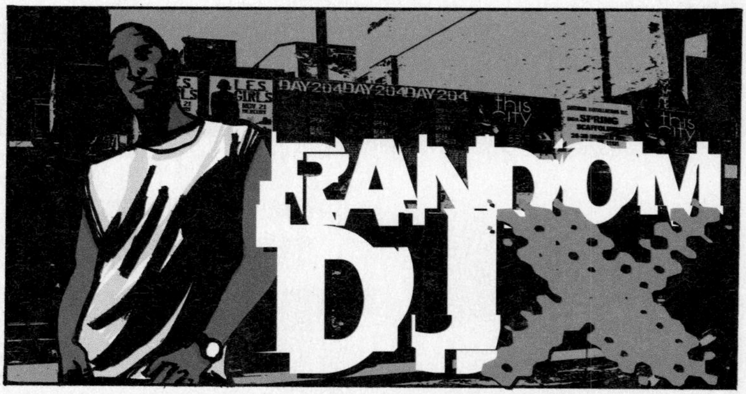
DAY204DAY204DAY204
RANDOM
DJ

RANDOM DJ X: Frequent fixture at Gulag. Kind of a Spooky/Shadow kind of sound by way of Hank Shocklee. Records a lot of street noise. Quiet, ambient stuff, lays it over this blistering shit that sounds like War. People like it. Random makes war sound cool.

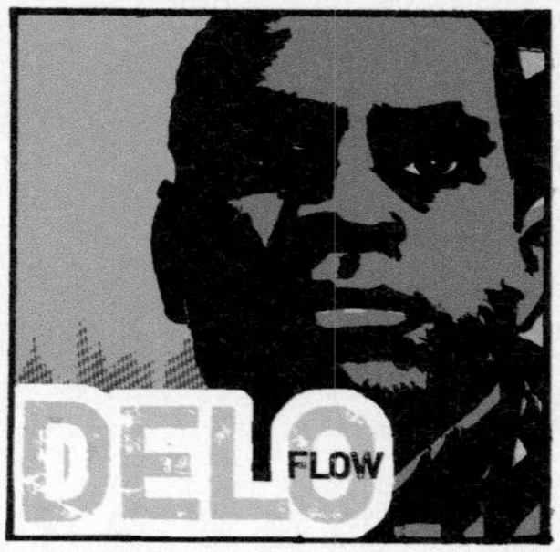
DELO
FLOW

DELO: One of several people who release CD's on a regular basis, found pretty easily on the street. Sounds like it was made with the built-in mic on his laptop and a midi keyboard, but the lyrics are genuine and his is one of the very few insights anyone here gets on what living above the park is like. Shit, most of us don't even go above 14th St. if we can help it. Again, compelling stuff that people really like.

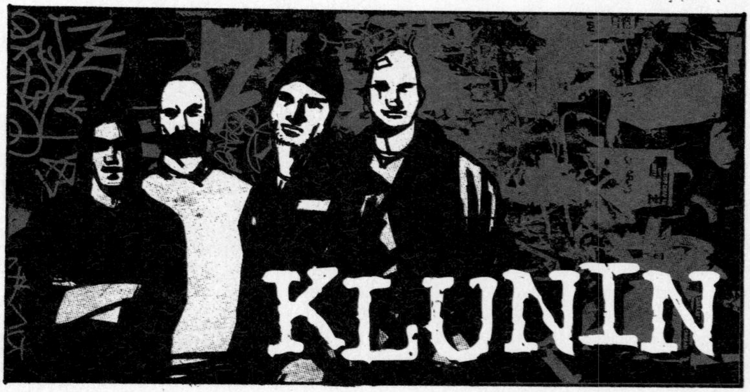
KLUNIN

KLUNIN: I firmly believe these are ex-fratboy NYU students who stayed here because they thought the war would be cool. Terrifying death metal with operatic, Scandinavian overtones. They've been performing with HELENA (pictured right), who really amps the Valkyrie vibe up, up, up. Catch them at Intercontinental, natch.

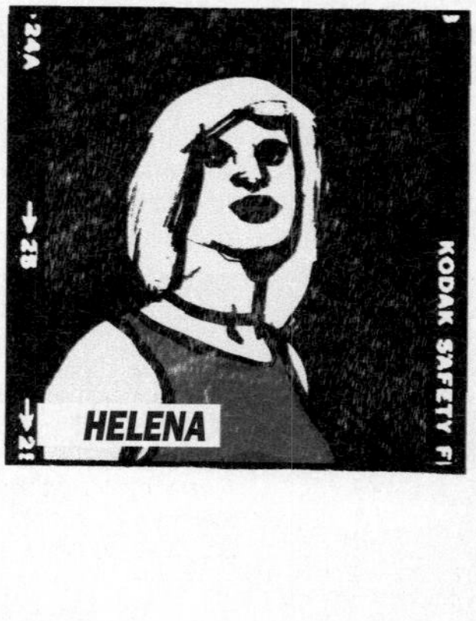
KODAK SAFETY F
HELENA

Occasionally real-world bootlegs get smuggled into the city, and based on what I've heard, the music is just as shitty out there as it is in here, but with one exception: There's no money to be made from music in the DMZ, so it feels more genuine on average.

ARTS

BOOKS/ZiNES

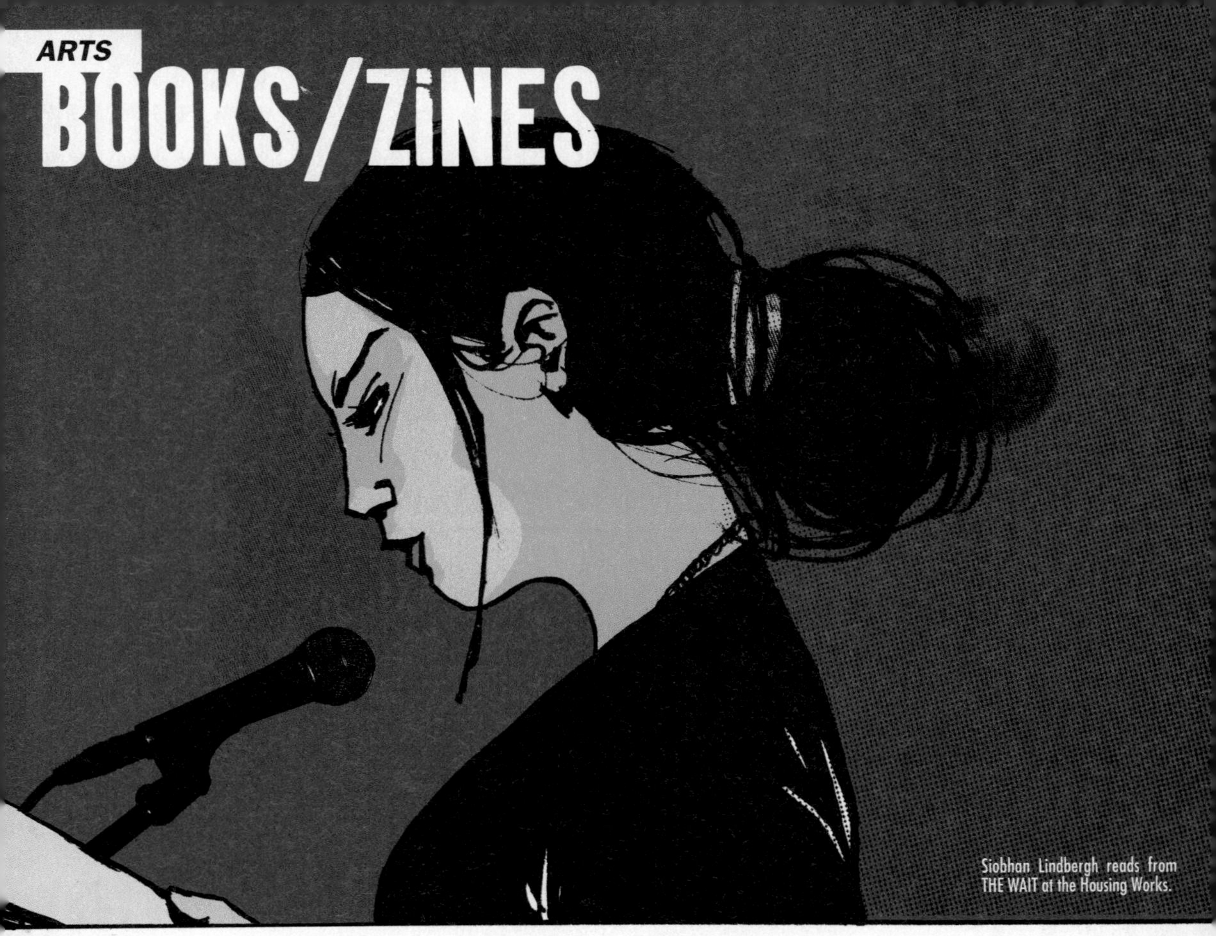

Siobhan Lindbergh reads from THE WAIT at the Housing Works.

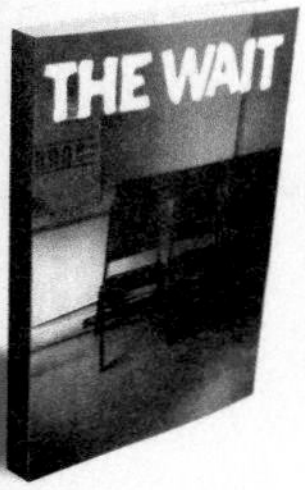
THE WAIT

THE WAIT by Siobhan Lindbergh

Ms. Lindbergh calls this book nonfiction, but I have my doubts. While I would never claim that life in the DMZ is easy for anyone, it's hard to imagine anyone having such a miserable time as she claims to have had. From the fantastically depressing to the harrowing and violent, it's truly amazing to think that the five-foot, soft-spoken writer who read with such confidence last week at the Housing Works is the owner of these experiences. But, putting that aside for the moment, the writing is good and could give outsiders an idea of what could potentially happen to people here. Put a copy of THE WAIT into the hands of the U.N. General Assembly and I bet humanitarian aid would triple.

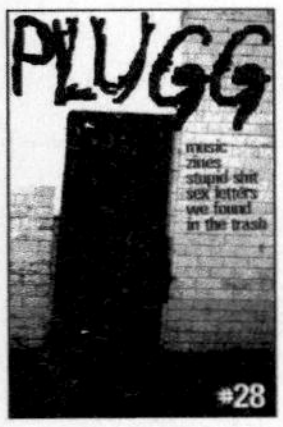
PLUGG
#28

PLUGG #28

If you're worried that you can't read PLUGG #28 until you've read the preceding 27 volumes, don't. PLUGG is a weird assortment of found objects and clippings from newspapers, often with snarky commentary. Good for quite a few laughs. How many more of these will be published? Rumor is the creators of PLUGG occupy an old Kinko's and have quite a stockpile of toner and paper.

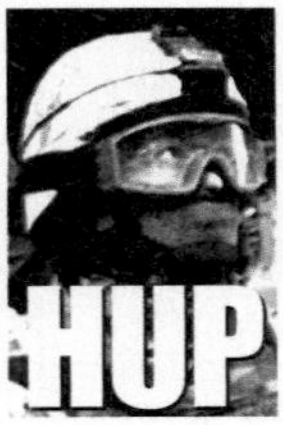
HUP

HUP

The creator of HUP, whoever he/she is, must be one of the most-wanted men in the city. A batch of G.I. mail, actual paper letters, was intercepted and reprinted, unedited, to make HUP. Hilarious, embarrassing, depressing, and offensive all at once. A spooky look into the minds of the people pointing weapons at us. Must read.

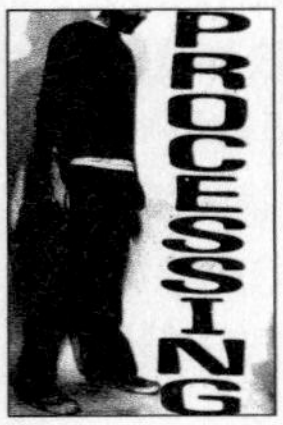
PROCESSING

PROCESSING

Menagerie of short fiction and poetry from a large group of people processing the war, never more than a single page each. Sounds horrible, but is strangely compelling. Open the book up at random and start reading.

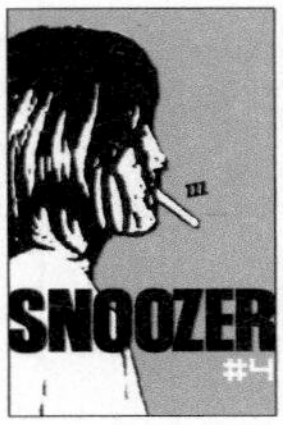
SNOOZER
#4

SNOOZER #4

Snoozer is determined to sleep through the war or die trying. She documents her efforts, mostly through sheer force of will, to sleep as much as humanly possible, and it's fascinating to read. The inner workings of a very clearly mentally ill woman, but she's charming and funny and bitter and extremely likable. I want to meet Snoozer.

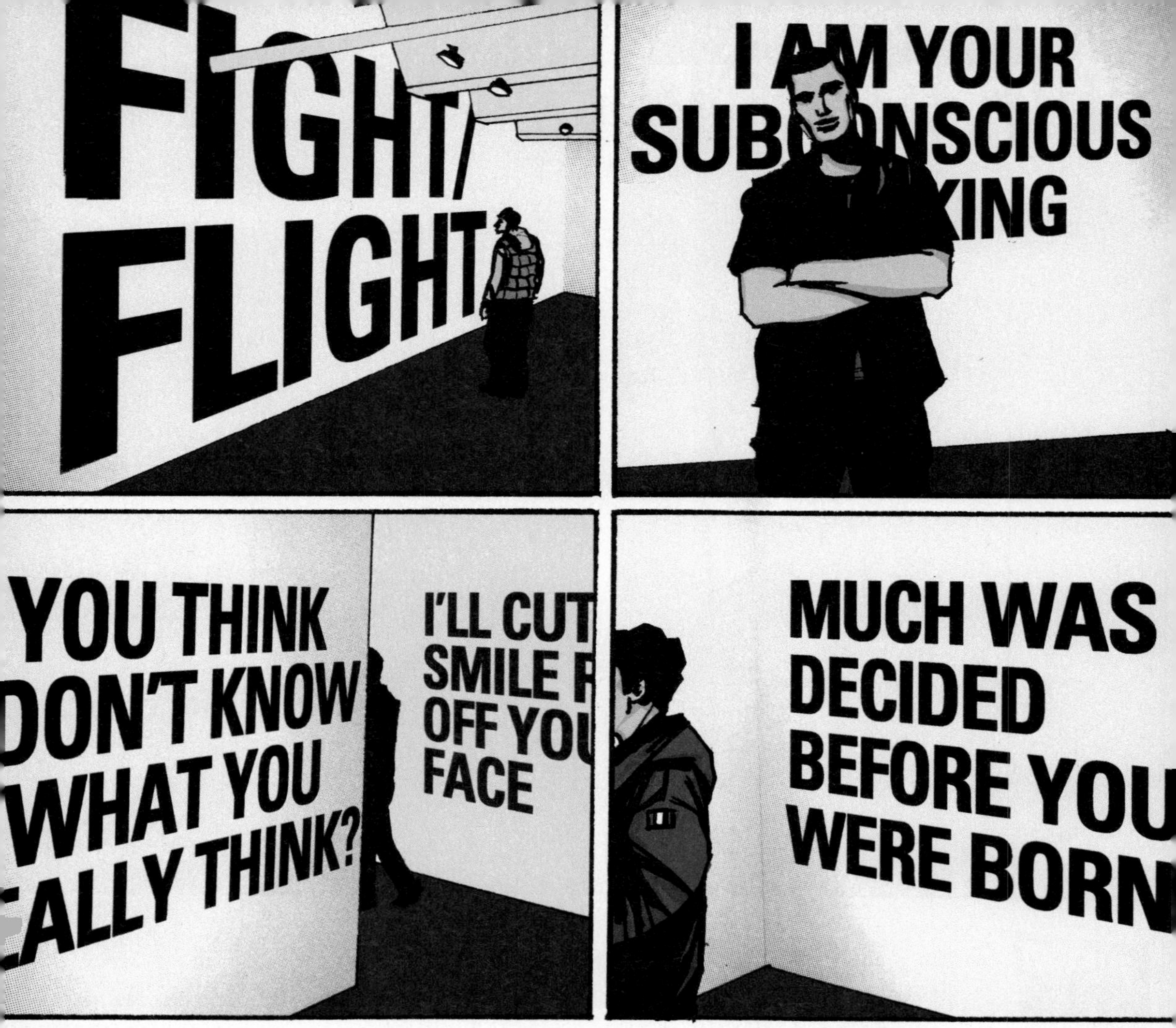

FIGHT/
FLIGHT
I AM YOUR
SUBCONSCIOUS
KING
YOU THINK
DON'T KNOW
WHAT YOU
ALLY THINK?
I'LL CUT
SMILE
OFF YOU
FACE
MUCH WAS
DECIDED
BEFORE YOU
WERE BORN

ARTS

GALLERiES

Walking firmly in the footsteps of Barbara Kruger, Jenny Holzer, and even de la Vega, the 44-yo artist who goes by the name Decade Later screens slogans on walls and gets away with it in every sense.

The first reaction you get after having the words I AM YOUR SUBCONSCIOUS TALKING is to say "fuck you!" because it's so assumptive and self-righteous. But it makes you want to walk around and see what else he claims you're secretly thinking, if only to say "fuck you!" a few more times. After a few minutes, though, you think he may be right.

I notice people silently mouthing the phrases to themselves as they read them, trying them out, seeing how they feel on their lips. They feel great. In a direct homage to Holzer, Decade tells us I'LL CUT THE SMILE RIGHT OFF YOUR FACE, which is incredibly satisfying to say. BETTER LUCK NEXT TIME (lower right) is a stream-of-consciousness rant of familiar clichés that don't sit well with residents of this city, too used to being manipulated and lied to by slimy politicians. FIGHT OR FLIGHT towers over you, intimidating you as the viewer can't help but mentally recall close calls and dangerous situations.

Decade Later isn't breaking new ground with anything he's doing, but by placing familiar words and phrases and clichés into a new setting, into the DMZ, they take on very specific meanings that we're all already thinking about.

BETTER RED THAN DEAD

I WASN'T BORN YESTERDAY. THERE'S A SUCKER BORN EVERY MINUTE, BUT THAT'S NOT ME. I DIDN'T JUST FALL OFF THE TURNIP TRUCK. YOU WON'T TRICK ME. FOOL ME NEVER. I SAW THAT COMING A MILE AWAY. DO I LOOK STUPID TO YOU? YOU'RE SO TRANSPARENT YOU MAKE WATER LOOK BAD. YOU NEED TO WAKE UP PRETTY EARLY. NICE TRY. GOOD ONE. YOU THINK YOU'RE PRETTY SLICK. CLOSE BUT NO CIGAR. BETTER LUCK NEXT TIME.

History: This is one of the craziest places in the city. A lot of people won't even talk about it, or they get really mad about it. Even the ones who don't care still don't have a lot to say. It feels like there's so much history, so many promises broken, so many people sick from the air and the dust, so much bullshit connected to it that it's just too much to process. So they pretend it's not here.

Except for the politicians. They talk about it. But they don't have to live with it.

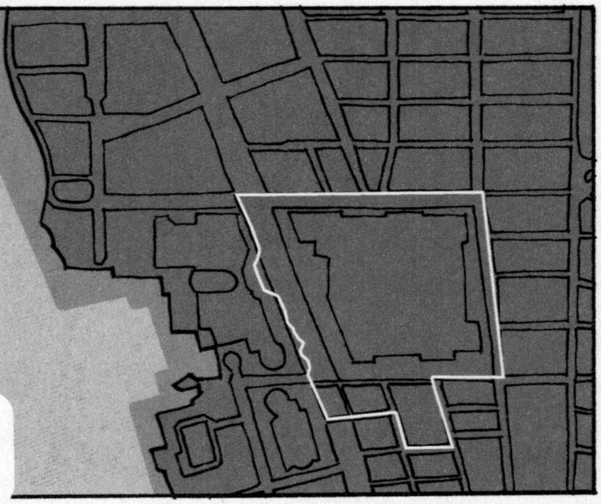

GROUND ZERO

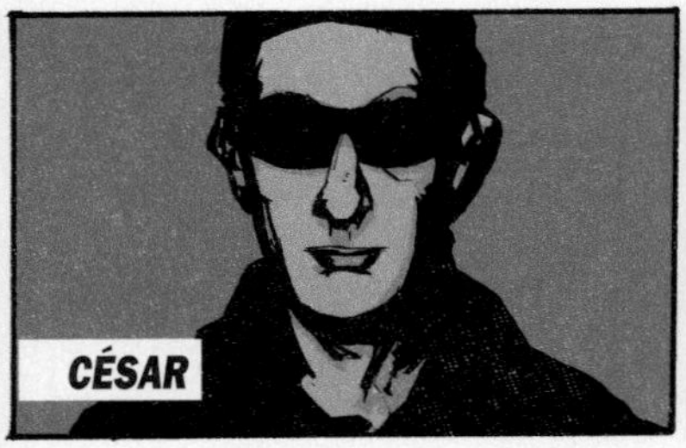
CÉSAR

Name: César

Age: 31

"People call it sacred. It's just four walls around a vacant lot. The rest of the world got over it – why can't we? I'm sick of having to watch what I say."

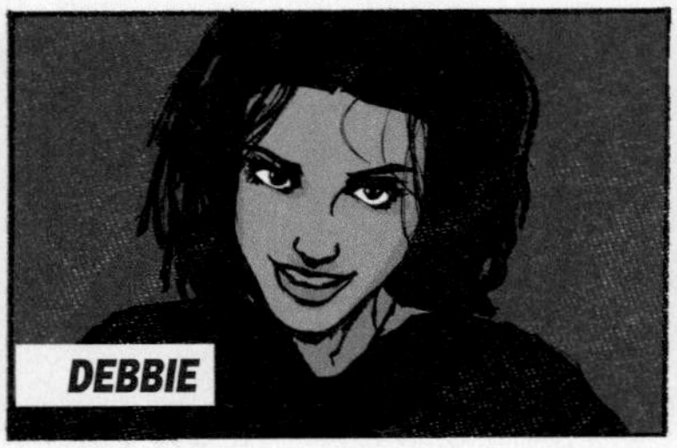
DEBBIE

Name: Debbie

Age: 23

"I heard that grass and trees are growing in there. I think that's nice. It should just be left alone. All the other open areas in the city are filthy and dangerous. We need clean spaces for later."

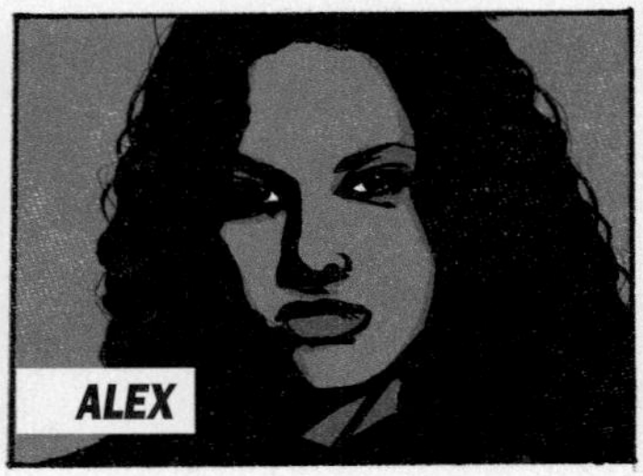
ALEX

Name: Alex

Age: 30

"I lost a cousin on 9/11, and I'm not afraid to talk about it. Where's the memorial? Where's the Freedom Tower? Why can't I go down there? I do and people shoot at me. I was born in this city."

The area around the site is actually controlled by U.S. troops. Feels political to me, like they need to have it in hand so the President can try and whip us up about the horrible tragedy of it all and justify their policies...

But what if it was just a field of grass and wildflowers behind those walls? I guess that wouldn't make people think about getting revenge.

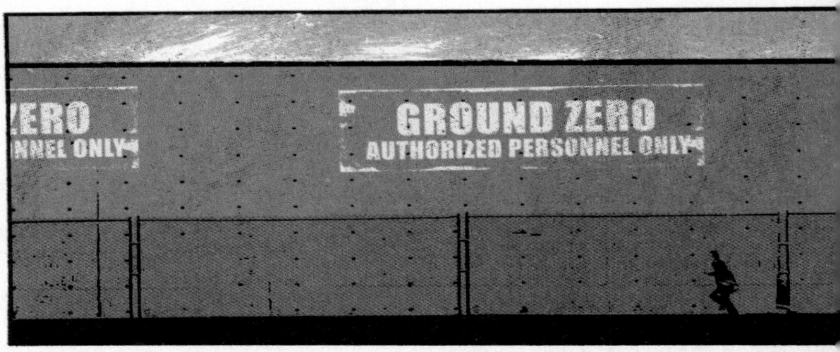
ZERO
NNEL ONLY
GROUND ZERO
AUTHORIZED PERSONNEL ONLY

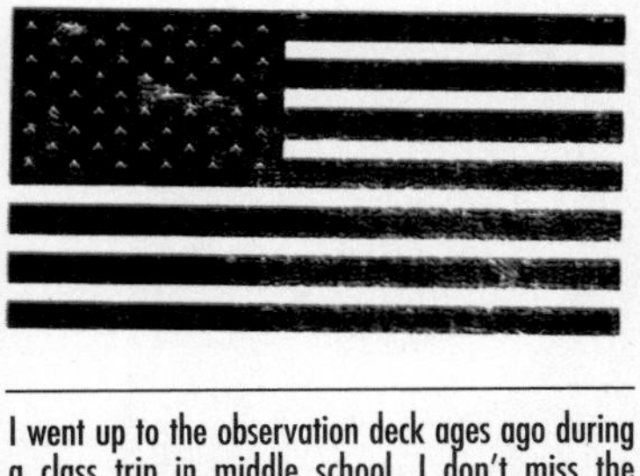

I went up to the observation deck ages ago during a class trip in middle school. I don't miss the towers, though. It's not "sacred ground." For people who actually live here, there's not a block in this city that doesn't have someone's blood staining it, so how can one thing be sacred and not another?

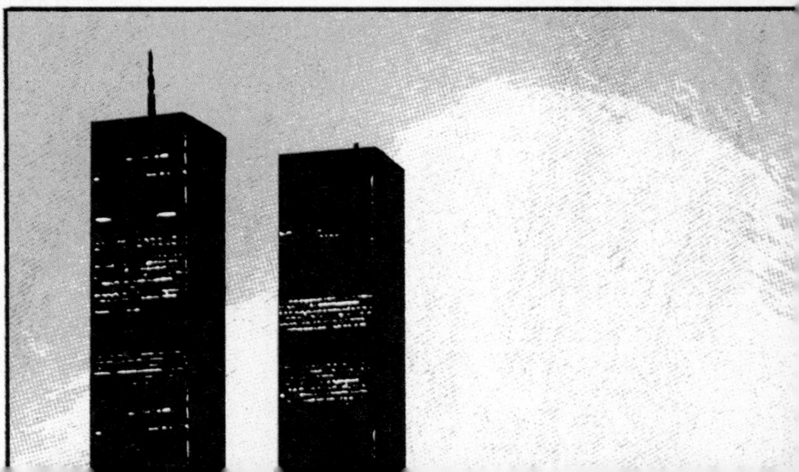

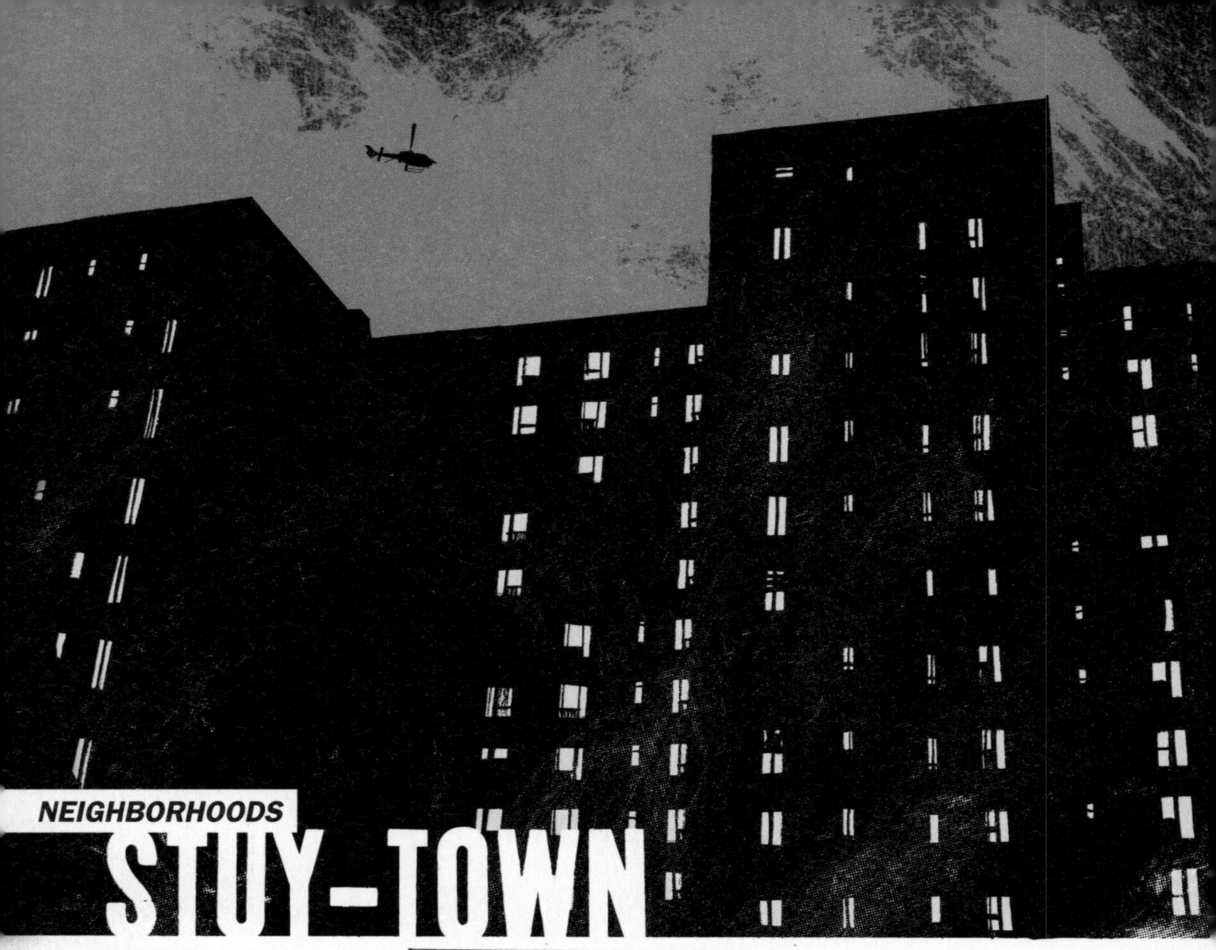

NEIGHBORHOODS

STUY-TOWN

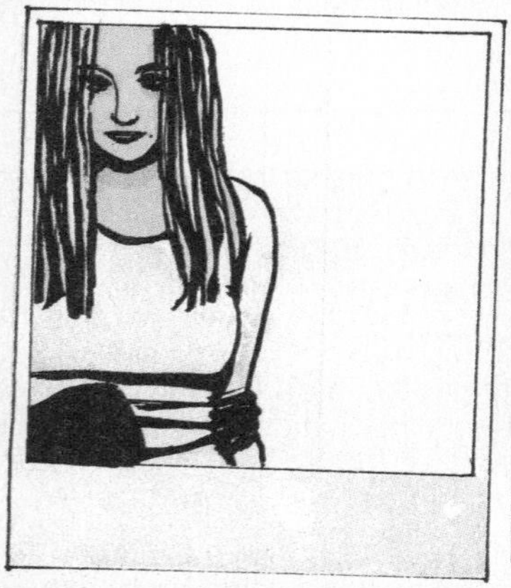

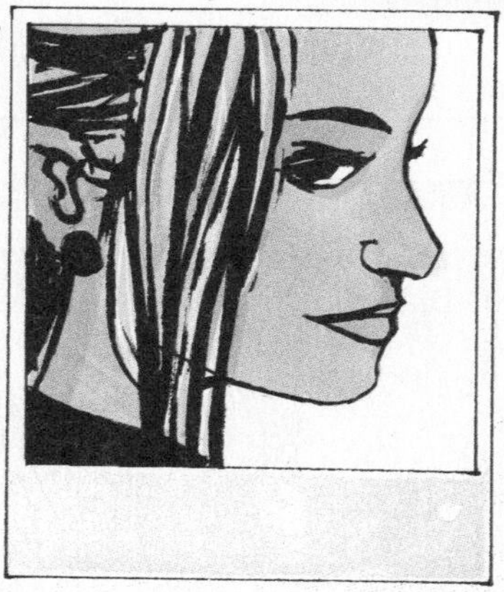

My apartment was given to me by one of The Ghosts, for me to watch over until the war ended and his family came back to claim it. I've taken good care of it, but it's time to move on. In light of recent events, I need to be not so easily found.

Stuy-town is one of the sanest places I've seen here. It's naturally defendable, and lucky for it the people who claim and protect it are decent. We all take care of it, help out with repairs, share food and resources and generally keep an eye out. The towers by Ave C are too exposed to the river for anyone to live in, so they plunder it for parts.

I have an older cousin who lived here years ago while she went to Hunter.

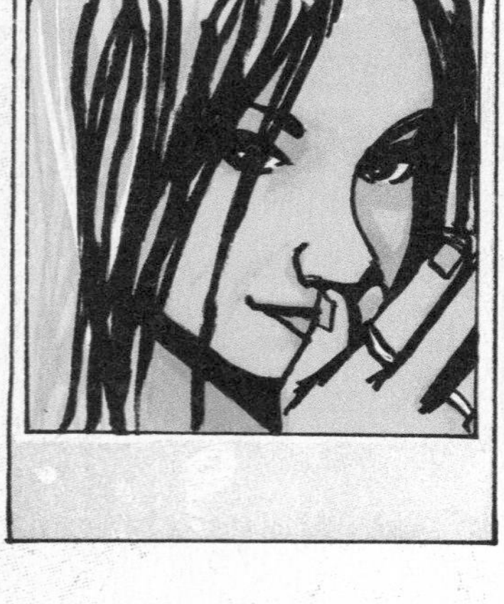

KELLY CONNOLLY

I met Kelly on a filthy, hot subway platform. She'd walked down from Midtown during active hostilities to find me. Suffice it to say neither of us was looking their best, but neither of us seemed to care.

Canadian citizen, reporter for IWN. I used to watch her on cable before I came to the city. Reminds me of home.

She visits me when she can, which isn't often enough.

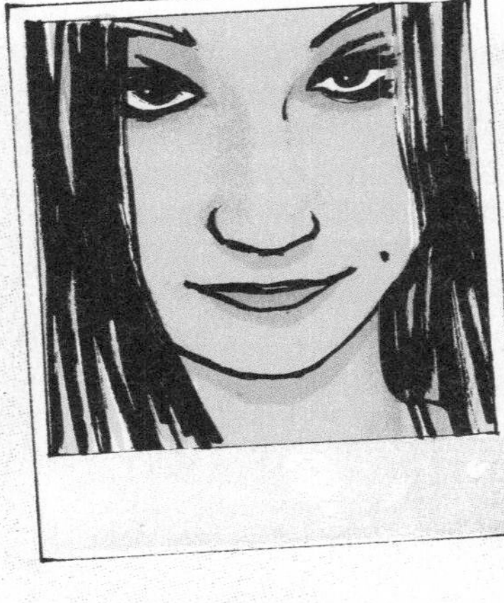

PEOPLE

ZEE

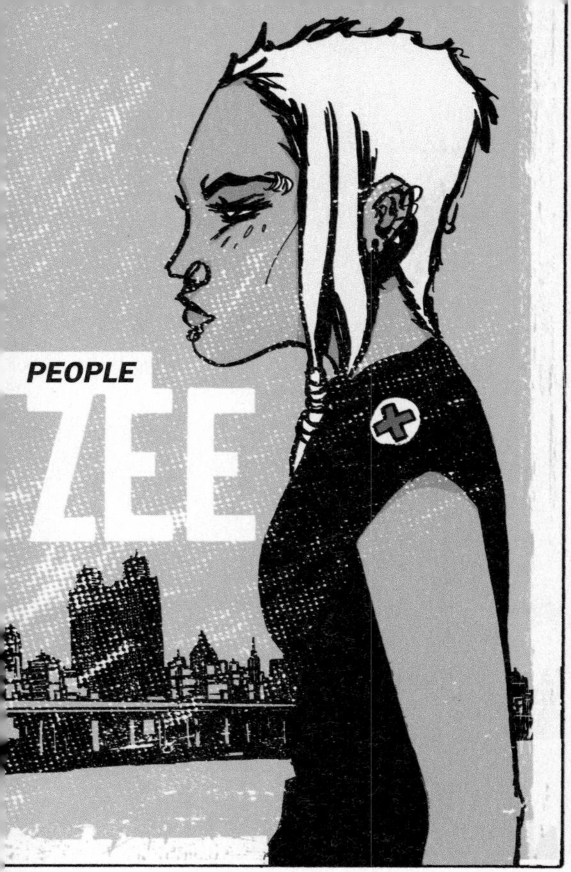

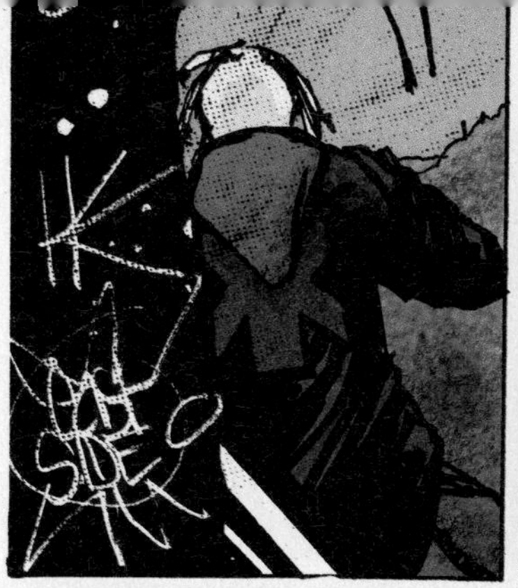

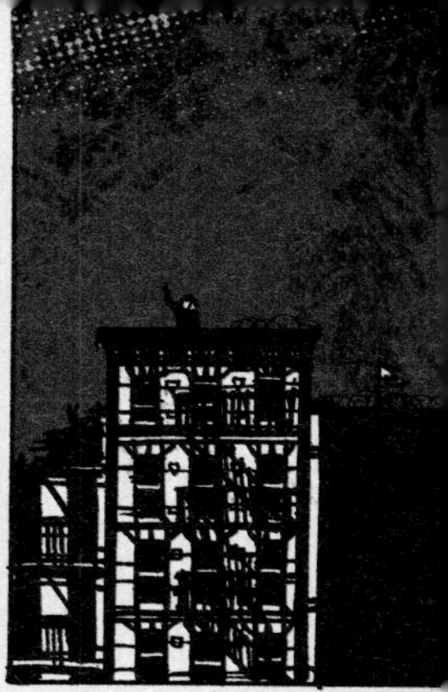

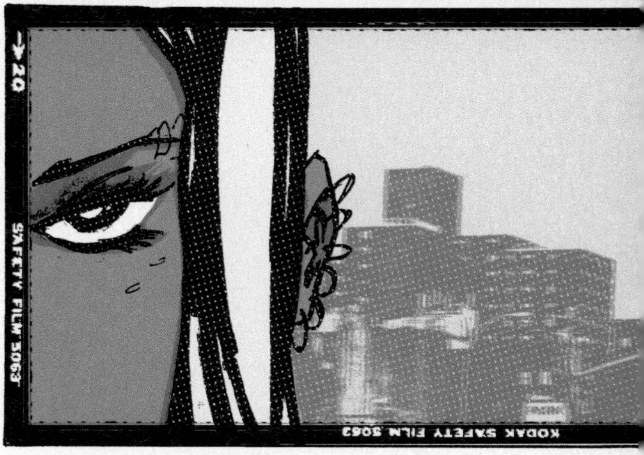
→20
SAFETY FILM 5063
KODAK SAFETY FILM 5063

My first night in the city, Zee put a gun in my face. Later she gave me breakfast and a guided tour of her neighborhood. She comes off all snarling and bitter, but I understand where some of that comes from now. She's a protector... she protects her friends, her block, her patients, and her right to be here.

Kelly says Zee likes me. I think Zee tolerates me, at best. She may trust me soon, but it will be a while yet before she *likes* me.

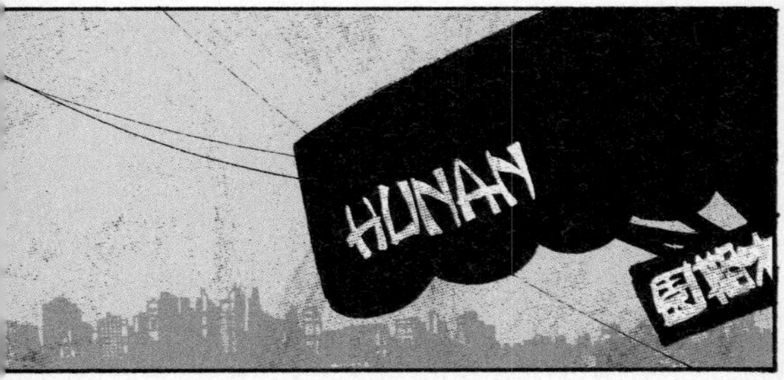
HUNAN

Zee's a hoarder and a thief. She runs a clinic, pretty much all by herself, and every day does rounds around the city. Whenever Red Cross or other relief supplies make it to the city, she's there and does whatever she can to personally receive medical supplies. What she isn't given, she steals. Better to get it directly, she tells me, because by the time it makes its way through the corrupt distribution network, everyone's siphoned off some of it for themselves and she's lucky to end up with a bottle of aspirin and a roll of gauze.

Having said all that, Zee's the most honest person I've met in the city. That gets in the way of her having a lot of friends, but her work is what matters most to her. I can respect that.

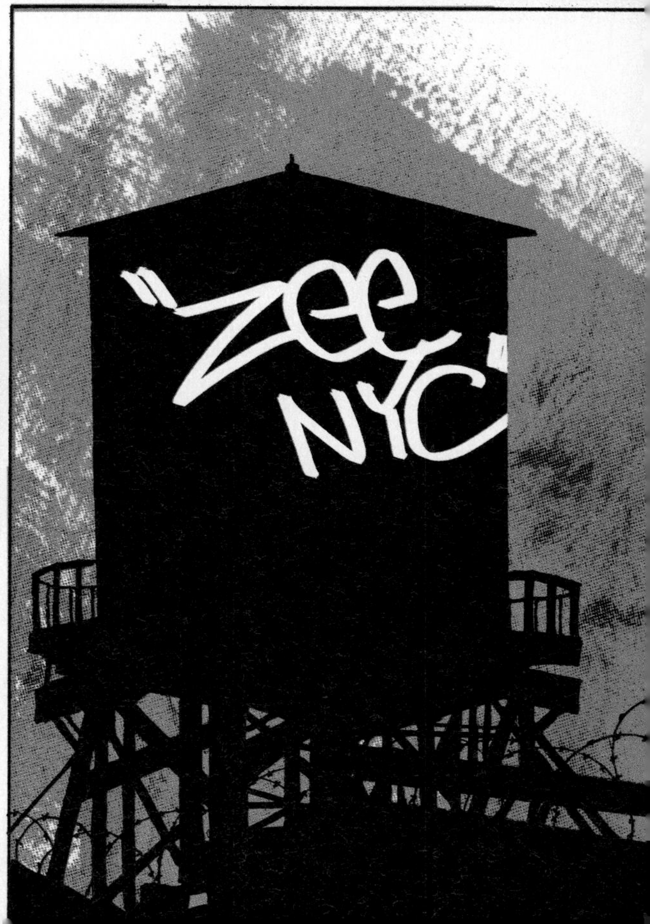
"ZEE NYC"

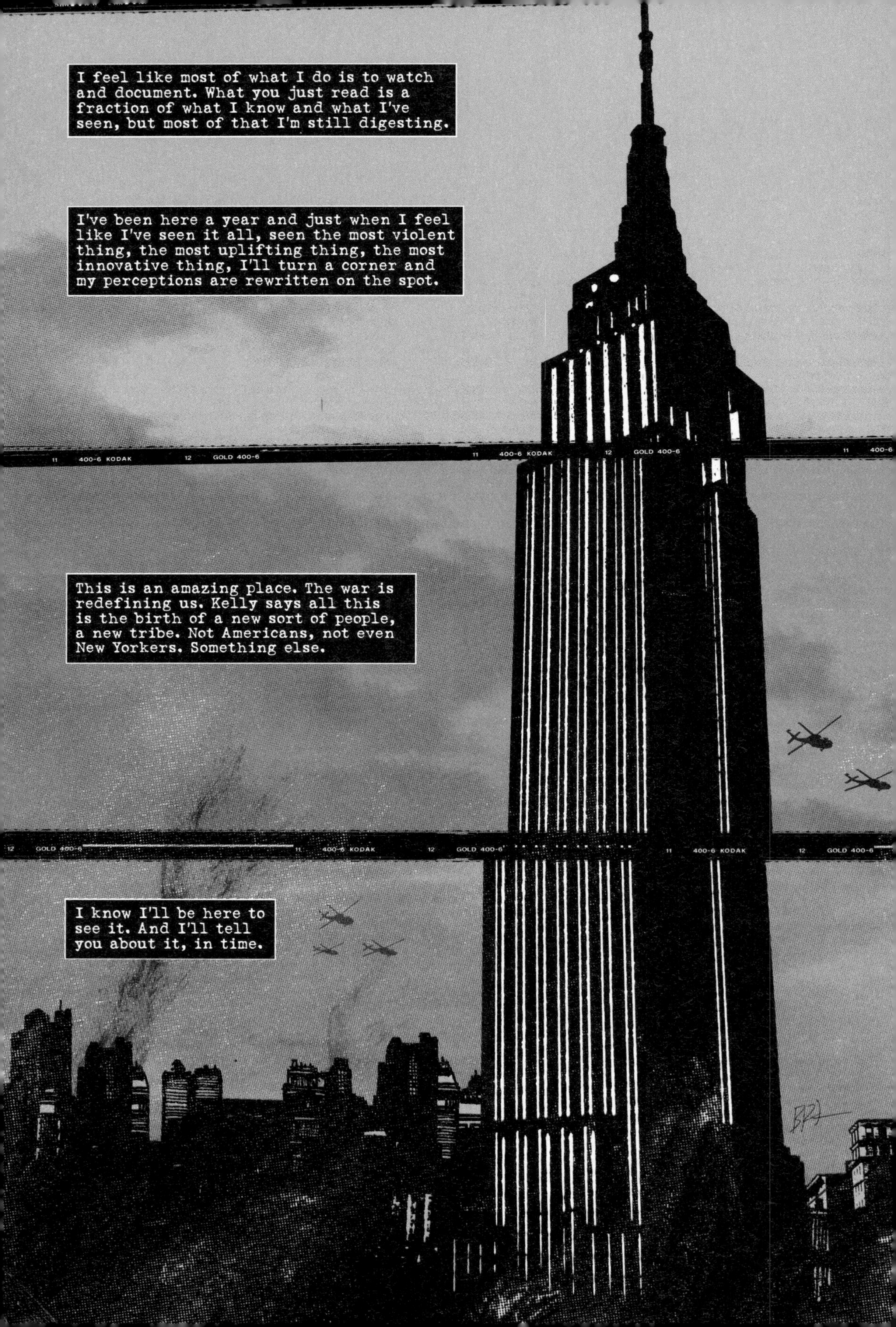

I feel like most of what I do is to watch and document. What you just read is a fraction of what I know and what I've seen, but most of that I'm still digesting.
I've been here a year and just when I feel like I've seen it all, seen the most violent thing, the most uplifting thing, the most innovative thing, I'll turn a corner and my perceptions are rewritten on the spot.
11 400-6 KODAK 12 GOLD 400-6
This is an amazing place. The war is redefining us. Kelly says all this is the birth of a new sort of people, a new tribe. Not Americans, not even New Yorkers. Something else.
12 GOLD 400-6 11 400-6 KODAK
I know I'll be here to see it. And I'll tell you about it, in time.

BOOK ONE

NEW JERSEY & INLAND

MANHATTAN ISLAND THE "DMZ"
POPULATION EST. 400,000

STATEN ISLAND "SNIPER HEAVEN"

BROOKLYN/QUEENS/LONG ISLAND
THE UNITED STATES OF AMERICA

THE DEMARCATION LINE

Justin Giampaoli is an award-winning writer at *Thirteen Minutes*, contributing writer at *Comics Bulletin*, guest contributor at *Fanboy Comics*, and created *Live From The DMZ*, the only site featuring extensive interviews and bonus content dedicated to Brian Wood's contemporary classic.

Brian, for this introductory installment, let's start at the top — what was the genesis for DMZ?

This is probably the most-asked question, in interviews, at conventions and signings, and you might think by now that if I hadn't thought up a genuine answer that I would have at least invented a fake one...but no. I don't know where it came from exactly. Well, a big part of it has to be the point of time in history...this was 2003, post-9/11, post-invasion of Iraq, and I was packing up my life to leave NYC for San Francisco. So I had war, politics, and my home city very much on my mind.

But how it all came together the way it did? Not sure. Once I was in SF, I did a bunch of artwork for WARTIME, which is what DMZ was originally called, as well as a map image that was an early draft of what became DMZ #1, page 1, panel 1. I had it in my mind that WARTIME was going to be a black and white, five-issue miniseries in the same way that Paul Pope's Vertigo projects were, although I wasn't in contact with Vertigo at that point. But I knew this was an important project for me, a return to a CHANNEL ZE-RO-esque point of view, and I kept slowly molding it during my time in SF.

I hated living in San Francisco, I'll add. I loved visiting it, I had a lot of friends there, and I really believed that I would be happy living there. I'm sure there were many reasons why I only lasted 18 months, but a big part of it was just not being ready to leave NYC after all, and I think that homesick feeling fueled both DMZ and LOCAL.

Do you recall how exactly you pitched it?

I do. I have the documents. The basic idea for DMZ came even before DEMO started shipping in late 2003. DEMO was more of a format experiment in its origins than anything else. With DMZ, I wasn't trying to innovate anything...I was trying to write what I always felt was a pretty commercial monthly comic. DEMO and LOCAL, in pitch form, looked like the perfect examples of a totally non-commercial comic book series.

You did a great Vertigo blog post about titling the NORTHLANDERS arc "The Plague Widow." Was there a similar process for this series or was it always going to be called DMZ?

WARTIME became DMZ simply because Vertigo had recently published a BOOKS OF MAGIC miniseries subtitled "Life During Wartime," and no one involved, myself included, wanted the similarity. So I was tasked with coming up with a new title. I just dug back into my e-mail from 2005 and found this, which I sent to my editor Will Dennis. We immediately decided DMZ was the one:

> EMBEDDED - you mentioned this once. I think it's a powerful word, and a word that has come to mean something in everyone's mind, so I think in that way it's a good choice. Downsides: already several books with that name about the Iraq war, and Matty isn't technically embedded (although pretty close to it)

> DMZ - also a word that immediately plants images in your head. I like short titles with impact. DMZ - huge letters across the top. I tried to make it tie in with New York a little bit, like DMZ NYC, DMZ, NY, but nothing seems to work. Haha, how about DMZ, 10012? (yeah, that's a joke)

> NO MAN'S LAND - also the name of an award-winning foreign film a couple years ago about the Serb-Croat war. Conflict there?

> THE NEW YORK WAR
> ON THE GROUND
> ROOKIE
> THE AMERICAN WAR
> UNDER FIRE
> LIVE FIRE
> THREE YEARS OF WAR
> LOST IN MANHATTAN
> WAR ZONE
> WITNESS TO WAR

You're a meticulous career planner. Was DMZ part of a larger strategy in your career portfolio?

Thanks for noting my career planning! I do that, at times to the annoyance of others, like editors, but I defend it because so far, knock on wood, I've made the right choices. Anyway, working for Vertigo was a career choice since day one, literally back in college in 1995 when I decided making comics was for me. But DMZ wasn't what I first pitched. I was holding on to that idea for myself...I was afraid to give it over to the DC Comics "machine," whatever that might have meant to me at the time. Loss of control, maybe. So I pitched him [Will Dennis] THE

TOURIST and SUPERMARKET and a few other things, but nothing was working. Finally, I wised up and e-mailed in DMZ and that was that. It was a good lesson learned, which is to always present your best idea.

I'm curious how much of Brian Wood exists in Matty Roth?

Ugh, not too much, I hope. Matty is pretty fictional overall, but there are aspects to his appearance, his backstory, and his general loser vibe that I did filch from a guy I worked with once. I think there is something to Matty's journey of sort of figuring himself out that I can relate to— moving to the city as a young guy, bouncing around from influence to influence, not really knowing who you are, and screwing up. I did that. But so did everyone else, which is why he's a character that a lot of people loathe. They see their own fuck-ups in him, same with Megan in LOCAL.

It always seemed to me that as Matty was being dropped into the unfamiliar world of the DMZ, there was some parity with you being dropped into your first ongoing series at Vertigo, both fleshing out an evolving identity. Matty and Brian, both 5 letters, Roth and Wood, both 4 letters, am I reaching?

Probably! Roth was literally picked at random in a pinch. I remember needing a last name and scanning the bookshelves lining my office walls, finally resting on a copy of GOODBYE, COLUMBUS by Philip Roth. As far as being dropped into an ongoing series, yeah, there may be something there. That was a pretty intimidating thing, especially since I went in with all the intention in the world of doing a little miniseries and staying out of the way of the big boys. Suddenly I'm being asked to plan my series out to the three- and four-year mark, and just trusting in myself and my editor that I'd be able to pull it off as I went. And no, that doesn't make my editor a stand-in for Zee!

Warren Ellis once referred to DMZ as "political sci-fi." Is that accurate?

I wouldn't have used the word "sci-fi," but I know what Warren means and I find that flattering. I've used that term a few times myself. I've also called it a war drama and a political action-adventure, depending on the context. Any story that runs for six years and 1,500 pages is bound to fit into several different labels.

Do you consider DMZ dystopian or post-apocalyptic? How do you describe it in genre terms?

I'd call it "war" before I would use either of those terms. I called CHANNEL ZERO dystopian so the same might apply to DMZ, but there's a problem with all of this that largely

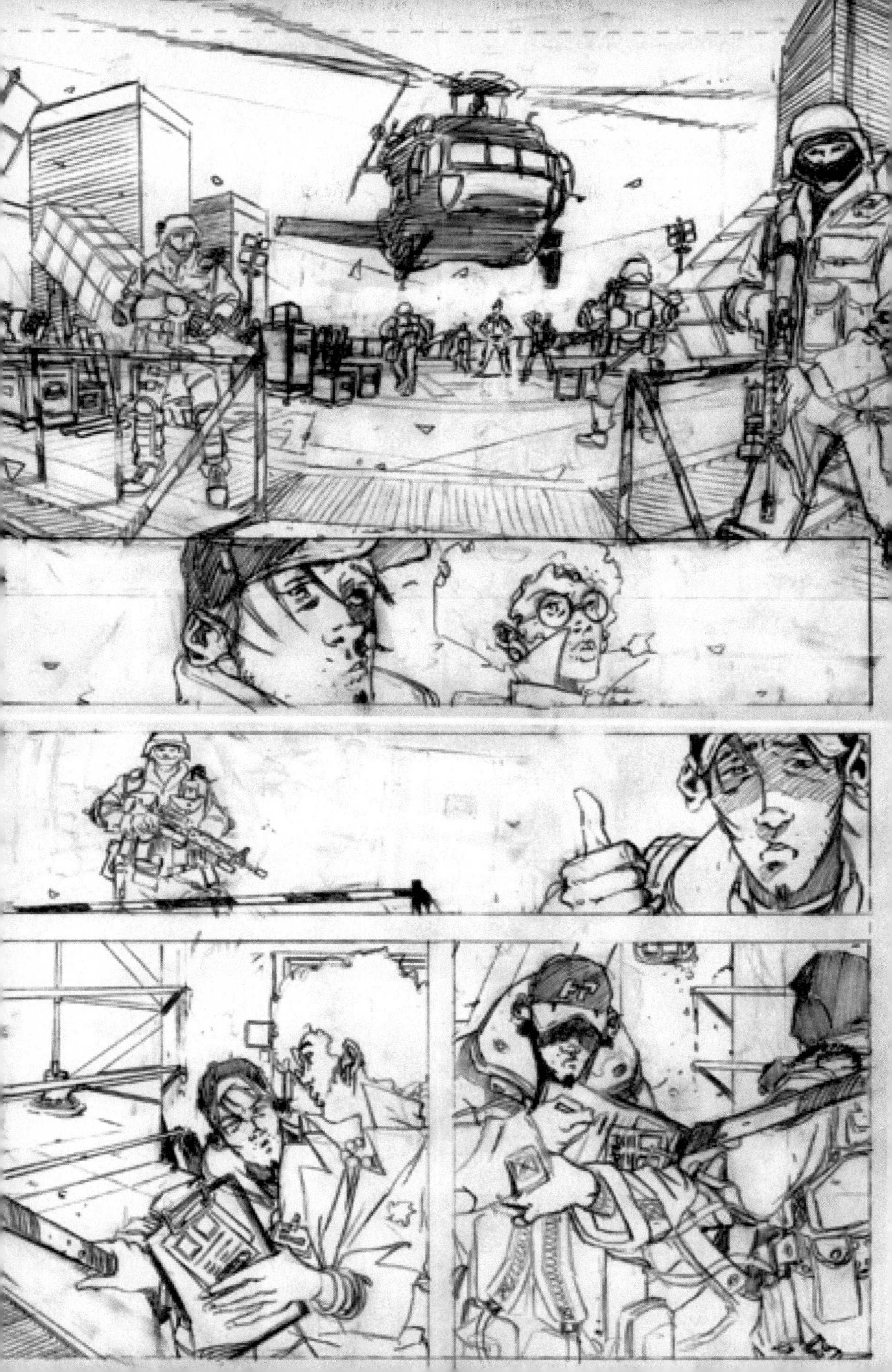

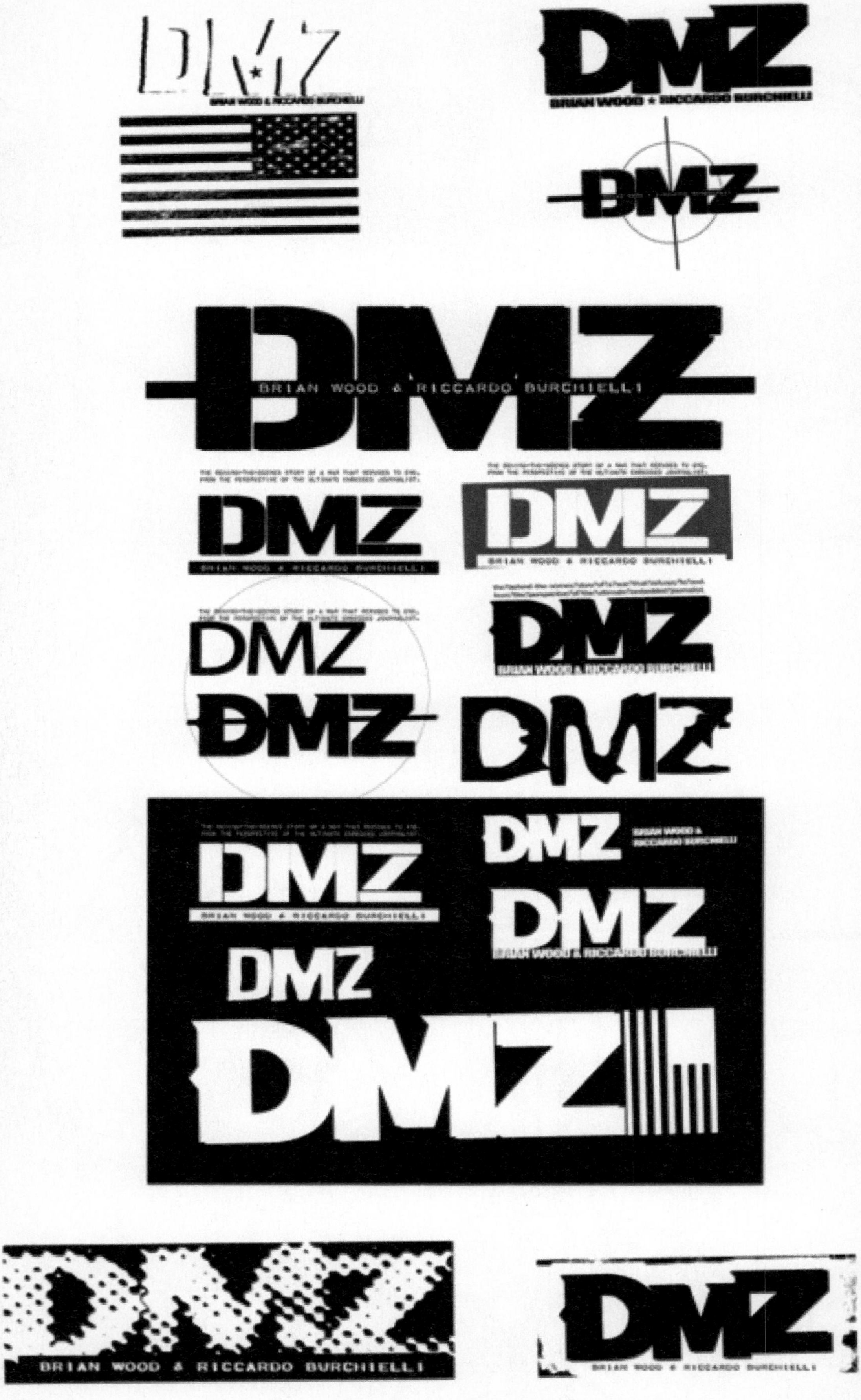
DMZ
BRIAN WOOD & RICCARDO BURCHIELLI
DMZ
BRIAN WOOD ★ RICCARDO BURCHIELLI
DMZ
DMZ
BRIAN WOOD & RICCARDO BURCHIELLI
DMZ
BRIAN WOOD & RICCARDO BURCHIELLI
DMZ
BRIAN WOOD & RICCARDO BURCHIELLI
DMZ
DMZ
BRIAN WOOD & RICCARDO BURCHIELLI
DMZ
DMZ
DMZ
BRIAN WOOD & RICCARDO BURCHIELLI
DMZ
BRIAN WOOD & RICCARDO BURCHIELLI
DMZ
BRIAN WOOD & RICCARDO BURCHIELLI
DMZ
DMZ
DMZ
BRIAN WOOD & RICCARDO BURCHIELLI
DMZ
BRIAN WOOD & RICCARDO BURCHIELLI

exists in my own head, which is, to me, DMZ is not set in the future. I mean, technically it is and most readers would say it is, but one of the "tricks" I use in writing it is to pretend like it's not, to never write anything that couldn't happen or exist right now (with the exception of a few bits of military technology). I never want to lose the relevancy of the story by making it too "future." An example of that is I tend to give Matty an older model film camera, rather than some cutting edge digital thing or the DMZ version of Spider Jerusalem's camera-glasses.

How did 9/11 impact you and the creation of DMZ?

It's true that 9/11 affected the creation of DMZ absolutely, that the book could not have existed without the event, but whatever thought processes that are involved with that must have happened almost entirely in my subconscious. At no point did I sit down and say, okay, now is the time I craft my response to 9/11 in comics form, or anything like that, and early on I would try to downplay the connection to avoid the book's being mis-categorized as a reaction piece or merely an anti-war rant. But yeah, there's an obvious and undeniable connection.

How did Riccardo become involved with the series?

It was as simple and as boring as finding his work in a stack of portfolios in my editor Will Dennis' office. Will makes trips overseas to conventions and collects samples from artists for that very reason. This is also how I "found" Davide Gianfelice for NORTHLANDERS. I liked the look of Riccardo's work, which was European in tone, but would occasionally blend in other stuff like manga speed lines. What clinched it, in the end, was that he drew a couple "fake" DMZ pages, some unscripted pages he made up based on a description of what the series was about. I think a combination of the strength of the work and the initiative of doing that without being asked made him the one.

How collaborative is it? How much input does Riccardo have with the design and direction of the series?

Storywise, the direction is purely mine. I'm not a co-writer type. I have zero interest in brainstorming with anyone on my work, be it another writer, an artist, an editor...unless it was deliberately planned from the start (I've said in recent interviews I had this idea to work on a book with David Lapham as a co-writer). But DMZ is so specifically me in concept, and developed by me in detail before we even started looking at artists; it's stayed that way. But, this isn't the same as me giving the artist freedom, or leeway, or leaving the design work up to them. Riccardo designed all the characters in the book. I had done a couple drawings of Matty, but Riccardo went another way. In the same way that I like to be left alone to write, I try

to leave the artist alone to do their thing. I try to limit my changes to the art to one instance per issue (usually a zoom or an angle change). So as we've progressed with the series, Riccardo's really put his visual stamp on the book in a huge way. The book is co-copyright him in the legal sense, and he's the co-owner in a very tangible sense as well. I love the guy, he's given six years of his life to this project, a real leap of faith for a guy who had never worked for a foreign company before.

You provided cover art for the first 34 issues; what can you share regarding your cover process?

I flew by the seat of my pants most of the time. I'm an illustrator in the sense that that's what I went to school for, but since I wrapped up CHANNEL ZERO in 1998, I barely drew anything. Maybe a dozen pieces per year, and I'm not very fast or versatile. The DMZ covers are what I do best, and I did them the only way I knew how.

An illustrator needs to be able to adjust and adapt and take notes and revise the work to fit the criteria of the job—all things I don't do well. So at times when my covers would be rejected by people at DC, for whatever reason, it was always a real struggle for me to accommodate what they wanted. I was really ready to be done by #34, and I think the book is much stronger with John Paul Leon taking over that role. He's incredibly talented. I remember him telling me he felt awkward at first, stepping into a job where he had to follow 34 covers that, for better or worse, were unique in their execution. But, I asked for JP to take over for his style, not for a version of what I do. I do enjoy making the covers for the trades, though.

You also did some of the interior art for those early issues, right?

I did a few pages in each of the first five issues, and then I did all of #12. It was a cool experiment, but never really gelled the way I think everyone thought it would. Time was also a factor for me. I was starting to pitch NORTHLANDERS, and LOCAL was struggling schedule-wise, so I decided it was better for me to spend my time on the writing and let Riccardo have those couple pages instead.

You crafted the DMZ title logo. What can you share about that piece of the business?

From 1999-2003, I worked as an in-house designer for Rockstar Games, and in that role I created dozens of logos and hundreds, maybe thousands, of logo variations, and for me this was easy. I whipped up a sheet of DMZ logos for Will Dennis in what was probably an hour and sent it over. We picked one, easy, much like picking the title "DMZ." (By contrast, the NORTHLANDERS logo was a huge, drawn-out struggle.)

What's the reception been like for the series from your perspective?

More than anyone expected. I talk about this with my editor from time to time. No offense intended to anyone, but who would have thought it would have lasted six years? Or even two years? That it would be translated into seven-plus languages and I'd be flown around the world to talk about it? (There was a brief minute when a massive Japanese publisher wanted to host Riccardo and me for a few months while we produced original DMZ content for that audience.) So on one hand, it's humbling and confusing, and as hard as everyone's worked, there were many other Vertigo books where everyone worked just as hard and their books didn't survive. So, yeah, humbling and very gratifying.

One reaction I thought we would get more of was from people accusing me of being anti-American or something like that. I thought for sure someone from the other end of the political spectrum would have some comments for me, but...nothing. Not sure if I'm happy about that or disappointed, to be honest.

I do remember reading a review that used the term "liberal fantasy" around the time we meet Soames and The Ghosts of Central Park. But, do you think it's just not on the radar screen of the people "from the other end of the political spectrum"?

My theory about this comes simply down to the timing of the book's release. It was pitched and accepted during the pretty intense first year of the Iraq invasion, and I grimly remember joking with my editor that, man, we better get this going quick, in case the war ends before we solicit it in Previews. This was early 2004. The book arrived in stores in November of 2005 and I really feel that public opinion had shifted to the point where most people had stopped being so rah-rah pro-war and any anti-war message in the book was falling on receptive ears. Or maybe it's just not that controversial? It got full-page write-ups in *The New York Times*, *The Chicago Sun-Times*, *The Independent*, etc., so clearly it passed in front of a lot of people's eyeballs, so if there were to be any drama it would have happened already. The worst I get is snarky stuff like the "liberal fantasy" comment you mentioned, from the comic book community.

How did you finalize "On the Ground" as the title of the first arc? I remember reading the singles and guessing you'd call it "Live From The DMZ," after Viktor's intended story (which I borrowed for the website!).

It wasn't even discussed. It was always "On The Ground." That was such a catchphrase at the time—and I remember

it was also during the first Gulf War—and I was really out to make that cultural connection. I would revisit that idea in later trades, using modern war slogans, like "Friendly Fire," "Hearts & Minds," or "War Powers."

You don't waste any time in the first issue; people are getting shot by page 15 and the chopper goes down on page 17. Was that lack of decompression calculated or more organic?

It was more about packing a whole bunch of stuff into the first issue as a common sense sort of "hook the readers!" thing. Looking back, we really do cover a lot of ground, from Matty being introduced, to the city being introduced, the crash, the death(?) of Viktor, Matty meeting Zee, her touring him around, and his failed extraction. I don't know if that sort of compression is the greatest thing. There's not a lot of depth to anyone. It's good for a first issue, but I'm glad I slowed down a little as I went.

Early on, there's a tight shot of a graffiti scrawl that says "Every Day is 9/11." Riccardo also delivered a two-page spread, which essentially looks like Ground Zero. Were you ever hesitant about those references being perceived as being made for shock value?

That little phrase really took off at the time, and got me some feedback both positive and negative. I guess I shouldn't be surprised, and we could have asked Riccardo to leave it off if we wanted, but we didn't. It really wasn't meant to be such a big deal, just a little bit of wall-scrawl that helped place the events of DMZ in the context of our own world. The first of several references to 9/11, actually. That line got picked up by, if I recall, marketing, and appeared on a couple house ads, and was also used extensively for this gallery exhibition we had in Lucca, Italy.

Looking back on it now, I'm glad we used it, but I can see how it might have helped, even just a little bit, if we hadn't, in terms of communicating to early readers that this is not a partisan series. It was never meant to be that, but it took me a little time to find the right balance walking that line. 9/11 was still really politically charged at the time, and any reference to it in any context other than one promoting the Bush Doctrine was suspect in the eyes of many.

Do you think there's such a thing as a post-9/11 aesthetic? Was that even in your lexicon when collaborating early on?

It was certainly not in mine. I think we'll be able to judge that some time in the future, at least a decade from now. I mean, I believe there is one, but it's still swirling around us and history needs to fix it in place. I remember being

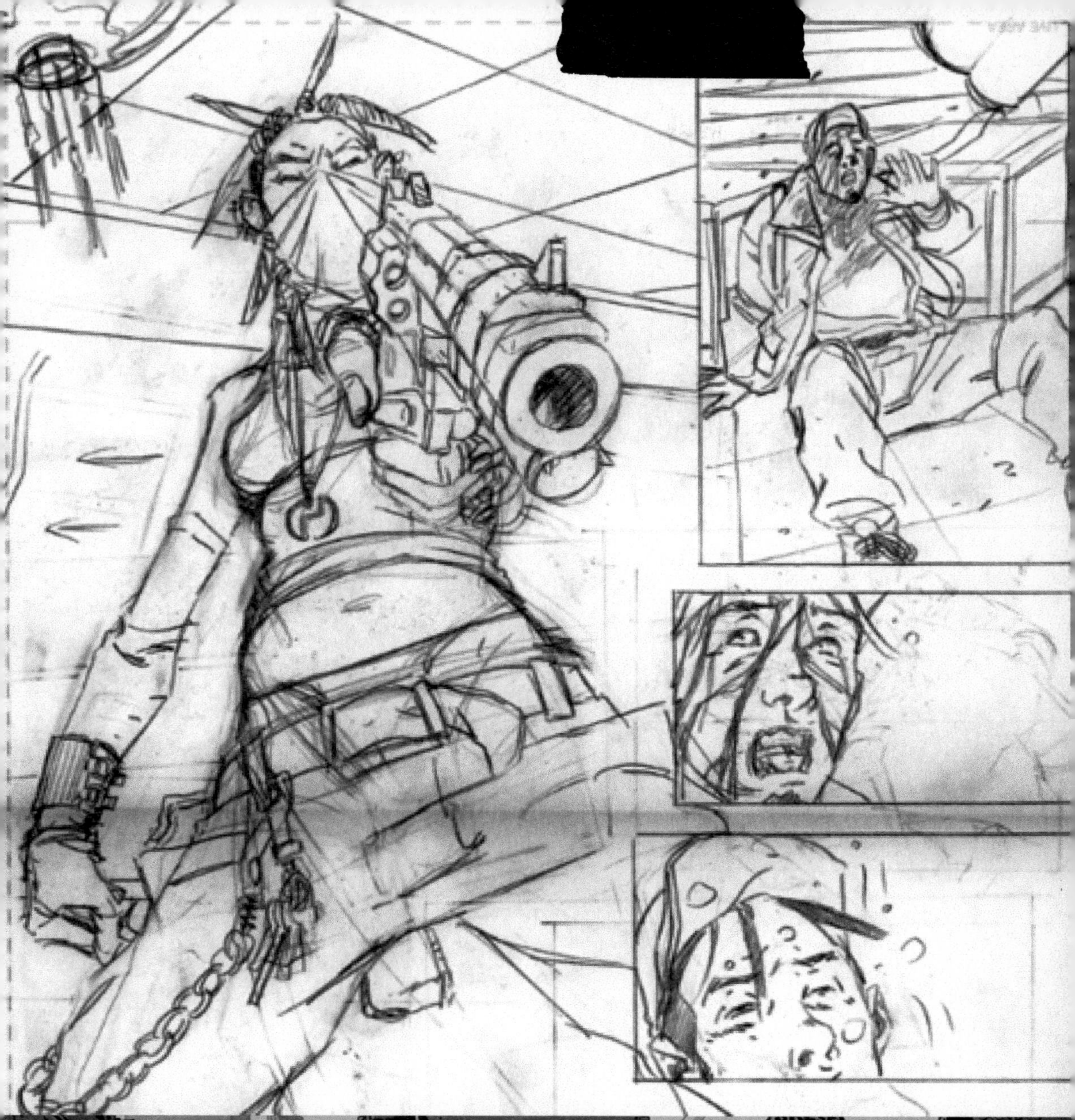

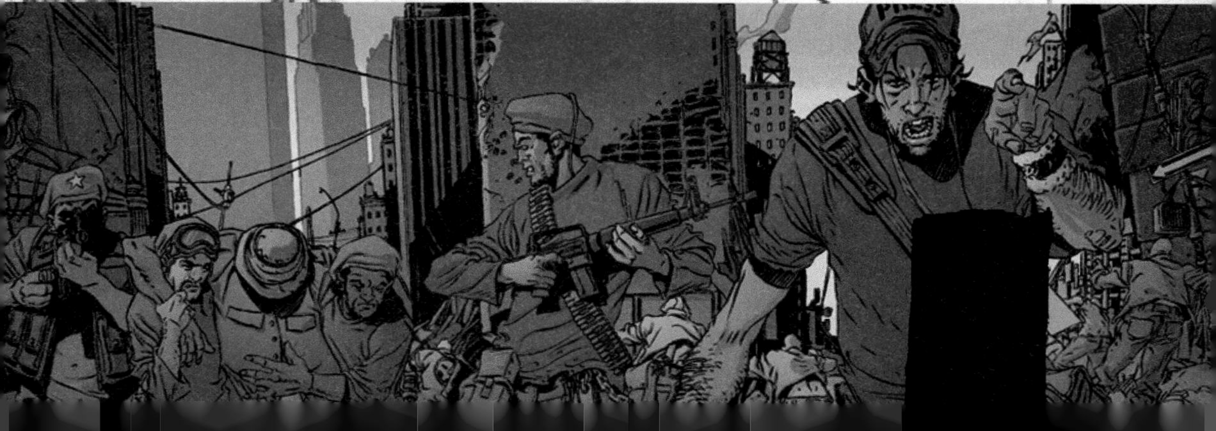
PRESS

on a Vertigo panel during the first year of DMZ, and some new books were being talked about: ARMY @ LOVE, UNKNOWN SOLDIER, LOVELESS, and HELLBLAZER: PANDEMONIUM, and someone commented how we were all heavy on the subject of war. This was not an editorial arrangement; this was what we all wanted to talk about, apparently.

The very first page of the series has the map of Manhattan and that lone soldier with his eyes glowing against the black silhouette. Do you recall what your thought process was for that image?

That was the first image of DMZ, back when it was WARTIME, a good two years before I would actually pitch the book. I can't recall the thought process in detail, but this was me, in NYC, in 2002. It's one of those cases where current events were heavy on the mind. I remember some concern when I wrote that into the first page.

There was minor pushback to my opening the book with dense Liberty News narration...actually my using news broadcasts at all was something a few people had problems with. I was told it slowed things down, it wasn't interesting or exciting to read, and was possibly pretentious (or would be perceived that way). It's also a hell of a lot of fun, to try to mimic the phrasing and tone of pundit-speak, an art form all on its own. As time has gone on, I found different ways to use it other than just as a stage-setting tool. But, to me, this was how I made comics, at least in the cases of CHANNEL ZERO and JENNIE ONE. And it's hard to imagine DMZ without it.

What does Viktor Ferguson's character embody?

He's simply The Establishment, the old way of looking at things, the conservative viewpoint (not meant in the political sense). He's the old guard to Matty's rookie. I handled it a bit bluntly, a bit two-dimensionally, but I figured that was called for.

Zee is obviously a really important character; where did she come from?

This is interesting. Zee didn't have an identity for several drafts of the proposal–she was referred to as "the girl," which at a glance is kind of obnoxious and more than a little misogynistic, like she didn't matter. But as time went on, and after the obvious was pointed out to me by a friend, I realized what the reason was: Zee is the city. An individual embodiment of the city, the soul of the city, and I had been subconsciously writing her in that role for years before I saw it. When Matty and the city are good, like in the "Body of a Journalist" arc, or the "Friendly Fire" arc, things are good with Zee as well. But when Matty and Zee have a falling out, it coincides perfectly with Matty's standing with the city, like during the end of the election story and in "Hearts & Minds."

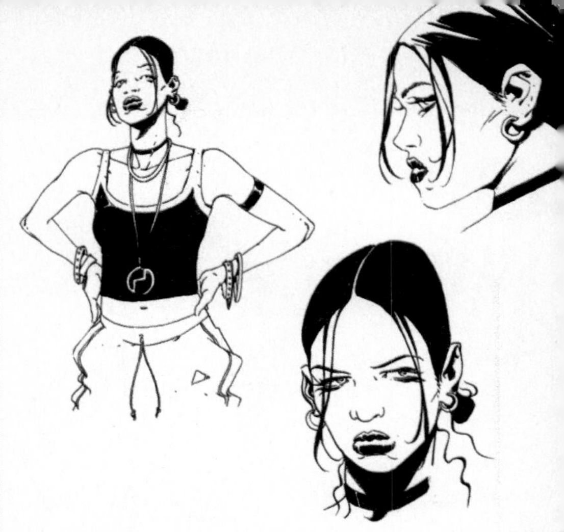

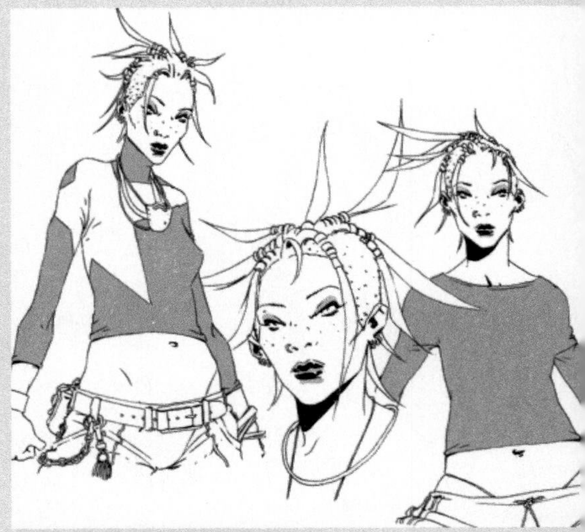

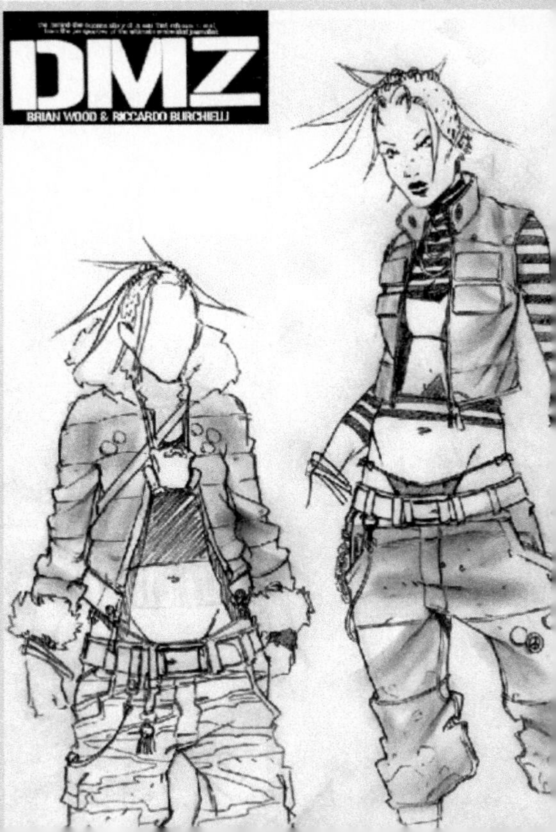
DMZ
BRIAN WOOD & RICCARDO BURCHIELLI

WARTIME

WRITTEN AND ILLUSTRATED BY

BRIAN WOOD

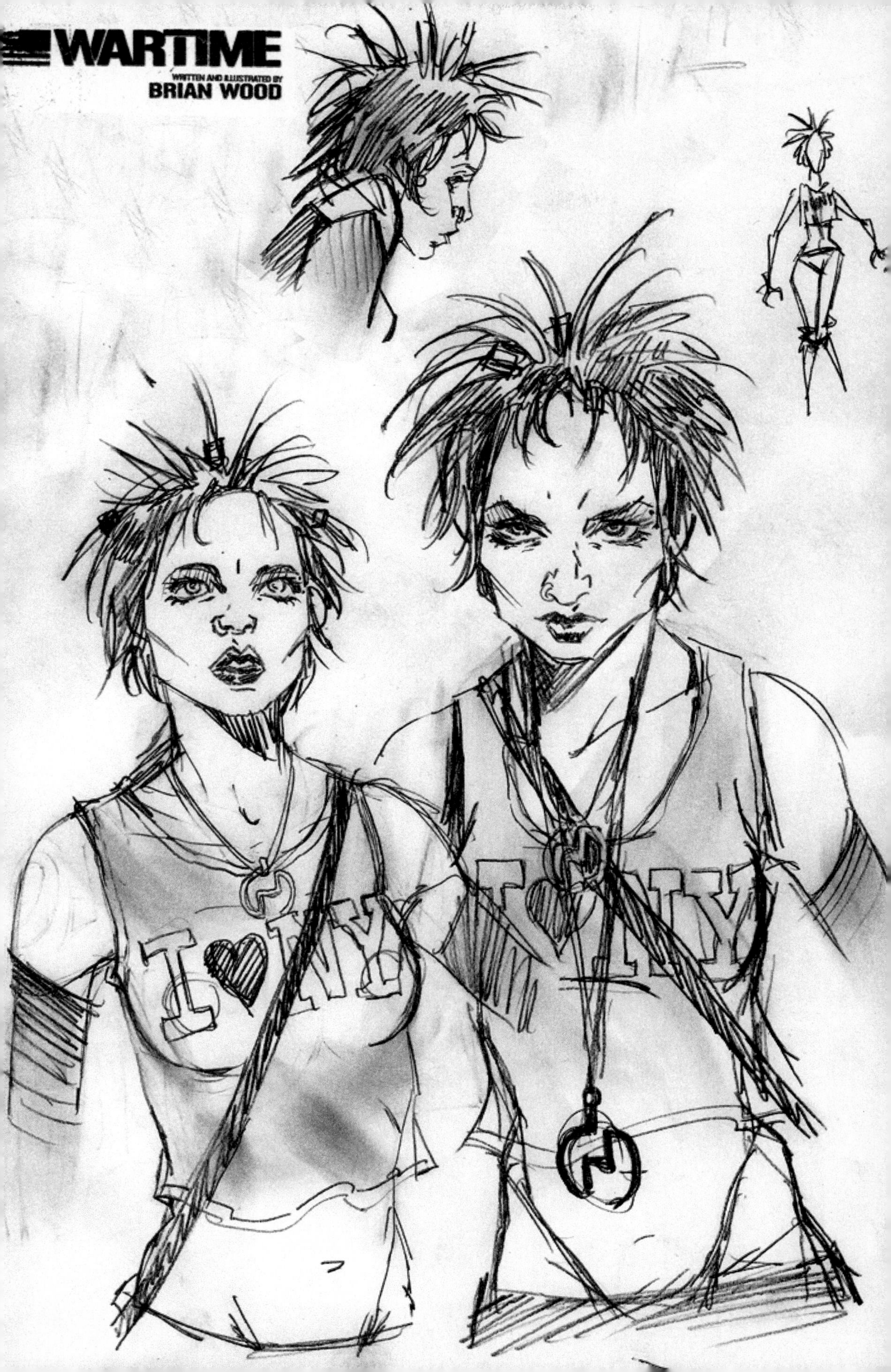
I ♥ NY
I ♥ NY

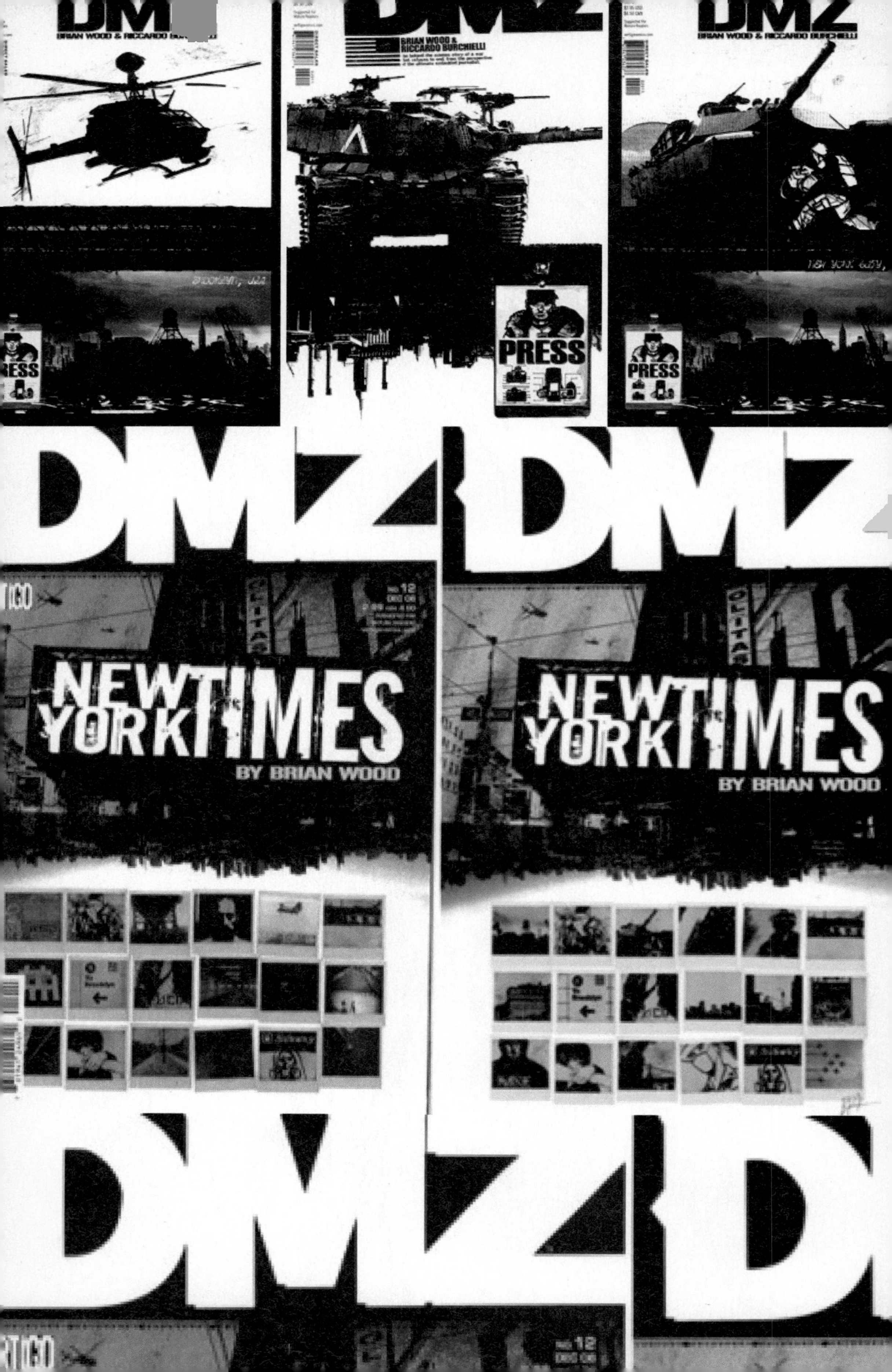
DMZ
BRIAN WOOD & RICCARDO BURCHIELLI
PRESS
DMZ
NEW YORK TIMES
BY BRIAN WOOD
NEW YORK TIMES
BY BRIAN WOOD
DMZ

Matty is an interesting ideological construct. One way to read him is that his naïvete is a sin, the chopper attack is the dark descent, and the DMZ becomes his hell. Does he initially represent the general public's political apathy?

He's certainly meant to be apathetic, not much of a thinker, certainly not someone particularly interested in politics in any meaningful sense. He's the sort of guy who gets his news from headlines only, probably the sort of headlines the *New York Post* prints.

There was a guy I worked with shortly after 9/11, and he's the person who most informed the creation of Matty, typically inspiring the worst traits in that character. At work we all used instant messenger to talk with each other, and in his little status space, where you could type a little tagline everyone could see, he wrote "Syria Next!" This was a few days after U.S. forces rolled into Baghdad. That's the sort of knee-jerk shit Matty Roth would think. I also used to imagine a pre-DMZ Matty Roth sitting on his couch in Long Island, eating Cheetos and playing Xbox.

The briefest glance at the comments section of most major news sites would make you think all of America is not unlike this Matty Roth, but clearly that's not the case. I do think that there are too many uninformed Americans when it comes to our wars and current events, but I chalk that up not to being naive, but our having access to too much information, too many opinions.

There's a very representational quality to your graphic design work, almost like street art stencils, a sense of re-appropriation of found imagery. You've slipped mentions of Jennie Holzer, Keith Haring, and Basquiat into your work. There's even an Invader mosaic on the cover of issue 12. Is this just personal interest or residual energy from your education at Parsons?

Yeah, it all comes from my time at Parsons. The art and design work I do on DMZ is a continuation, a refinement, of the CHANNEL ZERO "style," which was 100% analog. This was 1996-ish, I didn't own a computer, and Parsons had yet to really stress the value of computers as creative tools. Found imagery, stencils, fax, and photocopier effects—I did all that by hand. I ran art through my fax machine for visual effect, I bought hacked Kinko's cards to experiment with copy art, to scale my stuff up and down. I cut stencils and searched through the image library at school for stuff to use/steal/incorporate. I really, really miss those times. I used a lot of glue sticks. Now, I do all that digitally, but my goal is to always try to recreate that analog look.

You know, the cover of #12 that printed was just a sketch. I dropped in all those photos as placeholders for other images I would eventually draw, in order to get approval for the design of the cover. Then, since that and the final looked so similar, there was a mixup. I believe the real cover is in the trade, but here it is here. I'm sure that Invader image, along with several others, is a trademark violation, never my intention.

What was the title of the "Body of a Journalist" arc intended to convey?

Well, aside from a really vague reference to The Pogues song "Body of an American," which my editor appreciated, it's meant pretty literally—the body, living or dead, of the journalist Viktor Ferguson, last seen in issue #1.

This arc gives us Zee's origin, introduces Wilson, and mentions Decade Later and DJ Random Fire. Was fleshing out the world with more personalities one of your goals?

I think really early on, in the earliest days of proposal-writing, we all understood the potential in this fictional world for unlimited stories and characters. I didn't have much of a plan to roll them out, not beyond the core cast. I made Wilson up on the spot—the whole Chinatown Kingpin thing came later. All those people in issue 12, Decade Later and DJ Random Fire, I knew I was creating a potential pool of characters to use in the future, but at the time I was just having fun creating them.

DMZ#11
Zee - med student design + artist take on current design
prepared for Will Dennis   6-20-06
by Kristian Donaldson

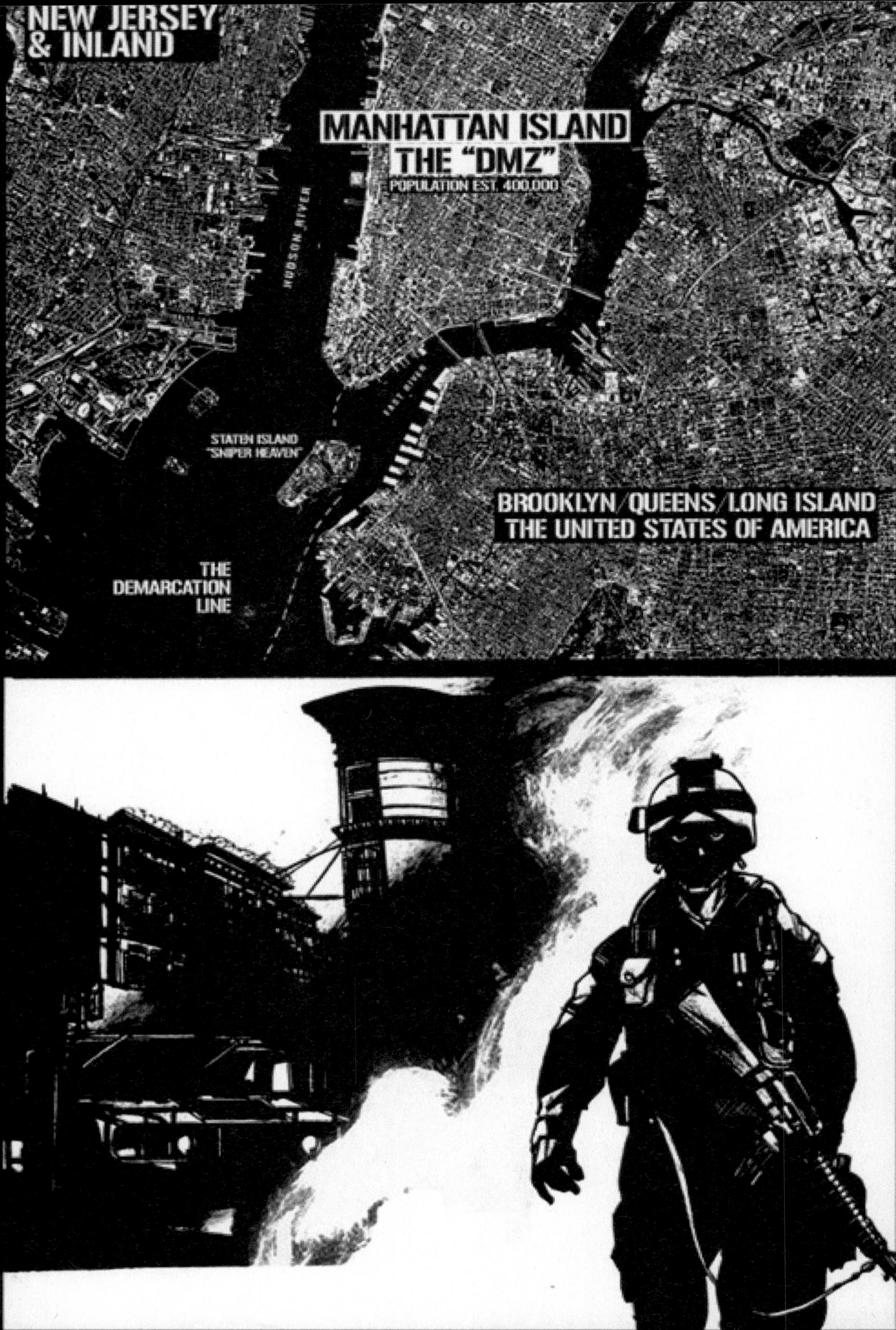
NEW JERSEY
& INLAND
MANHATTAN ISLAND
THE "DMZ"
POPULATION EST. 400,000
STATEN ISLAND
"SNIPER HEAVEN"
BROOKLYN/QUEENS/LONG ISLAND
THE UNITED STATES OF AMERICA
THE
DEMARCATION
LINE

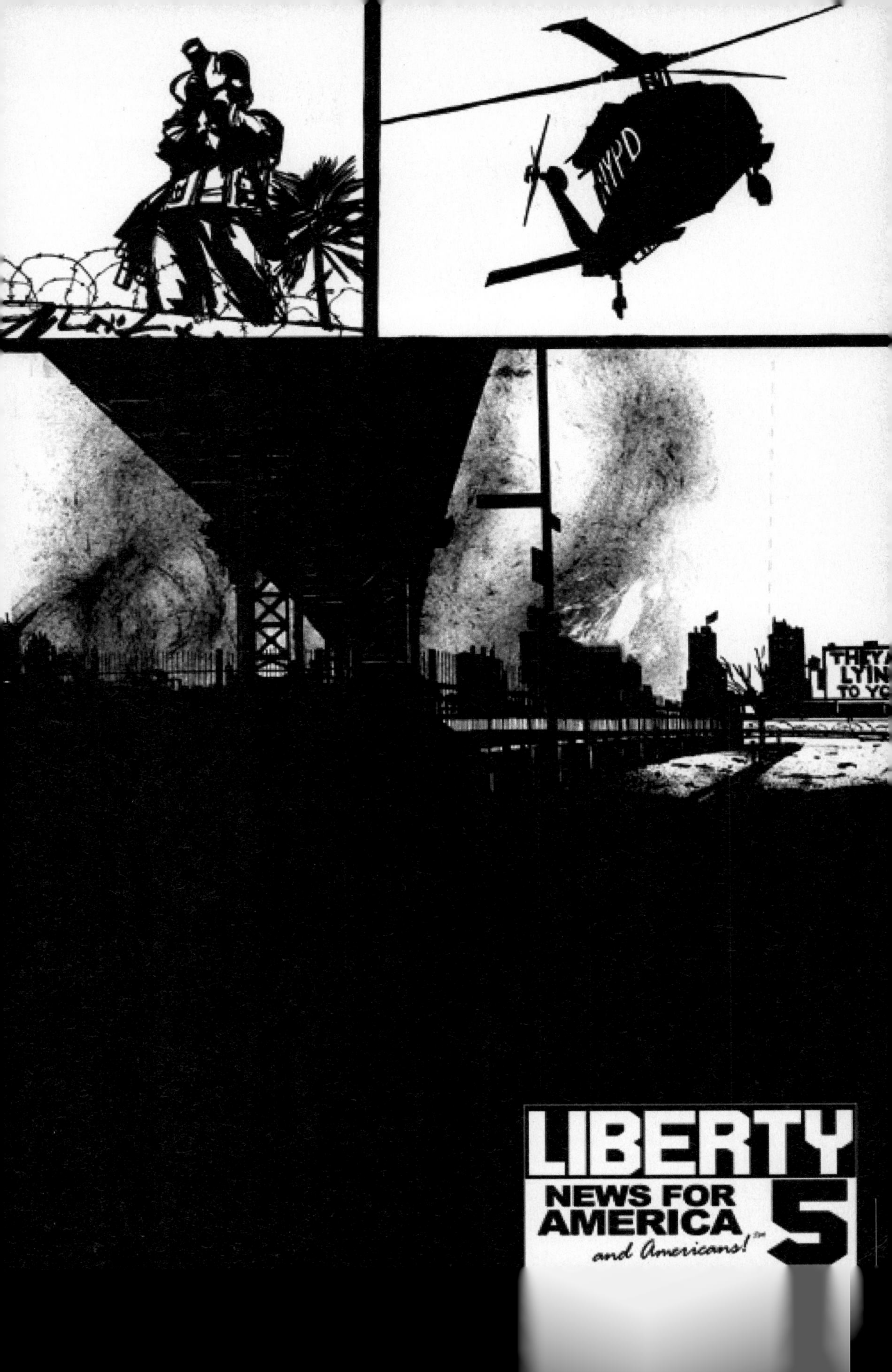
NYPD
LIBERTY
NEWS FOR AMERICA
and Americans!
5

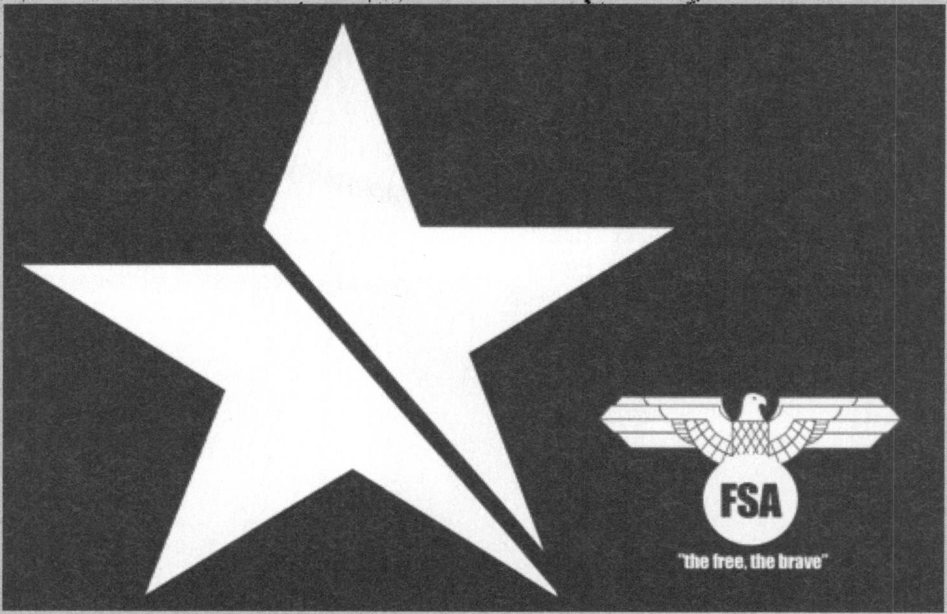
FSA
"the free, the brave"

Riccardo's portrayal of New York City is pretty convincing. Has he been to NYC or do you supply him with tons of reference photos?

It was a gradual thing, a process where I supplied reference in the early days. Riccardo lives in Florence, Italy, and his exposure to NYC was limited to films and TV, and whatever he could Google. So, the pencils for the first issue were way off the mark based on the needs of the script. Not his fault; it's not like I could draw Florence correctly either. So for those first few scripts, I went out and shot custom reference for him, for each page. I also started a habit that I continue to this day, for every artist and every script I write, where I put links to reference photos in the panel descriptions. I figure if I'm asking for something specific that needs to be accurate, it's the least I can do. The artist should spend his time drawing, not sifting through Flickr trying to identify what I'm talking about.

When Riccardo finally did visit New York, it was for NYCC about six months into the publication of DMZ. He brought his camera and took pictures of EVERYTHING, even things that would never occur to me, like manhole covers, traffic lights, hydrants, and stuff like that. The year after that, he moved to New York for several months, but at that point he was fully up to speed.

You'd worked with Kristian Donaldson previously on SUPERMARKET; how did you know he was right for DMZ?

I'm not sure I considered that question, to be honest. One of the best tools you have in comics is to work with a trusted partner, and Kristian is definitely that. If you look at *Supermarket*, past the pop coloring and cute girls, you see a rather shockingly high level of background detail, architecture, vehicles, and cityscapes. Not everyone can do that, and DMZ is nothing if not a book that demands a lot of environment from its artists. Kristian was great.

I love the iconography of the FSA split-star because it really captures the ethos of the movement. How did that symbol come about?

I think Riccardo designed that. It's perfect, simple in concept, but really unnerving to look at, vaguely fascist. I designed, more for laughs than anything else, a version of it that REEKS of Nazism. I had considered using that, to really throw readers off in terms of their assumptions about the personalities and motives of the Free States, but cooler heads prevailed.

Riccardo lives in Italy and doesn't go to many conventions or do interviews, and because DMZ is strongly branded as "a Brian Wood book," people might not realize to what extent he's formed the book. Aside from that FSA logo, Zee is entirely his design, as is Matty for the most part, and Wilson, etc. I put a lot of pressure on him, in terms of what sort of insanity he has to draw. I always joke that it takes me five seconds to type: "Page One. Splash page of NYC. Caption: The DMZ." Then the poor guy spends the next day and a half sweating over it. He's done that, I don't know how many times, for six years. Most comic book artists couldn't have done it. Some of the guest artists we have who draw a single issue tell me how murderous it was.

Wilson, "Ghost Protector of Chinatown," became a fan favorite character. Do you consider him a mentor to Matty?

I think he's Matty's friend, which is probably more important to him than a mentor. Matty's one of those guys who thrives off being around a charismatic person, who feels flattered when someone cool hangs out with him. Wilson's that guy, to a degree, but always a little removed. He's gives Matty advice and perspective in a non-threatening way, but it's really Parco who comes along and, to use an awkward expression, sweeps Matty off his feet.

Wilson's character changes drastically from his first appearance. Initially, he seems like he's just Matty's eclectic techie neighbor. Little do we know he's one of the most powerful figures in the DMZ. Was that shift intentional or a course correction?

It was a course correction. At first he was the oddball neighbor that Matty could talk to. One of the things I struggled with early on is that Matty had no friends and therefore, as a writer, it made things difficult because Matty couldn't verbalize a lot of what he was thinking. No wonder Brian K. Vaughan gave Yorick a monkey in Y: THE LAST MAN. At one point, it was suggested to me that Matty should have a dog, for this reason. With Wilson, I just saw an opportunity to expand the character. It sort of implies that Wilson misled Matty, posed as a fairly

innocent person and so maybe he was using Matty for some reason, but I like to think that Wilson needs a guy like Matty to talk to as well, someone who exists out of his crime boss world of sycophants and victims.

I'm curious how you'd describe Matty's relationship with the women in his life?

It's a disaster, basically. I used to make jokes about how Matty is doing what every guy in his 20s does in the city, or should do: date a lot of interesting women, but never take it anywhere beyond that. He's a bumbler, a fool. A few of them have come to tragic ends, though.

Speaking of, Eve Lindon was gut-wrenching. She seems like this small touch of warmth during a cold time, but Matty just learns he can't trust a soul.

Well, I had written that woman into the script as a sort of nameless functionary, and then it just seemed like an opportunity was there to build Matty's backstory, so I went back in and added the bit where she's part of his past. This reminds me, a few years back I was asked by DC, the west coast office, to write up a treatment for a DMZ TV show. That was a fun exercise (I use that word since no one ever did anything with my pitch) in trying to marry the existing story to the rules of a television show, as they were told to me. I tweaked a million things, but two very major changes were to bring Parco into the story right at the start, and to hugely expand the Eve Lindon character, and introduce her much, much sooner as well. I should really post that treatment online, but I feel like I only

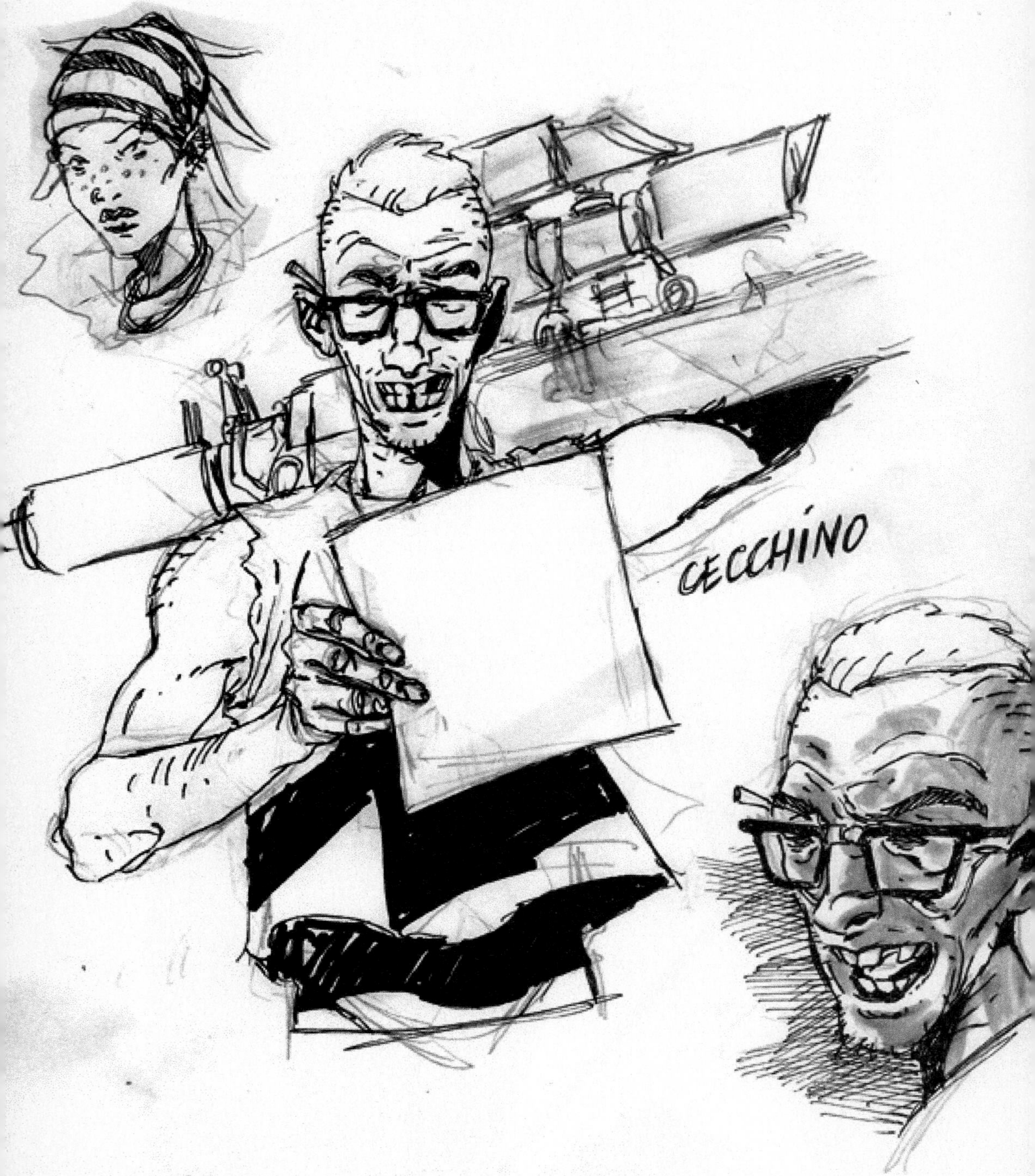
CECCHINO

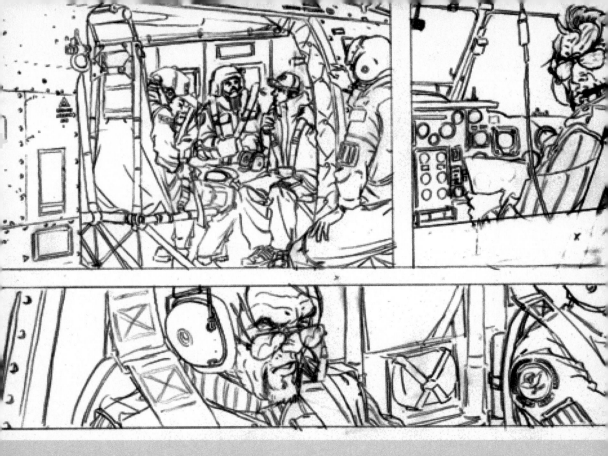

should if and when an actual DMZ adaptation is made.

The "Hawthorne Effect" in science suggests that the act of observing something changes it. Does that apply to Matty and his presence in the DMZ?

I think Matty's had a hugely disruptive affect. Sometimes it's deliberate, like with Viktor Ferguson, where he literally stops an invasion via blackmail, or when he partners with Parco, and other times it's more subtle, like in his interviews with Stevens, the soldier in "Friendly Fire." I think a lot of readers tend to miss all the really, really good stuff Matty accomplishes in those early days—he literally saves the city, before he screws it all up again. That was always the thing: here's this person who is supposed to be objective (but note: Matty was never a journalist), yet he sticks his nose into everything, meddles with everything.

We learn about the timeline of the war, with the Helena, Montana, uprising and the drive east to Allentown, PA. Do you have the entire war mapped out in notes?

No, that was actually meant to address the reader reaction, a lot of whom could not fathom, or accept, that the backstory was not available and was not the point of the story. I got a lot of mail, some of it really furious, about this. I really did believe that it was not, and is not, the point of the story, and I also knew that if I were to

map it out like a timeline, it would just be inviting these same sorts of readers to poke holes in it, to say "this or that could never happen." In other words, a nightmare. The story starts when the war is already far along, and it's about what happens now, not what caused it a decade in the past. But, I buckled a bit and wrote a couple pages to try to meet these people in the middle. I can't remember how it was received at the time. I think I name-dropped Allentown because that's where Becky [Cloonan] was living at the time, or she had lived there while drawing DEMO.

You said before that you continued to do the Zee one-shots because they were well-received, and now you're meeting a bit of the fan demand for the backstory. Some of your characters (I'm thinking of the lead singer from Theories & Defenses in LOCAL) have been very vocal about just putting it out there and not catering to expectations. So, will you adjust your writing plans based on fan feedback?

I have adjusted based on reaction, yeah. As far as when and why, I don't have any set rules. And while I think it's best for the story to never do this, in the case of DMZ, I was launching a series, my first, designed to run for years. I wanted it to run for years, so I was more sensitive to how readers were feeling about it. In hindsight, I've learned that it probably wouldn't have mattered. When it comes to creator-owned books, it's almost impossible to move the needle, to do something to affect change in orders or magnitude, short of having a film or TV adaptation to come out. DMZ would not have been cancelled if there was only one Zee one-shot, nor would sales have risen if Matty had a dog. So I still believe the wisest course of action is to write what you want, regardless of the voices on the Internet, but I know how easy it is to let those voices trigger self-doubt.

I'm reminded of this website, a fairly popular one run by a retailer, and in that first year of DMZ, he predicted that the series would crash and burn several times. When #3 shipped, he was critical of how that first arc concluded. He thought #12 was a total disaster, and so on. This is a guy who is a veteran, is a smart guy, and all his instincts were telling him what I was doing were terminal missteps. Not only was he wrong, but DMZ trades continue to place high in his "best of the year" sales lists. I say all this just to further underscore the point that the needle of the monthly sales trajectory is pretty hard to impact.

Talk to us about the intent of issue 12 and the process of creating art for an entire issue. The last time you'd done this was, what, CHANNEL ZERO?

Yeah, I've done a couple teeny things here and there, but DMZ #12 was the first full-length issue I'd drawn since the last CHANNEL ZERO in the late '90s. When DMZ started, the intention was that I would draw part of every single issue, as well as the covers. I'd pitched DMZ originally as something I would both write and draw, and while DC didn't want that (and I was probably foolish to think I could do it), this was a good compromise. Sure enough, I wasn't able to maintain that, due to time constraints. I am not a fast artist. DMZ #12 was my last hurrah, so to speak. I drew about 60% of it by hand, ink on paper. I scanned that in and finished it in Photoshop, color and all. It was hell. I mean, it was rewarding, but it just reminded me why I was not a monthly comic artist. Just that one issue beat the hell out of me, and I've never been more thankful for Riccardo.

End Transmission

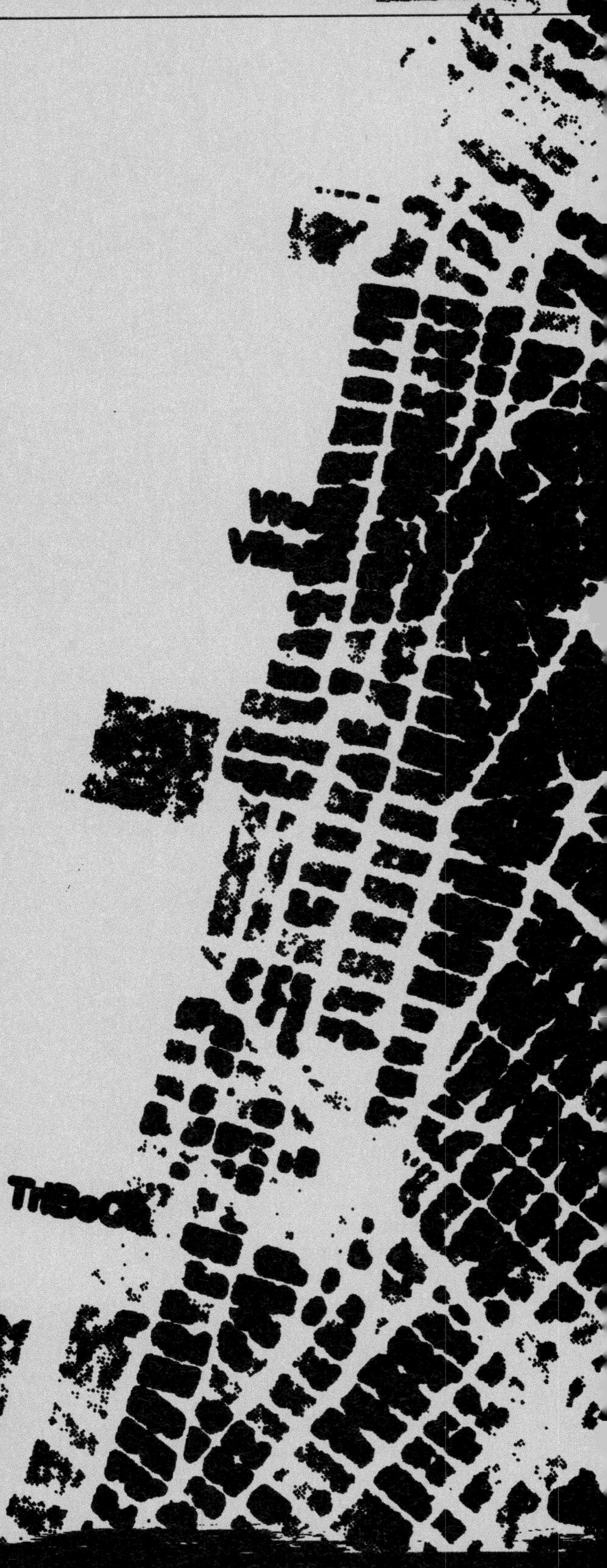